OXFORD MEDIEVAL TEXTS

General Editors

J. W. BINNS J. BLAIR

M. LAPIDGE T. REUTER

THOMAS OF MARLBOROUGH
HISTORY OF THE ABBEY OF EVESHAM

THOMAS OF MARLBOROUGH

HISTORY OF
THE ABBEY OF EVESHAM

EDITED AND TRANSLATED BY
JANE SAYERS and LESLIE WATKISS

CLARENDON PRESS · OXFORD

OXFORD
UNIVERSITY PRESS

Great Clarendon Street, Oxford OX2 6DP

Oxford University Press is a department of the University of Oxford.
It furthers the University's objective of excellence in research, scholarship,
and education by publishing worldwide in

Oxford New York

Auckland Bangkok Buenos Aires Cape Town Chennai
Dar es Salaam Delhi Hong Kong Istanbul Karachi Kolkata
Kuala Lumpur Madrid Melbourne Mexico City Mumbai Nairobi
São Paulo Shanghai Taipei Tokyo Toronto

Oxford is a registered trade mark of Oxford University Press
in the UK and in certain other countries

Published in the United States
by Oxford University Press Inc., New York

British Library Cataloguing in Publication Data

Data available

Library of Congress Cataloging in Publication Data

Data available

ISBN 0-19-820480-9

1 3 5 7 9 10 8 6 4 2

Typeset in Ehrhardt
by Joshua Associates Ltd., Oxford
Printed in Great Britain
on acid-free paper by
Biddles Ltd., Guildford and King's Lynn

PREFACE

THE present edition was commenced in 1993. JES has provided the historical annotation and the Introduction. LW has been responsible for all things pertaining to the Latin text and translation. Both editors have been involved in the general revision. Dr Teresa Webber has provided a section on the Rawlinson manuscript.

Since 1993 we have become indebted to several institutions for financial support and for access to manuscripts and archives, and to many individuals who have willingly answered queries and read sections of the text and translation.

First we both wish to thank the Twenty Seven Foundation for a grant which made it possible for us to have a microfilm and printouts of Bodleian MS Rawlinson A 287. Then JES wishes to express her gratitude to the Leverhulme Trustees for an emeritus professorship during the year 1999 to 2000 that enabled her to complete her part of the work and to track down and examine various Evesham sources. We would also wish to thank the staff of Duke Humfrey's Library in the Bodleian at Oxford, the Almonry Museum at Evesham, and the British Library Manuscripts department; and the following individual scholars who have been generous with their time in answering various queries, Julia Barrow, David Cox, Barrie Dobson, Othmar Hageneder, Katharine Keats-Rohan, Simon Keynes, Sister Maura O'Carroll, Kenneth Pennington, Olivia Robinson, Patrick Sims-Williams, Linda Voigts, Herwig Weigl, Ann Williams, and Reinhard Willvonseder.

We are indebted to the present general editors, James Binns, John Blair, Michael Lapidge, who lent us his unpublished transcript of Dominic's Book II, and especially to the late Timothy Reuter who read the whole of the text and of the translation. Two former general editors—Diana Greenway and Barbara Harvey—read significantly large portions of the text and translations, giving expert advice in their own specialist areas and we are very grateful to them also. We have been particularly fortunate in our critics, but we, of course, are responsible for all conclusions and statements *in errore* and otherwise.

The process of production has been helped by the expertise, wisdom, and common sense of John Cordy, the copy editor, by the

admirable professionalism of Joshua Associates, the typesetters, and
by the kind efficiency of Kay Rogers, the O.U.P. editor. We should
like to record our gratitude to them.

J.E.S.

L.W.

April and December 2002
London
Ferndown

CONTENTS

ABBREVIATIONS

AB	*Analecta Bollandiana*
acc.	acceded, accession
ANC	S. Kuttner and E. Rathbone, 'Anglo-Norman canonists of the twelfth century', *Traditio* vii (1949–51), 279–358
Ann. Mon.	*Annales Monastici*, ed. H. R. Luard (5 vols., RS xxxvi, London, 1864–9)
Ann. Wig.	'Annales prioratus de Wigornia' in *Ann. Mon.* iv
ASC	*The Anglo-Saxon Chronicle*, trans. D. Whitelock with D. C. Douglas and S. I. Tucker (London, 1961)
Bede, *HE*	*Bede's Ecclesiastical History of the English People*, ed. B. Colgrave and R. A. B. Mynors (OMT, corrected repr. 1991)
BIHR	*Bulletin of the Institute of Historical Research*
BL	British Library
BRUC	*A Biographical Register of the University of Cambridge to A.D. 1500*, compiled by A. B. Emden (Cambridge, 1963)
BRUO	*A Biographical Register of the University of Oxford to A.D. 1500*, 3 vols., compiled by A. B. Emden (Oxford, 1957–9)
C. & S.	*Councils and Synods with other Documents relating to the English Church*, i, pts. 1 (871–1066) and 2 (1066–1204), ed. D. Whitelock, M. Brett, and C. N. L. Brooke (Oxford, 1981); and ii, pts. 1 (1205–65) and 2 (1265–1313), ed. F. M. Powicke and C. R. Cheney (Oxford, 1964)
Cheney, *Letters*	C. R. and M. G. Cheney, calendared and ed., *The Letters of Pope Innocent III (1198–1216) concerning England and Wales* (Oxford, 1967)
Chron. Maj.	*Matthaei Parisiensis, monachi Sancti Albani, Chronica Majora*, ed. H. R. Luard (7 vols., RS lvii, 1872–83)
Code	*Codex Iustinianus, Corpus Iuris Civilis*, ii, ed. P. Krueger (Berlin, 1895; repr. Berlin, 1954)
comp.	compiled by
1 *Comp.*	*Compilatio Prima* in *Quinque Compilationes*, ed. E. Friedberg (Leipzig, 1882)

3 *Comp.*   *Compilatio Tertia* in *Quinque Compilationes*, ed.
                     E. Friedberg

4 *Comp.*   *Compilatio Quarta* in *Quinque Compilationes*, ed.
                     E. Friedberg

cons.   consecrated, consecration

Cottineau   L. H. Cottineau, *Répertoire Topo-Bibliographique des
                     Abbayes et Prieurés*, 3 vols. (Mâcon, 1935–70), i. A–L,
                     ii. M–Z, iii. References

CPL   *Calendar of the Entries in the Papal Registers illustrating
                     the History of Great Britain and Ireland*, ed. W. H.
                     Bliss, A. P. Fuller, and M. Haren (19 vols., HMSO,
                     London, 1893–1960, and Irish MSS Commission
                     1978–)

d.   died

DB Worcs.   *Domesday Book. 16 Worcestershire*, ed. F. and C.
                     Thorn (Chichester, 1982)

Decretum   *Decretum, Corpus Iuris Canonici*, i, ed. E. Friedberg
                     (Leipzig, 1879). [The *Decretum* is divided into two
                     parts *Cause* (C) and *Distinctiones* (D). The *Cause*
                     consist of *questiones* (q): p. c. means a dictum of
                     Gratian placed after the chapter]

Digest   *The Digest of Justinian*. Latin text ed. T. Mommsen
                     with the assistance of P. Krueger, trans. Alan Watson
                     (4 vols., University of Pennsylvania Press: Philadel-
                     phia, 1985)

EEA   *English Episcopal Acta* (Oxford University Press for
                     the British Academy, 1980–)

ed., edn.   edited by, edition

EHR   *English Historical Review*

el.   elected, election

Ep. Cant.   *Chronicles and Memorials of the Reign of Richard I*, ii.
                     Epistolae Cantuarienses, ed. W. Stubbs (RS xxxviii,
                     1865)

Foliot Letters   *Letters and Charters of Gilbert Foliot*, ed. A. Morey and
                     C. N. L. Brooke (Cambridge, 1967)

GEC   G. E. C., *The Complete Peerage of England, Scotland,
                     Ireland, Great Britain and the United Kingdom*, ed.
                     V. Gibbs *et al.*, (13 vols. in 14, London, 1910–59)

Gerald of Wales   *Giraldi Cambrensis Opera*, ed. J. S. Brewer (8 vols., RS
                     xxi, 1861–91)

Gervase   *The Historical Works of Gervase of Canterbury*, ed.
                     W. Stubbs (2 vols., RS lxxiii, 1879–80)

Greatrex, *Biog. Reg.*   J. Greatrex, *Biographical Register of the English Cath-*

	edral Priories of the Province of Canterbury c.1066–1540 (Oxford, 1997)
Greenway, *Fasti*	*Fasti Ecclesiae Anglicanae 1066–1300*, comp. D. E. Greenway, 7 vols.: i. *St Paul's London*; ii. *Monastic Cathedrals*; iii. *Lincoln*; iv. *Salisbury*; v. *Chichester*; vi. *York*; vii. *Bath and Wells* (London, 1968–2001)
HBC	*Handbook of British Chronology*, 3rd edn., ed. E. B. Fryde, D. E. Greenway, S. Porter, and I. Roy (Royal Historical Society Guides and Handbooks, ii: London, 1986)
Hemming	*Hemingi chartularium ecclesiae Wigorniensis*, ed. Thomas Hearne (2 vols., Oxford, 1723). Vol. ii begins at p. 319
HRH	*The Heads of Religious Houses, England and Wales*, i. 940–1216, ed. D. Knowles, C. N. L. Brooke, and V. C. M. London, 2nd edn. with new material by C. N. L. Brooke (Cambridge, 2001)
Institutes	J. A. C. Thomas, *The Institutes of Justinian*. Text, translation, and commentary (Amsterdam–Oxford, 1975)
JB	*Jocelin of Brakelond: Chronicle of the Abbey of Bury St Edmunds*, trans. D. Greenway and J. Sayers (Oxford World's Classics, 1998)
JL	*Regesta Pontificum Romanorum . . . ad annum 1198*, comp. P. Jaffé, rev. S. Loewenfeld, 2nd edn. (2 vols., Leipzig, 1885–8; repr. Graz, 1956)
Jo. Wo.	*The Chronicle of John of Worcester*, ii. 450–1066, ed. R. R. Darlington and P. McGurk, trans. J. Bray and P. McGurk; iii: 1067–1141, ed. P. McGurk (2 vols., OMT 1995–8)
KH	D. Knowles and R. Neville Hadcock, *Medieval Religious Houses England and Wales*, 2nd edn. (London, 1971)
Macray	*Chronicon abbatiae de Evesham*, ed. W. D. Macray (RS xxix, 1863)
Maleczek	W. Maleczek, *Papst und Kardinalkolleg von 1191 bis 1216* (Österreichische Akademie der Wissenschaften, Historisches Institut beim Österreichischen Kulturinstitut in Rom: Vienna, 1984)
MGH	*Monumenta Germaniae Historica*, ed. G. H. Pertz *et al.* (Hanover, Berlin, etc., 1826–)
M. O.	D. Knowles, *The Monastic Order in England*, 2nd edn. (Cambridge, 1963)

Mon. Angl.	Sir William Dugdale, *Monasticon Anglicanum*, ed. J. Caley, H. Ellis, and B. Bandinel (6 vols. in 8, London, 1846)
NMT	Nelson's Medieval Texts
Novels	*Novellae, Corpus Iuris Civilis*, iii, ed. R. Schoell and G. Kroll (Berlin, 1954)
n.s.	new series
OMT	Oxford Medieval Texts
P	A. Potthast, *Regesta Pontificum Romanorum ab 1198 ad 1304* (2 vols., Leipzig, 1885–). (All references are to numbers)
PL	*Patrologia Latina*, ed. J.-P. Migne (221 vols., Paris, 1841–64)
PN	English Place Name Society volumes
PRS	Pipe Roll Society
PUE	*Papsturkunden in England*, ed. W. Holtzmann (3 vols. in 4, Abhandlungen der Gesellschaft der Wissenschaften zu Göttingen, phil. hist. Klasse, new series xxv, 3rd series xiv–xv, xxxiii: Berlin, 1930, 1935–6; Göttingen, 1952)
Regesta	*Regesta Regum Anglo-Normannorum 1066–1154*, ed. H. W. C. Davis, C. Johnson, H. A. Cronne, and R. H. C. Davis (4 vols., Oxford, 1913–69)
Reg. Inn. III	*Die Register Innocenz' III.*, ed. O. Hageneder, A. Haidacher, W. Maleczek, Alfred A. Strnad, Andrea Sommerlechner, John C. Moore, and Herwig Weigl (5 vols. (continuing), Publikationen der Abteilung für historische Studien des Österreichischen Kulturinstituts in Rom: Graz–Cologne, Rome–Vienna, 1964-)
Reg. Malmesbury	*Registrum Malmesburiense*, ed. J. S. Brewer (2 vols., RS lxxii, 1879–80)
RS	The Chronicles and Memorials of Great Britain and Ireland during the Middle Ages, published under the direction of the Master of the Rolls ('Rolls Series') (99 vols., London, 1858–96)
RSB	References to the Rule of St Benedict are given with their chapter numbers. Justin Mc Cann's edition, *The Rule of St Benedict* (London, 1951), provides a translation.
Sawyer	P. H. Sawyer, *Anglo-Saxon Charters: An Annotated List and Bibliography* (London, 1968)
Sayers, *PJD*	J. E. Sayers, *Papal Judges Delegate in the Province of Canterbury (1198–1254)* (Oxford, 1971)

SLI	*Selected Letters of Pope Innocent III concerning England (1198–1216)*, ed. C. R. Cheney and W. H. Semple (NMT 1953)
trans.	translated by, translation
VCH	Victoria History of the Counties of England
Wendover	*Rogeri de Wendover Chronica sive Flores Historiarum*, ed. H. O. Coxe (4 vols., English Historical Soc., 1841)
X	*Decretales, Corpus Iuris Canonici*, ii, ed. E. Friedberg (Leipzig, 1881)

Abbreviations of English Counties

Berks.	Berkshire
Bucks.	Buckinghamshire
Cambs.	Cambridgeshire
Ches.	Cheshire
Derbs.	Derbyshire
Glos.	Gloucestershire
Hants.	Hampshire
Herefs.	Herefordshire
Herts.	Hertfordshire
Hunts.	Huntingdonshire
Lancs.	Lancashire
Leics.	Leicestershire
Lincs.	Lincolnshire
Middx.	Middlesex
Norf.	Norfolk
Northants.	Northamptonshire
Oxon.	Oxfordshire
Salop	Shropshire
Staffs.	Staffordshire
Warws.	Warwickshire
Wilts.	Wiltshire
Worcs.	Worcestershire
Yorks.	Yorkshire

N.B. Numbers given in bold type are references to the paragraph numbers of the text and translation.

SIGLA

Byrhtferth   'Vita S. Ecgwini', London, BL, Cotton MS Nero E i, pt 1, fos. 24^v–34^v; ed. J. A. Giles in *Vita Quorundum* [sic] *Anglo-Saxonum* (Caxton Soc., 1854), pp. 349–96

C   London, BL, Cotton MS Augustus II 11

DE   Dominic of Evesham, 'Vita S. Ecgwini'

DE i   Book I, ed. M. Lapidge in *Analecta Bollandiana*, xcvi (1978), 77–104, from two manuscripts: (H), Hereford Cathedral Library MS P 7 vi, fos. 234–49, and (D) Dublin, Trinity College MS 172, pp. 317–34

DE ii   Book II, not edited by M. Lapidge as above. Thomas follows it closely. The few variations that have been noted refer to M. Lapidge's unpublished transcript which he most generously lent us.

H   London, BL, Harley MS 3763

M   *Mon. Angl.* ii, nums. xxvii, xxviii, pp. 23–5. Original lost

R   Oxford, Bodleian Library, MS Rawlinson A 287

V   London, BL, Cotton MS Vespasian B XXIV

INTRODUCTION

I. THOMAS'S LIFE AND WORK

We should probably have little record of Thomas of Marlborough, who in all likelihood would have lived a reasonably uneventful life, had it not been for three events: the provision of an evil abbot, Roger Norreis, to the abbacy of Evesham by Archbishop Baldwin and King Richard I, in 1190; the arrival of a reforming bishop, Mauger of Worcester, to visit the community in 1202; and, as a result of this attempt, a sensational lawsuit which was pursued at Rome before Pope Innocent III.

These events provide the core of Thomas's *History*.[1] The *History* consists of three books. It is preceded by the *Life of St Odulf*, the *Acts of Worthy Men*, and the *Life of St Wigstan*.[2] These Lives and Acts of Evesham saints and worthies formed a prelude to Book I, the *Life of St Ecgwine*, and Book II, the *Miracles of St Ecgwine*. Ecgwine was Evesham's premier saint, the third bishop of Worcester, and the house's first abbot. Book III is divided into five parts. Part I is the history of the community and the *Lives and Deeds* of its abbots from the eighth century to Thomas's own lifetime. Part II opens with the proposed visitation by Mauger, bishop of Worcester, the diocesan. Part III records the proceedings before the papal curia, leading up to the high excitement of the declaration of the abbey's exemption from the bishop. Part IV is concerned with three matters: (1) the papal decision on Evesham's jurisdiction over the surrounding churches of the Vale, (2) the visit of the papal legate, John of Ferentino, cardinal deacon of S. Maria in via Lata, to investigate the state of internal affairs under Abbot Norreis, and (3) the consequent drawing up of an agreement between the abbot and the convent over the customs and disposition of the revenues of the monastery in 1206. Part V recounts

---

[1] Macray called the work a 'Chronicle'. It is in fact, however, not a chronicle in the sense of a chronological account of events, but rather a distinct 'History', with material arranged to argue and explain a particular theme.

[2] These works were printed by Macray as an Appendix, see below, p. lxiv. They are not an integral part of the *History*, which is concerned with the status of the abbey and its founding saint, Ecgwine, and so are not edited here. The first two are attributed to Prior Dominic, the third is Thomas's work, but he wrote it before embarking on the *History*.

the continuing tyranny of Abbot Norreis, his deposition by the legate Nicholas, bishop of Tusculum, in 1213, and the election of a successor, Randulf, prior of Worcester, as abbot. It is followed by a return (still within Part V) to the *Lives and Deeds* of the abbots of the house, first Randulf and then Thomas himself.[3]

The whole purpose of the *History* as conceived by Thomas was to support and boost the status of the abbey of Evesham. The plan was very carefully constructed. It needed first of all the firm foundation— the bedrock—of early saints. Before the opening of Book I, Thomas accordingly arranged the *Life of St Odulf*, the *Acts of Worthy Men*, and the *Life of St Wigstan*. In such an ambitious undertaking as his, the work of previous writers was necessarily included. The *Life of St Odulf* and the *Acts of Worthy Men* were the work of an Evesham prior of the twelfth century, Prior Dominic; the *Life of St Wigstan* he had composed himself.[4] These Lives and Acts, indeed, point the way towards the shining and essential figure of Ecgwine, the saintly founder of Evesham, whose Life and Miracles form the subject of the first two books. These two books were based on a *Life of St Ecgwine* by the same Prior Dominic, who in turn had built his account on earlier sources.[5] Thomas, for his part, abbreviated and altered Dominic's Book I to suit his own purposes. Between Books I and II he included twelve readings for the feast of the translation of St Ecgwine.[6] Then he proceeded to Dominic's second book, which, apart from some minor re-arrangement at the commencement, he preserved almost intact and word for word. Book III, with its five parts, is almost all Thomas's work down to the account of the election of a new abbot to succeed the deposed Roger Norreis and Thomas's final warning comments. The first part of Book III, however, was based on earlier accounts, mainly of the *Lives and Deeds* of the abbots before Thomas's time, some of which were probably written by Dominic in the early twelfth century.

From the end of Part I to the first few folios of Part V, it is all Thomas recording contemporary history that he had witnessed

---

[3] See below, p. lxv.

[4] Thomas specifically states that such an account had not been written before (44), but P. A. Hayward has argued from the manuscript tradition that there was an earlier source on which he based his work, possibly a *Vita* written by Dominic, cited in *William of Malmesbury: Gesta Regum Anglorum*, ii, ed. R. M. Thomson in collaboration with M. Winterbottom (OMT, 1999), p. 201.

[5] See below, pp. xxx and lxiv.

[6] See below, p. lxiv.

between the 1190s and 1213. Over this period Thomas had played a major role in the history of the Evesham community, its aims, aspirations, and achievements. The end of Thomas's work reiterates the personal nature of much of the account. By 1213 the community had acquired very considerable privileges: these Thomas was determined to maintain and protect. Hence his advice for the future when, as he sees it, the abbey might be vacant and threatened again by the diocesan. A new abbot, he says, was to be elected, confirmed—by the pope alone—and blessed, in accordance with the privileges that the monastery of Evesham had acquired. Thomas emphasized the importance of these newly won privileges. 'See that you do not lose the benefit of them. If you do so, God forbid, you will be reduced to slavery and be for ever wretched' (**509**). These are probably the last words he wrote. The *History* is thus very much a history of the importance of status, of an abbey that answered to the pope without an intermediary, whose privileges, so hardly won, had to be watched over and maintained.

How had Thomas come to be the author of such a book? What is known about him comes almost entirely from his own comments in the *History* itself, and from the *Lives and Deeds* of the abbots, which follows the *History* and recounts his progress through the monastic offices of dean, sacrist, prior, and finally abbot.[7] He studied first at Paris, most likely Arts, under the theologian, Stephen Langton, later archbishop of Canterbury (d. 1228). At that time, Richard Poore, who was to become a notable dean and bishop of Salisbury (d. 1235), was his fellow student: this was probably in the 1180s (**450**).[8] He went next to Oxford. He describes John of Tynemouth, Simon of Sywell, and Master Honorius as his 'masters in the schools' (**230**). The common bond between these three is that they were all lawyers and canonists, active at Oxford, so presumably it was canon law that he studied there. This could have been as early as 1188×1193. We also know that he taught at Oxford, before he was professed at Evesham (**522**). His teaching must have been in the growing university because there were no grammar schools of importance at Oxford, such as those attached to cathedrals. The statement that he taught also at

---

[7] The present edition includes the *Lives* down to the death of Thomas, as abbot of the house in 1236.

[8] J. Baldwin, *Masters, Princes and Merchants: the Social Views of Peter the Chanter and his Circle*, 2 vols. (Princeton, 1970), i. 26, 30, gives the dates 1180s to 1206 for Langton's period in Paris, with the earliest secure date for his lectures being between 1187 and 1193.

Exeter (which is in the section of the *History* which was re-copied in the fifteenth century) is likely to be the result of a miscopying or mishearing of the text.[9] He was thus no ordinary young novice when he arrived at Evesham to be professed in 1199 or 1200 (**516**).[10] There is evidence that he had some connection with the monastery at Evesham before this date, because Thomas informs us, before he writes of the 'intrusion' of Abbot Norreis in 1190, that the previous section, terminating with the abbacy of the Cluniac, Abbot Adam, who died on 12 November 1189, was 'a faithful account of these deeds as I either learned them or saw them myself, or as I heard and ascertained them from the trustworthy accounts of others' (**184**). Furthermore, in Thomas's *Life of St Wigstan*, there is a reference to his submitting the account to Archbishop Baldwin of Canterbury for his approval. Baldwin thought that Thomas had not put enough emphasis on the miracle of St Wigstan's growing hair. Accordingly, he sent two delegates, Paul, abbot of Leicester, and Baldwin, prior of Monks Kirby, to Wistow to verify the miracle of the growing hair.[11] As Archbishop Baldwin died in 1190, this has to mean that Thomas had a definite connection before that date with the convent at Evesham, whose brethren had asked him to write the account and to abridge the already existing life of St Ecgwine (**44**). By 1202, given his previous training and career, Thomas must have been at least in his thirties, so is likely to have been born between 1160 and 1170.[12]

It may be asked what Evesham had to offer to a well-trained clerk such as Thomas. Had he hoped to stay in the schools, for which he would have needed a patron and a benefice, or to enter the household

---

[9] The confusion is commonplace. It occurs also with William of Drogheda who appears in one of eight manuscripts (V) as *regenti in legibus Exonie*; in all the other texts the scribes have it correctly *Oxonie*; see J. E. Sayers, 'William of Drogheda and the English Canonists', in *Proceedings of the Seventh International Congress of Medieval Canon Law 1984*, ed. P. Linehan (Monumenta Iuris Canonici, ser. C, subsidia viii, Città del Vaticano, 1988), 205–22, at p. 205 n. 2, on the manuscripts. The mistake also occurs because of bad writing in BL Royal MS 9 E VII fo. 198ra. H. Kantorowicz (*Bractonian problems* (Glasgow, 1941), p. 17 n. 2) was the first to question the accuracy of the Oxford *and* Exeter comment. But H. G. Richardson ('Azo, Drogheda, and Bracton', *EHR*, lix (1944), 22–47, at p. 41 n. 3) did not accept the suggestion of inaccuracy in the text. While Exeter had had some importance in the study of law in its cathedral school, there is no evidence from any other source that Thomas was ever at Exeter, even as a schoolmaster. F. Barlow, however, in *EEA 11, Exeter*, p. lvii, and R. Bartlett, amongst others, have maintained a belief in the text as it stands.

[10] In 1202, he was said to be in his third year as a monk; see below, **516**.

[11] *Life and Miracles of St Wigstan*, printed in Macray, pp. 332–4.

[12] His contemporary, Richard Poore, may well have been born in or before 1167; see *EEA 18, Salisbury, 1078–1217*, ed. B. R. Kemp, p. lv.

of a high ecclesiastic, perhaps the archbishop? We do not know. As it developed, his career was much like that of Samson of Bury St Edmunds, who later regretted not staying in the schools and who had perhaps craved a career as a beneficed secular before he turned finally to the monastic life.[13] If, like Samson, Thomas had hoped for a more exalted position as a secular, there is no hint of it.

Thomas's family

There is remarkably little in the *History* about Thomas's origins. All we know is that he had a uterine brother—i.e. they shared the same mother, but had different fathers—whom he does not name, and who was not a monk. There is reference also to a cousin, Muriel (of Chepstow), who had a house in Evesham. The appellation 'of Marlborough' is found at least by the time he became prior (1218), presumably being used to distinguish him from other Thomases in the house. The first occurrences are in contemporary thirteenth-century rubrics in Book III Parts II and IV, fos. 150^r, 170^v (213, 395), where he occurs as 'de Merlebergia': the other occurrences are all in the replacement leaves in Part V, fos. 183^v, 184^r, and 185^r (516, 522, 531), written in the fifteenth century, in rubrics describing Thomas's work as dean and sacrist, then prior, and finally abbot. Clearly by this time he had become Thomas 'of Marlborough' or 'de Marlebarwe' in the house's historical memory. Marlborough in Wiltshire appears as 'Merleberge' in 1086 and 'Merleberga' in 1130 and is the most likely identification.[14] If Thomas did, in fact, come from Marlborough in Wiltshire, a royal borough, the nearest Benedictine abbey would have been Malmesbury. But the reasons for the choice of a particular community could be influenced by so many factors unknown to us that it is idle to speculate.

[13] Cf. R. W. Southern, *Robert Grosseteste: The Growth of an English Mind in Medieval Europe* (Oxford, 1986), ch. 3, esp. pp. 50–3; and for Samson, see *JB*, pp. 33, 40.

[14] Marlborough derives from Mærla's barrow, or mound, or perhaps, less likely, from *meargealla*, meaning gentian; PN *Wilts.*, pp. 297–8. Malborough, near Kingsbridge in Devon, is found as 'Merleberg' in 1275: it has the same possible derivation as Marlborough, PN *Devon*, Exeter, p. lvii. Neither it nor Mappleborough Green in Studley (Warws.), which occurs in an Evesham source of *c.*1200 as Mapellesborghe, and as Mabbelberwe in 1272, seem likely candidates for Thomas's toponym, though the later rendering may explain the 15th-cent. scribe's Marle*barwe*. Maugersbury (Glos.), which belonged to the monks' chamber, and is close to Stow-on-the-Wold, occurs as 'Malgaresburi' and 'Malgarisbury' (416, and Macray, p. 298): the *gar* element rules that out. There are no other place-names or local names that are possible contenders for Thomas's place of origin.

Proctor

Circumstances were to thrust Thomas into prominence. In 1202 the newly appointed Bishop Mauger of Worcester attempted to visit Evesham (Part II). From this point until the settlement of the case, Marlborough's activities were taken up with the convent's determined struggle to prove its exemption from the bishop. For its defiance in refusing entry to the bishop, the convent was excommunicated. The monks sought to bring the abbey's case before the archbishop of Canterbury. But the case was too complex for settlement by any other court than the final one and appeal was made to the pope. The main case over the exemption from the diocesan and the complementary case of the monastery's jurisdiction over the local area known as the Vale were fought out at Rome before the masterly Pope Innocent III and his advisers (Part III). Thomas went to Rome to present the abbey's case and during this time he attended the schools at Bologna. In the struggle against the bishop, the abbot and convent attempted to present a united front, although the infamous Abbot Roger Norreis had never been accepted by the monks. He had mercilessly tyrannized over them, keeping them short of food and clothing, calling them 'dogs', acting more like a layman than a priest, and wasting the convent's lands. He was a drunkard and a lecher, and reputed to be a murderer. But he was adept at making friends in influential places, which allowed him to be promoted and to survive for so long without censure. It was agreed that any charges against the abbot would not be raised at Rome, though the abbot's treatment of the convent's proctors at Rome was infamous. After the triumph in 1205, when the abbey's exemption was declared, and the judgment on jurisdiction over the Vale in 1207, the main struggle was to control Abbot Roger Norreis and to restore the monastery (Parts IV, V).

Dean of the Vale (1206)

In both the spiritual and the temporal improvement of the monastery, Thomas was closely involved, and from 1206 he acted as dean of the Vale (516, 520). The dean had jurisdiction over certain parishes within the vicinity of Evesham, acting as an archdeacon in the exempt area. This office was greatly enhanced by Thomas's efforts. Matters were made more difficult by the Interdict on the English Church from 1208 to 1214, and, indeed, by the newly won exemption from

any kind of correction by the diocesan. The convent was not finally relieved of Abbot Norreis until his deposition in 1213. As dean of the Vale, Marlborough attended the Fourth Lateran Council in Rome with the new abbot, Randulf, and while they were there the pope approved on 16 February 1216 the customs and disposition of the revenues of the abbey (521). In this remarkable document, Thomas doubtless had a hand.

Sacrist (1217)

In 1217 he was made sacrist. The biographer of the abbots is fond of detailing building works—the responsibility of the sacrist. According to him, Thomas, as sacrist, repaired much of the damage that had been caused to the windows and tombs in the presbytery by the collapse of the tower (519). He renewed the shrine of St Wigstan, had a reading-desk made for the choir, put a stove in the church underneath the clock, and had twelve albs made (521). All this he did in the year before he was appointed prior and much of it was paid for by his careful financial management as sacrist.

Prior (1218–29)

During his time as prior (522–30), Marlborough completed what has misleadingly been called his chronicle of the Abbey. It is in fact a *History* – a unique account of the lawsuit fought out at Rome, which he prefaced with an abbreviated edition of Prior Dominic's *Life of St Ecgwine* and the *Lives and Deeds* of the abbots up to the time of Abbot Norreis (1191). The whole of the description of the lawsuit is written with a frankness and a verve which makes the work remarkable on those counts alone. His vivid description of the journey to Rome, of the way in which the curia operated, of the pope and the cardinals, of the trials and tribulations of the petitioner, are without parallel at this date. He was observant and perceptive, and could tell a good story. There are small and important details: the advice of the pope to go to study at Bologna (which he did for six months) (274), Marlborough's collapsing with joy when the exemption was declared (316), and many other memorable vignettes of persons and places. The great speech made by Thomas nearly ten years later before the legate, Nicholas, bishop of Tusculum,[15] prefacing the final fall of Roger Norreis,

---

[15] Mistakenly identified as Pandulf by M. Bateson in *DNB* xiv (1909), p. 585, and G. G. Coulton in *Five Centuries of Religion*, 4 vols. (Cambridge, 1929–50), ii. 366.

evokes the drama of the occasion (461–84). Marlborough's subsequent career was taken up with paying off the debts consequent upon the lawsuit and maintaining every aspect of the abbey's rights, in the maintenance and possible extension of which he may perhaps have condoned forgeries. He did, however, submit the convent to archiepiscopal visitation.[16] The continuation of the *History* includes the *Lives and Deeds* of the abbots, and from here we learn that it was due to him that the customs and revenues were finally written down and approved at the time of the Lateran Council (518; cf. 239).[17] On entering office as prior, Thomas is recorded as possessing a considerable number of books, including law books, unfortunately not specified. There were also works on natural science, classical texts, sermons, commentaries, and books on grammar and music. He had several books produced, including what is now Rawlinson MS A 287 to fo. 181ᵛ (his *History*),[18] and he purchased others (522–3). He continued to embellish the church, particularly concentrating on the story of St Ecgwine in the stained glass of the presbytery and on Ecgwine's shrine, for which he built a throne.[19]

Abbot (1229–36)

On the death of Abbot Randulf, Thomas was elected abbot on 20 December 1229, confirmed by Pope Gregory IX in 1230, blessed by the bishop of Coventry, and finally, after the king had granted possession of the abbey, installed by the bishop at Michaelmas. He was to rule the abbey for almost seven years (531–46). The period during which the king had had possession was costly, as was the election process, so Thomas began his abbacy in debt. However, judicious management enabled him to enhance the dignity and appearance of the church, to construct comfortable quarters for the abbot, and to build his own marble tomb, which had superimposed on it an effigy of himself in pontificals. He died at Evesham on 12 September 1236, after suffering latterly some physical incapacity.[20]

[16] See App. IV.
[17] See below, p. liv fol.
[18] See below, pp. lxvi–lxxii.
[19] See below, p. lii.
[20] On 29 July 1236, Pope Gregory IX had ordered the bishop of Coventry, following the petition of Thomas to resign, owing to infirmity, to assign him a portion and to order the convent to proceed to the election of a new abbot, but Thomas died before any arrangement for the election of a successor had been made; *CPL* i. 156.

When was the *History* written?

The main evidence for the date of Thomas's writing is his own statement: 'I was made dean [in 1206] and have held that office continually until the present time of writing, even during my time as prior' (380). We also have the firm evidence of the author of the *Lives and Deeds* of the abbots, in speaking of Thomas as dean and sacrist, that Thomas composed (*composuit*) 'the book above', which contained the history of the great lawsuit, when he was prior (517). This author also states that Thomas as prior had the Haimo on the Apocalypse and the lives and acts of the patrons and abbots of Evesham bound up (*fecit*) in one volume (523), that is, the present Rawlinson volume as far as fo. 181^v (the election, confirmation and benediction of Abbot Randulf). Two replacement leaves which were written in the fifteenth century (one folio, 182^{r-v}, two-thirds down the second column) complete Thomas's own composition, reporting the payment of the Roman creditors for the privileges, and giving his advice on the importance of the preservation and use of these privileges (505, 509). The *History* then reverts to 'the works or actions of the abbots', first Abbot Randulf, and then Thomas himself, all copied in the fifteenth century.

The putting together of the volume undoubtedly took place under Thomas as prior. We should consider here the notes in the various parts of the text relating to Thomas's association with it.[21] We have the following descriptions—*editus* ('edited by'), *abbreviatus* ('abbreviated by'), *collectus et compositus* ('collected and compiled by'), and *fecit . . . in uolumine* ('had produced'). 'Edited' is found on fo. 121^r. Thomas 'edited' the life and miracles of St Wigstan (see 44–5).[22] Editing appears to have the meaning of authored. The First Book, the Life of St Ecgwine, is described as 'abbreviated' by Thomas the prior (fo. 124^r; 5).[23] Abbreviated means quite extensive revision. Then follow readings for the feast of St Ecgwine's translation: virtually the work of Thomas (fo. 130^r; 44). The Second Book, the Miracles of St Ecgwine, is said to have been 'edited', i.e. authored by Dominic, prior of Evesham: it was only very lightly edited in the modern sense of the word by Thomas (fo. 132^v; 65).[24] Book III, Thomas's own book, is

---

[21] See B. Guenée, 'L'historien par les mots', in Guenée, *Politique et histoire au moyen-âge* (Publications de la Sorbonne, Série Réimpressions 2: Paris, 1981), pp. 221–37, esp. 229–32. [22] See below, p. lxiv. [23] Ibid.

[24] Below, ibid. See M. Lapidge, 'Dominic of Evesham "Vita S. Ecgwini Episcopi et Confessoris"', *AB*, xcvi (1978), 65–104, at p. 104.

'collected and compiled' by Thomas the prior of Evesham 'from various charters, documents and manifest deeds' (fo. 140^r; **113**); and 'compiled' is used by the author of the life of Thomas in the *Lives and Deeds* of the abbots in describing what was undoubtedly this manuscript (fo. 183^v; **517**).

An examination of the manuscript shows immediately that it went through several stages of revision. Thomas may have written an account, at least in the form of notes, at the time of the case at Rome, or soon after the settlement of the main case and his return to England, that is, between 1206 and 1208.[25] The second stage in the work's construction must come after 1214, Abbot Randulf's election, confirmation, and blessing. And the last datable note of Thomas's activities as an author must come after 13 April 1214, the payment of the Roman merchants and the bringing of the privileges to Evesham on the second Sunday after Easter 'Misericordia Domini' (13 April 1214), for which Thomas as dean was so grateful that he made provision from the income of the deanery for a *caritas* of wine to be given to the convent on that day in future (**505**). The inclusion of the customs and disposition of the revenues of the house, in the name of Abbot Randulf, which is curiously placed in the middle of material for 1206, is clearly an addition by Thomas. But the legate did not confirm this text. The text he confirmed (in 1206) is of the less detailed arrangement made between the abbot (unnamed) and the convent, which is printed below in Appendix II A. Nor is Randulf's document as included in the *History* the exact text of what the pope confirmed after the Lateran Council in February 1216, for Thomas is recorded as prior, which he did not become until 1218, and mention is made of the Benedictine General Chapter not held until the same year, that is two years later. This, therefore, has to have been composed, as it stands in the book, after 1218.[26] We might argue that the final part on Abbot Norreis was perhaps not written until after Norreis's death in 1224,[27] in which case we are looking at a final

---

[25] The statement of A. Boureau ('How law came to the monks; the use of law in English society at the beginning of the thirteenth century', *Past and Present*, clxvii (2000), 29–74, at p. 29) that Thomas wrote the section dealing with the case at Rome 'about 1225' is not based on any precise evidence. The date of *c*.1225 presumably refers loosely to the statement that the book was 'composed' when Thomas was prior.

[26] See below, pp. lv–lvi, and lix.

[27] The details of the date of his reinstitution to Penwortham, and of his death are extremely vague: 'about five years after his deposition . . .', and 'he lived there for almost six years' (see **498–9**).

date between 1224 and 1230, when Thomas ceased to be prior, for when the Rawlinson text fos. 1^r–181^r were put together and used in the monastery at Evesham. There is nothing so far known to define that date more closely.

After the final folios of Thomas's 'authored' book comes a return to the *Lives and Deeds* of the abbots, starting with Abbot Randulf. We know from the biography of Thomas as dean that the book was all of one piece during the time he was prior (517, and see 523). In other words the 'works' of Abbot Randulf were securely there. But the present pages are replacements of the fifteenth century that would have allowed for adjustments to be made. Of the persons likely to have written the record of Abbot Randulf, Thomas, the prior, might seem the most likely candidate. The author, whoever he was, wrote it when Thomas was still prior, for so Thomas is referred to in connection with a maple-wood cup that Abbot Randulf bequeathed to the convent and *Prior* Thomas had coated with silver-gilt (515). Did Thomas even write his own biography as dean and sacrist, then prior, and finally abbot? The possibility is there. What is obvious is the unusual detail of the accounts. Whoever did write the account of Thomas as prior stated that 'we have combined the less important deeds of T. the monk with our description of his major deeds, so that you may by his example remedy at least minor faults'. The author clearly had been totally subjected to Thomas's aims and aspirations, providing a history that made the acts of later abbots look somewhat tame.

Thomas and the Law

Thomas's career took place at a time when the study of law began to develop in the Oxford schools. Throughout his work there are citations from the written laws: the canon law, the *canones*, and the Roman law, the *leges*, or *iura civilia*. He also displays a knowledge of the *ius commune* (the Roman law as applied in and adapted to most of medieval Europe) and of English feudal laws and customs.[28] He is

---

[28] For a brief description of the *ius commune*, see R. H. Helmholz, *The Ius Commune in England* (Oxford, 2001), pp. 10–15; P. Stein, *Roman Law in Medieval History* (Cambridge, 1999), pp. 42, 52, 61, 65; and for a survey of later views on the relationship between the English common law and the *ius commune* (the 'common law of Europe'), D. Ibbetson, *Common Law and the 'Ius Commune'* (Selden Society, 2001), pp. 3–6. The term *ius commune* has been retained in the translation below to save any confusion with the English common law. For Thomas's citations of the *ius commune*, see below, 245, 302–3, 357, 381–2, and for his citations of English feudal laws and customs, 229 at n. 2

thus one of a small and crucial number of witnesses to the development of the early English law schools. He is also an observer of the importance of procedural practice, especially at the curia. Finally, as we shall argue below, he was a primary influence in the reform and committing to writing of the customs of his house and the apportionment and control of the revenues, in accordance with the Benedictine Rule.

To begin with the canon law. A chance reference reveals that Thomas had received some instruction from the English canonists, John of Tynemouth, Simon of Sywell, and Master Honorius, which must have taken place in Oxford. Despite the efforts of major scholars, the early Oxford schools are still shrouded in mist.[29] In all likelihood the instruction was practical and procedural. However, by the 1150s, Englishmen were known at Bologna, the only university where the study of the two laws, Roman and canon, was advanced, and probably at the time of Thomas's arrival in 1205, at least two Englishmen, Alan and Gilbert, were at work there collecting recent decretals. Gilbert's collection had already appeared in 1203–4, and Alan's was circulating from 1206. It is possible, too, that John of Wales, who made a compilation out of Alan and Gilbert's work between 1210 and 1215,[30] was teaching in Bologna at this time.

How much Roman law Thomas was able to absorb in his six months at Bologna is difficult to assess. Although he makes reference to the teaching of Azo, it is noticeable that frequently his citations of Roman law are of texts that were commented on by his master, John

---

and **474**. Boureau's article, 'How law came to the monks', gives a general picture of the infiltration of legal knowledge into the monasteries, and includes a section on Evesham, but it needs to be treated with some caution, especially in the translation—for example *Sancte pater* (Holy father) is rendered as Saint Peter—and in some of the general assumptions. On feudal law, see W. Ullmann, *Law and Politics in the Middle Ages* (London, 1975), pp. 216–17.

[29] See esp. the sections by R. W. Southern, 'From schools to university', and L. E. Boyle, 'Canon law before 1380', in *History of the University of Oxford*, ed. J. I. Catto, i (Oxford, 1984), pp. 1–36, and 531–64; P. Stein, 'Vacarius and the civil law', in *Church and Government in the Middle Ages: Essays presented to C. R. Cheney*, ed. C. N. L. Brooke, D. E. Luscombe, G. H. Martin, and D. M. Owen (Cambridge, 1976), pp. 119–37; and F. de Zulueta and P. Stein, *The Teaching of Roman Law in England around 1200* (Selden Soc. supplementary series, 8: London, 1990), pp. xxii–xxvii, and xxxv–xxxvii.

[30] *Compilatio Secunda* of *Quinque Compilationes*, ed. E. Friedberg (Leipzig, 1882). The suggestion of J. C. Russell, *Dictionary of Writers of Thirteenth Century England* (*BIHR* special suppl. iii (1936), p. 78) that this is the same man as a monk proctor of Malmesbury, who appears in certain judge-delegate cases, is without any foundation.

of Tynemouth. However, his stay clearly enabled him to engage the very best legal advice for his case. Nor did he overlook the importance of those skilled in the rapidly developing court procedure in cases that were brought to the curia. He is one of only two known eyewitnesses whose recorded observations have survived, giving some detail of the procedure before the courts of *audientia* and of *audientia litterarum contradictarum.*[31]

Throughout the convent's struggle with Abbot Norreis over his depredation of the common property, Thomas also exhibits some knowledge of English feudal laws and customs as they affected assarts and encroachment. Over the part he played in the drawing up of the written constitutions he is quite boastful, realizing that this was as important to Evesham as its exemption. The 'law' of the legates, that is the declared decisions of the legates *a latere*, who represented the pope at the highest level, is as carefully recorded as the proceedings before the pope himself. It was the legate John of Ferentino who presided over the first written customs, and the legate Nicholas, bishop of Tusculum, who finally deposed Abbot Norreis after careful judicial proceedings. It may be thought from Thomas's account of the proceedings before the pope that Master Robert de Clipstone, his adversary as the proctor of the bishop of Worcester, was not as good a lawyer as Thomas himself, and that Thomas exaggerated Clipstone's weaknesses. The main difference between the two men, however, was that Thomas had the passion and imagination necessary in the winning of cases, while Clipstone, acting on behalf of the bishop, was much less engaged. As far as can be judged at a distance of nearly eight centuries, Thomas's reporting of the proceedings in his *History* seems fair and just. It has to be borne in mind, however, that the slant of his writing was always and not unnaturally towards Evesham.

---

[31] The other eyewitness account is *Chronicon Montis Sereni*, ed. E. Ehrenfeuchter, *MGH Scriptores*, xxiii (Hanover, 1874), pp. 130–226 at 200, but this is from considerably later, 1222–3, probably Feb. 1223, during the pontificate of Pope Honorius III.

II. THE ABBEY OF EVESHAM

A. STATUS AND EXEMPTION

The Evesham historians and the historic past

Legend has it from at least the early eleventh century[32] that on the banks of the River Avon, at the place where a shepherd had had a vision of the blessed Virgin Mary, Ecgwine, the third bishop of Worcester (the Hwicce),[33] established a religious community on the site given by King Æthelred, son of Penda of Mercia. According to the tradition held in the Benedictine abbey of Evesham in the twelfth century, in which presumably the young monks were instructed, these events took place early in the eighth century, as recorded in Ecgwine's foundation charter of 714 (27–33). To seal the house's promise and fortunes, the founder, accompanied by King Cenred of Mercia and King Offa of the East Saxons, who had contributed further to the endowment, set off for Rome to secure the approval of Pope Constantine and to place the abbey 'under his control and disposition' (29–30). Two papal privileges were supposedly issued by Constantine in 709 and 713 (318–23, 324–8), and addressed to Berhtwald, archbishop of Canterbury (693–731).[34] The foundations of the house were thus 'set' in these three documents.

Thereafter, the history of the abbey, like that of all institutions, religious and secular, was a history of triumphs and setbacks, of high points and low, which were produced by external conditions—social, political, and dynastic—as well as by internal factors. As the monks were taught to see it, the high points were the early days of the founder, which was the springtime of the endowments and privileges, and the period when Evesham's profile was high in the eleventh

---

[32] According to Byrhtferth of Ramsey (c.970–c.1020), see below, pp. xxix–xxx.

[33] The kingdom of the Hwicce was situated in the West Midlands with its episcopal see at Worcester. From the time of King Penda of Mercia in the early 7th cent., the Hwicce were subject to Mercian lordship, becoming subkings. On the Hwicce, see in general, D. Hooke, *The Anglo-Saxon Landscape: The Kingdom of the Hwicce* (Manchester, 1985), and P. Sims-Williams, *Religion and Literature in Western England 600–800* (Cambridge Studies in Anglo-Saxon England, 3: Cambridge, 1990). M. Lapidge (in *AB*, xcvi (1978), p. 102 at note 10.30) suggested that Alcester was possibly a royal residence of the kings of the Hwicce, but their chief centre is likely to have been Worcester.

[34] The texts of the two Constantinian privileges (JL 2147, 2149) are not included in Thomas's account of the foundation of Evesham, but are given later by him at the time of the hearing in the papal curia.

century under remarkable abbots (Ælfweard, Mannig, Æthelwig, and Walter), the days when pilgrims flocked to the tombs of the saints and a party of three set out from Evesham to re-kindle the religious life in the north of England, at Jarrow, Tynemouth, Wearmouth, and Whitby.[35] The low points were when seculars replaced monks between 941 and the end of the tenth century—except for a brief monastic restoration in the years 970–5—when King Æthelred gave the monastery to Bishop Ealdwulf of Worcester (c.996) and when Evesham properties were under attack from the neighbouring bishops of Worcester or from powerful lords such as Odo of Bayeux in the eleventh century. The monks knew about their past from the life of their patron saint, Ecgwine, and the account of his miracles, which were read on the appropriate feast days. They also knew about previous abbots from the *Lives and Deeds* of the abbots that existed in the house possibly from the eleventh century (included in Thomas's Book III Part I) and was continued up to the time Thomas was writing, and, indeed, beyond into the fifteenth century. The roll of abbots from Æthelwig's time included monks from Caen, Jumièges, Gloucester, Christ Church Canterbury, St Augustine's, and La Charité. Abbot Reginald Foliot, in particular, and Abbot Adam were abbots who were remembered for extending the abbey's rights. How much of this account is due to Thomas?

Thomas owed much to earlier Evesham historians and hagiographers. It is impossible to separate the two roles among the Evesham authors. The first historian of whom we have some evidence is Byrhtferth of Ramsey, the author of a *Life of Ecgwine*, written c.1020, for which we are told he had used 'ancient documents'.[36] Byrhtferth's work consisted of a prologue followed by four parts in which he outlined the story of Ecgwine, the third 'presul in regione Merciorum': how he had founded the monastery at Evesham, and had gone to 'the city of Romulus' bound in chains, where he had been miraculously released when the key that he had thrown into the Avon turned up in a fish in

---

[35] On the thrilling story of the Benedictine colonization of the North by the prior of Winchcombe and two monks of Evesham, see *Symeon of Durham, Libellus de exordio atque procursu istius hoc est Dunhelmensis ecclesie*, ed. and trans. D. Rollason (OMT, 2000), pp. 201–11.

[36] Byrhtferth's *Vita S. Ecgwini* is in BL Cotton MS Nero E I pt. 1, fos. 24ᵛ–34ᵛ. It is to be edited by Michael Lapidge for OMT. The sole printed edition is in *Vita Quorundam* [sic] *Anglo-Saxonum*, ed. J. A. Giles (Caxton Soc. London, 1854), pp. 349–96 (cited below as Byrhtferth; see above, Sigla).

the Tiber.[37] The third part described the verbal 'charter' (gift) in Ecgwine's name. It described how King Æthelred had given Flad-bury, the subking Æthelheard had given Stratford, Æthelheard's brother, Osweard, had given twenty hides at Twyford, and King Cenred, Æthelred's successor, eighty hides around Evesham, and how he, Ecgwine, had visited Rome a second time in the company of Kings Cenred and Offa. There 'liberty' had been acquired for the monastery in a document that bore the impression of the seal of the pope. At a council of great men held at Alcester, Berhtwald, archbishop of Canterbury, had composed, at the command of King Cenred, a privilege recording the endowment of 124 hides for the site of the abbey of Evesham: this privilege was then put on the altar. Byrhtferth's final section, IV, concludes with the death of Ecgwine, that is, his 'heavenly birth', and four miracles: that of the nine chains, of the seal that appeared swimming in the Avon on St Ecgwine's day, of the countryman who spilled his own brains, and how—when the church of Evesham was destroyed at the time of Abbot Osweard—the relics of St Ecgwine were miraculously unscathed.

The life of Ecgwine by Byrhtferth formed the basis of Book I of the work of the next historian-hagiographer, Dominic, prior of Evesham, writing about a century later.[38] Dominic's Life of Ecgwine, although based on Byrhtferth's, added significantly to Evesham's history. Dominic followed quite closely Byrhtferth's account of Ecgwine's preaching, rejection, the vision of the Blessed Virgin, and his two visits to Rome, first bound in chains, and then in the company of the kings, when the pope 'made that place (Evesham) free'. But Dominic was able to build on the basis of the information that Byrhtferth had provided. He was the first author to give details of the papal letter, which he dated to 709, and probably used the Liber Pontificalis to identify the pope concerned as Pope Constantine, and not Pope Boniface as Byrhtferth had it.[39] Next, on the basis of the information of the gifts recorded as made to the monastery in Byrhtferth's text, Dominic put these details into the framework of a foundation charter of Ecgwine. He added material that he found in Bede or the Anglo-

---

[37] This was a widespread and popular story that changed with the telling. Byrhtferth, Dominic, and William of Malmesbury, all have different versions; see M. Lapidge in AB xcvi, p. 100 n. to 6. 22.

[38] Dominic also wrote the Acts of Worthy Men and a Life of St Odulf, see above, and a small book on the Miracles of the Blessed Virgin Mary.

[39] Byrhtferth, p. 360. (Boniface V was pope from 619 to 625, and Boniface VI briefly in 896.)

Saxon Chronicle on Archbishop Theodore and King Wihtred of
Kent (not found in Thomas). It was Dominic, too, who provided the
date of 714 for the dedication of the church at Evesham and what he
described as the 'description of the gifts'. In the final part of his
Book I, leading up to the death of Ecgwine, which follows
Byrhtferth closely (including a digression), mention is made of a
'monachilis ordo' at Evesham, following the Rule of St Benedict—a
detail that is lacking in Byrhtferth. Dominic concluded his Book I
with the same four miracles that terminated Byrhtferth's *Life of St
Ecgwine.*

How does Thomas's account of the early years differ from that of
Dominic? The text of Dominic that Thomas had in front of him
must have posed certain problems. First of all, Thomas was anxious
to show that Ecgwine had resigned as bishop of the Hwicce on
becoming abbot of his newly founded community at Evesham (18)—
otherwise exemption for the thirteenth-century abbey would be
almost impossible to prove. He also made it clear that the pope
had confirmed the monastery under the rule of its own abbot, and
threatened anathema on anyone introducing clerks in their place.
While both Dominic and Thomas apparently speak of freedom from
episcopal exactions, Thomas also speaks of the liberties, immunities
and episcopal 'dignities' of the monastery, by which he presumably
means the abbey's jurisdictional and spiritual rights as they had
come to be by his time (19). Thomas attempted to sort out the
problems of the chronology of the early documentation to assuage
any fears that discrepancies might cause the documents to be
suspect. Before introducing the text of Ecgwine's charter of 714,
which he turns into a diploma with subscriptions and clauses of
blessing and sanction, he writes of the charter completed in Rome
and of the charter composed by Berhtwald. This was to demonstrate
that any possessions mentioned that were not in the first two
charters had been legitimately obtained and confirmed. Thomas
also faced the problem of providing dates for the sequence of events.
It was he who provided the dates for Æthelred's donation, 701, for
the visit of the kings to Rome, 709, and for Ecgwine's resignation as
bishop, 714.

Thomas also depended to some degree on the author of the Lives
of the Abbots, now only existing in the version found in his *History*.
In the *Lives and Deeds* of the abbots, the account of the *Life of Abbot
Æthelwig*, who died in 1077, is much more detailed than the accounts

of the other abbots that surround it.[40] In all probability Æthelwig's
Life is the work of the Evesham historian of the twelfth century, Prior
Dominic, which was completed between 1104 and 1110. Dominic
may have had a hand also in the next section on Abbot Walter
(d. 1104), which was added before 1129.[41] Dominic died in or before
1145—there is evidence for his attesting as prior after 1130—but he is
unlikely to have been the person who continued the lives of the abbots
after the death of Abbot Walter in 1104.[42] From then until 1189 they
are scrappy and not very informative and they omit entirely the
abbacy of Robert II (*c.*1121–4). Thomas was clearly not able to find
much on the lives and acts of previous abbots when he came to scour
the muniment room for his *History*.

It is the historian's task to find evidence and to interpret it. The
evidence that has been discovered must be verified, if possible, and
reconciled if it conflicts in any way. A chronology has to be imposed
in order to explain how things came to be as they are. It is in this light
that we should consider many monastic historians who worked on
forged evidence. In some cases Thomas knew that the evidence was
shaky—and in at least one case that it was forged. But certain
distinctions need to be made between fictitious content and forged
charter. In much of his writing he is trying to make sense of the
historic past. How had the community at Evesham come into being
and when exactly did it happen? Earlier historians at Evesham had
already supplied the charter of St Ecgwine—and like other monastic
foundation charters it had undoubtedly been added to and elaborated
over the course of time. It was not the medieval historian's task to cast
out but to explain. It has been remarked that our knowledge of
eighth-century Evesham is limited to 'a thirteenth-century list of
abbots and a mass of late forged charters'.[43] Some five centuries had
passed before Thomas began to write. Undoubtedly there was
considerable activity at Evesham in the early eleventh century,

---

[40] See R. R. Darlington, 'Æthelwig, abbot of Evesham', *EHR*, xlviii (1933), pp. 1–22,
177–98.
[41] On Dominic, see the important work of J. C. Jennings, 'Prior Dominic of Evesham
and the survival of English tradition after the Norman Conquest' (Oxford B.Litt. Thesis,
1958), and 'The writings of Prior Dominic of Evesham', *EHR*, lxxvii (1962), pp. 298–304.
For a list of Dominic's works, and their editions, see R. Sharpe, *Handlist of Latin Writers of
Great Britain and Ireland before 1540* (Publications of the Journal of Medieval Latin, 1:
Brepols, 1997), but Sharpe is wrong in saying that Dominic died in 1125.
[42] Jennings, 'Writings', p. 298, for the date of Dominic's death.
[43] Sims-Williams, *Religion and Literature*, p. 144.

when Byrhtferth, in his Life of St Ecgwine, provided an account of the gifts and endowments. Then in another burst of writing in the twelfth century, Dominic in his *Vita* drew up (or, just possibly, found) a charter for Ecgwine, the text of which was known to William of Malmesbury,[44] and included certain details about the death of Aldhelm, bishop of Sherborne, whose death was miraculously revealed to Ecgwine. Thomas then put this charter of foundation, including the gift of the castle of Chadbury (in Lenchwick), into an improved documentary framework. His redaction ends with the subscriptions of Kings Cenred and Offa and Archbishop Berhtwald and the note that many other chief men, bishops, abbots, and priests had subscribed 'as found in the authentic charter'. He then thought fit to add 'We have followed this almost word for word, just as the holy man set it forth in his charters which he wrote for the most part himself. And although the hand of the scribes is not the same [sc. as the original], we have transcribed faithfully and in summary fashion the narrative of that same hand and pen' (34). Thomas also pointed out that 'more possessions are indicated in this [Ecgwine's charter] than in the charter which had been completed in Rome, or in that charter which Berhtwald composed: I refer to those possessions which the holy man later acquired . . .' (26). Both accounts, Dominic's and Thomas's, draw attention to the part played by Archbishop Berhtwald in committing to writing details of the possessions and rights, as commanded by the pope, and undertaken at a royal assembly at Alcester (supposedly in 709).[45] This particular relationship between the archbishops of Canterbury and the community at Evesham was to be part of Evesham's argument as to its special status and will be examined later. It should also be noted that the claim to freedom from the demands of bishops, alluded to in both redactions of the charter, preceded Thomas's attentions to Dominic's text.

At what point in time the two privileges of Pope Constantine made their appearance it is difficult to say. Dominic had the first privilege of 709.[46] Thomas omitted it—and the later privilege of Pope Constantine of 713, of which Dominic appears to know nothing— in his revision, but included both privileges later in his Book III. He

[44] See William of Malmesbury, *De gestis pontificum Anglorum*, ed. N. E. S. A. Hamilton (RS lii, 1870), p. 384.

[45] See *HBC*, p. 587.

[46] Edited by M. Lapidge in *AB* xcvi, pp. 88–90 no. 11.

noted, however, in discussing the expulsion of the monks and the assaults of Godwine, ealdorman of Lindsey, in the late tenth and early eleventh centuries, that 'it is marvellous in our eyes that despite the many great tribulations and various sudden changes of persons who engaged in unjust rule here, the privileges of Pope Constantine, which our father Ecgwine acquired, were not completely destroyed by either the bishops of Worcester when they ruled over this church, or by the clerks when they were in charge here: this is especially marvellous since the privileges were formulated and written against the assaults of such people' (145). The survival was attributed naturally to the mercy of God and the mediation of the blessed Virgin. Whether the sentiments were Thomas's or an earlier writer's is not certain, but there was clearly a tradition of the existence of early documents within the abbey of Evesham.

The existence of such a tradition can be confirmed by the survival of copies of the texts of the two papal letters of Pope Constantine that come from the 1120s, to be copied again in the same form in the 1150s.[47] These texts exhibit no differences from those given by Thomas in his *History* as the documents shown to Pope Innocent III in the lawsuit at Rome. Furthermore, the first privilege shows no important differences between Dominic's text as given in his *Life of St Ecgwine* and Thomas's as included later on in the *History*. If we examine the two privileges, however, we have to ask why there was a need for a second privilege in 713, so soon after the first in 709, to accord with the story of the two visits and the dedication of the church in 714 (Dominic). Both privileges accord significant powers or duties of care and protection (*tuitio*) to the archbishop of Canterbury, thereby bypassing the diocesan, the bishop of Worcester. The significant differences between the first privilege and the second are that the second adds a section on the power and position of the abbot and condemns anyone introducing clerks in place of monks. While both inveigh generally against tyrants, the second privilege declares that the community shall be 'under the sole rule of its own abbot' (325). 'When the abbot dies, his successor is to be chosen by the brethren of that place, in accordance with canonical authority, either from the

---

[47] See J. Sayers, '"Original", cartulary and chronicle: the case of the abbey of Evesham', *Fälschungen im Mittelalter* (*MGH* Schriften xxxiii, 4, 1998), pp. 371–95, at 375–7. For the copies of the 1120s, see BL Cotton MS Cleopatra E I, fos. 34–5. For those of the 1150s, possibly intended to pass as originals, see Evesham Almonry Museum Accession no. 127 and BL Cotton MS Cleopatra E I, fos. 64–5; the latter is reproduced as pl. I in the above article.

monastery itself or from the diocese of the Hwicce. He is then to be consecrated in that church freely and canonically without any charge (i.e. financial exaction), and, out of reverence for the venerable Ecgwine, is to use the ring only in the celebration of mass, and on our authority always to hold the first place after the bishop of the Hwicce' (326). The bishop is being even more firmly removed from supervision of the monastery—sentiments that accord with the aspirations of ancient Benedictine monasteries in the twelfth century. Furthermore, the inveighing against tyrants and assailants of any rank who undermine the privileges instituted by God (324) leads up to the final sanction clause condemning anyone violating this privilege or attempting to introduce clerks in the place of monks—a concern that certainly goes back to the tenth century at Evesham, but not so far as we know earlier, and was to continue until the time of Thomas of Marlborough.

That Thomas recognized certain incompatibilities or had his suspicions about these documents is clear, because when the bishop's proctor at Rome declared them rank forgeries (299), he stated 'about the privileges of Constantine, I was entirely ignorant' (300). Although we are told that one of the privileges of Constantine did not arrive until after the sentence was passed (281), Thomas argued from both. His role as a lawyer was to examine the general statements in the Constantinian privileges that could be related to the concessions contained in the privileges and indults of later popes: Innocent II, Alexander III, Clement III, and Celestine III. His adversary, Master Robert de Clipstone, had also objected to the letters of the latter two popes, Clement and Celestine, which he said were associated with an official messenger of the curia who was known to be a forger of papal letters—an allegation of which Thomas says he was not ignorant 'although I personally had nothing to be guilty about' (300). No mention is made of suspicions raised about the authenticity of the privilege of Innocent II nor of the privilege of Alexander III. Thomas cites from both documents in his argument.

Of the seven English Benedictine houses claiming exemption from the diocesan, three, St Augustine's Canterbury, Malmesbury, and Evesham, based their claims on very early papal privileges.[48] (Of the

---

[48] In general on early papal privileges, see P. Wormald, 'Bede and Benedict Biscop', in *Famulus Christi: Essays in commemoration of the thirteenth centenary of the birth of the Venerable Bede*, ed. G. Bonner (London, 1976), pp. 141–69; on Malmesbury, see H. Edwards, 'Two documents from Aldhelm's Malmesbury', *BIHR*, lix (1986), 1–19.

remaining four, three—Bury St Edmunds, St Albans, and Westminster—owed their status to the actions of both kings and popes, while the fourth, Battle, was made exempt almost entirely through the exertions of the king.)[49] St Augustine's, Canterbury, purported to have a papal letter of Pope Boniface IV of 610, Malmesbury possessed a letter of Sergius I of 701,[50] and Evesham displayed the two letters of Pope Constantine of 709 and 713. Malmesbury and Evesham were the last two to receive the status of houses that answered *nullo mediante* to the pope, Malmesbury in 1191, and Evesham in 1205. Both these communities had sent to Rome in the time of Pope Innocent II to acquire privileges and on that occasion both produced their seventh- and eighth-century bulls, the new privileges making reference to them.[51] Whether the documents produced by Evesham prior to Innocent II's privilege of 1139 were the texts as we have them in the copies of the 1120s (i.e. as shown in 1205) we shall never know. However, John of Worcester, writing before 1140 (the grant of Innocent II to Evesham was of 1139), describes Evesham's document as acquired by Ecgwine as 'a letter of privileges, to protect the monastery which he had built in Worcestershire against the attack of evil men'.[52] It is therefore just possible to believe that some earlier papal document preceded the twelfth-century texts, because privileges of protection—some of which have been accepted as genuine— were issued by popes from the sixth century.[53] If the first privilege as we have it in the 1120s might be argued to rest upon some truth, the second relates clearly to events experienced in the late tenth century.

[49] Bury St Edmunds, St Albans, Westminster, Battle, and St Augustine's, Canterbury, had all achieved this status by the late 1170s. Bury St Edmunds was the only house to establish clear exemption in the eleventh century; the others followed in the decades between the 1150s and 1170s, St Augustine's being the last.

[50] H. Edwards, 'Two documents', pp. 1–19, especially 9–19, has argued that Sergius's letter, in spite of a dubious proem, is basically genuine. She edits the text, and also comments (at p. 13) on the 'privileges . . . secured by personal application at Rome'.

[51] For the text of Malmesbury's 'Vestigiis inherentes' of 1142, see *Registrum Malmesburiense*, 2 vols., ed. J. S. Brewer (RS lxxii, 1879–80), i. 346–8.

[52] *Jo. Wo.*, ii. 166–7.

[53] P. Wormald, in *Famulus Christi*, ed. Bonner, pp. 141–69, at 148, points out that the privileges of Gregory the Great were not so much of exemption as of protection against abuse of episcopal power. Privileges of Pope Constantine for Bermondsey and Woking (with which Evesham's documents may be compared) were to protect the *status quo*. There were new departures in the seventh century, however, in monastic exemption, limiting the episcopal power over monks, and allowing the monks to refuse episcopal masses unless by invitation, and to choose the officiating bishop. See also L. Falkenstein, *La Papauté et les abbayes françaises aux xie et xiie siècles: Exemption et protection apostolique* (Bibliothèque de l'Ecole des Hautes Études Sciences historiques et philologiques, cccxxxvi: Paris, 1997), p. 44.

There is no indication, however, that Evesham's first historian, Byrhtferth, knew much about papal privileges. On the other hand, we know that the two privileges were in existence in the time of Dominic, who chose in his Life of St Ecgwine to give the text of the first but not the second. It must remain a matter of conjecture as to whether it was Dominic or another who formed these privileges, but there can be little doubt that in an abbey such as Evesham there would have been enough knowledge to draw up something that might deceive a bishop and might even be used to effect at the papal curia in order to extract further privileges. The texts of the privileges of Pope Constantine produced in Rome by Abbot Reginald Foliot apparently satisfied Pope Innocent II when he issued a privilege for the abbey in 1139 (330).

Evesham's advances towards exemption in the twelfth century followed a pattern similar to that of Malmesbury. Both communities acquired privileges from Innocent II and Alexander III. Innocent II's grant to Evesham in 1139 allowed that no bishop was to celebrate in the abbey or the chapels a synod, chapters, ordinations or public masses, unless invited to do so.[54] Chrism was to be received from the bishop of Worcester, but the abbot might be blessed by any Catholic bishop of his choice. The privilege acquired by Malmesbury from Pope Innocent II in 1142 was similar, but it denied the abbot blessing from a bishop of his choice, and it demanded that payment should be made of an ounce of gold yearly as a sign of the abbey's liberty—a condition not required of Evesham. Pope Alexander III in 1163 allowed Evesham to receive the chrism, and the consecration of altars and the ordination of clerks from any bishop, granting burial rights and rights to celebrate during a general interdict.[55] For Malmesbury in the same year, he reiterated that chrism, the consecration of altars, ordinations of monks and clerks, and the blessing of the abbot was to be received from the diocesan bishop, provided that he did not charge for these things and that he was in communion with the apostolic see.

The significant differences were thus two: the payment of the ounce of gold yearly, putting Malmesbury theoretically in a very special position, and Evesham's greater freedom from the diocesan. All the documents that we have been discussing survive only in cartulary texts. We therefore cannot put too much weight on them as

---

[54] It is possible to see this as a development of Constantine's grants. For the text of Innocent II's privilege (JL 7999), see below, 329–31.

[55] For the text of Alexander III's privilege (JL 10877), see below, 332–6.

being the actual texts of the originals. However, there are no glaring anachronisms and, while they are not the genuine articles, they do not make claims that are inconsistent with privileges of this date. The key issue for both communities was 'libertas', which meant exemption from the diocesan's attentions. The monks of Malmesbury feared in 1117 that Bishop Roger of Salisbury would degrade their house to a priory, and seventy years later, in 1190, they were apprehensive that it would be reduced to a monastery belonging to the bishop. This cannot have been far from Thomas's mind in 1202.

The charters of the kings are only vaguely referred to by all the three Evesham historians. They play a shadowy, but nonetheless important, part in Thomas's account. At the beginning of Book III, after the two books on Ecgwine, Thomas was careful to note first of all the grants of King Æthelred of the site of Evesham itself in 701 and then of Chadbury, Fladbury, and Stratford in 703. These he follows with the grants of Offa in 703 of what was ostensibly the Vale and of Cenred in 709 who gave lands on either side of the Avon.[56] This was virtually the complete endowment. Neither Byrhtferth nor Dominic had ventured into these details. But nowhere does Thomas give the texts either of these royal charters concerning the land endowment or of any charters granting 'royal liberty'. The privileges of Pope Constantine had emphasized the granting of royal liberty, and in the course of the suit at Rome much was made of the liberty given by the kings, as recorded in their charters. Thomas had interpreted the liberty granted as like an 'imperial gift', shot through, perhaps, with a Roman law connotation, and a notion of the pope as true emperor. He argued that this liberty could not apply only to the small town of Evesham, but must extend also to the surrounding region— 'our monastery is . . . like a heart in the middle of the body' (362). The pope's decision to separate the hearing of the case of the exemption of the monastery from that of the jurisdiction over the Vale meant that detailed examination of the royal charters was not necessary until the hearing of the Vale case. At that point the pope delegated the scrutiny of the royal documents to judges in England. We do not know what they made of them. But Thomas at this juncture wrote: 'I am not setting down in writing here the privileges of the kings because, as you can judge from my preceding narrative, it is still doubtful whether those privileges are going to be of any benefit

[56] See below, 115, 117, and Sawyer no. 80.

to us or not' (377). We can only surmise what these documents may
or may not have included, but the tradition of charters of the kings
goes back to the early eleventh century where Byrhtferth records that
King Cenred at the council at Alcester ordered Archbishop Berhtwald to draw up a privilege, and what may have been landbooks for
the endowment of the 124 hides, probably on the basis of verbal
grants and promises made by the kings before the pope. Such stuff is
undoubtedly myth, but the tradition of documents is early, and
parchments purporting to be royal privileges are likely to have been
drawn up, certainly by the 1120s, when the privileges of Pope
Constantine were fabricated. Thomas inherited a rich tradition of
documents: whether he suspected what had perhaps survived from
eighty years earlier can only be an opinion. His statement, however,
suggests that in his view the privileges were not precise enough for his
purposes.

The archbishops of Canterbury

The course of events in the abbey of Evesham at the turn of the
thirteenth century was much influenced by the relationship between
the monastery and the archbishop of Canterbury—a relationship that
the Evesham historians traced back to the historic mission of
Archbishop Berhtwald as the pope's representative. At the time
of Bishop Mauger of Worcester's projected visitation in 1202 some
of the Evesham monks asserted that the care of their souls and the
powers of correction in the church of Evesham had been specially
entrusted by the pope to the archbishop of Canterbury. Their church,
they said, was 'betrothed already to the lord of Canterbury, the
protector of our church and our permanent legate' (255). It was
therefore to the archbishop that they went for help in times of
trouble.

What grounds are there for this claim? There are two points of fact.
First in 1197, and again in 1198, the monks of Evesham had
approached the archbishop of Canterbury, the metropolitan, rather
than the bishop of Worcester, the diocesan, about the behaviour of
Abbot Roger Norreis.[57] Archbishop Hubert Walter was at the time
papal legate. Second, in 1201, the archbishop (no longer legate at this
date) had visited the convent at Evesham to amend what needed
amending, because, as the papal privilege stated, and the monks

---

[57] See below, p. liv.

reminded him, 'the care for the souls of our church has been entrusted by the pope to you' (215). Among the letters of Peter of Blois, when archdeacon of London, and therefore probably of 1202 (possibly as early as June 1200),[58] is one which has every appearance of being genuine, and which was written in answer to an approach made to him by P. the prior and the convent of Evesham. In it Peter expresses surprise that they have not received some remedy in their troubles from the archbishop, a 'man of great prudence and counsel'.[59] Archbishop Hubert Walter, as legate, claimed to have the power to visit exempt houses, but Evesham, unlike Bury St Edmunds, never claimed an exemption, simply a special relationship with the archbishop as their guardian and protector. According to the chronicler Jocelin of Brakelond, the abbey of Bury St Edmunds resisted Archbishop Hubert's attempt to inspect them and procured from the pope in 1196 a letter stating that, as subject to the pope alone, they could be visited only by a legate who was the pope's direct personal representative, a legate *a latere*, which Hubert Walter was not.[60] Whether at this time the monks of Evesham were mindful of what was contained in their privileges and aware of their limitations, we cannot now say, but some of the monks held quite firmly that correction could come only from the archbishop, not the bishop, for 'our monastery is the only church in England which has been entrusted to the archbishop, and so it has a special claim on him after Canterbury' (256).

The hearing at Rome of the case for exemption from the bishop was the occasion of the discussion of all the privileges. The two letters of Pope Constantine, both addressed to Berhtwald, primate of the Britons, charged the archbishop with the protection of churches throughout Britain, particularly that founded by the venerable Ecgwine. From this Thomas assumed that 'our church was established by the authority of the pope, and was entrusted to the primate of the Britons as the pope's legate' (288). The next two major privileges for Evesham of 1139 (obtained by Abbot Reginald Foliot: 329–31) and 1163 (obtained by Abbot Adam: 332–6) were concerned more with the practicalities of exemption from the diocesan than with

---

[58] For the complex dating, see Greenway, *Fasti*, i. *St Paul's London*, p. 10.

[59] 'Afflictioni uestre totis', printed *Mon. Angl.* ii, num. xl, pp. 40–1, from Cotton MS Vitellius D III. 1, which did not survive the Cotton fire of 1731, and *PL* 207, no. cxlii, cols. 425–8.

[60] *JB*, pp. 72–5.

the powers of the archbishop, both taking the community under the pope's and St Peter's protection, but neither mentioning that Evesham was subject to the pope with no intermediary. They granted that no bishop was to celebrate chapters etc. without permission, that the blessing of the abbot was not to be restricted to the diocesan bishop, and that 'the special customs in the parishes' were to be observed. The third batch of papal letters produced consists of two indults of 1189 (obtained by Abbot Adam: 337–8) and 1192 (obtained by Abbot Roger Norreis: 339–41). Both declare the abbot and community 'to belong especially to the jurisdiction of the blessed Peter and ourself without any intermediary', a notion that would not have seemed strange to Abbot Adam, a Cluniac, and both conferring the use of the abbot's pontificals, the outward sign of exemption.

Innocent III's decision about the exemption of Evesham, enshrined in 'Ex ore sedentis' (342–55), lent credence to Pope Constantine's 'commission' to the archbishop of Canterbury as primate (with echoes of the Petrine commission), to act as protector of the church of Evesham, which was now declared to be free, wholly exempt from episcopal jurisdiction, and subject only to the Roman pontiff and the Roman church.

What part had the contemporary archbishops played in this? Hubert Walter, at least in the eyes of the monks of Bury St Edmunds, was anxious to extend his legatine powers. He was anxious, too, to build up the power of the see of Canterbury to protect appeals, that is, the tuitorial appeal, whereby the archbishop's court protected an appeal to the papal court until the case was heard. The protection of the archbishop of Canterbury, however, while necessary for the confirmation of the fact that an election to the abbacy had been properly carried out, was to go no further. Thomas warned the community that confirmation of an abbot of an exempt house must come from the pope alone and not from the archbishop of Canterbury. This he stated clearly in his final section, where the copyist added in the margin, 'Note concerning the archbishop' (507).

The story was not quite over, for in 1233, after he became abbot, Thomas submitted to annual visitation by the archbishop or his delegates in a charter recorded in Canterbury archiepiscopal sources but not in Evesham sources.[61] What lay behind this we do not know. The document of submission was copied into the archiepiscopal

---

[61] Printed below as Appendix IV.

cartulary, but a marginal note added that this letter was revoked by a letter of Pope Innocent IV dated 18 December 1249, declaring that Evesham should not be visited, as it was subject *nullo mediante* to the pope alone. Had the archbishop of Canterbury been seeking to extend his rights at Evesham's expense?

The bishops of Worcester

From the first, relations between the two Benedictine communities of Evesham and of Worcester, which lay within twenty miles of each other, were close. In liturgical practice they had much in common, and they shared St Ecgwine, who was both bishop of Worcester and founder of the community at Evesham, in later terms its abbot. The *History* is keen to show, however, that Evesham was in no way dependent on the bishopric of Worcester, making it clear that Ecgwine had founded the abbey on an estate given him by King Æthelred in 701—the date supplied by Thomas. It is stressed, too, that Ecgwine had become the first abbot of this community and had at that time resigned as bishop of Worcester. The house therefore did not belong to the see of Worcester. Evesham is, of course, unlikely to have had the sort of freedom it later claimed—in any case freedom (and its opposite, subjection) were not real concepts in the very loose diocesan arrangements of the early eighth century, in which monasteries were highly regarded. Nor did the bishops of Worcester have the kind of diocesan rights feared by exempt communities in the twelfth century.

At the end of the tenth century (995×6) Ealdwulf, bishop of Worcester, had obtained the abbey of Evesham from King Æthelred and subjected it to his jurisdiction, and from this nadir in the fortunes of the community it is possible to discern the beginnings of the contest over the possession of certain lands and endowments between the abbey of Evesham and the bishops of Worcester. Until this point Evesham posed no threat to episcopal authority.[62] The revival in the abbey's fortunes under Abbot Ælfweard, the kinsman of King Cnut, consisted in the building up of the central estates, claiming properties that had been lost and also others to which they had no clear previous claim. Evesham, perhaps, sailed past the Norman Conquest in calmer waters than any other Benedictine house, as Abbot Æthelwig was left as the Conqueror's agent in the West Midlands. Particularly at issue

---

[62] Sims-Williams, *Religion and Literature*, p. 176.

between the bishopric of Worcester and the abbey of Evesham were the properties at Hampton and at Bengeworth, which were on Evesham's doorstep. It is less easy to determine the origins of the jurisdictional dispute, in so far as it was distinct from the territorial issue.

By the early twelfth century, however, the quarrel over Evesham's status and position within the diocese of Worcester had found its expression in more prolific documentary form. It had been sharpened by the central reform movement in the Church that sought to give diocesans greater powers over their dioceses. But such centralizing tendencies were at odds with the powerful and ancient institutions that claimed exemption, the pope presenting himself as the protector of monks, a position much furthered by the rise of the great abbey of Cluny. The papacy was shifting its position from protecting the monks, especially from lay aggressors, to exempting them from outside interference from clerics.[63] The bishops of Worcester in the twelfth century seized every opportunity to enforce what they saw as their rights, visitation being the key. The documents suggest that they were determined in their quest—from the Evesham point of view nothing short of aggressive. Opportunities for asserting their position were during vacancies in the abbey and just after a new election when the convent's resistance would have been at its weakest. The monks' only real ally was the pope, but he was far away, and molestation and persecution might well take place even after appeal. A letter of Gilbert Foliot to Godfrey, archdeacon of Worcester, asking him to restrain his bishop from persecuting the monks of Evesham, dates probably from the very early days of William de Andeville as abbot in 1149–50.[64] Some years earlier a remarkable letter written by Abbot Reginald to his nephew, Gilbert Foliot, abbot of Gloucester, had referred sadly (and despairingly) to the hostility from the bishop of Worcester in the light of his recently acquired papal privilege of 1139. In the past, Abbot Reginald says, 'Worcester considered us as free citizens, never as slaves.' It is no coincidence that this letter—undoubtedly genuine—was copied into Thomas's manuscript at the point where the monks were discussing Mauger's visitation and a case was being made for resistance.[65]

---

[63] For an excellent summary of the development of exemption, see Falkenstein, *La Papauté et les abbayes françaises*, pp. 217–24.

[64] Printed in *Foliot Letters*, no. 90.

[65] The letter is printed below as App. III.

The prologue

It was the declared intention of Prior Thomas, stated in his prologue, to record the distinguished deeds of good men and the evil actions of wicked men, the high points and the low points of human actions. Learning from example was a common sentiment expressed in prologues. Orderic Vitalis says in the prologue to his *Historia ecclesiastica*, 'Our predecessors . . . have recorded the good and evil fortunes of mortal men as a warning to others . . .'. [66] John of Salisbury writes in the prologue to his *Historia pontificalis*, 'men may by examples of reward or punishment be made more zealous . . . nothing, after the grace and law of God, teaches the living more surely and soundly than knowledge of the deeds of the departed'; citing Cato, he says, 'the lives of others are our teachers'.[67] Thomas traced the writing of history in this manner back to the Greeks. 'In order that evil men should not enjoy the same standing in society as good men', the Greeks had introduced a literary remedy. The Romans copied the Greeks in the perpetuation of virtue by making written record, but they also erected statues to the virtuous. In this way, he says, they reminded men of their ancestors and challenged their descendants to great deeds and glorious acts. The message of imitating the good and shunning evil acts had been incorporated in the lives of the holy fathers for all to read and hear, and 'had not the Lord made it clear both through the writings of the New Testament and the Old what men should shun and what imitate?' (112). This then is Thomas's task. Both benefactors and despoilers are to be recorded. There is a strong emphasis on material possession and on the duty to recover alienated lands that imperilled the souls of the alienators.

Contemporary history

The major part of Thomas's work is contemporary history, but contemporary history that has to be linked closely to the past. Part I therefore opens with the outline history of the abbey and abbots of Evesham up to what he calls 'the intrusion' of Abbot Roger Norreis. Thomas's observations of Abbot Norreis are first-hand and continue right through the description of the lawsuit at Rome until Norreis's

---

[66] *The Ecclesiastical History of Orderic Vitalis*, ed. M. Chibnall (6 vols., OMT, 1969–80), i. 130–1.

[67] Cato, *Distichs*, iii. 13; *The* Historia pontificalis *of John of Salisbury*, revised ed. M. Chibnall (OMT, 1986), p. 3.

deposition in 1213. Norreis is therefore woven into the account. Abbot Randulf is also treated as part of the main story. Again Thomas was an observer, writing over a period of sixteen years up to Randulf's death. While Norreis has his history in the attempted 'destruction' of the abbey of Evesham, Randulf belongs to the history of the rebuilding of the religious life and a fresh start for the beleaguered community. Before we look at other aspects of the community's life, essential to the *History*, we need to consider briefly these two abbots.

Abbot Roger Norreis

The abbot imposed on the convent by King Richard I on the advice of Archbishop Baldwin had been deposed as prior of Canterbury, to which office Baldwin had appointed him, just eighteen days after the death of Abbot Adam of Evesham on 12 November 1189. Virtually all the parts of Thomas's Book III are concerned with Abbot Norreis, from his 'intrusion' in Part I (185) to his death which is mentioned in Part V (499). Norreis first comes to notice as treasurer at Christ Church, Canterbury, in 1187, when he was sent by the convent to the king to complain about the archbishop's plans to establish a college of secular clerks—an action that the monks found threatening. The king and Archbishop Baldwin were abroad at the time, at Alençon, and there it appears that Baldwin made Roger Norreis cellarer of the convent—an action that was seen by the Canterbury monks as 'buying off' Roger. Worse was to follow, and in September 1189, Archbishop Baldwin made him their new prior, giving him certain conventual manors. His reputation among the monks of Christ Church, Canterbury, as a supporter of Baldwin, was as a traitor, and one who had impinged on the convent's rights and properties. This reputation would have hummed through Benedictine parlours and, allowing for the natural passion of the two monastic writers who have painted lurid pictures of his character, Baldwin's action in persuading the new king, Richard I, to give Roger Norreis the abbey of Evesham seems irresponsible. It is possible that the first few years at Evesham were uneventful and that Baldwin perhaps had hoped that Norreis would sort out the finances of the house, but it was all too apparent before very long that there were flaws in his character and that he had vices not suitable to an abbot of one of England's foremost Benedictine houses. The dramatic story has been told by G. G.

Coulton[68] and by Dom David Knowles,[69] using Thomas as the source. As argued above, it seems likely that Thomas of Marlborough had some connection with the community at Evesham before 1199 (his first year as a monk), perhaps dating back to the last days of Abbot Adam who died in 1189. After 1200 it is certain that he writes as a first-hand witness, and as such he was vital in the process of the deposition of Abbot Norreis by the legate, Nicholas, bishop of Tusculum, in 1213. For Thomas, Norreis was the very epitome of the bad abbot. He had appropriated and squandered the property of the abbey and he had abandoned the Rule both in his personal conduct and in his failure to provide for the convent's observance of it.

Abbot Randulf

The abbot chosen to succeed Roger Norreis was Randulf, a monk and prior of Worcester. In 1202, together with Walter de Broadwas, he had headed a party of Worcester monks who went to Rome to promote the canonization of Wulfstan.[70] The following year, 1203, he was elected prior on Christmas Eve.[71] As prior his time seems to have been successful, for on 2 December 1213, following the death of Bishop Mauger of Worcester, he was unanimously elected bishop[72]— a choice satisfactory no doubt to the monks, but not to the king, who wished to give the bishopric to his chancellor, Walter de Grey, recently rejected at Coventry. The legate, Nicholas, bishop of Tusculum, was prevailed upon to seek Randulf's withdrawal. Accordingly, he quashed the election and advised the monks of Evesham to elect Randulf as their new abbot, which they duly did on 20 January 1214 (**502**).

Misunderstanding of the text of Thomas's *History* has led several writers to assume that Randulf had been a monk at Evesham.[73] In fact the statement that he was a monk of the house refers to the confraternity between the two Benedictine houses of Worcester and of Evesham, whereby a monk of either community had a place in

---

[68] *Five Centuries of Religion*, ii. 347–78 (chs. xxiv and xxv).
[69] *M. O.*, ch. xix, pp. 331–45.
[70] *Ann. Wig.*, p. 391.   [71] Ibid. 392.
[72] *Rotuli litterarum clausarum*, ed. T. D. Hardy, 2 vols. (1833–4), i. 148; *Ann. Wig.*, p. 402.
[73] C. R. Cheney, *Pope Innocent III and England* (Päpste und Papsttum, ix: Stuttgart, 1976), p. 162; *HRH*, pp. 48, 84; Greatrex, *Biog. Reg.*, p. 8; and Greenway, *Fasti* ii. *Monastic Cathedrals*, 103—all state that he was a monk of Evesham.

chapter and a stall in choir in both houses, arrangements that were common from the mid twelfth century. However, the phrase 'natione Eveshamensis' obviously means that Randulf was born in the Evesham area (502). Although it is clear that the legate would have imposed Randulf on the convent if they had not agreed to elect him, Randulf in many ways seemed the ideal successor to Abbot Roger Norreis. The author of the *Lives and Deeds* of the abbots suggests, with the word *mitissimus*, that he was a mild man, a placator (510). He was perhaps the perfect foil for the more quixotic and passionate Thomas, who went with the abbot to the Lateran Council the year after the abbot's election (521). The task facing Abbot Randulf, if complex, was at least clear. He had to restore the house both spiritually and economically. According to the biographer, his first good work was to pay off the debt incurred in the lawsuit in Rome to the abbey's Roman creditors (510). His second good deed was that he reclaimed, by an exchange, the pension of sixty shillings from the church of Ombersley that had been paid to the legate Nicholas's clerk, Humfrey. This money was now diverted for the use of the poor for the Maundy, which formerly had to be provided by the abbot (511). His third good work was to transfer the revenues of one obedientiary to another when necessary, if one was over-provided and the other had insufficient funds. He abolished the custom of the abbot's coming to the sacrist's manor of Bretforton for one day's lodging, thereby causing considerable expense to the sacristy, assigning instead from the sacristy three marks to be paid to the infirmary and two to the pittancery (512). These reforms were included in the customs and disposition. He restored buildings, bought mills, made fishponds, constructed dovecots, and made assarts, giving some lands, rather than licence to assart. (His biographer was critical of his granting of the assarts rather than of licence to assart.) Within the precinct at Evesham he constructed a watch chamber next to the hall in the great court. He left the high table a silver cup and a maple-wood cup, and the convent other bowls, spoons, and two gold rings. He gave vestments, including a mitre, two albs, and a cope, and a fine ring for Mass, and vestments for the altar of the Lady chapel. The mitre was presumably for his own use and he also had three abbatial seats made (513–15). Protective of his status as a mitred abbot, he insisted on his place beside the bishop at the synod of Worcester in 1219.[74] In the sixteen

[74] *Ann. Wig.*, p. 411. For the statutes see *C. & S.*, ii. 1, pp. 52–7. A mitred abbot had quasi-episcopal jurisdiction over the territory of his abbey.

years of his abbacy he appears to have restored the observance of the religious life at Evesham, eleven of them with Thomas as his prior.

B. CULT AND BUILDINGS

Both Benedictine communities at Evesham and Worcester were active in the cult of saints. Their calendars show such close connections in the observance of saints' days that assignment of their origin is often difficult. Two of the calendars pre-dating 1100 have been attributed by some scholars to Worcester and by others to Evesham.[75] Both communities had contact with the continent that was reflected in the saints in their calendars.

Evesham's own saints

For a monastery claiming high status, it was essential to have its own saints. Both saints' lives and their corporal remains became important to reformers. How early Ecgwine was accorded the rank of a saint at Evesham and at Worcester, we do not know. Bede does not mention Ecgwine. In all likelihood he made his reappearance on the Evesham scene when Evesham's fortunes began to rise, and Michael Lapidge's suggestion that the *Vita* of Ecgwine by Byrhtferth of Ramsey was perhaps written at the invitation of Abbot Ælfweard, himself a monk of Ramsey before he came to Evesham, is an attractive one.[76] It was certainly Abbot Ælfweard who presided over the revival at Evesham. As a relative of Cnut (perhaps through a relationship with Ælfgifu of Northampton), it was at his instigation that the remains of St Wigstan—a ninth-century royal Mercian martyr—were translated from Repton to Evesham.[77] Wigstan was important to Evesham as a descendant of their royal patron, King Cenred. It was also Abbot Ælfweard who purchased for Evesham, from merchants in London, all the relics of the ninth-century Brabantine saint, Odulf (146). Along with Credan, said to be the eighth abbot of Evesham (after Ecgwine), who was at some point accorded the position of a saint,

---

[75] *English Kalendars before A.D. 1100*, ed. F. Wormald (Henry Bradshaw Soc. lxxii, 1934), calendars 16 and 18; and see V. Ortenberg, *The English Church and the Continent in the Tenth and Eleventh Centuries* (Oxford, 1992), pp. 248 n. 157 and 19 n. 66.

[76] M. Lapidge, 'Byrhtferth and the Vita S. Ecgwini', *Mediaeval Studies*, xli (1979), 331-53, at 342, repr. in Lapidge, *Anglo-Latin Literature 900-1066* (London and Rio Grande, 1993), pp. 293-315, at 304.

[77] On Wigstan, see D. Rollason, *Saints and Relics in Anglo-Saxon England* (Oxford, 1989), pp. 59, 117, 157-8, and 175; and see below, 146 and nn. 5 (p. 150), 1 (p. 152).

Ælfweard had thus assembled at Evesham a number of saints and shrines. His successor, Abbot Mannig, a goldsmith of repute, whose fame had spread as far away as France, made shrines for Saints Ecgwine, Odulf, and Credan (**149**). The stage was set for the coming of the pilgrims 'from Aquitaine, Ireland and many lands', referred to under his successor Abbot Æthelwig (**160**). There were also three hermits at Evesham under Abbot Mannig, of whom one, Wulfsige, a layman from Crowland, was regarded as a saint probably soon after his death. Wulfsige is described by Dominic in his *Acts of Worthy Men* as a hermit for seventy-five years. He acted as the spiritual adviser of Earl Leofric of Mercia and his wife Godgifu, and it was he who prevailed upon Wulfstan to accept the bishopric of Worcester in 1062.[78] His tomb is referred to by Thomas when he was sacrist. Wulfsige had another particular claim to fame in the eyes of Thomas—he had returned Badby and Newnham to the abbey's possessions.

Thomas and the development of the cults

Thomas chose to preface his *History* with the Lives and Miracles of the Evesham saints, Odulf, Wigstan, and, of course, Ecgwine. The *Life of St Odulf* was that written after 918 by Cappidus Stavrensis to which Dominic apparently added the *Miracles*: neither Thomas nor Dominic had seen fit to alter it much.[79] Thomas personally had authored the *Life and Miracles of Wigstan*, attributing his sources mistakenly to Bede: clearly he was using a copy of Bede with additions based probably in part on John of Worcester.[80] He added certain pieces of information to what was the original account of Wigstan's life and miracles. He recorded that the fall of the tower at Evesham (in 1207, see **436**) broke not only the feretory, or shrine, of the saint, but also the crown of the head, which had been placed in a cloth along with the other bones 'as is the custom'. Hearing of this event, the canons of Repton asked the abbot and monks of Evesham for some relic of the saint who was also their patron. Their request was granted by Abbot Randulf and a small portion of the head and an arm bone were transferred to Repton. Thomas also reported, from personal knowledge, the account of Archbishop Baldwin's investigation into the miracle of St Wigstan's hair that was said to occur

[78] Dominic in his *Acts of Worthy Men* (Macray, p. 322) mentions the other two hermits also, and see below, **146** and n. 6. For Wulfsige's influence on Wulfstan, see *Jo. Wo.*, ii. 590–1.
[79] Printed by Macray, in Appendix, pp. 313–20. See Jennings, 'Writings', p. 301.
[80] See Macray, pp. 333, 337; *Jo. Wo.*, ii. 262–3 and n. 6.

annually on the day of his death. This enquiry must have taken place between 1188 and 1190. Baldwin had appointed Paul, abbot of St Mary de Pré, Leicester, and Baldwin, prior of Monks Kirby (Warws.) to go to Wistow (Leics.) to observe this phenomenon and to certify its veracity or otherwise. At the appointed hour the grass round the chapel turned into a man's hair, which they touched, kissed, and marvelled at, and then after a short time only grass was to be seen there. They hastened to Canterbury to inform the archbishop.[81]

Ecgwine is central to Thomas's *History*, never far from Thomas's thoughts. Thomas's abbreviation of the first book of the *Life and Miracles of St Ecgwine* enabled him to undertake some revision of the stories. For the most part, Thomas was content to leave Dominic's arrangement of Book II of the *Life and Miracles of St Ecgwine* in its original order. But he did see fit to follow Dominic's prologue with two of the four miracles that were originally in Byrthferth and thence in Dominic Book I. These were the miracles of the unharmed shrine during the time of the collapse of the church under Abbot Osweard, and the miraculous death of the man who claimed land belonging to the abbey (**68, 70–1**). Sandwiched between these two was the tale of the countryman who in swearing a false oath lost his beard (**69**). This slight alteration in the order may have been made by Thomas in order to impose a stricter chronology. As rearranged, the two stories coming from the time of Abbot Osweard are now put together. Henceforth the sequence of miracles exactly follows Dominic's Book II. The other two of the original four miracles recorded in Byrhtferth and Dominic—the miracle of the seal in the Avon and the miracle of the nine chains—Thomas thought appropriate to include in the twelve readings, 7–8 (**55–6**) and 9–11 (**57–60**), for the night vigils of the feast of the translation which he had been asked to provide in a shortened form.[82]

Cults needed to be associated not only with the written word but also with the growth and embellishment of buildings and the provision of suitable shrines and reliquaries. The church of Evesham

---

[81] The *Life and Miracles of St Wigstan* are printed in Macray, Appendix pp. 325–37. On the points made here, see esp. pp. 334, 336. For the date of the enquiry see *HRH*, p. 170, the accession of Paul in 1188, and *HBC*, p. 232, the death of Archbishop Baldwin in 1190. On the manuscripts and textual tradition of the Life of St Wigstan, see P. A. Hayward, 'The idea of innocent martyrdom in late tenth- and eleventh-century English hagiology', *Studies in Church History*, xxx (Oxford, and Cambridge, Mass., 1993), 81–92, at pp. 81–2 nn. 3–4.

[82] Those readings for St Wigstan's feast, which Thomas had been asked to provide, if ever completed, do not survive.

as Thomas first knew it was a Norman fabric, largely constructed under Abbots Walter and Reginald.[83] Doubtless the crypts and the upper part of the church as far as the nave that Walter built called to mind the great Romanesque churches of Normandy, with which he would have been familiar as Lanfranc's chaplain. In this church presumably there were shrines from which Abbot Walter took the relics of the Evesham saints that he had submitted to the ordeal by fire, from which they had emerged unscathed—indeed, the head of St Wigstan had miraculously shed beads of sweat—for Walter, convinced of the sanctity of both Credan and Wigstan, is said to have placed the relics in raised feretories.[84] Abbot Reginald Foliot continued the construction of the nave walls 'as they can be seen today', commissioned arm-reliquaries for St Ecgwine and St Oswald, and made good St Ecgwine's shrine which the goldsmith, Abbot Mannig, had made, and which had been stripped of its gold, silver and precious stones by the monks during the Anarchy (178). This shrine is described as of gold, silver, and precious stones, three of which illuminated the church at night (149). Whether Mannig's shrines built for Saints Odulf and Credan had survived to this time, we do not know.

Abbot Adam undertook much building work. As a former Cluniac he valued grand and spacious buildings, gorgeous vestments, and works of beauty, of which the lectern for the chapter house may be the one surviving at Norton; and it is said that in his time the shrine of St Ecgwine was completed. Also under Abbot Adam, the cloister—which Abbots Maurice and Reginald had begun—was completed, as was the nave of the church with the assistance of Dean Richard of Wells (182). This assistance was possibly assistance in the design as well as financial help. With the collapse of the church tower in 1207 Thomas (? as dean) was instructed by Abbot Norreis to undertake the task of restoration. The *History* says that within two years he had renewed the walls of the presbytery and built them to provide an

[83] For a summary of the building works and excavations at Evesham, see D. C. Cox, 'The building, destruction, and excavation of Evesham abbey: a documentary history', *Transactions of the Worcestershire Archaeological Society*, 3rd ser. xii (Worcester, 1990), 123–46.

[84] See Dominic's *Acts of Worthy Men*, printed in Macray, Appendix, pp. 320–5, at 323–4; and *Life and Miracles of St Wigstan*, Macray, pp. 335–7. See also P. A. Hayward, 'Translation narratives in post-Conquest hagiography and English resistance to the Norman Conquest', in *Anglo-Norman Studies*, xxi (1999), ed. C. Harper-Bill, pp. 67–93, who makes the point at 91–3 that only those relics about which there was doubt were put to the test. Notably St Ecgwine's relics are not mentioned as being included in the trial.

ambulatory around the presbytery, no doubt to provide for festive occasions and the movement of pilgrims (519, 524). After 1217, when he became sacrist, and hence the obedientiary who was usually in charge of building works, he replaced the stained-glass windows broken by the collapse of the tower, repaired all the damaged shrines, renewing the shrine of St Wigstan that had suffered considerably (521). Later he had a throne and a 'royal image' made for it (529). Further work on the fabric continued under him as prior (from 1218). The *History* refers now to the second collapse of the tower (524). It is not clear whether these two accounts can be compressed into one or not, for they seem to repeat one another, but it is clear that Thomas cared deeply about the Evesham saints and their shrines. He repaired St Ecgwine's shrine, renewing 'the flowers and precious stones' on it, and built a throne for it. In homage to St Ecgwine, and doubtless to instruct the pilgrims, he put a glass window in the presbytery to illustrate the saint's story. He made provision also for the reliquaries of Saints Wigstan and Credan to be brought before the high altar at the time of their feasts and for candles to burn before them during this time, presumably the octave (524–7). Some of the building works seem to have been in the area of the crypt, possibly to strengthen the choir and the presbytery (519).

The Virgin had shown herself to Ecgwine, as well as to the swineherd, and her cult at Evesham was not neglected. The altar of St Mary in the crypt and its maintenance, especially the provision for its lighting, were the responsibility of the sacrist. Here, too, from the accounts in Thomas's acts, he took a particular interest (521, 525–7).

C. CUSTOMS AND REVENUES: THE DEFINITION OF RIGHTS

Part of Thomas's *History* is concerned with the extended and bitter quarrel between Abbot Norreis, on the one hand, and the community headed by the prior, on the other. Such disagreements about the administration of the revenues and the relative rights of abbot and convent were not new, nor confined to Evesham, but took place in many Benedictine abbeys at this time.[85] What is remarkable about Evesham, however, is the high degree of independence that the prior

---

[85] On the development of the separation of the lands and revenues between the abbot and the prior and convent in general, see E. U. Crosby, *Bishop and Chapter in Twelfth Century England: A Study of the 'Mensa Episcopalis'* (Cambridge, 1994), ch. 3.

and convent attained in a settlement made with the abbot on the
authority of the legate, John of Ferentino, in 1206. This written
settlement recognized that the prior and convent had a portion of
lands and revenues virtually separate from those of the abbot. The
document (cited as M) dealt not only with the disposition of the
revenues but also with the customs of the house.[86] It was confirmed
by the legate, as consisting of statutes made by common consent for
the good estate of the monastery and accepted by both the abbot and
the monks, before he left in November 1206 (430). It gave the prior
and convent an independence in running their own estates and affairs
that was on the same scale as the jurisdictional and spiritual powers
granted to both the abbot and the convent in 'Ex ore sedentis'
(342–55).

A second document, dealing with the customs and apportionment,
dates from the abbacy of Randulf, who succeeded Roger Norreis in
1213 (399–429). Pope Innocent III confirmed a forerunner (now lost)
of the text of the Randulf document, as we now have it, after the
Lateran Council, at which both Abbot Randulf and Thomas were
present (431). That document may have been closer in some ways to
the written agreement confirmed by the legate, but in other ways it
may have been more favourable to the abbot. There is no doubt that it
was 'renegotiated'. The seal of direct papal approval and protection
put the arrangements at Evesham on an even more secure footing.

It is not the purpose of an introduction to the texts to do more than
outline their significance. But before we go on to an examination of
their development and date, some short explanation is needed. It is
clear that these two documents—and another redaction of Abbot
Randulf's charter surviving as Cotton MS Augustus ii 11 (cited as
C)[87]—incorporate arrangements made over a considerable period of
time and they reflect changes and further definition. All the documents are divided into two parts: a section that deals with the customs
of the house and a section dealing with the disposition of the
revenues. As we have already seen, in his history of the development
of the Evesham endowment, Thomas was anxious to point out that it
was not static, that more had been acquired as time wore on. It is clear
that by the time Thomas was writing, the text of the 1206 arrangement had been reworked and was now seen by him as superseded, and
that after the departure of Abbot Norreis, against whom there was

---

[86] See below, App. II A.   [87] See below, App. II B.

undoubtedly personal animus, demands may have been toned down; for instance the reproving of monastic officials by the brethren has been altered to 'by the abbot and the brethren' by the time of Abbot Randulf.

For this reason the text of the document of 1206 did not find a place in Thomas's *History*, but it survives in a transcript made for Dugdale's *Monasticon* (edition of Caley, Ellis, and Bandinell).[88] The original, from which the text was taken, probably by John Caley, who was keeper of the Records in the Augmentation Office, is described as an 'autographum sub sigillis in curia Augmentationis'. It presumably survived among the records of the court of Augmentations until at least 1819, the date of publication of vol. ii of *Monasticon*, but is now lost. It is printed below in Appendix II A; the text is based on that in *Monasticon*.

This document, which we shall call M (*Monasticon*), had its origins no doubt in the desire of the convent to protect the assignment of revenues to particular obedientiaries, to curtail the abbot's authority over all the monastery's income and endowments, and what is more to restrict the abbot's activities by a written agreement.

According to Thomas's testimony, it was Archbishop Hubert Walter who first ordered the customs of Evesham to be put into writing. This instruction from Archbishop Hubert did not follow the convent's first two complaints about the abbot's appropriation of the convent's rents for himself, his squandering of their properties, and his giving away of assarts, which were made to the archbishop in 1197 and probably the following year, 1198 (191–3). Nor did it take place when the archbishop came to Evesham again, most likely in 1201. On that occasion details concerning the archiepiscopal rights over the monastery had been put into writing, but the question of defining the customs and revenues had not been broached. That followed Thomas's return from the papal curia after his first visit in 1202–3 when the archbishop came to Evesham in 1203. Thomas informs us later on in the *History* that he had first learned at the papal curia about the possibility of putting the customs and details of the revenues in writing, and on his return gave advice on this, emphasizing the sealing of the document by the abbot, the convent, the legate, and even the pope.[89] This does not exactly square with Thomas's

[88] Printed in vol. ii, nums. xxvii–xxviii, pp. 23–5.

[89] The account of Thomas's life later in the *History* says that 'when Thomas returned from the Roman curia he gave advice about something which he had learned was practised

statement that Hubert Walter was involved (239). It is possible that the initiative came from Thomas, though Hubert Walter's importance in the making and keeping of written records is well known. However that may be, the drawing up of the document was not effected under Archbishop Hubert, who died on 13 July 1205.

The beginnings of the actual process of codification rested until the legate John of Ferentino came to Evesham in 1206 to investigate the state of affairs there. With the previous allegations no doubt in mind, he conducted a careful scrutiny into the behaviour and conduct of the abbot and of the monks. He also commenced an enquiry into the revenues of the obedientiaries and the customs of the house with a view to providing a written record. But he departed without completing either the scrutiny or the 'dispositio' of the revenues. He reserved to himself the completion of the 'scrutiny' or enquiry into the behaviour and conduct of the abbot and of the monks, and he delegated the settlement of the 'dispositio' to the abbots of Lilleshall and Haughmond. As a result of the activities of the two abbots, as Thomas records, 'All the revenues assigned to our offices and all the customs relating to the cellary were put in writing. This document we sent to the legate and he confirmed it' (393). It can thus be dated before the legate's departure in November 1206. The order of the offices in M is prior, precentor, sacrist, chamberlain, kitchener, pittancer (there is no refectorer), infirmarer, almoner, and master of the fabric; finally come the customs of the cellarer. The only anniversaries of abbots mentioned are those of two twelfth-century abbots, Reginald (d. 1149) and Adam (d. 1189). It will also be noted that when compared with our other two texts, there is no entry for the dean's office.

Following the deposition of Abbot Roger Norreis in 1213, it is almost certain that there would have been reference to the customs and disposition, and the new abbot, Abbot Randulf, when elected on 22 January 1214, would doubtless have been required to promise observance of the arrangements.

The redaction of the customs and disposition of the revenues as copied into Thomas's *History*, which we shall call R (*Rawlinson*), is, indeed, in Randulf's name (399–429). This text, Thomas states, was confirmed by Pope Innocent III at the time of the Fourth Lateran

elsewhere in other churches, and this was that the customs and revenues belonging to the convent should be put in writing and confirmed with the seals of the abbot, the convent, and the papal legate, and even of the pope himself' (518).

Council (1215).[90] This cannot be strictly correct because it was confirmed by Innocent on 16 February 1216, by which time the Council had ended, but there is no doubt that the confirmation took place while Abbot Randulf and Thomas were in Rome or very soon after they had left. The *History* also states that when Abbot Randulf 'gladly' confirmed the disposition, he 'enhanced it with many additional revenues, as inspection of the documents reveals' (398). Furthermore, Randulf's document, which Thomas purports to copy, includes the statement that what follows is the record 'not only of those revenues which we had at the time of the confirmation (i.e. by the pope), but also of those we acquired afterwards', adding that Pope Innocent II and Pope Alexander III had conceded and confirmed not only the revenues that the abbey of Evesham held in their time, but also those acquired later by just means (400).

Reference is made in R to Abbot Randulf's action in accordance with a statute of the Benedictine general chapter (418). The first Benedictine chapter for the Southern Province cannot predate September 1218, so the main text (R) must be later than that date. R also refers to the anniversary of Abbot Randulf (409, 419), but this does not necessarily mean that it must date after his death on 17 December 1229, as it was not unusual practice to provide for an anniversary during a lifetime.

Our third text is a text of the disposition of Abbot Randulf, closely comparable with the copy in Rawlinson, but not identical. It survives in a *copie figurée* (an elaborate but unsealed copy)[91] in the British Library, Cotton MS Aug. II. 11 (C). C is printed as Appendix II B, below (the sections that are not in R are printed in italics). It opens in the name of Abbot Randulf and with the same preamble as R. There are some grounds for arguing that it predates R. Firstly, certain 'wearisome customs' at Bourton-on-the Water, which are described in C, are not present in R, and a pension from Ombersley, mentioned in C, is called an 'old' pension in R. Secondly, certain marginal additions in R are found in the text of C, notably in the entries concerning the almonry and the kitchen. The order of the entries in C is exterior cellarer, prior, dean, precentor, sacrist, altar of St Mary in the Crypt (part of the sacristy), almoner, refectorer, infirmarer, pittancer, kitchener, chamberlain, master of the fabric, guest-house

---

[90] There were three sessions of the Lateran Council on 11, 20, and 30 November.

[91] See *Vocabulaire International de la Diplomatique*, ed. M. M. Cárcel Ortí, Commission Internationale de Diplomatique (València, 1994), p. 33 no. 56.

master, and finally, customs of the cellarer. C includes a separate entry for the pittancer, as does the earliest text M. C also has under the pittancery a comment about the church of Ombersley and the legate's clerk, Humfrey, which is not found in R, namely that Abbot Randulf assigned 20s. for the celebration of the feast of St John before the Latin gate from the pension of 60s. from the church of Ombersley, which, because the abbot had given this to his own clerk, the papal legate, Nicholas, in 1213, gave to his clerk, Humfrey. The author of the *Lives and Deeds* of the abbots, under the deeds of Abbot Randulf, comments that the abbot later reclaimed this pension, diverting it to the use of the poor, with the consent of the legate (**511**).

However, C (the charter) cannnot be earlier than R, for there is the startling revelation in the text of C that Abbot Randulf had conferred two marks from a pension of 60s. from the church of Ombersley on the almonry, 'as written in the chapter on the good works of Abbot Randulf'. This is a reference to the *Lives and Deeds* of the abbots, as found in Part V of the *History*, and must put C's compilation close to the death of Abbot Randulf. In R it occurs as a marginal addition (**419** and n. 3). Its incorporation into the text of the charter (C) has, of course, to mean that C *must* post-date the writing of the *Life* of Abbot Randulf.

It seems unlikely, if not impossible, that the *Life* would have been written before the death of the abbot in question, and, if this assumption is correct, then the text, which is not dated or sealed, but simply ends with the triple Amen, must date from after 17 December 1229, the day of Abbot Randulf's death.[92] But the charter, as already pointed out, is in the name of Abbot Randulf. Can its compilation be squared with a date after his death, and why would it have been compiled?

In the aftermath of Abbot Randulf's death, there would have been considerable concern in the monastery about his successor. In view of the recent history of the house and its struggles, a successor who

[92] The date of the death of Abbof Randulf is not given in the *Lives and Deeds* of the abbots, but is recorded in H and in other later sources—Harley MS 229, fo. 17ᵛ, printed in *Mon. Angl.* ii, num. xxxii, p. 27; Cotton MS Vespasian B XV (from H), and Lambeth MS 589 (from Cotton MSS Vitellius E XII and XVII)—as 16 kal. Jan. (17 Dec.) 1229. The Patent Rolls (*Patent Rolls of the Reign of Henry III A.D. 1225–1232* (HMSO London, 1903), p. 320) record in the royal licence granted to elect a successor that Adam, the subprior, and Walter, the cellarer, notified the king on 'the Wednesday before St Thomas's day' (19 December) of Abbot Randulf's death. The licence is not dated but obviously post-dates 19 December.

would advance its position and observe its customs was essential. The inevitable vacancy made it imperative that the division of funds between abbot and convent should be clearly set out and observed, particularly so if the new abbot was not to be Thomas. It was by no means certain that the successful candidate would be Thomas, and indeed, although he was elected abbot three days later on 20 December and was admitted by the king on or before 7 January 1230 (532), the election did not run smoothly. The pope ordered a new election in a letter to the convent of 2 May (533). Thus the most likely explanation for the making of C is that it was drawn up on or very close to 17 December 1229, the death of Abbot Randulf, perhaps before 6 January, and probably well before 2 May, the date of the pope's letter. Thomas was not blessed until 12 July 1230 (534), and did not receive possession of the abbey until some twelve weeks later, on 29 September 1230 (536), but it is unlikely that a further redaction took place at that date, for why would the name of Randulf have been retained? The obvious answer to this question is that the text in Randulf's name had had papal confirmation, which it was essential to preserve. If our suggestion about the date of the compilation of C is correct, it gave Thomas or someone in his circle the chance to update the customs and disposition, just as they had been updated from time to time after the pope's confirmation in 1216.

The evidence from the charter, C, is that it has to be later than R. It is, of course, clear that both C and R were not compiled (as opposed to copied) at any one specific date. They were subject to numerous changes and additions. It is clear, too, that neither text has a direct dependence on the other. The variations between the texts indicate either an intermediary or different sources. While C and R share many sections, there are differences within the sections. R, for example, provides for twenty-five paupers on Prior Thomas's anniversary from land at Bengeworth (this is a late thirteenth-century over-writing of the text), while in C the subprior is to feed thirty poor people in the parlour on that day, the writer stating that Thomas had increased the rent by an exchange. In one instance in R eight principal feasts are provided for, as opposed to seven in C.[93] There is little doubt that under Thomas as prior there was much rewriting of R. R also omits the whole section in C on the income of the altar of

---

[93] On another occasion (fo. 174ra), R refers to seven principal feasts, suggesting a possible slip, but an increased number of feasts might not necessarily indicate a later development.

St Mary in the Crypt with which Thomas was closely associated as sacrist and as prior. As sacrist 'he had it decreed in chapter that lamps should be kept perpetually burning before the high altar and in the crypt before the altar of St Mary' (521); and as prior he bought two sites for shops in Evesham and some land, and used this income for the altar lights (525).

When was R copied into Thomas's *History*? For the date of when this particular version of the disposition of the revenues and customs of the house was completed and copied into Part IV (fos. 171^r–4^v) of the book now known as MS Rawlinson A 287, we have to return to the question of the date of the compilation of Thomas's *History*. This particular redaction cannot have been put together before 1218 because of the reference to the General Chapter and to Thomas as prior, an office he did not hold until that year. Its inclusion in the middle of the events of 1206 is apparently because of its connection with the earlier arrangement that the legate had confirmed. Thomas no longer wished to include the text of 1206, as it was now outdated, but he did need to provide a text of the customs and disposition of the revenues as they were at the time of writing, most likely in the early years of his priorate which began in 1218. He also needed the pope's letter of confirmation though in fact that took place in 1216 and did not confirm the text that Thomas included. Dating this particular redaction of the customs and disposition of the revenues unfortunately does not narrow the possible dates for the completion of Thomas's book. The date has to be after 1218 and before 1230: it could be at any point in the interim period of the 1220s.

The significance of the written customs and disposition of the revenues

Evesham was probably among the first Benedictine houses in England to establish a regular system of accounting and audit. The circumstances of the legate's intervention in the domestic arrangements, both at St Mary's, York, and at Evesham (failing houses), possibly put them at the forefront of reform. On the other hand, it may well be that the fortuitous survival of the texts has accorded these two houses an innovative position, which in fact reflected a new devolved system of accounting that was becoming popular among Benedictines in the early thirteenth century. According to the provisions, each obedientiary was to appear before the abbot or his delegate and render an account four times a year in the presence of the prior and six monks,

three of whom were chosen by the abbot and three by the convent. The kitchener, or cook, was to account weekly. Whether these accounts were written or verbal, supported by tallies, cannot be stated with certainty.

What we can say with certainty, however, is that the customs were committed to writing and that these clauses were included. They were supported by further decrees stating that no monk was to have two offices, although a fellow helper, acting also in the capacity of an overseer, could be appointed. Furthermore, the abbot was to appoint the obedientiaries only in chapter and on the advice and with the consent of the chapter. The obedientiaries were listed. They were to be appointed from amongst the convent. The bestowing of churches and revenues, the alienating of lands, the initiation and termination of lawsuits, the freeing of villeins, and the appointment of the abbey's servants, were to take place only in chapter and with the convent's consent. Provisions for transferring funds from an obedience in surplus to an obedience in debt were to be transacted by the abbot in consultation with the chapter. Nor was the abbot to accept or expel monks without the consent of the convent and again this had to be done openly in chapter. While the abbot's authority was undoubtedly safeguarded in the customs, he was now obliged to seek approval in chapter, even if he might act without it. While the consent to all major transactions may have been somewhat theoretical, Evesham's written customs are the spearhead of a movement away from vague precedent to written law. Anyone reading these stipulations cannot but see them as the antidote to the wayward practices of Abbot Norreis, who had alienated the monks' property and taken their obediences into his hands 'to do as he pleased with them' (189). But they also echo practices and problems in other houses, where abbots and convents were not in agreement about management, and where, in some cases, as at Bury St Edmunds, secular clerks had been appointed by the abbot and brought in to manage estates and money more efficiently and to supervise the monks.[94]

The importance of the chapter as a place of council as well as of edification and correction is paramount. Here in future all appointments were to be made of the officers of the convent, in the case of Evesham the obedientiaries, the prior, the subprior, the third prior, the masters of order, and the prior of the dependency of Penwortham.

---

[94] *JB*, pp. 70–2, 79.

The late Dom David Knowles saw these customs as reflecting extremely democratic views.[95] This might be seen as the judgement of a brilliant historian revealing attitudes of his own day, but it is also clear that to Thomas the definition of rights represented a notable advance in Evesham's quest for status.

Evesham's relations with other Benedictine houses

As pointed out above, relationships between the Benedictine priory at Worcester and the Benedictine abbey of Evesham were close and we should not see the struggle between Evesham and the bishop of Worcester as initiating a period of hostility between the two communities. It is likely that there would have been interchange of books and that Thomas and others at Evesham knew of the works of the Worcester chroniclers. In 1077 Bishop Wulfstan of Worcester had established a confraternity agreement between Worcester, Evesham, Gloucester, Winchcombe, Pershore, Chertsey, and Bath.[96] At some point in the twelfth century the two communities had entered into a confraternity arrangement. Confraternity arrangements were at first for reciprocal prayers for the dead. Later they allowed monks of the other house equal rights in both communities, with a place in chapter. The election of Randulf, monk and prior of Worcester, as the successor to Abbot Norreis, no doubt furthered contacts. Evesham also had confraternity arrangements with Whitby, St Mary's, York, Malmesbury, and Odense, its daughter-house in Denmark. Evesham and Whitby were historically and sentimentally connected by the mission of 1073–4, and the arrangement between the two houses, declaring that 'the two congregations were to be as one', took place before 1125.[97] The mission of Evesham monks to Whitby indirectly formed the link with St Mary's, York, to which house some Whitby monks migrated. Pacts of confraternity between the two houses date from the decade of the 1150s, that of 1159–60 stating that 'monks of Evesham shall be for all things as monks of York'. [98] The connection with St Mary's, York, may be closer than the documents now allow us to demonstrate, and there may be some direct relationship between the constitutions the legate suggested for St Mary's, York, in 1205,

[95] *M. O.*, pp. 414–15.

[96] See B. Thorpe, *Diplomatarium Anglicum aevi Saxonici* (London, 1865), pp. 615–17.

[97] *HRH*, p. 78. H fo. 86ʳ; V fo. 16ʳ.

[98] H fo. 85ᵛ (incorrectly rubricated 'Witebi'); V fo. 15ᵛ. On St Mary's, York, see also J. Burton, 'A confraternity list from St Mary's abbey, York', *Revue Bénédictine*, lxxxix (1979), 325–33, esp. 326–30.

and those for Evesham. It was at St Mary's, York, that Abbot Randulf
was blessed as abbot by the legate in 1214.

There was probably considerable solidarity with the Benedictine
community at Malmesbury, Evesham's nearest neighbour after
Worcester, with whom they shared much in common in the struggle
against the diocesan. The confraternity agreement between Malmesbury and Evesham was made comparatively late by Abbot Robert II
with Abbot Roger Norreis between 1190 and 1205, and declared that
the abbot or any brother of the other house had the right to enter the
chapter, to seek refuge in the house, and generally to share in all the
benefits, bodily and spiritual, as if he were a monk of that house.[99]
Delinquent monks were to be received not as prisoners, but as monks
of the cloister, and in some cases rights of voting in an abbatial
election (as well as the right to receive votes) were conceded, though
this is not stated in any of the Evesham arrangements and some of
these privileges may never have been used.[100] The convent of
Evesham also had a confraternity agreement with its daughter-
house, Odense, in Denmark, whereby any monk of Evesham, who
went to Odense with permission, was to be treated as a monk of the
house, and the same was the case for any Odense monk coming to
Evesham.[101]

The legacy of Thomas of Marlborough

As we have seen, Thomas's purpose in writing was not to provide a
record of a legal action brought before the papal curia in the
pontificate of a reforming pope, but to establish a written account
of the history of the community at Evesham so that its rights should
never again be lost. This was the driving force. Under the challenge
of a threat, and with disagreement as to how the threat should be met,
opinions come to be defined more exactly and rights become firmer.
There is no doubt that Evesham's rights were advanced by Thomas.
They could not have stayed static but they might well have declined.
Thomas improved the house's status in three ways. The opportunity
came to him in virtually three roles, first as proctor at Rome, secondly

[99] H fo. 84^r; V fo. 14^r. Printed *Mon. Angl.* ii, p. 19, num. xvi, from Cotton MS
Vitellius E XVII.

[100] Knowles in *M. O.*, pp. 474–5: he commented specifically on the Evesham
confraternities.

[101] H fos. 88^v–9^r; *Mon. Angl.* ii, p. 25, num. xxix, printed from V fo. 16^a. On Odense,
see P. King, 'English influence on the church of Odense in the early middle ages', *Journal
of Ecclesiastical History*, xiii (1962), 145–55.

as monastic official (most importantly as dean and sacrist), then finally as prior and as abbot. As the abbey's proctor he was directly involved in the legal process which had become so important for the maintenance of ancient rights. As dean of the Vale he was immediately concerned with the abbey's jurisdiction over the parishes in the Vale and as sacrist he had administrative responsibilities including the care for the abbey's buildings. To restore the community to its former status the cults of the Evesham saints and their shrines were important—matters that had concerned Thomas from his earliest associations with Evesham in the writing of the lives of Wigstan and Ecgwine. As prior, and later as abbot—both offices of great power and authority within the convent and the wider community—he was concerned in the business of the estates and in the government of the house. The restoration of good relations between the abbot and the convent and the building up of the community in numbers and resources were the tasks of his priorate and abbacy. At the time of Abbot Norreis's attempt to expel Thomas of Marlborough and Thomas de Northwich in 1206, thirty monks left with them on 25 November in that year. As old and infirm monks were left in charge of the sacred relics and the treasure of the church, we may presume the full number of the community to have been in the region of forty to fifty monks (see App. V, and **395**). We do not know, however, how many left during the Interdict: certainly recruitment is likely to have been at a low ebb prior to Norreis's deposition in 1213. The abbey had to be made vital again. It might be that the institution Thomas was so vigorously defending would face further challenges to its position in future. For this reason it was essential that there should be a written record so that the community should know its status and so that there should be no backsliding for lack of evidence. Thomas had witnessed the vulnerabilty of a house without adequate written records. His *History*, however, was for the purposes of the community alone. There was no idea of circulation and there is no evidence that there were other copies of the manuscript or that it circulated in thirteenth-century Benedictine houses or indeed anywhere else. That it has survived is a miracle of history.

III. THOMAS'S HISTORY

A. THE MANUSCRIPT: RAWLINSON MS A 287 (R)

Outline of the manuscript

1. Haimo of Auxerre *Expositio in Apocalypsim beati Ioannis*
   fos. 1^r–116^r

2. *Vita S. Odulfi*
   a. fos. 116^v–118^r (not edited by Macray)
   b. fos. 118^r–19^v Translation and Miracles of St Odulf (Macray, pp. 313–20)

3. *Acta Proborum Virorum*
   fos. 119^v–120^v (Macray, pp. 320–5)

4. *Vita S. Wistani*
   fos. 121^r–123^v 'editus a Thoma priore Eveshamie' (Macray, pp. 325–37)

5. *Vita beati Ecgwini et Miraculi*
   Prologue 'editus a Dominico priore Eveshamie' (Macray, pp. 1–2)
   fos. 123^v–124^r
   Liber Primus 'abbreviatus a Thoma priore Eveshamie': in the form of 12 'lectiones'
   (Macray, pp. 3–27); Explicit (Macray, pp. 27–9)
   fos. 124^r–130^r
   Translation of St Ecgwine: in the form of 12 'lectiones' (Macray, pp. 30–8)
   fos. 130^v–2^v
   Prologue of 'Liber Secundus' on the miracles, 'editus a Dominico' (Macray, p. 39)
   fos. 132^v–3^r
   Liber Secundus
   fos. 133^r–9^r (Macray, pp. 40–67)
   Liber Tercius
   fos. 140^r–82^v (Macray, pp. 69–260)
   fos. 182^v–94^r Continuation of the Lives and Deeds of the Abbots (Macray, pp. 260–310)

[fo. 187^r: the present edition ends here with the death of Abbot Thomas of Marlborough]

The first four sections have not been included in the present edition.

The Latin text of 2b, 3, and 4, however, is printed by Macray as Appendices (pp. 313–37), and the Continuation of the Lives and Deeds of the abbots after Thomas (from fos. 187^r–94^r) is on his pp. 278–310.

Quiring of Thomas's History

Four quires of 10 fos., + 2 additional fos. (180^r–181^r), of a large volume measuring 430×321 mm
Written space 296 mm×202–210 mm
Ruled for 41 lines; but fos. 141rb, 146vb, 179va, and 181rb are of 42 lines

(1) fos. 140^r–149^v Pars Prima
            fo. 148^r Pars Secunda begins

(2) fos. 150^r–159^v Pars Secunda
            fo. 155^v Pars Secunda ends
            fo. 155^v Pars Tercia begins

(3) fos. 160^r–169^v
            fo. 166^r Pars Tercia ends
            fo. 166^r Pars Quarta begins

(4) fos. 170^r–179^v
            fo. 176^r Pars Quarta ends
            fo. 176^r Pars Quinta begins
            [fo. 179^v—catchword *benedictum*]

Two folios, 180, 181
            fo. 181^v Pars Quinta ends
                                    End of 13th cent. hand

Fos. 182^r–194^r replacement leaves of the fifteenth century
     fo. 182^v end of Thomas's *History*
                                    later part of the Lives of the abbots
                                    begins (with Abbot Randulf)
     fo. 187^r death of Thomas
     fo. 194^r MS ends

B. THE MAKING OF THE MANUSCRIPT
(TERESA WEBBER)

The account of Thomas of Marlborough's deeds, which comprises one of the continuations of his *History*, states that among the books Thomas had caused to be made ('fecit') whilst prior of Evesham (1218–29) was 'Haymonem super Apocalypsim et uitas et gesta patronum et abbatum Eueshamie in uno uolumine' (Oxford, Bodleian Library, Rawlinson MS A 287, fo. 184^r; below, 523). This statement almost certainly refers to Rawlinson A 287 itself, a large, handsome manuscript (430×321 mm) which contains Haimo of Auxerre's commentary on the Apocalypse (fos. 1^r–116^r), Dominic of Evesham's *Vita S. Ecgwini* (fos. 123va–139^r; below, 1–111), and Thomas's *History* (fos. 140^r–194^v; below, 112–509, 510–46).[102] The entire manuscript (with the exception of fos. 182–94 which are fifteenth-century replacement leaves) was produced at Evesham during the early decades of the thirteenth century.

The physical characteristics of the manuscript suggest that it was not originally planned as a single unit but was probably compiled in two stages, the *Vite* and the *History* being added to an existing copy of Haimo's commentary which now occupies the first twelve quires. These twelve quires are the only ones that have quire signatures, and the quality of their parchment and the standard and consistency of ruling are much higher than that of the remainder of the manuscript. Although the *Vita S. Odulfi* begins on the final verso of quire 12, it is written in a different hand, and, given the difference in the quality of the parchment and the ruling of both the following quire in which the text is completed and those of the remainder of the manuscript, it seems likely that the *Vita S. Odulfi* and the other texts were added subsequently, and that Haimo's commentary was originally intended to be the only item in the manuscript. Nevertheless, the similarity of layout, script, and decoration throughout the manuscript not only points to a common origin for both the Haimo and the additions (as does the preference in both the Haimo and the *History* for quires of ten leaves rather than the more usual eight) but also suggests that the additional texts were intended to be viewed as having some form of textual relationship with the Haimo and that they were added not piecemeal, but as a group. All the texts are written in two columns

---

[102] Paragraphs 510–46 are a continuation of the *Lives and Deeds* of the abbots, incorporated earlier in Thomas's *History*.

with the same or very similar size of written-space ($c.296 \times 202$–210 mm), and the same or almost the same number of lines per column (41 lines for Haimo and the *History*, 42 for the *Vite*, with the first line of text written above the first ruled line). The major decoration throughout comprises very similar, well-executed pen-drawn initials in red and blue, with pen-flourishing. The visual presentation of the *History* differs from the rest of the manuscript in just one respect. Whereas rubrication for the Haimo and the *Vite* had been planned from the outset, the scribe of the *History* left no space other than for the opening brief rubrics introducing the prologue and the text proper. Running titles in the upper margin, dividing the text into five 'Particule', may have been included as part of the original scheme, since they may be in the same hand as that of the elaborate initials to the prologue and the text proper on fo. 140^r (the pen-flourishing added to the numeral 'III' on fo. 165^v is similar to that of the initials), but the text scribe left no space for rubrics within the text to indicate the beginning of each new *particula*, nor for any other text divisions. Instead, a different scribe subsequently added appropriate rubrics in the margins. This, coupled with the fact that the *History* begins at the start of a new quire, and is perhaps in a different hand from that of the *Vita S. Ecgwini*, might suggest that the *History* had originally existed as a separate unit. Other evidence, however, indicates that it was copied with the intention of following on directly from the *Vita S. Ecgwini*, since what is probably the original hand has rubricated both the prologue to the *History* and the beginning of the text proper as 'Liber tercius' and 'Liber secundus'. The refinements made subsequently to the apparatus of rubrics provided for the *History* may, therefore, be attributed to the likelihood that its exemplar had been in a less finished state than those of the other items of Rawlinson A 287.

Text scribes

The statement in the account of Thomas's deeds that he 'fecit . . . Haymonem super Apocalypsim et uitas et gesta patronum et abbatum Eueshamie in uno uolumine' led some scholars to assume that he produced the manuscript himself, or was at least its main scribe. It is now thought, however, that the term 'fecit' usually denotes responsibility for production rather than necessarily the actual process of copying.[103] Given the different stages in which the manuscript was

[*See p. lxviii for n. 103*]

put together, this statement may rather be interpreted as indicating Thomas's responsibility for bringing all the items of the manuscript together into a single volume.

The manuscript is written throughout in the same style of hand-writing: a formal book hand which displays to varying degrees some of the characteristics of Textualis (the general name given to the stylized formal book hands that evolved during the late twelfth and early thirteenth centuries), such as a tendency towards lateral compression, the shortening of ascenders, the breaking of curved strokes at the apex of letters such as m and n, the addition of lozenge-shaped serifs at the tops of minims, the fusion of facing curved strokes (such as b and o), and a preference for the 7-shaped tironian *nota*, d with an angled shaft, and an almost vertical 2-shaped r after o in place of respectively the ampersand, d with a vertical shaft, and either a rounder form of 2-shaped r or the upright minuscule form.

Despite the general similarity of the script throughout the manu-script, it is not all the work of a single scribe. Nevertheless, identifying the number of text scribes and distinguishing their stints is not easy. The manuscript was produced during a period in which handwriting, both for formal and informal purposes, was undergoing various developments, with the consequence that the handwriting of individual scribes can exhibit a wide degree of variation both in general appearance and in matters of detail. Thus, as in the first ten or so leaves of the *History*, portions of handwriting several leaves apart may exhibit a number of differences, yet it is impossible to detect a change of hand between those two points. The hand at the beginning of the *History* displays more of the character-istics of Textualis than any other part of the manuscript, yet, very gradually and with no obvious change of hand, the letter forms become less laterally compressed and the incidence of other Textualis characteristics becomes less frequent. Likewise, for the first 71 folios of Haimo's commentary, 'et' is represented by the ampersand; on fos. 71^v and 72^r both the ampersand and the tironian *nota* are employed, then from fo. 72^v onwards, the ampersand is rarely used. But there are no other indications that the change in scribal practice was the result of a change of hand. I would, therefore, tentatively conclude that the Haimo and the *History* are each the work of a single scribe. It is more difficult to establish whether both texts are the work of the

[103] H. Hoffmann, *Buchkunst und Königtum im ottonischen und frühsalischen Reich*, *MGH* Schriften xxx (1986), i. 42–6.

same scribe. The opening leaves of the *History* are written in a hand the proportions of which are much closer to that of fully developed Textualis than is the case with the hand of the Haimo, although well before the end of the text the proportions are the same as those of the Haimo. Furthermore, throughout the *History*, the scribe makes a greater use of the fusion of facing curves than does the scribe of the Haimo. Such differences, however, might be attributed to the fact that the *History* was produced some time after the Haimo, and that the scribe may have come to adopt (albeit not consistently) new scribal practices. It is possible, therefore, that the same scribe wrote the Haimo and the *History*.

The *Vita S. Odulfi* can more confidently be identified as the work of a different scribe. Although he wrote in the same style, his hand is much less fluent and appears to be a somewhat studied (and not always successful) attempt to write the kind of script employed by the scribe or scribes of the Haimo and the *History*. His activity in the manuscript is confined to this one text. Another scribe copied both the *Vita S. Wistani* and the *Vita S. Ecgwini*; his hand bears a close resemblance to that of the Haimo and the more 'conservative' style of the scribe of the *History*, but there are some differences, such as the position of the tie-marks used at the end of lines to indicate word-division, which prevent a more positive identification.

Corrections and additions

The *Vita S. Odulfi, Vita S. Ecgwini*, and the *History* all were subsequently corrected and revised to differing extents. A contemporary scribe whose hand I have not identified with certainty elsewhere in the manuscript rewrote over erasure a large portion of text at the end of the *Vita S. Odulfi* (fos. 119ra, line 3–120^{v}, with the exception of fo. 119rb, lines 34–7 which were not erased). Another contemporary scribe made three additions to the rubrics of the *Vita S. Ecgwini*, noting that the prologues to Books I and II had been 'editus a Dominico priore Eueshamie' and that Book I had been 'abbreuiatus a Thoma priore Eueshamie'. The *History* was much more extensively revised at various times and by different scribes. Apart from corrections probably made by the text scribe himself (usually over erasure), the earliest stage of revision may well have comprised the addition of a more detailed apparatus of rubrication and subject headings. This was, for the most part, added by a contemporary scribe who wrote a distinctive, somewhat

uncalligraphic hand, characterized by a backwards slope (most evident in letters formed with ascenders or descenders, such as b and p) and the forking of ascenders. This scribe also made at least five substantial corrections over erasure (fos. 146vb, lines 15 'modo est et kingleyam'–20 'molendino remisit' and 24 'molendinum de Samburna'–32 'eius tamen tempore'; 169ra, lines 7 'Quam rationem'–17 'cogeremur eosdem'; 169rb, lines 21 'Audistis etiam'–41 'extremo tempore'; 179rb, line 38 'Quare dixi'–179va, line 4 'a lite cessauimus'). He may also have added the letter from Abbot Reginald to Gilbert Foliot found in the lower margin of fo. 148^{v}. Another scribe, who wrote a more formal and practised book hand, added rubrication on fos. 160^{v}–164^{r} and 168^{v}. He may also have added the correction in the left-hand margin of fo. 158^{v} and the addition in the lower margin of fo. 169rb, following on directly from the correction over erasure made by the other rubricator-corrector. A later thirteenth-century corrector made one correction over erasure on fo. 172rb (lines 21 'pascere uiginti quinque'–26 'feretris eorum'), and several thirteenth-century hands supplied numerous corrections and additions on fos. 172^{v}–173^{v} concerning the revenues due to Evesham obedientiaries.

The original text of the *History* now ends abruptly in mid-sentence at the end of fo. 181^{v}. The remainder of the work of the original scribe and any subsequent piecemeal continuations have been removed and were replaced *en bloc* during the fifteenth century, the narrative being continued until the death of Abbot Roger Zatton. These replacement leaves (fos. 182–194) conceal the number of stages in which the *History* was added to between the original production of the manuscript and the supplying of the final thirteen leaves sometime after 1418. However, there is no evidence in the form of annotation to suggest that the manuscript received detailed attention during the fourteenth century. Other than the several thirteenth-century corrections and additions made on fos. 172^{v}–173^{v} to the account of revenues in Abbot Randulf's Disposition of the Revenues and Customs, the annotations found in the manuscript are in fifteenth-century hands, and, for the most part, are the work of Richard Pembroke (*BRUO* 1456), a monk of Evesham by 1428, who was elected abbot in 1461 and died in 1467. He made numerous short marginal annotations, chiefly drawing attention to subject matter in the adjacent text, not only in the *History* but throughout the entire manuscript.

Rawlinson A 287 is an important localizable and datable example of early-thirteenth century monastic manuscript production, and, like the manuscripts associated with Matthew Paris that were produced a little later at St Albans, testifies to the high standards of book production that could still be found within a monastic milieu during the first part of the thirteenth century. It gives physical substance to the documentary evidence concerning manuscript production at Evesham and the provisions made for it during the early thirteenth century. Abbot Randulf's Disposition of the Revenues (see below, 409, 411) assigned revenues to the prior for the purchase of parchment and for the provision of scribes to copy books and to the precentor for the purchase of ink and pigments. The account of Thomas's deeds in the *History* records his acquisitions of books for the abbey and distinguishes betweeen those he brought with him and those made by scribes at Evesham whilst he was prior and whilst he was abbot. The account also distinguishes between the liturgical books made by monastic scribes and the rest, presumably made by the paid scribes for whom revenues had been assigned to the prior in Randulf's Disposition. Unfortunately, Rawlinson A 287 is the only one of these books which can be identified with certainty. Very few other early thirteenth-century books with an Evesham provenance are known to survive, and I have not identified in them any of the hands found in Rawlinson A 287. But closely similar book hands to those in Rawlinson can be found in two contemporary (or perhaps slightly earlier) cartularies : BL Cotton MS Vespasian B XXIV and BL Harley MS 3763, fos. 58–94. These manuscripts are the work of a number of scribes employing different types and grades of script, and also contain numerous additions made at various times during the thirteenth century and later. Both contain the texts of a number of Anglo-Saxon diplomas (for the most part forged), written in formal book hands of the same type as found in Rawlinson A 287 (though not identifiable as the work of any of the Rawlinson scribes). The employment of formal book hands for the Anglo-Saxon diplomas by contrast with the more current hands used for most of the other documents in the two cartularies was almost certainly intended to convey the formality of the book hands employed in original Anglo-Saxon diplomas. The work of these scribes not only indicates a sense of decorum with regard to script but also reinforces the evidence of Rawlinson A 287 of the presence at Evesham of a number of scribes skilled in writing formal book

hands in the decades when monasteries are generally thought to have been giving way to urban localities as the main centres of manuscript production.

C. THE EVESHAM CARTULARIES AND OTHER SURVIVING RECORDS

Little of the abbey of Evesham survived the Dissolution. Many of its buildings were put to other uses, allowed to decay, or rifled for their stone, its library and archives destroyed or dispersed. There is unfortunately now no magnificent medieval archive, as there once was, and such as is still to be found at Canterbury, Durham, and Westminster. There are, however, two surviving cartularies of quality.

1. **British Library Cotton MS Vespasian B XXIV** (cited as V) is a fine, general cartulary, compiled in the twelfth and thirteenth centuries, which was in the possession of Dr Samuel Fell (1584–1649), dean of Christ Church, Oxford, from 1638. Where Fell got the manuscript from is unknown, but it is possible that it had arrived at Christ Church when the deanery of the Vale passed to the dean and chapter in 1546.[104] On the other hand, Fell may have acquired the manuscript from a Worcester source. From 1626, when he was appointed Lady Margaret professor of divinity, he held a canonry of Worcester and he had married into a Worcester family, the Wylds.[105]

The manuscript has no formal arrangement. It consists of 79 folios,[106] mainly concerning Evesham's rights and properties. The properties were mainly in the vicinity, in Worcestershire (including Ombersley, Hampton, Childswickham, and Bengeworth), Gloucestershire, and Oxfordshire, but also further afield in Northamptonshire (Badby), Middlesex (Hillingdon), and Lancashire (Penwortham). There are some details of rents and tenants. Charters of the donors, royal charters, and episcopal charters are found throughout the book under the relevant properties. The manuscript also includes the Domesday text, Evesham A (fos. 6–7^v), edited by Peter

---

[104] See Sayers, 'The proprietary church in England: a note on *Ex ore sedentis* (X. 5. 33. 17)', in *Zeitschrift der Savigny-Stiftung für Rechtsgeschichte, kan. abt.*, lxxiv (1988), 231–45, at p. 243.

[105] On Samuel Fell and the family, see *DNB* vi. 1162–3; and 1157–9, for his son also dean of Christ Church.

[106] First (paper) page numbered 1.

Sawyer.[107] The text begins on fo. 3 with a list of the feasts. On fo. 4 there is an incomplete document, followed by the grant of a corrody by Abbot Randulf and the convent. Fos. 4–5 is an excerpt from 'the good works of Prior Thomas' (to be found in the *Lives and Deeds* of the abbots), as described in Rawlinson, and on fo. 6 the *Lives* is continued, some of it a repeat, perhaps copied from R. The manuscript is contemporary with Thomas, and some sections are especially connected with him: his advice on privileges, the oaths of the officials and deans, and of the chaplains (fo. 74), and the report of a bond encashed by him and another proctor at Rome in 1205 (fo. 52^v). The latter is printed below as Appendix I. Interspersed among the general charters concerning Evesham's properties are agreements with other religious houses (Malmesbury, Winchcombe, Kenilworth, St Mary's, York, and Whitby) (fos. 14–15), charters concerning the Danish dependency of Odense (fos. 19, 22, 48),[108] and details of the number of monks and servants at Evesham in the early twelfth century (printed below as App. V). On fos. 76–80 there are full texts of some of the house's important papal letters which are found in R.

1. fo. 76^v First privilege of Pope Constantine, 709 (JL 2147) = R fo. 162rb (318–23)
2. fo. 76^v Second privilege of Pope Constantine, 713 (JL 2149) = R fo. 162vb (324–8)
3. fo. 77 Alexander III 'Pie postulatio uoluntatis', 1163 (JL 10877) = R fo. 163va (332–6)
4. fos. 78^v–9 Innocent II 'Sicut iniusta poscentibus', 1139 (JL 7999) = R fo. 163ra (329–31)
5. fo. 79 Clement III 'Largitione nostri muneris', 1189 (JL 16426)= R fo. 164rb (337–8)
6. fo. 80 Innocent III 'Ex ore sedentis', 1205 (P 2660) = R fo. 146va (342–55)

A rough description of 'the principal instruments', as Dugdale calls them, is given in *Mon. Angl.* ii, pp. 11–12 note a, with asterisks by those he prints *in extenso*.

---

[107] 'Evesham A, a Domesday Text', *Miscellany*, i (Worcs. Hist. Soc., 1960). Both cartularies have been extensively used by Dr H. B. Clarke, 'The Early Surveys of Evesham Abbey: an investigation into the problem of continuity in Anglo-Norman England' (Birmingham Ph.D. Thesis, 1977).

[108] Printed *Diplomatarium Danicum*, 1st ser. ii, 1053–1169, ed. L. Weibull (1963), nos. 24, 66, 67; and iii, no. 48.

2. The present **Harley MS 3763** in the British Library (cited as H) was in the possession of Henry Fleetwood of Penwortham before he disposed of it to Lord Harley, retaining the right to borrow it (fos. 1 and 2). Penwortham in Lancashire was a cell of Evesham, but, although this particular cartulary contains documents relating to Penwortham,[109] it is in the main a composite general cartulary of the thirteenth and fourteenth centuries, which may not have been bound up till after the Dissolution, and is unlikely to have been at Penwortham throughout the medieval period.

The manuscript consists now of 201 folios. Much of the material is also to be found in V.[110] The first section contains material relating to Ombersley church (to fo. 21^v), and various tracts, forms of libels, and procedural treatises (to fo. 44^v).[111] There are then charters concerning the general business of the convent, including ordinations of vicarages, presentations, appropriations (to fo. 54^v), Evesham's property (to fo. 59), Anglo-Saxon royal charters (fos. 62–7), knights and free tenants (fo. 68), properties, especially Penwortham, and agreements (fos. 70^v–94). Transcripts of the papal privileges occupy fos. 95–115^v. Here are recorded 68 letters, the earliest Pope Constantine's grants of 709 and 713, the latest a letter of Urban V of 1362. In between are all the major letters and privileges acquired by the abbot and the community in the intervening centuries. The compiler, or possibly a later annotator, noted whether the documents survived in the abbey's treasury or not. Royal charters from Henry III to Richard II are copied on fos. 119–149^v, and charters of the abbots and of the abbot and convent occupy fos. 153^v–163^v.

Some sections of the *History* and the *Lives and Deeds* of the abbots (fos. 169–79) are also to be found in this manuscript. They have been copied from R. Thomas's strictures on the conservation of privileges are copied (also from R) on fo. 116^v. Part of the confirmation of the legate, John of Ferentino, of the first disposition of the revenues of the abbey (printed below in App. II A, from a charter which is now lost) is on folios 69–70, and extracts from Abbot Randulf's disposition of the revenues and customs of the house are on fos. 150–3^v,

---

[109] Some printed as *Documents relating to the Priory and other Possessions in Lancashire of the Abbey of Evesham*, ed. W. A. Hulton (Chetham Soc., xxx (1853)).

[110] The contents are roughly described in *Mon. Angl.*, ii, pp. 10–11 note f.

[111] For an analysis of the first section of the manuscript, containing the legal material, see J. Sayers, 'An Evesham manuscript containing the treatise known as "Actor et Reus" (British Library Harley MS 3763)', *Bulletin of Medieval Canon Law*, n.s. vi (1976), 77–9, repr. in J. E. Sayers, *Law and Records in Medieval England* (Variorum, 1988).

perhaps taken from the Rawlinson manuscript or from the Cotton charter (see App. II B for the collated text). Amongst the miscellaneous material at the end of the manuscript, characteristic of a general cartulary, are 'Reasons to support the argument that the dean of Evesham's office is a dignity' (fo. 186), followed by fourteenth-century material connected with the dean, mortuaries, notes concerning the obedientiaries, and pensions.

Papal letters in V and H

As noted above, both the major Evesham cartularies include the important papal privileges of the house. The conspectus below shows their relationship with R. In general where one can check, H follows V. H, as mentioned above, comments on the originals surviving.

R	V	H
Innocent III 'Constitutis in presentia' (Ferentino 22 May 1203) (Not in P) fo. 153^{rb-vb} (245–7)	——	——
Constantine I [709] (JL 2147) fo. 162^{rb-va} (318–23)	——	fo. 95^r no original
Constantine I (713) (JL 2149) fos. 162vb–163ra (324–8)	——	fo. 95^v no original
Innocent II 'Sicut iniusta poscentibus' (Lateran, 16 April 1139) (JL 7999) fo. 163^{ra-va} (329–31)	fo. 78^v	fo. 95^v no original
Alexander III 'Pie postulatio uoluntatis' (Tours 5 June 1163) (JL 10877) fos. 163va–164rb (332–6)	fo. 77^r	fo. 96^r original
Clement III 'Largitione nostri muneris' (Lateran 10 July 1189) (JL 16426) fo. 164rb (337–8)	fo. 79^r	fo. 98^v no original
Celestine III 'Largitione nostri muneris' (St Peter's 13 Jan. 1192 (JL 16801) fo. 164va (339–41)	fo. 79^v	fo. 99^r original

Innocent III 'Ex ore sedentis' (St Peter's
18 Jan. 1206) (P 2660)
    fos. 164va–166ra (342–55)   fo. 80^r fo. 99^v
                                                      original

Innocent III 'Auditis et intellectis' (St
Peter's 3 Feb. 1206) (P 2681)
    fos. 168$^{ra–va}$ (372–4)   ——   fo. 101^r
                                                        original

Innocent III 'Presentium uobis auctoritate'
(St Peter's 7/8 Feb. 1206) (Not in P)
    fos. 168$^{va–vb}$ (376)   ——   ——

Innocent III 'Cum a nobis' (Lateran 16 Feb.
1216) (Not in P)
    fos. 174$^{va–vb}$ (431)   ——   fo. 102^r
                                                     no original

Gregory IX 'Cum dilecti filii' (Lateran 2
May 1230) (Not in P)
    fo. 185va (533)   ——   ——
(Gregory IX issued H fos. 97^v–8^r 'Licet singuli archiepiscopi' on the
same day as the above letter)

Variations between the texts

Alexander III
H and V use 'subscripsi', while R uses 'subscribo'. V has only a single
Amen, but V gives more details of cardinals' titles. H also gives the
details of the cardinals' subscriptions, but omits two. The subscriptions are positioned differently in R and V.

Innocent II
'Sicut iniusta poscentibus' 16 Apr. 1139. H has (incorrectly) as 'Sicut
iniusta petentibus'

Clement III
V gives Roger as the addressee, the other two state Adam. H omits
the triple Amen

Celestine III
Both V and H omit the triple Amen

H and V probably used the originals of Alexander III and Celestine
III, and H, perhaps, of Clement III

Other Evesham sources

British Library

Cotton MS Augustus II 11 (printed Appendix II B).

Cotton MS Cleopatra E I fos. 34^r–5^r: copies of first and second privileges of Pope Constantine

Cotton MS Cleopatra E I fos. 64^r–5^r: copy of second privilege of Pope Constantine (713)

Cotton MS Nero D III (fos. 1^r–218^r, cartulary of St Leonard's hospital, York). Evesham material, listed in the contents as no. 2, 14th–15th cent., with added notes. Eight folios, fos. 219^r–226^r (formerly fos. 242^r–9^r), much of it printed *Mon. Angl.* ii, pp. 21, 22, 31–3, num. xvi, xxi, and xxxiv. William de Cheriton, agreement concerning Ombersley and Badby (fo. 219); judicial material (fos. 219^v–20^r, heriots and mortuaries, perhaps from Harley 3763 fos. 186^r–7^r); sacrist's rents (fos. 220^r–1^r); charter of Henry duke of Lancaster, concerning Penwortham; verses on the bells, 1354 (fo. 223^r); charter of Abbot John and the convent of Evesham, 1450 (fo. 226^r); additional note concerning Prior Thomas of Marlborough and heriots in the Vale (fo. 222^v).

Cotton MS Titus C IX fos. 1^r–38^r Register of Abbot Richard Bromsgrove (1418–35). Includes letters concerning his election (fos. 1^r–3^r); the Benedictine general chapter and visitation (fos. 16^r, 25^v); ordinations (fos. 17^r, 33^v–4^r); royal letters, including the king to the pope and the Council of Basle (fo. 24^v); indulgences for Syon abbey (fos. 30^v–1^r); the charter of Abbot Thomas of Marlborough concerning visitation, 1233 (fo. 22^v: see App. IV— which, however, is printed from Lambeth MS 1212).

Cotton MS Vespasian B XV 16th-cent. fos. 19–22 (formerly fos. 17^r– 20^r), 'Ex chronico monasterii Eueshamensis', Lives and Deeds of the Abbots to Abbot Clement Lichfield, 1539, from Harley MS 3763, fos. 169^r–79^r, printed *Mon. Angl.* ii, pp. 36–9 num xxxvi, fo. 21^v (beginning with Abbot Richard Bromsgrove, 1418) to fo. 22^r (the end) printed Macray App. II B, with incorrect foliation.

Cotton MS Vitellius D III 1 fo. 131^r: letter of Peter of Blois, archdeacon of London, to the prior (P.) and the convent of Evesham; as recorded by Dugdale and printed *Mon. Angl.* ii, pp. 40–1 num. xl. This was destroyed in the Cotton fire of 1731. It is printed also in *PL* 207, no. cxlii, cols. 425–8.

Cotton MS Vitellius E XVII fos. 224^r–50^r. Fragment of a late

14th-cent. register, damaged in the Cotton fire of 1731, containing miscellaneous material: agreements between Malmesbury and Evesham, and Evesham and Whitby (fo. 224^r), rents and payments from obedientiaries (sacrist, especially, also almoner and chamberlain), leaves from a calendar (fos. 241^r–6^v), anniversaries (fos. 227^v–8^r, 239^r), obits (fos. 248^r–9^r, extremely damaged). Some material printed *Mon. Angl.* ii, p. 19, num. xvi; pp. 34–6, num. xxxv; pp. 39–40, num. xxxviii–ix; and 'Summa decimarum spiritualium et temporalium Eveshamie' (fo. 238^r) printed p. 39, and the office of the precentor (fo. 250^r) printed p. 39, num. xxxvii (much damaged).

Harley MS 229. Chronicles belonging to Evesham, including Eusebius of Caesarea. 3 folios (fos. 17^r–19^r): abbots of Evesham, from the Conquest to Abbot Zatton (1379–1418) printed *Mon. Angl.* ii, pp. 26–7, num. xxxii.

Harley MS 744. Noted by Macray, but of minor interest. 17th-cent. transcripts from records in the Tower of London. Under letter E, fos. 137^r, 154^v, 164^v. A 19th-cent. hand has noted 'This book would be much more useful if the names of the counties were *always* put in the margin'.

Lambeth Palace Library, London SE1

MS 1212 fo. 48^v: charter of Abbot Thomas and the convent concerning visitation by the archbishop of Canterbury (see below, App. IV).

MS 589 pp. 40, 41: Wharton's notes of the succession and deaths of the abbots to the Dissolution, from the two Evesham obituaries, Cotton MSS Vitellius E XII and XVII (the former burned and the latter much damaged in the 1731 fire).

MS 585 pp. 230, 665: further notes by and of Wharton.

Wellcome Library for the History and Understanding of Medicine, London NW1

MS 209, four endpapers (two at the front and two at the back), incomplete and much cut down: 13th-cent. text of certain legal cases, decisions, arguments, and procedural points; glossed 13th–14th cent. Reference is made to the case over the Vale which identifies the leaves as certainly from an Evesham manuscript. The last pope to be mentioned is Pope Gregory IX (1227–41).

Bodleian Library, Oxford

MS Tanner 223 fo. 53^v, see Lambeth MS 1212 (above).

Gough MS Worcestershire (notes and extracts made by Tindal from V, H, and Harley MS 744)

MS Chs. Worcs. A 2 no. 2: chirograph between Abbot Thomas and the convent of Evesham and Prior Nicholas and the convent of Daventry concerning Badby.

Worcestershire Record Office 899: 49 BA 8746: forged papal letter of Pope Gregory IX

Evesham Almonry Museum Accession no. 127. (Purchased at Sotheby's sale of Monday 6 July 1964) Copy of first privilege of Pope Constantine (709)

D. PREVIOUS EDITION

Bodleian Library, Oxford, MS Rawlinson A 287, fos. 118–194, was edited as *Chronicon abbatiae de Evesham, ad annum 1418*, by the Reverend William Dunn Macray for the Rolls Series and published in 1863.[112] He included the Translation of St Odulf, the Life of St Wigstan, and Dominic's *Acta Proborum Virorum* in Appendices. Macray, a special assistant in the Bodleian Library, was responsible for many catalogues of various collections in the Manuscripts Department, and for the two-volume *Calendar of Charters and Documents relating to Selborne and its Priory* (Hants Rec. Soc. 4 and 8, 1891–4), to be found in the muniment room at Magdalen College, of which he became a Fellow. He contributed extensively to the Reports of the Royal Commission on Historical Manuscripts (see Reports 11, 13, 14, 15). He was also the editor of two other volumes in the Rolls Series: *Chronicon abbatiae Rameseiensis* (RS 83, 1886), and *Charters and Documents illustrating the History of . . . Salisbury*, selected by W. H. Rich Jones (RS 97, 1891).

Macray was a careful scholar and a good classical Latinist, who naturally preferred classical Latin spellings and endings. We have not found significant errors of transcription in his text. There is one

[112] Macray matriculated at New College, Oxford, in 1844. At the time of the publication of his Evesham volume, he was chaplain of Magdalen College and curate of St Mary Magdalen. He became rector of Ducklington (near Witney) in 1870 and a Fellow of the Society of Antiquaries in 1873. In 1890 his *Annals of the Bodleian Library* was published. For his career, see J. Foster, *Alumni Oxonienses: 1715–1886* (4 vols., Oxford, 1888), iii. 899.

example of annotation leading to a misunderstanding:[113] otherwise Macray did not err. He did not, however, note marginalia. As a manuscript cataloguer and archivist, he took care to examine other Evesham sources both within the Bodleian and outside in the British Library, including V and H.[114] Since Macray's edition, no further manuscripts of Thomas's *History* have come to light, but modern research has been able to use resources that were non-existent or difficult to use nearly 140 years ago and has provided new opportunities for the re-examination of the text.[115] We hope that we have added to the enlightenment of the meaning and to the greater understanding of this unique text.

E. THIS EDITION

Every attempt has been made to collate the key and only manuscript of Thomas's *History* (R) with related sources, such as V and H.

The manuscript went through some re-formation during the time that Thomas was supervising it, as Dr Webber has shown above. This is clear from the contemporary deletions and overwriting of important single words, phrases, and, in some cases, whole sections. The longer corrections belong to the author. They are either made to fit the erased area or extended into the margins, that on fo. 147ra extending down into the bottom left-hand margin by seven lines and continuing at the top of fo. 147rb, where it adds two lines. Another instance on fo. 169rb shows eleven lines added below the text, which had been ruled for only 41 lines, making a total of fifty-two. In the bottom margin of fo. 148^v is a letter of Gilbert Foliot in a neat thirteenth-century charter-hand, the content of which it was clearly thought relevant to insert at that particular point. The text of the letter has been printed below as Appendix III.

---

[113] When he came to editing the text of 'Ex ore sedentis' in R, Macray (pp. 179–83), rightly gave variant readings in H and V, but on p. 183 he did not explain that the *consensu* for *consilio* (and the *nulli omnino* for the plain *nulli*) in the 'Ex ore' in H came from the fact that he was reading a much later confirmation of Innocent VI of 12 Nov. 1360.

[114] On one occasion Macray confused V fo. 13^r with H fo. 113^r (old foliation, now fo. 116^r).

[115] Unfortunately digitization was not able to bring up readable underlying texts in two instances, but we are most grateful to Dr Natalie Tchernetska of Trinity College, Cambridge, for trying to do this for us.

In the seventeenth century, expressions such as *papa, sedes apostolica, summus pontifex, apostolica auctoritate*, and the like, were expunged or struck through. Having no useful significance, these erasures and strikings out have not been noted.

Marginalia and Notes

Marginalia and notes show the use of the manuscript throughout its history. Those of the thirteenth, fourteenth, and fifteenth centuries have been recorded, but not those of the sixteenth and seventeenth centuries. In the main these notes were made alongside the account of the legal proceedings at Rome and in the margins surrounding Abbot Randulf's disposition and constitutions, both of which clearly engendered much interest.

Editorial conventions

Headings

The contemporary red headings that are provided in the margins (sometimes with crosses against the text to show where they belong) have in all cases been brought into the text as headings without comment.

Spelling

As the manuscript is very close to the author and, indeed, has some of his corrections, the original spelling has been retained throughout, with only the following exceptions. R consistently uses excercere etc. for exercere etc., cecessi for secessi, and sanccimus for sancimus. Because these renderings may cause confusion to the modern reader, they have been silently emended.

Word separation

Words that have been separated, e. g. quam diu, quam uis, quo aduixit, pro culdubio etc. have been silently emended.

Capitalization

The capitalization of the manuscript has not been followed. Capitals have been used only for names of persons, places, the Deity.

Punctuation

The punctuation has been modernized.

Personal names

In the translation Old English personal names have been rendered in standard West-Saxon spelling. The name Ecgwine has always been given in the form Ecgwinus in the Latin, though there are many variations, viz. Eguuinus, Egwinus, and Ecgwinus. Latin personal names have not been translated where there is no obvious synonym.

Place names

Latin place names have not been extended unless the extension is certain. Suspension marks have been used where there is doubt. The Vale (of Evesham) is always given a capital to distinguish it from any other vale.

In the translation, places that are *not* identified by county are within Worcestershire. All other places, with the exception of county towns and significant cities, are identified by their counties within square brackets. In the Index, *all* places (including those in Worcestershire) have been identified with their counties. The counties are those as before the redefinition of 1 April 1974.

Dates

Dates have also been supplied in square brackets in the translation where necessary. All dates have been given in New Style.

Brackets

Pointed brackets indicate editorial additions in the Latin text, in accordance with OMT style.

Paragraphs

In order to facilitate use of both the Latin text and the translation, the paragraphs have been numbered in bold type throughout.

Translation note

Indulgentia. The chronicler uses this word in two slightly different but significant senses. Firstly he employs it for the *indulgentie*, the concessions, granted by Popes Clement III and Celestine III, allowing the abbot of Evesham the use of the pontificals. Where the word occurs in this type of document it has been translated as indult. Its use in this sense is found in paragraphs **281**, **290**, **299**, **337**, **339**, **344**, **349**, **350**, **387**, **395**, **397**. (The translation, indulgence, has been avoided because it has come to be associated with the remission of

punishment due to sin which is not what is intended here.) Secondly, Thomas uses this word to signify the papal grant or concession to the bishop of Worcester of the power to visit the abbey. This is more difficult to translate with exactitude, and where *indulgentia* occurs in this sense we have chosen to call it an empowerment; see paragraphs 195, 196, 204, 245, 268, 271, 278, 500.

Ius commune. This phrase has not been translated but left in the Latin so as to avoid any confusion with the English Common Law. The *ius commune* was an amalgamation of Roman law and of canon law as developed in medieval Europe. For Thomas's citations, see below, 245, 302, 303, 357, 381, 382.

The word *dominus*, an indeterminate term of respect before names, has been ignored in the translation except where it means the Deity, on one occasion where it is used for St Ecgwine (viz. my lord and saint), and where it is used in an address, e.g. my lord bishop, my lord abbot, etc. The lord of Canterbury, Worcester, etc. has been translated as archbishop or bishop as appropriate to the see.

IV. CHRONOLOGY

A. FICTION AND FACT: SIGNIFICANT DATES IN EVESHAM'S HISTORY BEFORE 1190
(dates in italics are uncertain)

701   King Æthelred of the Mercians gives the site of Evesham ('Æthomme') to Ecgwine, bishop of the Hwicce (source Thomas, following Byrhtferth and Dominic: Thomas supplies the date (13, 27, 115).

703   He also gives Stratford, Chadbury castle (Thomas only), and the monastery of Fladbury (28, 115)

704   Foundation of the monastery at Evesham by Ecgwine (18)
King Cenred of the Mercians and King Offa of the East Saxons give 84 hides round Evesham (28)

709   Kings Cenred and Offa go to Rome (source Thomas, from Bede probably, *HE* v. 18–19 (pp. 516–17) and v. 24 (pp. 566–7, for date)). Ecgwine accompanies them (*JW* ii. 166–7) (15, 29)

	Æthelwig becomes abbot of Evesham (**151**)
1066, post	King William I entrusts him with control of most of the Midlands (Worcs., Glos., Oxon, Warws., Herefs., Staffs., and Salop) (**156**)
1073–4	Three monks (two of Evesham and one of Winchcombe) set out to revive monasticism in the north of England at Jarrow, Melrose, Wearmouth, and Whitby (Symeon of Durham, *Libellus de exordio atque procursu istius, hoc est Dunelmensis ecclesie*, ed. and trans. D. Rollason (OMT, 2000), pp. 200–11)
1077	Death of Abbot Æthelwig. He is succeeded by the first Norman abbot of Evesham, Abbot Walter (**171, 173**)
1077	Odo of Bayeux obtains lands belonging to the abbey of Evesham (**173–4**)
1100	Writ of King William II: no bishop is to hold ordinations or synods or confer orders at Evesham, unless requested by the abbot (V fo. 29^v; *Regesta Regum Anglo-Normannorum*, ed. H. W. C. Davis, i (Oxford, 1913), no. 429)
1104	Death of Abbot Walter (see *HRH*, p. 47)
	Dominic, historian and hagiographer, is a monk of Evesham by this date, and prior by 1125. He writes the Life of St Ecgwine (**1, 40, 65**), the Life of St Odulf (text Macray, pp. 313–20), the Acts of Worthy Men (text Macray, pp. 320–5), and the Miracles of the Virgin. He dies in the 1130s or 1140s and before 1145 (see Jennings, *EHR* lxxvii (1962), pp. 298, 301, 323–4)
1130	Reginald Foliot becomes abbot (**178**)
1139	Privilege 'Sicut inusta' obtained from Pope Innocent II (**178**, text **329–31**; JL 7999)
?1149–50	William Beauchamp and Roger, earl of Hereford, plunder Evesham lands (**180**)
1161	Abbot Adam becomes abbot (**182**)
1163	Privilege of Pope Alexander III (**183**, text **332–6**; JL 10877)
1189	Death of Abbot Adam (see *HRH*, p. 47)

B. CHRONOLOGICAL SUMMARY OF THOMAS'S LIFE
AND THE MAJOR EVENTS OF THE YEARS
1202–1236

1160×70?	Thomas born. His parents are unknown (see above, pp. xviii–xix)
1180s	Thomas studies at Paris, probably Arts, under Stephen Langton, later archbishop of Canterbury. His fellow students include Richard Poore, later bishop of Salisbury (450)
1188×93	Thomas studies law at Oxford, under Masters John of Tynemouth, Simon of Sywell, and Honorius of Richmond, and later teaches there (230, 522)
1189 12 Nov.	Death of Abbot Adam of Evesham (see *HRH*, p. 47)
before 1190	Thomas has some contact with the abbey of Evesham: begins to write the Life of St Wigstan and to abridge Prior Dominic's Life of St Ecgwine (44)
1190 Jan.	Roger Norreis, prior of Christ Church, Canterbury, is made abbot of Evesham (185)
1190 19 or 20 Nov.	Death of Archbishop Baldwin of Canterbury (see *HBC*, p. 232)
1197 probably	First complaint of the convent about the behaviour of Abbot Norreis made to the legate, Archbishop Hubert Walter (191)
1198	Second complaint to the archbishop who was no longer legate (as Pope Celestine III had died in Jan.) (193)
1199 or 1200	Thomas is professed as a monk of the abbey of Evesham (516)
?1200 or 1201	Archbishop Hubert Walter comes to Evesham (see 193)
1202 15 Aug.	Mauger, bishop of Worcester, makes first attempt to visit Evesham (195)
17 Aug.	The convent refuses to accept his visitation (204)
23 Aug.	Bishop Mauger excommunicates the convent (210)

1203 ?Spring	Archbishop Hubert Walter comes again to Evesham (238)
	First written record of the customs and revenues made (239)
1203 22 May	Enquiry into the bishop's rights over the abbey committed to judges delegate, the pope reserving judgment for himself (245–7)
1204 Sept–Nov.	Abbot Norreis and Thomas of Marlborough, as proctor, set out for Rome to appeal against the bishop. (Thomas left on 29 Sept.) (261–3)
1204 Nov.–mid March 1206	Thomas is at the Roman curia (263, 390), except for the half year spent at Bologna (see below)
1205 18 Apr.	Thomas goes to Bologna for six months to brush up his law (274)
24 Apr.	Report of the papal commission in England, granting immediate jurisdiction over the abbey to the bishop, but referring the long-term decision to the pope, as requested by the terms of their mandate (244–50, 254, and see 243 for date)
after 29 Sept.	Thomas returns to the Roman curia (280)
24 Dec.	Pope Innocent III declares the abbey's exemption. Thomas all but faints for joy (314–17)
1206 18 Jan.	The papal sentence ('Ex ore sedentis') is put into writing (text 342–55)
Jan.	The case concerning jurisdiction over the Vale commences in Rome (356 fol.)
3 and 7/8 Feb.	Papal mandate to the bishops of Ely and Rochester, and to Master Benedict of Sawston, canon of St Pauls's, who are required to establish the facts in the case over the Vale (372–4)
May–Autumn/Winter	Legation of Cardinal John of Ferentino to England (C. & S. ii. 1, p. 4)
(perhaps Aug.)	He visits Evesham (392). He also visits St Mary's abbey, York, with which Evesham has a confraternity arrangement, and advises written customs there (see Cheney, EHR, xlvi (1931))

1206 (perhaps Aug.)	The legate confirms the agreement between the abbot and convent (**393, 430**)
	Thomas is made dean of the Vale (the officer who had archidiaconal powers over the area) (**576**)
25 Nov.	Many of the monks, including Thomas, unable to put up with Abbot Norreis's persecution any longer, leave the convent (**395**)
1208 23 Mar.	The papal Interdict on England is pronounced (**437**; see *C. & S.*, ii. 1, p. 11)
1213 20 Sept.	The papal legate, Nicholas bishop of Tusculum, arrives in England (**447**)
	He was to confirm King John's surrender of the kingdoms and to secure the right conditions to lift the Interdict. He was also to fill vacant abbeys and to punish those who had damaged the Church (see *C. & S.*, ii. 1, pp. 20–1)
Nov.	He comes to Evesham and begins an enquiry into the conduct of Abbot Norreis (**459**). Thomas gives evidence (**461–84**)
22 Nov.	The legate deposes Roger Norreis as abbot of Evesham (**493, 510** for the date)
1214 20-22 Jan.	Election of Randulf, prior of Worcester, as abbot (**502–3**)
2 July	The papal Interdict is finally relaxed (**447**; see *C. & S.*, ii. 1, p. 11)
1215	Thomas attends the Fourth Lateran Council with Abbot Randulf (**521**)
1216 16 Feb.	Papal confirmation of the disposition of the revenues and the customs of the house (**431**)
1217	Thomas becomes sacrist, in charge of building works (**516, 521**)
1218	Thomas is appointed prior (**521–2**). As prior, he composes his *History* of the abbey (see above, pp. xxi, xxiii–xxv)
1229 17 Dec.	Death of Abbot Randulf (**531**)
20 Dec.	Election of Thomas as abbot (**532**)
1230 2 May	Pope Gregory IX orders a new election. Thomas is re-elected (**533**)

12 July	Thomas is blessed as abbot by the bishop of Coventry at Chester (**534**)
29 Sept.	Thomas gains possession of the abbey (**536**)
1236 12 Sept.	He dies and is buried in the abbey of Evesham in the tomb that he had prepared for himself (**539, 546**)

TEXT AND
TRANSLATION

⟨LIBER I⟩

fo. 123va **1.** *Incipit prologus in uitam beati Ecgwini episcopi et confessoris et de miraculis que Deus per eum dum hac mutabili luce adhuc[a] frueretur operari dignatus est,[b]editus a Dominico priore Eueshamie[b][1]*

fo. 123vb Diuinorum series et altitudo misteriorum, quanto sepius recitatur, attentius auditur, diligentius consideratur, tanto audientis animus auditu expauescit, admiratione obstupescit, magnitudinis consideratione euanescit; unde Psalmista, 'Accedet homo ad cor altum, et exaltabitur Deus'.[2] Quanto enim homo accedere et accedendo ascendere ad Deum nititur, tanto Deus exaltari et exaltando elongari conspicitur. Nam cum seuus furor Caldaici regis tres illos ex Iudea gente pueros in fornacem misisset, ipsamque fornacem pice ac ceteris ignium fomentis succendi omnimodis elaborasset, quanta diuine fuit eminentia glorie quod illi per flammas illesi deambulabant, ymnum Deo canebant, tamque morosa et ordinata[3] supputatione uniuersa Dei opera ad ipsius laudem prouocabant! Ipsa tyranni rabies id contuendo exterrita pertimuit.[4]

2. Denique alius eiusdem imperii tyrannus, cum Danielem in lacum leonum misisset et ipsos leones longa dierum inedia seuientes in ipsam pene rabiem conuertisset, quanta uirtus diuina emicuit, quod leones fame prorsus addicti coram se uirum expositum uidebant et nullo eum morsu attingere audebant! Ipse tyrannus id condigna extollens admiratione, in uocem laudis atque confessionis potentie superne erupit.[5] Quemadmodum uero sub temporibus legis que, sicut ait apostolus, 'iram operabatur',[6] terroris et comminationis Deus

---

[a] *written over an erasure, and* adhuc *has been corrected and squeezed in* [b-b] *written in a different hand?, over an erasure, and an additonal line has been taken for* priore Eueshamie

---

[1] Dominic's *Vita S. Ecgwini* Book I (before it was edited and abbreviated by Thomas) is edited by M. Lapidge in *Analecta Bollandiana*, xcvi (1978), 65–104, at pp. 77–104. It is cited here as DE i. DE ii refers to Lapidge's transcript of Book II. For details, see above, p. xiv, Sigla.

For Byrhtferth's Life of St Ecgwine, written in the early 11th cent., see M. Lapidge, 'Byrhtferth and the *Vita S. Ecgwini*', *Mediaeval Studies*, xli (1979), 331–53, repr. in *Anglo-Latin Literature 900–1066* (Hambledon: London, 1993), pp. 293–315. Byrhtferth's Life of St Ecgwine was known to Thomas.

[2] Ps. 63: 7–8.

[BOOK I]

1. *Here begins the Prologue to the Life of Ecgwine, bishop and confessor, and the account of the miracles which God deigned to perform through him, while he was still enjoying this transitory life, written by Dominic, prior of Evesham*[1]

The more often one recites the frequency and greatness of divine mysteries, the more attentively men listen to such stories, and the more diligently they contemplate them, all the more do their minds experience fear and, becoming struck with wonder, feel their puniness as they consider the greatness of such mysteries. Hence, the Psalmist writes: 'A man will search even the depths of his heart, and God will be exalted'.[2] Indeed, the more a man strives to approach God and to reach him, as he attempts this, the more God is seen to be exalted, and in being thus exalted is observed to be high above mankind. As when the Chaldean king, in his fierce anger, cast those three young men of the Jewish race into the furnace, and did all he could to stoke that furnace with pitch and other kinds of fuel for the fire, how great and excellent was God's glory, when they walked about unharmed amidst the flames, singing a hymn to God, and despite so deliberate a calculation which had been ordered,[3] they stirred all God's creation to his praise. The very madness of the tyrant changed to terror as he gazed at this, and became a great fear.[4]

2. Then again, when another tyrant of that same empire cast Daniel into the den of lions, and had made those lions almost mad, ravenous as they were from lack of food for days, how greatly did divine power show itself, when the lions, which had suffered such hunger, saw a defenceless man in their midst, but did not dare to savage him with their teeth. That very tyrant in his great amazement, applauded what had happened, and broke out into words of praise and confession of the power of the Lord above.[5] As in the times of the law, which, as the apostle says, 'brought retribution',[6] God exercised the judgements of

---

[3] Nebuchadnezzar had ordered that the furnace be made seven times as hot as usual; Dan. 3: 19. The reference and the comparison come straight out of Byrhtferth.

[4] For the story of the Chaldean king (Nebuchadnezzar) and the three men (Shadrach, Meshach, and Abed-nego), see Dan. 3: 8–30.

[5] This tyrant is King Darius. For the story, see Dan. 6.

[6] Rom. 4: 15.

exercebat iudicia, ita sub temporibus gratie tanquam filiis suis sue benignitatis euidentiora demonstrat indicia. Quanta enim gratia quod supra pectus tante maiestatis, ipsius scilicet omnipotentie, discipulus tanquam in sinu matris recumbebat! Merito humana debilitas ad tante magnitudinem uirtutis exclamat, 'Domine, audiui auditum tuum | et timui',[1] consideraui opera tua et expaui.

fo. 124ra

3. Nec solum in anterioribus, uerum et modernis temporibus multa et multum preclara dignationis sue circa nos Deus aliquando prebet insignia. Diuerso quippe temporum successu tanquam diuersis noctium horis per orbem sydera producit, uiros equidem religione approbatos, scientia preclaros, sermonis facundia et dignitate adornatos, signorumque magnificentia ubique admirandos, quibus nulla hereticorum uersutia, nulla Stoichorum, nulla Achademicorum, nulla denique philosophorum contraire potest astutia. Sicut enim sol aureus suo exortu uniuersa noctis nubila exturbat, ita ueritas per eos ubique falsitatis machinamenta subuertit et dissipat.

4. Inter quos, memoria nostra, uelut sydus conspicuum exortum est in Brittannie partibus, sub regibus Merciorum Aedelredo et Kenredo, beatus uir Ecgwinus, cuius actibus digne scribendis ipse uix sufficeret, si adesset, Homerus. Quantus proinde ego, qui eius uitam scribere presumo, longe prorsus infra pedes aliorum positus, et digne illius excellentiam stilo commendare omnino impotens atque nescius? Verum si per me uita illius aliis utcumque innotescit, optinenda est uenia, quoniam in templo Dei sunt phiale, sunt et sciathi.[2] Eorum itaque auctoritate coactus et oratione adiutus, quorum preceptioni me parere et morem gerere expedit, Deo opitulante, conabor pro uiribus meis describere,

aquis ille uir fuerit tantus, quo stemate sanguinis ortus,
quos habuit mores, demum quos edidit actus.a

Explicit prologus.

---

a–a If fuerit is om. this can be read as two hexameters

1 Hab. 3: 2.

terror and threats, so now in these times of grace he shows clear signs of his mercy, as it were to his own children. What grace it is that allows a disciple to recline upon the breast of such majesty, I mean that of the almighty, as upon the breast of his mother! With good reason human weakness proclaims the greatness of such goodness: 'O Lord, I have heard of your fame, and have been fearful';[1] I have considered your works, and stand in awe.

3. Not only in times past, but also in modern times God sometimes shows many great and wonderful signs of his grace towards us. As He brings forth stars at different times, as season succeeds season, so he brings forth men highly regarded for their religion, distinguished in knowledge, endowed with eloquence and dignity, admired everywhere for the greatness of their miracles, men who can be contradicted by none of the ravings of heretics, by none of the cleverness of the Stoics, Academicians, or indeed of any philosophers. For just as the golden sun at its rising chases away all the clouds of darkness, so truth, through such men, destroys and scatters in all places the devices of false teaching.

4. One such man, like a bright star, has risen within our memory in the region of Britain, governed by Æthelred and Cenred, the kings of the Mercians: this was the blessed Ecgwine, to whose deeds even Homer, if he lived now, could scarcely do justice in words. Who am I, then, who presume to tell the story of his life? I am far inferior to others, and utterly lack the ability or knowledge to extol sufficiently well with my pen the sublime qualities of that man. Yet, if in some way his life can be made known to others by me, I shall obtain pardon, for in God's house there are ignoble vessels as well as noble.[2] Hence, impelled by the authority and helped by the words of those men whose teaching it is right that I should obey and whose way of life to live, I will try, with God's aid, to describe as best I can how great a man he was, to relate his family origins, his character, and the deeds he wrought.

Here ends the Prologue

---

[2] Cf. 2 Tim. 2: 20.

5. *Incipit liber primus de uita sancti Ecgwini, episcopi et confessoris, et miraculis que Deus per eum dum hac mutabili luce frueretur operari dignatus est, abbreuiatus a Thoma priore Eueshamie.*

| LECTIO PRIMA

Temporibus Ethelredi atque Kenredi, qui Merciorum regimen optinuerunt, in territorio Wigornensi extitit religiosus uir cui nomen erat Ecgwinus, regali ex prosapia ortus.*ᵃ* Qui postquam adolescentie tempus transegit, gratiam Dei multam optinuit, illustratione ueri luminis et sancti spiritus aspiratione irradiatus, sicut bonorum actuum subsequens comprobauit effectus.*ᵇ* Quantum enim in eo crescebat successus temporis, tantum excrescebat totius intentio et studium probitatis. Assiduus erat in lectione, cordis sui agrum peruigili excolebat sollicitudine, auellando que nociua noscebat et inserendo que salubria esse dinoscebat.*ᶜ* Iustus, fortis, constans et prudens, cuique quod suum est exibere satagebat; ratione considerata labores et pericula non segniter suscipiebat, perseuerantemque in eis animi tolerantiam ferebat, ac rerum singularum fines diligentissime attendebat. Vnde omnia opera sua uerendo, iuxta illud beati Iob, 'Verebar omnia opera mea, sciens quia non parceres delinquenti',*ᵈ* ¹ ad exequenda Dei mandata pium ac mite cor gerebat;*ᵉ* in exterioribus quidem causis sciens ac discretus, fortis et ad omnia consideratus, in diuinis autem intelligentia preditus, sapientia plurimum excellebat. Igitur*ᶠ* postposita secularis fastus ambitione et bonorum temporalium iocunditate, paupertatem uoluntariam propter Deum appetiuit, et ecclesiastico cultui diuinisque officiis se omnino mancipauit. Per singulos itaque ordinis ecclesiastici gradus ad sacerdotium usque prouectus, mox totam uitam suam ita in contemplationem diuinam conuertit, quatinus in actiua conuersatione Deum pre oculis semper haberet, illius recordatus*ᵍ* quod scriptura dicit, 'Timenti Deum bene erit in extremis'.²

ᵃ *DE i.1 ll. 5–7 om.* R   ᵇ *DE i.1–2 ll. 10–16 om.* R   ᶜ *DE i.2 ll. 5–8 om.* R
ᵈ timidus *add. DE i.2 l. 14*   ᵉ subdebat *DE i.2 l. 15*   ᶠ beatus Ecgwinus *add. DE i.3 l. 1*   ᵍ recordans *DE i.3 l. 7*

¹ Job 9: 28 (*Vulgate* quod *for* quia).

5. *Here begins the first book of the Life of St Ecgwine, bishop and confessor, and the account of the miracles which God deigned to perform through him, while he enjoyed this transitory life. This is abridged by Thomas, prior of Evesham.*

FIRST READING

In the times of the kings Æthelred and Cenred, who occupied the throne of the Mercians, there lived a holy man in the district of Worcester whose name was Ecgwine, sprung from royal lineage. After he had passed the years of youth he received an abundance of God's grace, and was enlightened by the light of truth and by the inspiration of the Holy Spirit, as the following story of his good deeds proves. As he matured with the passing of time, all the more did his concentration and study of all that was honest grow. He was zealous in his reading, and cultivated the field of his heart with watchful concern, plucking out whatever he knew to be harmful, and sowing what he knew to be wholesome. He was just, brave, steadfast, and learned, and endeavoured to render to each his own and, giving due consideration to everything, he undertook dangerous tasks with vigour; his mental perseverance in these things was long-lasting, as he waited with great patience for the outcome of every single affair. Accordingly, he had a deep respect for everything he did—as the blessed Job said, 'I had a deep respect for all my works, knowing that Thou dost not spare the wicked'[1]—and he behaved with a good and gentle heart when obeying the commands of God. In worldly matters he was knowledgeable and discreet, brave and considerate in everything; in divine matters he was endowed with perception, and greatly excelled in wisdom. Therefore, putting aside the striving of worldly pride, and the delights of temporal possessions, he sought a willing poverty in the service of God, and committed himself utterly to the life of the church and to divine services. So, advancing through each of the grades of the church orders to the priesthood, he soon turned his whole life into the contemplation of divine things, to the extent that in his active life he always had God before his eyes, recalling what scripture says: 'All will be well in the end for the man who fears God.'[2]

---

[2] Cf. Eccles. 8: 12.

6.   LECTIO SECUNDA

Vbi uero Wictiorum*a* sedes pontifice orbata est,[1] clamat clerus, petit
fo. 124va populus, beatum uirum pro sanctitatis merito ad epis|copalem
dignitatem sullimandum. *b*Igitur, licet multum reluctans diuque
renitens, eligitur ab omni clero in episcopum. Rogantibus primoribus*c*
et principibus Ethelredi regis Merciorum, quo concedente, immo
etiam plurimum cogente, primate etiam Brittannie[2] consentiente et
confirmante, ad episcopatum prefate urbis cum canticis et ymnis*d*
assumptus est.*bi* Positus igitur in pontificio, statim diuini uerbi factus
est inclitus predicator, bonisque exinde actibus omni conamine
operam dedit, tanto humilior quanto altiori sullimatus erat officio.
*e*Pater orphanorum, sustentator uiduarum,[3] iustus iudex[4] oppres-
sorum et consolator erat desolatorum; unde carus Deo et hominibus
effectus est.*e*

7. Beatus itaque Ecgwinus, 'supra firmam petram fundatus',[5] armis
diuinis accinctus, doctrinis celestibus imbutus, potenter eos redar-
guebat qui sane fidei resistebant, leniter uero eos demulcebat qui
suaui iugo[6] Christi obediendo colla subdebant. Prauis erat sermo eius
quasi stimulus,[7] mansuetis uero quasi oleum. *f*Fortibus erat durus,
humilibus erat mitis et mansuetus.*f* Fortissimus itaque ueritatis
assertor *g*uir Dei,*g* populos nouiter conuersos et gentilitatis *h*plurimum
adhuc*h* sapientes et errore antiquo in multis deceptos illicitisque
connubiis contra Christianam sectam inuolutos, a faucibus diaboli
abstrahere cupiens atque ab errore paterni delicti et ab squalore
uetuste gentilitatis conuertere desiderans, sepe*i* luculenter quidem de
talibus uiciis ad eos locutus est. *j*Cumque esset mitissimus ut Moyses,
zelatus est legem Domini ut Finees,[8] tremendi iudicii et sempiter-
norum tormentorum crebris tonitruis retundens lapidea corda,
arguens, obsecrans, increpans in omni patientia et doctrina, instans
oportunitate*k* oportuna.[9]

---

a Wigornensis *DE i.3 l. 9*   *b–bi* *DE i.3 ll. 11–16 recast R*   *c* primatibus *DE i.3 l. 13*
d triumpho glorie *DE i.3 ll. 15–16 for* canticis et ymnis *R*   *e–e* *DE i.3 ll. 19–22 recast R*
f–f sentence of *R om. 2 scriptural quotations of DE i. 4 ll. 6–9*   *g–g* sanctus Ecgwinus *DE
i.4 l. 10*   *h–h* ad huc plurimum *DE i.4 l. 11*   *i* sepenumero *DE i.4 l. 15*   *j* *R om.
here a long quotation from Bede's 'De die iudicii' which DE included at this point (i.4 ll. 16–52)
following Byrhtferth*   *k* importunitate *DE i. 4 l. 56*

---

[1] On the diocese of the Hwicce (i.e. Worcester), which presumably corresponded with
the territory of the kings of the Hwicce, see D. Hooke, *The Anglo-Saxon Landscape: The
Kingdom of the Hwicce* (Manchester, 1985), p. 12.

[2] This is Thomas's phrase: it is never used by Dominic. The primate of Britain is

6. SECOND READING

When the see of the bishop of the Hwicce became vacant,[1] the clergy pleaded and the people requested that this blessed man, who merited it because of his holiness, should be elevated to episcopal dignity. Although he put up considerable resistance to this, and objected to it for a long time, he was elected by all the clergy as bishop. When all the leading men and athelings of Æthelred king of the Mercians requested this, the king agreed, nay insisted, with the primate of Britain[2] consenting and confirming. With canticles and hymns, he [Ecgwine] was admitted to the bishopric of that city. After his appointment to the bishopric he at once became a renowned preacher of the divine Word, and henceforth strove with all his might to achieve good deeds, all the more humbly because of his more elevated office. He was father to the fatherless, sustainer of widows,[3] a just judge[4] of the oppressed, and consoler of the desolate; and so he became beloved of both God and men.

7. Thus the blessed Ecgwine, 'founded upon a firm rock',[5] girt about with the armour of God, imbued with heavenly wisdom, strongly rebuked those who opposed sound faith, but gently consoled those who bowed their necks in subjection to the easy yoke[6] of Christ. To the wicked his speech was, as it were, a goad,[7] to the gentle it was as oil. To the strong he was harsh, to the humble he was mild and gentle. He was a strong advocate of the truth, a man of God, who desired to snatch from the jaws of the devil persons newly converted, but still very wise in the ways of the heathen, and deceived by ancient heresies of many kinds, or involved in unlawful marriages contrary to the way of Christ. He longed to turn them away from the error of the sin they had inherited, and from the wretchedness of their long-time paganism, often speaking with clarity to them of such evils. Though he was as gentle as Moses, he was as zealous for the law of the Lord as Phinehas,[8] striking their stony hearts with his frequent tirades of fearful judgement and eternal torments, reproving, exhorting, rebuking, with great patience and good teaching, acting with urgency when the time was right.[9]

Berhtwald, archbishop of Canterbury, elected 1 July 692, cons. 29 June 693, d. or trans. 13 Jan. 731; *HBC*, p. 213. [3] Cf. Ps. 67: 6 (68: 5).
[4] From the *Dies Irae*, sequence of the mass for the dead.
[5] Cf. Matt. 7: 25 and see also Matt. 16: 18.
[6] Cf. Matt. 11: 30. [7] Cf. Eccles. 12: 11.
[8] Cf. Num. 25: 11. [9] Cf. 2 Tim. 4: 2.

8.   LECTIO TERCIA

Verum quia insanabilibus morbis plerumque officit medicina et
ratione obuia augetur insania, ab inuidis et persecutoribus*a* Christiane
fo. 124vb religionis seua tempestas *b*contra sanctum Domini*b* excita|tur, *c*et
ueritatis inimici in ueritatis assertorem seditiosa peste*c* grassantur et
in eius angelicam uitam falsis figmentis armantur; unde ei dominica
uoce beatitudo potius cumuletur: 'Beati', inquit, 'qui persecutionem
patiuntur propter iusticiam'.[1] *d*Vulgus enim et populus, cuius uita et
intentio erat procliua ad malum omni tempore,*e* [2] *f*uidens sibi illicita
non licere, et assueta uicia relinquere oportere, unde proficere debuit.*f*
Inde contra athletam sanctum Dei in iram et odium et scandalum
exarsit, eumque paulatim coniecturis et adinuentionibus et rumoribus
malis diffamans, inueterata*g* simultate prodita, ab episcopatu eum
expulit. Permisit *h*potestas primatis,*h* et admisit hoc excitatus contra
eum liuor regius. De eo nempe non solum apud regem *i*delatio, set
etiam apud Romanum antistitem ab inimicis et insidiatoribus perlata
fuerat accusatio.*i* Tum uero athleta Domini ewangelicis exemplis
imbutus, cum se uidisset ad certamen uocari, pro salute*j* errantis
populi et pro adnichilandis inimicorum figmentis ad apostolicam
sedem intrepidus ire disponit, exemplum Domini et magistri sui
sequens qui, 'sciens omnia que uentura erant super eum',[3] retrorsum
non abiit nec faciem suam ab increpantibus auertit, set processit, et
querentibus hostibus ultro se tradidit.

9.   LECTIO QVARTA

Beatus itaque Ecgwinus, quia iamdudum causa uisitandi apostolos*k*
decreuerat Romam ire, nunc Raphaele archangelo fretus comite,
proficiscitur, et felix exul ac penitens beatus suppremam iuris
ecclesiastici sedem adiit. Et quamuis coram hominibus se immunem

---

a inimicis *DE i.4 l. 58*   *b–b* persecutionis *DE i.4 l. 59*   *c–c* atque seditiosa in
sanctum domini *DE i. 4 ll. 59–60*   *d* R om. *3 scriptural quotations at the end of DE i. 4*
ll. 63–7   *e* R om. *DE i.5 ll. 2–4*   *f–f* R corr. *DE i.5 l. 4; see note in AB*   *g* adulta
DE i. 5 l. 7   *h–h* magistratus *DE i.5 l. 8*   *i–i* R transposes delatio *and* accusatio
j sanctus Ecgwinus, fide munitus, diuina consolatione roboratus, angelico consilio fretus,
gladio spiritus sancti accinctus *DE i.5 ll. 12–13, om. R*   *k* uisitandis apostolis *DE i.5*
ll. 20–1

---

[1] Matt. 5: 10.
[2] Cf. Prov. 29: 22.
[3] John 18: 4.

8.   THIRD READING

But as medicine generally makes incurable diseases worse, and madness is increased by reason used against it, so a fierce storm was stirred up against the holy one of the Lord by the enemies and persecutors of the Christian religion, and those hostile to the truth raged like a pernicious plague against the champion of truth, and were incited against the angelic life of this man by untrue fabrications. So, may happiness be heaped upon him, as in the words of the Lord, who said: 'Blessed are they who endure persecution for the sake of righteousness.'[1] For the common mob and the people, whose lives and thoughts were at all times inclined towards evildoing,[2] saw that they were not allowed to do what was wrong, and that they must abandon the vices they practised, necessary for their own advantage. Accordingly, they burned with anger and hatred against the holy champion of God and stirred up slander against him. Little by little they maligned him with false suggestions, lying stories, and malicious rumours, and by propagating an ancient dispute, they had him expelled from the bishopric. This was allowed on the primate's authority, and royal envy stirred up against Ecgwine permitted this to happen. Further, an accusation was brought against him by hostile and treacherous men not only before the king but also before the bishop of Rome. Then the champion of the Lord, well-versed in the persecutions related in the Gospels, seeing that he was being challenged to a contest, bravely decided to travel to the apostolic see, for the salvation of his wayward people, and to confute the fabrications of his enemies. Thus he followed the example of his Lord and Master, who, 'knowing everything which was to happen to him',[3] did not withdraw from the fray, or shrink from those who accused him, but went forth, and voluntarily surrendered himself to his enemies who were looking for him.

9.   FOURTH READING

Therefore, the blessed Ecgwine, who for some long time had intended to go to Rome to visit the apostles, put his trust now in the companionship of the archangel Raphael, set out on his journey, and as a happy exile and a blessed penitent he arrived at the supreme judgment-seat of ecclesiastical law. Although he knew that he was innocent before men of the things brought against him, and said so,

ab illatis sciret et confiteretur, tamen quia coram Deo peccatis se obnoxium esse non diffitebatur, necnon et pro peccatis plebis sue errantis profecturus in superni arbitrii et diuini examinis iudicio, pedes suos uinculis ferreis astrinxit que claue poterant firmari*a* ac reserari, ipsamque clauem in fluuium Auene proiecit. Vinctus igitur seruus Iesu Christi Domini nostri Ecgwinus, emulatus Petrum fluctus

fo. 125ra   calcantem et Paulum in uinculis gloriantem,[1] tanta difficul | tate tantisque laboribus peruenit ad apostolicam urbem de uinculis apostolicis gloriantem.*b* ʻO fortissimum uictorem laborum, O contemptorem humanarum exprobrationum, O hominem angelis et hominibus admirandum, et tot populis et gentibus spectaculum factum! O uirum cunctis imitabilem, nec terroribus concussum, nec blandimentis seductum, nec laboribus uictum, qui inter corporis sui pressuras et abiectiones nec mundanas laudes captauit, nec aspectus hominum recusauit!

10.   LECTIO QVINTA

Denique*d* ferro uinctis pedibus Romam ingreditur, et, quod maxime quesierat, in ecclesia beati Petri apostolorum principis, ad orationem prosternitur.*e* Quod dum uir sanctus uigilanti cura peragit, omnipotens Deus pro seruo suo uigilare nec desistit. Interim namque famuli eius pro cibis emendis ad flumen pergunt, quibus uenditores piscem offerunt, quo empto et asportato et ex more condiendi exenterato, omnipotentis Dei ma⟨g⟩nificentia*f* compedum clauiculam quibus uir sanctus pedes suos astrinxerat in uisceribus piscis inueniunt, ferrumque quod Anglicus fluuius absorbuerat, Romanus Tiberis exalat.[2] Pro antiquo igitur statere piscantis Petri, coram multis redditur clauicula famulo Christi, qua se sciret soluendum gratia ipsius celestis clauigeri. Intelligens igitur uir Dei peregrinationis assumpte inesse fructum et optate exauditionis effectum, per omnia uoluntati Dei se subiciens, coram cunctis clauem accepit et uincula

---

a ligari *DE i.6 l. 28*   *b* triumphantem *DE i.6 l. 4*   *c* *top margin*: sanctus quoque Ecgwinus Romam profectus est uinculatus compedibus. Campane urbis ut fertur in eius aduentu per se sonuerunt secundum cronicon Cistress libro q(uinto) c. 23; *see Ranulf Higden, Polychronicon, ed. C. Babington and J. R. Lumby, 9 vols.* (RS xli, 1865–86) vi. 202, 203   *d DE i.6 ll. 11–13 om. R*   *e DE i.6 ll. 15–16 om. R*   *f* mirificentia *DE i.6 l. 21*

---

[1] Cf. 1 Cor. 7: 22, *seruus Cristi*; Matt. 14: 28–9, for St Peter walking on the water; and Acts 26: 29, for St Paul in chains.

[2] Cf. Matt. 17: 26. This ancient story, which is in Byrhtferth, can be traced as far back as Herodotus. Versions of it were common in hagiography, and can be found, for example,

yet in the presence of God he did not deny that he was guilty of sins. Indeed, as he was about to set out to plead for the sins of his erring people at the judgment-seat of the heavenly court and the divine judge, he bound his feet with iron fetters which could be shut and opened with a key, and this he threw into the river Avon. Bound therefore as the slave of Jesus Christ our Lord, Ecgwine, emulating Peter who walked on the water, and Paul who gloried in his chains,[1] reached the city of the apostles only with great difficulty and great toil, but glorying in his apostolic chains. O bravest victor of toils, despiser of human reproach, admired by angels and men, who has become a wonder to so many peoples and races! O man to be imitated by us all, who, not troubled by terrors, or seduced by flattery, or overcome by toil, amidst the pains suffered in his body and in his banishment, did not grasp at worldly praise, or object to the gaze of men!

10.   FIFTH READING

Eventually he reached Rome, his feet bound with fetters, and in the church of the blessed Peter, prince of the apostles, he prostrated himself in prayer, which he had particularly desired to do. When the holy man had spent the night in prayer, almighty God did not cease to be watchful for his servant. In the mean time his servants went to the river to buy provisions, and the sellers offered a fish to them. After buying this and bringing it back, they gutted it as was usual for seasoning a fish, and then by the power of almighty God, they found in the entrails of the fish the key of the chains with which the holy man had secured his feet, so the iron key which the English river had swallowed, the Roman Tiber disgorged.[2] Therefore, instead of that ancient coin of Peter when he was fishing, the key was returned to Christ's servant in the presence of many people, and he knew that he was to be freed with it by the grace of the key-bearer in heaven. Hence, the man of God, realizing that there was benefit in this for the journey he had undertaken and advantage for the audience he desired, submitted himself in everything to the will of God, received the key in the presence of them all and released the bonds with which he was

in the lives of St Benno of Meissen, St Ambrose of Cahors, St Maurilius of Angers, and St Gerbold of Bayeux. The story was altered slightly in its telling: Dominic's account differs from Byrhtferth's, and William of Malmesbury's in his account of St Ecgwine (*De gestis pontificum Anglorum*, ed. N. E. S. A. Hamilton (RS lii, 1870), pp. 296–7) is different again; see Lapidge, *Anglo-Latin Literature*, pp. 307–8.

quibus astringebatur reserauit.[a] Tanta miraculi nouitas in omnes
erupit, Romam implet. Qui miserabilis ac noxius putabatur, sanctus
et uenerabilis comprobatur. Quis illum uidere non certabat? Quis ab
eo benedici non festinabat? Ipse etiam uenerandus papa Constantinus,[b][1] cognito sancti uiri aduentu et solutionis compedum miraculo
prelibato, auditis etiam laboribus eius et angustiis in itinere perpes-
sis, [c]illum ad se uenire fecit, uolentem sibi prosterni digna reuerentia
detinuit et quem auctoritate apostolica benedixit propter sanctitatis
fo. 125[rb] meritum | ab eo benedictionem suscepit.[c]

11.   LECTIO SEXTA

Condigna[d] itaque a pontifice Romano beatus Ecgwinus exceptus
honorificentia, [e]ad celebrandum ante illum missarum solempnia,[e] et
ad eius singulare colloquium et consilium frequenter acciebatur et
gratiose audiebatur. Non enim erat sermo eius fatuus uel inutilis, set
'sale spirituali conditus';[2] sane fidei doctrinam et Christiane morali-
tatis formam sapiebat.[f] Paterno ille hunc affectu amplectebatur; hic
per omnia illi debita[g] reuerentia subditus obsequebatur. Tandem
controuersie sue et itineris causa coram ipso Christianitatis summo
iudice recitata[h] et omnimoda uentilatione examinata[i] et ad uotum
diffinita, cum apostolica benedictione et litteris apostolica consignatis
auctoritate, in quibus magnorum dignitas priuilegiorum continebatur,
[j]cum gloria triumphi[j] ad propriam sedem remeauit in Angliam.

12. Vbi uero nuntii de illius reditu ad regis audientiam peruenerunt,
auditis miraculis[k] que Deus per seruum suum dignatus est operari,
plurimum gratulatus iocunda illum suscepit exultatione, et[l] auctoritate apostolica [m]a Brittaniarum primate[m][3] restitutus est in propria
sede. Quo in cathedra pontificali restituto, sicut 'lux orta est iustis et
rectis corde letitia',[4] sic 'obstructum est os loquentium iniqua',[5] et
'omnis iniquitas opilauit os suum'.[6] Sic dicit scriptura: 'Cum iustus
resurgit, impius emoritur',[7] sic aduersarii eius aut confunduntur aut

---

[a] DE i.6 ll. 29–38 om. R   [b] om. DE, who does not name the pope here, following
Byrhtferth, but DE identifies later (i. 11)   [c–c] Recast by R from DE; auctoritate apostolica
add. R   [d] debita DE i.7 l. 13   [e–e] paraphrase of DE   [f] DE i.7 ll. 18–20 om. R
[g] dulcedinis add. DE   [h] discussa DE   [i] om. DE   [j–j] add. R   [k] et uirtutibus
add. DE   [l] cum add. DE   [m–m] add. R

---

[1] Constantine I was pope from 25 March 708 to 9 Apr. 715.
[2] Col. 4: 6.
[3] Berhtwald; see above, 6 n. 2.
[4] Ps. 96: 11 (97: 11).   [5] Ps. 62: 12 (63: 11).

bound. Such an unheard-of miracle amazed everybody, and was the talk of Rome. The man who was thought to be wretched and guilty, was applauded as holy and venerable. Who did not strive to see him? Who did not hasten to be blessed by him? Even the revered pope Constantine,[1] when he learned of the arrival of the holy man and of the miracle that set him free from the fetters, and heard also of his toils and difficulties suffered on the journey, had him come to him. When Ecgwine wished to prostrate himself before him, the pope prevented him with due respect, and from the man whom he blessed with apostolic authority he himself received a blessing through the true holiness of the man.

11.   SIXTH READING

The blessed Ecgwine was therefore received by the Roman pontiff with well-deserved honour. He was frequently invited to celebrate solemn mass before him, to converse and consult with him alone, and he was listened to graciously. For his conversation was not silly or pointless, but 'seasoned with spiritual salt';[2] he was knowledgeable in the teaching of sound doctrine and in the nature of Christian behaviour. The pope embraced him with fatherly affection, and Ecgwine, submitting to him with due reverence, was obedient to him in all matters. Finally the reason for the dispute and for his journey was related before the supreme judge of Christianity himself, and investigated with every kind of inquiry. A decision was made which accorded with his wishes, having the pope's blessing and letters sealed with apostolic authority, in which was enshrined the dignity of great privileges. So he returned to England to his own see with glorious success.

12. When news of his return reached the ears of the king [Æthelred], and he heard of the miracles which God deigned to perform through his servant, he congratulated him warmly, receiving him with very great joy. Ecgwine was therefore restored by apostolic authority to his own see by the primate of the British [Berhtwald].[3] Thus restored to his episcopal seat, as 'the light rises on the just and the righteous with a joyful heart',[4] so 'the mouth of those who speak evil was stopped',[5] and 'all their iniquity stopped them speaking'.[6] As scripture says, 'When the just man is restored, the wicked man dies'.[7] So Ecgwine's opponents were either confounded or converted. He was received

[6] Ps. 106: 42 (107: 42).   [7] Cf. Prov. 24: 16.

conuertuntur.*ª* In ampliorem igitur a rege susceptus amoris gratiam et
*ᵇ*familaritatem specialem*ᵇ* *ᶜ*ex amico amicissimus ex familiari famili-
arissimus apud regem effectus, que uolebat apud illum facile
optinebat.

13.   LECTIO SEPTIMA

Hiisdem sane temporibus locus erat in territorio Wigornensi dumis ac
uepribus condensis incultus, qui a modernis Eueshamia appellatur,
tunc uero temporis Hethomme nuncupabatur.¹ *ᵈ*Hunc uir Dei
*ᵉ*concupierat quia ibi clauem in aquam proiecerat;*ᵉ* et a rege Merciorum Aethelredo² expetiit ac optinuit, in quo*ᶠ* pastores gregum ad
uictualia seruorum*ᵈ* | Dei nutrienda constituit. Ex quibus unus Eoues
nomine plura portenta et signa *ᵍ*in eodem loco*ᵍ* sepe cernens,
*ʰ*quadam die uidit ibidem uirginem preclarissimam ipsius solis
fulgorem sui splendore deuincentem, librum in manibus tenentem,
et cum aliis duabus uirginibus celestia cantica psallentem. Quod cum
idem pastor domino suo beato Ecgwino intimasset, uir Domini rem
tacitus considerabat,*ʰ* et secum in animo reuoluens Dominum Iesum
Christum de sacra uirgine natum prius pastoribus gregum per
angelum annuntiatum et eisdem in presepi demonstratum, quod a
paruo homine audierat non paruipendebat, set per se ipsum, inuocato
Iesu Christi nomine cum ieiuniis et precibus, id inuestigare studuit.
14. Quadam igitur die, expletis nocturnis officiis et uigiliis, summo
mane, adiunctis secum tribus sociis, cum psalmodiis et precibus ad
designatum locum nudus pedes pergit, eminusque relictis sociis ipse
interius processit, diutiusque terre accubans, cum lacrimis et gemitu
implorabat respectum misericordie redemptoris cum interuentu
ipsius sancte genetricis.*ⁱ* Surgenti igitur illi ab oratione tres uirgines
non minoris splendoris et glorie quam prius apparuere, quarum que
media eminebat precelsior omnique nitore splendentior aliis pre-
fulgebat, liliis candentior, rosis uernantior, odore inestimabili fra-
grantior, librum quoque manibus preferens et crucem aurea luce

fo. 125ᵛᵃ

ª *DE i.7 ll. 39–44 om. R*   *ᵇ⁻ᵇ* admirationis excellentiam *DE*   *ᶜ* *DE i. 7 ll. 45–55*
om. R   *ᵈ⁻ᵈ* [fo. 125ʳᵇ] *written over an erasure?*   *ᵉ⁻ᵉ* add. R   *ᶠ* *Instead of* in quo *R*,
iure sibi concesso super predictam siluam, quattuor per eam *DE i. 8 ll. 5–6*   *ᵍ⁻ᵍ* eadem
silua *DE*   *ʰ⁻ʰ* *DE i. 8 ll. 9–18 paraphrased R, with omissions*   *ⁱ* *DE i.8 ll. 32–6,
biblical quotations, om. R*

---

¹ The origin of the name is from *hamm* (the great bend in the river, from which
'Homme'), to which the prefix 'Et' (OE *æt*) was added, so 'Hethomme'. It is also associated

into greater and more affectionate favour by the king, and became the friendliest of friends, the most intimate of subjects to the king, and with the king he easily obtained whatever he desired.

13.   SEVENTH READING

At that same time there was a place in the district of Worcester, overgrown with thickets and dense bushes, which these days is called Evesham, but then was known as 'Hethomme'.[1] The man of God had desired this place, because it was there that he had thrown the key into the water. He therefore asked Æthelred, the king of the Mercians,[2] for it and obtained it. Here he put herdsmen to maintain it for providing victuals for the servants of God. One of the herdsmen, called Eoves, who often saw many signs and wonders in that very place, one day saw there a brilliantly shining virgin who outshone the brightness of the sun by her own splendour. The virgin was holding a book in her hand, and with two other virgins was singing heavenly hymns. When the shepherd told his master, the blessed Ecgwine, of this, the man of God considered the matter quietly, turning it over in his mind that a proclamation was once made by an angel to shepherds that the Lord Jesus Christ had been born of a holy Virgin, and was shown to them in the crib. He did not think light of what he had heard from a lowly man, but, invoking the name of Jesus Christ with fasting and prayer, made it his very own business to investigate the story.

14. One day, therefore, after the night offices and vigils were over, at the first light, he took three associates with him, and made his way bare-footed to the place indicated; then, leaving his associates some distance off, he himself went on further into the region, sat on the ground for some time, and with tears and groans prayed that by the intercession of His holy mother the Redeemer would show mercy. As he rose from prayer, three virgins appeared to him, no less splendid and glorious than previously. The virgin in the middle of these stood out taller, shining more brightly than the others, whiter than lilies, more verdant than roses, with a fragrance that could not be described: she carried in her hands a book and also a Cross which shone with a

with the name Eof, who was said to be the shepherd, or herdsman, to whom the Virgin Mary miraculously appeared (hence 'Eofeshamme'), and is sometimes found as 'Cronuchhamme', from the cranes or herons seen no doubt by the river; see PN *Worcs.*, pp. 262–3.
    [2] Æthelred, king of Mercia, the son of Penda, acceded 675, d. ?716, abdicating in 704, according to Bede (*HE* v. 24); *HBC*, p. 16.

radiantem. Cumque cogitaret hanc Domini genitricem esse, uirgo precellentissima, quasi fauens tam pie estimationi, adorantem pretensa quam tenebat cruce benedixit, et cum tali ualefactione disparuit.[a]

15.   LECTIO OCTAVA

Gauisus itaque uir sanctus super hiis,[b] intellexit esse diuine uoluntatis ut locus ipse Dei cultibus conseruaretur et propitiationi seculorum ipsius beate genitrici consecraretur. Vouerat enim ab olim inter uarias temptationum angustias, si Dominus prosperum faceret desiderium suum, edificaturum se Domino | templum; unde modo nactus locum tanto indicio a [c]beata Maria[c] preelectum, Deo et ipsi Dei genetrici ad soluendum uotum eundem deputauit locum. Ipsum igitur protinus emundauit, opus a Deo presignatum inchoauit et decenter ad finem perduxit, possessionibus[1] etiam multis a regibus Anglie impetratis eundem locum ditauit. Modico post hoc tempore, Kenredus rex Merciorum, anno uidelicet quinto regni sui, et Offa rex Orientalium Saxonum, Romam ire pergentes,[2] cenobii quod construere ceperant auctorem beatum Ecgwinum et magnam itineris sui causam, ueluti testem tam manifeste ostensionis beate uirginis Marie, socium eiusdem itineris sibi acciuerunt. Hunc uero laborem beatus Ecgwinus libens subiit, ut ecclesia[d] quam extruxerat a Romano pontifice omnimodam libertatem ab episcoporum subiectione optineret. Quod et ipse Kenredus rex, ad quem ius patronatus eiusdem ecclesie pertinebat, omnimodis procurabat.

16. Igitur Romam amica itineris societate profecti, coram summo pontifice Constantino, qui tunc apostolice sedi presidebat,[3] causas itineris sui aperuerunt, et plurima de beneficiis suis regia libertate

fo. 125[vb]

---

[a] *DE i.8 ll. 44–6 om. R*   [b] et debitas Deo gratias ad soluens *add. DE i.8. l. 47*
[c–c] Deo *DE i. 8. l. 53*   [d] ecclesie *R*

[1] At this point (DE i. 8 l.56), R omits a long passage, including Ecgwine's foundation charter, which is put in later. The letter of Pope Constantine is also omitted, but, unlike the charter, it does not appear elsewhere in Book I. R departs significantly from DE, recasting the story of the visit to Rome, until Lectio XI. Thomas notes that Cenred went to Rome in the fifth year of his reign, which is unknown to Dominic, and talks of the 'primas Britanniarum', a term not used by Dominic. Dominic prefers 'ad limina sanctorum apostolorum' to describe the journey to Rome, and he gives the place Alcester [Warws.] for the synod held on the return. Thomas does not name the place of the synod in Lectio IX.
[2] The fifth year of Cenred's reign was 709: Thomas takes this date from Bede, *HE* v. 24

golden light. When Ecgwine realized that this was the Mother of the Lord, the virgin who surpassed all the others, as if showing favour to him for his pious thoughts, blessed him with the cross which she held out as he worshipped her, and then, after a gracious farewell, she disappeared.

15.   EIGHTH READING

So it was that that holy man rejoiced over these things, understanding that it was the divine will that that very place should be preserved for the worship of God, and be consecrated to His blessed Mother for the redemption of the world. For he had once vowed amidst varied trials and temptations, that if the Lord would prosper his desire, he would build a temple to the Lord. Hence, having now obtained through this sign the place already chosen by the blessed Mary through such a sign, he set it aside as the place to discharge his vow to God and the very Mother of God. He at once cleansed the place therefore from defilement, began the work appointed by God, and brought it to an honourable end, endowing the place also with many possessions[1] obtained from the kings of England. A short time after this, Cenred, king of the Mercians, in the fifth year of his reign [709], and Offa, king of the East Saxons, set out on a journey to Rome.[2] They summoned the blessed Ecgwine to accompany them on that journey, as the founder of the monastery which they had begun to build and the chief reason for their journey, and as the witness of so clear a vision of the blessed Virgin Mary. The blessed Ecgwine gladly submitted to this hardship, in order that the church which he had constructed should obtain from the pope complete freedom from subjection to bishops. King Cenred himself, to whom belonged the right of patronage over this church, procured this freedom in full.

16. So they travelled to Rome enjoying one another's company on the way; and came before Pope Constantine, who at that time occupied the apostolic see.[3] They explained the reason for their journey, and bestowed many of their lands with royal freedom in the

(pp. 516–17), according to whom he abdicated and went to Rome in 709, dying *c*.709. Cenred's companion, Offa, king of the East Saxons, acceded between 694 and 709 and d. in or after 709, when he, too, abdicated and went to Rome.

[3] Bede, *HE* v. 19, gives the whole story of the journey of the two kings, Cenred and Offa, to Rome during the reign of Pope Constantine. Both kings received the tonsure at Rome and died there. Bede, however, does not mention anything about Ecgwine accompanying them.

contulerunt in loco ostense uisionis, immo manifeste ostensionis beate Virginis, sicut ipse summus pontifex in priuilegio suo asserit,[1] et de ipsa ostensione eque ita certum esse tenendum precepit quemadmodum de beati Ecgwini bonitate non dubitauit. Ipsas uero donationes et beneficia prefati reges in ipsorum priuilegiis nominatim determinauerunt et apostolica auctoritate corroborari fecerunt; et eundem locum sub testimonio tante auctoritatis ita ampliatum, totum liberum quoad temporalia, Deo et sancte eius genetrici et beatis apostolis Petro et Paulo contulerunt. Summus[a] uero pontifex locum illum ut sibi donatum, quem regia potestas regie libertati donauit, et ipse auctoritate | Dei et sanctorum apostolorum et sua quoad spiritualia donauit, sicut in ipsius priuilegio continetur. Omnibus igitur itineris sui causis rite peractis et ad uotum completis, cum benedictione apostolica, prospero gressu, in Angliam sunt regressi. Quo dum uenissent, secundum formam mandati apostolici a Britwaldo, Britanniarum primate, illis in partibus in quibus manifestatio habita fuisse refertur, concilium tocius Anglie,[2] episcoporum uidelicet sacrique ordinis religiosarum personarum optimatumque regni cum proceribus suis, coactum est.

fo. 126ʳᵃ

17.   LECTIO NONA

Concilio itaque de grege dominico ex mandato apostolico in nomine Domini coadunato, et priuilegiis tam summi pontificis quam regum in communi perlectis, cuncti laudem et gloriam Deo dederunt, et clamantes dixerunt, 'Benedictus Deus qui per seruos suos talia operatur et preparat in terris unde anime saluentur in celis. Nos uero quicquid in hac constitutione papa uenerabilis exercet et imperat, suscipimus et laudamus; quidquid uero reges et principes nostri in loco "Ethomme"[3] contulerunt, concedimus et confirmamus'. Hiis uero ita expletis, et soluta in pace uniuersa que illuc conuenerat contione, sicut sancta synodus decreuerat beatus Ecgwinus et Wilfridus episcopus[4] ad locum prefatum perrexerunt, et ipsum

---

[a] written over an erasure

[1] See below, 319–20.
[2] See C. Cubitt, *Anglo-Saxon Church Councils c. 650–c.850* (London, 1995), App. I, p. 263, who, citing Lapidge, considers the council fictitious. See also below, 40.
[3] See above, 13 n. 1.
[4] This is Wilfrid, bishop of Worcester, not Wilfrid, archbishop of York. Dominic (DE i. 10 l. 32) had included a passage stating that Archbishop Wilfrid of York was at the Council of Alcester with Archbishop Berhtwald, and this passage has confused some historians. Thomas

place where the vision had been revealed: the manifest appearance of the blessed Virgin, as the pope himself asserted in his privilege,[1] the nature of the manifestation itself, the fact that he considered it to be completely acceptable, and had no doubt about the reliability of the blessed Ecgwine. They then had the very endowments and benefences, which these kings specified by name in their privileges, ratified by apostolic authority; and conveyed that place, thus enhanced by the testimony of such authority, wholly free with respect to its temporalities, to God, His holy Mother, and the blessed apostles Peter and Paul. The supreme pontiff thus took that place as donated to him—which royal power gave in royal freedom—and himself on the authority of God, the holy apostles, and his own, gave it its spiritualities, as set out in his privilege. Therefore all the reasons for that journey were duly fulfilled and completed according to their wishes, so they returned with papal blessing and a favourable journey to England. When they arrived back, a council of the whole of England,[2] made up of the bishops, of the holy order of the religious, magnates and nobles of the realm, was summoned by Berhtwald, primate of Britain, in that region where the vision is said to have taken place.

17.   NINTH READING

When the council of the Lord's congregation had been assembled in the name of the Lord in accordance with the apostolic command, and the privileges of both the pope and the kings were scrutinized in common, all gave praise and glory to God, and exclaimed aloud, 'Blessed be God who performs and prepares such things on earth through His servants, by which their souls may be saved in Heaven. Whatever the venerable pope enacts and commands, we accept and approve; whatever endowments our kings and princes have bestowed upon the place called "Ethomme",[3] we allow and ratify'. When this business had been completed, and the whole assembly which had met there had been dismissed in peace, the blessed Ecgwine and Bishop Wilfrid,[4] as the holy synod had decreed, proceeded to the said place,

makes no mention at all of Archbishop Wilfrid of York. Bishop Wilfrid means the bishop of Worcester whom John of Worcester (*Jo. Wo.* ii. 174–5) speaks of as being chosen to succeed Ecgwine during the latter's lifetime, but it is impossible to say whether the dedication took place in 709, shortly after the Council of Alcester, as seems to be suggested by Thomas, or in 714, as Dominic states in a passage which Thomas pointedly omits, see below, 33. The chronology is very confused and there may well have been more than one dedication.

in honore Dei et beate eius genetricis et apostolorum Petri et Pauli et
omnium sanctorum in festiuitate eorundem dedicauerunt.

18. Et ex precepto apostolico constituta est ibidem congregatio
monachorum que minus in illis partibus tunc habebatur, ouile
uidelicet diuinitus preostensum, apostolica auctoritate fultum,
regia libertate donatum, cleri et populi benedictione sancitum.
Postquam uero beatus Ecgwinus optatum diem uidit quod locus
quem extruxerat dedicaretur, et monachilis ordo ad seruiendum Deo
inibi constitueretur, iam exinde omissis terrenorum negotiorum
fo. 126rb   curis, se ad contemplatiuum ui|te contulit statum. Exemplum
etiam Domini secutus se humiliando,[1] episcopale sede dimissa,
inibi effectus est abbas. Et iccirco iustum uidebatur summo
pontifici, sicut ipse testatur, ut eadem ecclesia ampliorem dignitatem
a sede apostolica merito sui optineret. 'Constituit ergo in nomine
Domini ut isdem locus sub monarchia proprii abbatis liber existeret',[2] et ut omnis qui hec que ipse statuit 'destruxerit aut male
contaminauerit'[3] uel infringere uoluerit, seu in loco monachorum
clericos inmittere temptauerit, sit maledictus et anathema coram
Deo et angelis eius inperpetuum; ille uero qui hec 'conseruauerit et
adauxerit quod benedictionibus repleatur'[4] et a Deo in eternum
conseruetur exorauit.

19.   LECTIO DECIMA

Multas etiam alias libertates et inmunitates et episcopales dignitates,
quibus idem monasterium usque in hodiernum diem excellentissime
pollet, contulerunt postmodum Romani pontifices eidem loco, tum ut
sancto et sibi donato, tum ad honorem beate Dei genitricis Marie que
eundem sibi elegit, tum ob reuerentiam beati Ecgwini episcopi. Que
in priuilegiis eiusdem cenobii expresse continentur, et cum summa
reuerentia et cautela diligentissima et cura exactissima ibidem obser-
uantur. Indutus igitur monachum uir Dei Ecgwinus cepit amplius
uerbis et doctrinis pluere, uirtutibus et miraculis choruscare, curas
mundi postponere, dampna rerum temporalium simplici animo
tolerare: ut de eo ueraciter posset dici quod antea dictum fuerat in

---

[1] Cf. Phil. 2: 8.
[2] Cf. the text of the second privilege of Pope Constantine, see below, 325.
[3] Cf. the first privilege of Pope Constantine for certain similarities of a general kind, see
below, 322.
[4] Ibid.

and dedicated it in honour of God and of His blessed Mother, and of the apostles Peter and Paul and all the saints, in a festival honouring them all.

18. In accordance with the apostolic command a community of monks was established there, which did not at that time exist in that district, and the flock divinely foreshadowed was supported by apostolic authority, endowed with royal liberty, affirmed by the blessing of clergy and people. When the blessed Ecgwine saw that longed-for day when the place which he had built would be consecrated, and a monastic order established to serve God in that place, he then abandoned all concerns for worldly matters, and devoted himself to a contemplative way of life. Following the example of the Lord by humbling himself,[1] he resigned his bishop's see, and became abbot of the monastery. Indeed, because of Ecgwine's merit, it seemed right to the pope, as he himself bore witness, that that same church should obtain from the apostolic see greater dignity. 'He decreed therefore in the name of the Lord that that place should be free under the rule of its own abbot';[2] that anyone who 'refuted these rights which the pope himself established or wished wickedly to misuse or infringe them',[3] or attempted to introduce clerks in place of monks, should be accursed and an anathema before God and his angels for ever; but he prayed that the man who 'preserved these rights and augmented them should be blessed to the uttermost'[4] and saved by God eternally.

19.   TENTH READING

After that, popes at Rome bestowed upon that place many other liberties, immunities, and episcopal dignities, with which the monastery to this day is most excellently empowered, not only because it had been given to the saint and to them, in honour of the blessed Mary, Mother of God, who chose the place for herself, but also to show reverence to blessed Ecgwine as bishop. These are contained in detail in the privileges of the monastery, and are observed in that place with the greatest respect, with the most diligent circumspection, and with punctilious care. And so clothed in the monk's habit, the man of God, Ecgwine, began to give greater expression to good doctrine, to stand out amongst men for his virtues and for miracles performed, to put the cares of the world behind him, and to endure the loss of temporal things with a sincere heart; so that it could be

prophetis, 'Qui sunt isti qui ut nubes uolant et quasi columbe ad fenestras suas?'[1] Et sicut dicit apostolus, 'Nostra autem conuersatio in celis est',[2] ita iste sanctus conuersabatur in terris, ut animus et intentio eius semper esset in celis. Sacre insistebat lectioni; debitis castigabat corpus inedia et uigiliis. Humilis erat in habitu, in

fo. 126ᵛᵃ   sermone | iocundus, in predicatione deuotus, in moribus uenerabilis, in orationibus peruigil, in lectione assiduus, in uultu angelicus, in affectu pius, in uirtutibus admirabilis, in bonitate amabilis, in pietate laudabilis, multis etiam fulgens miraculis. Nam, ut cetera omittamus, inter lacrimas et singultus que nocte ac die indesinenter omnipotenti Deo fundebat, sepe angelorum uisitationibus demulcebatur, et aliorum sanctorum qui de hoc seculo excesserant continuis consolationibus refouebatur. Beatam uero Dei genetricem Mariam ita toto affectu et spiritu, toto corde et amore amplectebatur, ut numquam a memoria eius excideret, numquam in uerbis ipsius deesset. Cuius uisitatione et consolatione seruus Dei recreatus, omnia que mundi erant omittebat, et que Dei erant indesinenter exercebat. Miseris condolebat, pauperes recreabat, esurientes pascebat, sitientes potabat, nudos uestiebat, infirmos uisitabat, mortuos sepeliebat, orphanis et uiduis, secundum apostolum, solamen exibebat, et 'ab hoc seculo immaculatum se custodiebat'.[3]

20.   LECTIO VNDECIMA[a]

Virtutum itaque uniuersarum auidus executor et uitiorum insectator beatus Ecgwinus, ubi ad cigneam etatis speciem peruenit, [b]omnipotentis Dei nutu, qui sanctos suos salubriter uerberat, in monasterio quod construxerat in diutinam decidit egritudinem. Quam cum patientissime amplecteretur,[b] mortemque sibi iam instare persensisset, coram fecit adesse filios quos Deo genuerat, et eos hac extrema monuit adortatione. '"Vixi, fratres, apud uos, nec pudet uixisse."[4] Feci enim quod potui, quamuis omnino exiguum sit quod feci. Quid agere et a quibus uos oporteat declinare dixi, quibuscumque modis dicendum esse existimaui. Ostensa igitur rectitudinis uia precor ut gradiamini. Que enim in futuro retributio? Si gaudium, erit eternum;

---

[a] R returns to DE i.17   [b-b] om. DE (at i.17 l. 3)

[1] Isa. 60: 8.   [2] Phil. 3: 20.   [3] Jas. 1: 27.
[4] Paulinus, Life of Ambrose; see Vita di Cipriano, Vita di Ambrogio, Vita di Agostino, ed. and trans. into Italian A. A. R. Bastiaensen (Vite dei Santi, iii: Milan, 1975), cap. 45, p. 112, ll. 10–11.

truly said of him what was once said in the Prophets, 'Who are these who fly like a cloud, and like doves to their roosts?'[1] And as the apostle says, 'Our habitation is in the heavens',[2] and that saint so lived on earth that his mind and his gaze were always upon the heavens. He applied himself to reading sacred literature; he chastized the body by obliging himself to fast and spend nights in prayer. He was humble in nature, cheerful in his conversation, devout in preaching, reverential in behaviour, ever watchful in prayer, assiduous in his reading, angelic in countenance, pious in disposition, admired for his virtues, beloved for his goodness, praised for his holiness, and illustrious because of the many miracles he performed. To say nothing of his other qualities, amidst the tears and sighs which he poured forth ceaselessly night and day before almighty God, he was often consoled by visitations of angels, and refreshed by the continual comfort given by other saints who had departed this earthly scene. Further, he so cherished the blessed Mary, Mother of God, with the whole of his mind and spirit, with the whole love of his heart, that she was never out of his thoughts, never absent from his speech. So this servant of God was refreshed by her presence and comfort, he eschewed all that was worldly, and ceaselessly practised the things of God. He consoled the wretched, restored the poor, fed the hungry, gave drink to the thirsty, clothed the naked, visited the sick, buried the dead, gave comfort to orphans and widows as the apostle enjoined, and 'kept himself spotless from the world'.[3]

20.   ELEVENTH READING

The blessed Ecgwine, eager to accomplish all the virtues and to attack all the vices, reached the final stage of his life, and it was the will of God, who chastens His saints for their good, that he should suffer a long illness in the monastery which he had founded. He embraced this with great patience, and realizing that death was now imminent, summoned before him the sons whom he had begotten for God and counselled them with these last words of exhortation. ' "I have lived amongst you, my brothers, and have not been ashamed to have done so."[4] I have done what was in my power, though it is very little indeed that I have done. I have told you, by whatever means I thought it best to speak to you, the things it behoves you to do, and the things to avoid. Therefore I beseech you to walk in the way of righteousness that I have shown you. What will be your reward in the future? If joy,

si tormentum, erit perpetuum. Nil uero inter utrumque medium. |
Nec uos decipiat presentis umbra felicitatis.[1] "Fugit enim uelut
umbra, et numquam in eodem statu permanet."[2] Ipse qui "uia est,
ueritas et uita", "uiam iniquitatis a uobis amoueat", "uiam iustifica-
tionum suarum uos instruat",[3] illamque amouendo et hac instruendo
felici perseuerantia uos ad uitam perducat eternam.'

21. Et Patri eos immortali commendans, accepto uiatico, plenus
dierum et plenus uirtutum uita excessit tercio kalendas Ianuarii.
Quantus uero exinde ^{a}meror fuerit in fratribus monasterii, quantus
in principibus et optimatibus patrie dolor,^{a} quanta tristitia in clero,
quanta desolatio in populo, quanta in uiduis et orphanis et pauperibus
acclamatio, supersedemus dicere quia non possemus edicere. Perdi-
derant enim principes regni optimum in secularibus consiliarium,
clerus doctorem et magistrum precipuum, populus rectorem et
iudicem^b iustissimum, pupilli et orphani dispensatorem largissimum.

22.   LECTIO DVODECIMA^c

Concurrit igitur ordo monasticus, occurrit et clerus ad beati uiri
exequias, ruunt cateruatim populi utriusque sexus ad tanti uiri
exuuias. Vna ex parte funebria personabant; alia ex parte cantica
letitie resonabant. Hinc luctus et lacrime quia defunctus erat, inde
gaudium et exultatio quia celum optinebat. Triumphi quodammodo
celebritas uidebatur, non funeris. Celebratis ergo missarum solemp-
niis et aliis ex more peractis obsequiis, positum est corpus eius cum
debito honore in loco quem prius elegerat sibi. Apposuit epithaphium
scriptor, non leonina dictatum cantilena, set simplici commendatum
stilo et descriptione non ficta.

    Rupe sub hac uili tegitur uir summus, et urna
    Clauditur angusta, quem subuehit alta per orbem
    Veri fama uolans. Genus hic spectabile duxit,
    Et mores habuit preclaros magnaque gessit.
    Ecclesiam ^{d}fecit Eouesham quam modo dicunt,^{d}
    Ditauit terris, et multa nobilitauit
    Libertate locum. Qui regni iura tenebat
Omni|modam scripsit; subscripsit curia regni,

$^{a-a}$ meror *and* dolor *reversed, and* fuerit . . . monasterii *om. DE* ^{b} et iudicum *om. DE*
^{c} *DE i.17 at l. 25* $^{d-d}$ fecit quam nunc dicunt Eouesham *DE i. 17 l. 40*

---

[1] This may be a quotation, but we have been unable to identify it.   [2] Job 14: 2.
[3] Cf. John 14: 6; Ps. 118: 29 (Ps. 119: 29); and Ps. 118: 27 (Ps. 119: 27).

it will be eternal; if torment, it will be for ever. There is no way which leads between them. Let not this shadow over your present happiness deceive you.[1] "For it will flee as a shadow does, never remaining in the same position."[2] May He, who "is the Way, the Truth and the Life", "keep from you the way of iniquity", "teach you his ways of judgement",[3] and by so instructing you, may lead you with happy perseverance to the life eternal.'

21. Commending them thus to the immortal Father, he received the last communion, and full of days and full of virtues he departed this life on 30 December [717]. How great was the mourning among the brethren in the monastery, the sadness among the leading men and nobles of the land, the sorrow among the clergy, the distress among the people, and the weeping among widows, orphans, and the poor! But we will refrain from speaking further of what we cannot fully express. For the leaders of the realm had lost the best of counsellors in secular matters, the clergy had lost a preacher and an exceptional teacher, the people had lost a guide and a most just judge, dependants and orphans had lost a generous provider.

22.   TWELFTH READING

All the monks assembled, and the clergy met for the funeral of the holy man. The people hurried together in throngs to the remains of this great man. On one side there was the sound of lamentation, on the other songs of joy rang out: the grief and tears amongst the former were for his death, the joy and delight on the other were that he had attained heaven. In a way it seemed the celebration of a triumph, not of a funeral. Therefore, when solemn mass and other customary obsequies had been carried out, his body was laid to rest with due honour in the place which he had previously chosen for himself. An epitaph was written and placed there, not a composition in Leonine verse, but the offering of a simple pen, faithfully recorded:

'Beneath this base rock is buried a man of distinction, and enclosed in a narrow urn is he whose reputation for the truth was carried throughout the world on the high wings of fame. He was the head of an illustrious family, his manner of life was highly esteemed, and his deeds were great. He founded the church which is now called Evesham, endowed it with lands, ennobled the place with great liberty. He who possessed the rights of the kingdom put in writing every kind of liberty, confirmed by the king's court, and the pope of

Et qui Romanam sedem tunc papa regebat
Confirmauit eam proprio testante sigillo.
Vita migrauit cum solis per Capricornum
Tercius ac decimus medians existeret ortus.[1]

23. Multis miraculorum signis *in eodem loco* Deus euidenter
postea monstrauit quanta sanctus uir Ecgwinus apud eum gratia in
celis eminebat. Orbatis lumine lumen ad eius nominis inuocationem
restituebatur, auditu priuatis auditus reddebatur, debilibus uirtus*b*
amissa reformabatur, et omne ab eis infortunium amouebatur. Nec
solum ab incommodis exterioribus per eius merita consilium optine-
batur, uerum et ab interioribus animarum incommoditatibus auxilium
diuinitus adipiscebatur. Super hiis ergo uiri sancti fama per patriam
diuulgata, *ad impetranda tam corporis quam anime remedia frequentia populorum ad eundem locum ueniens, multa ipsum cele-
britate longe lateque in sullime attollebat, ad gloriam et laudem ipsius
qui cum patre et spiritu sancto uiuit et regnat Deus per omnia secula
seculorum. Amen.*c*2

24. *d*Attollant igitur poete quanta uelint amplificatione Babilonem
mirifice turritam, Niniuen trium dierum itinere[3] spatiosam; nos ista
iure attollimus et attollendo preferimus edificiorum menia. De illis ad
inanem seculi pompam extructis ait Ecclesiastes, 'Vanitas uanitatum
et omnia uanitas':[4] de istis testatur scriptura, 'Gloriosa dicta sunt de
te, ciuitas Dei'.[5] Non solum enim ex insensibili materia ibi Deo edes
constituuntur, uerum ex rationali atque immortali animarum substantia gloriose et perennes domus ibi edificantur. Illorum magistratus, quia in armis, in curribus et in equis confidit, obligatur et
cadit: horum ducatus, in nomine Domini spem sibi totam affigens, ad
certamina expeditus assurgit erectusque persistit. Nulla hunc exerci-
fo. 127rb tum uiolencia superare potest; 'quis enim', | secundum apostolum,
'separabit eum a caritate Christi?'[6] Nulla prorsus tribulatio, seu ferri,
seu inedie, seu algoris, seu cuiuslibet terreni furoris. Nulla denique
hunc astutia subuertet, quoniam hec acies spiritualiter die ac nocte in
excubiis suis perstat, sicut in Canticis Canticorum dicitur, 'Vnius-
cuiusque uiri ensis super femur suum propter timores nocturnos'.[7]

---

a–a ad eius tumulum *DE i. 18 l. 1*   *b* ualitudo *DE i. 18 l. 5*   *c–c* only *R*   *d* *R*
reverts to DE i.14

[1] Ecgwine died on 30 December, i.e. the tenth day into Capricorn, not the thirteenth.
[2] A common end to a collect.
[3] The 'poeta' is in fact Byrhtferth (p. 382: beginning of his part IV). Dominic added the

that time who ruled the Roman see confirmed it, and ratified it with
his own seal. Ecgwine passed from this life when the thirteenth rising
of the sun was moving through Capricorn.'[1]

23. God afterwards showed clearly by the evidence of many miracles
in the same place how much the holy man Ecgwine excelled in grace
in His presence in the heavens. At the invocation of his name sight
was restored to the blind, hearing to the deaf, strength was restored to
the weak, and every misfortune was removed from them. Through his
merits not only was guidance obtained to deal with worldly troubles,
but also aid was gained from heaven to face the spiritual difficulties of
the soul. Because of these things, therefore, the fame of this holy man
spread throughout the country, and to obtain these benefits for both
the body and the soul a throng of people came to that place. Men far
and wide extolled this man to the skies, because of his great renown,
to the glory and praise of the Lord Himself, who, with the Father and
the Holy Spirit lives and reigns as God for ever and ever. Amen.[2]

24. Poets may extol Babylon with its amazing walls as extravagantly
as they wish, or Nineveh, a vast city three days' journey[3] across, but
we rightly praise those things we have mentioned and prefer that to
praising the walls of buildings. *Ecclesiastes* says of these things built
for the world's empty glory, 'Vanity of vanities, all is vanity';[4]
scripture testifies to these things, 'Glorious things are spoken of
thee, O city of God.'[5] For not only are dwellings for God constructed
there of inanimate material, but glorious, eternal houses are built
there from the rational and immortal substance of souls. The ruler of
the former, because his confidence is put in arms, chariots, and
horses, is bound to them and falls; the leader of the latter, fixing all
hope for himself in the name of the Lord, armed for battle rises up
and continues upright. No violence can overcome such an army, for
as the apostle says, 'Who will separate us from the love of Christ?'[6]
Certainly no affliction, either of sword, or of starvation, or of cold, or
of any earthly rage. Finally, no cunning will overthrow this army, for
this column stands firm day and night on spiritual watch, such as is
spoken of in the *Cantica Canticorum*, 'Let a man's sword be ready at
his loins for the terrors of the night.'[7] What more can I say? It has as

scriptural quotations; Jonah 3: 3 for Nineveh, and cf. Jer. 5: 58 for Babylon's walls. See
Lapidge, *AB* xcvi (1978), p. 103 note to 14. 1.

[4] Eccles. 12: 8.
[5] Ps. 86: 3 (87: 3).
[6] Rom. 8: 35.
[7] S. of S. 3: 8.

Quid plura? Eum habet tutelam et propugnatorem qui suos milites ad hec bella mittens et adortans, ait: 'Confidite, ego uici mundum'?[1] Quem ambitum ciuitatis et murum? Qui nullo ariete labari, nullo aduersariorum impulsu potest impelli, quoniam ipse 'saluator ponetur in ea murus et antemurale'.[2] Nulla suffodi potest fraudis machina, quia 'non dormit neque dormitat qui custodit Israel'.[3] Horum ergo Christi pugionum castra sunt ista beati Ecgwini edificia et alia per orbem monachorum cenobia. *Hec autem scripsimus* propter poeticas in secularibus gestis acclamationes et propter eos qui rei geste simplicem anullare solent stilum nisi uariis uerborum fucis ueritas depingatur; depingendo uarietur, uariisque immutata figuris ueritas non esse uideatur.

25. *Nunc autem redeamus* ad ea que, ut uite historiam seriatim texeremus, in uita sancti Ecgwini interserere pretermisimus. Nulli enim umquam sacrorum dogmatum scriptori contigisse legimus, tum ob sui ipsius insufficientiam, tum ob rei scribende ineffabilitatem, tum ob lectorum fastidium, quin aliqua memoria digna in suis scriptis inserere obmiserit. Vnde beatus Iohannes ewangelista, 'Multa alia signa fecit Iesus in conspectu discipulorum suorum que non sunt scripta in libro hoc.'[4] Sic et nos cum caritati uestre uitam sancti Ecgwini scriberemus, ne fastidiosis lectoribus tedium generaret prolixitas, multa obmisimus, que hic stilo commendare dignum duximus, quorum quedam in eius sacra depositione, quedam uero tantum in eius sanctissima translatione sunt legenda.

fo. 127ᵛᵃ 26. Et primum cartam be|ati Ecgwini scribamus quam post dedicationem ecclesie Eueshamensis dictauit.[5] Vnde plures in ea denotantur possessiones quam in illa que Rome confecta erat uel in illa quam Brithwaldus dictauit, ille uidelicet quas beatus uir medio tempore inter cartarum confectionem adquisiuit. Multas enim postea beatus Ecgwinus ecclesie Eueshamensi adquisiuit possessiones, que omnes sub eadem libertatis forma a regibus eidem ecclesie sunt collate sub qua et ille quas Rome fecerat confirmare. Est autem forma carte huiusmodi:

---

a–a hiis per digressionem dictis *DE i. 14 l. 29*   *b–b* redeamus unde digressi eramus *DE i. 14 end. R leaves DE here, reverting to DE i. 9 for Ecgwine's charter two paragraphs below*

[1] John 16: 33.
[2] Isa. 26: 1.
[3] Ps. 120: 4 (121: 4).
[4] John 20: 30.

its defender and protector the One who, sending his soldiers to such battles, addresses them with these words: 'Have confidence, I have overcome the world.'[1] How great is the circumference of that city and its wall! No battering-ram can break through this wall, no enemy assault destroy it by any attack, since 'the Saviour Himself will stand in that city as a wall and a bulwark'.[2] No treacherous engine can undermine it, because 'He that guards Israel, neither slumbers nor sleeps'.[3] Therefore the house of the blessed Ecgwine and other monasteries throughout the world are fortresses housing the weapons of Christ. We have written these things because of the praises given by poets to secular exploits, and because of those who are accustomed to despise a simple style of narrative, unless truth be portrayed in a variety of colourful expressions, be distorted by such depiction, and not even appear to be the truth when changed by distorting metaphors.

25. Let us now return to those matters which we have omitted to include in the life of St Ecgwine in order to construct the story of his life in due order. Indeed, we read that no writer of sacred teaching has ever avoided omitting to mention some matters in his writings that ought to have been included, on account of his own inability, the inexplicable nature of the matter he is writing, or the boredom of his readers. So it was that the blessed John the Evangelist wrote, 'There are many other signs which Jesus performed before the eyes of his disciples which have not been written in this book.'[4] So even we, when writing our account of the life of St Ecgwine out of love for you, lest excessive long-windedness should create weariness in apathetic readers, have omitted many things which we thought merited being commended to writing now, some of which are to be read at his holy deposition, others only at his most holy translation.

26. First let us write down blessed Ecgwine's charter, which he drew up after the dedication of the church of Evesham.[5] More possessions are indicated in this than in the charter which had been completed in Rome, or in that charter which Berhtwald composed: I refer to those possessions which the holy man acquired in the time between the completion of those charters. For the blessed Ecgwine later acquired many possessions for the church of Evesham, all of which were bestowed by the kings upon the same church under the same provision of liberty as those possessions which he had had confirmed at Rome. The form of the charter is as follows:

[5] See above 17 and n. 4, and below, 33 and n. 5.

27. *Charta beati Ecgwini episcopi*[1]

*a*In nomine Domini nostri saluatoris Christi.*a* Ego Ecgwinus Wictiorum humilis episcopus uolo manifestare *b*in ista carta*b* qualiter ego
primum per sancti spiritus inspirationem istum locum elegi et
monasterium edificaui in nomine ⟨et⟩*c* in honore omnipotentis Dei
et sancte Marie*d* uirginis. Contigit quodam tempore, *e*ut ego breuiter
hic narro,*e* quod ego sepe*f* in laboribus multarum*g* uisionum ductus
fui. Qua de re arsit michi in animo per sancti spiritus inspirationem,
quod ego, *h*si Dominus prosperum faceret desiderium meum,*h* unum
locum edificare deberem ad laudem *i*Domini mei*i* et sancte Marie
uirginis et omnium Christi electorum, et etiam michi ad eternam
retributionem antequam ab ista mutabili uita discederem. *j*Postquam
igitur ab urbe Roma reuersus fui ubi clauem in uentre piscis inueni
quam in fluuium iuxta Hethomme proieceram,[2] cogitans locum illum
sanctum, concupiui eum, et cum tunc maxime florerem in diebus
Aelredi regis Merciorum, cepi eum benigne precari ut michi concedere dignaretur eundem locum qui Ethomme uocabatur.[3] Satis ille
libenti animo quod poscebam concessit, quia et Dei amicus et salutis
anime sue erat studiosus.

28. In quo loco cum beata uirgo Maria cuidam pastori gregum, Eoues
nomine, comparuisset, ob cuius uiri sanctitatem eundem locum
Eoueshamiam nuncupaui, et ipse eandem apparitionem michi intimasset; statim, subiunctis ieiuniis et orationibus, ad eundem locum
nudus pedes, adiunctis michi peccatori tribus sociis, accessi, et
eandem gloriosam uirginem clara luce ibidem manifeste uidere
fo. 127vb merui, et cum cruce aurea | quam manu gestabat michi benedixisset,
disparuit. Tanto itaque indicio nactus locum proposito meo congruentem, statim illum emundaui, et opus a Deo presignatum
inchoaui. Ad quod complendum dedit michi Aelredus rex Stratfor-
dam et castellum de Chadelburi,[4] et illud uetus monasterium quod
Fladeburi nominatur,[5] quod sibi euenit ex hereditate uxoris sue,

---

a-a *not in DE*   *b-b* omnibus fidelibus Dei *DE i.9*   *c* *The scribe at first wrote* in
Homme (*the original name for Evesham*), *but then he or another contemporary has corrected this
to* in nomine; *if the latter case is the correct meaning,* et *would need to be added to make sense*
d perpetue *add. DE*   *e-e* non sine omnipotentis Dei dispositione *DE*   *f* *om. DE*
g et magnarum *add. DE*   *h-h* *a repeat from Lectio Octaua, above, where it is DE i. 8 l. 51*
i-i et gloriam omnipotentis Dei *DE*   *j-j* Postquam igitur . . . notata sunt (*p. 34*). *At this
point R begins to leave DE and does not return until the end of the next paragraph. It re-orders
the sequence, and begins with the story of the donation of Æthelred, followed by Eoves' (the
shepherd's) vision of the Virgin Mary; the latter om. DE*

---

[1] Sawyer, no. 1251. The only complete copy of the charter is the present text, the

27. *The charter of the blessed bishop Ecgwine* [1]

In the name of Christ, our Lord and Saviour. I, Ecgwine, the humble bishop of Worcester, wish to show in this charter the way in which I first chose this place through the inspiration of the Holy Spirit, and built the monastery in honour of Almighty God and Mary the Holy Virgin. There was a time, as I shall describe briefly, when I was often led to experience the pains of many visions. For this reason the thought was stirred within me by the inspiration of the Holy Spirit, that, if the Lord prospered my desire, I should build a place to the praise of my Lord, to Mary the Holy Virgin, and to all Christ's elect, and also as an eternal recompense for myself before I departed this transient life. Therefore, after my return from Rome, when I found in the belly of the fish the key which I had thrown into the stream near Hethomme,[2] considering that place to be holy, I set my heart on it. Then, when I prospered greatly in the days of Æthelred, king of the Mercians, I began to beseech him kindly to deign to grant me that very place called 'Hethomme'.[3] He very willingly granted what I requested, because he was both a friend of God and eager to achieve the salvation of his own soul.

28. When the blessed Virgin Mary appeared in this place to a certain herdsman called 'Eoves'—I called this place Evesham because of the holiness of this man—he himself had informed me of that appearance. After praying and fasting, I went immediately to that place barefooted with three companions who had joined me sinner as I was, and I was honoured to see in a brilliant light the same glorious Virgin in that very place. When she had blessed me with the golden cross which she was carrying in her hand, she disappeared. Therefore, having obtained through such a sign the place that accorded with my purpose, I immediately cleansed it of any defilement, and began the task preordained by God. To enable its completion, King Æthelred gave me Stratford-upon-Avon [Warws.], the walled town of Chadbury,[4] and that ancient monastery which is called Fladbury:[5] this last

original of which is now lost. See Lapidge's comments on Byrhtferth's spurious version of the Ecgwine charter in *Anglo-Latin Literature*, pp. 305–6.

[2] This story is not in DE's charter, but cf. Lectio VII, above 13.

[3] DE and Byrhtferth (p. 363) mention the gift of 'Aethomme' itself from King Æthelred, but not in the context of the charter.

[4] The gift of the *castellum* (walled town) of Chadbury does not appear in either Byrhtferth or DE. For the meaning of *castellum*, see *Dictionary of Medieval Latin*, fasc. ii. 294.

[5] For the minsters of Fladbury and Stratford, see Sims-Williams, *Religion and Literature*, esp. pp. 140–2.

Ostriŏ uocate, et ego illud uetus monasterium dedi Aethilhardo Wictiorum subregulo pro terra que erat in Stratforda quam iniuste occupauerat.[1] Postquam uero Aethelredus rex factus est monachus,[2] Kenredus, qui successit ei in regnum Merciorum, et Offa, rex Orientalium Anglorum,[3] de hereditate que illum contingebat in regno Merciorum, dederunt eidem ecclesie octoginta quatuor mansas in circuitu loci illius qui dicitur 'Homme',[4] in utraque parte fluuii illius qui uocatur Auena, in possessionem ecclesie, pro remedio anime sue et successorum suorum. Post paruum denique tempus a predicti reguli fratre, Oswardo nomine, aliam terram optinui, id est, uiginti mansas in loco qui Twiford appellatur.[5] Et post hec Aelthilricus, Osheri regis filius, et Balterius,[6] religiosus sacerdos, uterque eorum .viii. mansas pro diuina religione; et ita complete sunt ecclesiastice possessiones .cxx. manse, sicut infra scriptum est, et in libro[7] manifestatur terra et termini eius quem scripsit Brythwaldus archiepiscopus et dictauit consensu principum quorum nomina infra notata sunt.$^{j'}$

29. ^{a}Post duos annos Aldelmus religiosus episcopus migrauit ad Dominum.[8] Quod ego per reuelationem agnoscens, conuocatis fratribus et obsecundariis meis, excessum uenerandi patris eis aperui, concitoque gradu ad locum ubi sacrum corpus eius iacebat, quinquaginta ferme milibus ultra Meldunense monasterium positum deueni, et ad sepulturam adduxi et honorifice sepeliui, mandans ut in quocumque loco sacrum corpus in asportatione pausauerat sacre crucis erigerentur signacula.[9] Post non multum tempus famosus rex et michi plurimum | amicus, Kenredus, et Offa rex Orientalium Anglorum, Romam ire disponentes, rogauerunt me ut comes et socius itineris eorum existerem. Quod negotium, tum quia omnino eramus obnoxii ad inuicem, libens concessi, tum quia ceptum opus ad optatum finem iam expleueram, ipsumque opus apostolica confirmari

fo. 128ra

---

^{a} R returns to DE i. 9 at l. 43

---

[1] On the kings and kingdom of the Hwicce, see Hooke, *Anglo-Saxon Landscape*, pp. 3–23, and *HBC*, pp. 11–12.
[2] He became a monk at Bardney in 704; Bede, *HE* v. 24 (pp. 566–7).
[3] For dates, see above, nn. to 13, 15   [4] See above, 13 n. 1.
[5] Twyford is in Norton-and-Lenchwick.
[6] Thomas notably follows Byrhtferth here, while DE has Walter. Oshere, king of the Hwicce, had acceded by 693: his son Æthelric was ruling in 736 and in 723×737; see *HBC*, p. 11.
[7] That the charter was in the form of a landbook is stated by both Dominic and Thomas.

he had inherited from his wife, Osthryth, and I gave that ancient monastery to Æthelheard, subking of the Hwicce, for the land which was in Stratford which he had wrongfully seized.[1] After King Æthelred became a monk,[2] Cenred, who succeeded him in the kingdom of the Mercians, and Offa, king of the East Angles,[3] gave to that same church from the inheritance which fell to them in the kingdom of the Mercians eighty-four hides situated around the place which is called 'Homme',[4] on both sides of the river called the Avon, and this was to be a possession of the church for the salvation of their souls and for the souls of those who succeeded them. Finally, after a short time, I obtained from a brother of the above-mentioned subking, named Osweard, other land, namely, twenty hides in a place called Twyford.[5] After this Æthelric, son of King Oshere, and Balterius,[6] a priest and monk, each gave eight hides as a token of their religious devotion. Thus the total ecclesiastical possessions were one hundred and twenty hides, as recorded below, and the land and its bounds is described in a landbook[7] which archbishop Berhtwald [693–731] wrote, dictating it with the assent of the leading men whose names were noted at the end.

29. After two years Aldhelm, bishop and monk, went to be with the Lord.[8] I gained knowledge of this through a revelation, so summoning my brethren and assistant priests I revealed to them that the reverend father had died. We made haste to the place where his holy body lay, which I discovered was lying almost fifty miles beyond the monastery of Malmesbury [Wilts.]. I carried the body to a place to be buried, and gave it an honourable burial, ordering that in whatever place the holy body stopped during the time it was being carried a holy crucifix should be erected.[9] Not long after this [709] the famous king and very great friend of mine, Cenred, also King Offa, king of the East Angles, decided to go to Rome, and asked me to be their companion and associate on the journey. I gladly agreed to this proposal, both because we were absolutely bound to each other in friendship, and because I had now brought the task I had begun to its desired end, but I particularly wished that deed to receive apostolic

---

[8] Aldhelm, abbot of Malmesbury and bishop of Sherborne, died in 709 or 710. From the 10th cent. onwards his cult was celebrated at Malmesbury. There is no evidence that he and Ecgwine were known to one another. On Aldhelm, see M. Lapidge in *Blackwell Encyclopedia of Anglo-Saxon England*, pp. 25–7.

[9] This passage, from the beginning of the paragraph, is quoted in William of Malmesbury's *De gestis pontificum Anglorum*, p. 384. William had direct knowledge of Ecgwine's charter.

auctoritate optabam, et ab ipso in posterum eidem ecclesie omnimo-
dam libertatem ab episcoporum exactionibus optinere satagebam.
Volebat, monebat etiam ut id procurarem rex Kenredus, ad cuius
hoc patrocinium attinebat.

30. Igitur Romam amica itineris societate profecti, ad limina sanctorum apostolorum conscendimus ac debitas Deo gratias exsoluimus,
quia tam nos quam omnia nostra incolumes et iocundi ieramus. Dein
Romane et apostolice apicem dignitatis debita cum reuerentia
adeuntes, coram eo ingressi, benigne satis et ad uotum ab eo
fuimus excepti. Postulata et accepta coram eo dicendi licentia, itineris
et laboris nostri causam sibi aperuimus, eiusque consilium et auxilium
exquisiuimus. Audiuimus optata dignationis eius responsa, et ex
condicto que disposueramus uota et dona Deo sub testimonio tante
auctoritatis offerentes, donauimus Deo et sanctis apostolis eius *et
ecclesie Romane* sub manu et dispositione Romani pape cenobium
Eoueshamense quod extruxeramus *multis possessionibus ampliatum;* totumque liberum[1] coram Deo et sanctis apostolis eius et
coram summo Christianitatis pontifice ipsum locum esse concessi-
mus, fecimusque apostolica et regia corroborari auctoritate donationes
et priuilegia que illi loco concesseramus.

31. Presidebat tunc Romane sedi reuerendus papa Constantinus;
cuius litteras et auctoritatem et confirmationem super hac donatione et libertate cum impressione ipsius sigilli suscipientes,
admodum letati sumus. His ita omnino ad libitum nostrum
expletis, expetita ab apostolico benedictione, summo cum tripudio
fo. 128rb reditum aggressi, arridente nobis | felici fortuna, prosperrimo
rerum omnium nostrarum statu, in Angliam sumus reuersi.

32. *Deinde post paruum tempus reuersionis nostre, ex mandato
apostolico fuit sapientium conuentus in loco qui Alneceastre uocatur.[2]
Et Kenredus rex omnibus quod Rome feceramus notificauit nobis ad
eternam retributionem et successoribus nostris, et omnes bene
salutauimus et apostolicam benedictionem sub pape sigillo dedimus,
et ipsi leti illud idem confirmauerunt uerbi et fidei iussione; et
Bryhtwaldus archiepiscopus ex ore omnium et terram loci et

ᵃ⁻ᵃ et ecclesie Romane *om. DE i. 9 l. 72*   *ᵇ⁻ᵇ* multis possessionibus ampliatum *om.
DE i. 9 l. 74*   *ᶜ End of DE i.9. For this paragraph, R uses some of DE i. 10 and 13, but
very loosely*

---

[1] It was, of course, important that Ecgwine, as bishop of Worcester, should be shown to
have conceded in his charter that Evesham should be wholly free.
[2] ?709. See above, 15 n. 1, 16 n. 2.

confirmation, and was endeavouring to obtain from the pope himself complete freedom for the church of Evesham from the demands of bishops for posterity. King Cenred wished this, and advised also that I should procure this, as it belonged to his protection.

30. Therefore, having made our way to Rome on a journey of friendly companionship, we came to the threshold of the Holy Apostles and expressed our thanks to God that not only we ourselves had arrived safely and in good heart but also that our possessions were intact. Then approaching with due reverence the high place of Roman and apostolic authority, and entering the presence of the pope, we were very kindly received by him as we wished. Having requested and received permission to speak before him, we explained to him the reason for our arduous journey, and asked for his advice and help. We received the desired reply of his highness, and, in accordance with the agreement which we had drawn up, we offered vows and gifts to God under the testimony of this high authority, and gave to God, to His holy apostles, and to the Church of Rome, the monastery of Evesham which we had built, and was now enlarged with many possessions, to be under the control and disposition of the Roman pope. In the presence of God and His holy apostles, and before the High Priest of Christianity we conceded that this place should be wholly free,[1] and we had the endowments and privileges which we had conceded to that place confirmed by apostolic and royal authority.

31. At that time the reverend pope Constantine presided over the Roman see; we were overjoyed to receive his letters, and authority and confirmation of this endowment and liberty, which were given the impression of his very own seal. So, since matters had been fulfilled entirely to our wishes, we asked for the apostolic blessing, prepared for our return with great jubilation with good fortune smiling upon us, and then returned to England with our affairs in a very prosperous state.

32. Shortly after our return, in accordance with the apostolic command, an assembly of councillors was called in a place called Alcester.[2] King Cenred informed everyone of what we had achieved at Rome for the eternal salvation of ourselves and our successors, and greeting them all gladly we gave them the apostolic benediction contained in the letter under the pope's seal. They confirmed this joyfully with a command expressed in words of trust. From the oral testimony of them all, Archbishop Berhtwald recorded in detail in a

libertatem in carta descripsit.[1] Tunc elegerunt sapientes ut domnus Wilfridus episcopus et ego priuilegium idem ad locum eundem afferremus. Eadem autem die qua illuc peruenimus omnium sanctorum erat festiuitas,[2] et eadem die Wilfridus episcopus et ego[a] ecclesiam quam construxeram Deo et sancte Marie et Christi electis omnibus consecrauimus,[3] et cartam .cxx. mansarum et loci libertatem que hic continetur super altare posuimus,[4] et sic coram omnibus locuti fuimus: 'Domine Deus, qui in celis habitas et omnia creasti, conserua illum qui locum istum pacificabit et conseruabit, et hanc Dei hereditatem et hanc libertatem confirmabit quam Deo optulimus. Nos etiam precipimus in Dei omnipotentis et omnium uirtutum celestium nomine, ut neque rex, neque princeps, neque minister, nec ullius ordinis homo, id presumat ut locum istum sanctum diminuat, aut sibi in priuatam potestatem aliquid uendicet, set sit locus hic, ut nos optamus, gregibus et Dei pastoribus eiusdem loci in usum, et bene dispositus in potestate proprii abbatis secundum regulam Dei et beati Benedicti. Si autem aliquis—quod absit—auaritie spiritu arreptus uertere uelit, iudicetur ante tribunal Dei, et numquam in Christi ueniat memoriam, set nomen eius deleatur in euum de libro uiuentium, et ligetur eternarum penarum nodis in inferno, nisi in hac uita penitens emendet. Si quis autem has res bene conseruare uoluerit, Dominus Deus et omnes sancti eius conseruent eum, et letificent animam eius in terra uiuentium, et dent eternam | mercedem in hac uita et in futura.'[b]

fo. 128[va]

33. Huius 'priuilegii descriptio scripta[c] fuit ab incarnatione dominica anno .dccxiiii. Horum testimonio quorum nomina infra scripta uidentur, post paruum tempus migrationis beati Guthlaci de hoc seculo.[5] [d]Ego Kenredus, rex Dei dono Merciorum, uenerando

---

[a] _marginated and_ episcopus et _corrected ?_ donationum descriptio patrata _DE i. 13 l. 48_   [b] futuro _R_   [c-c] ecclesie dedicatio et   [d-d] (p. 40) om. _DE_

---

[1] If the Byrhtferth story is to be accepted, this is presumably the basis for Sawyer, no. 80, which is found in V fos. 68–9—a conglomerate of Evesham's properties probably amounting to _c._120 hides.

[2] The feast of All Saints became established in the West after 609 or 610 under Pope Boniface IV. Its observance on 1 November dates from the time of Pope Gregory III, d. 741; see _Oxford Dictionary of the Christian Church_, 3rd edn., ed. E. A. Livingstone (Oxford, 1997), p. 36.

[3] This suggests a date of 709 again.

[4] The grant of the 120 hides was said earlier to be the product of a number of

charter,[1] both the territory of the place and its liberty. All the councillors then decided that Wilfrid, the bishop, and I should bring the privilege to that place. The day we arrived there was the feast of All Saints,[2] and on that same day Bishop Wilfrid and I consecrated the church which I had built to God, the Blessed Mary, and to all Christ's elect,[3] and we placed on the altar the charter for the one hundred and twenty hides[4] and for the liberty of the place which was contained in it. These were the words we spoke in the presence of them all: 'Lord God, who livest in the heavens and hast created all things, preserve the man who will protect and keep this place safe, and who will confirm this inheritance of God and this liberty which we have offered to God. We further direct, in the name of almighty God and all heavenly virtues, that neither king, nor nobleman, nor official, nor man of any rank, should dare to take anything away from that holy place, or claim for himself any part of it for his personal property; but let this place be, as we desire it, for the use of God's flock and pastors in this place, and be properly maintained under the rule of its own abbot in accordance with the rule of God and of the blessed Benedict. But if anyone, God forbid, seized with a spirit of greed should wish to change this, let him be judged before God's judgment-seat, and never be remembered by Christ; rather let his name be deleted for ever from the Book of Life, and he be confined in Hell with the bonds of eternal punishments, unless he repent and reform in this life. But whoever is willing to preserve these things virtuously, may the Lord God and all His saints preserve that man, give his soul joy in the land of the living, and grant him an eternal reward in this life and in the life to come.'

33. The account of this privilege was written down in the year 714 after our Lord's incarnation, a short time after the passing of the blessed Guthlac from this world.[5] The names of those men witnessing it are seen written below.

'I, Cenred, by God's gift, king of the Mercians, bestowing this gift

---

donations. On the placing of charters on the altar, a practice to secure God's (and frequently a particular saint's) protection, see M. Clanchy, *From Memory to Written Record: England 1066–1307*, 2nd edn. (London, 1979), pp. 156, 256. Charters might also be offered at a shrine or copied in Gospel books which remained on the altar.

[5] Dominic, followed by Thomas, got the date of Guthlac's death, 714, presumably from the Anglo-Saxon Chronicle, see *ASC* p. 26. Thomas omits Dominic's date for the dedication (see textual note c–c), but sticks to 714 for the charter, perhaps because he wanted the second privilege of Pope Constantine (713) to precede it.

episcopo Ecgwino hanc libertatis donationem concedens, dono et signo agye crucis Christi[1] munio. Ego Offa, rex Orientalium Anglorum, hanc prefatam donationem in nomine sancte et indiuidue trinitatis sub crucis sigillo concessi et subscripsi. Ego Brythwaldus archiepiscopus hanc donationem sub sigillo sancte crucis confirmans subscripsi. Et multi alii subreguli, episcopi, abbates et presbiteri subscripserunt, sicut in autentico habetur.[d1]

34. [a]Hec nos pene uerbum ex uerbo subsecuti sumus, sicut ipsemet uir sanctus in cartis suis ex maxima parte scribendo est prosecutus. Et licet scriptorum non sit eadem manus, eiusdem manus et stili seriem fideli relatione summatim transcripsimus.[a]

35. Ecce audistis, fratres mei dilectissimi, in ista carta, 'ne lucerna accensa sub modio absconderetur, set, ut luceret omnibus qui in domo Domini sunt, super candelabrum poneretur',[2] et uidentes bona opera beati Ecgwini glorificemus patrem nostrum qui in celis est, quanta per eum Dominus clara opera et miraculosa, dum adhuc ista mutabili luce frueretur, operari dignatus est. Quorum quedam, quia in uita eiusdem ea uobis plenius scripsimus, dilucidare hic non oportet. Set 'hoc est mirabile in oculis nostris',[3] quod beatus Ecgwinus in hac peregrinatione positus tam per multa locorum interualla longe distantia quam prope posita in spiritu cognouit. Ecce enim audistis qualiter excessum religiosi antistitis Aldelmi per reuelationem cognouerit. Cum enim gloriosi presules, beatus uidelicet Ecgwinus et sanctus Aldelmus, ita mutuo karitatis uinculo se ad inuicem diligerent et sibi confederarentur, ut non solum eedem fo. 128ᵛᵇ dignitates, cum uterque esset episcopus et abbas | et uterque binas regeret ecclesias,[4] set et morum grauitas et uite sanctitas uere faceret spirituales esse germanos; tanta circa eos karitas effulserat, quod sicut in uita sua dilexerunt se, ut quamuis corpore separarentur, tamen in morte spiritus eorum non sunt separati. Quis ergo non credat eorum spiritus coniungi in celis, quamuis eorum corpora separentur in terris, quorum in mortis articulo, ut frater fratri funeris obsequia exhiberet,

---

[a-a] DE i. 10 ll. 1–4. R then summarizes in the following paragraph

[1] For the very unusual agie crucis, see Dictionary of Medieval Latin, iv (Oxford, 1989), under 'hagius'.
[2] Cf. Matt. 5: 15.
[3] Ps. 117: 23 (118: 23); Matt. 21: 42; and Mark 12: 11.
[4] Ecgwine was bishop of Worcester (693×?–30 Dec. 717) and abbot of Evesham, and Aldhelm was bishop of Sherborne (c.705–9) and abbot of Malmesbury; HBC, pp. 222–3. Thomas here is connecting the two Evesham and Malmesbury saints, Ecgwine and

of liberty upon the venerable bishop Ecgwine, give it, and ratify it with the sign of the holy cross[1] of Christ.

I, Offa, king of the East Angles, have conceded and subscribed this aforesaid gift in the name of the holy and indivisible Trinity under the seal of the cross.

I Berhtwald, archbishop, have subscribed, confirming this gift under the seal of the holy cross.'

And many other subkings, bishops, abbots, and priests subscribed it, as found in the authentic document.

34. We have followed this almost word for word, just as the holy man set it forth in his charters which he wrote for the most part himself. And although the hand of the scribes is not the same, we have transcribed faithfully and in summary fashion the narrative of that same hand and pen.

35. Look, my most beloved brethren, you have heard in that charter of the great and marvellous deeds that the Lord deigned to perform through Ecgwine, while he was still enjoying the light of this transitory life, 'lest that light which has been kindled should be hidden under a meal-tub rather than put upon the lamp-stand, so that it may shine upon all who are in the house of the Lord',[2] and they, seeing the good works of the blessed Ecgwine, may glorify our Father who is in heaven. Some of these deeds we do not need to elucidate here, as we have written about them more fully for you in our Life of Ecgwine. But 'it is marvellous in our eyes'[3] what understanding in spirit the blessed Ecgwine possessed when engaged in this pilgrimage, whether he was vast distances away or near at hand. Indeed you have heard how he knew by revelation of the death of Aldhelm, the bishop and monk. The renowned prelates, the blessed Ecgwine and St Aldhelm, loved each other and were bound to each other so much by a mutual bond of affection, that not only the same high offices— for each was a bishop, abbot, and ruler of two churches[4]—but also their sobriety of character and holiness of life truly made them spiritual brothers; in fact so bright a light of love shone around them that, loving each other so much in this life, though separated in body, their spirits were not separated in death. Who could doubt therefore that their spirits were united in the heavens, though their bodies were separated on earth since, at the very moment of death, when the one brother was conducting the funeral service of the other,

Aldhelm, perhaps to highlight the exempt status of the two abbeys whose founders had been both bishop and abbot.

tam subito et tam miraculose spiritus at corpora coniungebantur. Set in hiis, sicut in beatis Ambrosio et Martino,[1] omnipotentis Dei sunt collaudanda magnalia, circa quos consimile miraculum contigisse non ambigitur, ad eius laudem et honorem qui in sanctis suis semper et ubique est gloriosus. Qui uiuit et regnat per omnia secula seculorum. Amen.[2]

36. *Qualiter beatus Ecgwinus aquam de terra produxerit*[3]

Denique non pretereundum esse decreuimus memorabile miraculum quod per seruum suum beatum Ecgwinum hoc itinere Romano *manifeste operari dignatus* est Dominus. Quadam itaque die, cum sanctus uir et qui cum eo erant per abrupta montium iter agerent, uenerunt in terram in qua non erat aqua. Populo igitur pre angustia laboris et feruore caloris sitiente, nec unde sitim releuaret habente, quia beatus Ecgwinus in tanta ueneratione a compatriotis habebatur, quidam, sanctitatis uiri Dei increduli similes populo quondam Israelitico, quasi ab altero Moyse a beato Ecgwino petierunt aquam ad bibendum.[4] Alii uero fideles, incredulos increpantes, de uiri sanctitate plenam fiduciam reportantes, ex fide plena, caritate non ficta et spe certissima ut sic pastorali cura eis subueniret, hoc idem a beato uiro postulabant. De quorum fide confisus beatus Ecgwinus simul cum ipsis in orationem se prostrauit, et facta oratione cum lacrimarum flumine, ecce subito in medio illorum ex arida terra fons erupit aque limpidissime. Igitur prius increduli, uiso miraculo, ad ueritatem conuersi, credentes uero in fide roborati, uoces ad sidera fo. 129ʳᵃ tollentes laudes altis|simo dederunt, et, tam diuino miraculo confortati quam aqua diuinitus data cum paucis cibariis que secum habebant refocillati, in fortitudine cibi et potus illius dietam alacriter peregerunt. Factumque est sic ut qui prius a multis iustus ignorabatur tunc ab eisdem sanctissimus haberetur, simul omnibus qui aderant Deum collaudantibus qui 'in sanctis suis semper est et ubique

---

ᵃ⁻ᵃ written over an erasure

[1] Martin, like Ecgwine and Aldhelm, was both bishop and abbot. However Thomas's connection of him with Ambrose is, perhaps, that both are said to have died in 397. The comparison between Ecgwine and Aldhelm, on the one hand, and Ambrose and Martin, on the other, is nowhere in DE, who simply reports Aldhelm's death.

[2] A common ending to a collect.

[3] This paragraph is modelled on DE i. 10, and records the same miracle, but it is elaborated by Thomas. The miracle probably orginates with Dominic: it is not in Byrhtferth; see Lapidge in *AB* xcvi, p. 102 note to 10. 6.

their spirits and bodies were so suddenly and so miraculously joined? But in the case of these men, as in that of the blessed Ambrose and Martin,[1] almighty God must be praised for these miracles, for around these latter saints it cannot be doubted that a similar miracle occurred, to his praise and honour, who is at all times and in all places glorified amongst his saints. Who lives and reigns for ever and ever. Amen.[2]

36. *The blessed Ecgwine produces water from the earth*[3]
Finally, we have decided not to neglect mentioning the memorable miracle which the Lord deigned to perform manifestly through his servant, the blessed Ecgwine, during his journey to Rome. One day when the holy man and his companions were making their way through precipitous mountains they came to a land in which there was no water. The people, being in great distress and suffering from thirst in the fierce heat, had no means of relieving their thirst. Some of them, therefore, because the blessed Ecgwine was so highly revered by his countrymen, though, like the people of Israel long ago, they had no trust in the holiness of this man of God, asked the blessed Ecgwine for water to drink as if he were another Moses.[4] Other faithful men, rebuking their unbelief, showed their complete trust in the holiness of Ecgwine, and out of their complete trust, with unfeigned love and sure hope, they made this same request of that blessed man, that with pastoral care he would bring them help. The blessed Ecgwine, trusting their good faith, at the same time prostrated himself in prayer with them, and suddenly, after he had offered his prayer with a stream of tears, a spring of the clearest water burst forth in their midst from the parched earth. Those who had previously disbelieved were converted to the truth when they saw the miracle and, believing what was true, were strengthened in their faith, and raising their voices to the heavens they gave praises to the almighty; indeed not only were they invigorated by the divine miracle, but were also refreshed by the water divinely provided and the few morsels of food which they had with them, so, strengthened by the food and that water, they proceeded eagerly with their daily work. The result was that he who previously was unknown by many as a just man was then considered by them to be a most holy man, and everybody there at the same time praised God, who at all times and in all places works wondrous things through his saints. And

---

[4] For the story of Moses providing water for the Israelites, see Exodus 17: 1–6.

mirabilis'.[1] Et condigne satis. Futurum enim erat ut, eo reuerso in patriam, ex ore eius fluerent aque uiue, 'salientes in uitam eternam',[2] et per uerbi eius attractum ex montuosis et saxosis cordibus auditorum diuini gratia amoris et spiritualium dulcedo prosiliret uirtutum, ad eius gloriam. Qui uiuit et regnat per omnia secula seculorum. Amen.

37. *De subuersione Alecestrie, et quare fabri ibi uigere non possunt* [3]

Quoddam miraculum per beatum Ecgwinum dum adhuc luce hac frueretur perpetratum, stilo perfectius commendandum nostris temporibus est reseruatum. Quod ideo in uita sua neminem predecessorum nostrorum scripsisse credimus, quia per ipsius facti euidentiam et publicam noticiam eiusdem miraculi dignam adhuc habeamus memoriam, nec ab hominum recedat memoria quod adhuc probatur fide occulata. Set quia fugacis eui longinquitas gestorum solempnium memoriam abolet, et que publice facta fuerunt profunda obliuione sepeliendo tamquam infecta reddere festinat, longeuo ueracis scripti testimonio illud posterorum memorie tradendum dignum duximus. Tale quid circa illum diuinorum secretarium, beatum uidelicet Iohannem, ewangelistam contigisse legitur. Cum enim tres ewangeliste prius eo scripsissent ewangelium, nullus illorum in serie sui ewangelii illa duo precipua, immo, quamuis mirabilia uniuersa Domini opera, pre ceteris tamen excellentiora mirabilia, de ceci nati illuminatione et de quatriduani Lazari scripsit resuscitatione. Quamuis tamen beato Ieronimo mirabilius uideatur quod Dominus noster Iudeos | ementes et uendentes in templo, ubi idem Iudei dominabantur, flagello ex funiculis facto de eodem templo eiecerit, quod immensus exercitus facere non poterat.[4] Set hoc, quod de ceco illuminato et Lazaro resuscitato scribenda beato Iohanni sunt reseruata,[5] non solum ob beati Iohannis prerogatiuam factum esse credimus, immo etiam propter ipsorum miraculorum excellentiam et publicam noticiam. Hec enim duo Domini facta inter ea que gessit in corpore pre ceteris lucencia propter sui magnitudinem et facti solempnitatem in tantam admirationem et uenerationem, ut a seculis

fo. 129rb

---

[1] Ps. 67: 36 (68: 35).   [2] John 4: 14.

[3] This miracle does not come from Dominic. Thomas introduced it, perhaps, to show the importance of the events in the council at Alcester in Evesham's history.

[4] Pseudo-Jerome, *Expositio quattuor euangeliorum*, PL xxx, 578–9 (John 2: 15): '*flagellum de resticulis*, id est, vindicta pro variis peccatis, inde ejiciuntur de Ecclesia'.

[5] John 9: 1–7, and 11: 17–44.

rightly so. For it was to happen that, when Ecgwine returned to his country, living waters would flow from his mouth, 'springing up into eternal life',[1] and through the influence of his words, the grace of the divine love and sweet spiritual virtues would spring forth from the hard, rocky hearts of those who listened to him, to the glory of the One who lives and reigns for ever and ever. Amen.

37. *The destruction of Alcester and the reason why craftsmen are unable to flourish there* [2]

A certain miracle was performed by the blessed Ecgwine while he was still enjoying the light of this world which was left to our times to be recorded more fully in writing. It is our belief therefore that none of our predecessors wrote about it in their lifetime, for we still remember the miracle well through the evidence of the deed itself and people's general knowledge of it, nor has it receded from men's memories, but is still acknowledged as eye-witness testimony. However, because length of time, fleeting as it is, effaces the memory of illustrious deeds, and, by burying them in its profound oblivion, soon causes things which were done publicly to appear not to have been done, we have thought it right to hand the story down for posterity's sake, by the lasting testimony of a truthful document. One reads that such happened in the case of that writer of the divine word, St John the Evangelist: for although the three evangelists had written their gospels before him, not one of them in the course of their Gospel wrote about those two particular stories, the giving of sight to the man born blind, and the raising of Lazarus from his four days of death, which, though all the Lord's works were marvellous, were miracles more wonderful than all the others. However, it seemed more wonderful to St Jerome that our Lord made a whip out of ropes, and drove out from the temple Jews who were buying and selling in that place, when those very Jews were the masters there, a thing which a huge army was unable to do.[3] But the fact that the stories of the restoration of sight to the blind man and of the raising of Lazarus were reserved for St John to tell,[4] we believe happened not only because of the special authority of St John, but also because of the very special nature and the general knowledge of those very miracles. For these two deeds of our Lord, which he performed amongst other deeds while he was alive in the body, are more conspicuous than his other miracles because of the greatness and solemnity of what was done. They caused such wonder and reverence, being unheard of

inaudita hominibus facta sunt, quod tribus ewangelistis necessarium
non uidebatur ea per scripturam memorie hominum commendare,
que se per sui prerogatiuam omnium mentibus inscribebant.

38. Set ille uere theologus, non solum memor preteritorum set etiam
cognitor occultorum et presagus futurorum, Iohannes uidelicet
ewangelista, ⟨in⟩ futurum certissimus quod 'superhabundaret iniquitas, et multorum refrigesceret caritas',[1] quamuis et ille multa scribere
omisisset, sicut idem testatur, dicens, 'Multa et alia signa fecit Iesus
in conspectu discipulorum suorum que non sunt scripta in libro hoc',[2]
tamen hec propter ipsorum et sui ipsius prerogatiuam et priuilegii
dignitatem ewangelio suo interseruit, ne, refrigescente caritate, eorum
ab hominum mentibus memoria recederet, quod et tunc pro parte
apud quosdam accidisse conspexerat. Vnde et nos, uix preterita uel
pauca ad memoriam reuocantes, presencia non intelligentes, futura
penitus ignorantes, posteris super ignorancia precauentes, miraculum
illum stilo commendamus quod nos futuros prius caritati uestre
promiseramus.

39. Cum igitur beatus Ecgwinus operibus caritatis totus afflueret et
indesinenter insisteret, maxime tamen totis uiribus predicationi
operam dedit, sciens quia 'qui conuerti fecerit peccatorem ab errore
uie sue saluabit animam eius et operiet multitudinem peccatorum'.[3]

40. Erat itaque iuxta Euesham castrum, Alnecestre nomine, tunc |
fo. 129va temporis Anglie famosissimum, regale uidelicet mansum, et regie
mansioni aptissimum, ueluti nemoribus consitum, fluminibus piscosis
et riuulis iocundis circumdatum, necnon muris et turribus uallatum.
Set quia multotiens 'ex adipe prodit iniquitas',[4] quanto magis rerum
terrenarum opulentia et temporalium bonorum habundantia eiusdem
loci habitatores affluebant, tanto magis gule et luxurie dediti, uacantes
uentri et lateri, studentes auaricie et cupiditati, misericordissima Dei
clementia se indignos efficiebant. Horum siquidem perpetue ruine et
animarum iacture compatiens beatus Ecgwinus, eorum opinioni et
errori succurrendum putauit. Feruebat namque beati uiri circa idem

---

[1] Matt. 24: 12.   [2] John 20: 30.
[3] Jas. 5: 20.   [4] Ps. 72: 7 (73: 7).

before in living memory, that it did not seem necessary to the three evangelists to commit the stories to the memory of men by writing about them, when the very miracles impressed themselves on the minds of everybody because of their special importance.

38. However, that true theologian, John the evangelist, not only mindful of things past, but also having insight into hidden depths, and aware of future events, was certain that in future 'iniquity would abound, and that the love of many would grow cold',[1] so, although he would have to leave out many things from his narrative—as he himself testified, 'there were many other signs that Jesus performed in the presence of his disciples which are not written in this book'[2]— he nevertheless included these stories in his Gospel because of the special authority and the great privilege they, and he himself, possessed, so that they might not slip from men's memories when their love grew cold, for he had seen this happen to some extent in the case of some men even in his own time. Hence, even we, who can scarcely recall to mind even a few past events, or understand present happenings, and are utterly ignorant of the future, want to prevent posterity from suffering ignorance, and must therefore commit to writing an account of that miracle, which we had previously promised we would do out of love for you.

39. Although the blessed Ecgwine gave himself entirely to his works of charity and never ceased to pursue them, he nevertheless put every effort he could into his preaching, knowing that 'he who makes a sinner turn from the error of his ways will save that man's soul and obliterate a multitude of sins'.[3]

40. Near Evesham there was a fortress called Alcester, the most famous one in England at that time, a royal dwelling, and most suitable for a royal household, being planted about with woodlands, surrounded by rivers full of fish and pleasant streams, and fortified with walls and towers. However, because many times 'iniquity comes forth from fatness',[4] the richer the inhabitants of that place became in worldly things and the greater its abundance of material possessions, all the more addicted were its inhabitants to gluttony and extravagance, spending their time eating and lounging about, and wholly greedy and lustful, so that they made themselves unworthy of God's abundant mercy. However, the blessed Ecgwine, deeply concerned about the everlasting destruction of these men and the loss of their souls, decided that help should be given to them to change their minds and the error of their ways. The love of this holy man burned

castrum ardentius caritas eo quod in eodem loco ex mandato apostolico, a Brithwaldo Brittaniarum primate, concilium tocius Anglie, episcoporum uidelicet sacrique ordinis religiosarum personarum optimatumque regni cum proceribus suis, fuit pro eo et per eum non multo prius coadunatum; et ibidem in nomine Domini, priuilegiis tam summi pontificis quam regum in communi perlectis, Eoueshamense cenobium sit liberum denuntiatum, et, ex precepto apostolico, ab inde progredientibus episcopis, in ecclesia Eoueshamensi sit congregatio monachorum constituta, que minus in illis partibus tunc habebatur; ouile uidelicet diuinitus preostensum, apostolica auctoritate fultum, regia libertate donatum, cleri et populi benedictione sancitum, sicut priuilegia eiusdem ecclesie testantur.

41. Ad hunc ergo locum accedens beatus Ecgwinus, obsecrando, increpando, uerbum Dei annuntians *opportune, importune,* in omni mansuetudine et pietate, in omni patientia et doctrina,[1] illis gentibus predicauit regnum celorum, et non tacuit uicia eorum. Set gens illa absque consilio et sine prudentia, et ceruicis dure, immo indurate, nec assueta uicia relinquere nec saluberrimis monitis sancti uiri uole|bat adquiescere, set nec eius salutifere doctrine aliqua ratione obuiare, neque sapientie et spiritui qui in eo loquebatur poterat resistere. Vnde, et cum palam nec posset nec auderet dicere, 'Recede a nobis quia uias tuas nolumus',[2] ne uerbum Dei disseminaretur uarias discurrit ad artes. Cum enim castrum illud, ueluti nemoribus undique consitum, conflandi ferrum locus esset aptissimus, et fabris et ferri exclusoribus maxime repleretur, gens incredula detestabilior populo qui in predicatione beati Stephani ne audirent uerbum Dei aures suas opturabant,[3] incudes ferreis malleis quibus maxime habundabat per plateas et uicos castri circumquaque tanto strepitu continue percutiebat, ut beati uiri sermo non audiretur et ut a castro recedere cogeretur.

42. Beato igitur Ecgwino castrum exeunte, immo iam longe a castro agente, pre concussione, immo confusione, malleorum et incudum

_{fo. 129vb}

---

a–a cf. DE i.4 l. 56, and the variant given

[1] 'oportune, importune', 'in omni . . . doctrina': 2 Tim. 4: 2.
[2] Job 21: 14.
[3] Acts 6 and 7.

all the more fervently for the men of this fortress, because in that very place, in obedience to the apostolic mandate, a council of the whole of England had only a short time before this been called by Berhtwald, the primate of Britain, of bishops, of ecclesiastical dignitaries, of magnates in the realm and its nobles on account of that mandate. It was there that the privileges of both the pope and of the kings were read out for all to hear: it was proclaimed that the community at Evesham was to be free, and that, in accordance with the apostolic command and with the bishops following on from that, a congregation of monks should henceforth be established in the church of Evesham, which had previously been rare in those regions; hence a flock was divinely appointed, supported by apostolic authority, granted royal liberty, and sanctioned with the blessing of the clergy and the people, just as the privileges of that church testify.

41. The blessed Ecgwine visited this place, therefore, imploring them and berating them, proclaiming the word of God in season and out of season, in all gentleness and goodness, patiently and with sound teaching,[1] and preached to those people about the kingdom of heaven, and he was not silent about their sins. But those people were without wisdom or good sense, stubborn and obdurate, having no wish to abandon the vices they were used to practising nor to listen quietly to the wholesome teaching of that holy man; yet they were not by any means able to oppose his teaching, which would bring them salvation, nor to resist his spiritual wisdom which he spoke among them. Hence, when they could not openly dare to say 'Depart from us, for we do not want to know your ways',[2] they nevertheless had recourse to various cunning devices, lest Ecgwine should sow the seed of God's word in their hearts. That fortress, situated in a place surrounded by woods, was eminently suitable for smelting iron, and was especially occupied by craftsmen and miners of iron ore. They were an unbelieving race of people, more loathsome than the people who shut their ears lest they should hear the word of God when the blessed Stephen preached.[3] So these men began to beat their anvils continuously with their iron hammers, of which the place had a great abundance, wherever it was possible throughout the streets and highways of the fortress, making so great a din that the sermon of the blessed Ecgwine could not be heard, and he was compelled to withdraw from the fortress.

42. When the blessed Ecgwine left the fortress, in fact when he was some considerable distance away, both his ears were still ringing from

adhuc tinniebant ambe aures eius ac si percutientes incudes eum sequerentur; et respiciens neminem uidit nisi solum discipulos suos, et leuatis in celum oculis, flexis in terra genibus, contra arcem fabrilem castri illius Dominum imprecatus est. Res mira et omni admiratione digna. Dominus, dicti sui non inmemor, 'Qui uos spernit me spernit',[1] se in seruo suo contemptum et repulsum reputans, non tantum castri illius arti fabrili maledixit, set et ipsum castrum subuertit. Nam castrum ipsum terra absorbuit, ita quod, nouo super ueteri qualitercumque reedificato usque in hodiernum diem in constructione nouarum domorum in fundamentis earum antiqua edificia reperiuntur. Iusto etiam Dei iudicio, qui ipsum locum et eius habitatores in eo in quo deliquerunt puniuit, per quingentos annos et amplius usque ad tempora nostra penam eis inflixit, duraturam quamdiu ei qui inflixit placuerit, uidelicet, quod numquam postea in eodem loco aliquis artem fabrilem recte exercuit, nec aliquis eam excercere uolens ibi uigere potuit, quamuis multi | hoc temptauerint facere, nec usque in hodiernum diem profecerint, cum usque nunc castrum illud ab arte fabrili suspensum permanserit, ut uere de eo dici possit, 'Culpa demi potest, perhennis erit.'[2]

fo. 130ra

43. Nam ad delendam culpam illius loci et placandam iram beati Ecgwini, uel in signum reconciliationis federis inter beatum uirum et eundem locum, uel nescimus quo alio Dei iudicio, locus in quo ylium quondam eiusdem castri fuerat datus est ecclesie Euesha-mensi, ut, quasi per principale domicilium quod sanctus Ecgwinus in eodem loco optinet, omnibus sit liquidum beatum uirum quondam per predicationem suam in bello illo spirituali in eodem loco contra aereas potestates optinuisse,[3] quamuis tunc hoc liqui-dum constet non fuisse. Si uero alicui hec predicta que diximus incredibilia uidentur, ad locum prefatum accedat, et fide oculata per ipsam rei euidentiam et facti noticiam et famam publicam, hec ita pro certo inueniens,[4] beatum Ecgwinum, immo Deum, laudabit, qui in sanctis suis semper est gloriosus per omnia secula seculorum. Amen.

---

[1] Cf. Luke 10: 16.

[2] Cf. Ovid, *Epist. ex Ponto*, i. 1 ('Pena potest demi, culpa perennis erit').

[3] Cf. Eph. 2: 2 for the powers of the air.

[4] John Blair comments on the folkloric character of this story and suggests that the redevelopment of the site and the discovery of Roman remains—in fact Alcester had been a Roman industrial centre—may explain its origin.

the beating and the clatter of the hammers and the anvils, as if the
beating of the anvils was pursuing him. Looking back, he saw no
one except his disciples, and raising his eyes to heaven, and kneeling
upon the ground, he invoked the Lord to curse the craftsmen's art
in that fortress. Then an amazing thing happened that deserves
great admiration. The Lord, not unmindful of his words, 'Whoever
rejects you, rejects me',[1] believing Himself to have been despised
and rejected in His servant, not only cursed the art of the craftsmen
in that fortress, but destroyed the fortress itself. For the earth
swallowed up the very fortress, so that whenever any sort of new
building work has been carried out upon the old building, even up
to this present day, during the construction of new houses ancient
buildings are found among their foundations. Also by God's just
judgment, who punished that place and its inhabitants in it, where
they had done wrong, for five hundred years or more up to our
present time, he has inflicted a punishment upon them, destined to
last as long as it please the God who inflicted it, namely that since
that time no one has ever plied his craftsman's skill in that place,
and no one wishing to do so has ever been able to prosper there,
though many have tried to do so, nor have they been successful up
to the present time, for up to now the fortress has remained devoid
of the craftsmen's skill, so that it could truly be said of that place:
'The reproach can be removed, but the punishment will be for
ever.'[2]

43. To remove the offence of that place and to placate the anger of
the blessed Ecgwine, the place in which the heart of the fortress had
once been was given to the church of Evesham, either as a sign of a
renewal of a bond between the holy man and that place, or because of
some other judgment of God. The purpose of the gift was that it
should be crystal clear to everybody throughout the main dwelling
place which St Ecgwine holds in that place, that the blessed man had
through his preaching gained a victory in that same place in the
spiritual war against the powers of the air;[3] though it is accepted that
at the time this was not clear. Should this story which we have told
seem unbelievable to anyone, let him go to that place; and after he has
examined at first hand the evidence for the event, the information
about what happened, and the public knowledge of it, he will
assuredly discover that the story is true,[4] and will indeed give
praise to the blessed Ecgwine, or rather to God, who dwells for
ever among his saints, for ever and ever. Amen.

Explicit liber primus de uita sancti Ecgwini et de miraculis que
per eum Dominus operari dignatus est dum hac luce frueretur.

44. *De compositione legende in translatione sancti Ecgwini*[1]
Hec que sequuntur usque ad secundum librum non legantur nisi
in translatione tantum.

Rogatus fui aliquando a fratribus ut uitam eximii martiris Wistani
aduocati nostri sine soloecisimo et alio uicio, quod nondum factum
fuit, stilo commendarem prolixiori; necnon et uitam sanctissimi
patroni nostri beati Ecgwini episcopi, que prolixius tractabatur,
saluo per omnia historie tenore, in tantum abbreuiarem ut fastidiosi
auditores tedio non afficerentur, ita uidelicet stilum temperans, quod
utraque pro temporum qualitate nataliciorum eorundem in eisdem
festiuitatibus ad legendam in nocturnis uigiliis sufficeret.[2]

45. Magis itaque de eorum sacra circa eosdem sanctos deuotione
quam de mea confisus eloquentia, immo omnem spem ponens in eo
fo. 130ʳᵇ qui 'linguas infantium facit disertas',[3] fratrum uoluntati ue | lut
precepto obtemperaui, et utrumque opus, non prout uolui sed
prout potui,[4] Deo adiuuante compleui. Que cum domino Cantuariensi[5] corrigenda legissem, et ipse ea approbando commendasset, et
cum eadem fratribus placuissent, iterum crebro pulsauerunt me
precibus suis ut in translatione eiusdem patroni nostri beati Ecgwini
tante festiuitati congruentem et specialem legendam ad nocturnas
uigilias, que minus apud nos adhuc habebatur, eis componerem.

46. Ego uero, quamuis peticionem illorum ueluti ratione nitentem
intelligerem exaudiendam, cum etiam sepe puduisset me quod in
tanta festiuitate de tanto patrono nichil speciale ad nocturnas uigilias
legebatur, tamen uidens tantum opus supra me esse, diu distuli
prebere eis assensum. Et hoc ideo maxime quia cum miracula
sanctorum in eorum translationibus legi consueuerint, putabam in
legenda infra octabas omnia que de eodem patrono nostro scripta
erant, esse consummata et expensa. Fratribus tamen in uoluntate sua

---

[1] There were two feasts of the translation, 10 Sept. and 11 Jan.
[2] i.e. the anniversary of the saint's death. From the end of the 2nd cent., the saint's
natalitia or *natalis* (his heavenly birthday) was kept as a feast with liturgical celebrations at
his tomb. The first incontrovertible evidence of this practice is the 'Martyrium Polycarpi'
(*c.*156), where St Polycarp's followers express their intention of celebrating the birthday of
his martyrdom in days to come; see *Oxford Dictionary of the Christian Church*, pp. 1046,
1131, 1445. The feast of St Ecgwine was celebrated on 30 December, that of St Wigstan on
1 June.
[3] Wisd. 10: 21.

Here ends the First Book of the Life of Saint Ecgwine, and of the miracles which the Lord deigned to perform through him while he enjoyed life in the light of this world.

44. *The composition of the reading on the translation of St Ecgwine* [1]
The following words preceding the Second Book are only to be read on the feast of the translation of St Ecgwine.
I was once asked by the brethren to write a full account, to be without fault or error, of the life of that renowned martyr and protector of ours, Wigstan, because this had not yet been done. Also that I should abridge the Life of our most holy patron the blessed bishop Ecgwine, already treated at great length, providing the gist of all the events of the story. I was to abbreviate my account so that disdainful listeners should not become bored, and to modify my style so as to be sufficient for reading in the nightly vigils during the festivals celebrating the birthdays of these men. [2]
45. And so trusting more in the holy devotion of the brethren towards those saints than in my own eloquence, indeed putting all my trust in him who 'makes the tongues of infants fluent', [3] I accepted the will of the brethren as a command, and with God's help I completed each work, not as I wished but as I was able. [4] And when I had read these out to the archbishop of Canterbury [5] for him to correct any errors, and he had put the seal of his approval on both works, the brethren were pleased about this, and again entreated me with persistent prayers that I should write for them a lection on the translation of that same patron of ours, the blessed Ecgwine, specially appropriate for such a festival, to be read out at nightly vigils, something which we did not have at all up to that time.
46. Although I realized that their request should be heeded, for it was clearly reasonable, and had often felt ashamed myself that nothing special was read at the night-time vigils on that feast-day in honour of so great a patron, yet I saw that so great a task was beyond me, and delayed for a long time before agreeing to their request. I delayed for this reason in particular that the miracles of saints were accustomed to be read at their translations, and I thought that in the things set to be read within the octave everything which had been written about that same patron of ours had been completed and used up. However, as the brethren persevered in their desire, wishing to satisfy their desire,

---

[4] Cf. Terence, *Andria* 805: 'ut quimus . . . quando ut uolumus non licet'.
[5] Baldwin, archbishop of Canterbury from 1184 to 1190; see above, p. xviii.

perseuerantibus, sepe et multum mecum cogitare cepi, uolens eorum uoluntati satisfacere, unde sermonis sumerem materiam et exordium, postulans ab eo auxilium cuius 'spiritus ubi uult spirat',[1] et qui dat omnibus affluenter et non improperat.

47. Interim autem librum qui de eiusdem beati uiri miraculis scriptus est legens et relegens, tandem duo tantum miracula inueni que in legenda infra octabas posita non erant.[2] Quibus lectis et perspicaciter intellectis, inueni ea maxime proposito meo conuenientia et operi prelibato aptissima, uidelicet, de foca magno pisce contra solitum modum talium piscium in flumine Auene apud Eouesham in festiuitate predicti uiri beati ad esum seruorum Dei inuento, et de homine ferreis uinculis astricto a sanctis apostolis Petro et Paulo ab urbe Roma Eoueshamiam transmisso et a beato fo. 130va Ecgwino soluendo.[3] Que cum mente | concepissem et plenius intellexissem, ultra quam credi possit admiratus sum, et quasi in extasi pre gaudio factus sum eo quod clauis Dauid[4] aperire dignata est, et introductus sum in cellam uinariam[5] in qua michi tam egregium demonstratum est exemplar. Quis unquam non credat hec diuina facta dispositione? Vel quis dubitet hec tam solempnia miracula in tam solempni solempnitate legenda, diuino reseruata esse iudicio? Credat qui uoluerit, quia ego credo, Dei prouidentia ita factum esse. Nam 'omne datum optimum et omnem donum perfectum de sursum est, descendens a patre luminum.'[6] Igitur de casu tam admirabili obstupefactus, per rei tamen tante euentum confortatus, opus michi iniunctum aggrediens, ad finem qualemcumque usque perduxi, illo adiuuante sine quo nichil est sanctum, nichil ualidum. Qui cum patre et spiritu sancto uiuit et regnat Deus per omnia secula seculorum. Amen.[7]

---

[1] John 3: 8.

[2] The book is almost certainly Byrhtferth's Life of St Ecgwine; see note below.

[3] The miracle of the seal is in Byrhtferth's *Vita S. Ecgwini*, iv. 9, and the miracle of the man bound in chains, who was sent from Rome to Evesham to be freed by St Ecgwine, is in both Byrhtferth (iv. 7–8) and Dominic (DE i. 18). Both miracles are described by Thomas in more detail in Readings 7–11. For the chain miracle, cf St Kenelm: *Three Anglo-Saxon Saints' Lives*, ed. and trans. R. C. Love (OMT, 1996), pp. 82–3. The other miracles included in Byrhtferth's Life of St Ecgwine, which are discussed by M. Lapidge, *Anglo-Latin Literature*, pp. 307–9, are the miracle of the rustic, 70, below, the miraculous

I began to think much and often about where I might get the introduction and the matter of my speech from. I begged help from him whose 'spirit blows where it wills',[1] who gives abundantly to everyone and does not reproach us.

47. Meanwhile I read and re-read the book which was written about the miracles of that holy man, and at last found two miracles alone which had not been put in the stories to be read during the octave of the feast.[2] After reading them and understanding them thoroughly, I found those matters especially pertinent to what I had in mind and most suitable for the work I have mentioned. The first miracle concerned the seal, a large fish different from the sort of fish usually found, which was discovered in the River Avon at Evesham, and intended to be eaten by the servants of God on the feast-day of the holy man. The second miracle concerned the man who had been tied with iron chains and sent from the city of Rome to Evesham by the holy apostles Peter and Paul, and then freed by the blessed Ecgwine.[3] When I first began to think about these miracles and realized their full import, I was amazed beyond belief, and became, as it were, beside myself for joy, for the key of David[4] had deigned to open a door, and I was introduced into a wine cellar[5] in which that excellent model was revealed to me. Who could ever disbelieve that this occurred through divine intention? Or who could doubt that such celebrated miracles as these had been reserved by divine wisdom to be read at so solemn a service? Let him believe who wishes, as I believe, that this has occurred by the providence of God. For 'every good and every perfect gift is from above, and comes down to us from the Father of lights.'[6] Therefore, stunned by so wonderful an occurrence, and strengthened by an event of such moment, I embarked upon the task enjoined upon me, and have now brought it to some sort of conclusion, with the help of the One without whom nothing is holy, nothing effective. Who reigns with the Father and the Holy Spirit as God for ever and ever. Amen.[7]

---

preservation of the relics, **68**, below, and Ecgwine and the key found in the fish's belly, **10**, above. The miraculous appearance of the Virgin is also in Byrthferth.

[4] Cf. Isa. 22: 22.
[5] S. of S. 2: 4.
[6] Jas. 1: 17.
[7] A common ending to a collect.

48. *In translatione sancti Ecgwini*

LECTIO PRIMA

Cum uirtus diuina, fides preclara, et uita immaculata sanctos efficiat Christi confessores, occulto quodam Dei iudicio quorundam coram hominibus clarescentibus miraculis ita lucent bona opera quod uidentes glorificent patrem suum qui est in celis,[1] et illos per quorum merita talia fiunt miracula uenerantur in terris; quorundam uero ita in occulto fiunt opera bona, quod solus pater eorum celestis qui uidet in abscondito[2] sit eorum retributor et retributio. Dominus enim et saluator noster qui solus nouit quos elegerit pro locorum, temporum et personarum qualitate, quibusdam ad uitam predestinatis et fidelibus, ad morum edificationem et fidei ipsorum roborationem signa et prodigia ostendit, ut suorum uita et opera seruorum inperpetuum ecclesie sue sit in exemplum. Quibusdam uero ad mortem precitis et reprobatis 'ut generationi male et peruerse nullum signum nisi Ione dandum'[3] pronuntiauit.

49.   LECTIO SECVNDA

fo. 130vb Merito ergo in sanctorum natalitiis[4] eorum uita, | per quam Deo qui uidet in corde probantur accepti, legitur; in eorum uero translationibus eorum opera et miracula recitantur, per que eorum sanctitas hominibus qui uident in facie manifestatur. Gaudeamus igitur, fratres dilectissimi, qui talem ac tantum meruimus habere protectorem et patronum, beatum uidelicet Ecgwini episcopum et confessorem, qui pro innocentia pura, uita honesta, et recte fidei doctrina cum sanctis Dei meruit coronari in celis, et propter opera preclara et miracula manifesta que pro eo Deus operari dignatus est, inter sanctos confessores honoratur in terris. Quia ergo eiusdem patroni nostri uitam in eiusdem depositione legendam pro temporis qualitate caritati uestre prolixius transcripsimus, nunc aliqua de eius operibus et miraculis in eius translatione legenda pro temporis angustia breuiter perstringamus.

---

[1] Cf. Matt. 5: 16.
[2] Cf. Matt. 6: 6.
[3] Cf. Luke 11: 29; Matt. 12: 39 and 16: 4, and for 'generatio perversa' Luke 9: 41 and Matt. 17: 16.
[4] See above, 44 n. 2.

48. *On the translation of St Ecgwine*

FIRST READING

While divine goodness, a pre-eminent faith, and an unblemished life may produce holy confessors of Christ, the good deeds of some men, through a certain hidden judgment of God, are manifested before men in miracles, and shine so brightly that men, seeing their good deeds, glorify their Father who is in heaven,[1] and venerate on earth those men through whose merits such miracles are performed. Some men's good deeds are done in secret, so that their Father in heaven alone, who sees in secret,[2] may be their rewarder and reward. For our Lord and Saviour, who alone knows whom he has chosen to suit the nature of the places, the times, and the persons, has revealed, to some who are faithful and predestined for life, signs and wonders for the building up of their morals and the strengthening of their faith, in order that the lives and the deeds of these his servants should be an everlasting example to his Church. But he has proclaimed to those who have been condemned and predestined for death 'that no sign be given to such an evil and perverse generation, except that given to Jonah'.[3]

49.   SECOND READING

On the birthdays of saints[4] there is good reason for reading about their life, through which they have proved acceptable to God, who sees into the heart. At their translations their deeds and miracles are recited, through which their holiness is manifested to men, who see the outward appearance. Let us rejoice, therefore, my most beloved brethren, who have been privileged to have as good and great a protector and patron as the blessed bishop and confessor, Ecgwine. He is a man who earned his crown with the saints of God in the heavens because of his undefiled innocence and goodness of life, and for his teaching of sound doctrine; and he is honoured amongst holy confessors on earth for his excellent deeds and the manifest miracles which God deigned to perform for him. It is for these reasons that we copied out more fully, out of our love for you, the life of our patron to be read at the commemoration of his burial, to suit the essential nature of that occasion; but now let us restrict other stories of his deeds and miracles to a shorter account, to be read at the time of his translation to suit the restraint of that time.

50. Beatus itaque Ecgwinus episcopalis officii cura suscepta, non tam honorem quam onus se suscepisse intelligens, magis prodesse quam preesse concupiuit.[1] Immo magis operarium in orto dominico se constitutum cognouit ut operaretur et custodiret illud.

51.   LECTIO TERCIA

Excoluit igitur beatus Ecgwinus ortum dominicum remouendo nociua et apponendo utilia, sicut Dominus dicit: 'Ecce', inquid, 'posui te ut dissipes et euellas et edifices et plantes. Dissipes et euellas uicia, edifices et plantes uirtutes.'[2] Dissipes arbores infructuosas, euellas herbas inutiles. Edifices arbores fructuosas, plantes herbas utiles. Sic et beatus Ecgwinus assumpsit arma dissipandi, securim uidelicet aspere increpationis, et posuit eam ad radicem arboris infructuose, et falcem acutam ut herbas nociuas eradicaret; ut 'pro saliunca ascenderet abies et pro urtica cresceret mirtus'.[3] Accepit etiam instrumenta edificandi, putatorium uidelicet uere instructionis et fossorium saluberrime admonitionis, et usus est potenter opere et sermone, secutus Iesum qui cepit facere et docere.

52.   LECTIO QVARTA

Sciuit namque beatus Ecgwinus quia 'qui fecerit et docuerit sic homines hic | magnus uocabitur in regno celorum',[4] et qui ' parce seminat parce et metet, et qui seminat in benedictione, de benedictionibus metet'[5] in uitam eternam. Set beati uiri 'semen aliud cecidit secus uiam et conculcatum est, et uolucres celi comederunt illud. Et aliud cecidit supra petram et natum aruit, quia non habebat humorem. Et aliud cecidit inter spinas, et simul exorte spine suffocauerunt illud.'[6] 'Expectauit tamen ut faceret uuas, fecit autem labruscas',[7] et terra mala 'spinas et tribulos'[8] protulit ei, et uinea sua, 'conuersa in amaritudinem',[9] odore suo malo a cella uinaria eum expulit. Videns igitur uir sanctus quia 'hoc genus demonii non nisi in

fo. 131ra

---

[1] *RSB* cap. 64. See A. De Vogüé, *Community and Abbot in the Rule of St Benedict*, trans. C. Philippi and E. R.Perkins, 2 vols. (Cistercian Studies Series, v: Kalamazoo, 1979–88), ii. 329, where 'magis prodesse quam preesse' is traced to St Augustine.

[2] Cf. Jer. 1: 10. This quotation, presumably selected by Thomas, was much used by Pope Innocent III in the letters of his first year; see *Reg. Inn. III*, i Indices, p. 17.

[3] Isa. 55: 13. The whin is a thorny shrub.

[4] Matt. 5: 19.

[5] 2 Cor. 9: 6.

50. When the blessed Ecgwine undertook the responsibility of his episcopal office, he recognized it not so much as an honour, as a burden, and desired rather to be of use than to be a person in authority.[1] Indeed he knew that he had been set in the Lord's garden rather as a labourer, that he might work in it and guard it.

51.   THIRD READING

The blessed Ecgwine, therefore, cultivated the Lord's garden by removing the weeds and planting good seed, as the Lord says in these words: 'See, I have set you there so that you may destroy and uproot, build and plant. You are to destroy and uproot vices, build and plant virtues.'[2] You must destroy unfruitful trees, and uproot useless plants. You must establish fruitful trees, and plant beneficial herbs. So it was that the blessed Ecgwine took up weapons for destruction, his axe of fierce rebuke, and he placed it at the root of a fruitless tree, and used his sharp sickle to uproot noxious plants, so that 'the fir tree should spring up in place of the whin and the myrtle grow instead of the briar'.[3] He also received the tools for building, the pruning-knife of sound instruction and the spade of wholesome admonition, and he made powerful use of deed and word, following Jesus who had begun his ministry with deeds and teaching.

52.   FOURTH READING

The blessed Ecgwine knew that 'the man who is a doer of deeds and a teacher of men will be called great in the kingdom of heaven',[4] and 'he who sows sparingly will also reap sparingly, whereas he who sows bountifully will also reap bountifully'[5] unto life eternal. But 'some seed of the holy man fell on the pathway and was trampled under foot, and the birds of the air ate it up. Some fell upon rocky ground and as it sprang up it withered because it had no moisture. Some fell among thistles, and the thistles grew up and choked it.'[6] 'However, he expected it to produce choice grapes, but it produced wild grapes',[7] and the poor ground brought forth 'thistles and thorns'[8] for him, and his vineyard 'changed into a place of bitterness',[9] and he was driven from his wine cellar because of its evil smell. The holy man, therefore, seeing that 'this kind of demon is cast out only by prayer

[6] Luke 8: 5–7.   [7] Isa. 5: 2.
[8] Cf. Heb. 6: 8.   [9] Cf. Amos 6: 13.

ieiunio et oratione eicitur',[1] de episcopatu conuersus est in exilium, de predicatione in peregrinationem.

53.   LECTIO QVINTA

Cum igitur de propriis meritis non presumeret, post beatam Dei genitricem summo opere beatos apostolos Petrum et Paulum quibus Dominus potestatem non solum corpora set etiam animas et mentes hominum 'ligandi et soluendi'[2] tradiderat, in auxilium inplorandos credidit, ut uelamen a cordibus plebis sue errantis amoueretur. Vt ergo facilius per eos a Domino exaudiretur, eorum limina petenda decreuit. Et ut corpus inter eundum attenuaret, uinculis ferreis pedes suos astrinxit que claue poterant firmari ac reserari, et clauem in fluuium Auene proiecit. O uere prelati erga subditos caritas ineffabilis, qui se ipsum uinculis ferreis astrinxit ut subditi a uinculis peccaminum soluerentur! O fides constantis hominis fidei Abrahe comparabilis,[3] qui per corporis sui mortificationem filios a morte anime credidit suscitandos! O beati uiri spes admirabilis, qui ut sciret an misericors Deus peccata plebis sibi commisse dimitteret in terris, humano auxilio se destituens, diuine pietati se commisit soluendum a uinculis!

54.   LECTIO SEXTA[4]

Arrepto itaque itinere tot regionum digito gentium est demonstra-
fo. 131ʳᵇ tus, aliis dicentibus quia bonus est, aliis non, set se|ductor et criminosus. Tandem tanta difficultate tantisque laboribus peruenit ad apostolicam urbem de uinculis apostolicis gloriantem. Denique ferro uinctis pedibus Romam ingreditur, et, quod maxime quesierat, in ecclesia beati Petri apostolorum principis ad orationem prosternitur. Quod dum uir sanctus uigilanti cura peragit, omnipotens Deus pro seruo suo uigilare non desistit. Interim famuli eius pro cibis emendis ad fluuium pergunt, quibus uenditores piscem offerunt. Quo empto et asportato et ex more condiendi exenterato, omnipotentis Dei magnificencia compedum clauiculam quibus uir

---

[1] Matt. 17: 20.
[2] Cf. Matt. 16: 19; another allusion favoured by Pope Innocent III.
[3] Cf. Gen. 15: 6, and Romans 4: 12.
[4] This reading has echoes of the fifth reading in Book I above.

and fasting',[1] left his bishopric for exile, and his preaching for pilgrimage.

53.   FIFTH READING

Since, therefore, he would not lay claim to any merits of his own, he believed that after the holy Son of God he should beseech the help of the apostles Peter and Paul, to whom the Lord gave the power 'of binding and releasing'[2] not only the bodies of men but also their souls, in order that the veil should be removed from the hearts of his erring people. So that he should more easily be heeded by the Lord through their intercession, he decided to make a journey to the threshold of the apostles. Also, so that his body should be weakened during the journey there, he bound his feet with iron chains which could be locked and unlocked with a key, and then threw this into the River Avon. What truly unspeakable love of a prelate towards his subjects, who bound himself with iron chains that his subjects should be released from the bonds of their sins! What faith, comparable to that of that man of faith Abraham,[3] for he believed that by the mortification of his own body his sons could be rescued from the death of the soul! What wonderful hope that holy man had, who, depriving himself of human help that he might know whether the merciful God would cancel on earth the sins of the people committed to his care, entrusted himself to the divine goodness to release him from his bonds!

54.   SIXTH READING[4]

So he set off on his journey. Many of the people in the regions he passed through pointed their finger at him, some saying that he was a good man, others that he was not, but a wicked deceiver. Eventually, after great difficulty and great hardship he arrived at the apostolic city glorying in his apostolic bonds. Then he entered Rome with iron chains binding his feet, and,—a thing he most wanted to do— prostrated himself in prayer in the church of St Peter, prince of the apostles. While that holy man continued watching and praying, almighty God did not cease to keep watch over his servant. In the mean time his servants went to the river to buy provisions, and the vendors offered them a fish. Having purchased it and brought it back, they gutted it in the usual way to season it: then, through a mighty act of almighty God, they discovered in the entrails of the fish the key to

sanctus pedes suos astrinxerat in uisceribus piscis inueniunt;
ferrumque, quod Anglicus fluuius absorbuerat, Romanus Tyberis
exalat. Pro antiquo igitur statere piscantis Petri coram multis
redditur clauicula famulo Dei qua se sciret soluendum gratia
ipsius celestis clauigeri. Intelligens igitur uir Dei peregrinationi
sue inesse fructum et optate exauditionis effectum, per omnia
uoluntati Dei se subiciens, coram cunctis clauem accepit et uincula
quibus astringebatur reserauit.

55.   LECTIO SEPTIMA

Quis iam non dixerit beatum Petrum ad artem suam ueterem,
uidelicet piscatoriam, reuersum, qui quasi in reti suo piscem ad
urbem per tot maria traxit ut fratrem suum a uinculis corporis
absolueret? Ne itaque alicui hec quia inusitata iam impossibilia
uideantur, conferantur ista hiis que propter ipsum Deus post beati
uiri depositionem mirabiliter operari dignatus est; et si uidebuntur
mirabilia, desinent tamen uideri impossibilia, quia ea que euentus
assiduitate didicimus quasi quodam usu sepe in habitum mentis
uertimus.[1] Sancita igitur a patribus dies annua qua beatus Ecgwinus
adiit celestia regna,[2] quot annis post depositionem eius illuxerat
festiua, sepe superius miraculis illustrata. Que inter natalicia
Domini solempnia duplicata populi et familie sue refulget letitia,
quasi corona aurea sole repercussa. Accurrit solito populosa frequen-
tia ad celebria tanti patris | gaudia. Nox ipsa luciflua et dies preclara
cantu et laude continuatur excelsa cum iocunditate festiua. Nec
desunt solita Christi beneficia seruitoribus uel hospitibus suis
parata, nec desunt post missarum solempnia competentia refectionum
insignia. Sed modo piscium deerat copia, ut mirabilior appareret Dei
gratia.

fo. 131va

---

[1] This may be a quotation, but we have not been able to identify it.
[2] i.e. 30 Dec., the day of his death, and therefore of his spiritual birth.

the fetters with which the holy man had secured his feet. The iron key, which the English river had swallowed, the Roman Tiber disgorged. Instead, therefore, of that ancient coin of Peter when he was fishing, in the presence of many people, the key was returned to God's servant, and he knew that he was to be freed with it by the grace of the One in heaven who provided it. Hence, the man of God, realizing that here was the reward for the journey he had undertaken and the means of obtaining the audience he desired, submitted himself in everything to the will of God, received the key in the presence of them all, and released the bonds with which he was bound.

55.   SEVENTH READING

Who could now deny that the blessed Peter had returned to his ancient occupation of fishing, dragging the fish, as if in his own net, through so many seas to Rome in order to free his brother from his bodily chains? But lest these remarkable events should now seem impossible to anyone, let them be compared to those marvellous miracles which God deigned to perform on Ecgwine's account after the funeral of that holy man; and if they should seem marvellous, they will nevertheless cease to seem impossible, for the things we have learned from the repetition of an event we turn into a habit of mind, as it were, by the frequent observance of it.[1] Therefore, an anniversary was established by our fathers on the day when the blessed Ecgwine entered the heavenly realms,[2] for every year after the day of his funeral a feast-day had illumined the story, the day often being made more illustrious by miracles. This is repeated during the solemn feast of our Lord's birthday and the joy of the people and of Ecgwine's community shines brightly like a golden crown when struck by the sun's rays. Great throngs of people pour in to the accustomed place for the joyous celebrations of our great father. Night itself is bright and the day made splendid with singing and praise as the festival continues with its lofty expressions of joy. There is no lack of the accustomed benefits of Christ prepared for his servants and his guests, and after the celebration of mass, no lack in the provision of excellent refreshments. All they lacked was the abundance of fish, so that the grace of God might appear all the more wonderful.

56.   LECTIO OCTAVA[a]

Cum ergo super hoc ipso mane pastoris officiositas fratres deuota
alloqueretur caritate, superuenit quidam qui dixit se mire magnitudinis piscem conspexisse in ipso quod subterfluit monasterio flumine.
Continuo illuc concurritur; spiculis, iaculis, et cunctis armamentis
preda obruitur, capitur, extrahitur, atque coram pedibus ministrorum
domini exponitur, qui piscis a scolasticis foca nominatur.[1] Extollit
populus uisum miraculum, et clamosa laude cunctorum glorificatur in
sancto suo Ecgwino largitor omnium bonorum. Numquam enim
antea uisus est huius generis piscis in hoc flumine, set neque in
tota patria inuentus est tante magnitudinis in hoc genere, qui
distributus largiflue et domesticis et aduenis suffecit gratifice.
Nonne pium est credere ob meritum sancti Ecgwini beatum
Petrum, quasi arte sua piscatoria, eadem potestate qua prius a flumine
Anglico piscem ad refectionem conserui sui beati, uidelicet Ecgwini,
Romam traduxerat, nunc eadem uirtute piscem hunc a mari magno ad
idem flumen Anglicum, contra solitum cursum huiusmodi generis
piscium, ad sustentationem seruorum et ueneratorum eiusdem
coepiscopi sui transmisisse?

57.   LECTIO NONA[b]

Adhuc aliud miraculum post depositionem beati Ecgwini per eius
merita a Domino patratum, ad superioris quod Dominus pro eo dum
in hac uita esset operari dignatus est confirmationem, in medium
deducamus. Quodam itaque alio tempore uir quidam scelerosus,
quasi alter ille latro qui a dextris crucis Dominice in cruce dependebat
et scelera sua Domino confitebatur,[2] pro suis reatibus Deo sponta-
fo. 131[vb] neam ultionem exhiben|do, nouem uinculis ferreis se astrinxit in
diuersis corporis sui membris. Qui, non Dominum temptans[3] set
diuine uoluntati per omnia se subiciens, apud semetipsum decreuit se
numquam ab hiis uinculis absolui nisi Dominus illum a uinculis
peccatorum ostenderet absolutum. Digna igitur pro factis se subire

---

   [a] *This miracle is in Byrhtferth, Vita S. Ecgwini, iv. 9, and DE i. 21*   [b] *This miracle,*
which is described in readings 9 to 11, is in Byrhtferth, Vita S. Ecgwini iv. 7–8, and also in DE
i. 18

---

   [1] This suggests that Byrhtferth had a bestiary to hand. It was, perhaps, an Atlantic grey
seal.
   [2] Cf. Luke 23: 33, 39–43, for the robber crucified with Jesus confessing his sins.
   [3] Cf. Matt. 4: 7.

56.   EIGHTH READING

The next morning, when the abbot was carrying out his duty of
addressing the brethren with godly love about this very matter, one
of the monks intervened, saying that he had seen a fish of amazing
size in the very river which flowed below the monastery. The monks
immediately ran there, and attacked their prey with darts, spears,
and all kinds of weapons; it was caught, dragged out of the river, and
laid before the feet of their lord's servants: this fish is called by
scholars a seal.[1] The people applauded the miracle they had seen and
with the loud praise of them all the Bestower of all good things is
glorified in their own blessed Ecgwine. For never before had a fish of
this kind been seen in this river; indeed, there was not found in the
whole country a fish of this kind, which was of such a size. It was
divided up generously, and pleasantly satisfied the monks of the
house and its visitors. Is it not right to believe that, because of the
merits of St Ecgwine, the blessed Peter, with the same power with
which he had previously brought the fish from the English river to
Rome to refresh his fellow-servant, the blessed Ecgwine, had now,
with his skill as a fisherman, as it were, sent this fish from the ocean
across waters not usually frequented by fish of this sort, to that same
English river, for the sustenance of the servants and venerators of his
fellow bishop?

57.   NINTH READING

But we must now bring to light yet another miracle that occurred
after the funeral of the blessed Ecgwine, wrought through his merits
by our Lord, as a confirmation of the miracle mentioned above, which
our Lord had deigned to perform while Ecgwine was alive. It was on a
certain other occasion that an evil man—a man comparable to that
other robber who hung on a cross on the right hand of our Lord's,
and confessed his sins to the Lord[2]—dispensed his own voluntary
punishment for his guilty deeds, by binding himself with nine iron
chains in different parts of his body. He was not putting the Lord to
the test[3] but, submitting himself in all things to the divine will, had
decided in his own mind that he would never be freed from these
chains unless the Lord showed that he had been absolved from the
bonds of his sins. Admitting that he was suffering a punishment
worthy of the evils he had done, he had put no trust in his own

confessus, non de suis meritis confisus, set laboribus desudans, ieiuniis et orationibus insistens, meritis et precibus sanctorum se commendans, ferri hoc pressus pondere per diuersorum limina sanctorum pergens, ut a uinculis tam corporis quam anime absolueretur deuotissime postulabat. Cuius fidem et spem, necnon cordis contritionem, laborem et operis satisfactionem, Dominus ex alto prospiciens, iam per diuersorum sanctorum merita, quos idem penitens in circumiacentibus et longe positis regionibus per multa temporum curricula adierat, octo circulos ferreos quibus fuerat astrictus dissoluerat.

58.   LECTIO DECIMA

Nono uero circulo durius astringebatur, carne uidelicet circumquaque intumescente, super quo dissoluendo principalem potestatem habentes tam corpora quam animas ligandi et soluendi, beatos uidelicet apostolos Petrum et Paulum, credidit adeundos. Quorum limina cum adiisset et eorum suffragia postulasset deuotissime, tale in sompnis recepit responsum: 'Vade in Angliam, et beati presulis Ecgwini locum debito uenerationis cultu require, et misericordiam optinebis.'

59. Surgens itaque a sompnis beatus penitens gaudet se pro parte accepisse quod quesierat. Exaudierant enim eum apostoli ut consilium darent, non ut ⟨in⟩ presens plene liberarent. Accepta itaque spe certissima eorum sibi non abfuturum auxilium quorum receperat consilium, quem cogebat necessitas dilationem tam grauem patientissime sustinuit, quia non aliter potuit optinere quod expetiit; et cum tali ualefactione itinere arrepto, edem sancti Ecgwini adiit, in cuius basilica cum per multos dies ieiuniis et orationibus expetitam et fo. 132ra expectatam misericordie opem | prestolaretur, quadam die, hora tercia a fratribus monasterii deuotissime decantata, et missa, ut moris est, celeberime subsecuta, hora perceptionis diuini misterii uere penitenti diuinum non defuit ministerium.

60.   LECTIO VNDECIMA

Nam uirtute diuina tante ui nonus[a] ille circulus dirumpitur ut ipse fragor in choro a fratribus audiretur, ac si ferrum malleo percuteretur.

---

    [a] nouus R

merits, but laboured under these hard toils, devoting himself to prayer and fasting, and entrusted himself to the merits and prayers of the saints. Oppressed by the weight of the iron chains, he made his way through the thresholds of various saints, and implored them most devoutly to free him from the bonds not only of his body but also of his soul. The Lord, seeing from on high his faith and hope, as well as the contrition of his heart, his labour, and the penance of his action, now through the merits of the various saints, whom the man in his repentance had approached over a long period of time in districts near and far away, had freed him of eight of the iron chains with which he had been bound.

58.   TENTH READING

The penitent was bound more harshly by the ninth shackle, and the surrounding flesh was swollen. He believed that to be released from this he needed to approach the apostles Peter and Paul, who possessed above all others the power of binding and freeing both body and soul. When he approached their threshold and besought them most devoutly for their aid, he received this reply in his sleep: 'Go to England, and, observing due reverence, seek out the place of the holy bishop Ecgwine, and you will obtain mercy.'

59. Rising from sleep, therefore, the blessed penitent rejoiced that he had in part received the help he had requested. For the apostles had given heed to him in that they were giving him advice, but were not freeing him entirely for the present. Accepting with confident hope that the apostles whose advice he had received would not deny aid to him, he endured with great patience the grievous delay which necessity forced upon him, for he could not otherwise obtain what he desired. So it was with this farewell that he set off on his journey. He came to the shrine of St Ecgwine, and when he had spent many days in Ecgwine's church in prayer and fasting, awaiting the act of mercy that he had requested and hoped for, one day at nine o'clock in the morning, when the brethren of the monastery were singing and mass was being celebrated with great devotion, as was their custom, at the moment the holy sacrament was received, divine aid was truly at hand for the penitent.

60.   ELEVENTH READING

That ninth shackle was severed by divine power with such force that the noise it made was heard in the choir by the brethren, as though

Et ipso inpetu fractionis a loco ubi secus altare penitens orabat ferrum illud in chorum deiciebatur ac si manu hominis iactaretur, ut diuine miserationis opitulatio omnibus manifestaretur. Euentus igitur ordine facti serie et rei ueritate a fratribus monasterii diligentius inquisitis, pulsantur classica, et clara uoce cum gratiarum actione attolluntur Dei magnalia. O quam ueridica Domini sententia, qua secutos se hiis que ipsi eum fecisse uiderant similia, immo maiora, facturos promiserat. Ecce enim omnibus pie credentibus patet luce quidem clarius, quod Dominus beato Ecgwino, quem mirabiliter soluerat a uinculis, potestatem contulerit mirabilius soluendi alios a nexibus tam anime quam corporis. Ad illum namque quem ab Anglia Romam traduxit a uinculis ferreis ab apostolis soluendum, de eadem urbe in Angliam per eosdem apostolos misit istum penitentem a circulo ferreo ab eodem liberandum. Celebramus^a igitur, fratres dilectissimi, deuotissime tanti patris translationem, quem Dominus omnipotens tot, tantis, et tam mirandis uirtutibus glorificat in terris et nobis manifestat glorificatum in celis.

61.   LECTIO DVODECIMA[1]

Gaudeat precipue ecclesia Eoueshamensis et cum summa deuotione et spirituali gaudio letetur, que tot eius beneficiis honoratur, tot possessionibus ab eo sibi adquisitus ditatur, tot libertatibus exaltatur, et priuilegiis per eum et propter eum sibi collatis munitur. Maxime autem corde et ore simul Christum ueneretur, quod propter uite eius honestatem et fidei meritum beata uirgo Maria in eodem loco per manifestam ostensionem et corporalem presentiam se manifestauit fo. 132rb eidem; et quia ibi steterunt | beate uirginis sacratissimi pedes, idem locus sanctificatur et a summo pontifice Constantino locus sanctus nominatur. Extollant uocem in beatissimi uiri laudem specialius monachi Eueshamensis cenobii, qui per ipsum a summo pontifice ouile diuinitus preostensum, apostolica auctoritate fultum, regia

---

^{a} *Perhaps* celebremus *intended*

[1] Twelve lections implies monastic use; see J. Harper, *The Forms and Orders of Western Liturgy from the Tenth to the Eighteenth Century* (Oxford, 1991), pp. 91–5.

iron was being struck with a hammer. And then, at the impact of the blow that severed it, the iron shackle was hurled from the spot near the altar, where the penitent was praying, into the choir, as if it had been thrown by a man's hand, so that the aid provided by divine mercy should be made manifest to everyone. When the reason for what had occurred and the truth of the matter had been carefully examined in detail by the brethren of the monastery, the bells were rung and the miracles of God were extolled in loud cries accompanied by thanksgiving. How true is the Lord's judgment by which he has promised those who followed him that they would perform miracles similar to those which they had seen him do, in fact even greater miracles! For see, to all who believe devoutly in him he makes it clearer than daylight that the Lord bestowed upon the blessed Ecgwine, whom He had miraculously freed from his bonds, the more wonderful power of releasing others from the bonds of both the body and the soul. For it was to Ecgwine, whom He had brought from England to Rome to be freed from his chains by the apostles, that he sent that penitent from Rome to England through those same apostles to be set free from that iron shackle by Ecgwine. Let us therefore celebrate, my beloved brethren, most devoutly the translation of so great a father, whom the almighty Lord glorifies by so many great and marvellous acts of goodness on earth and reveals him to us glorified in the heavens.

61.   TWELFTH READING[1]

Let the church of Evesham especially rejoice and express its gladness with great devotion and spiritual joy, for it is honoured by so many benefits of Ecgwine, enriched by so many possessions acquired for it by him, exalted by so many liberties, and protected by the privileges bestowed upon it by and through him. It should also venerate Christ greatly with heart and voice because, through the virtue of Ecgwine's life and the excellence of his faith, the blessed Virgin Mary manifested herself in Evesham to Ecgwine in a clear revelation and bodily appearance. Because those most holy feet of the blessed Virgin had stood there, that place is sanctified, and called a holy place by Pope Constantine. Let the monks of Evesham monastery more specially raise their voices in praise of that most blessed man, for it was through Ecgwine that they are called a monastery by the pope, divinely foreshown, supported by apostolic authority, endowed with

libertate donatum, cleri et populi benedictione sanctitum, appellantur, sicut priuilegia eiusdem cenobii testantur; ad gloriam et laudem Domini nostri Iesu Christi, 'cui est honor et imperium'[1] cum patre et spiritu sancto per omnia secula seculorum. Amen.

62. *Qualiter sit constitutum festiuitatem translationis sancti Ecgwini hoc tempore solempniter esse celebrandam* [a]

Magnifico rege Canuto de hac uita decedente,[2] optimates Anglie ut iurauerant et fidem sibi dederant fieri statuere; accitisque quibusdam baronibus[3] iusserunt ut pro filio regis Eardecanuto quantotius irent, eumque ad Angliam deducerent.[4] Qui, precepto obtemperantes, maturant propter quod missi erant explere. Aderat tunc inter eos quidam episcopus nomine Aeilwardus, qui sub eisdem temporibus binas ecclesias regebat, scilicet episcopatum Lundonie ciuitatis et abbaciam sancti Ecgwini.[5] Is dum in medio mari cum ceteris legatis nauigaret, repente aduenit turbidus auster, nec defuit frigidissimus boreas, eurus etiam zephirusque uidebantur adesse. Ita nempe huc illucque uagabunda nauis flatibus ferebatur, ut putares omnes uentos inter se uicissim inisse certamen. Nunc naui[b] uersus etherea fluctibus sublata, nunc ad ima eisdem deiecta, omnem spem salutis perdiderant.[c] Exoritur nauticus clamor, stridor rudentum, undique letalis dolor accumulatur. Tandem tempestate deuicti et pene in ultimam desperationem deducti, post pacem in commune perlatam, Deo omnipotenti se suasque animas lacrimose commendauere. Cum ecce uenerabilis pontifex Æilwardus, recordatus merita sancti Deoque dilecti patris Ecgwini, geminas ad sidera palmas extendens, | talia refert: 'O dilecte pater, Ecgwine, tui serui nunc miserere, nosque pariter a presenti periculo mortis eripe.' Vouit etiam huiusmodi uotum: 'Si Deus omnipotens per tua dulcissima merita dignatus fuerit seruos suos inpresentiarum liberare, scrinium tibi "ex auro et argento"[6] faciam preparare,[d] et sanctam solennitatem tuam amplius quam antea fuerat iubebo cum honore frequentari.' Vix uerbum compleuerat, cum mox, non paulatim uerum gregatim, precipiente

fo. 132va

---

[a] *This section is taken from Dominic's Book II* (*DE* ii. 2)   [b] nauis R   [c] perdiderat *DE*   [d] prepari *DE* (*D*)

[1] 1 Tim. 6: 16.
[2] Cnut, king of England from 1016 to 1035, and king of Denmark from 1019 to 1035, died at Shaftesbury in 1035 and was buried at the Old Minster, Winchester; *HBC*, p. 28.
[3] The use of the term barons is, of course, anachronistic in an Anglo-Saxon context.
[4] Harthacnut arrived in England in June 1040; *HBC*, p. 28.

royal liberty, and affirmed by the benediction of the clergy and people, as the privileges of that monastery testify; to the glory and praise of our Lord Jesus Christ, 'who possesses honour and power'[1] with the Father and the Holy Spirit for ever and ever. Amen.

62. *How it was decided that the festival of the Translation of St Ecgwine should be solemnly celebrated at that time*

After the great king Cnut departed this life,[2] the nobles of England decided that the action they had sworn and promised to undertake should be carried out. They therefore summoned certain barons[3] and commanded them to go as soon as possible to the king's son, Harthacnut, and bring him to England.[4] Obeying this command, they made haste to fulfil the mission upon which they had been sent. Among them was a bishop named Ælfweard who had jurisdiction over two churches at that time, the see of the city of London and the abbey of St Ecgwine.[5] While he was sailing with the other envoys in mid-ocean, a fierce wind from the south suddenly assailed them, but it also seemed that a very cold north wind, as well as east and west winds were blowing. So the ship was blown by these blasts this way and that off its course, so that it might have been thought that all the winds were vying with one another in their assault upon it. One moment the ship was lifted high in the sky by the waves, the next moment hurled to the depths by them, so that the men lost all hope of safety. There was a loud cry from the sailors, a creaking of the rigging, and everywhere a distressing fear of death was building up. At last, overwhelmed by the storm and brought almost to utter despair, they achieved some peace of heart amongst them and tearfully commended themselves and their souls to almighty God. But see, the venerable bishop Ælfweard, recalling the merits of St Ecgwine, the father beloved of God, raised both hands to the heavens, and uttered these words: 'O beloved father Ecgwine, have pity now on your servant, and rescue all of us from the present danger of death.' He also made a vow in such words as these: 'If almighty God deigns through your sweetest merits to rescue his servants from our present plight, I will have a shrine made ready for you "made of gold and silver",[6] and will command that your holy eminence be visited with honour more regularly than before.' Scarcely had he finished speaking, when immediately at the Lord's command, everything

---

[5] Ælfweard was bishop of London from 1035 to 1044; *HBC*, p. 220.
[6] Exod. 31: 4.

Domino, tranquillitas redire, solaris radius illucescere, simul omnia in prosperum cedere; naute uero cum gaudio cursum extendere, ac cum summa uelocitate terram petere. Et statim ad Flandrense litus appulsi, nimium 'optata potiuntur arena'.[1]

63. Inde ad Heardecanutum peruenientes, qui ea tempestate cum matre sua apud comitem Flandrie hospitabatur,[2] communem assensum populi sibi per omnia pandunt. Sicque ut futurum regem Anglie illum cum ueneratione assumentes, cum ingenti letitia in Angliam repedarunt, eumque regem, ut mos est, constituerunt. Prelibatus ergo episcopus Aeilwardus, non immemor sponsionis sue, statim ut ad propria uenit opus quod uouerat accelerari iussit. Perfectoque scrinio cum auro et argento adornato in quo nunc ossa patris nostri sancti Odulfi[3] honorifice recondita seruantur, indixit omni populo, cum pontificali auctoritate, ut cum summa frequentia undique conuenirent ad celebrandam solennem translationem reliquiarum sanctissimi patris nostri Ecgwini, .iiii. idus Septembris.[4] Seruabantur namque reliquie eiusdem patris hisdem temporibus in quodam scrinio quondam precioso fuluoque metallo bene adornato, set iam pridem a Dacis circumcirca expoliato. Veniente igitur die sancito, suffragia sancti cuncti efflagitare, omnes pari uoto quoquo modo poterant seruitio tanti patris insudare, festinabant. Denique statuto tempore adueniente quo reliquie in scrinium sibi paratum transferrentur, conueniunt cum pontifice alii uenerandi sacerdotes, parantur cruces
fo. 132vb et | cerei, multaque honestas omnimodis condecorata cumulatur. Ordinata itaque processione maxima cum reuerentia, in hymnis dulcisonis Deum predicantes, uoces attollunt in excelsis letantes. At postquam ad locum reliquiarum uentum est, libantes incensum cum turribulo, multo metu ac modestia cum maxima dignitate transferunt reliquias sancti patris et protectoris nostri Ecgwini in scrinium sibi officiosissime preparatum.

---

[1] Virgil, *Aen.* i.172.

[2] Harthacnut's mother, Emma, the second wife of Cnut and the widow of King Æthelred the Unready, was a daughter of Count Richard I of Normandy; see *HBC*, pp. 27, 28, 29. The visit of Harthacnut and Emma to the count of Flanders probably took place in 1035. The count of Flanders at the time, if the date of the trip is correct, was Baldwin IV, who died on 30 May 1036; see A. Capelli, *Cronologia, Cronografia e Calendario Perpetuo*, 6th edn. (Milan, 1988), p. 473.

[3] Odulf (d. 855), monk and missionary in Frisia, whose relics were stolen by Vikings and brought to England to London. There they were purchased by Bishop Ælfweard, who gave them to his abbey of Evesham; see above, **62**, and below, **146**; and D. Farmer, *Oxford Dictionary of Saints*, 4th edn. (Oxford, 1997), pp. 373–4.

[4] The feast of the translation of St Ecgwine on 10 Sept. is recorded in a calendar,

happened, not gradually, but suddenly at the same time, for calm returned, the rays of the sun shone brightly, and everything was suddenly all right again. The sailors with true joy set course, and made for land with all speed. Immediately on landing on the coast of Flanders, 'they take possession of the beach they had longed for so greatly.'[1]

63. They then came to Harthacnut, who at that time was being entertained with his mother by the count of Flanders,[2] and informed him of their people's general acceptance of his rule over them in all matters. Thus taking him with reverence as the future king of England, they returned to England with great joy, and made him their king in their customary way. Therefore, bishop Ælfweard, not forgetful of his promise, immediately on his arrival home gave orders for the work which he had vowed to be completed as soon as possible. The shrine, in which the bones of our father, St Odulf,[3] are now preserved and honourably buried, was completed and adorned with gold and silver, and with his episcopal authority the bishop enjoined upon all the people that as many as possible should meet there from all districts to celebrate the solemn translation of the sacred relics of our most holy father Ecgwine on 10 September.[4] The relics of father Ecgwine were at that time being preserved in a shrine once beautifully adorned with precious stones and yellow metal, but which had some time before been plundered by the Danes who lived round about. When the appointed day arrived, the whole congregation hastened to implore the saint's help, and all of them to toil with like zeal in whatever way they could in the service of so great a father. Finally when the appointed time came for the relics to be translated to the shrine prepared for them, other reverend priests met with the bishop, the crosses and candles were prepared, and great honour, graced by every means possible, was added to the occasion. And so, in ordered procession, with the greatest reverence, and in the sweet harmony of their hymn-singing, they praised God, and, rejoicing, raised their voices to the heavens. After they had arrived at the place of the relics, they dispersed the incense with the censer, and with great fear and humility, with the greatest of dignity, they translated the relics of our holy father and protector Ecgwine to the shrine most dutifully prepared for them.

probably from Evesham, of the latter half of the 11th cent., no. 16 in *English Kalendars before AD 1100*, ed. F. Wormald (Henry Bradshaw Society lxxii: London, 1934), p. 206. It also records the Deposition on 30 Dec. (p. 209).

64. Hec fuit causa qua primum translatio sancti Ecgwini constituta est. Tunc namque a prefato pontifice est statutum, ut cum frequentia populari, uti hactenus fit, altissime eadem translatio quot annis celebraretur.

64. This was the reason why the feast of the Translation of St Ecgwine was first established. For it was at that time that it was decreed by the afore-mentioned bishop that the feast of the Translation should be celebrated every year in the most exalted manner and be attended by a large congregation, as it has been up to this time.

⟨LIBER II⟩

65. *Incipit prologus libri secundi de miraculis sancti Ecgwini que Deus per illum operatus est postquam ab hac mutabili luce decessit, editus a Dominico priore Eweshamie*[1]

Cum diuina*ᵃ* omnipotentis Dei miracula per sanctos uiros mirabiliter ostensa uarios et multiplices fructus ea pie considerantibus proferant, non incommodum duximus pauca breuiter prelibare, quatinus mens tam dulci memorie intenta, uirtutem huiusmodi considerationis ualeat secundum rationem perpendere. Magnum namque fructum legentibus et audientibus, si digne id egerint, perspicue manifestant, quoniam et placidior a mundanorum fantasmate memoria custoditur, et sepenumero tantorum patronorum exemplis celeste regnum non negatur. Inde enim exit quamplurima dulcedo laude diuinitatis, arduus etiam amor, sanctorum gloria, fauor preteritorum, emendatio presentium, spes futurorum bonorum.

66. Vnde, quia multa que Deus per beatum patrem nostrum sanctum Ecgwinum dignatus est operari, negligentia et incuria scriptorum scimus obliuioni tradita esse, proinde congruum uidetur memorie litterarum tradere ea que a fidelibus et credulitate dignis uiris potuimus secundum rei ueritatem indagare. Id enim ut ageremus, fo. 133ᵃ multarum instantia precum | et obedientia precipientium fratrum et maxime amore sancti compulsi sumus. Preclare igitur uirtuti obedientie animum summittentes, illa precipue studuimus depromere que ab ipsis a quibus sunt uisa percepimus, prout gesta constant in ipsa ueritate. Nullo modo quippe decet preterire singula, licet non possimus tanti uiri explicare uniuersa. Sit ergo, sancto spiritu opitulante, principium narrandi quod cognouimus sanctum Dei Ecgwinum in antiquo tempore fecisse per uirtutem Dei.

ᵃ cuncta *DE*

---

[1] R now returns to DE which it reproduces more or less verbatim. However, some changes were made in the order of Book II by incorporating two chapters (19 and 20) of DE i. Thomas moved DE i. 20 in to follow the prologue, which is entirely Dominic's. He then reverted to DE ii.1, and followed it by DE i. 19. (He had already moved DE ii. 2 up into Book I to follow reading 12.) From DE i. 19 onwards, the sections 3 to 25 all follow Dominic. Because the textual changes were minuscule, M. Lapidge in *AB* did not reproduce a full text of Dominic's Book II. He did, however, complete the edition in typescript and has very kindly lent this to the present editors. References henceforth to DE ii are to this source.

[BOOK II]

65. *Here begins the prologue of the second book of the miracles of St Ecgwine, which God performed through him after he departed this changeable world, related by Dominic, prior of Evesham* [1]

Since the divine miracles of almighty God, wonderfully revealed through holy men, produce for those who contemplate them devoutly many different kinds of benefit, we have thought it well worthwhile to mention a few of them briefly, so that the mind that is intent upon remembering such joyous events may be able to consider with reason the virtue of such contemplation. Those who read or hear of these things clearly reveal that they have derived great benefit from doing so, if they have done this with good intent, for the mind is more at peace and protected from the superficiality of earthly events, and the heavenly realm is time and again confirmed by the miracles of such patrons. Indeed, how much sweet pleasure from the praise of God comes from the praise of heavenly things, even a deep love, glory of the saints, the support of past events, correction of present behaviour, and hope of future blessings.

66. Hence, because we know that many of the miracles which God deigned to perform through our blessed father, St Ecgwine, have been assigned to oblivion because of the negligence and carelessness of writers, it seems fitting for us to hand down a written account of those miracles of which we have been able to gain a truthful account from trustworthy men whose word can be believed. We have been impelled to do this by the urgent prayers of many, by complying with many brethren who have urged us to do this, and especially by our love for St Ecgwine. Therefore, submitting our mind entirely to the great virtue of obedience, we gave thought especially to declaring those miracles which we ascertained from those who had actually seen them, insofar as there was agreement that they had in very truth occurred. It is not right that we should in any way neglect recording individual miracles, though we cannot give a full account of all the miracles of so great a man. Let us, therefore, with the help of the Holy Spirit, make a beginning by narrating what we have learned that this saint of God did in ancient times by the power of God.

67. *Incipit liber secundus de miraculis sancti Ecgwini que Deus per illum operatus est postquam ab hac mutabili uita decessit* [1]

Qualiter feretrum sancti Ecgwini sub ruina ecclesie illesum sit conseruatum [a]

Regnum Anglie pater sancti Eadwardi regis et martiris rex Eadgarus obtinuit, rex iure uocandus.[2] Rex enim Eadgarus Deo erat humilis ac deuotus, Christianis sanctionibus obtemperans existebat et subditus. In armis strenuus et fortis, hostibus erat ferox et immanis, equitatis iustissimus executor, set cum moderamine pietatis, suis erat, salua imperii maiestate, mansuetus et mitis. Felix ea tempestate Anglia, felix, inquam, ea tempestate Anglia. Ecclesiarum status integerrime uigebat ubique; sacri ordines diuinis mancipati solummodo misteriis, uacabant scripturis et aliis actionibus ecclesiasticis. Ipse laicalis ordo libens ac promptus debite institutum religionis exequebatur. Opima tellus ad uotum respondebat omnibus in rebus.

68. Preerat tunc cenobio Eouesham abbas Oswardus, quantum ad humanam attinet estimationem uir approbandis moribus.[3] Sub cuius regimine, occulta animaduersione diuina, ecclesia ipsa ruit quam beatus Ecgwinus exstruxerat. Ruit ergo, ac secum uniuersa subruit, subruens confregit, confringendo comminuit. Magnus igitur exinde apud omnes timor, meror ac dolor, set pro reliquiis beati uiri supremus ac pene solus apud omnes timor, meror ac dolor. Vere |-

fo. 133rb bantur quippe quod beati uiri reliquie sub strage tanta omnino essent comminute, minutatimque in puluerem coacte iam nulla possent discerni certitudinis assertione. Verum ubi mundantes locum ad id uentum est, tam disposite inter saxa circumiacentia locatum adeoque sanum et incolume uas illud repertum est, quod fractura in eo nulla, nulla prorsus ulla in parte in eo uideretur lesura. Quibuscumque enim sue animaduersionis Deus intentaret uindictam, circa hunc beatum

---

[a] *DE i. 20 and Byrhtferth iv. 11*

[1] There are some similarities between the miracles of St Ecgwine recounted here between 67 and 72 (as to what happened to those who falsely claimed the saint's lands) and the miracles of St Kenelm of neighbouring Winchcombe, as R. Love points out, *Three Anglo-Saxon Saints' Lives*, p. 75 n. 3. A. Thacker also comments on Ecgwine's cult in general and on the saint's protection of his territorial rights, 'Saint-making and relic collecting by Oswald and his communities', in *St Oswald of Worcester*, ed. N. Brooks and C. Cubitt (London, 1966), 244–68, at pp. 260–2.

[2] Edgar acceded in. 957 as king of the Mercians, and in October 959 as king of England. He died in 975; *HBC*, p. 27.

67. *Here begins the Second Book of the miracles of St Ecgwine which God deigned to perform through him after he departed this changeable life*[1]

The shrine of St Ecgwine is preserved unharmed under the ruins of the church

King Edgar, the father of St Edward king and martyr, occupied the realm of England and is justly called a king.[2] For King Edgar was a humble and devout servant of God, obedient and submissive to the law of Christ. He was vigorous and strong in warfare, fierce and formidable to his enemies, a most just judge of equity and, guided by his religion, was gentle and merciful to his subjects, saving the imperial majesty. England was fortunate at that time, I say again, fortunate at that time. The state of the churches was flourishing and intact everywhere; the clergy were committed solely to the divine mysteries, and spent all their time in reading the scriptures and in other activities of the church. The laity carried out freely and promptly the due requirements of religion. A prosperous land was returning to its pledges in all matters.

68. Abbot Osweard ruled the monastery of Evesham at that time,[3] a man of praiseworthy character so far as human estimation goes. But during his rule, by a secret judgment of God the church, which the blessed Ecgwine had built, collapsed. It fell and demolished everything with it, and in its demolishing, it shattered the church, and in its shattering, reduced it to dust. Everybody then experienced great fear, sorrow, and grief; but the fear, sorrow, and grief were felt most of all by everybody, almost solely in fact, for the fate of the relics of the blessed Ecgwine. For they feared that these relics of this holy man had been utterly reduced to dust beneath such destruction, and since they had been crushed into tiny pieces of dust, no one would now be able say with any certainty which were the relics. However, when it came to the business of clearing the place, that vessel was found so well placed among the rocks that were lying all around, and so safe and sound, that there seemed to be no fracture in it, and absolutely no harm done to any part of it. Hence, whatever men God intended to suffer the penalty of His vengeance, so far as this blessed man was

---

[3] Thacker, 'Saint-making', p. 261, suggests that Abbot Osweard revived Ecgwine's cult in the early 970s, though by the end of the century it was largely forgotten.

uirum gratie et acceptationis sue magnam ostendebat ubique euidentiam, ipse super omnia Deus benedictus in secula. Amen.

69. *Item de quodam rustico qui dum reliquias sancti Ecgwini de terra
tollere debuit, propriam barbam auulsit*[a]

Rege Ætelredo,[b] Eadgari magni regis filio, fecundissimum Anglie
regnum deuote gubernante,[1] uiro plurimo uirtutum flore redimito,
fuit quidam auaritie pesti supra modum deditus, ac per hoc salutis sue
nimium incuriosus, qui ad hoc, inimico humani generis instigante,
prorupit, ut de terra sancti Ecgwini magnam partem laboraret
inuadere, quatinus inuasam iuxta sui iuris libitum ualeret possidere.
Contradicitur a multis sanctum locum tueri cupientibus, et precipue
ab eiusdem loci abbate nomine Oswardo. Controuersia multiplicatur,
et uariis obiectionibus causa diatim aggrauatur, donec, iudicum
sententia, in commune decernitur dies ad hanc causam finiendam.
Igitur die constituta fiunt preces studiosius, Deus et eius sancti
deposcuntur attentius. Peracta supplicatione et missis ex more
celebratis, ad locum designatum cum reliquiis sancti Ecgwini pro-
peratur; ab omnibus in adiutorium sanctus Domini uocatur.[c] Adest et
rusticus cum suis barbarice frendens, confertur in medio procerum
questio,[d] uerum finis nullus poterat adesse huic[e] negotio. Tandem lite
terminata, a iudicibus statuitur ut manu propria rusticus reliquias
fo. 133[va]   sancti Ecgwini de terra quam calumniabatur | tollens, sibimet
eandem[f] terram iurando adquireret. Erat uero isdem rusticus uir
grandeuus, barba ualde prolixa barbatus. Assurgens itaque, ueste
deposita in medio, barbam propriam concludit palmo: 'Per istam',
inquit, 'barbam sanctum auferam, quia mea est terra, et ego eam
possidebo iure hereditario.' O mira Dei uirtus! Vix emissum euo-
lauerat[g] uerbum, et ecce totam barbam coram cunctis lapsam ita
proiecit ad terram ac si apposita esset, non naturaliter nata. Obstu-
puere omnes; uident annosum rusticum sine barba uniuersi, quosdam
ira, alios dolor, omnes demum commouet risus. Sic qui alienam
iniuste cupierat inuadere terram, iure cum ipsa terra propriam

---

[a] *DE ii. 1 and Byrhtferth iv. 10*   [b] Aethelstano *DE, wrongly*   [c] aduocatur *DE*
[d] questio *om. DE*   [e] huius *R, DE*   [f] tandem *DE (H)*   [g] uoleuerat *DE*

---

[1] Æthelred the Unready, acceded March 978, died 1016. He was dispossessed of the
kingdom for some months in 1013/14 by Swegn Forkbeard, king of Denmark; *HBC*,
p. 27.

concerned He showed everywhere great evidence of His grace and favour, so may God Himself be blessed above all else for ever. Amen.

69. *The story of a countryman who plucked out his own beard, when he should have been lifting the relics of St Ecgwine from the ground*
When King Æthelred, son of the great king Edgar and a man of surpassing virtue, was devoutly governing the prosperous kingdom of England,[1] there was a man who was excessively addicted to the curse of avarice, and consequently too careless of his own salvation. Hence, urged on by the enemy of the human race [the devil], he threw himself into a plan to appropriate a great part of the land of St Ecgwine, with the intention of being able to hold on to the land he had appropriated as his by right. He was opposed by many who desired to protect that holy place, and especially by the abbot of the place, called Osweard. The dispute increased and the case became more serious day by day as various charges were made, until a day was decided in common, by decree of the judges, when the case must finish. Therefore on the appointed day prayers were said more assiduously, and God and His saints were entreated more earnestly. When the prayers of supplication were over, and Mass had been celebrated according to the custom, they make haste to the designated place with the relics of St Ecgwine. The help of the Lord's saint was invoked by everyone. The countryman was present with his supporters raging like a savage. An inquiry of leading men was convened in public, but there was no end to this business. Eventually, the suit was terminated, and the judges decreed that the countryman should lift with his own hands the relics of St Ecgwine from the earth which he was claiming, and gain for himself the land by swearing an oath. The countryman was an elderly man, who had a very long beard. He stood up, laid his cloak down on the ground, and grasped his beard with his hand, saying, 'I swear by this beard of mine, I will remove the saint, because it is my land, and I will possess it by right of inheritance.' O the wonderful goodness of God! Scarcely had these words been uttered, when, see! he pulled out his beard so that it fell to the ground as if it belonged there, and had not grown naturally. Everyone was stunned when they saw the aged rustic without his beard: some were moved to anger, others to grief, but all of them finally to laughter. So it was that the man who had wrongfully desired to appropriate the land, justly lost his beard with the land itself. May

perdidit barbam. Per omnia benedictus Deus, qui in sanctis et per sanctos suos talia operatur.

70. *De alio rustico qui cum periurio terram sancti aufe(r)re uellet proprium cerebrum effudit* [a]

Quidam in uicino rusticus erat, ut id hominum genus sepius se habet, moribus agrestis et intemperanti cupiditate, parui lucri gratia ad omne malum pronus atque infrenis. Exarsit illi animus ad inuadendam iuris ecclesie beati presulis Ecgwini terrulam. Appetiuit, appetendo surripuit, surripiendo inuasit, et inuasam iuris sui iam esse rustica peruicacitate iurare cepit. Calumniatur, peierat, ac peierare [b] non cessat. Tandem in causam res ponitur, et altercationi huic audiende ac definiende dies statuitur. Sanxerunt ergo iudices ut die statuto rusticus ille super calumniose inuasam terram ueniret, suamque illam terram esse in qua consistebat iuraret. Concessit arridenti animo rusticus, pluris habens obolum quam abiurande fidei sue periculum.

71. Ad diem ergo statutum qua controuersiarum finis habendus erat, uterque ad locum accessit, subituri sententiam quam super hac re iuris ac legis periti decreuerant.[1] Summo mane ipsius diei prior ecclesie, uir morum uenerandus honestate et actuum probitate, fo. 133vb nomine Wire|dus, ante sancti reliquias humi prostratus, obnixe diu orauit, orans Deo et sancto causam suam commendauit, commendando septem psalmos quos ex more penitentiales dicunt,[2] lacrimose omnino decantauit. Peroratis supplicetur psalmis, fratres ut hoc ipsum agerent summopere admonuit, et cum reliquiis beati Ecgwini ad subeundam iudicii censuram pergit ipse, et cum eo plurima fratrum multitudo. Affuit ex parte alia rusticanus cum multo rusticorum tumultu, atque tergiuersationibus populosis rem turbare ac uerum inquietate conantur. Tandem compulsus est ad sacramentum accedere rusticus. Sumpserat de domo sua puluerem et eo subtulares suos impleuerat, ut tuto iurare posset quod supra terram

---

[a] *DE i. 19. From now on the sections follow DE ii. 3–25, and only very minor changes are made by R in the wording*   [b] *pegerare R*

---

[1] For some comments on the case, see P. Wormald, *The Making of English Law*, i (Oxford, and Cambridge, Mass., 1999), pp. 158–9.

[2] Psalms 6, 31 (32), 37 (38), 50 (51), 101 (102), 129 (130), and 142 (143). These were said prostrate after Prime and before the Litany during Lent; see *The Monastic Constitutions of Lanfranc*, ed. and trans. D. Knowles, rev. C. N. L. Brooke (OMT, 2002), pp. xxii, and 30–3. Their use by Prior Wiredus at this time was presumably because of the solemnity of the occasion.

God be blessed in all things, who works such wonders in and through His saints.

70. *Another countryman, who wished to misappropriate land of the saint through perjury, spilt his own brains*

There was a countryman in the vicinity of Evesham who, being of a boorish nature and inordinately greedy, as is often the case with that kind of man, had an unbridled propensity for everything evil for the sake of little gain. His mind burned to appropriate a small piece of land that rightfully belonged to the church of the blessed bishop, Ecgwine. He desired it, and in desiring it stole it, and after stealing it, appropriated it, and no sooner appropriated than he began to swear on oath with boorish obstinacy that it was his by right. He laid a claim to it, caused trouble, and did not cease to make matters worse. At last the case came to trial, and a day was appointed for the dispute to be heard and decided. The judges therefore declared that on the appointed day the countryman was to come to state his case about the land disputatiously appropriated, and to take an oath that that land on which he was staying was his own. The man agreed in good heart, having more regard for a halfpenny than for the danger of perjuring himself.

71. When the appointed day arrived on which an end was to be brought to the dispute, each side came to the place, to receive the decision of the men who were knowledgeable in the law and justice.[1] At the dawn of that day the prior of the church, named Wiredus, a man respected for his honourable character and for his virtuous deeds, prostrated himself before the relics of the saint, praying earnestly for a long time, and in his prayers commending his cause to God and the saint; in doing so he tearfully chanted in their entirety the seven psalms which are customarily called the penitential psalms.[2] When these had been sung with humility, he earnestly pleaded with the brethren to do the same. He then stepped forward himself with the relics of the blessed Ecgwine to submit to the judgment of the court, and with him a large number of the brethren. On the other side was the rustic, accompanied by a noisy following of many other countrymen and, with numerous people lagging behind, they tried to disturb the proceedings and subvert the truth. At length the countryman was compelled to come forward to take the oath. He had picked up some dust from his own home and filled his shoes with it, so that he could safely swear that

suam consisteret.[1] O uere rustica, non dico astutia set stultitia, uel fortasse satis condigne rustica dicetur astutia! Arbitrabatur fortassis quod Deum latere posset fraus que in tellure[a] lateret; at etiam in subtulari Deus fraudem rustici comprehendit. Nam ubi rusticus ipse ad reliquias iuraturus manum porrexit, ferreo falcastro quod in manu gestabat, nescio quo casu, ·in cerebro percussus, subito ad terram mortuus ruit; et ignominiosa, set quali illum decebat, morte uitam cum terra sancti coram omnibus amisit. Hoc diuine comminationis terrore et qui aderant et qui longe lateque audiebant exterriti, exinde locum uenerando, metuendo et amando nil omnino aduersus illum forisfacere tunc erant ausi. Itaque benedictus Deus mirabilis existens in sanctis suis.[2] Gloriosus enim in se, gloriosa in sanctis suis et per sanctos suos operatur ubique. Qui uiuit et regnat per omnia secula seculorum. Amen.

72. De quodam artifice[b]

Tempore pacifici regis Eadwardi, summi et ultra communem ualentiam laudabilis principis, dominus abbas Mannius cenobium sancti Ecgwini deuotissime regebat,[3] uir Deo karus et omnibus subiectis | amabilis. Hic inter cetera que multum extollenda operatus est, scrinium sancto Odulfo fieri decreuit, quod opus ut uidit in melius ire studuit sancto Ecgwino dedicare.[4] Aderant tum quam plures artificiosi, quorum omnium magister erat quidam, pater uidelicet domni Clementis postmodum Eoueshamensis prioris. Is cum, sicut huiusmodi opus exigit, sepius fundendo et tundendo ac cum scalpro incidendo labori insisteret, quadam die more solito sedens et cum scalpro paruas imaginulas diligentissime coaptans, subito casu tam grauiter manum sinistram cum ferro quod tenebat uulnerauit ut per mediam manum gutta sanguinis alia ex parte stillaret. Commotus itaque tam repentino casu: 'O sancte', inquit,

fo. 134[ra]

---

[a] telluri R   [b] DE ii. 3

[1] Comparable folktales are found in Stith Thompson, *Motif-Index of Folk-Literature*, 6 vols. (Copenhagen, 1955–8), iv. 80 (J. 1161.3), the trespasser's defence, the man who puts earth from his own land in his shoes, and 491 (K. 2319.1), earth of two countries (Scotland and Ireland) is put in the shoes to define the wearer's whereabouts.

[2] Cf. Ps. 67: 36 (68: 35).

[3] For Mannig, blessed as abbot on 10 Aug. 1044, resigned in 1058 because of paralysis, and died in January 1066 (*HRH*, p. 47), see below, 149–54. Edward (II, the Confessor, 1042–66), resided from 1041 with the household of King Harthacnut, his half-brother,

he was standing on his own land.[1] What true rustic—I will not say
guile but stupidity—though perhaps it may quite properly be called
rustic guile! He thought perhaps that trickery could conceal from
God what he was concealing on earth, but God also knew of the
man's trickery in his shoe. For when the countryman himself
stretched out his hand to the relics to take the oath, somehow or
other he was struck on the head by an iron bill-hook which he was
carrying in his hand, and immediately fell dead upon the ground.
Thus by an ignoble death, but one that he deserved, he lost his life
along with the saint's land in the presence of them all. Both those
who were present, and others from near and far who heard of it,
were terrified by a fear of divine punishment. After that they
reverenced the place, feared it, and loved it, and at that time
made no attempt whatsoever to offend against it. So, blessed be our
marvellous God who lives in His saints.[2] He is glorious in Himself,
glorious in His saints, and performs glorious deeds in and through
His saints everywhere. Who lives and reigns for ever and ever.
Amen.

72. *A story about a craftsman*

At the time of King Edward, the peace-maker, who was an extra-
ordinarily valiant and renowned prince, the abbot Mannig, a man
beloved of God and loved by all his subjects, was ruling the
monastery of St Ecgwine most devoutly.[3] Mannig, amongst other
things that he did deserving high praise, decided to have a shrine
made for St Odulf, and when he saw that the work was going very
well, he was eager to dedicate it to St Ecgwine.[4] There were at that
time many craftsmen, and the master of them all was the father of
Clement, later prior of Evesham. One day, as this kind of work
requires, he was concentrating upon the task, frequently casting,
hammering, and cutting with a chisel, and was sitting in his usual
manner, very carefully shaping some small images with his chisel,
when it suddenly happened that he cut his left hand so severely with
the iron tool which he was holding, that a stream of blood gushed
from one place all over his hand. Alarmed by this sudden accident, he

who associated Edward with himself in the kingship, hence the 'peace maker'; see *HBC*,
p. 29.
   [4] On Mannig as a goldsmith and painter, see C. R. Dodwell, *Anglo-Saxon Art: a New
Perspective* (Manchester, 1982), pp. 65–7, 80, and 200, who describes Mannig as 'the
greatest master craftsman of the Confessor's reign'. Later in his life Mannig perhaps acted
more as an overseer with lay professionals actually exercising the craft.

'Ecgwine, nonne hic assum in tuo seruitio? Si quicquam de seruitio miseri peccatoris curas, iam ostende'. Dixit; et statim diuina medela accedente, et dolore et uulnere per sancti uiri merita caruit. O uirum mirabilem, omniumque ore predicandum! Non interposuit tempus medele,[1] set ad exemplum Marci euangeliste,[2] mox post dolorem uulneris sanitatem per Deum superinfudit.[3]

73. *De reliquiis sancti Ecgwini furatis et reuocatis, furibus infirmitate percussis*[a]

Matrona quedam, Algitha nomine, dum sepius tempore predicti regis Eadwardi ecclesiam sancti Ecgwini frequentaret, uenit ei in mentem ob amorem sancti omnimodis temptare, si quicquam de reliquiis eius ualeret adquirere.[4] Cepit igitur callide uolutare qualiter desiderium suum posset facilius perpetrare. Accitis itaque secreto pueris loci eisque, ut fertur, dona tribuens et ampliora promittens, rogauit quatinus sibi de reliquiis sancti Ecgwini uel modicum quid clam perquirent,[b] ut per hoc maiorem mercedem ab ea perciperent. Sciebat enim illam etatem minus habilem intelligentie, leuiusque posse decipi. Prebent assensum pueri, et cepere querere tempus et horam qua[c] sine noticia aliorum implerent promissum.

fo. 134[rb] 74. Verum quid non audet ardens cupiditas? Per | infirmam etatem perficit auaritia suum officium; pergunt nocte pueri ad sancti Ecgwini feretrum, apertoque uelociter[d] scrinio, furto[e] auferunt magnum thesaurum, omni margarita preciosiorem.[5] Proh dolor! Temerariis manibus irreuerenter tractant membra sancti, et, sublata[f] parte brachii cum uno dente, matrone studuere clanculum deportare. Verum enimuero super tam incredibili audatia non diu distulit, ut in sequenti patuit, uindictam[g] sumere ultio diuina. Nam sumens predicta matrona diu desideratum thesaurum, leta repedauit ad propria. Locatis igitur honorifice secundum suum posse reliquiis sancti Ecgwini in mundissimo locello, credebat se diutius gauisuram de furto. Cum ecce! sanctus Domini Ecgwinus per uisionem matrone noctu apparens, iubet eam se ipsum proprium reportare ad locum, dicens se iniuste ab ipsa inde fuisse sublatum. Negligit illa imperata,

---

[a] *DE* ii. 4   [b] perquirerent *DE ii*   [c] quo *R, DE*   [d] uiolenter *DE*   [e] inde add. *DE*   [f] sublate *R*   [g] uidictam *R*

---

[1] Cf. Jer. 8: 15.   [2] Cf. Mark 5: 29.
[3] Cf. *Acta Sanctorum*, 25 April (St Mark), p. 348.
[4] On relic-theft, see P. J. Geary, *Furta Sacra*, rev. edn. (Princeton, New Jersey, 1990).

said, 'St Ecgwine, am I not here in your service? If you have any concern for the service of a poor sinner, show it now!' Such were his words; at once divine healing occurred, and the pain and the wound disappeared through the merits of the holy man, Ecgwine. How wondrous a man, worthy to be praised by the lips of everyone! No time intervened before the healing took place,[1] but like the story of Mark the evangelist,[2] the saint sent healing by God's power immediately after the pain of the injury.[3]

73. *The relics of St Ecgwine are stolen and recovered, and the thieves are stricken with illness*

A certain lady named Ealdgyth used to visit the church of St Ecgwine frequently during the time of the above-mentioned King Edward. One day because of her affection for the saint she thought about trying by every means she could to acquire something from his relics.[4] She therefore began to ponder a cunning plan as to how she could most easily achieve her desire. She secretly summoned some boys of the place and, giving them, it is said, some presents, and promising greater rewards, she asked them to obtain secretly any small item they could from the relics of St Ecgwine, and so receive from her this greater reward. She knew that boys of that age were less capable of understanding a situation, and could be more easily deceived. The boys agreed to the task, and began to look for the best time for fulfilling their promise without others finding out.

74. What will a burning greed not dare! Avarice carries out her duty through people of impressionable age. So the boys set off at night for the shrine of St Ecgwine, quickly open the reliquary, and steal a great treasure, more precious than any pearl.[5] Alas! With their audacious hands they irreverently handled the limbs of the saint, stealing a part of the arm and one tooth, and were eager to carry their secret possession back to the lady. But divine punishment was not delayed long for this unbelievable audacity, as the following reveals. For picking up her long-desired treasure, the lady returned home rejoicing. She placed the relics of St Ecgwine with as much honour as she could in the most fitting place for them, and believed that she would long rejoice over her theft. But see! The Lord's saint, Ecgwine, appeared to the lady in a vision during the night, and commanded her to take him back to the place that belonged to him, saying that he had been wrongfully removed by her from there. She ignored the

[5] Cf. Matt. 13: 44–6.

et identidem secunda admonita est eiusmodi uisione. Set cum nec sic optemperaret, uerum ob nimiam cupiditatem habendi uisiones fantasie deputasset, tercia demum uisione uenit sanctus Ecgwinus, ⟨et⟩ ualde commotus, iubet*ᵃ* ut se reduceret. Qua negante, 'Prius', inquit sanctus, 'quam crastinus Titan solito refulserit, uelles meis optemperasse preceptis.'

75. Quid moras nectimus? Matrona diluculo exurgit apertis oculis ceca, sicque dum presenti usa est uita, pulcherrimos habens oculos, permansit in perpetua cecitate. Misit tamen postea, licet sero, ad Mannium, ea tempestate abbatem monasterii sancti Ecgwini, querens licentiam habendi reliquias, et promittens se feretrum ex auro et argento adornatum ob honorem reliquiarum facturam. Spopondit etiam ipsum scrinium cum reliquiis, et insuper terram propriam que Suella¹ ab incolis uocitatur, cum uita decederet, procul dubio sancto Ecgwino eiusque seruis daturam. Quam sponsionem, licet peccato filii sui prepedita per se implere nequiret, impleuit tamen postea omni-
fo. 134ᵛᵃ potens per dominum ac prudentissimum Agelwi|num abbatem, successorem uidelicet domni et artificiosissimi Mannii abbatis.² Nam idem abbas et predictam uillam, que sibi in uadimonium tradita fuerat, ob difficultatem reddende pecunie iudicio optinuit, et etiam scrinium cum apud Wigorniam recognouisset per Dei adiutorium suo dominio mancipauit, quod usque inpresentiarum in monasterio sancti Ecgwini seruatur. Hactenus de matrona. Pueri uero supra commemorati qui prefati furti auctores extiterunt, iudicio Dei demum grauiter subiacuerunt. Nempe quidam ex eis in aqua necatus est, quidam uero quoad uixit molestia corporali pene sine intercapedine grauissime detentus est.

76. *De quodam muto loquele restituto*ᵇ
Clarissimum omnipotentis Dei miraculum per beatum confessorem suum Ecgwinum mirabiliter seruis suis insinuatum, ad medium censemus deducendum. Erat tempore prefati regis quidam homo in Anglia apud Cantiam qui, pro causa soli Deo cognita, mutus in hanc lucem materno utero profusus, dolorem parentibus maximeque sibi diatim exaggerabat. Is tandem in iuuentute, diuino admonitus instinctu, per memoriam sanctorum uersus Romam ire disposuit.

ᵃ iubens *DE*   ᵇ *DE ii.5*

¹ For the manor of Swell (Glos.), see below, 169.
² For Æthelwig, abbot from 1058 to 1077 (*HRH*, p. 47), see below, 151–71.

command, and again she was warned in a second vision. She again disobeyed it, and because of her extreme desire of possession, considered that the visions were her imagination. Finally, St Ecgwine appeared in a third vision very perturbed, and ordered that she should take him back. When she refused, the saint said, 'Before tomorrow's sun has finished its accustomed course, you will wish you had obeyed my command.'

75. Why do we contrive to delay? At daybreak the lady rose and opened her eyes, but she was blind, and while she lived her life here, despite having beautiful eyes, she remained in perpetual darkness. Afterwards, though some time later, she sent to Mannig, at that time the abbot of the monastery of St Ecgwine, asking permission to keep the relics, promising that she would adorn the reliquary with gold and silver in honour of the relics. She also promised that when she departed this life she would certainly give a reliquary with the relics to St Ecgwine and his servants, and her own land as well, which is called Swell[1] by those who live on it. Although her promise could not be fulfilled because the sinful action of her son prevented this, yet the Almighty later fulfilled it through the efforts of that wise abbot dom Æthelwig, successor to the astute abbot, dom Mannig.[2] For abbot Æthelwig obtained both the above-mentioned vill, which he acquired in a judgment because of a difficulty over paying dues, and also the reliquary, which he took into his own possession by God's help when he recognized it at Worcester, and it has been kept safe in the monastery of St Ecgwine up to the present time. So much for the lady. As for the boys we have mentioned above, who were responsible for the theft, they finally succumbed severely to God's judgment. One of them drowned, and another was severely crippled by a physical disability that gave him hardly any rest as long as he lived.

76. *Speech is restored to a dumb man*
We are now of the opinion that we should make it generally known that a spectacular miracle of almighty God was wonderfully revealed to His servants through His blessed confessor Ecgwine. During the time of the above-mentioned king Edward there was a man in England, living in Kent, who for reasons known to God alone, had been born into this world dumb, and this, as time went on, caused increasing grief to his parents, but especially to himself. Eventually, when he was in his youth, spurred on by a divine impulse, and mindful of the saints, he decided to go to Rome. So he set off on the

Incipiens ergo iter constitutum, Romam usque perueniens, tribus ibidem annis ad limina apostolorum deuote pro infirmitate sua supplicans permansit.

77. Cui cum nichil remedii pro uoto occurrisset, post trinam reuolutionem annorum meditabatur maximo cum merore si quippiam sibi posset fieri in salutem. Ecce[a] quadam nocte per dulcem quietem astitit sibi quedam persona albis uestibus induta, huiusmodi depromens oracula: 'Quid hic', inquit, 'tam diu iacens frustra consumeris? Reuertere ad patriam tuam Angliam. Quere inibi monasterium sancti Ecgwini, illucque uadens cum oblatione Dei et illius sancti misericordiam deprecare, statimque sanaberis.' Optemperans igitur mutus diuino mandato, extim | plo ad natale solum repedauit.

fo. 134[vb]

78. Veniens autem in Angliam, indicio ductus, per diuinum auxilium recto itinere ad monasterium sancti Ecgwini peruenit. Erat uero tunc dies sabbati.[1] Igitur cunctis fratribus in choro astantibus, uenit predictus uir candelam manu gestans cum uespertina sinaxis decantaretur, pergensque ante altare diutius orauit, sicque candelam optulit.[2] Qua oblata, rursus ad orationem stetit. Res mira et uehementer stupenda! Cum coram cunctis astaret mutus, subito cadens riuum sanguinis ex ore cepit excreare, nimiaque pre angustia in pauimento circumquaque uolutare. Finita ergo uespertina prece, accessit ad illum qua excreans iacebat domnus Aeuicius, ea tempestate prior loci, cum quibusdam senioribus, interrogans quid haberet, aut cur sanguinem excreans sic iaceret. Surgens itaque homo in medio fratrum, oculosque cum manibus ad Deum intendens, demum lingua resoluta, hanc primam ita cepit uocem formare: 'Sic me adiuuet omnipotens Deus, meusque dominus sanctus Ecgwinus, per cuius meritum in me misero tale miraculum operatus est Christus, sicut uobis uera dixerim.' Sumensque principium orationis omnia seriatim pandit, ut supra habetur comprehensum. Qua narratione finita, fratres exhilarantur, conuocatur etiam populus, ora relaxantur in summis Dei laudibus; incipientesque 'Te Deum laudamus', classicum sonant diutius, extollentes Dei miracula quam poterant dulcius, qui est super omnia benedictus Deus.

---

[a] autem *add.* DE

[1] Although in the Middle Ages 'dies sabbati' was Saturday, the context suggests that it may in fact have been a Sunday.

journey he had resolved on, and having reached Rome, stayed there for three years, praying devoutly at the threshold of the apostles for his disability.

77. When, after the passing of three years, there was no sign of the cure he desired, he began to ponder with considerable sadness whether anything at all could be done to heal him. But see, one night during the peaceful silence, a person dressed in white raiment stood before him, giving him advice as follows, 'Why do you spend so much time lying here to no purpose? Return to your country England. There seek out the monastery of St Ecgwine, and go there with an offering; pray for God's mercy, and that of the saint, and you will immediately be cured.' The dumb man immediately obeyed the divine command, and at once made his way back to his native soil.

78. He arrived in England, and was led by a sign; with God's help he took the right road and reached the monastery of St Ecgwine. It was now the sabbath.[1] Therefore, all the brethren were standing in the choir, when the man arrived carrying a candle in his hand as vespers was being sung: advancing before the altar he prayed for a long time, and then offered his candle.[2] Having made his offering, he again stood in prayer. Then, a wonderful and amazing thing happened! As the dumb man was standing before them all, suddenly he fell, and began to cough up a stream of blood, and, through extreme distress, thrash around in all directions on the floor. Evening prayer being over, Æfic, prior of the place at that time, came over with certain older monks to where the man was lying and coughing; they asked what was the matter, and why he was lying there in this way coughing blood. Rising in the midst of the brethren, and raising his eyes and his hands to God, his tongue was finally loosed, and he began to make this first utterance: 'May almighty God help me as may my lord St Ecgwine, by whose merit Christ has wrought such a miracle in one so wretched as I, that I might tell you the truth.' Starting with his prayer, he revealed the whole story in detail, as has been recounted above. When his story was ended, the brethren were overjoyed, the people were also summoned, their mouths were opened in loud praises of God, beginning with the 'Te Deum Laudamus'; they rang the bells for a long time, extolling as sweetly as they could the miracles of God, who is God blessed above all things.

---

[2] The candle represents the man's prayer.

79. *De quodam contractu reformato*[a]

Illud etiam non uidetur pretereundum quod sub eodem tempore in quodam homine cunctis apud Eoueshamium notissimo per beatissimum patrem nostrum sanctum Ecgwinum credimus patratum. Erat enim isdem miserando infirmitatis genere detentus, qui nec surgere quidem poterat[b] nisi dextra leuaque baculis sustentaretur, ambulans uero uno pede suspenso quasi tripes miserabiliter | gradiebatur. Tali autem infirmitate diutius possessus, nullo genere medele poterat mederi. Nam pes eius cum tibia et coxa in tanto fuerat tumore conuersus ut quasi monstrum quoddam fere ad instar humane medietatis intumescens, miserabile preberet spectaculum.

80. Veniens igitur quadam die ad locum ubi sancti Ecgwini reliquie conseruantur, humiliter coram altare[c] suspirare, intimo ex corde gemere, ac cum magna intentione dominum sanctum Ecgwinum cepit deprecari. Fratres autem eadem hora per Dei prouidentiam in choro erant presentes, quorum presagam mentem cerneres ex uultuum indicio quodam modo trepidare, spem futuri miraculi concipere, sanctum Ecgwinum deuotius exposcere, in commune Dei ineffabilem misericordiam expectare. Infirmi sanitatem, sancti gloriam, sui loci honorem opperiebantur. Quam uera prophetica admiratio! ⟨Quam⟩ mirabilis Deus in sanctis suis![1] Dum enim cunctorum astantium corda diuinitus tacta ad futuri prestolationem uiderentur arrecta, ecce! uident infirmum dextra leuaque baculos sue miserie adiutores abicere, ipsum in terram cadere, pedem infirmum extendere, donec omni passione solutus, gaudens exurgeret cum Dei laudibus. Accurrere uniuersi, singuli quasi rei ignari hominem interrogare, plaudere, admirari, Dominum et sanctum Ecgwinum collaudare ceperunt. Fit strepitus in ecclesia, sonantur classica, attollantur cantica diuina, omnium in Dei laudibus reserantur corda. Prelibatus uero uir, tantarum laudum materia, proprios coram altari sancto relinquens baculos, cunctis spectantibus, sanis pedibus remeauit ad propria, clara uoce 'benedicens Dominum qui regnat in secula'.[2]

81. *De quodam leproso sanato*

Eisdem temporibus quidam leprosus uisu horrendus, dolore pene intractabilis, uniuerso corpore deformis, memoriam sancti Ecgwini

---

[a] *DE ii. 6*   *[b]* possit *DE*   *[c]* astare *R*

[1] Cf. Ps. 67: 36 (68: 35).   [2] This is a common end for a prayer or collect.

fo. 135[ra]

79. *A cripple is made whole again*

It does not seem right to us to neglect mentioning the miracle which we believe was wrought at the same time by our blessed father St Ecgwine in the case of a man who was well known to everybody in Evesham. He was crippled by a pitiful kind of disability, and could not get up unless supported with crutches on his left and his right, so that he walked along with one leg hanging, as if he were pathetically taking steps on three legs. He had possessed this disability for a long time and no remedy of any sort had been successful. His foot, shin, and thigh had coalesced into so great a swelling, that this was like some monstrosity, being almost half the size of a man, and making him a miserable sight to behold.

80. One day this man came to the place where the relics of St Ecgwine are preserved, and here he sighed humbly before the altar, with a groan coming from the depths of his being. He began with great feeling to pray to his lord, St Ecgwine. By God's providence the brethren were at that hour in the choir, and from the looks on their faces, one could have perceived a sort of agitation in their expectant minds, which had conceived a hope of an impending miracle and were devoutly entreating St Ecgwine, awaiting in common the ineffable mercy of God. They were anticipating the healing of the disabled man, the glorification of the saint, and the honouring of their place. What a truly prophetic state of wonder! How wonderful is God in his saints![1] For while the hearts of all of them standing there were divinely touched, and they seemed on tiptoe in their anticipation of what was to happen, they saw the disabled man throw away the crutches on his left and right, those supports of his wretchedness, then fall on the ground, stretch out his affected foot until, free of all pain, he stood up with joy, praising God. They all ran to him, and one by one, as though they were unaware of what had happened, began to question him, applaud him, wonder at him, and to praise the Lord and St Ecgwine. The church resounds, the bells ring out, voices are raised in divine singing, the hearts of all are unlocked in their praises of God. The man who had been the subject of such praises left both of his crutches before the holy altar and, watched by everyone, returned to his own home on healthy feet, blessing with a loud voice the Lord who reigns for ever.[2]

81. *A leper is healed*

At that same time there was a leper who was horrifying to look at, and almost impossible to deal with because of his affliction, the whole of

deuotus expetiit, et ab imo pectore gemitus effundens, sanctum Dei ut sui misereretur cum spe salutis creberrime deprecabatur. |

Tandem diu desiderata aduenit meritis beati uiri miseratio diuina; condonatur petenti infirmo sanitas laudibus plena. Posses namque uidere scabiem ueluti quoddam scutum de corpore cadere, uirum undique sanum effectum quamplures Deo et sancto gratias agere, infirmitatem comminus depositam quid fuerit testari, ipsum uero hominem quid sit omnibus cernentibus uoce clarius corpore sanato ostendere. Vnde uoces et cantica, plausus et iubilamina Deo magnifice libantur, qui a seculo facit mirabilia.[1]

82. *De multiplici genere languentium sanatorum per sanctum Ecgwinum* [a]
De miraculis sancti Ecgwini multa inquirentes, et super his sepe numero colloquentes cum personis fide dignis et ueneranda bonitate adornatis, id a compluribus compertum memorie studuimus mandare quod in antiquo tempore ante aduentum Normannorum in Angliam, Dei operante clementia, tanta miraculorum frequentia monasterium sancti uiri illustrabatur, ut raro dies[b] sabbati solares radios occuluerit quo non qualicumque infirmitate uel molestia detentus gratam per sanctum Ecgwinum medelam aliquis eger optinuerit. Videres plerumque si adesses nunc unum, nunc duos, nonnumquam plures egrotantes causa salutis aduentasse, coram altare modo accedere, modo ab aliis delatos adesse, in terram uolutare, preces effundere, gemitum emittere, in commune salutem sperare. Hos cecos, illos uero claudos, quosdam surdos, alios autem mutos, nonnullos leprosos siue paraliticos uel molestia ferri astrictos, aut qualibet alia infirmitate obsessos, cerneres adesse. Demoniaci uero in tam miseranda conglobatione non defuere. Verum in tali cuneo sepe gratia diuina per sancti Ecgwini merita adesse, cecos illuminare, claudos erigere, surdis auditum reddere, mutis linguam restituere, leprosos mundare, paraliticos sanare, ceterosque egrotantes non differebat curare, plures etiam ferro pro criminum[2] | abolitione grauiter deuinctos meritis sancti Ecgwini mirabiliter liberare. Nam cum quidam huiusmodi

---

[a] *DE ii. 8*   [b] *DE*; die R

[1] Cf. Ps. 135: 4 (136: 4).
[2] It is not certain whether these were criminals bound in chains for their crimes, or persons who like Ecgwine had shackled themselves for penitential purposes. Most likely they were the latter, as *crimen* can be used for sin.

his body being deformed. This man devoutly sought out the shrine of St Ecgwine and, groaning from the depths of his heart, again and again pleaded with the saint of God to have pity upon him, in the hope of being healed. At last the divine pity, long desired, came through the merits of that blessed man. Healing was granted to the disabled man in answer to his prayers, healing that led to abundant praises. You could see the scab fall from his body like some sort of shield, and the man, healed in every part of his body, expressing a multitude of thanks to God and the saint; for his affliction, which he had just been rid of, testified what he had been, while the man himself demonstrated in a loud voice to everyone who saw him what he was now that his body had been healed. Hence voices and hymns, applause and jubilation were magnificently expressed to God, who performs miracles evermore.[1]

82. *Many different kinds of sick people healed by St Ecgwine*
Having conducted many investigations into the miracles of St Ecgwine and frequently discussing them with trustworthy people highly esteemed for their honesty, we have made it our business to write an account of what we have discovered from many sources. It is a fact that in ancient times before the coming of the Normans to England, by God's mercy the monastery of that holy man became so famous for its many miracles that rarely did a sabbath day see the sun's rays disappear without some sick person, afflicted by disability or illness, obtaining a gracious cure through St Ecgwine. You could generally see, if you were there, now one invalid, now two, often more, who had come for healing sometimes approach the altar, at other times come because they had been carried by others and would grovel upon the ground, utter prayers, and groan, hoping for healing in common with the others. You could observe some present who were blind, others who were lame, some deaf, others dumb, some with leprosy or paralysis, others bound with painful fetters, or distressed with some other illness. In that miserable throng there was no lack of those possessed by devils. But in that company the divine grace was present through the merits of St Ecgwine: the blind received their sight, the lame walked, hearing was restored to the deaf and speech to the dumb, lepers were made clean, the paralysed made whole, there was no delay in healing others who were sick, and many who were bound with heavy iron chains for their sins[2] were wonderfully set free by the merits of St Ecgwine. There was one

passione pressus ad sancti Ecgwini patrocinium expetendum se
deuote optulisset, et circa sanctorum memoriam frequentius incubans
Dei et eius sancti misericordiam expetisset, adeo quadam die suam
pietatem magnifice declarauit omnipotens ut tanta ui ferrum ab
infirmo excusserit, quod longius a propria sede resiliens, totam
ecclesiam tinnitu intentam reddiderit, cunctis qui aderant mirantibus,
et Deum una dulcimode laudantibus, qui tanta et tam mira in sanctis
et per sanctos suos manifestare dignatur miracula.

83. *Qualiter Sperckulfus monachus uidit beatam Mariam apud Euesham in criptis*[a]

Ea tempestate solennitas sancti Ecgwini maxima cum ueneratione
honorificentissime celebrabatur, populi etiam multitudo certatim
affluebat, ingens apparatus, maxima frequentia, copiosa letitia pari
modo renitebant. Tum globus monachorum aliunde aduentantium
non minimo decori[b] fuisse priuatus[c] uidebatur. Inter quos quidam
religiosus et ualde uenerabilis uite monachus Couentrensis,[1] nomine
Sperckulfus, solitus erat monasterium sancti[d] frequentare, in sanctorum festiuitatibus aduenire, altaria circuire, in orationibus pernoc-
tare, lucubrando ⟨et⟩ animum supernis intendendo, matutinos cantus
cum psalmodia preueniendo, omnimodis deuote agendo Dei sibi
misericordiam coaptare.[e]

84. Is cum in quadam sancti Ecgwini festiuitate solito more adueniens,
nocturnales ymnos in uigiliis cum psalmodia persistens preoccuparet,
in cripta Deo sanctoque Ecgwino consecrata quo tum rite solitarius
residebat, admirabilem uisionem conspexit. Nam cum Dauiticum
canticum ex ordine deuotius reuolueret, uidit primo limina cripte
diuina uirtute recludi, dehinc paulatim domum in[f] qua sedebat
superno lumine illucescere, demum quamplurimo fulgore eiectis
tenebris irradiari. Cumque ad hoc spectaculum territus animum et
una oculos conuertisset, ecce con | spicit processionem quam maximam
sanctorum spirituum aduenientem, que, maxima pulchritudine ac
summa honorificentia digesta, mirabile specimen intuenti prestabat.
In qua quidam pueri luminum portitores cum candelabris precede-
bant, dehinc ephebi sequebantur, post quos seniores ueneranda canitie

fo. 135[vb]

---

[a] *DE ii. 9*   [b] decore *DE*   [c] *DE*; priuatis *R*   [d] Ecgwini *add. DE*   [e] *Marg.*
Monachus Couentrensis Sperkulphus *?s.xiii*   [f] *inserted R*

---

[1] This miracle story almost certainly dates from after 1043, when a papal letter
confirmed Earl Leofric's foundation; see below, **146**.

man oppressed with pain of this sort who devoted himself to seeking the protection of St Ecgwine. He would frequently make his bed near the shrine of the saints, and ask for the mercy of God and His saint. One day the Almighty responded to his piety with great power, so that He shook the chains from the disabled man with such force that, being flung so far from where the man was resting, they made the whole church take notice of the sound, and all who were there marvelled and praised God with sweet singing, who deigns to manifest such great and wonderful acts in and through His saints.

83. *A monk named Sperckulf sees the blessed Mary in the crypt at Evesham*

At that time the feast of St Ecgwine was being celebrated with very great reverence in a most honorific fashion, a large crowd of people too was eagerly flocking to it; great magnificence, the huge number present, and abundant happiness alike shone forth. And then the throng of monks coming from elsewhere seemed to have been deprived of no small splendour. Amongst these was a monk of Coventry,[1] a devout man, highly revered for his holy life, named Sperckulf. He was accustomed to visit the monastery of the saint frequently, to attend the feasts of the saints, to go round all the altars, to spend the night in prayer, to seek out for himself the mercy of God, by working at night, and setting his mind on heavenly things, to precede his morning chants with the singing of psalms, and to act with devotion in every way he could.

84. On the occasion of one festival of St Ecgwine he came in his usual manner, and was occupied in singing the night hymns and psalms during the eve of the festival, when, duly sitting alone in the crypt dedicated to God and St Ecgwine, he experienced a wonderful vision. He was devoutly reciting the psalms in order when he saw at first the doors of the crypt shut by divine power, and then the place where he was sitting gradually become bright with a heavenly light, until, banishing the darkness, it shone with a most brilliant light. When, awestruck, he turned his mind as well as his eyes towards this sight, then indeed he saw a mighty procession of holy spirits arriving who, set apart by their great beauty and high distinction, displayed a wonderful sight to the beholder. At the head of this procession certain boys processed, carrying lamps with candelabras; these were followed by youths, and after them came venerable older men with gleaming

renitentes gradiebantur. Hi omnes albis stolis induti mirum spectaculum prebuere. Ad ultimum quedam persona pontificali habitu[1]—supra
quam dici potest 'mira uenustate'—redimita aduenit, quam dextra
leuaque bini seniores simili habitu adornati deducebant. Accedentes
ergo coram altare sancti Ecgwini, plurima cum modestia astantes
matutinale officium exordiuntur.[2] Quo cum summo honore expleto,
unus ex eis ad missam decantandam se preparauit. Mira res! Missa
incipitur, ac mirabili dulcedine more solito decantatur. Solenni uero
missa finita, horisque canonicis honorifice decantatis, haud secus quam
intrauerat totum illud collegium seriatim procedendo domum egredi-
tur. Dehinc, modico interuallo expleto, ante matutinale officium
classica pulsantur.

85. Ad hec credenda, licet iusiurandum tam uenerabilis uiri corda
audientium autentica ueritate confirmauerit, non minimum tamen
ueneranda illius uita ad omnem dubietatis caliginem detergendam
proficit. Omittentes ergo quam constans et infatigabilis in oratione et
in*a* uigiliis, quam alacer diuini uerbi auditor, quam frequens in Dei
seruicio perstiterit, illud dicendum arbitramur: quod tante fuerit
abstinentie ut raro quarta uel sexta feria cibum sumpserit. Vnde,
quia Deo fidelis permansit, eius secreta conspicere meruit. Non solum
enim predictam uidit uisionem, set, quod est mirabile dictu, cum
idem monachus quadam nocte in ecclesia Dei genitricis,[3] que tunc
temporis miro decore constructa habebatur, in illius solennitate
fo. 136ra uigilans pernoctaret, ecce uni | uersis ecclesie ianuis sponte reclusis,
cum inestimabili claritate et decore conspicit simili modo processionem uenientem, sanctumque Ecgwinum cum alia quadam reuerenda
persona, totius mundi lumen, miserorum et peccatorum omniumque
Christianorum refugium *b*et solatium, Dei scilicet genitricem*b*[4] et
semper uirginem Mariam, sullimissime, ut digna est, deducentem.
Peruenientes igitur ante altare sancte Marie, uenerandus pontifex
sanctus Ecgwinus, post matutinale officium honorifice decantatum,
missarum solennia maxima uenustate exorditur. Cerneres monachum
ista tuentem mente deductum trepidare, animo fluctuare, ac secum
talia alternatim reuoluere: 'Quid est istud uidere? Num sensum
meum perdidi? Putasne istius ecclesie monachi hic suum officium

---

a add. R   *b-b* om. DE

[1] Probably chasuble, cope, and mitre.
[2] Matins is the service after Nocturns, which took place at daybreak.
[3] The abbey church at Evesham was dedicated to the Virgin.

white hair. All these were clad in white stoles, a wonderful sight to behold. At the end a person in bishop's robes arrived,[1] of whom it could be said he was crowned with a wonderful loveliness, and was escorted on his left and his right by two elders adorned in similar garments. They approached the altar of St Ecgwine, and standing by it with great humility, they began the office of Matins.[2] When the service had been brought to an end with great honour, one of them made preparations to sing Mass. How wonderful was this vision! Mass was begun, and sung in the usual manner with great sweetness. And when this solemn service was over, and the canonical hours had been honourably sung, the whole of that congregation left the place just as they had entered it, and made their way home in due order. Then, after just a short time had elapsed, the bells began to ring before the office of Matins.

85. Although the oath of so respected a man convinced those hearing the story that it was absolutely true, no less effective in dispelling any mists of doubt was the holy life of that man. Without recounting how persistent and tireless he was in spending nights in prayer, how zealous a hearer of divine scripture, how assiduous and steadfast in the service of God, we consider that mention must be made of his great austerity of life, so that he rarely took food on a Wednesday or a Friday. Hence, because he remained faithful to God, he was deemed worthy of perceiving His mysteries. But not only did this monk see the vision we have described but, marvellous to relate, one night in the church of Mary,[3] mother of God, a church of surpassing beauty built at that time, he was praying in the solemnity of the church, when suddenly all its doors opened of their own accord and he saw a procession similar to that of his previous vision moving towards him with incredible splendour and beauty: St Ecgwine, with another revered person, leading sublimely, as was most fitting, Mary, the mother of God,[4] the everlasting virgin, the light of the whole world, the refuge and solace of poor sinners and of all Christians. The reverend bishop St Ecgwine, coming to the altar of the blessed Mary after the office of Matins had been reverently sung, began most graciously the solemn service of Mass. You could have seen the monk trembling as he watched intently, agitated in mind, pondering over one thought, then another such as, 'What is this I am seeing? Surely I have not lost my senses? Are the monks of this church carrying out

[4] As part of this clause is not in DE, it may indicate that Thomas had a better text than that found in either of the two surviving manuscripts of DE.

peragunt? Set hic neminem *recognosco ex illis.* An spiritus sunt uel corpora que uideo? Nonne hic quidam assunt, quos diu ex hac luce subtractos intelligo?' Viderat namque in illo globo quosdam quos et Eoueshamensis monasterii monachos et iam defunctos nouerat. Hac igitur ambiguitate compulsus, accedit secreto ad quendam, et que esset cui missa decantaretur inquirit. Ad quem paucis: 'Tace; num ignoras dominum nostrum sanctum Ecgwinum beate Dei genitrici et semper uirgini Marie sacrum mysterium celebrantem?' Territus ille huiusmodi responsione, locum repetens rei exitum prestolabatur. Itaque peracta missarum celebratione, horisque sancte Marie ex ordine decantatis, iterum duo episcopi celi reginam et mundi dominam humillime dextra leuaque assumentes, eodem modo quo prius induxere, cum processione et summa gloria reduxere.[1] Istius-modi uero rei exempla late suppetunt.

86. *De quodam canonico Turonensis ecclesie*

Compertum quippe habemus quendam canonicum olim Turonis Deo sanctoque Martino seruientem quodam modo uniformem uidisse uisionem.[2] Qui cum stultitia inductus glisceret rescire causam cur fo. 136rb in ordinati|one seu translatione sancti Martini que in estate cele-bratur,[3] nullus hominum post decantatum completorium ecclesie auderet remanere, studuit se ipsum subtus quoddam altare clanculo occulere donec, cunctis pro more discedentibus, eius rei causam quiret explorare. Quid amplius? In conticinio noctis, cum solus uastam ecclesiam uagabundis oculis perambularet, subito uidet ecclesie limina patefacta, intrantemque mirabilem processionem, sanctum uero Martinum portam salutis et, post Deum, primam spem Christianorum sanctam Mariam honorifice dextra ducentem. Que, cum in medio ecclesie constitisset, incepit hanc antiphonam,

---

a–a ex illis recognosco *DE*

[1] This miracle indicates the size and grandeur of the abbey church at the time, with its extensive crypt. For the architectural revival of the period, see E. Fernie, *The Architecture of the Anglo-Saxons* (London, 1983), pp. 112–61.

[2] This vision does not seem to be recorded in any other surviving source. Evesham was the centre of a cult of the Virgin Mary, and the story of the canon of Tours was included by Dominic here amongst the miracles of St Ecgwine because it made a useful comparison with Dominic's other stories of the appearance of the Virgin at Evesham. To the Evesham compiler it had the added attraction that St Martin of Tours, like St Ecgwine, was both monk and bishop. Dominic knew of this Vision story, possibly from a written source or perhaps from an oral tradition. J. C. Jennings assigns it to 1039–66; see J. C. Jennings, 'Prior Dominic of Evesham and the survival of English tradition after the Norman

their duties here, do you think? But I do not recognize any of them here. Are they spirits or bodies that I see? Surely, there are some of these here whom I know departed this life long ago?' For he had indeed seen some in that company whom he had known as monks of the monastery of Evesham, and who had then died. Impelled by this uncertainty, therefore, he approached one of them secretly, and asked him what the reason was for Mass being sung? The monk replied briefly, 'Be silent! Surely you are not unaware that our lord St Ecgwine is celebrating the sacred mystery for the blessed mother of God, Mary, ever virgin?' Awestruck by such a reply, he resumed his place and awaited the outcome of the proceedings. Therefore, when the celebration of the Mass was over, and the Hours of the Blessed Mary had been sung in due order, the two bishops, most humbly taking their places again on the left and right of the queen of heaven and mistress of the world, and escorting her in the same way as before, led her from the place in procession and with great glory.[1] Similar examples of such visions are widely found.

86. *A canon of the church of Tours*

Indeed we have discovered that a canon of Tours, a servant of God and St Martin, once saw a similar kind of vision.[2] Impelled by a foolish impulse, this man yearned to discover the reason why, during the celebration of the ordination or the translation of St Martin, which is celebrated in the summer,[3] none of the men dared to stay behind in the church after compline had been sung. He therefore made it his business to hide secretly under one of the altars until all had left in the usual way, so that he might investigate the reason for this. What more? During the silent hours of the night, he was wandering alone through the huge church looking everywhere, when suddenly he saw the doors of the church open, and a wonderful procession with St Martin himself entering this portal of salvation, honourably escorting on the right the Blessed Mary who, after God Himself, is the primary hope of Christians. When she came to the centre of the church, she stood there and began this antiphon, 'I have

---

Conquest' (Oxford B. Litt., 1958), pp. 35, 99, who discusses in detail the work of Dominic as a hagiographer. The story from Tours may have arrived at Evesham through a pilgrim to the Evesham shrines. Dominic did not include it in his collection of the Miracles of the Virgin which was compiled before 1130, for which see J. C. Jennings, 'The origins of the "Elements Series" of the miracles of the Virgin', *Mediaeval and Renaissance Studies*, vi (1968), 84–93, and R. W. Southern, 'The English origin of the "Miracles of the Virgin"', ibid., iv (1958), 176–216, at pp. 178–83.   [3] 4 July.

'Non uidi iustum derelictum nec semen eius querens panem',[1] eamque sola mira cum dulcedine modulando ad finem usque perduxit. Post hec ad sepulchrum sancti Martini cum processione pergit, peractoque propter quod uenerant, respexit sancta Maria clericum ista cernentem, et statim ad sanctum Martinum quasi commota subinfert, 'Quis est hic clericus solus ausus hac ecclesia temere remanere?' Cui sanctus Martinus ad eius genua se prouoluens, 'Mitissima domina, miserere, noster est clericus; iube quod placet.' 'Tui causa', inquit angelorum regina, 'huic ignosco; uerum precipe ut se preparet, quoniam post triduum temporale seculum perdet.' Quod ut dictum, sic factum.

87. Cum igitur his et aliis quampluribus exemplis intelligamus Deum et eius sanctos ecclesias sanctas frequentare, qua instantia bonis operibus et Dei seruitio condecet omnipotentis famulos insudare; cum quanta reuerentia debet Christianus in domo creatoris sui persistere! Dilecta etenim Deo ualde sunt loca ad que ipse cum sanctis dignatur sepius uenire uisitanda. Verum quoniam tempus expostulat, ad miracula patris et protectoris nostri Ecgwini unde paululum digressi sumus, stilum uertamus. Debemus enim tanto operi morem gerere, ut in futuro mercedem a Domino queamus percipere.

fo. 136va 88. | *De quodam sanato et quodam fure de mortis articulo misericorditer liberato*[a]

Reuerentissimo abbate domno Aegelwino Eoueshamensium rectore prudentissimo huius uite modum faciente, uiro quo post sanctum Ecgwinum coram seculo nullus utilior et insignior ipsa in ecclesia extitit, tempore magni Willelmi regis Anglorum et ducis Normannorum, domnus Walterus Eoueshamensem abbatiam regendam suscepit.[2] Is cum esset uir peritie multoque decore et omni facetia condecoratus, nouis rebus, ut fieri solet, animum tradidit. Ecclesiam namque recenti opere delectatus incepit, et antiquum opus quod tum temporis ex pulcherrimis in Anglia extitit, paulatim destruxit. Cerneres, mirum dictu! tam magnum antiquitatis opus in solam criptam insimul congestum; ceterum, deficiente copia operandi, in magna angustia procuratorem operis fore. Difficultate namque rerum

---

[a] *DE ii. 10*

[1] Ps. 36: 25 (Ps. 37: 25).
[2] Walter had been a monk of Cerisy. He was made abbot of Evesham in 1077. William

not seen one just man abandoned, nor his seed seeking bread',[1] and she alone sang this to the very end with wonderful sweetness. After this she made her way to the tomb of St Martin with the procession, and when she had finished what she had come to do, the blessed Mary looked at the clerk who was observing her and immediately addressed St Martin, as though she were angry, 'Who is this clerk who alone has dared to remain boldly behind in this church?' Kneeling before her, St Martin replied to her, 'Most gentle lady, have mercy! He is our clerk. Command what you will.' 'For your sake', said the queen of the angels, 'I pardon him; but tell him to prepare himself, for in three days he will forfeit his life in this world.' And what she said actually happened.

87. Hence, we learn from these and many other examples that God and his saints visit the holy churches, so that it is fitting for the servants of the Almighty to do their utmost to act virtuously and to serve God. How reverent the Christian ought to be in the house of his creator! How beloved of God are those places to which He deigns to come with his saints on frequent visits! But as the time demands it, let us now turn our pen again to the account of the miracles of our father and protector Ecgwine, from which we have digressed for a short while. For our behaviour with respect to a task of this magnitude ought to be such that we may be able in the future to receive a reward from our Lord.

88. *A man is healed, and a thief mercifully escapes the moment of death*
The most revered abbot Æthelwig made it his way of life to be a wise ruler of Evesham, and there was no man, after St Ecgwine, who in worldly matters was more competent or more distinguished in that church than he. In the time of William, the great king of the English and duke of Normandy, he was succeeded by Walter as ruler of Evesham abbey.[2] He was a man of experience, displaying great charm and refinement, who set his mind upon introducing changes, as usually happens [with a new man]. Delighted by recent architecture he began to build a church, and gradually demolished the ancient building, which at that time was one of the most beautiful in England. You could see, marvellous to relate! pieces of this great work of antiquity piled up together in the one crypt. However, as there was a lack of material to work with, the steward responsible for the work was having a difficult time. The place was fraught with troubles, first

of Malmesbury (*De gestis pontificum Anglorum*, p. 137) says that he was a monk of Caen, but Evesham's History is more likely to be accurate; see below, 173.

isdem locus cingebatur, tum petrarum, tum lignorum, tum, quod maxime in humanis necessitatem iuuat, pecuniarum. Qua necessitate compulsus, domnus abbas Walterus, conuocatis ad se binis fratribus loci, honorifice omnibus necessariis sufficienter dispositis, cum reliquiis sancti patris nostri Ecgwini illos per Angliam direxit. Qui precepto spiritualis patris obedientes, cum aliquotiens Angliam peragrassent, tanti patroni meritis adiuti, pecuniam plurimam sue ecclesie adquisierunt, et etiam multorum saluationis ac sanitatis emolumentum per sanctum Dei ab omnipotente concessum nobis ueraci stilo transcribendum tradiderunt. Proferamus ergo in medium pauca de multis, ad declarandum uirum uirtutis.

89. Cum predicti fratres ad Oxinefordiam, fulti reliquiis sancti Ecgwini, letabundi peruenissent, et uerbum Dei, populo spectante, predicassent, quidam uir magne, ut postmodum claruit, fidei, ad feretrum sancti Ecgwini inter ceteros humiliter accessit, ternas orationes coram cunctis deuotissime compleuit, | et per singulas preces manum ad marsupium mittens indeque triplicem oblationem sumens, sancto Dei fideliter optulit. Verum antiquus hostis haud talia passus: quendam ex suis, qui uti 'palea inter triticum'[1] aderat, ardenti cupiditate instigauit, ut fideli uiro in sacris orationibus intento, clandestino dampnum inferret. O mira insania! Omnibus fere ad superna intentis, ipse infelix, ut membrum diaboli, prope uirum approximat, et de eius marsupio denarios quot preualet latenter abstrahit. Dupplicat nefarium opus, et identidem tertio instaurat simile facinus. Set sanctus Ecgwinus non diu distulit damnare furantis manus. Nam cum infelix tertio manum iniecisset marsupio, exaruit continuo, et ueluti clausa retenta est in eodem loculo. Videres furem trepidare, pallescere, ueluti dementem oculos circumiacere, omnimodis mortem suspectam habere. Tandem causam intelligentes qui aderant, furem comprehendere, factum mirari, sanctum Dei sullimi uoce collaudere, ceperunt. Fit plausus circumquaque, iudicant furem interitum ire, ex statuto maturant perficere. Monachi uero reliquias sancti secum deferentes non prius desistunt a precibus

_{fo. 136vb}

[1] Jer. 23: 28.

over stone, then over wood, and then over that essential element in human affairs in times of necessity, money. Impelled by this necessity, Abbot Walter summoned two of the brethren of the place to him, and making sufficient provision for all the necessary arrangements, sent them throughout England with the relics of our father, St Ecgwine. They obeyed the command of their spiritual father, and when they had journeyed up and down England several times, they acquired a good deal of money for their church, aided by the merits of such a patron. They also gave us information, to be written down in a truthful account, of payments made by many in hopes of salvation and good health being granted by the almighty through Ecgwine, the holy man of God. Let us therefore set out a few stories out of many which show a man of virtue.

89. When these brethren, sustained by the relics of St Ecgwine, reached Oxford, they were full of joy, and they preached the word of God to onlookers. One man, of great faith, as later events proved, humbly approached the feretory of St Ecgwine amongst others, and prayed most devoutly three prayers in front of them all. During each one of the prayers he put his hand into his purse and took from it an oblation, doing this three times, faithfully offering it to Ecgwine, the saint of God. But the old enemy [the devil], that inveterate enemy of God, did not permit such things to happen. One of his followers, who was there like 'chaff amongst the wheat',[1] he tempted with a passionate desire to inflict loss upon that faithful man while he was intent upon his holy prayers. What an amazing madness! While almost everybody was intent upon heavenly thoughts, this unfortunate man, as a disciple of the devil, drew near the man, and furtively stole as many pennies as he could from his purse. He then repeated his wicked act, and did the same again a third time. But St Ecgwine did not long delay in inflicting just punishment on the hands of the thief. For when the unfortunate man had dipped his hand a third time into the purse, it instantly withered, and was held fast in the little bag as if imprisoned in it. You could see the thief all of a tremble, growing pale, looking all around him like a madman, and imagining all sorts of death. Eventually all those who were there realized the reason for this, and began to arrest the thief, to marvel at what had happened, and to raise their voices in praise of God's saint. There was applause all around; the judgment made was that the thief should suffer death, and they hastened to carry this out in accordance with the law. However, the monks, carrying with them the relics of the saint, did

quam, adiutorio sancti Ecgwini, instantia precum uincunt iudicum[a] statutum. Sicque in una re duplicem benignitatem per sanctum suum ostendit omnipotens, cum et seruum suum de furto, et furem misericorditer liberauit de mortis articulo.

90. *De quodam puero sanato*[b]

Plerique fidelium uirorum, audientes famam uirtutum sancti Ecgwini, in seipsis sunt experti quam proximus Deo et quam efficax adiutor se in necessitate deuote inuocantibus beatus uir habeatur. Nam quidam diues, Iuo dictus, homo Hugonis de Grantemainilo,[1] cum suus filius grauissima infirmitate decoctus in articulo mortis iamiamque detineretur, ipsemet pro filio suo sanctum Ecgwinum fo. 137[ra] deuote supplicaturus, comperta ipsi | us fama, cum candela et oblatione ad eius monasterium accessit. Indixit tamen suis hominibus antequam a domo qua infirmus iacebat discederet, ut si interim puer moreretur sibi cum festinatione statim nuntiaretur. Veniens igitur ad ecclesiam sancte Dei genitricis Marie sanctique Ecgwini, coram altare accedere, caput humillime in terram declinare, oblationem offerre, Deum supplicetur adorare, sanctumque Ecgwinum cum lacrimis deuote pro filio exorare studuit.

91. Ibique tota die cum sequenti nocte in uigiliis et orationibus ardentem candelam manibus gestando permansit, sepius humi se prosternens et pectus tundens, donec mane facto ad reuisendam prolem eum animus compulisset. Oblata ergo portione candele et licentia a sancto petita,[2] cum spe iter assumptum relegebat. Et ecce unus ex suis in medio itineris occurrens, renuntiauit domino proprium filium sanissimum effectum. Miratur pater; iubet ut quando uel quomodo id sit factum edicat. Cui famulus, 'Cum lutea aurora hodie claresceret et lucem solitam per celi centrum diffunderet, qualitatem facti nobis ignorantibus sanus apparuit uester filius.' Audiens hoc pater, ardentius iter agressus, ad dilectam sobolem peruenit quantotius.

---

[a] iudicium *DE*   [b] *DE ii. 11*

---

[1] Judith Green, *English Sheriffs to 1154* (PRO Handbooks xxiv, 1990), p. 53, suggests that Hugh was sheriff of Leicester before 1093, to be followed by Ivo (de Grandmesnil), his son, some time between 1093 and 1102. The text makes it clear that the Ivo mentioned here is not Hugh's son. On Ivo de Grandmesnil and Ivo, the knight, see D. Greenway, 'Conquest and colonization: the foundation of an alien priory, 1077', in *The Cloister and the World: Essays in Medieval History in honour of Barbara Harvey*, ed. J. Blair and B. Golding (Oxford, 1996), 46–56, at pp. 53–6. The Ivo, knight, mentioned here, is probably the Ivo referred to in this miracle. The story has obvious parallels with the story of the centurion's

not cease from praying until, with St Ecgwine's help and the earnestness of their prayers, they had overruled the decree of the judges. So, at one and the same time the Almighty showed a double kindness through his saint, when he mercifully saved his servant from theft, and the thief from the moment of death.

90. *A boy is healed*

Most men of faith, who heard of the reputation of St Ecgwine's powers, experienced in their own lives how close he was to God, and how real a helper that blessed man was considered to be to those who devoutly invoked him in their times of trouble. There was a certain rich man named Ivo, a man of Hugh de Grandmesnil,[1] whose son had a wasting disease and was on the very point of death. Ivo, having heard of Ecgwine's reputation, went to his monastery with a candle and an offering to pray to him devoutly for his son. However, he had given instructions to his men before he left the house where the invalid lay that, if the boy died in the mean time, they were to make haste and tell him at once. Therefore, when he arrived at the church of the Blessed Mary, mother of God, and of St Ecgwine, he took care to approach the altar, to bow his head to the ground in great humility, to make his offering, to worship God in supplication, and to pray to St Ecgwine with devotion and tears on behalf of his son.

91. He remained there for the whole of the day and the following night, watching and praying, and holding the burning candle in his hands. He often prostrated himself and beat his breast, until morning came and his mind compelled him to visit his son again. He therefore offered up what was left of the candle and, requesting the permission of the saint to depart,[2] he began to set off on the journey he had undertaken in hope. But look what happened, one of his men meeting him in the middle of his journey, gave his master the news that his son had been made well again. The father marvelled. He bade the man to tell him when and how this had happened. The servant replied, 'When today's golden dawn began to grow bright and to spread its accustomed light throughout the vault of heaven, your son appeared before us well, though we did not know the nature of what had happened.' Hearing this the father took to the road more eagerly, and arrived home as fast as he could to his beloved child.

servant in Matt. 8: 5–13 and Luke 7:1–10 (noted by Jennings, 'Prior Dominic' (B.Litt., 1958), pp. 34–5).
[2] This action expressed the hope that the saint would continue praying on his behalf.

92. Accurrens igitur filius obuiam, patrem sanus et incolumis amplectitur. Funduntur cum gaudio lacrime, sancti Ecgwini magnalia predicantur utrobique. Hic*a* pater cum filio, illinc omnis presens familia, maximo tripudio resonabat. Ad ultimum sciscitatur*b* filium pater quomodo ei sanitas adueniret. 'Nouit', inquit filius, 'omnipotens Deus me sanum esse, set qualiter michi sanitas acciderit ignorare.'[1] Tunc iterum omnes benedicebant Dominum et sanctum Ecgwinum, per quem tale miraculum insigniter est propalatum.

93. De quodam in expeditione liberato*c*

Sub isdem diebus duobus monachis cum reliquiis sancti Ecgwini pergentibus, uentum est ad maximam ciuitatem Anglie, fo. 137rb Lundoniam. | In qua cum fecissent uerbum Dei ad populum, adstabat cum ceteris quidam miles Petri de Valonia,[2] Willelmus Spinetus nuncupatus. Qui cum intente semina uerbi Dei in agro cordis[3] sumpsisset, talem ibidem radicem fixit unde postea in necessitate maxima dulcem fructum percepit. Succedenti enim tempore, dum cum domino suo in citeriorem Brittanniam in expeditione aduersus Walenses pugnaturus equitasset,[4] quadam die cum sociis dolose ab hostibus insidiis circumseptus pene morti est addictus. Nempe uniuersis coequitibus suis telis inimicorum obrutis et neci traditis, ipse solus in medio hostium positus, cum nec se posset defendere nec manus inimicorum euadere, in ultimam horam prope deuenerat miserabili certamine. Nam tanta lassitudine ipse et sonipes super quem sedebat opprimebantur, ut nec idem manibus et armis pugnare nec equus eum quoquam ualeret deferre.

94. Reminiscens ergo uirtutum que de sancto Ecgwino apud Lundoniam audierat, ex intimo pectore ingemiscens: 'O Domine', inquit, 'qui semper in tribulatione te inuocantibus[5] presto es, si uera constant que de sancto Ecgwino episcopo audiui, iam nunc per eius merita a presenti periculo mortis me libera.' Continuo, oratione finita, aduenit repente fortitudo tanta, ut et ipse uirtutem insolitam et equus cui presidebat uelocitatem perciperet permaximam, statimque per sancti uiri merita ab inimicis mirabiliter ereptus, Deo et sancto Ecgwino

---

a hinc *DE*   *b* stipulatur *DE*   *c* *DE ii. 12*

---

[1] Cf. John 9: 20–25.
[2] Peter de Valognes was sheriff of Essex and sheriff of Hertfordshire in 1086 and probably earlier; see Green, *Sheriffs*, pp. 39, 47.
[3] Cf. Mark 4: 15.

92. His son, running to meet him, embraced his father, fit and sound in body. They wept tears of joy, and both of them extolled the great miracles of St Ecgwine. The house resounded with great jubilation, here with the father and the son, there with the whole family present. Eventually the father asks his son how it was that his health returned. The son replied, 'Almighty God knows that I am healed, but I do not know how health came to me.'[1] Then again they all blessed the Lord and St Ecgwine, through whom such a miracle was wonderfully revealed.

93. *A soldier is healed during a campaign*
At about the same time two monks, who were travelling with the relics of St Ecgwine, came to London, the largest city of England. When they had preached the word of God to the people there, a knight of Peter de Valognes,[2] named William Thorn, was standing listening with others. He eagerly received 'the seeds of the word of God in the soil of his heart',[3] and these took so firm a root there that he later reaped a rich harvest in a time of great need. For subsequently, when he had gone on an expedition into the Welsh Marches to fight the Welsh,[4] he was one day cunningly ambushed by the enemy along with his comrades, and barely escaped being killed. Indeed every one of his fellow knights was struck by the enemy's weapons and slain, while he himself, being surrounded all alone by the enemy, and unable to defend himself or to escape from their attack, was facing almost certain death in that lamentable combat. For he and the horse which he was riding were so overcome with fatigue, that neither he himself had the strength to fight with his hands or his weapons, nor the horse to carry him anywhere.

94. However, remembering the power of St Ecgwine, of which he had heard in London, and groaning in the depths of his heart, he cried, 'O Lord, who are ever at hand "to help those who call upon you in trouble",[5] if what I have heard in London about St Ecgwine the bishop is really true, even now rescue me by his merits from the present peril of death.' The instant he finished praying such courage suddenly came upon him, that he himself received extraordinary strength, and the horse he was controlling amazing speed. At once, by the merits of that holy man, he was miraculously snatched from his foes, and thereafter he remained a devout servant of God and St

---

[4] The campaign against the Welsh presumably took place under the Conqueror and dates this before his death in 1087.   [5] Cf. Ps. 80: 8 (81: 7); 117: 5 (118: 5).

exinde mansit deuotus. Veniensque postmodum ad sancti uiri monasterium, promissum reddit*ᵃ* uotum, offerens super altare oblationem et deuotam sancto fundens ex imo affectu precem. Conuocans
autem priorem loci, a principio enuntiat fidem uerbi, sicut ex ordine
habetur comprehensum in superiori.

95. *Qualiter feretrum sancti Ecgwini in flumine submersum, siccum
permanserit; et qualiter seruiens cum brachio eiusdem in eodem flumine
submersus euaserit*ᵇ

Res admonet ut quoddam mirum per sanctum Ecgwinum coram
fo. 137ᵛᵃ multis insinuatum | lectori offeramus legendum. Reliquie sancti uiri
quocumque deportabantur, maximo honore cingebantur, summaque
diligentia custodiebantur. Dum igitur quadam die custodes sanc-
tarum reliquiarum ad flumen quod Trenta ab accolis*ᶜ* uocitatur
peruenissent, et rapidam ipsam aquam transmeare necessarium
duxissent, monachus quidam ex ipsis nomine Heremannus,[1] timens
fluminis immanitatem et tremendam precipitationem maximeque pro
sanctis reliquiis sollicitus, ipsemet ante se super equum scrinium
sancti Ecgwini deportare studuit, ut si quid periculi accidisset meritis
sancti uiri protegeretur. Cuidam uero ministrorum precepit ut
brachium sancti Ecgwini[2] de collo suspensum maxima cum reuerentia
conseruaret. Post hec, ductore precedente, primum monachus cum
reliquiis sancti, postmodum ceteri quaquauersum sequebantur.
Verum*ᵈ* monachus, Dei prouidentia, a recto uado paulatim aberrans
et in profundum fluminis cum magno timore equitans, circumfusio-
nem aque ad pectora usque patiebatur. Ea ad enucleationem uirtutum
sancti Ecgwini prouenere, ut quanti meriti apud Deum sit sanctus
facillime possis peruidere. Nam cum prefatus monachus flumen (ut
diximus) transmeasset, in tantum sanctum suum clarificauit omnipotens, ut nec in theca scrinii nec in aliquo uestimento monachi una
saltem gutta aque quiret reperiri, set ueluti per fluctuantes segetes seu
siluas in autumnali tempore equitatum isset, ita a natura elementalis
aque discriminatus appareret.

ᵃ reddidit *DE*   *ᵇ* *DE ii. 13*   *ᶜ* incolis *DE*   *ᵈ* Vere *DE*

---

[1] A Lotharingian name, possibly illustrating Evesham's close ties with the continent in
the 11th cent. On the contacts see V. Ortenberg, *The English Church and the Continent in
the tenth and eleventh centuries* (Oxford, 1992), pp. 57–9, and 106.

[2] For a fine example of an early 12th-cent. arm-reliquary, see plate 10 and p. 16 of R. Ó
Floinn, *Irish Shrines and Reliquaries of the Middle Ages* (National Museum of Ireland,

Ecgwine. He came later to the monastery of that holy man and, fulfilling a vow that he had made, he placed an offering upon the altar and with deep feeling uttered a prayer of devotion to the saint. He then summoned the prior of the monastery, and from that moment proclaimed his trust in the word of God, as has been recounted in detail above.

95. *The feretory of St Ecgwine sinks in a river, but remains dry; a servant sinks in the same river with an arm of the saint, and escapes*

The subject urges us to bring to the reader's attention a particular miracle which occurred in the presence of many people. Wherever the relics of the holy man were carried they were encompassed with great honour, and guarded with the greatest diligence. One day, therefore, when the guardians of the holy relics arrived at a river called the Trent by those living near it, and considered that it was necessary to cross its fast-flowing water, one of them, a monk named Heremann,[1] was alarmed at the height of the river and its frightening speed of flow, and especially anxious about the holy relics. He therefore determined himself to carry the reliquary in front of him on horseback, so that if any danger occurred he would be protected by the merits of St Ecgwine. He told one of the attendants to hang the arm of St Ecgwine[2] from his neck, and to keep it safe with the greatest of reverence. After this, with the guide in front, the monk went first with the relics of the saint, and after him the rest followed as and when they could. The monk, however, by the providence of God, strayed gradually from the straight route over the shallows, and with great fear rode his horse into the deep water, thus causing the swirling water to flow up to his breast. This had happened so that the power of St Ecgwine might be revealed, and that you might more readily perceive how important the saint is to God. For when the monk crossed the river, as we have said, the Almighty raised his saint's fame to such heights, that not a single drop of water could be found either in the inside of the reliquary or in any of the monk's clothing: it was as though he had gone riding through the waving cornfields or the woods in autumn, and so that it appeared to be shunned by the nature of the watery element.

1994); and for a 13th-cent. example, *Liturgical Objects in the Walters Art Galley* (Baltimore, 1967), plate 25. By the time of Dominic's writing, St Ecgwine's arm may have been encased in a metal reliquary with a hollowed out wooden core to take the arm bone, such as that of St Lachtin.

96. Quis astantium et tam mira uidentium secundum posse non laudabit*ª* Dominum? Quis tam insigne prodigium minus predicabile estimauerit quam si super aquas ierit? Vtrunque etenim contra legem nature fieri certum est. Quis scientium tam clarum miraculum quoad uixit non aliis in opportunitate predicare studuit? Veruntamen omnipotens non in hoc solummodo facto mo | dum declarandorum meritorum sancti uiri statuit, set statim in eodem loco haud multum dissimile miraculum per dilectum suum sanctum Ecgwinum manifestauit.

fo. 137ᵛᵇ

97. Minister enim, cui brachium sancti Ecgwini superius commendatum diximus, dum cum eodem brachio non recto tramite uadum attemptaret, in gurgitem incidit permaximum, in quo pridie nauis una demersa fuerat. Quod cum in littore astantes cernerent pallescere, trepidare, cum ingenti tumultu et dolore ad Dominum exclamare, sanctumque Ecgwinum cum lacrimis inuocare ceperunt. Monachi uero tum pro famuli periculo, tum pro brachio sui protectoris in maxima angustia extitere: omnes in commune nomen sancti Ecgwini cum clamore inuocauere. Cum ergo diu multumque sub aquarum mole uir prelibatus latuisset, omnesque qui aderant hunc iam necatum existimarent, tandem super aquas uiuus apparuit, et tertio immersus tertioque super liquidum elementum uisus, demum per uirtutem sancti ad terram extraitur fessus, ubi tam insigne miraculum cunctis astantibus est ostensum, ut nec in theca brachii sancti Ecgwini nec in uexillo quod infra positum seruabatur uel una solummodo aque gutta apparuerit, neque quicquam in eo madidum repertum fuerit. Opstupuere uniuersi; pariter collaudant magnalia sancti Ecgwini; eiusque ministrum apprehendentes et ad domum deducentes leti prope eum permanent, curam impendentes. Qui cum plurimum aque ab ore dimisisset, postera die sanus et incolumis ceptum iter accelerat cum ceteris.

98. *De cereis sine adiutorio hominis accensis*ᵇ

Alio tempore dum reliquie sancti Ecgwini a monasterio sancti Pancratii deferrentur,[1] processione precedente cum cruce et ardentibus cereis, repente ui uentorum cerei extincti sunt. Set cum uno pene

---

ª laudauit *DE*   ᵇ *DE ii. 14*

---

[1] St Pancras, Lewes, a Cluniac house, was founded in 1077 by William de Warenne and his wife.

96. Who among the bystanders, seeing such marvellous events, will not give as much praise to God as they can? Who could think so amazing a miracle as being less estimable than if he had ridden above the waves? For there is no doubt that each is an event contrary to the laws of nature. Who amongst those who know of so extraordinary a miracle has not made it his aim, while he is alive, to tell others about it when the opportunity occurs? Yet the Almighty decided that the manner of declaring the merits of this holy man should not rest with this miracle alone, but immediately displayed another very similar miracle through his beloved St Ecgwine.

97. The attendant we mentioned above, to whom the arm of St Ecgwine had been entrusted, in attempting to cross the shallow water with the arm by the wrong course, fell into very deep water, where the previous day a ship had sunk. When those standing on the shore saw this, their faces turned pale and their bodies trembled, they began to cry aloud with great clamour and sorrow to the Lord, and to call upon St Ecgwine tearfully. The monks were in great distress both over the danger to the servant and over the arm of their protector, and all of them as one called loudly upon the name of St Ecgwine. When the man, therefore, had been a very long time under the deep water, and all who were there thought he had now been drowned, he at last appeared above the water alive. He sank three times, but appeared on the surface of the river again three times, and at last through the goodness of the saint was dragged to the bank exhausted. It was here that the extraordinary miracle was revealed to all the bystanders: namely, that not a single drop of water was to be seen either in the bag carrying the arm of St Ecgwine, or on the banner which had been put into it to keep it safe, and no dampness was found at all in it. Everybody was amazed, and together they praised the great deeds of St Ecgwine; and leading the servant by the hand, and joyfully escorting him back home, they stayed near him, and looked after him. When he had expelled most of the water from his mouth, he was well the following day, and set off speedily with the others on the journey they had begun.

98. *Candles are lit without human assistance*
At another time when the relics of St Ecgwine were being carried from the monastery of St Pancras [Lewes],[1] and a procession was making its way with cross and burning candles, the candles were suddenly extinguished by a gust of wind. However, when they had

miliario processissent, rursus cerei diuinitus accensi, ardentes cunctis mirantibus uisuntur.

99. De muliere cuius infans ex utero rupto fuerat extractus[a]

fo. 138[ra] Preterea multi diuersarum infirmita|tum morbo detenti, cum de aqua benedicta unde brachium sancti Ecgwini lotum fuerat hausissent, celerem sanitatis effectum maturius percepere. Quedam etenim mulier cuius infans infra materna uiscera morti addictus fuerat, nec, sicut plerisque, abortiuus exierat, uerum in materno utero computruerat. Dum de aqua unde sancti Ecgwini brachium erat lotum cum spe salutis sumpsisset, statim in sequenti nocte uigilando cum cognatis et amicis ante feretrum sancti, dirupta est aluus illius, uenienteque aurifabro cum forcipe[1] et infantilia ossa [b]iam fere medio anno putrescentia[b] a maternis uisceribus extrahente. Que prius iugi dolore et maximo fetore torquebatur postmodum sanitati reddita est.

100. De altera muliere sanata[c]

Altera item mulier, cuius brachium miserrime fuerat contractum, per beatum Ecgwinum coram multis sanata est.

101. De uirtute sancti Ecgwini pacificandi homines[d]

Omnibus autem pie intuentibus liquet sanctum Dei Ecgwinum filium pacis extitisse, cuius reliquiis tam miram Dominus gratiam conferre dignatus fuerit ut quantacumque quilibet discordie peste discissi fuissent, presentibus eius reliquiis mox in pacis gremio filiis pacis consensissent. Nam cum quidam ita nece karorum indurati essent ut, neque auctoritate regali seu episcopali uel cuiuslibet dignitatis deuicti, paci assensum preberent, aduenientibus in id locorum sancti Ecgwini reliquiis, confestim ianua pacis[2] in commune omnibus patefacta est. Omnes presentes in hoc facto obstupescere, nonnulli etiam pre gaudio flere cepere.

---

[a] DE ii. 15   [b-b] om. DE   [c] DE ii. 16   [d] DE ii. 17

[1] The goldsmith was called because his tools included forceps, or pincers, used for intricate work; see J. Cherry, Goldsmiths (London, 1992), p. 27, and Theophilus, The Various Arts: De diversis artibus , ed. and trans. C. R. Dodwell (OMT, 1986), p. 68.

[2] A possible reference to John 10: 1–2.

processed for almost a mile, the candles were lit again by divine power, and to everyone's amazement were seen burning.

99. *A woman's baby is delivered from her burst womb*

Besides this there were many who were disabled by different kinds of illness, but when they had drunk from the blessed water in which the arm of St Ecgwine had been washed, they soon began to feel the swift effect of good health again. There was a certain woman whose baby was doomed to death in its mother's womb, but had not, as in the case of many others, been aborted, and so it had begun to decay in the mother's womb. However, after the mother had drunk from the water in which St Ecgwine's arm had been washed, in the hope of being healed, the following night, when she was praying with relatives and friends before the shrine of the saint, her belly burst, and a goldsmith arrived with forceps[1] to remove from the mother's womb the baby's bones, which had now been decaying for almost six months, from the mother's abdomen. So the woman who before this had been tormented by perpetual pain and the greatest stench, was afterwards restored to health.

100. *Another woman is healed*

Another woman, whose arm had been pitifully deformed, was also healed through the blessed Ecgwine in the presence of many people.

101. *The power of St Ecgwine to bring men peace*

It is obvious to everyone who contemplates the matter piously, that God's saint Ecgwine was a son of peace, through whose relics the Lord deigned to bestow such wonderful grace that any who had been torn apart by the bane of strife, however great it might be, were soon in the embrace of peace, and one with the sons of peace, when the relics of the saint were at hand to help. For when there were any who had been so hardened by the death of those they loved, that though they could not be subdued by royal or episcopal authority or by that of any person of position, they would show their willingness to be peaceful, if the relics of St Ecgwine arrived in the place where they were staying, and the door of peace[2] was immediately opened to everyone alike. All who witnessed this fact were amazed, and some even began to weep for joy.

102. De eodem[a]

Rursus in ciuitate Wintonia uir quidam, acerbitate interfecti filii prope in amentiam uersus, ita indeuincibilis permanserat, ut nulla precum instantia multo temporis ad pacis concordiam potuerit inflecti. Ventum est ad illam ciuitatem cum reliquiis sancti Ecgwini, fo. 138rb et finito | sermone pro quo uenerant, admonentur sanctarum reliquiarum custodes quatinus paci studerent. Cumque sermo pacis exortus esset, et preces ad predictum uirum pro amore sancti inflectendum subiuncte fuissent, non ualens ille ulterius presentiam reliquiarum et uim uerborum sufferre, coram cunctis fugam iniit. Cerneres illum a multis insequi, nec a quoquam posse comprehendi. Mox uirtute sancti Ecgwini spontanee reductus, ante sanctas reliquias corruit, sine mora omnia indulgens firmissima pace concessa. Quo facto, quam multorum ora in Dei laudibus relaxata sunt!

103. De muliere a graui infirmitate sanata[b]

Mulier quedam in Dorobreui triennio grauissima infirmitate detenta est. Hec cum cognouisset reliquias sancti Ecgwini illuc aduentasse, misit per manus nuntiorum suam oblationem ad feretrum, ampliora promittens si Deus per sancti uiri merita sibi optate sanitatis concederet gaudia. Sequenti uero die ipsa mulier leta et incolumis propriis manibus ad sanctum Ecgwinum suam oblationem detulit, collaudans Dominum et eius fidelem seruum sanctum Ecgwinum.

104. De homine uincto, soluto et liberato a morte[c]

Solennis dies sancti Ecgwini erat in proximo cum quidam eius minister comprehensus in latrocinio morti adiudicatus est. Impositus ergo miser ille super uile iumentum, uinctis manibus post tergum, deducebatur iuxta monasterium sancti Ecgwini ad locum suo capiti periculosum. Qui recordatus[d] futuri diei magnam solennitatem et sancti Ecgwini miram benignitatem, de iumento cui insidebat sponte cecidit, et ad monasterium sancti fugiendo peruenit. Inueniensque hostium apertum statim ingreditur, et coram altare sancti Ecgwini adiutorium postulans prosternitur. Mirum dictu! continuo manice dissolute liberas manus hominis reddidere. fo. 138va Ita per merita sancti Ecgwini et a | ligamine manuum et ab

---

[a] DE ii. 18   [b] DE ii. 19   [c] DE ii. 20   [d] recordans DE

102. *A similar miracle*

Again, in the city of Winchester [Hants] there was a man who almost went mad with anger when his son was killed. He had remained so impossible to subdue, that for a long time he could not be influenced by any earnestness in prayer to calm down and be at peace. When men arrived in that city with the relics of St Ecgwine, and after the discussion for which they had come there was over, the guardians of the holy relics were admonished to concentrate their minds on achieving peace. Talk of peace began, and prayers were added to influence the above-mentioned man to a love for the saint. Unable to endure any longer the presence of the relics or the force of the sermon, he took to flight in the presence of them all. You could have seen him being pursued by many people, but unable to be apprehended by anyone. But through the power of St Ecgwine he was soon escorted back of his own accord, and he fell prostrate before the holy relics. In no time he accepted everything, and was granted an assured peace. Whereupon the lips of many were opened in praise of God.

103. *A woman is healed of a serious illness*

A woman of Rochester [Kent] had been disabled by a very serious illness for three years. When she learned that the relics of St Ecgwine had arrived in that city, she sent by the hands of messengers her offering to the reliquary, promising larger gifts if God would grant her through the merits of St Ecgwine the joys of the good health she longed for. On the following day the woman, now healed, joyously brought her offering in her own hands to St Ecgwine, praising the Lord and his faithful servant St Ecgwine.

104. *A man is bound, freed, and rescued from death*

It was soon a sad day for St Ecgwine when one of his servants was caught stealing and sentenced to death. The wretched man was put on a decrepit nag, his hands bound behind his back, and brought near the monastery of St Ecgwine to a place perilous to his life. Aware of the great solemnity of that day to come, and the wonderful kindliness of St Ecgwine, he fell of his own free will off the nag on which he was sitting, and taking to flight, came to the monastery of the saint. Finding the entrance open he immediately entered, and falling before the altar of St Ecgwine, implored his help. Wonderful to relate! the manacles immediately loosened and the man's hands were freed. So it was that by the merits of St Ecgwine he was freed from the bonds on

insectatione persequentium inimicorum liberatus, sancto amodo proinde gratias agens permansit.

105. *De illeso cadente ab ecclesia Eweshamie*[a]

Nec pretereundum remur quod multis oppido mirum uisum est, neminem in destructione monasterii sancti Ecgwini de uita periclitatum. Quadam namque uice cum tigna presbiterii studuissent deicere, astabat quidam operarius in media domo super trabes, molitus quomodo ad tigna deicienda ualeret insistere. Cum repente omnia insimul tigna ruinam maximo fragore dedere et pariter ruentia[b] mortem uicinam in medio trabium astanti intentauere. Quid faceret miser, quo se uerteret, subita ruina interceptus ignorabat. Tempus consilii aberat, proiciens ergo se inter binas trabes nequaquam interlaqueatas, ipsasque hinc et illinc geminis manibus apprehendens, superueniens pondus ita illesus sustinuit. Tunc qui astaret potuisset[c] uidere omnes presentes ueluti exangues effectos trepidare, pre timore uociferari, una sanctum Ecgwinum ab omnibus inuocari. Compresso igitur tanto clamore, prefatus uir mirabili sinuamine ad superiora reductus, exurgit incolumis et letus, Dominum collaudans et sanctum Ecgwinum humillimis uocibus cunctique id cognoscentes gratias retulerunt pro diuinis mirabilibus.

106. *De quodam raptore percusso infirmitate, et, pecunia restituta, sanato*[d]

Pandendum uero cunctis pie legentibus uidetur mitissimum Dei seruum sanctum Ecgwinum non solum subiectis et eius tutelam humiliter expetentibus adiutorem benignissimum, uerum enimuero etiam eum eique commissa contempnentibus uindicem durissimum. In multis enim necessitatibus maximis et diuersis semper presto fuit suis seruis se inuocantibus. Sepe etiam in grauissimis placitis expetitus, mirum adiutorium prebuit exposcentibus. Plerumque fo. 138vb uic|toriam affuturam per euidentissimas uisiones multifariam tremebundis insinuauit. Quas ob nimiam copiam omittentes, fastidioso lectori breuitati studentes morem gerimus.

---

[a] *DE ii. 21*   [b] *corr. Macray*; ruentes *R, DE*   [c] potis esset *DE*   [d] *DE ii. 22*

his hands, and from the pursuit of his enemies who were chasing him. From that moment he continued to give thanks to the saint.

105. *A man is hurt falling from the church of Evesham*
We consider that we should not overlook relating a miracle that seemed to many absolutely amazing, when nobody's life was endangered during the demolition of St Ecgwine's monastery. It was on a particular occasion, when the monks had set their minds on removing the timbers of the presbytery, one of the workmen was standing in the centre of the building above the beams, working out how he could take up a position to remove the timbers, when suddenly all the timbers came down at the same time with an enormous crash, and as they fell together, they threatened imminent death to the man standing amidst the timbers. Caught by the sudden fall, the poor man did not know what he was to do, or where to turn. There was no time to think about it, and so hurling himself between two beams which were in no way connected, and clutching them with both hands, he thus held up the weight as it fell unharmed. Then anyone standing there could have seen that everybody present was in a state of agitation, drained as it were of their blood, and calling out in fear, while St Ecgwine was invoked by them all as one. But then all the great clamour was silenced as the man by amazing contortions was brought up again, and emerged joyfully safe and sound, praising God and St Ecgwine in words of great humility. When everybody learned what had happened they rendered thanks for divine miracles.

106. *A robber is struck by illness, and after returning the money, is healed*
It seems right to us to reveal to all devout readers that St Ecgwine, that most merciful servant of God, was not only the kindest of helpers to his servants and to those who humbly sought his protection, but was also a most severe punisher of those who scorned the powers entrusted to him. In their many times of great and varied need, he was always ready to help his servants who called upon him. But often he received requests also on most important occasions, and provided wonderful help to those requesting it. He generally conveyed information of many kinds of future victory by clear visions to those who were of a fearful nature. Although we are omitting some of the accounts of these visions, because of their large number, we will nevertheless gratify the reader who is hard to please with a brief account.

107. Id autem cunctis tam sanctum uirum cognoscentibus liquet, raro quempiam eum impune contempsisse, uel iniuriam sibi suisque sine uindicta irrogasse. Vnde licet multimoda et magnifica suppetant exempla in mediocribus et inspectandis etiam personis, unum tamen ex compluribus, magis summatim tangentes quam narrantes, causa breuitatis, subnexuimus.

108. Quidam auaritia et tipo superbie distentus, improbitate magis quam ui, aliquot nummos a ministris sancti Ecgwini haud equa lance adquisiuit. Quamobrem sanctus uir iniuria suorum commotus, per uisionem hominem alloquitur, iubens ut quod iniuste de se adquisierat reportaret. Minatur insuper dampnum grauissimum, *ni optemperatum ierit,* affuturum. Sed cum ille paululum*b* credulus minime obsecundaret, de equo cadens detrimentum corporis incurrit. Admonetur iterum; et nec sic obaudiens simili damno grauius percellitur. Verum sanctus Ecgwinus non prius destitit quod suum erat tertio expetere, donec predictus uir, grauissima infirmitate decoctus, uellet nollet, per quendam reuerendum archidiaconum denarios quos iniuste adquisierat ad altare sancti Ecgwini remitteret. Venit ergo archidiaconus ad monasterium sancti Ecgwini, conuocans ad se priorem loci cum ceteris fratribus, coram altare rem gestam ex ordine pandit. Nec mora indulgent fratres misericordiam poscenti, nummi offeruntur, reus absoluitur, infirmus a sancto Dei diuinitus curatur.

109. *De uirtute sancti Ecgwini circa incendia extinguenda*c

fo. 139ra Inter cetera que sanctus ac dilectus Dei Ecgwinus multa et mi | ra seruis suis dignatus est intimare, omnem facundiam ea uidentur excellere que in igneo elemento ualde admiranda nouimus eum misericorditer egisse. Hec licet tam multa sint ut uix quisquam studiosorum omnia comprehendere sufficiat, ad declaranda tamen cetera tria in medium breuiter proferamus consideranda. Apud monasterium sancti Ecgwini predium quoddam ditissimarum domorum a domino Aelfwardo episcopo et abbate fuerat edificatum,[1] quod maximo honori deditum a multis diuitibus frequentabatur per

---

a-a in . . . iri *DE* (*H*)   *b* paulum *DE* (*H*)   *c DE ii. 23*

---

[1] This estate appears to have been like the sort of 'urban manor' identified, for example, at Winchester and at Oxford in the 10th to 11th cent.; see J. Blair, *Anglo-Saxon Oxfordshire* (Stroud, 1994), pp. 151–2. For the development of the town of Evesham, a classic monastic borough, from the mid-11th cent., see R. H. Hilton, 'The small town and urbanisation—

107. It is clear to all who know this holy man that seldom did anyone scorn him with impunity or inflict injury upon him or his servants without being punished. Hence, although there are many kinds of wonderful miracles to choose from that relate to both ordinary and distinguished persons, for the sake of brevity we have included just one of many, more summarizing than narrating.

108. It is about a man who was very greedy and puffed up with a sort of pride, who had, dishonestly rather than violently, gained possession of several coins from servants of St Ecgwine by devious means. Because of this the holy man was angered by this wrong done to his servants, and addressed the man through a vision, telling him to take back what he had wrongfully gained from them. He further threatened him that he would be severely harmed if he did not obey. When the man, hardly believing him, did not in the least obey him, he fell off his horse and suffered an injury to his body. He was warned a second time, and similarly disobeyed, so he was stricken with a similar but more severe injury this time. St Ecgwine did not cease yet a third time to seek what was his own, until the man, softened by his severe disability, whether he wished it or not, sent back to the altar of St Ecgwine, by a revered archdeacon, the pennies which he had wrongfully acquired. The archdeacon came to St Ecgwine's monastery, and summoning the prior of the place with the other brethren, revealed in detail before the altar what had happened. Without delay the brethren granted forgiveness to the man at his request, the coins were offered up, the accused absolved, and the sick man was divinely healed by God's saint.

109. *The power of St Ecgwine to extinguish fire*
Amongst the many other miracles which St Ecgwine, beloved of God, deigned to make known to his servants, those really amazing deeds in the element of fire, which we know he mercifully performed, seem beyond our eloquence to describe. Although these are so many that scarcely any of his devotees has the ability to retain them all in his memory, let us briefly bring forward for consideration three of them to exemplify the rest. Near the monastery of St Ecgwine an estate of very costly houses had been built by Ælfweard, bishop and abbot.[1] This was greatly honoured and visited by many wealthy people

Evesham in the Middle Ages', *Midland History*, vii (1982), 1–8, and T. R. Slater, 'Medieval town-founding on the estates of the Benedictine Order in England', in *Power, Profit and Urban Land*, ed. F.-E. Eliassen and G. A. Ersland (Aldershot, 1996), pp. 70–92.

annum. Hoc, peccatis exigentibus, igne inuasum, miserabile cunctis uidentibus prestabat spectaculum. Commoti qui aderant uniuersi ad patrocinium currunt sancti Ecgwini, asportant eius feretrum ad locum periculi, et per medium unius domus ad quam maxime ignis uergebat deferentes reliquias sancti, rei exitum prestolantur, de uirtute sancti pontificis confisi. Mira dicturus sum! Statim ut ad illam domum ignis peruenit, unam medietatem consumpsit, aliam dimisit; nec ultra ausus est ignis suum protelare incendium quam quo sancti Ecgwini deportatum fuerat feretrum.[1] Sic sanctus pontifex et suam ecclesiam liberauit et preclarum miraculum ostendit, et uoces Deum confitentium in sullimi extulit. Huiusmodi uero miraculum bis demonstratum est per sanctum Dei Ecgwinum.

110. De eodem[a]

Nec minus illud erat quod in eodem elemento per sanctum Ecgwinum operatus est Christus. Circa ecclesiam sancti uiri quedam altissima et maxima sepes de spinis in uicino fuerat constructa,[2] quam cum ignis ex uicinis domibus emissus inuasisset, maximum timorem seruis sancti pontificis incussit. Timebant enim omnes ne per uicinam sepem monasterium sancti Ecgwini ab igne corriperetur. Concurrunt igitur ad ecclesiam, arripiunt scrinium sancti, deferunt quantotius ad ignem, ac super sepem prope incendium ponentes, fo. 139rb ta | lia efferunt uociferantes, 'Domine sancte pater Ecgwine, si uis, te ipsum ab incendio defende.' Vix emissum est uerbum cum, ecce! tantum crepitum reddidit incendium quasi super ignem aquam infunderent utres centum. Mox uiribus exemptis, insimul totum consopitum est incendium. Quis cernentium in tam mirabili facto non laudauit Dominum? Omnibus etenim est patefactum multum apud superos posse beatum Dei confessorem Ecgwinum.

111. De ecclesia[b]

Monasterium[c] sancti patris nostri Ecgwini sepe, ut retulerunt qui uiderant, incendio consumptum foret, nisi hoc uirtus sancti pontificis

---

[a] DE ii. 24   [b] De ecclesie R. DE ii. 25   [c] Nonasterium for Monasterium R

[1] Cf. a miracle recorded in Bede, HE iii. 17 (pp. 204–5), where a buttress, against which Aidan had been leaning when he died, survived during a fire, while all around burned down.
[2] D. C. Cox, 'The building, destruction, and excavation of Evesham abbey: a documentary history', Transactions of the Worcestershire Archaeological Society, 3rd ser. xii (Worcester, 1990), 123–46, at pp. 132–3, notes the similarity of the story of the hedge

throughout the year. However, because of men's sins, the estate was invaded by fire and provided a miserable sight to all those who saw it. All who were there were alarmed, and hastily sought the protection of St Ecgwine. They carried his reliquary to the place of danger, and bringing the relics of the saint through the middle of one house to which the fire was making its way, awaited the outcome, trusting in the power of the holy bishop Ecgwine. What a wonderful story I am about to relate! Immediately on reaching that house, the fire consumed half of it and left the other half, and it did not dare extend its flames beyond the place to which St Ecgwine's reliquary had been carried.[1] Thus the holy bishop both rescued his church and displayed a significant miracle, and raised to the heavens the voices of those who trusted in God. A miracle of this sort was twice demonstrated by God's saint, Ecgwine.

110. *A similar miracle*
No less wonderful was that miracle which Christ performed in the same element of fire through St Ecgwine. Around the church of the holy man at no great distance a very high and extensive thorn hedge had been grown.[2] When the fire from the nearby houses spread it attacked this hedge and struck great fear into the servants of the holy bishop. They were all afraid that St Ecgwine's monastery would catch fire from the hedge. They therefore hurried together to the church, seized the reliquary of the saint, and took it as quickly as they could to the fire and, placing it upon the hedge near the fire, they uttered words such as these, crying, 'O lord and holy father Ecgwine, if it is your will, defend yourself from the fire.' Scarcely had these words been uttered when, indeed, the fire made a loud crackling noise, as if they were pouring water from a hundred buckets upon the flames. Soon, its strength spent, the whole fire died down at once. Who of those who saw this did not praise the Lord for so wonderful a deed? It was made manifest to all, that God's blessed confessor, Ecgwine, had great power in heaven.

111. *The church*
The monastery of our holy father Ecgwine, as those who witnessed it have reported, would often have been destroyed by fire, had not the

with that told in Stephen of Ripon's Life of Bishop Wilfrid (*The Life of Bishop Wilfrid by Eddius Stephanus*, ed. B. Colgrave (Cambridge, 1927), pp. 146–7), and suggests that Dominic may have taken it from there.

pia defensione protegeret. Allatis namque ad locum incendii sancti uiri reliquiis, plerumque uis uentorum aliorsum retorquebatur, nonnumquam uero ipsum incendium consopiebatur. Nam cum quodam tempore maximo prope monasterium flagrante incendio, sancti Ecgwini scrinium per angustissimum tramitem inter duas domos a fratribus deferretur, continuo ut in id locorum est uentum, omne pariter incendium cessauit consopitum. Nec plus erat spatii quo sanctus fuerat delatus quam longitudo pedis unius. Remansit ergo una domus ab igne illesa, alia uero periit consumpta. Hinc itaque rogemus Dominum uirtutum, ut per tantum patronum Ecgwinum soluat uincula peccatorum nostrorum, et pascat nos gratia beneficiorum suorum, et conuertat aut excidat capita aduersariorum, et in die belli et in ruina mundi obumbret nos scuto bone uoluntatis et uelamento*a* alarum suarum, et liberet ab igne uastationum et a flamma uitiorum et a suppliciis eternorum incendiorum, perducatque nos ad huius patris nostri consortium, cum quo ipsum auctorem omnium laudemus in secula seculorum. Amen.[1]

---

a inuelamento *DE* (*H*)

holy bishop defended it by his power and devoted protection. For when the relics of the holy man had been brought to the place of the fire, the force of the winds was generally turned to some other direction, and sometimes the very fire died down. On one occasion when there was a large fire burning near the monastery, the reliquary of St Ecgwine was carried along a very narrow path by the brethren between two houses, and immediately on its arrival at that place, it caused the whole fire everywhere to die down. The width of the passage down which the saint was carried was no more than a foot. One house had been unharmed by the fire, the other was completely destroyed. Hence, therefore, let us ask the Lord of all goodness to free us through our great patron Ecgwine from the bonds of our sins, and nourish us with the grace of his benefits; to convert or destroy the lives of his enemies, and in the day of war and the downfall of our world to protect us with the shield of his good will beneath the shelter of his wings; to rescue us from the fire of destruction, from the flames of vice, and from the punishment of the eternal fires; and to lead us into the fellowship of this our father, Ecgwine, with whom we may praise Him, the creator of all, for ever and ever. Amen.[1]

---

[1] A common ending to a collect.

⟨LIBER TERCIVS⟩

PARTICVLA PRIMA

112. *Incipit prologus libri tercii*

Ne bonorum et malorum post mortem apud homines eadem sit conditio, bonorum uidelicet egregiis actibus cum factoribus suis commorientibus et malorum prauis operibus cum actoribus suis consepultis, ueteres Grai scripti remedium obiecere prudenter, et scriptores suos, quos dixere historiographos, ad conscribendas rerum historias studiosius exciuerunt, ut uocis uiue silentium uox scripta suppleret. Romani uero Grecorum emuli perpetuande uirtutis causa non solum stili assumpserunt offitium set et statuas adiecerunt, et sic, tam ueteres representando quam prouocando posteros, uirtutis amorem, tum per oculos tum per aures, ad interiora multipliciter demissum, imitantium mentibus firmius impresserunt. Porro patrum gesta sanctorum, quos frequentius commemorat et commendat ecclesia, neminem ad imitandum accenderent, si conscia ueritatis antiquitas legendam nobis hystoriam non reliquisset. Et nisi Dominus tam in Nouo quam in Veteri Testamento que sint fugienda et que imitanda tum scribendo tum aliis scribenda expressisset, nullus bona a malis distinxisset. Hiis et aliis exemplis instructi, ut benefactorum ecclesie Eueshamensis a tempore fundationis sue memoria sit in benedictione, et ut gloria eorum tractu temporis non marcescat nec eximia eorum gesta obliuio posteritatis extinguat, set ut quod ab eis magnifice factum fuit posteri sumant in exemplum, eorum gesta stilo commendare dignum duximus. Necnon et eorum qui eiusdem ecclesie bona distraxerunt malefacta denotabimus, ut nos bonorum exemplis informati a malis male alienata reuocare studeamus et que ab eis fuerunt dispersa congregare nitamur.[1] Ad quod faciendum tanto facilius prouocabimur et artius astringemur, quanto magis in periculum anime sue ipsos ea fecisse, et possessores non minus

---

[1] Cf. Isa. 11: 12. On the writing of the prologue, see above, p. xliv.

[BOOK THREE]

PART ONE

112. *The Prologue*

The ancient Greeks, in order that evil men should not enjoy the same standing in society as good men, wisely introduced a literary remedy. That the distinguished deeds of good men should not die with their doers, nor the evil actions of wicked men be buried with their perpetrators, they made a determined effort to stir their writers whom they called historians to record their history, so that the written word might be substituted for the silence of the spoken word. The Romans, emulating the Greeks in their desire to perpetuate virtue, not only employed the service of the pen but also erected statues, so, as much by reminding men of their ancestors as by challenging their descendants, they implanted deep within men in many ways, through both the eye and the ear, a love of virtue, and strongly influenced the minds of those seeking it. Furthermore, the deeds of the holy fathers whom the church frequently commemorates and commends would not have enthused any man to imitate them if antiquity, aware of the truth, had not left us a history for us to read. And had not the Lord made it clear as much through the writings of the New Testament as of the Old what men should shun and what imitate, in addition to making it clear through the works of other writers, no one would have distinguished good from evil. We have thus learned from these and other precedents; and in order that the memory of the benefactors of the church of Evesham from its very foundation should be blessed, and that their glory should not grow dim through the passage of time, or posterity's forgetfulness obliterate their great deeds but rather take their brilliant achievements as their example, we have thought it good to write an account of what they did. Likewise we shall also record the evil deeds of men who pillaged the property of this church in the hope that, encouraged by the example of good men, we may strive to recover what has been wrongfully alienated by evil men, and endeavour to gather in what has been scattered by them.[1] We shall be the more easily stirred to do this and the more strictly obliged to achieve it, the more aware we are that those men committed their acts in peril of their souls and that the

periculose, immo pernitiosius et magis iniuriose et sine ratione, ea possidere, cognouerimus.

Explicit prologus.

fo. 140rb | **113.** *Incipit liber tercius de constitucione Eueshamensis cenobii, et benefactoribus et malefactoribus et abbatibus eiusdem ecclesie, et operibus eorum bonis et malis, collectus et compositus a Thoma priore Eweshamie ex uariis cartis et scriptis et factis manifestis.*

Anno igitur ab incarnatione Domini septingentesimo quartodecimo, sanctus ac Deo dignissimus antistes Ecgwinus postquam ecclesiam Wigornensem ueluti pastor bonus tercius gloriosissime rexerat, sextodecimo episcopatus sui anno, cum longo confectus fuisset senio, prefatam sedem pontificalem ex toto reliquit, constituto pro eo, secundum suum uelle et electionem, uenerabili uiro Wilfrido episcopo.[1] Ad locum istum primitus ab eo Eouesham appellatum quem, Sancti Spiritus reuelatione et beatissime Dei genitricis semper uirginis Marie manifesta apparitione confortatus, diligentissime primus in honore ipsius angelorum et hominum regine per sex annos construxerat, mente et corpore pariter rediit, atque in magna contemplatione Dei, ueluti in uita sua plenissime habetur, usque ad ultimum diem transitus sui nouem annis sanctissime uiuens hic permansit.[2]

114. Sciant ergo omnes huius sancte ecclesie filii atque amici[3] perfecte eam diligentes tam presentes quam futuri, quod locus iste tunc temporis nichil pertinebat ad Wigornensem ecclesiam cui ipse episcopus preerat, set, ut prefati sumus, diuino admonitus instinctu, a rege Æthelredo filio Pendan regis, cuius meminit Beda uenerabilis presbiter in gestis Anglorum, illum optinuit, et monachilem congregationem, pro amore Dei atque salute anime sue, primus omnium hic constituit.[4] Hic autem nomina possessionum quas

---

a-a rubricated in R

[1] Wilfrid succeeded Ecgwine as the fourth bishop of Worcester. His dates are uncertain: *HBC*, p. 223, gives 718 to 743×745, ?29 Apr. 744. See next note.

[2] The earliest source for the date of Ecgwine's death is *Jo. Wo.*, ii. 174–5, who says that Ecgwine died on 30 Dec. 717 (in one MS, 716). John of Worcester also says that Wilfrid was chosen 'during Ecgwine's lifetime to fill his place, and received the church of Worcester'. Thomas dates Ecgwine's resignation as bishop to 714. By saying that Ecgwine remained at Evesham for nine years before his death (presuming that he accepted the 717 of John of Worcester), Thomas brings the date of Ecgwine's arrival at Evesham to 708–9. In saying that Ecgwine resigned as bishop of the Hwicce in his sixteenth year, Thomas makes Ecgwine's accession 698–9. This does not contradict any charter evidence, but it does conflict with John of Worcester's statement (156–7) that Ecgwine succeeded Oftfor in

owners of property alienated are in no less danger, indeed that their possession of these things is more pernicious, even more damaging, and is without entitlement.

The end of the prologue

113. *Here begins book three: the establishment of the monastery at Evesham; its benefactors, despoilers, and abbots: their deeds, good and bad, collected and composed by Thomas, prior of Evesham, from the various charters, documents and manifest deeds*

In the year AD 714 the prelate Ecgwine, a holy and very godly man, after he had ruled the church of Worcester gloriously as its third good shepherd, frail by reason of old age, resigned in the sixteenth year of his episcopate, and by his wish and nomination the venerable Wilfrid was appointed as his successor.[1] He retired in body and mind alike to that place first called by him Evesham. Encouraged by a revelation of the Holy Spirit and a clear vision of the eternal virgin Mary, the most blessed mother of God, he was the original builder of this place over a period of six years, in honour of the very Queen of angels and men. He remained there for nine years till the day of his death, living a holy life and meditating much upon God, as is fully revealed in his life. [2]

114. Let all sons and friends of this holy church,[3] who love it perfectly now and in the future, know that this place in no way belonged at that time to the church of Worcester, over which the bishop himself ruled. No, as we have said already, led by divine inspiration, Ecgwine received Evesham from King Æthelred, son of King Penda, who is mentioned by the venerable priest Bede in his *Deeds of the English*, and for love of God and for the salvation of his own soul, he was the very first to establish there a congregation of monks.[4] It seems right to us at this juncture to catalogue the

692; see Sims-Williams, *Religion and Literature*, p. 142 n. 124. Thomas had, indeed, provided a perfect chronology to fit with the visit to Rome, and the consequent documents. Thomas seems sure that Ecgwine resigned, with which John, a Worcester source, does not disagree in his statement that Wilfrid was appointed bishop during Ecgwine's lifetime. It was supremely important to the Evesham case for exemption to establish that Ecgwine had indeed resigned because although the idea of being both bishop and abbot was acceptable in the 8th cent., it would clearly have meant by Thomas's lifetime that the abbey was subject to the bishop. The 'Life' is Book I, above.

[3] This phrase is based on an opening form of a 12th-cent. ecclesiastical charter.

[4] On Æthelred, son of Penda king of Mercia, see *HBC*, p. 16, and Bede, *HE* v. 24, pp. 566–7. According to Bede, Æthelred of Mercia abdicated in 704 and became a monk. Bede, however, has nothing to say about Ecgwine and Evesham. William of Malmesbury in his notice of Evesham (*Gesta Pontificum*, pp. 296–8) pointed out Bede's ignorance of the bishop and his abbey.

idem reuerendus pater noster beatus Ecgwinus huic ecclesie adquisiuit, et eorum nomina a quibus eas optinuit, ut eorum memoria sit
in benedictione, denotanda dignum duximus.

115. *Nomina benefactorum Eueshamensis cenobii et possessionum eiusdem*
Anno igitur ab incarnatione Domini septingentesimo primo, rex
Merciorum Æthelredus, filius Pende, in honore beate uirginis
Marie, dedit uiro uenerabili Ecgwino episcopo Hethomme.[1] Anno
fo. 140va incarnati uerbi septingentesimo tercio dedit idem | rex ecclesie beate
Marie constructe in Hethom, postquam beata uirgo Maria in eodem
loco comparuerat, beato Ecgwino Chadelburi, Fladeburi et Stredfort,
quam postea, mortua Ostritha regina, occupauit Æthellardus Wicciorum subregulus, donec beatus Ecgwinus daret eidem pro ea
Fladeburi. Eodem anno dedit Offa rex eidem ecclesie in Hethom,
Huffam, tres Littletonas, Potidenho,[2] Huniburne, Aldintone, Badde-
seie, Bretfortone et Wikewane. Set Oswardus, mortuo Æthellardo
subregulo fratre eius, occupauit postea eandem terram uiginti
mansarum in Thuiforde donec beatus Ecgwinus tradidit ei Stredford.
116. Anno ab incarnatione Domini septingentesimo sexto, Æilwar-
dus Wicciorum subregulus, consentiente rege Kenredo, dedit ecclesie
beate Marie in Hethomme Ambresleiam.[3] Eodem anno Ailricus,
Osheri regis filius, consentiente rege Kenredo, dedit ecclesie beate
Marie in Hethomme Childeswikewane,[4] et Walterus ⟨filius⟩ Dudde,
sacerdos, Suelle maiorem.[5]
117. Anno ab incarnatione Domini septingentesimo octauo,[6] Kenredus rex Merciorum, filius Wlferi, dedit ecclesie beate Marie in
Hethomme ex una parte Auene, Nortonam, Echeslench, Chirchlench,
Mortonam, Biuintonam, Husebarewe, Witheleiam, Samburne, Kine-
wartune, Salford et alteram Salford;[7] ex altera parte Auene, Hamtone,
Bengwithe, Willerseie, Dunnintone, Bradewelle, Tetlestrope,
Stowam, Malgaresburi, Burthtone.[8]
118. Anno ab incarnatione Domini septingentesimo undecimo, rex
Merciorum Chelredus, filius Æthelredi regis, dedit ecclesie beate
Marie in Hethomme,[9] Raggeleiam, Arewe, Eccleshale, Wileshale,

---

[1] Thomas normally uses the early form 'Hethomme' (OE *æt Homme*, 'at the bend') for
the site of the monastery at Evesham; see below, 116–18.

[2] For Poden in Church Honeybourne, see D. Hooke, *Worcestershire Anglo-Saxon
Charter-Bounds* (Woodbridge, 1990), pp. 382–3.

[3] Sawyer, no. 54: V fos. 25^v–26; H fo. 67^r–v.

[4] Sawyer, no. 1174; V fo. 33^r; H fo. 66^v.

[5] Glos. Sawyer, no. 1175; H fo. 67^v.

possessions which our reverend father Ecgwine acquired for this church, and to give the names of those from whom he received them, so that their memory may be blessed.

115. *The names of the benefactors of the church of Evesham and of its possessions*

In the year AD 701 Æthelred, king of the Mercians and son of Penda, gave Evesham[1] to the venerable bishop Ecgwine, in honour of the blessed Virgin Mary. In 703 Æthelred gave Chadbury, Fladbury, and Stratford-upon-Avon [Warws.] to Ecgwine for the church of the blessed Mary, which had been built in Evesham after the blessed Virgin had appeared in that place. Afterwards, following the death of Queen Osthryth, Æthelheard, subking of the Hwicce, occupied these lands until the blessed Ecgwine exchanged them for Fladbury. In the same year King Offa gave Offenham, the three Littletons, Poden,[2] Church Honeybourne, Aldington, Badsey, Bretforton, and Wickhamford, to the church of Evesham. Osweard, after the death of his brother Æthelheard the subking, later seized possession of the same land, consisting of twenty hides in Twyford, until Ecgwine gave him Stratford [Warws.].

116. In the year AD 706 Æthelweard, subking of the Hwicce, with the agreement of King Cenred, gave Ombersley to the church of the blessed Mary in Evesham. [3] In the same year Æthelric, son of King Oshere, with the agreement of King Cenred, gave Childs Wickham to the church of the blessed Mary in Evesham.[4] The priest Walter Dudde gave it Lower Swell.[5]

117. In the year AD 708[6] Cenred, king of the Mercians, son of Wulfhere, gave to the church of the blessed Mary in Evesham, Norton, Atch Lench, Church Lench, Abbots Morton, Binton [Warws.], Hilborough, Weethley, Sambourne, Kinwarton, Salford and the other Salford,[7] on the one side of the Avon; and on the other side, Hampton, Bengeworth, Willersey [Glos.], Donnington, Broadwell, Adlestrop, Stow-on-the-Wold, Maugersbury, and Bourton-on-the-Water.[8]

118. In the year AD 711 Ceolred, king of the Mercians, son of king Æthelred, gave to the church of St Mary in Evesham,[9] Ragley,

---

[6] 709 (Cenred with Offa); see Hooke, *Charter-Bounds*, pp. 46–57. Source V fos. 68^r–9^r, with further properties mentioned (noted H fo. 59^r), regarded as spurious. Cf. Sawyer, no. 80.   [7] From Binton on in Warws., but the 'other Salford' is Oxon., formerly Glos.

[8] The properties from Willersey onwards are all in Glos.

[9] Sawyer, no. 81 (710); H fo. 62^r.

Addrichestone, Dorsintone, Brome, Mulecote,[1] Buuintone, Hilde-
buruurche, et unam hidam in Budifordia.[2]

119. Anno ab incarnatione Domini septingentesimo sextodecimo
Ethelbaldus, filius Alewi, rex Merciorum, dedit ecclesie beate
Marie et domino Ecgwino primo abbati de Eouesham,[3] Hactone,
Brainesford, Hamptone iuxta Wictium emptorium, Houptone, Wit-
fo. 140vb tone, et Lench Bernardi, | Westone, Hudicote, Stoke.[4] Hec autem
fuit causa commutationis supradictarum uillarum de Fladeburi,
Stradford et Tuiford.[5] Æthelardus Wictiorum subregulus, cognatus
Ostrithe regine et regis Offe,[6] ea mortua sine liberis, quia Chelredus
non erat filius eius, et rege Ethelredo facto monacho,[7] dicens regem
non posse hereditatem uxoris sue alicui conferre, occupauit Stredford
quia ibi fortior erat donec beatus Ecgwinus redderet ei Fladeburi quia
erat heres regine Ostrithe. Quo defuncto sine liberis, Oswardus frater
eius occupauit iniuste uiginti mansas in Tuiford, ut heres Offe regis
de terris eius in regno Merciorum, donec beatus Ecgwinus reddidit ei
Stredford, dicens fratrem suum illam iuste tenuisse, et iniuste pro
propria hereditate de Fladeburi ei contulisse. Set episcopi Wigornie,
fortiores nobis, ut suo predecessori datas postea eas adquisierunt, et
ecclesia nostra cui date erant illis iniuste caret.

120. Post decessum uero beati Ecgwini quas possessiones huic
ecclesie alii contulerint et nomina conferentium, ut et eorum in
orationibus nostris perpetua habeatur memoria, hic subnectendum
bonum et utile putauimus.

121. Anno igitur ab incarnatione Domini septingentesimo uicesimo
primo, predictus Ethelbaldus rex dedit ecclesie beate Marie in
Eouesham unam portionem quam accole Sele nuncupant, cum statu
trium mansium in loco ubi salse aque ebulliunt,[8] que debet reddere

---

[1] Milcote was a hamlet near the confluence of the Avon and the Stour containing that
part of Weston-upon-Avon which is in Warws., Weston itself being chiefly in Kiftsgate
hundred (Glos.), but also in Barlichway hundred (Warws.). There were actually two
Milcotes, see below, 169, 174.

[2] All the identified places are in Warws. with the exception of Dorsington, which is in
Glos.

[3] Sawyer, no. 83; H fo. 62^v.

[4] Stoke is almost certainly Larkstoke in Ilmington, Warws.

[5] The name, Twyford, is preserved in Twyford House and Farm. The ford was across
the Avon from Offenham to Evesham. For identification, see Hooke, *Charter-Bounds*,
pp. 23–4, 48–9 (map), and 408–17; and PN *Worcs.*, p. 265.

[6] The passage might be taken to read kinsman of Queen Osthryth and of King Offa.
Osthryth was the wife of King Æthelred of Mercia and daughter of Oswiu, king of
Northumbria. She was murdered by her own Mercian nobles in 697; see Bede, *HE* iv.
20–2 (pp. 400–1); v. 24 (pp. 564–5). King Offa is the king of the East Saxons.

Arrow, Exhall, 'Wileshale', Atherstone, Dorsington, Broom, Milcote,[1] Binton, Hilborough, and one hide in Bidford.[2]

119. In the year AD 716 Æthelbald, son of Alhwih, king of the
Mercians, gave to the church of St Mary and to Ecgwine, the first
abbot of Evesham,[3] Acton Beauchamp, Bransford, Hampton Lovett
near Droitwich, Upton Warren, Witton in Droitwich, Sheriff's
Lench, Weston-upon–Avon [Glos.], Hidcote [Glos.], and Stoke.[4]
Now this was the reason for the exchange for the above-mentioned
vills of Fladbury, Stratford-upon-Avon [Warws.], and Twyford.[5]
Æthelheard, subking of the Hwicce, and kinsman of Queen Osthryth
and King Offa,[6] on the death of the queen, who left no heirs, as
Ceolred was not her son and Æthelred had become a monk,[7] said that
the king could not bestow his wife's inheritance upon anyone, and
seized possession of Stratford where he had a strong force, until the
blessed Ecgwine returned Fladbury to him because he was an heir of
Queen Osthryth. Since Æthelheard died without children, his
brother Osweard wrongfully seized possession of twenty hides in
Twyford as the heir of King Offa to his lands in the kingdom of the
Mercians, until Stratford was returned to him by the blessed
Ecgwine. Osweard said that his brother had held rightful possession
of Stratford and had wrongfully bestowed it upon Ecgwine in
exchange for his own inheritance of Fladbury. However, the bishops
of Worcester, being stronger than we were, later acquired those
possessions as they had been given to their predecessor, and our
church to whom they had been given was unjustly deprived of them.

120. After the death of the blessed Ecgwine, other men bestowed
certain possessions upon this church, and we have thought it right
and beneficial to include their names here, so that we may remember
them for ever in our prayers.

121. In the year AD 721 the above-mentioned King Æthelbald gave to
the church of the blessed Mary in Evesham a plot of land which its
inhabitants call 'Sele', with three dwellings situated in the place
where salt water bubbles up:[8] it should produce 360 measures of salt

---

[7] Her husband, Æthelred entered the monastery of Bardney and became its abbot, *HE*
v. 19 (pp. 528–9), v. 24 (pp. 566–7), and see 498n, 368n. It is generally assumed that
Ceolred was Osthryth's and Æthelred's son, but Bede *HE* v. 19 does not actually say so.

[8] 'Sele' is probably Sale Green in Droitwich. This may bear some relation to Sawyer,
no. 97; V fo. 27ᵛ, which calls it 'Saltwich'. On the importance of the ancient brine springs
at Droitwich and on the production of salt, which was used as a preservative and was thus
a very lucrative commodity to possess, see D. Hooke, 'The Droitwich salt industry: an
examination of the West Midland charter evidence', *Anglo-Saxon Studies in Archaeology
and History*, ii (1981), 123–69.

annuatim trescentas sexaginta mittas salis. Dedit etiam capellas sancti Albani[1] et sancte Margarete in Wigorn', cum pluribus domibus circumiacentibus.

122. Anno ab incarnatione Domini septingentesimo quinquagesimo septimo Thingfrith[2] rex Merciorum dedit ecclesie beate Marie et sancti Ecgwini in Eouesham, Eunlade, Deillesforde, Chesteltune, Cornewelle, Salford, Derneford,[3] Schiptone.[a]

123. Anno ab incarnatione Domini septingentesimo septuagesimo quarto Bertulfus[4] rex Merciorum dedit ecclesie beate Marie Virginis et beati Ecgwini, Pebewrtham, Quentonam, Sloptram.

124. Anno ab incarnatione Domini nongentesimo septuagesimo tercio Huue þe Huuede, comes Warewikie, dedit ecclesie beate Marie et beati Ecgwini, consentiente rege Eadgaro, Witlakesforde | et Greftone Minorem.[5]

fo. 141ra

125. Anno ab incarnatione Domini nongentesimo octogesimo sexto Ethelredus rex Anglie, frater beati Ædwardi, dedit ecclesie beate Marie in Eouesham et ecclesie beati Eadwardi in Stowia unam mansam sitam iuxta Malgaresburie. Quod ius antiquitus quidam raptor, Wlfric Ripa uocamine, a prefato monasterio inique abstulit, set prefatus rex Ethelredus hoc[b] eidem monasterio postea reddidit.[6]

126. Anno ab incarnatione Domini millesimo octauodecimo Kanutus rex Anglie dedit ecclesie beate Marie et beati Ecgwini Baddebi et Newham.[7] Idem Kanutus dedit quinque terras in Gloucestre et duas in Winchelcumbe et unam in Norhamtone.[8]

127. Anno ab incarnatione Domini millesimo quinquagesimo quinto Eadwardus rex Anglie dedit ecclesie beate Marie et beati Ecgwini Suuellam minorem[9] et Graftone maiorem, et concessit quod porth et mercatio essent apud Eouesham.[10]

128. Alio uero tempore Warinus Bussel dedit ecclesie de Euesham

---

[a] S[chip]tone: chip *written into the margin* (s. xv): *the same hand in a different ink has gone over the 'd' and 'e' of* Deillesforde, *above*   [b] h *inserted over an erasure*

---

[1] For this chapel, see Wulfstan's 'synod' of 1092, *C. & S.*, i, pt 2, no. 100: there is no mention of St Margaret's. On the veracity of the '1092 synodal document', see J. Barrow, 'How the twelfth-century monks of Worcester perceived their past', in *The Perception of the Past in Twelfth-Century Europe*, ed. P. Magdalino (London, 1992), pp. 53–74, at 60–9.

[2] Thingfrith is a mistake for his son Offa. Offa ruled from 757 to his death in July 796; *HBC*, p. 16.

[3] Cf. Sawyer, no. 112; H fo. 63[r]. Offa, king of Mercia, to Evesham, 777. Dornford is more likely to be Dorn in Blockley, Glos. (formerly Worcs.), a hamlet west of the Fosse Way, than Dornford in Wootton (Oxon.); see VCH *Oxon.*, xi. 267–8, and PN *Worcs.* p. 98.

[4] Berhtwulf was not king of the Mercians until 823. Cf. Sawyer, no. 191, of 840,

per annum. Æthelbald also gave to the church the chapels of St Alban[1] and St Margaret in Worcester along with several houses situated around them.

122. In the year AD 757 Offa,[2] king of the Mercians, gave to the church of the blessed Mary and St Ecgwine of Evesham, Evenlode [Glos.], Daylesford [Glos.], Chastleton [Oxon], Cornwell [Oxon], Salford [Oxon, formerly Glos.], Dornford,[3] and Shipston-on-Stour [Warws., formerly Worcs.].

123. In the year AD 774 Berhtwulf,[4] king of the Mercians gave to the church, Pebworth, Quenington, and Slaughter [all Glos.].

124. In the year AD 973 Ufa 'the Huuede', earl of Warwick, gave to the church of St Mary and St Ecgwine, with the assent of King Edgar, Wixford [Warws.] and Grafton Minor [Warws.].[5]

125. In the year AD 986 Æthelred, king of England, brother of the blessed Edward, gave to this church and to the church of the blessed Edward in Stow [Glos.], one hide situated near Maugersbury [Glos.]. The monastery [of Evesham] was formerly robbed of this property by a thief called Wulfric Ripa, but King Æthelred later restored it to this monastery again.[6]

126. In the year AD 1018 Cnut, king of England, gave Badby and Newnham [both Northants] to the church of the blessed Mary and the blessed Ecgwine.[7] He also gave it five tenements in Gloucester, two in Winchcombe [Glos.], and one in Northampton.[8]

127. In the year AD 1055 Edward, king of England, gave to the church of the blessed Mary and the blessed Ecgwine, Upper Swell,[9] and Grafton Major [Warws.], and granted Evesham borough status and a market.[10]

128. Subsequently, Warin Bussel gave to the church of Evesham the

---

Berhtwulf granting Evesham, Quinton (Warws.), Pebworth (Glos.) and Mappleborough in Studley (Warws.); H fo. 63[v].

[5] Sawyer, no. 1214 (with the date 962); H fo. 64[r]. The charter was probably forged at Evesham between 1097 and 1104; see C. Hart, *Early Charters of Northern England and the Northern Midlands*, p. 79. On Ufa, the sheriff, see below, 135. The meaning of 'the Huuede' is unknown: the scribe reproduces the Anglo-Saxon thorn.

[6] In 1016. Sawyer, no. 935; H fo. 64[v]. *Domesday Book*, i (Record Commission, 1783), fo. 165b, records that Evesham has 'Malgeresberie ad Eduuardestou', where there had been eight hides TRE, 'et nona hida iacet ad ecclesiam S. Edwardi: Rex Adelredus quietam dedit ibi'.

[7] Sawyer, no. 957 (1020); H fo. 65[r].

[8] No charters of Cnut for these properties have survived.

[9] Glos. Cf. Sawyer, no. 1026, probably spurious.

[10] On the development of the town from this date, see Slater, 'Medieval town-founding', pp. 78–81; and Hilton, 'Small town and urbanisation', p. 1.

ecclesiam de Penwrtham et terciam partem decimarum de dominico de Lailonde et de Meoles et Farintone cum pertinentiis suis.[1] Ricardus Bussel dedit ecclesie *ᵃEoueshamensi sex bouatas terre in Longeton et totam ecclesiam de Lailonde et quartam partem piscarie de Penwrtham et unum rete liberum[2] et capellam de Meoles.ᵃ* Albertus frater eius dedit duas bouatas terre in Lailonde et assartum de Blakesha[m].ᵇ[3] Ricardus uero episcopus Conuentrensis[4] per cartam suam hec omnia cum prioratu nobis confirmauit. Comes autem Rogerus Pictauensis dedit nobis ᶜ Hocwike;[5] hanc tenemus de rege. Nigellus constabularius Cestrie medietatem de Thelewelle et unam piscariam et unam hidam in Goldhore.[6] Milo Crispin dedit dimidiam hidam in Hildendone;[7] Brien filius Comitis dedit ecclesiam de Hildendone;[8] Alnod sacerdos dedit ecclesiam beati Michaelis in Cornhulle, London'.[9] Rodbertus de Stafford dedit Wrottesleiam et Liuentonam.[10] Willelmus Fossard dedit ecclesiam de Huntintun.[11]

ᵃ⁻ᵃ two lines written over an erasure   *ᵇ two or three letters illeg.; ins. over an erasure* *(s. xv)*   *ᶜ dedit nobis ins. marg. (s. xv)*

---

[1] Penwortham was founded as a cell of Evesham some time between 1104 and 1122 (see KH, pp. 56 and 73, and VCH *Lancashire*, ii (1908), p. 104), the dates of Abbot Robert of Evesham's abbacy, by Warin Bussel, baron of Penwortham (1102–49). The charter printed in W. Farrer, *The Lancashire Pipe Rolls . . . also Early Lancashire Charters* (Liverpool, 1902), pp. 320–1 (from H fo. 89ʳ) appears to be a composite piece of work, covering gifts made piecemeal, including land in Martin, not mentioned here. For the Bussels, see *Mon. Angl.* iii. 417–21, where Dugdale includes some of the family's charters and the confirmation of Pope Alexander III. It is likely that the cell was served by Evesham monks from the beginning. The reason why Warin Bussel chose to favour the abbey of Evesham appears to have been that his wife, Matilda, had property in Evesham: her gift of two bovates of land in Evesham is recorded in a charter of her son, Albert Bussel; see *Documents relating to the Priory of Penwortham and other possessions in Lancashire of the Abbey of Evesham*, ed. W. A. Hulton (Chetham Soc. xxx, 1853), pp. xvii–viii, and 5–6 (no. vi).

[2] Hugh Bussel's charter (see next note) states that this net was in the river Ribble.

[3] Probably Blacklache (meaning 'black pool') which is in Leyland: the name is perpetuated in Blacklache House; E. Ekwall, *The Place-names of Lancashire* (Publications of the University of Manchester, English ser. xi, 1922), p. 133. Hugh Bussel, son of Albert, confirmed these three gifts of his grandfather, Warin, his uncle, Richard, and his father, Albert, in a charter copied into V fo. 75ʳ, and witnessed by Warin, his heir, Henry, his brother, and Antigonia, his wife. The texts of all four charters are in H fos. 89ʳ–90ʳ.

[4] Richard Peche, cons. after 18 Apr. 1161, resigned 1182, d. 6 Oct. 1182. His confirmation is noted in *EEA* xvi (1998): *Coventry and Lichfield 1160–1182*, ed. M. J. Franklin, no. 34.

[5] In *c.*1149, Earl Ranulf (II), earl of Chester, confirmed this gift of Howick (in Leyland), made by Count Roger at the time of Earl Ranulf (I; 1120–9) of Chester, his father; V fo. 75ᵛ: printed in *Charters of the Anglo-Norman Earls of Chester c.1071–1237*, ed. G. Barraclough (Record Soc. of Lancashire and Cheshire, cxxvi, 1988)), no. 90, who failed to note that this was a confirmation. See Judith Green, 'Earl Ranulf II and

church of Penwortham [Lancs.], and a third of the tithes of the demesne of Leyland, Meols and Farington [all Lancs.], with their appurtenances.[1] Richard Bussel also gave the church of Evesham six bovates of land in Longton [Lancs.], the whole of the church of Leyland, a quarter of the fishery of Penwortham, one free net,[2] and the chapel of Meols. His brother Albert gave it two bovates of land in Leyland and the assart of 'Blakesham'.[3] Richard, bishop of Coventry,[4] by his own charter confirmed all of these properties for us with the priory [of Penwortham]. Count Roger the Poitevin gave us Howick,[5] and we hold this of the king. Nigel, the constable of Chester, gave us half of Thelwall [Ches.], as well as a fishery and a hide of land in Golborne.[6] Miles Crispin gave us half a hide in Hillingdon [Middx.];[7] Brian Fitz Count gave us the church of Hillingdon;[8] the priest Alnod gave us the church of the blessed Michael in Cornhill, London. [9] Robert of Stafford gave us Wrottesley [Staffs.] and Loynton;[10] William Fossard gave us the church of Huntington;[11] Hugh fitz

Lancashire', *The Earldom of Chester and its Charters*, ed. A. T. Thacker (Journal of the Chester Archaeological Society, lxxi, 1991), p. 103.

[6] Possibly in Winwick (Lancs).

[7] Miles Crispin was probably a younger son of William Crispin. The family came from Neaufles in Normandy. He had substantial estates in England by 1086, including lands in Oxfordshire. He married the daughter of Robert d'Oilly; see J. A. Green, *The Aristocracy of Norman England* (Cambridge, 1997), pp. 35, 38, 77, 274.

[8] Brian Fitz Count, illegitimate son of Count Alan of Brittany, created lord of Abergavenny by Henry I, and a staunch supporter of the Empress Matilda, married Matilda, the widow, or more likely daughter, of Miles Crispin, heiress to the lordship of Wallingford; see Green, *Aristocracy*, pp. 132, 145, 285, 373.

[9] All three gifts are noted in V fo. 12ᵛ. Miles Crispin apparently received some of the lands of Roger of Montgomery after they were forfeit, including Hillingdon. For the text of Brian Fitz Count's charter, see V fo. 17ʳ, also in H fo. 87ʳ⁻ᵛ.

[10] 'Liventon' appears to be Loynton (Staffs.), a township in the parish of High Offley. Robert of Stafford was by 1086 the most important lay tenant-in-chief in Staffs., and probably the sheriff. A younger son of Roger de Tosny, he acquired land from a number of antecessors, the most important of whom was a thegn called Wulfgeat. This gift of land at Wrottesley to Evesham abbey is noted by Green (*Aristocracy*, p. 76) as being very early for a Norman giving land to a Benedictine house and is also of interest because it is witnessed by two members of a thegnly family, Æthelwine the sheriff and Turchil (of Arden) his son, which leads her to suggest that Robert may have married into that family; see R. W. Eyton, *The Staffordshire Cartulary*, Collections for a History of Staffordshire, ii (1881), p. 178.

[11] *Early Yorkshire Charters*, ii, ed. W. Farrer, (1915) no. 1058, purports to be the confirmation by William Fossard I of the gift of the church of Huntington (Yorks.) made by (Robert) his father to the church of St Ecgwine of Evesham, dated c.1140–59. The following charter, no. 1059, is the grant of the church by Roger, the abbot, and the convent of Evesham to Richard, abbot, and the convent of Whitby, for an annual pension of 10s. Roger was only abbot for one year, 1159–60, so the charter can be precisely dated. The source for both charters is the Whitby cartulary. For the Fossard pedigree, see *Early Yorkshire Charters*, ii. 327–8.

Hugo filius Rogeri dedit nobis Suleston[1] et unam carrucatam terre de hereditate Margarete uxoris sue ad petitionem eiusdem, et Paganus de Nauers dedit eidem loco insulam que dicitur Serpham.[2] Willelmus de Harewecurt dedit nobis quinque solidos in molendino de Westun.[3]

fo. 141ʳᵇ Robertus de Kikeswic dedit nobis decimas de Pikerleye.[4] | Isti fuerunt huius ecclesie principales et primi benefactores, quibus pro misericordia sua magna benefaciat Deus et retribuat eis secundum retributionem quam retribuerunt nobis, respondens ipsis secundum benefacta eorum, 'ut centuplum accipiant in regno celorum'.[5]

129. Set quia tum per uarias temporum incommoditates et bellorum incursus, tum per malignorum hominum impugnationes et inuasiones, tum per prelatorum et subditorum huius ecclesie insufficientiam, malitiam et negligentiam, a pluribus maleuolis Dei et ecclesie huius inimicis diuersis temporibus hec bona multimodis direpta et subtracta dinoscuntur, et iterum, per gratiam Dei, per sufficientiores, diligentiores et magis que Dei erant quam carnis et sanguinis diligentes, malignorum prelatorum et subditorum bonos successores, pro magna parte reuocata et redintegrata consistunt, tam malefactores quam benefactores, tam dispersores quam redintegratores ut utrique dignam remunerationem et mercedem, iusticiam et misericordiam consequantur, stilo, licet insufficienti, commendabimus.

130. Hoc etiam in subsequenti opere diligens lector attendat quod si aliquando alium a predictis aliqua ex predictis huic ecclesie contulisse scriptum inuenerit, magis reuocasse quam de nouo contulisse intelligat, quamuis adquirenti, conseruanti, et dispersa reuocanti, eadem merces a Domino debeatur.

131. Igitur omnes possessiones a sanctissimo patre nostro beato Ecgwino adquisitas integerrime sine diminutione et cum summa libertate decem et octo abbates post eius depositionem possederunt, quorum nomina sunt hec: Primus ab eo Æthelwold abbas; secundus, Aldbore abbas; tercius, Aldbath; quartus, Aldfefert;

---

[1] Southstone is in Stanford-on-Teme. Hugh Fitz Roger has not been further identified.

[2] Gilbert Foliot's confirmation of these two grants, dated 1148×1163 (*Foliot Letters*, p. 363 no. 298) reveals that Southstone was intended as a cell of Evesham, and that Payne de Noyers' grant of the island of 'Serpham' (presumably in the river Teme) was for the same cell. The cell was dedicated to St John the Baptist, but no more is heard of its existence. It probably failed soon after the grants were made. Payne de Noyers was possibly the Payne, brother of Alexander *de Nuariis*, both of whom attested a charter of Richard Fitz Pons giving his wife the manor of Leach in Gloucestershire in *c*.1127; see *Ancient Charters Royal and Private prior to A.D. 1200*, part 1, ed. J. H. Round (Pipe Roll Society, x: 1888), no. 12.

[3] William de Harcourt is presumably the William, son of Robert Fitz Anschetil, whose

Roger gave us Southstone[1] and a carucate of land from the inheritance of his wife Margaret at her request, and Payne de Noyers gave us an island called 'Serpham';[2] William de Harcourt gave us five shillings revenue from the mill of Weston-upon-Avon [Glos. and Warws.];[3] and Robert de Kikeswic gave us the tithes of Pixley [Herefs.].[4] These were the principal and original benefactors of this church. May God bless them for their great mercy, and reward them according to the gifts they have made to us; may He answer their prayers according to their good deeds, 'that they may receive a hundredfold in the Kingdom of Heaven'.[5]

129. However, it is well known that these possessions have in many ways, and at different times, been plundered or removed by many ungodly men who were hostile to this church. This happened sometimes during periods which were prejudicial to the interests of the church or when enemies invaded, sometimes through the assaults or encroachment of men of ill-will, and sometimes through the incompetence, malice, or neglect of the rulers or servants of this church. But then again, by the grace of God, because of the competence and the diligence of the good men who succeeded those bad rulers and servants, who cared more for the things of God than the things of flesh and blood, these possessions have for the most part been restored or renewed. We shall therefore entrust to our pen, unworthy though it be, the prayer that malefactors and benefactors, those who have squandered our resources and those who have restored them, may each receive their due reward, recompense, justice and mercy.

130. The attentive reader should note that if he finds it written in any later record that someone other than the above-mentioned persons bestowed some properties upon this church, he should be aware that that person had restored property to the church rather than bestowed new property upon it, though the Lord grants the same reward to those who acquire, those who preserve, and those who gather up what has been scattered.

131. All the possessions acquired by our most holy father, the blessed Ecgwine, were held wholly without diminution, and with absolute freedom, by the eighteen abbots who followed after his death: the first was Æthelwold, the second Aldbore, the third Aldbeorth, the fourth

family were prominent tenants of the Beaumont twins. He attested from the 1120s to 1149; see D. Crouch, *The Beaumont Twins* (Cambridge, 1986), pp. 124–6 and n. 80.
    [4] Robert de Kikeswic has not been further identified.   [5] Cf. Matt. 19: 29.

quintus, Tildbrith; sextus, Cutulf; septimus, Aldmund; octauus, Credanus sanctus; nonus, Thincferth; decimus, Aldbald; undecimus, Ecbrith; duodecimus, Elferd; terciusdecimus, Wlfard; quartusdecimus, Kinelm; quintusdecimus, Kinath; sextusdecimus, Ebba; septimusdecimus, alter Kinath; octauusdecimus, Eduuinus abbas.[1] Isti omnes pariter per ordinem hanc abbatiam integram atque indiuisam cum terris | et possessionibus et magna libertate ueluti pater Ecgwinus dereliquit quamplurimis annis tenuerunt.

fo. 141va (in margin)

132. *De prima destructione Eueshamensis ecclesie, et dispersione monachorum et substitutione canonichorum, per Alchelmum et Wlricum laicos et Osulfum episcopum*

Deinde uero defuncto abbate Eaduuino, et rege Ædmundo,[2] non illo sancto, regnante, quidam nefandissimus princeps huius patrie, Alchelmus nomine,[3] a rege eodem iuuenili etate minus sapiente hanc abbatiam optinuit, et quasi lupus rapax,[4] primus raptor huius ecclesie, gregem Christi dispersit, seruos Dei monachos inde fugauit, terras et possessiones sibimet accepit, quosdam canonicos in loco monachorum, quibusdam terris sibi relictis, constituit, et quamdiu uixit contra Deum et omnes sanctos eius iniquissime tenuit. Post eius denique mortem diuersi homines sub diuersis regibus laicali potentia locum istum possederunt, ueluti erat quidam sancte ecclesie raptor iniquissimus nomine Wlfricus,[5] et episcopus quidam nomine Osulfus,[6] et ita de una potestate in aliam potestatem contrariam res huius monasterii miserrime distrahebantur, quoadusque rex pacificus Ædgarus in regno confortatus,[7] sapientium consilio et maxime sancti Dunstani archiepiscopi,[8] sinodum totius Anglie fecit congregari,[9] in qua prefatus archiepiscopus Dunstanus et sanctus Osuualdus

---

[1] Very little is known about these early abbots. They appear in charters and records, many of which cannot be verified, and which reveal little more than their names. There are, however, two notable exceptions with the fourteenth and fifteenth abbots in the list, Abbots Cynelm and Cynath, who were deduced by Armitage Robinson to have been trained in the Worcester *familia* of the scholarly bishop Waerferth, and who continued to be associated with the bishop's entourage after they became abbot of Evesham. Indeed, it is not unlikely that Abbot Cynath accompanied Bishop Cenwald of Worcester on his visit to certain German monasteries in 929; see J. Armitage Robinson, *The Times of Saint Dunstan* (Oxford, 1923), pp. 38–40. Thomas is likely to have copied this list from a source presumably drawn up in the mid to late tenth century.

[2] Edmund I, son of King Edward the Elder, b. 921, acc. Oct. 939, cons. ?28 Nov. 939, d. 26 May 946. Not St Edmund, king of the East Angles, acc. 855, d. 20 Nov. 869, whose popularity as a saint, especially in the eleventh and twelfth centuries, presumably explains this comment; *HBC*, pp. 9, 26.

[3] Ealdorman, 940–56.

Aldfrith, the fifth Tilhberht, the sixth Cuthwulf, the seventh Aldmund, the eighth the holy Credan, the ninth Thingfrith, the tenth Aldbald, the eleventh Ecgberht, the twelfth Ælfrith, the thirteenth Wulfweard, the fourteenth Cynelm, the fifteenth Cynath, the sixteenth Ebba, the seventeenth another Cynath, and the eighteenth Edwin.[1] All of these abbots alike, for all these years, held this abbey intact and undivided, with its lands and possessions, and in complete freedom, just as father Ecgwine left it.

132. *The first destruction of the church of Evesham; the dispersal of the monks and the substitution of canons by the laymen, Ealhhelm and Wulfric, and Bishop Oswulf*

After the death of Abbot Edwin, when King Edmund was ruling[2]— not the saint—a certain nefarious chief man of this country, named Ealhhelm,[3] gained possession of this abbey from the king when he was young and lacking in wisdom. Like a ravening wolf[4] the first despoiler of this church scattered Christ's flock, and drove the monks, God's servants, from this place. He appropriated their lands and possessions, and in place of the monks he installed some canons, keeping some lands for himself. As long as he lived he held these lands without right, against God and all His saints. After his death various men under different kings possessed this place with lay power. One of these despoilers of the holy church was called Wulfric,[5] and another was a bishop named Oswulf.[6] So the possessions of this monastery were shamefully dragged from one form of power to another which differed from it, until the peace-maker, King Edgar, was confirmed in his kingdom.[7] On the advice of his witan, and especially of the archbishop, St Dunstan,[8] he convened a synod of the whole of England.[9] At this synod Archbishop Dunstan and St

---

[4] Cf. Gen. 49: 27.

[5] This is presumably the Wulfric who held land at Bourton-on-the-Water, Maugersbury, and Daylesford (Glos.), given to him by King Eadred in 949; see Sawyer, no. 550. It has been suggested by P. Sawyer, *Charters of Burton Abbey* (London, 1979), p. xlviii, that this was Wulfric *pedisequus*, a possible kinsman of Wulfric *spot*, whose family had connections with the West Midlands. C. Hart, however (*Early Charters of Northern England and the North Midlands* (Leicester, 1979), pp. 371–2), identifies him as Dunstan's brother; see n. 8 below.

[6] Oswulf, bishop of Ramsbury from 949×51 to his death in 970; *HBC*, p. 220.

[7] Edgar I, son of King Edmund I, b. 943, acc. 957 as king of the Mercians, Oct. 959 as king of all England, cons. ?960/1, d. 8 July 975; *HBC*, p. 27.

[8] Archbishop of Canterbury, acc. 959, d. 19 May 988; *HBC*, p. 214.

[9] The synod must have been held between 971 (the accession of Oswald to York) and 975, the death of Edgar, if the Evesham writer is correct in stating that Oswald was

archiepiscopus[1] ac beatus Ætheluuoldus Wintoniensis ecclesie antistes,[2] omnesque alii episcopi et abbates et principes huius patrie
affuerunt, ibique decreuerunt ut omnes ecclesie que destructe fuerant
a monastica religione restaurarentur.[3]

133. *De reformatione eiusdem ecclesie et reuocatione monachorum et
amotione canonicorum per beatos Dunstanum et Ethewoldum[a] et per
Oswardum abbatem*

Qua de re sanctus Atheluuoldus iussu regis et beati Dunstani et
aliorum magnatum communi decreto ad plures ecclesias transiens,
abbates et monachos constituens, tandem ad istum locum uenit et
Osuuardum abbatem hic constituit, commendans ei terras et possessiones quas Alchelmus Christi aduersarius post mortem Eadwini
abbatis abstulit.

134. *De secunda dispersione[b] monachorum et substitutione canonicorum
per Alferum et Godwinum laicos et Algesium episcopum*[4]

Deinde uero, defuncto rege pio Eadgaro, et filio eius Eaduuardo, qui
postea martir effectus est, iuuenili nimium etate et sensu simplici
regnante,[5] et ideo parum fortiter regno suo dominante, dux quidam
fo. 141[vb]   sceleratissi | mus, Alferus nomine, potentissimus huius patrie domi-
nator, monachos iterum de multis ecclesiis expulit. Hic namque ad
istum locum pergens monachos iterum hinc expellens, canonicos
paucos constituens,[6] hanc uillam Eouesham et Vffenham et reliquas

---

[a] *MS* Ethewoldum *? written over*   [b] b *MS* dispersitione

archbishop of York at this time, and was probably the Synod of Winchester held in 970×3;
see below, n. 3. John of Worcester, under the year 969 (*Jo. Wo.*, ii, p. 419, and in a passage
based on Byrhtferth's *Vita S. Oswaldi*), mentions that Edgar ordered Dunstan of
Canterbury, Oswald of Worcester (not of York—he received the archbishopric in 971),
and Æthelwold of Winchester to expel secular priests from the greater monasteries.
Byrhtferth says that this was in a council at Easter but he does not mention Oswald as
being present; *C. & S.*, i. pt. 1, pp. 113–18, 114 n. 4. This (and the present account)
appear to be the only sources for the action taking place in a synod and neither Byrhtferth
nor the Evesham writer can be deemed wholly reliable. In a general context, and for a
critical examination of the sources, see Hanna Vollrath, *Die Synoden Englands bis 1066*
(Paderborn, 1985), pp. 259–60.

[1] Bishop of Worcester from 961–71, when he was translated to York, but he retained
the see of Worcester, dying on 29 Feb. 992; *HBC*, p. 224. On the possible tampering with
this and the next passage in an attempt to write out the part played by Oswald, as bishop of
Worcester, in the reform of Evesham—which would perhaps have suggested a certain
subjection to the see later—and for the consequent boosting of the importance of
Æthelwold in the revival, see D. Cox, 'St Oswald of Worcester at Evesham Abbey:

Oswald, archbishop,[1] the blessed Æthelwold, bishop of Winchester,[2] and all the other bishops, abbots, and chief men of this country were present. There they decreed that all churches whose monastic religion had been suppressed should be restored as monasteries.[3]

133. *The re-establishment of this church, the restoration of the monks, and the removal of the canons by the blessed Dunstan and Æthelwold, and Abbot Osweard*

After the general decree had been made on this matter, St Æthelwold, by order of the king, the blessed Dunstan, and the other magnates, visited several churches and reinstated abbots and monks. At last he came to this place and here reinstated Osweard as abbot, entrusting to him the lands and possessions which Christ's enemy, Ealhhelm, had taken from the abbey after the death of Abbot Edwin.

134. *The second dispersal of the monks and substitution of canons by the laymen Ælfhere and Godwine, and by the bishop, Æthelsige*[4]

Then the pious King Edgar died, and his son Edward, who later became a martyr, reigned when he was too young and naive.[5] His control of his kingdom was consequently weak, and a certain unscrupulous man called Ælfhere, who was a powerful lord in this district, again expelled monks from many churches. He came to this place and again expelled the monks from here, and installed a few canons.[6] He took this vill of Evesham, Offenham, and other vills

Cult and Concealment', *Journal of Ecclesiastical History*, liii (2002), 1–17, at pp. 2–4, 15–16. The rewriting could be the work of either Dominic or Thomas.

  [2] cons. 29 Nov. 963, d. 1 Aug. 984; *HBC*, p. 223. See next note, and below, **133, 325**.

  [3] Æthelwold appears to have drawn up the *Regularis Concordia* 'in the wake of a synod held in Winchester some time between 970 and 973'; see *Wulfstan of Winchester, Life of St Æthelwold*, ed. M. Lapidge and M. Winterbottom (OMT, 1991), p. lviii. Monasteries were to be restored, and lay overlordship over monasteries was condemned; see *Regularis Concordia*, ed. T. Symons (NMT, 1953), pp. 1–2, and 7 (cl. 10). On Æthelwold's part in the restoration of the monks, see *Wulfstan of Winchester, Life of St Æthelwold*, pp. xlv–li. On the view that Oswald at Worcester did not totally eject the clerks, but put in monks alongside them, see J. Barrow, 'How the monks of Worcester perceived their past', in *The Perception of the Past in Twelfth-Century Europe*', ed. P. Magdalino (London, 1992), pp. 53–74, at 56–7, and the references cited there.

  [4] Æthelsige I of Sherborne, acc. 978×979, d. or trans. 991×993; *HBC*, p. 222.

  [5] Edgar died in 975. His son, Edward, was born *c*.962, acc. July 975, d. 18 March 978; *HBC*, p. 27.

  [6] On the second dispersal, see D. J. V. Fisher, 'The anti-monastic reaction in the reign of Edward the Martyr', *Cambridge Historical Journal*, x (1950–2), 254–70, esp. p. 265: 'When, as at Evesham, ejection was followed by a redistribution of monastic lands and the restoration of secular clergy, it is easy to see why the movement was popular.'

hic in circuitu sibi in dominio assumpsit, fratri suo, Alfuuardo nomine, Ambresleie dedit, et octo hidas apud Biuintone quibusdam militibus suis tradidit, presbiteris uero quicquid sibi placuit de terris ecclesie concessit.[1]

135. Hiis temporibus quidam potens homo Vfa nomine, uicecomes uidelicet super Wareuuicscire, reddidit huic loco cum corpore suo defuncto uillam Withlagesford, quinque hidas.[2] Set presbiteri qui tunc temporis prefuerunt nimis incauti postea filio suo, Wlfgeato nuncupato,[3] ipsam terram eo tenore dederunt ut post mortem eius ecclesia iterum cum tota substantia que ibi tunc reperta fuisset eam reciperet. Set hec donatio ad ecclesie dampnum longo tempore durauit, scilicet usque quo abbas Ageluuius, tempore sancti Eaduuardi regis, a Wigodo regis barone[4] digno pretio eam comparauit. Quandam etiam uillam nomine Mapeldreboreh, quinque hidas habentem, ipsi presbiteri cuidam uiro nobili, Agelmaro nomine,[5] similiter suo die concesserunt, sed ita iniuste concessa usque in hodiernum diem ea caret ecclesia. Has et alias de hiis terris quas habebant potentibus hominibus iccirco dederunt ut adiutores plures haberent, ne monachi eos iterum ex hoc loco expellerent. Set, Dei gratia, 'in uanum laborauerunt'.[6] Igitur dux Alferus, de quo superius prefati sumus, in egritudine constitutus, de uita sua desperatus est.

136. De Fredegaro abbate

Quapropter uocauit ad se quendam monachum, Freodegarum nomine, qui cum eo conuersabatur, et dedit ei abbatiam, Eouesham uidelicet et Vffenham, et alias terras simul quadraginta hidas quas ipse habebat. Reliquas uero terras ecclesie presbiteris et aliis amicis suis prius dederat.

137. Set ipse abbas Freodegarus ad locum istum perueniens, pauco
fo. 142ra tempore hic | potuit commorari, quia clericos fortiores se inueniens nullo modo ualuit eos hinc expellere. Qua de re quendam potentem hominem adiit, Godwinum nomine,[7] qui tunc temporis terram habuit

---

[1] Priests probably indicates canons, and the word *miles* is not contemporary with the acts described.

[2] For Ufa, the sheriff, see above, 124.

[3] He has not been further identified.

[4] Wigod held Wixford in King Edward's day; by 1086 it was in Evesham's hands; see *Domesday Book*, published by the Record Commissioners, 2 vols. i (1783), fo. 239^r. There is nothing to connect him with Wigod of Wallingford, a considerable landowner, holding property in at least seven shires, and possibly as many as eleven, for whom see M. K. Lawson, *Cnut: The Danes in England in the Early Eleventh Century* (London and New

which were in this neighbourhood, and made them part of his own demesne; he gave Ombersley to his brother Ælfweard, handed over eight hides of land at Binton [Warws.] to some of his thegns, and gave his priests whatever lands of this church he pleased.[1]

135. It was during these times that a powerful man named Ufa, the sheriff of Warwickshire, restored to this church, to be received with his dead body, the vill of Wixford [Warws.] which consisted of five hides.[2] However, the priests in charge at that time were most imprudent, for they subsequently gave that land to Ufa's son Wulfgeat[3] on condition that the church received it back again on his death along with the property that had been found on it. In fact this gift to Wulfgeat, to the detriment of the church, lasted for a long period of time, until, indeed, Abbot Æthelwig in the reign of St Edward bought it from the king's baron Wigod[4] at a fair price. Similarly those priests granted a nobleman named Æthelmær[5] the vill of Mapleborough [Warws.] which consisted of five hides, and so injurious was the grant that the church does not possess Mapleborough even today. The priests made gifts of these and other lands to influential men in order to secure more helpers to prevent the monks expelling them again from this place. But by the grace of God 'they laboured in vain'.[6] Indeed, the ealdorman Ælfhere, of whom we have spoken above, fell sick and despaired of his life.

136. *Concerning Abbot Freodegar*

He consequently summoned to his side a monk called Freodegar, with whom he was associated, and gave him the abbacy, Evesham and Offenham, and other lands he possessed amounting to forty hides altogether. He had previously given the remaining lands of the church to priests and others of his friends.

137. Abbot Freodegar came to Evesham but was able to stay for but a short time as he found that the clerks were stronger than he, and he could in no way expel them. He therefore went to see a man of great influence named Godwine[7] who at that time held land called

---

York, 1993), pp. 172, 180. The term baron is not contemporaneous, but it perhaps captures Wigod's standing in post-Conquest terms.

[5] The name is too common to make any satisfactory identification. The one Æthelmaer we know connected with Evesham, who was leasing land for three lives in Norton from Abbot Ælfweard and the convent in 1016×23 (Sawyer, no. 1423), seems too late for this account.

[6] Ps. 126 (127): 1.

[7] Godwine, ealdorman of Lindsey; see below **144** n. 1.

Tofecestre appellatam, et optinuit ab eo ut mutuo sibi daret hanc terram pro ista abbatia. Placuit autem id prefato principi, atque ad regem Æthelredum, fratrem beati Ædwardi martiris,[1] accessit, donans sibi trescentas mancusas auri eo tenore ut sibi abbatiam hereditario iure perpetuo donaret. Rex igitur cupiens habere illud aurum stulte concessit sibi hunc locum. Protinus ille huc pergens presbiteros sibi subiecit, omnique abbatia iniuste res et possessiones eius diripiens sicut uolebat dominari cepit.

138. Deinde post aliquantum tempus rex predictus dedit hanc abbatiam cuidam episcopo, Agelsio nomine. Set is iterum[a] post non multum tempus iram regis incurrens, ab episcopatu deiectus mare transiit et nunquam reuersus est.[2] Deinde rex dedit eam cuidam alio[b] episcopo, Æthelstano uocato.[3]

139. *De secunda reuocatione monachorum et prima subiectione Eueshamensis ecclesie episcopis Wigornie per Aldulfum episcopum et Aluricum abbatem*
Quo defuncto, Aldulfus episcopus Wigornie[4] a rege eam optinuit, et primus libertate sua fraudauit et sue iurisdictioni[c] subiecit. Ille autem constituit hic abbatem, Alfricum nomine.[5]

140. *De Algaro abbate*
Post cuius etiam mortem Alfgarus abbas prefuit. Inter hos omnes quoque semper Goduuinus quadraginta habuit hidas, uidelicet hanc uillam Eouesham et Vffeham, Ambresleie, Burhtun, Lencwike,[6] ita ut nec episcopi nec abbates plus possent habere quam solummodo ecclesiam et reliquas terras quas presbiteri tenuerunt.

141. *De redemptione terrarum a Godwino per Brihtmarum abbatem*
Defuncto iterum isto abbate Alfgaro, Britthmarus quidam abbas prefuit huic loco. Qui uir uenerabilis super Goduuinum coram

---

[a] is iterum *over an erasure*   [b] *MS* alii   [c] et sue iurisdictioni *over an erasure*

[1] Son of Edgar, b. ?968/9, acc. Mar. 978, cons. 979, d. 23 Apr. 1016; *HBC*, p. 27.

[2] Æthelsige I of Sherborne, acc. 978×979, d. 991×993; *HBC*, p. 222. Dorothy Whitelock has shown that the story of his incurring the king's wrath and crossing the sea never to return is due to a misunderstanding. Instead the bishop went in 991 on a royal embassy to Richard of Normandy, after which no more is heard of him; D. Whitelock, *Some Anglo-Saxon Bishops of London*, Chambers Memorial Lecture 1974 (H. K. Lewis for University College London, *c.*1975), p. 23 n. 3.

[3] ?Ælfstan of London 959×64–995×996 (*HBC*, p. 220). He may have held the abbacy of Evesham from 991 until his death *c.*995; Whitelock, ibid., p. 23 and n. 3.

Towcester [Northants]. He was successful in arranging with him an exchange of Towcester for the abbey. Godwine, pleased with the transaction, then approached King Æthelred, brother of Edward the martyr,[1] and gave him three hundred gold mancuses on condition that the king made him a gift of the abbey to be his by hereditary right forever. The king, being eager to have the gold, foolishly granted him this place. Godwine came here straightway and, having established control over the priests, unjustly robbed the whole abbey of its property and possessions, and began to rule it just as he pleased. **138.** Then after some time King Æthelred gave this abbey to a certain Bishop Æthelsige. But again, he soon incurred the wrath of the king and, after being deprived of his bishopric, he crossed the sea never to return.[2] The king then gave the abbey to another bishop called Ælfstan.[3]

139. *The second restoration of the monks, and the first subjection of the church of Evesham to the bishops of Worcester by Bishop Ealdwulf and Abbot Ælfric*

When Ælfstan died the king gave Ealdwulf, bishop of Worcester,[4] possession of the abbey. He was the first to rob it of its liberty and to subject it to his own jurisdiction. However, he did install an abbot here named Ælfric.[5]

140. *Concerning Abbot Ælfgar*

When Ælfric died, he was succeeded by Abbot Ælfgar. During the abbacies of all these men Godwine always remained in possession of the forty hides comprising the vill of Evesham, Offenham, Ombersley, Bourton-on-the-Water [Glos.], and Lenchwick.[6] Consequently, the only land the bishops or abbots could hold was the church and the other lands which the priests held.

141. *Abbot Brihtmær redeems the lands from Godwine*

When Abbot Ælfgar died an Abbot Brihtmær succeeded him here. A godly man, he repeatedly sued Godwine before many chief men of

---

[4] Abbot of Peterborough; bp of Worcester 992–4 June 1002 (d.). He was translated to York in 995, but retained the bishopric of Worcester (*HBC*, p. 224).

[5] During the excavations begun in 1811, a burial was discovered in the north transept with a lead plate inscribed, 'Hic requiescit domnus abbas Ælfricus huius loci anima sua requiescat in pace Amen'; see VCH *Worcs.*, ii. 388.

[6] See above, **136.**

multis principibus huius patrie frequenter placitauit,[1] eo quod iniuste terras ecclesie possideret. Qua de re diiudicatum est ei, ut tantum aurum quantum regi dederat sibi redderet, et ipse terras ecclesie iure reciperet. Quod et ipse libenter fecit, et quadraginta hidas ecclesie restituit.

142. De primo [Ageluui]no abbate[2]

Huic uero abbati quidam nomine Ageluuinus abbas successit, et suo tempore abbatiam istam ut decessor eius reliquirat | integram conseruauit.

fo. 142rb

143. De secunda inuasione possessionum huius abbacie per Godwinum

Quo etiam ex hac luce instabili migrante sepedictus Goduuinus sancte ecclesie aduersarius per potentiam suam abbatiam istam iterum inuasit, terras et possessiones diripuit, suoque dominio contra Deum miserabiliter mancipauit. Et hoc sine iussione regis fecerat, eo quod ipse eodem tempore mare transiens adiit comitem Normannie Rodbertum, cuius filiam habebat uxorem,[3] fugiens namque quasi imbellis uerecundose[a] persecutionem Sueinonis regis fortissimi Danorum, qui tunc temporis maximam partem huius patrie cum maximo exercitu inuaserat.[4]

144. De plena reuocatione possessionum huius ecclesie et particulari reformatione libertatis eiusdem, et plena expulsione Godwini per Eilwardum abbatem, et aliis operibus eius

Set eodem pagano duce secundo aduentus sui anno diuinitus extincto, rex Æthelredus patriam reuersus[5] quendam monachum Ramesiensem, Alfuuardum nomine, constituit abbatem in hoc loco.[6] Qui uir uenerabilis huc adueniens, fretus auxilio Dei atque regis, peruasorem iuris huius sancte ecclesie, Goduuinum uidelicet, cum magna fortitudine hinc expulit, et terras abbatie huius sicuti melius fuerant antiquitus, Dei gratia annuente, uiriliter omnes adquisiuit. Goduuinus uero qui eas iniuste habuit, eodem anno Dei nutu in

---

[a] se over erasure extends into the margin and is written again in the next line and expunged (s. xv)

---

[1] This may mean the shire court. The word patria is used.

[2] Æthelwinus (Æthelwine or Æthelwig) called 'the first' to distinguish him from Abbot Æthelwig (1058–77), on whom see below, 151 f.

[3] The chronicler is mistaken. Emma (Ælfgifu), who married Æthelred as his second wife, was the daughter of Count Richard I of Normandy, not Robert. She later married Cnut of Denmark, the son of Swegn. Robert I, duke from 1027–35, was the father of William the Conqueror (HBC, pp. 27, 28, 34).

this district[1] on the grounds that he had no right to possess lands of this church. In this matter judgment was given in the abbot's favour, namely, that he should pay Godwine as much gold as he had given the king, and himself receive rightful possession of the church. He gladly did this, and Godwine restored the forty hides to the church.

142. Concerning the first abbot Æthelwig[2]

Brihtmær was succeeded as abbot by a man named Æthelwig who during his period of office preserved the abbey intact, just as his predecessor had left it.

143. Godwine's second assault upon the abbey's possessions

When Æthelwig departed this mortal life, this Godwine I have so often mentioned, who was an adversary of the church, used his great power to make a second assault upon the abbey. He robbed it of its lands and possessions and deplorably alienated them for his own demesne, contrary to God's will. He had done this without mandate from the king because the king at that time was abroad visiting Count Robert of Normandy, whose daughter he had married.[3] King Æthelred, who was no soldier, had fled shamefully from the pursuit of Swegn, the powerful king of the Danes, who at that time had invaded a large part of this country with a very large army.[4]

144. The full restoration of this church's possessions and the partial recovery of its liberty; the complete expulsion of Godwine by Abbot Ælfweard; and other of his deeds

The pagan leader was killed by divine intervention within two years of his accession, so King Æthelred returned to his own country.[5] He installed a monk of Ramsey named Ælfweard as abbot of Evesham.[6] When this godly man arrived here, relying on the help of God and of the king, and with considerable courage, he expelled from this place the man Godwine who had invaded the rights of this holy church. Also, by God's grace, he manfully regained all the lands of this abbey as they had been more fully held in antiquity. But in fact that same Godwine, who held these lands wrongfully, was by God's

---

[4] Æthelred was in exile in Normandy from Jan. 1014 until Lent of that year; *HBC*, p. 27.

[5] The pagan leader is Swegn. Following his death in 1014, King Æthelred began his second reign which lasted until his death in 1016; *HBC*, p. 27.

[6] Ælfweard was abbot from *c.*1014 to 1044; see *HRH*, p. 47, and *Jo. Wo.* ii. 540–1.

bello contra regem Danorum, Cnutonem Sueinonis filium, facto occisus est.[1]

145. Ita denique post mortem abbatis Eaduuini a tempore regis Ædmundi, non illius qui uere sanctus appellatur sed alterius,[2] usque ad finem fere regni regis sepedicti Æthelredi, quod laboriosissime triginta annis tenuit, diuersi huic loco prefuere prelati, laici uidelicet, presbiteri, episcopi, et abbates, et ideo nimirum res et ornamenta*a* huius sancte ecclesie que pater noster Ecgwinus uel alii qui post eum pacifice eidem prefuerunt direpta atque in diuersis locis distracta dinoscuntur. Et multa digna memoria hic facta profunde obliuioni traduntur, de quibus aliquid magis pie arbitrari elegimus quam aliquid presumtuose diffinire; quamuis ob tocius loci sanctificationem, locum sanctum diuidendo et loca a locis distinguendo, strictius et discretius loca in quibus facta sunt specificari non
fo. 142va curemus, cum tamen ea infra ambitum huius | cenobii facta nequaquam*b* dubitemus. Set hoc 'est mirabile in oculis nostris'[3] quod in tot et tantis tribulationibus et tam uariis et subitis personarum hic iniuste dominantium mutationibus, priuilegia Constantini episcopi*c* que reuerendus pater noster beatus Ecgwinus adquisiuit,[4] uel ab episcopis Wigornie cum huic ecclesie dominabantur, uel a clericis quando huic loco prefuerunt, maxime cum talium contra incursus concepta et scripta sint, omnino non fuerint demolita. Set hoc per Dei misericordiam et interuentum eiusdem gloriose genitricis Marie factum esse credimus, que sicut locum quem elegit penitus periclitari passa non est, sic eius iura et iuris confirmationes ad eiusdem ecclesie reformationem illesa conseruare dignata est.

146. Vir uero prudens Æluuardus abbas, qui etiam sub Cnutone rege Londoniensis ecclesie episcopus effectus est, non tamen huius loci gubernationem deserens, laboriose, ueluti prefati sumus, omnes terras ante habitas reuocauit, et Bradewellam pro sex marcis auri redemit a consanguineo suo rege Cnutone.[5] Qui rex

---

a marg. Nota de rebus et ornamentis ecclesie dirept. (s. xv²)   *b* erasure here of one word (?pape)   *c* episcopi has been written over ?pape. Marginal note beside the entry reads Nota de priuilegiis Constantini episcopi non sunt demolit (s. xv²)

[1] Godwine, ealdorman of Lindsey was killed at the battle of Ashingdon in 1016; see ASC (s.a. 1016), p. 96, version C, and Jo. Wo., ii. 490–1.
[2] See 132 n. 2 (p. 140), above.
[3] Ps. 117 (118): 23.
[4] For the privileges, see below, 318–28.
[5] Ælfweard was appointed bishop of London in 1035; see HBC, p. 220. For him, see M. Lawson, Cnut, pp. 149–50, 155, 193. Ann Williams has suggested that he was perhaps a

will killed in the battle he fought against the Danish king Cnut, son of Swegn.[1]

145. To sum up then. After the death of Abbot Edwin in the reign of King Edmund [I]—not St Edmund, but the other king of that name[2]—until almost the end of the reign of the frequently mentioned King Æthelred, who ruled with great vigour for thirty years, different kinds of rulers, viz. laymen, priests, bishops, and abbots, governed this place. It is not surprising therefore that the property and treasures of this holy church, which were given to it by our father Ecgwine and others who ruled the same church peaceably, were pillaged and are known to have been dispersed to various places. Many things which have happened here deserve to have been recorded, but have been consigned to utter oblivion. We have preferred to treat these deeds with respect rather than to describe them in any way presumptuously. Because of the holiness of the whole place, we would not want to make too specific or too distinctive mention of the places where these deeds occurred by dividing up a holy place, or by differentiating one place from another, though we should not doubt in the least that they took place within the precincts of this monastery. Indeed, 'it is marvellous in our eyes'[3] that despite the many great tribulations and various sudden changes of persons who engaged in unjust rule here, the privileges of Pope Constantine, which our revered father Ecgwine acquired,[4] were not completely destroyed by either the bishops of Worcester when they ruled over this church, or by the clerks when they were in charge here: this is especially marvellous since the privileges were formulated and written against the assaults of such people. We believe that this was achieved through the mercy of God and the mediation of his glorious mother Mary: just as she did not allow the place which she had chosen to be completely endangered, so she chose to keep its rights and confirmations of privilege intact in order to effect the restoration of this church.

146. The wise Abbot Ælfweard, who was also appointed bishop of London in the reign of King Cnut, did not abandon his rule of this place, but with great vigour, as has already been said, recovered all the lands previously held by this church, and for six marks bought Broadwell [Glos.] back from King Cnut, who was his kinsman.[5] The

kinsman of Ælgifu of Northampton, in ' "Cockles amongst the Wheat": Danes and English in the Western Midlands in the first half of the eleventh century', *Midland History*, xi (1986), 1–22, at p. 8.

reliquias beati Wistani[1] et nigram casulam meliorem cum aliis
ornamentis ad eam pertinentibus huic ecclesie contulit.[a] Iste etiam
rex dedit huic ecclesie Baddebi et Neueham.[2] Idem uero Æluuardus episopus et abbas sanctissimas corporis reliquias fere omnes
beati Odulfi confessoris a mercatoribus eas Londonias portantibus
mercatus est digno pretio, id est, centum marcis, atque ad istum
locum quem maxime dilexerat transmisit, laudabiliter reseruandas
hic perpetuo.[b][3] Libros etiam plurimos tam diuinos quam grama-
ticos de Londonia transmisit. Iste etiam abbas, postquam Aldulfus
episcopus Wigornie[4] hanc abbatiam sibi et successoribus suis
subiecerat, primus abbatum in libertatem proclamauit, et in
tantum optinuit quod uenerabilem uirum Auitium huius ecclesie
priorem decanum Christianitatis tocius uallis constituit, quam
nunquam libertatem ecclesia ista postea amisit.[c][5] Qui prior et
decanus[d] fuit a rege Cnutone et ab aliis principibus huius patrie
fo. 142[vb] plurimis ualde dilectus et honoratus pro sua sanctitate. | Iste prior
quasi ex paterna hereditate duas uillas Baddebi et Neueham huic
sancte ecclesie reddidit. Hoc idem fecit postea beatus Wlsius[6] cum
parentes sui easdem uillas iterum iniuste occupassent; de una enim
erant parentela. Eius etiam ortatu Leoffricus comes et Godgiua
comitissa, eo quod pater erat confessionum suarum, prudentissime
mundum in plurimis spernentes, elemosinis et orationibus diligenter instantes,[7] Couentreiam abbatiam[8] pluresque alias ecclesias pro
amore Dei gloriose edificantes, terris et possessionibus et plurimis

---

[a] *marg.* Nota de reliquiis beati Vlstani (*s. xv²*)   [b] *marg.* Nota de reliquiis beati Odulfi
(*s. xv²*)/ emptis et datis ecclesie (*s. xvii*)   [c] *marg.* Nota de primo decano istius loci
(*s. xv²*)   [d] ualde *deleted*

[1] Wigstan, prince of the royal house of Mercia, was murdered (probably at Wistow,
Leics.) in 849 for opposing the marriage of his mother, whom he had asked to rule as
regent, to Beorhtric, his cousin, on the grounds that the marriage would be incestuous. He
was buried in the royal monastery at Repton, the mausoleum of the Mercians, with his
father and grandfather. In 1019, Ælfweard asked Cnut for the relics of his cult; see *Acta
Sanctorum*, 1 June, cols. 85–6; *AB* lviii (1940), 90–103; Jennings in *EHR*, lxxvii (1962),
298–304.
[2] Sawyer, no. 957 (1020). The tradition of the Benedictine abbey of Crowland, to which
Badby belonged at the time of Domesday, was somewhat different, namely that Badby had
been given on a hundred-year lease to Northman, brother of Leofric. On Northman's
death it passed to Leofric, who gave it to Evesham. Sawyer, no. 977, is the grant by King
Cnut of Newnham (Northants, not Notts. as Sawyer) to Æfic the monk of Evesham and is
likely to be genuine; Lawson, *Cnut*, pp. 155, 240. It is easy to see how the two
Northamptonshire possessions of Evesham were brought together in this way.

king granted this church the relics of the blessed Wigstan[1] and a fine black chasuble with other precious things belonging to it. He also gave it Badby and Newnham [Northants].[2] That same bishop and abbot Ælfweard purchased all the holy relics of the body of the blessed Odulf at a fair price of one hundred marks from the merchants who were bringing them to London, and he sent them to the place for which he had the greatest affection, to be lovingly preserved here for ever.[3] He also sent from London a large number of books, not only sacred works but also grammars. Ælfweard was the first abbot, after Ealdwulf, bishop of Worcester,[4] had subjected this abbey to himself and his successors, to proclaim its liberty; and so successful was his rule that he was able to appoint the venerable Æfic, prior of this church, as dean of Christianity in the whole of the Vale, and this church never again lost its liberty.[5] As prior and dean Æfic was highly respected and honoured for his godliness by King Cnut and most of the other leading men of this country. As prior he restored to this holy church, as if from his patrimony, the two vills of Badby and Newnham. The blessed Wulfsige[6] did the same thing afterwards, when his relatives had once again wrongfully taken possession of these same vills; for they were from the same kindred. Persuaded by Wulfsige, their spiritual father, Earl Leofric, and Countess Godgifu, wisely rejecting the world for the most part, and assiduous in almsgiving and prayer,[7] magnificently built the abbey at Coventry[8] and many other churches in their love for God, and enriched them with lands, possessions, and many beautiful

---

[3] The relics of Odulf, the monk and missionary to Frisia, who died in 855, which came to rest in Evesham, had been stolen by Viking pirates from Staveren, but Odulf died at Utrecht, which makes their authenticity dubious. See *Acta Sanctorum*, 12 June, cols. 591–5; for their later history, see below, 149. There were two feasts of the translation, 10 Oct. and 24 Nov.

[4] See above 139.

[5] On the liberty, the Vale, and the dean of the Vale, see Sayers, 'The proprietary church in England: a note on "Ex ore sedentis" (X 5. 33. 17)', *Zeitschrift der Savigny-Stiftung für Rechtsgeschichte, kan. Abt.* lxxiv (1988), 231–45, at pp. 234–5, 238–40. The older Benedictine houses claimed exempt areas, administered later as deaneries, or more frequently archdeaconries, under the abbot; for Bury St Edmunds, St Albans, Glaston-bury, and Westminster, see Sayers, 'Monastic archdeacons', in *Church and Government in the Middle Ages: Essays presented to C. R. Cheney*, ed. C. Brooke *et al.* (Cambridge, 1976), pp. 177–203, repr. in *Law and Records in Medieval England* (London, 1988), ch. vi.

[6] Wulsi [Wulfsige], a hermit saint (and monk of Crowland before he became a monk at Evesham). According to John of Worcester, Wulfsige, who had led the solitary life for more than forty years, was instrumental in Wulfstan's acceptance of the bishopric of Worcester in 1062, reproving him for his obstinacy and disobedience (*Jo. Wo.*, ii. 590–1).

[7] Cf. Rom. 12: 12.

[8] Founded in (?)1043: in that year a papal confirmation was granted; KH, pp. 53 and 63.

ditabant ornamentis honestissimis.*ᵃ* Hanc etiam abbatiam ualde diligentes honorabant, facientes hic honorabilem ecclesiam in honore sancte Trinitatis,*ᵇ*¹ in qua fecerunt constitui crucem non modicam et ymaginem sancte Dei genitricis Marie sanctique Iohannis Euangeliste argento et auro honorabiliter fabricatas; necnon etiam uillam quandam, Shuocham nomine, et uiridem casulam et minorem nigram capam et multa alia ornamenta preciosa huic loco contulerunt.

147. Supra namque retulimus hoc quod in priuilegiis patris nostri Ecgwini reperimus, uidelicet, quod ipse centum uiginti hidas huic loco ex utraque parte fluminis huius quod dicitur Auene adquisiuit,² hanc uillam uidelicet Eouesham et Lencwike ex parte ista, Hamtune quoque et Beningwrthe ex alia; set hee due Hamptone et Beningwrthe cum aliis terris plurimis ablate et a diuersis hominibus, sicut superius dictum est, sunt possesse a tempore Ædmundi regis usque ad tempora Cnutonis regis sub hoc Ailuuardo episcopo et huius loco abbate. Ipse igitur rex Cnuto in primo anno regni sui³ quendam ducem super omnes potentiorem huius terre pro causis quas nouerat fecit occidi, Edricum nomine, cum quo etiam et aliis plurimis militibus suis quidam potens homo Normannus uocabulo, frater uidelicet huius Leofrici comitis, perimitur eius iussione.⁴ Quapropter rex, quoniam Leofricum plurimum dilexerat, ut emendaret erga eum propter*ᶜ* mortem fratris sui, fecit eum comitem et principem super omnes terras, ab ista Wigornensi prouintia usque ad Sco | tiam, insuper et terras fratris sui, que plurime erant, sibi concessit. Inter has namque uillam supradictam Hamtune quinque hidas Leofricus accepit, quam frater suus Normannus donante rege Æthelredo plurimis annis possedit. Cum autem aliquot annis ipse comes eam possideret, et frequenter huc ueniendo amicitiam atque noticiam prefati prioris Auitii et aliorum fratrum, ecclesiam illam quam prediximus edificando multaque beneficia peragendo, ex toto haberet, tandem cognoscens quod pater noster Ecgwinus primitus eam huic ecclesie obtineret, rogatu omnium fratrum pro alia terra quam prius dederat, Suocham nomine, ita omnino liberam huic ecclesie perpetualiter

fo. 143ʳᵃ

ᵃ marg. Nota de ecclesia de Couentre (*s. xv²*)   *ᵇ marg.* Nota de ecclesia in honore sancte Trinitatis facta (*s. xv²*)   *ᶜ* propter *inserted* (*s. xv*)

---

¹ This church of Holy Trinity is somewhat puzzling, as there is no further mention of it: it seems likely that it was actually attached to the abbey as a chapel, either from the time of its construction or perhaps later as a result of further building having taken place. There is no evidence that Holy Trinity was a previous dedication of either of the two parochial

treasures. They lovingly honoured this abbey by building here a noble church in honour of the Holy Trinity.[1] In it they had a large cross erected as well as an image of St Mary, Mother of God, and another of St John the Evangelist, beautifully fashioned in silver and gold. They even bestowed upon this abbey a vill named Southam [Warws.], a green chasuble, a small black cope, and many other precious treasures.

147. We have referred above to something that we found in the privileges of our father Ecgwine, that Ecgwine himself acquired for this place 120 hides on each side of the river Avon,[2] comprising the vill of Evesham and Lench on the one side, and Hampton and Bengeworth on the other. However, the two vills of Hampton and Bengeworth with many other lands were taken away and possessed by various men, as related above, from the time of King Edmund till that of King Cnut under Bishop Ælfweard who was also abbot of Evesham. During the first year of his reign,[3] King Cnut had one of the most powerful leading men in this land, named Eadric, put to death for reasons best known to himself. Executed along with him and many others of his thegns was an influential man called North-man, brother of Earl Leofric.[4] However, as the king had a very high regard for Leofric, in order to compensate him for the death of his brother he made him an earl and chief man over all the territories from the region of Worcester north to Scotland, and granted him in addition his brother's lands, which were numerous. Amongst these Leofric received the above-mentioned Hampton which consisted of five hides that his brother Northman had possessed for many years as a gift of King Æthelred. The earl himself held possesssion of this land for several years, but he came to know Prior Æfic and other brethren very well, and became their friend during his frequent visits to this place, because of his building of the church we have mentioned, and through the benefits he bestowed. Eventually he learned that our father Ecgwine had originally held that land for this church, so, at the request of the brethren and in exchange for Southam [Warws.]—the other land which he had previously given to the church—he granted it to this church to be held completely free for ever, just as he had

chapels of St Laurence and All Saints, which stood (and still stand) close to the abbey; see Cox, 'Building, construction, and excavation', p. 124.

[2] See above, 28.

[3] i.e. 1017.

[4] On this whole episode, see *ASC* F; *Encomium Emmae Reginae*, ed. A. Campbell (Royal Historical Society, Camden 3rd ser. lxxii, 1949), ii.15, pp. 30–2; Hemming, i. 259, 281. See also *Jo. Wo.*, ii. 504–5.

concessit, quemadmodum ipse, rege donante, longo tempore possedit, et ueluti in carta sua que in fine huius operis habetur per scripta apertissime demonstratur.[1]

148. Venerabilis igitur prior iste Auicius anno ab incarnatione Domini millesimo tricesimo octauo ex hac luce discessit, et in eadem ecclesia sancte Trinitatis coram eadem religiosa comitissa Godgiua uenerabiliter sepultus extitit, cuius et memoriam habuit quamdiu uixit. Postea uero gloriosus Ailuuardus Londoniensis ecclesie, ut prediximus, antistes, huius ecclesie pastor piissimus, in egritudine constitutus, iussit suis ut huc eum deducerent, cupiens, si Deus disponeret, in hoc loco quem plurimum ante dilexerat, menbra sua fragilia perpetualiter requiescere. Set quidam fratres atque laici quos ipse antea diuitiis et honoribus plurimum exaltans huic loco prefecerat, diabolico instinctu ad maximum dampnum huius sancte ecclesie contra eum rebelles effecti, per legatos sibi mandauerunt quod si huc ueniret omnes monachi discederent.[2] Quo audito, uir ille uenerabilis plus quam dici ualet contristatus, et pro hiis nefandissimis traditoribus suis nimium huic loco iratus, toto animo ad Ramesiensem ecclesiam conuersus, ubi prius fuerat monachus fecit se deduci, et

fo. 143ʳᵇ omnia ornamenta que secum portabat, uidelicet casulas, | capas, pallia plurima multaque alia ornamenta que huic loco offerre cogitabat, uersa uice prefate ecclesie Ramesie omnia condonabat. Et ita millesimo quadragesimo quarto anno ab incarnatione Domini uitam temporalem finiens, ibi sepultus requiescit.[3]

149. *De abbate Mannio et sanctis operibus eius*
Eodem anno, facto consilio apud Londonias,[4] Mannius huius ecclesie monachus abbas a rege Æduuardo, secundo uidelicet anno regni eius, eligitur, atque ad istum locum quarto idus Augusti consecratur.[5] Hic uir ualde uenerabilis et sacris litteris aliisque plurimis artibus fuerat imbutus, uidelicet cantoris, scriptoris, pictoris aurique fabrilis operis scientia pollens, super omnes alios fere huius patrie magister optimus habebatur. Apud Cantuariam uero atque ecclesiam Couentreiam

---

[1] Charter of Leofric giving Hampton; Sawyer, no. 1223 (1033×1038). The text is in V on fo. 30ʳ⁻ᵛ: it no longer survives as part of R.

[2] The chronicler does not point out that Ælfweard had leprosy. At least, this was the gloss put on what John of Worcester described as Ælfweard's infirmity (*Jo. Wo.*, ii 540–1) by the Ramsey chronicler; see *Chronicon abbatiae Rameseiensis*, ed. W. D. Macray (RS lxxxiii; London, 1886), pp. 157–8.

[3] Cf. the account in *Jo. Wo.*, ii. 540–1, who gives the date of Ælfweard's death as 25 July.

possessed it for a long time as a gift from the king: this is clearly shown in his charter which is to be found at the end of this work.[1]

148. However, the venerable prior, Æfic, departed this life in the year of our Lord 1038, and was honourably buried in the same church of Holy Trinity in the presence of the devout Countess Godgifu who remembered him as long as she lived. After this the blessed Ælfweard, who was bishop of London as we have said, and the most devoted shepherd of this church, fell ill. He commanded his men to bring him here, for he desired, God willing, to rest his frail limbs for ever more in this place which he had previously loved so much. However, some of the brethren and laymen whom he himself had given authority over this place, after first exalting them with abundant riches and high honours, objected to this. With evil intent, and to the greatest detriment of this holy church, they rebelled against him and told him through their messengers that all the monks would leave if he came here.[2] When that venerable man heard this he was saddened beyond words and, very angry with this place, because of those who had unspeakably betrayed him, he turned with all his heart towards the church of Ramsey [Hunts.] where he had previously been a monk, and had himself taken there. All the treasures which he was carrying with him, such as chasubles, copes, a large number of altar-frontals, and all the many other treasures which he was intending to offer this place, he now gave to the church of Ramsey. And in the year of our Lord 1044 his life on this earth ended, and he was buried there.[3]

149. *Abbot Mannig and his holy deeds*

That same year at a Council held in London,[4] Mannig, a monk of this church, was appointed abbot by King Edward in the second year of his reign, and was consecrated abbot of this place on 10 August.[5] This venerable man had been well educated in both sacred literature and many other arts, so that he was an accomplished cantor, scribe, painter, and goldsmith; he was also considered to be the best master before all others in the whole of this country. He produced many highly acclaimed works at that time at Canterbury and at the church of

---

[4] See *C. & S.*, i pt 1, p. vii n. 2. No record of this Council (which took place in 1044) is known other than the references to Mannig's appointment at it in *ASC* (D), p. 108 (s.a. 1044) and *Jo. Wo.*, ii. 541. The editors of *C. & S.* surmise that Robert of Jumièges may have been appointed to the see of London at this Council.

[5] *ASC* (D), p. 108 (s.a. 1044) also.

sicuti in multis aliis locis plurima opera tunc temporis ualde laudabilia operatus est. In isto denique loco ecclesiam maiori opere quam antea fuit construere cepit, et usque ad bonum finem consummando consecrari fecit. Villa que appellatur Chirichlench suo tempore reddita est huic ecclesie. Similiter et Witheleia primitus a patre nostro Ecgwino adquisita, et tempore Ædmundi regis ueluti plures alie usque ad sua tempora ablata, iterum, Dei gratia, sibi est reddita.[1] Feretrum etiam sancti Ecgwini ex argento, auro et lapidibus pretiosis composuit, in quo erant tres lapides magnam partem ecclesie de nocte illuminantes, in quo opere quoddam miraculum contigit diuinitus, ut credimus, peractum. Nam quidam inter aurifices post abbatem magister aliorum, Godricus nomine, cum sculperet quandam ymaginem que deberet poni in illo scrinio, contigit ut manum sinistram cum artificiali subula mediam perfoderet; at ille, statim sanguinem extergens nichilque doloris sentiens, set quodam ligamine uulnus manus sue ligans, crastina die surgens de lecto, repperit ipsam plagam ex omni parte curatam. Quam rem mox ostendit abbati, qui simul cum fratribus gratias et laudes |

fo. 143va referunt Deo omnipotenti sanctoque Ecgwino suo patri. Idem artifex Godricus postea, tempore Walteri abbatis, monachus factus, plurimis annis uiuens in bona conuersatione sancto fine quieuit in pace.[2] Fecit etiam idem abbas Mannius feretra beati Odulfi et sancti Credani;[3] missalem librum atque psalterium magnum propria manu descripsit ac laudabiliter depinxit, necnon et plura alia opera huic ecclesie laudabiliter operatus est.

150. Ante septem fere annos[4] ex hac luce sue transmigrationis, iustissima Dei clementia, patientiam eius uolens probare sicut et sancti Iob, permisit eum incurrere grauissimam atque insanabilem corporis infirmitatem quam Greci paralisin appellant, ita ut, dissolutis omnibus menbris, ultra non ualeret aliquid disponere de ista abbatia.

---

[1] Mannig also supposedly received a confirmation of the abbey's privileges and of Leofric's grant of land at Hampton (for which see Sawyer, no. 1398; V fo. 31^r) from Bishop Lyfing between 1042 and 1046. Bishop Lyfing says that he confirmed the gift 'with his writ and seal' at the command of the king [Edward].

[2] This story is included also in 72 above, where Godric is said to be the father of the monk Clement who later became prior.

Coventry, as he did in many other places. In Evesham he began to build a church of larger proportions than before, and when he had completed the work successfully he had it consecrated. During Mannig's time the vill of Church Lench was returned to this church. Similarly Weethley [Warws.], which had been first acquired by our father Ecgwine and during the time of King Edmund had been alienated like many other vills up to this time, was again restored to this church by God's grace.[1] Mannig also had a shrine of St Ecgwine set up, made of gold, silver and precious stones. In this there were three gems which illuminated a large part of the church at night, and upon this shrine a miracle occurred which, we believe, was wrought by God. The story is that one of the goldsmiths named Godric—who was master of the others after the abbot—was carving an image which had to be placed upon that shrine when he happened to stab the middle of his left hand with the awl with which he was working. He immediately wiped away the blood, thought nothing of the pain, but tied a bandage around the gash on his hand. However, when he got up the next morning, he found that the wound had completely healed. He straightway showed this to the abbot who, along with the brethren, gave thanks and praise to Almighty God and to their father St Ecgwine. That same smith, Godric, later in the time of Walter, became a monk: he lived a godly life, and after a holy end, rested in peace.[2] Abbot Mannig also built shrines to the blessed Odulf and St Credan.[3] With his own hand he copied a missal and a large psalter, beautifully illuminating them; and he produced many other works for this church in praiseworthy fashion.

150. About seven years[4] before Mannig passed from this world God, by His just mercy, wishing to test his ability to endure suffering as He had the blessed Job, allowed Mannig to suffer a serious incurable disease which the Greeks call 'paralysis'. As a result he could not move his limbs, and so was no longer able to administer any of the business of the abbot's office.

---

[3] Credan was an 8th-cent. abbot of Evesham in the time of King Offa. Virtually nothing is known about him, except that his relics were put to the ordeal by Abbot Walter in 1077, along with those of Evesham's other saints, and that his tomb was saved when the tower collapsed in 1207 (see Farmer, *Oxford Dictionary of Saints*, p. 117, and below, 436). For St Odulf, see above, 146 and n. 3 (p. 153).

[4] This was in 1058: Mannig survived until Epiphany 1066; see below, 154 and n. 4.

151. *De ampliatione huius cenobii per Ælwinum abbatem et magnificis eius actibus*

Qua de re prudenti usus consilio quendam de suis monachum elegit ad id officium honestis moribus ualde probatum, tam generis nobilitate quam diuina lege ac seculari prudentia plurimum ualentem, nomine Ageluuinum, qui multo antea tempore episcopatum Wigornensis ecclesie sub Aldredo archiepiscopo laudabiliter rexerat,[1] et nunc sub eo iure prepositi tocius abbatie huius curam agebat. Misit quoque eum cum quibusdam fratribus et honorabilibus secularibus personis ad regem Aeduuardum,[2] grauibus morbis demonstrans se esse oppressum, orans et multum supplicans ut huic uiro abbatiam istam ex toto traderet et abbatem pro eo faceret.

152. Quod rex prudens cognoscens eiusque pie peticioni annuens, fecit eum apud Glocestre, ubi tunc curiam suam tenebat, coram multis principibus huius patrie ab Aldredo archiepiscopo honorabiliter in Paschali sollempnitate die festiuitatis sancti Georgii martiris consecrari,[3] et ab illo tempore tam sibi quam cunctis baronibus suis carus, et inter primos necessarios consiliarius habebatur.

153. Reuersus namque domum cum multis optimatibus, ex parte regis grandi honore atque amore suscipitur tam a fratribus quam ab fo. 143vb omnibus huius sancte ecclesie populis. | Quamdiu uero abbas suus Mannius superuixit maximam ei curam gerebat, constituens duos de melioribus personis cum quibusdam seruientibus qui die noctuque ei humiliter deseruirent. Ipse autem frequenter eum uisitans, que uolebat humili deuotione obediendo perficiebat, nec unquam quamdiu supererat in loco abbatis causa humilitatis stare uolebat.

154. Transiit quoque uir ille Mannius^a eadem nocte et hora, ut fertur, qua rex gloriosus Æduuardus, festiuitate uidelicet sancte ephiphanie Domini,[4] quorum animas, ut credimus, angeli suscipientes deduxerunt in gaudium Domini sui.

155. Viuente autem isto Dei cultore rege Æduuardo septem annis abbas Ageluuius huic loco preerat,[5] pluresque terras tam ab eo quam

---

^a Mannius *over an erasure* (s. xv)

---

[1] Æthelwig was elected abbot in 1058 and died in 1077; *HRH*, p. 47. Ealdred, bishop of Worcester from 1047 to 1062, also held the archbishopric of York from 1061 to 1069 (*HBC*, p. 224).   [2] Edward the Confessor, acc. 1042, d. 5 Jan. 1066 (*HBC*, p. 29).
[3] F. Barlow, *Edward the Confessor* (London, 1970), p. 209 n. 3, argued that this was 23 April 1058 rather than 1059 (as Macray, p. 87) because Easter day in 1059 fell on 4 April, hence 23 Apr. was hardly Eastertide, whereas in 1058 Easter day was 19 Apr. The statement that Abbot Æthelwig ruled Evesham for seven years during the reign of King Edward the Confessor (see below, p. 161 nn. 4, 5) would be correctly reckoned from 1058

151. *The enlargement of the monastery by Abbot Æthelwig, and his great deeds*

After taking wise advice about his condition, Mannig appointed one of his monks to that office, a man highly recommended by his own virtuous character. He was a man not only of great nobility of family but of considerable knowledge in divine and secular law. His name was Æthelwig, who a long while back had admirably administered the bishopric of Worcester for Archbishop Ealdred,[1] and now under him by right of the provostship took on the care of the whole abbacy. Mannig also sent him with some brethren and reputable lay persons to King Edward,[2] explaining that he was very ill, and earnestly entreated him to hand over the office of abbot entirely to Æthelwig, making him abbot in his stead.

152. The king gave wise consideration to this and assented to his respectful petition. He had Æthelwig duly consecrated by Archbishop Ealdred at Gloucester, where he was at that time holding his court, in the presence of many leading men of this country on the festival of St George the martyr during Eastertide.[3] From this time on Æthelwig was as beloved by the king as he was by his [the king's] barons, and was regarded as a counsellor amongst his closest friends.

153. He returned home with many great men, and on the king's behalf was received with great honour and affection not only by the brethren but also by all the people associated with this holy church. While Mannig, his abbot, survived he showed him the greatest possible concern, appointing two of his best men with some servants to serve him respectfully day and night. Æthelwig himself visited him frequently, and with humble devotion obediently carried out whatever he wished. In his humility he never wished to occupy the position of abbot as long as Mannig lived.

154. Mannig is said to have passed away on the same night, and at the same hour, as the blessed King Edward, during the festival of the Holy Epiphany of the Lord,[4] and we believe the angels received their souls and led them into the joy of their Lord.

155. Abbot Æthelwig ruled this place for seven years during the reign of King Edward,[5] that devoted servant of God, and held many

rather than 1059 if the chronicler preferred a period of just under seven years, i.e. 7 years less 3 months, rather than a period of nearly eight years (7 years 9 months).

[4] Edward the Confessor is said to have died on 5 Jan. (*HBC*, p. 29), and Mannig *circa* Epiphany—his obit was kept on 6 Jan. (*HRH*, p. 47). Since the feast began with the vigil on the previous day, 5/6 Jan. would explain the statement.

[5] i.e. from 1058 to 1066 (Jan.).

ab aliis bonis hominibus optinebat, quarum nomina inferius demon-
strabimus. Defuncto nempe rege isto et Haraldo regnum accipiente,[1]
quicquid uolebat ab eo impetrauit. Deinde rege Willelmo ipsum
Haraldum Dei iudicio expugnante,[2] totaque Anglia secundum uelle
suum ex toto dominante, tam episcopi quam abbates multique nobiles
huius patrie latitabant, eius persecutionem atque ferocitatem
fugientes. Iste tamen abbas Ageluuius confidens in Domino[3] ad
eum accessit, Deique gratia donante super omnes fere huius Anglice
gentis barones maximam amicitiam apud eum obtinuit, quam usque
ad ultimum diem sui obitus idem rex erga eum fideliter seruauit.

156. Plures itaque abbatie alieque ecclesie terras et possessiones illo
tempore Normannis inuadentibus perdiderunt, set ipse Dei nutu non
solum nullas perdidit set maioribus opibus et honoribus abbatiam
istam multipliciter adauxit.[4] Et quoniam rex sapiens cognouerat eum
⟨esse⟩ uirum prudentem, pene omnes huius gentis homines seculari
sapientia precellentem, commisit ei curam istarum partium terre,
uidelicet Wirecestrescire, Glouecestrescire, Oxenefordscire et Ware-
uuikescire, Herefordschire, Stafordscire, Scrobschire, ita ut omnium
huius patrie consilia[5] atque iudicia fere in eo penderent. Et non solum
fo. 144ra in istis partibus, set etiam per totam An|gliam ubicumque ueniebat,
tam Franci quam Angli[6] pro iustissima lege tenebant quicquid ipse
legibus secularibus dicebat. Quotienscumque ad placita uel ad sciras
pergebat undique concursus populorum eum frequentabat, quisque
pro sua necessitate consilia atque auxilia contra aduersarios humiliter
postulabat: unde comites et uicecomites cunctique regis barones
optimum consiliarium naturali scientia preditum eum cognoscentes,
quasi dominum illum uenerabantur. Et ubicumque ueniebat uel ad
curiam regis seu alicubi ad placita semper nobilitas hominum
sequebatur eum, atque humili obsequio ei famulabatur.

157. Isdem namque temporibus erat uir religiosus, 'simplex et

---

[1] Harold had acceded to the throne on 6 Jan. 1066. He died at Hastings on 14 Oct. of
the same year; see HBC, p. 29.

[2] See previous note.

[3] Cf. e.g. Ps. 10: 2 (11: 1); Rom. 14: 14; and numerous other references.

[4] The considerable achievements of Æthelwig in gaining lands for Evesham (see below,
166–70) gave him an almost saintly character in the eyes of the Evesham historians. From
the Worcester viewpoint, Æthelwig was nothing short of a 'devil figure', classed in the
same category as Urse d'Abetot; see P. Wormald, 'Oswaldslow: an "immunity"?', in St
Oswald of Worcester: Life and Influence, ed. N. Brooks and C. Cubitt (Leicester, 1996),
pp. 117–28, at 125; and E. Mason, St Wulfstan of Worcester (Oxford, and Cambridge,
Mass., 1990), p. 127, 'To the Worcester writers . . . any unavoidable mention of him in
their works was unfavourable.' For the two contrasting narratives about the lands at issue,

lands both from him and from other good men, and we shall mention their names below. After the death of King Edward, Harold succeeded to the throne, [1] and Æthelwig obtained from him whatever he wished. Then King William, as a judgment of God, defeated Harold himself in battle,[2] and subjected the whole of England completely to his own will. As the result, bishops, abbots, and many noblemen of this country went into hiding, fleeing his fury and persecution. However, Abbot Æthelwig, trusting in the Lord,[3] went to see him and, as a gift of God's grace, was received at William's court with great friendship, greater than that accorded to almost all the barons of English race; and William maintained that friendship towards him faithfully to the very end of Æthelwig's life. **156.** Many abbeys and other churches lost lands and possessions at the time the Normans invaded, but Æthelwig by God's will not only lost no possessions but in many respects enhanced his abbey with more extensive buildings and greater honours.[4] The king was shrewd enough to recognize that he was a prudent man, with more worldly wisdom than almost all other men of his race, so he entrusted him with care of the following areas: Worcestershire, Gloucestershire, Oxfordshire, Warwickshire, Herefordshire, Staffordshire and Shropshire. Hence, the councils[5] of all the men of this region and the judgments depended almost entirely on him. Indeed, it was not only in those regions but also throughout the whole of England that wherever he went both Frenchmen and Englishmen[6] considered any pronouncements he made on secular laws to be the most just law. Whenever he proceeded with the hearings at the shire courts, crowds of people thronged him on every side, and every man would abase himself and ask for his counsel and assistance in his needs against his adversaries. Hence, earls, sheriffs and all the king's barons acknowledged him as the best of counsellors, endowed with common sense, and revered him as though he were their lord. So wherever he went, to the king's court or to moots elsewhere, a group of nobles always followed him and served him in humble obedience.

157. In those days there was a bishop of Worcester called Wulfstan, a

see *English Lawsuits from William I to Richard I*, ed. R. C. van Caenegem (Selden Soc. cvi, 1990), no. 10, pp. 29–32.

[5] What seems to be meant here is the shire courts.

[6] The use of the term 'French and English' is characteristic of royal writs of the 12th cent. rather than the 11th and reflects an author of that date, not earlier; see *Regesta Regum Anglo-Normannorum: The Acta of William I* (1066–1087), ed. D. Bates (Oxford, 1998), p. 64.

rectus', Wigornensis ecclesie antistes, Wlstanus nomine.[1] Hic cognoscens abbatem Ageluuium uirum prudentem tam apud regem
quam apud omnes principes eius seculari prudentia et fortitudine
plurimum ualere, sepissime ad se conuocans*ᵃ* et ipse ad illum ueniens,
eius consilio atque auxilio utebatur in multis utilitatibus ecclesie sue.
Qua de re uir ille uenerabilis eius fretus iudicio ac fortitudine quam
plurimas terras antea perditas adquisiuit.

158. Contigit autem eo tempore Willelmi regis ut Thomas archiepiscopus Eboraci, prudens homo, episcopatum Wigornensis ecclesie
uellet subicere sue ecclesie.[2] Ad hanc rem defendendam duas marcas
auri abbas sibi accomodauit et unam dedit, et ita, Deo opitulante et
abbate uerbo et opere consilium et opem ferente, libertatem ecclesie
sue seruauit. Et quoniam episcopus erat uir bonus et pater suarum
confessionum, quasdam terras sibi dedit quarum nomina ista sunt,
uidelicet, Bisepesdun'[3] et Cagecote, et ipse sibi mutuo concessit
uillam que uocatur Milecote. Non solum autem huic ecclesie set et
omnibus ubicumque fuerat aduocatus beneficiorum suorum suffragia
gratanter impendere studuit. Nam quadam uice uocatus ab archiepiscopo Lanfranco, quasdam terras diu ablatas Cantuariensi ecclesie
Christi ipse iudex et testis adquisiuit. Pro qua re usque in hodiernum
diem anniuersarius depositionis | eius dies ibi in ecclesia illa
obseruatur.[4] Abbatia etiam de Gloecestre in primis, uenerande
memorie Serlone abbate[5] ibi ueniente, tunc temporis erat pauperima,
set, eodem abbate humiliter rogante, multimoda frequenter ei sua
impendit leuamina. Rex etiam Willelmus tollens abbatem Wincel-
cumbensem, Godricum nomine,[6] fecit constitui in captiuitate apud
Gloecestre moxque*ᵇ* huic abbati Ageluuio suam abbatiam commisit,
quam fere per*ᶜ* tres annos quasi propriam in cunctis gubernando
seruauit. Deinde rex donauit illam cuidam abbati Galando nomine, et,

fo. 144ʳᵇ

ᵃ con *over an erasure (s. xv)*   *ᵇ* que *interlined (s. xiii¹)*   *ᶜ* per *interlined (s. xiii¹)*

[1] Job 1: 1. Wulfstan II, el. 29 Aug., cons. 8 Sept. 1062, d. 19 or 20 Jan. 1095. See the
account of the devout Wulfsan and his election to the see of Worcester in *Jo. Wo.*, ii.
588–93.
[2] For Thomas of Bayeux's designs on Worcester, see *Jo. Wo.*, iii. 13, 17. Thomas's
predecessor, Ealdred, bishop of Worcester, had retained that see when he became
archbishop of York. On Ealdred's death in 1069, Bishop Wulfstan of Worcester claimed
the Worcester lands. The case was not settled until after the consecration of Thomas in
1170 or in 1171 when York's claims to make Worcester 'its handmaiden' were quashed.
[3] In the north-west part of Stratford-upon-Avon.
[4] See Christ Church, Canterbury, obits, BL Cotton MS Nero C IX fo. 5ᵛ (14 kal. Mar.
= 16 Feb.); printed J. Dart, *History and Antiquities of the Cathedral Church of Canterbury*

'guileless, upright man'.[1] He saw that Abbot Æthelwig was an intelligent man having considerable influence not only over the king, but also over the king's leading men because of his worldly wisdom and influence, so he would often ask him, therefore, to visit him, or would himself go and see him, and ask his advice and help on many practical issues concerning his church. As a consequence, that venerable man, relying on Æthelwig's advice and influence, regained all the lands he had previously lost.

158. It was in the time of King William that Thomas, archbishop of York and a knowledgeable man, wanted to make the see of Worcester subject to his own church.[2] To assist Wulfstan in protecting his interests, the abbot lent him two marks of gold and gave him one mark, so with God's help and with the advice and assistance which Æthelwig gave him by word and deed, Wulfstan preserved the liberty of his church. As the bishop was a good man and Æthelwig's spiritual father, Æthelwig gave him certain lands which were called Bishopton[3] and 'Cagecote', and the bishop granted him in exchange a vill called Milcote. He sought freely to bestow the assistance of his good deeds not only on this church but on all on whose behalf he had acted. On one occasion, in fact, when he was summoned by Archbishop Lanfranc, he regained for Christ Church Canterbury, as both judge and witness, certain lands which had long been alienated. Because of this service the anniversary of his demise is still observed in that church to this day.[4] There is also the particular case of Gloucester Abbey: at the time Serlo[5] of blessed memory came there as abbot it was very poor, but when he respectfully asked Æthelwig for help he often received from him all sorts of assistance. Then, when King William removed Godric, abbot of Winchcombe, from office,[6] keeping him in captivity at Gloucester, he soon entrusted that abbey to Abbot Æthelwig, and for almost three years he administered it and looked after it in all respects as if it were his own. The king then gave it to a certain Abbot Galandus, and when this man died a

(1726), p. xxxiv, and R. Fleming, 'Christchurch's [*sic*] sisters and brothers; an edition and discussion of Canterbury obituary lists', in *The Culture of Christendom. Essays . . . in Commemoration of Denis L. T. Bethell*, ed. M. A. Meyer (London and Rio Grande, Oh., 1993), p. 134. This service rendered by Æthelwig does not appear to be recorded elsewhere.

  [5] Serlo, abbot from 1072 to 1104, had been previously a canon of Avranches and then a monk of Mont-S.-Michel; *HRH*, p. 52.

  [6] Godric, son of Godeman, royal chaplain, and abbot from 1054, was removed by the Conqueror in 1066 and retired to Evesham; *HRH*, p. 79. The source for his retiring to Evesham is *Diplomatarium Anglicum aevi Saxonici*, ed. B. Thorpe (London, 1865), p. 617.

eo post modicum tempus ex quo eam accepit defuncto, iterum isti abbati Ageluuio committitur, qua longo tempore postea uti propria dominabatur.[1]

159. Pater quoque pauperum, iudex uiduarum, pupillorum, orphanorum, peregrinorum,[2] omnium miserorum consolator erat piissimus, elemosinas largifluas ubicumque pergebat fecit distribui benigniter omnibus. Nam in primis temporibus sui regni rex Willelmus fecit deuastari quasdam sciras istis in partibus propter exules et latrones qui in siluis latitabant ubique, et maxima dampna pluribus hominibus faciebant, uidelicet Eoueruuicscire, Ceastrescire, Scrobscire, Stafordscire, Deorbiscire, unde maxima multitudo senum, iuuenum, mulierum cum paruulis suis famis miseriam fugientes dolentissime huc ueniebant,[3] quos omnes ille uir miseratus pro posse suo alebat. Plures namque diu absorti durissima fame, dum cibum auidius sumerent moriebantur. Iacebant miseri homines per totam uillam tam in domibus quam deforis, necnon et in cimiterio isto languidi, huc antequam uenirent fame consumpti, et iccirco ut cibum corporis sentiebant plurimi uita deficiebant. Qua de re facta est magna mortalitas multo tempore de talibus hominibus, ita ut cotidie fere quinque uel sex homines, aliquando plures, miserabiliter morientes, a priore huius loci sepeliebantur. Et quoniam plurimi pueruli inter eos habebantur, unicuique seruienti uel ministro huius ecclesie necnon et fo. 144va quibusdam fratribus ad hoc posse habentibus, | unum puerulum dompnus abbas ut alimento corporis sustentarentur commendabat. Quorum nonnulli probi uiri postea effecti, in multis officiis fratribus honeste seruiebant.

160. Erat quippe tunc temporis quidam prior hic, iuuenis quidem corpore set tamen morum probitate etatem transiens, Alfricus nomine, qui fecit dorsellos capituli. Hunc abbas constituit, ut omnes superuenientes peregrinos et pauperes deuote susciperet, atque necessaria uite sollicite administra⟨r⟩et eis. Precepit etiam celerario et omnibus prepositis abbatie huius ut ei in omnibus obedirent, et quicquid ad opus egenorum constituerat, uidelicet,

---

[1] The abbey was in Æthelwig's custody until 1068/9, when Galandus was made abbot; HRH, pp. 79, 257. If Galandus did not cease to be abbot until 1075, 'the many years' of Æthelwig's rule seems an exaggeration on the part of the author (whether Dominic or Thomas at this point), as Æthelwig died in 1077.

[2] Cf. Ps. 67: 6 (68: 5), 'patris orfanorum et iudicis viduarum'.

[3] On the harrying of the north, for which this is a major source, see John Palmer, 'War and Domesday waste', in Armies, Chivalry and Warfare in Medieval Britain and France (Harlaxton Medieval Studies, vii (1998), ed. M. Strickland, pp. 256–75. Ann Williams,

short time after accepting the appointment, he again entrusted the abbey to Abbot Æthelwig, who ruled over it for many a year after this as though it were his own. [1]

159. Furthermore, Æthelwig was a father to the poor, a judge of widows, wards, orphans, and foreigners,[2] and with great gentleness consoled all who were wretched; he had an abundance of alms lovingly distributed to everybody wherever he went. Indeed, in the early years of his reign, King William had some shires in these regions of England laid waste because of the exiles and outlaws who were hiding in the woods everywhere, and he inflicted enormous damage upon many people: counties affected were Yorkshire, Cheshire, Shropshire, Staffordshire, and Derbyshire, and from these regions a large number of young and old, and women and children, came fleeing to Evesham in great distress from the misery of famine.[3] In his concern for them all Æthelwig gave them all the sustenance he could. Many who had long been oppressed by severe hunger died through eating the food too ravenously. Throughout the whole vill wretches lay languishing either in the houses or in the streets, even in the cemetery itself, being exhausted by hunger before they got there, and therefore when they tasted food for the body most of them died. For this reason there was high mortality among such people, so almost every day five or six people, sometimes more, perished miserably and were buried by the prior of this place. As these people included many young children, the abbot entrusted to every servant or official of this church, and even to some brethren who had the resources for this, the responsibility of sustaining one child each with bodily nourishment. Some of these children grew up to be men of high integrity who served the brethren honourably in many spheres of duty.

160. At that time there was a prior here called Ælfric, a man of youthful strength of body, but older than his years in holiness of character, who had had hangings made for the chapter-house. The abbot appointed him to the duty of welcoming cordially all pilgrims or poor persons who came to them, and of providing them with the necessities of life. He also commanded the cellarer and all the reeves of this abbey to obey Ælfric in every respect and to provide him fully and promptly with everything that he wanted for the work amongst

The English and the Norman Conquest (Woodbridge, 1998), pp. 40, 53, says that many of the refugees fleeing from the north to Evesham were the men and families of Earl Edwin of Mercia.

omnem decimationem suam et insuper quicquid necessarium haberet sine dilatione habundanter ei redderent. Solebant illis temporibus multi peregrini de Aquitannia, de Hibernia, ac de aliis terris plurimis huc uenire, quos omnes iste suscipiens necessaria prebebat. Et quoniam pater Benedictus in regula iubet ut mensa abbatis cum peregrinis et hospitibus fiat,[1] semper de mensa quoque sua ipse abbas cotidie tredecim pauperes largiter reficiebat; preter istos, ad mandatum duodecim pauperes siue esset domi seu foris specialiter usque ad diem obitus sui habebat, qui uictum et uestitum in omnibus ueluti unus monachus semper habebant. Quorum pedes et manus aut per se aut per priorem suum, qui maxime hanc curam sub eo gerebat, cotidie lauari aqua calida humiliter uolebat. Inter hos namque pauperes quidam erant leprosi, quorum manus et pedes sicuti aliorum libenter lauando osculabatur. Isti namque omni nocte ad matutinos, et in die ad utrasque missas et ad omnes horas debebant sine dilatione uenire, nec alicui licebat uel domum aut alicubi licebat uel domum aut alicubi remeare uel discedere sine licencia prioris qui, ut diximus, maximam curam super eos gerebat. Hyemis quoque tempore, uidelicet a festiuitate omnium sanctorum[2] usque ad Pascha, uenientes ad matutinos in ecclesia remanebant usque ad diem, orationibus

fo. 144vb uacantes, et ita primo | mane aut ipse abbas aut prior faciebat ad eos sicut supra dictum est mandatum Domini cotidie. Omnibus noctibus principalium festiuitatum pro abbate et fratribus debebant tota nocte in ecclesia uigilare usque ad mane. A festiuitate omnium sanctorum usque ad natale Domini et iterum a septuagesima[3] usque Pascha, ter in ebdomada, uidelicet die Dominica, quarta et sexta feria, unusquisque eorum, abbate donante, accipiebat singulos denarios. Similiter ipsis primis diebus natalis Domini, Pasche, Pentecostes, et omnibus summis festis per annum, denarii tam illis quam aliis pauperibus misericorditer ab eo erogabantur. Et quando aliquis eorum moriebatur protinus prior in loco suo alium constituebat. Erant nempe pauperes ceci, claudi, et ita debiles ut tamen possent ad ecclesiam uenire et secundum quod dictum est uiuere, nisi maior infirmitas aliquem eorum impediret. Preter istos suprascriptos et preter omnes aduenientes pauperes et peregrinos, quinquaginta habebat egenos qui cotidie sibi constitutum accipiebant cibum.

161. Et non solum talibus pauperibus, set etiam pluribus nobilibus ad

---

[1] *RSB* cap. lvi.
[2] I Nov.
[3] Septuagesima Sunday is the third Sunday before Ash Wednesday.

the needy; this included the whole of his tithe and also anything else he considered necessary. In those days many pilgrims used to come to Evesham from Aquitaine, Ireland, and many other lands; all of these he would welcome and provide with necessities. Since Father Benedict commands in the Rule that the abbot's table should include pilgrims and guests,[1] the abbot always fed thirteen poor persons lavishly at his own table also. Besides those, he made a special point of having twelve poor persons for Maundy up to the day of his death, whether he was at home or abroad, and they always received food and clothing, just as if they were monks. It was the abbot's wish in all humility that their feet and hands should be washed in warm water every day, either by himself or by his prior who used to deputize for him especially in this duty. There were some lepers amongst these poor persons whose hands and feet he would wash and kiss just as he did those of others. All of these had to attend matins promptly every night as well as the two daytime masses and all the daily offices: none of them was allowed to go home or anywhere else, or to leave the monastery, without the permission of the prior who, as we have said, took very great care of them. During the winter-time, from the feast of All Saints[2] until Easter, they would come to matins and then stay in the church until dawn, spending their time in prayer; then, in the early morning every day, either the abbot himself or the prior would administer the Lord's Maundy to them, as we have stated above. Every night during the principal feast days they had to spend the whole night in the church until the morning in prayer for the abbot and the brethren. From the feast of All Saints until Christmas, and again from Septuagesima[3] until Easter, each one of them received three times a week, on Sunday, Thursday, and Saturday, a penny which was given to them by the abbot. Similarly, on the first day of Christmas, Easter, Pentecost, and all the principal festivals throughout the year, pennies were generously given by the abbot not only to them, but to other poor persons as well. When any of them died the prior immediately substituted another poor person. Indeed, some of the poor, though blind, lame, or weak, were nevertheless able to come to the church and live in the manner described unless the infirmity of any of them was so great as to prevent him from doing so. Apart from those described above, and all the poor or pilgrims who came to the abbey, the abbot had fifty needy persons who every day received food which had been appointed for them.

161. But it was not only to the poor such as those to whom he became

eum confugientibus, paterna hereditate omnique substantia miserabiliter sublata rege Willelmo iubente, factus est refugium et adiutor[1]
piissimus in maximis necessitatibus.

162. Quocienscunque ad curiam regis uel alicubi iter ageret et aliquis
pauper nudus occurreret, mox aliquem de suis hominibus expoliabat
et pauperi uestimenta eius dabat, set suo postea 'duppliciter red-
debat'.[2] Omni namque anno quatuor uel quinque dies ante natale
Domini et iterum post diem palmarum tota ebdomada ante Pascha
quasi excercitus magnus pauperum et peregrinorum huc solebant
uenire, quibus omnibus tam per se quam per monachos uel fideles
laicos elemosinas largiter ministrando erogare, mandatum Domini
faciendo manus et pedes lauare, quibusdam uestimenta, plurimis
calciamenta, multis studuit denarios benigniter erogare, omnes
quoque letos fecit hinc recedere.

fo. 145[ra]   163. Cunctis etiam noctibus precipuarum solennitatum per annum
ad honorem Dei et sanctorum eius, coram uno quoque altari fecit
candelam ardere tota nocte usque mane. Plures namque missas
secundum quod tempus habebat cotidie solebat libenter audire, et
ad unamquamque earum, sacerdoti sacra sollennia celebranti unum
uel plures denarios cum magna cordis compunctione studebat offerre.

164. Et quoniam erat tam diuitibus quam pauperibus erogator
largissimus, dedit ei diuina clementia copiam rerum maximam in
omnibus. Ornamenta quoque adquisiuit plurima, uidelicet casulas,
cappas, pallia,[3] crucem magnam, et quoddam altare auro et argento
pulcherrime operatum, necnon etiam quandam capellam ualde
honestam in honore sancti Nicholai construi et consecrari laudabiliter
fecit.[4]

165. Ante suum tempus duo fratres huius loci diabolico instinctu
seducti, quasdam reliquias de feretro furati sunt sancti Ecgwini patris
nostri, et tradiderunt eas cuidam matrone nobilissime Aldithe
nomine, set alter eorum, Alfricus uocabulo, qui auctor erat sceleris,
uolens huc redire, diuino iudicio cadens in isto flumine periit de terra
uiuentium pro tanto crimine. Apparuit ergo uir Dei sanctus Ecgwinus
ipsi matrone in uisione semel et iterum et tercia nocte, iubens
minando ut suas reliquias quantocius huc ad ecclesiam reportaret.
Set illa, feminea decepta cupiditate, nullo modo uolens id perficere,

---

[1] Cf. Ps. 9: 10 (9: 9).   [2] Cf. Job 42: 10; Zech. 9: 12.

[3] The word *pallia* is used generally for cloths that cover something: here it is likely to
mean altar-cloths, chalice-covers, crozier-covers, or funeral palls, rather than cloaks.

[4] On the cult of St Nicholas, see D. Greenway, 'Conquest and colonization: the
foundation of an alien priory, 1077', in *The Cloister and the World: Essays in Medieval*

a refuge and a devoted helper[1] in their great necessity, but also to many nobles who fled to him for protection when King William commanded their family inheritances and all their property to be ruthlessly taken from them.

162. Whenever Æthelwig journeyed to the king's court or anywhere else and was met by a poor man having no clothes, he would immediately take the clothes from one of his men and give them to that man, but he would later 'restore to his own man twice what he had taken'.[2] Every year, four or five days before Christmas, and again after Palm Sunday for the whole week before Easter, a great army, as it were, of paupers and pilgrims would come here; to all of these he would himself give generous alms, or would delegate monks or devoted laymen to do this. Then he would carry out the Lord's Maundy, and wash their hands and feet. He sought generously to provide some with clothes, more with footwear, and many with pennies, and so caused all to depart joyfully from here.

163. Every night of the year when there were church feasts to the honour of God and his saints he had a candle kept burning all night before every single altar until the morning. Every day he gladly heard as many masses as he had time for, and at each of these, greatly pricked in his conscience, he gladly offered one or more pennies to the priest celebrating that solemn service.

164. Since he was as generous a benefactor of the rich as he was of the poor, God in his mercy gave him a great abundance of everything. He acquired many treasures also, such as chasubles, copes, altar-frontals,[3] a large cross, an altar beautifully worked in gold and silver, and, to his further praise, he had a fine chapel built, and dedicated to St Nicholas.[4]

165. Before Æthelwig's time two brethren of this monastery, led astray by the wiles of the devil, stole some relics from the shrine of our father St Ecgwine, and gave them to a certain noble lady Ealdgyth. One of them called Ælfric who instigated the crime wanted to return here, but by God's judgment he fell into the river and passed from the land of the living for his dreadful crime. Then the man of God, St Ecgwine, appeared to the lady in a vision, first on one occasion, then a second time, and finally a third time at night, when he commanded her to take his relics back to this church as soon as she could. However, beguiled by feminine greed, she utterly refused to do this,

History in Honour of Barbara Harvey, ed. J. Blair and B. Golding (Oxford, 1996), pp. 46–56, at 51, and esp. n. 27.

Dei iudicio mox percussa est perhenni oculorum cecitate. Qua de re plusquam dici ualet timore perterrita, ueniens huc ad abbatem Mannium et fratres, clamans se ream et culpabilem et impetrans ab eis indulgentiam, obtinuit ab eis ut quamdiu uiueret eas possideret, fecitque statim honorabiliter fieri auro atque argento hoc minus feretrum sancti Ecgwini et reliquias intus re | poni. Set post mortem eius filius suus, Arnisius uocabulo, paterne hereditatis effectus heres, quasi imprudens uiuendo luxuriose atque insipienter perdidit cuncta que habebat, et istud feretrum sancti Ecgwini cuidam potenti homini custodiendum commendabat. Quod ut abbas Ageluuius cognouit, protinus adueniens, recto iure illud debere esse proprium huius sancte ecclesie adplacitauit, et ita, Dei gratia opitulante, suum uelle impetrauit, et ad istum locum cum magna reuerentia, processione maxima contra facta tam fratrum quam populorum, reportari fecit.[1]

fo. 145rb

166. Hactenus de isto dompno abbate Ageluuio plura locuti sumus, set testis est Deus,[2] testes omnes angeli et sancti eius sunt, quia quicquid tam de illo quam de aliis supra retulimus, ueracem narrationem ad noticiam tam presentium quam sequentium fratrum et amicorum huius sancte ecclesie fideliter fecimus. Partim namque in antiquis cartis huius loci reperimus, partim a fidelissimis uiris audiuimus, partim nos ipsi oculis nostris perspeximus. Nunc igitur in fine huius operis uolumus per ordinem terras demonstrare quas ipse a rege Æduuardo et ab aliis bonis hominibus laboriosissime maximaque pecunia redimendo adquisiuit huic sancte ecclesie, et usque ad mortem absque omni questione in pace tenuit magna cum libertate.

167. In Wiricestrescire: Beningwrthe, Heamtune; ultra Wiricestre: Uptun, Wittune, Leinch, Eacesleinc, Ciricleinc.[3] Cum erat prepositus sub Mannio abbate,[4] Biuintune, Dailesford, Eunilad, Brainesford, Actune. Hec fuit terra patris sui: has duas uillas dedit Vrsoni[5] pro

---

[1] For roughly the same story, see above, 73–5. A. Gransden (*Historical Writing in England c.550–c.1307* (London, 1974), p. 113) has pointed out the differences between the two accounts, the most important of which are that firstly, according to the *Miracles* (above), Ealdgyth promised to return the relics and make a gift of the manor of Swell (while in the *History* there is no mention of Swell in this context), and secondly that, on Ealdgyth's death, the relics went to Worcester from which Abbot Æthelwig recovered them by legal process. This is at odds with the above account, and the omission of the relics being taken to Worcester is significant, though it may not be due to Thomas.

[2] Cf. I Kgs. (I Sam.) 12: 5.

[3] The Lenchs were actually to the east of Worcester.

[4] See above, 151. Sawyer, no. 1238 (probably spurious), is the restitution of Daylesford

and so, by God's judgment, she was soon struck permanently blind. She was unspeakably distressed by what happened to her, so she came here to Abbot Mannig and the brethren proclaiming her guilt and sin, and pleading for their forgiveness. She was allowed by them to retain possession of the relics for the rest of her life, and she at once took measures to have a shrine of St Ecgwine made, smaller than the monastery's shrine, adorned with gold and silver, and to have the relics placed inside it. However, after her death, her son Arnisius became heir to his father's estate and, through living extravagantly and imprudently like the foolish man he was, he lost everything he possessed, and he entrusted that shrine of St Ecgwine to the protection of a certain magnate. When Abbot Æthelwig learned of this he went straightway to see him, contending that the shrine ought by rights to belong to this holy church. The result was that, with God's help, he obtained Arnisius' agreement to this, and had the shrine brought back to the church with great reverence, with a procession of the monks and people going out to meet it.[1]

166. We have now spoken a good deal about Abbot Æthelwig, but God is witness,[2] as are all his angels and saints, that everything we have hitherto stated about him and others has been truly and faithfully written for the edification of both present and future brethren and friends of this holy church. Some facts we have found in the ancient charters of this place, some we have learned from trustworthy men, and others we have ourselves witnessed with our own eyes. So now, at the end of this work we would like to provide a catalogue of the lands which Æthelwig recovered and acquired for this church with great effort and at great expense from King Edward and other good men, lands which he held peaceably, without any dispute and with considerable immunity until his death.

167. In Worcestershire: Bengeworth and Hampton; beyond Worcester: Upton Warren, Witton, Lench, Atch Lench, and Church Lench.[3] When he was Abbot Mannig's deputy,[4] he acquired Binton [Warws.], Daylesford [Glos.], Evenlode [Glos.], Bransford, and Acton Beauchamp: this was his father's land, and these last two vills he exchanged with Urse[5] for Bengeworth which Urse had

---

(1061×5) by Ælfgar, earl of Mercia, to Abbot Æthelwig. For the benefactions of the Mercian earls to Evesham, see Williams, *The English and the Norman Conquest*, p. 24 and n. 3.

[5] Urse d'Abetot, sheriff of Worcester *c.*1068/9–1108; see J. A. Green, *English Sheriffs to 1154* (PRO Handbooks, no. 24, 1990), p. 87.

Beningwrthe quam iniuste occupauit, sicut medietatem iterum postea fecit et omnes tres iniuste detinet.[1]

168. In Wareuuicscire: Witlakesford, Aruue, Ecleshale, Rageleia, Eatherichestun, Brome, Graftun et alia Graftun,[2] Hildesburguurthe, Saltford.

169. In Gloecestrescire: Suelle, Ceasteltun et alia Ceasteltun, Cornuuelle, Quenintun, Sciptun, | Saldford, Deorneford, Stoke, Westun, Hudicote, Peppeuurthe, Dorsintun, Mulecote et alia Mulecote.[3]

fo. 145va

170. De hiis terris quasdam optinuit ab ecclesia Wigornensi quas prelati eiusdem ecclesie iniuste occupauerant, s⟨c⟩ilicet Actun et Benenguurthe, Mulecote et Westun, Eunilade et Dailesford, et plures domos in Wigornia,[4] set Stredford et Fladeburi non reuocauit. De hiis terris quas, ut diximus, suo tempore adquisiuit, quibusdam bonis hominibus pro magna necessitate et honore ecclesie dedit, et inde Deo et sibi fideliter quamdiu uixit seruiebant. De aliis terris quas antecessores sui adquisierunt nichil omnino dedit, set in manu sua usque ad obitum ad necessitatem fratrum honorabiliter tenuit. Nec unquam alicui parenti de hiis uel de aliis terris aliquid concessit, set terras parentum suorum quascumque poterat habere ecclesie tradidit.

171. Omni tempore uite sue non continue set frequenter dolorem pedum grauissimum quem Greci 'podagra' appellant,[5] patiebatur. Et hac infirmitate ante finem suum diutissime fatigatus, tandem anno Dominice incarnationis millesimo septuagesimo septimo plenus dierum in uera confessione sanctoque uiatico corporis et sanguinis Domini percepto, coram fratribus et filiis eum nimio dolore plangentibus, quos paterno amore dilexerat, quartodecimo kalendas Martii hominem exiuit et quo diuine clementie placuit spiritum transmisit. Cuius anime succurrat et misereatur summa pietas Dei: Amen.

172. Quando enim ipse primitus abbas effectus est, non erant hic nisi duodecim fratres; tunc uero cum obiit triginta sex dimisit,[6] quibus abbatiam maiorem et habundantiorem terris et possessionibus quam unquam antea fuit, omnibus bonis plenissimam, dereliquit. Et quinque archas plenas argento ad nouam ecclesiam construendam quam facere disposuerat, reliquit.

---

[1] viz. Hampton, Upton, and Witton.

[2] viz. Grafton Major and Grafton Minor.

[3] Chastleton [? two], Cornwell, and Salford are all now in Oxon. in the area roughly between Moreton-in-Marsh and Chipping Norton.

[4] The Worcester source (Hemming) mentions Acton, Eastbury, Bengeworth, Milcote, and Weston as belonging to the convent of Worcester, Evenlode and Daylesford as the property of the bishop; printed *English Lawsuits*, ed. van Caenegem, p. 31.

wrongfully seized; but later Urse again took a moiety of the land and wrongfully held on to all three places.[1]

168. In Warwickshire he acquired Wixford, Arrow, Exhall, Ragley, Edstone, Broom, Grafton and the other Grafton,[2] Hilborough, and Salford.

169. In Gloucestershire he acquired Swell, the two Chastletons, Cornwell, Quenington, Shipston-on-Stour, Salford, Dornford, Stoke, Weston-upon-Avon, Hidcote, Pebworth, Dorsington, and the two Milcotes.[3]

170. Some of these lands he obtained from the church of Worcester whose bishops had wrongfully seized them: these were Acton Beauchamp, Bengeworth, Milcote, Weston-upon-Avon [Glos. and Warws.], Evenlode, Daylesford [both Glos.], and many dwelling-houses in Worcester,[4] though he did not recover Stratford [Warws.] or Fladbury. He gave some of these lands, which, as we have said, he acquired during his lifetime to certain good men to pay for the needs of the church and to maintain its good name; they then faithfully served God and the abbot for as long as he lived. He gave nothing whatsoever away of any of the lands which his predecessors had acquired, but kept them in his possession to provide for the needs of his brethren while he lived. Nor did he ever grant any of these or other lands to any relative; indeed, he handed over to the church such lands as he was able to get from his own kinsmen.

171. Throughout his life Æthelwig suffered, not all the time but frequently, with a painful foot complaint which the Greeks call 'podagra'.[5] Worn out by this affliction for a considerable time before his end, he finally departed this mortal life on 16 February AD 1077 at a good age. He made a true confession, received the last sacrament of our Lord's Body and Blood in the presence of his brethren and sons who mourned him deeply, for he had loved them as a father, and he entrusted his spirit to God's divine mercy. May God in his great pity succour him and have mercy upon his soul. Amen.

172. When Æthelwig first became abbot here [1059] there were no more than twelve brethren: when he died he left thirty-six to whom he bequeathed an abbey which was larger and richer in lands and possessions than it had ever been, enjoying an abundance of every-thing.[6] He also left five caskets full of silver for the erection of a new church which he had planned to build.

---

[5] 'Podagra' is gout.
[6] On the number of monks at Evesham, see below, App. V.

173. *De operibus abbatis Walteri bonis et malis, et de amissione terrarum quas Ælwinus abbas congregauerat, et constructione huius ecclesie ex pecunia ab eodem Ailwin⟨o⟩ ad hoc congregata*

fo. 145ᵛᵇ Tercio | quoque mense post discessum patris huius Ageluuii, misit rex huc quendam monachum de monasterio quod uocatur Cerasia, Walterum nomine,¹ litteris tam liberalibus quam gra⟨m⟩maticis undecumque eruditissimum, qui fuit capellanus Lanfranci archiepiscopi.² Hic uero abbas effectus, omnem abbatiam hanc sicuti antecessor suus habebat suscepit. Set quia tunc temporis iuuenis erat etate, minus seculari prudentia preditus quam oporteret, sequens consilia quorundam iuuenum parentum suorum ad maximum dampnum ecclesie, noluit homagium a pluribus bonis hominibus quos predecessor suus habuerat suscipere, eo quod terras omnium si posset decreuit auferre.³ Qua de re in iram et odium contra eum conuersi, ad Odonem fratrem regis, Baiocensis ecclesie episcopum, qui tunc temporis sub rege quasi quidam tirannus prefuit huic patrie, miserunt, falsa accusatione dicentes abbatem Ageluuium per fortitudinem, non recto iure, tantas terras adquisisse. Quapropter presul prefatus, nefandorum hominum consilio deprauatus, cupiditate etiam iniquissima res ecclesie habendi nimium illectus, regem fratrem suum adiit, et tam peccunia quam iniquis suis accusationibus terras sancti monasterii huius sibi dari optinuit.⁴

174. Protinus ergo quasi lupus rapax⁵ consilia malignantium in loco qui dicitur Gildenebeorge⁶ iubet congregari, quinque uidelicet sciras,⁷ ibique plus per suam iniquam potentiam quam recto iure ex triginta sex terris quas abbas Ageluuius per dignam peccuniam ecclesie adquisiuit, uiginti octo uillas fecit eidem abiurari et suo iniquo dominio usurpari. Quarum nomina hic subtitulantur: Beningwrthe, Heamtun, Vptun, Wittun, Aruue,

---

¹ Æthelwig died 16 or 17 Feb. 1077, so the third month is presumably April or May. Walter was abbot from 1077–1104; *HRH*, p. 47. William of Malmesbury says that he was a monk of Caen (*Willelmi Malmesbiriensis monachi de gestis pontificum Anglorum*, ed. N. E. S. A. Hamilton (RS lii, 1870), p. 137), a mistake possibly arising from his association with Archbishop Lanfranc, who had been abbot of St Étienne, Caen (see next note). Cerisy-la-Forêt was an ancient Benedictine house restored about 1030 by Robert, duke of Normandy; Cottineau, i, col. 656.

² See M. Gibson, *Lanfranc of Bec* (Oxford, 1978), pp. 171 n., 183–4; and *The Letters of Lanfranc Archbishop of Canterbury*, ed. and trans. H. Clover and M. Gibson (OMT 1979), no. 54. For his famous testing of Evesham's pre-Conquest relics, see the miracles following the *Vita S. Wistani* (Macray, pp. 335–7).

³ Cf. below, 180 and n. 1, for his creation of hereditary tenures.

⁴ On Odo of Bayeux's reputation and his large estates, see David R. Bates, 'The character and career of Odo, bishop of Bayeux (1049/50–1097)', *Speculum*, l (1975), 1–20. For

173. *The deeds of Abbot Walter, good and bad; the loss of lands which Abbot Æthelwig had accumulated; and the erection of this church from the money accumulated for this purpose by the same Æthelwig*

In the third month after the death of father Æthelwig, the king sent here a monk named Walter from a monastery called Cerisy.[1] A man of extensive learning in letters, as much in the liberal arts as in grammar, he was the chaplain of Archbishop Lanfranc,[2] and received the whole of the abbey just as his predecessor had left it. However, being a young man at that time, he was endowed with less worldly wisdom than he should have been and, to the great detriment of the church, he followed the advice of some youthful relatives of his. He refused to receive homage from many good men whom his predecessor had received, because he intended to confiscate the lands of all these men if he could.[3] Turning hostile and resentful towards him, therefore, they sent to the king's brother Odo, bishop of Bayeux, who ruled that church at that time under the king like some tyrant, and they made false accusations that Abbot Æthelwig had acquired many lands by force rather than by legitimate means. The result was that this prelate, corrupted by the counsel of wicked men and enticed by an inordinate passion to appropriate this church's property, went to the king, his brother, and by bribery and false accusation was successful in having the lands of this holy monastery given over to him.[4]

174. So, like a ravening wolf,[5] he straightway summoned from the five shires[6] councils of men hostile to us, to gather in a place called Gildenebeorge.[7] There, more by his own evil influence than by legitimate means, he had this abbey deprived of twenty-eight vills from the thirty-six territories which Abbot Æthelwig acquired for the church by his honest money, and seized them for his own unjust lordship. Here is a list of their names. Bengeworth, Hampton, Upton

---

four hides in Lench, which Odo took from Evesham and gave to Urse d'Abetot, see *DB Worcs.* 11.

[5] Gen. 49: 27; cf. Matt. 7: 15; Acts 20: 29.

[6] Worcs., Glos., Oxon., Warws., and the former Winchcombeshire. For the four-shire stone in the parish of Evenlode which stands where these shires met, see A. Mawer and F. M. Stenton, *The Place-names of Worcestershire* (PN vol. iv, Cambridge, 1927), p. 124. In a 12th-cent. copy of a charter of 969 the bounds of Evenlode at one point on their circuit run from one stone to another and so on and mark the northern extremity of the parish. For the lost county of Winchcombeshire, see J. Whybra, *A Lost English County: Winchcombeshire in the Tenth and Eleventh Centuries* (Studies in Anglo-Saxon History, 1: Woodbridge, 1990).

[7] Ildeberga (now lost), probably in Evenlode; see *Place-names of Worcestershire*, pp. 124–5; *DB Worcs.* notes (not paginated) to ch. 10 (the abbey of Evesham) nos. 11 and 12 (VCH *Worcs.*, i. 307); Hemming, i. 213–15.

fo. 146ra Ecleshale, Raggeleie, Saltford, Eatheristun, | Brome, Graftune, Ceasteltun, et alia Ceasteltun, Cornuuelle, Quenintun, Sciptun, Saltford, Deorneford, Stoke, Hudicote, Peppeuurthe, Dorsintun, Milecote, et alia Milecote, Actun, Branesford, *a*Wiuleshale, Biuinton', Budiford,*a* Eunilade, Deilesford, Westune, Leinch quam Vrsini tenent contra rotulum Winton.[1] De hiis uero Walterus abbas Westune *b*Hamptun' et medietatem de Beningwrthe, quam Ernegrim tenuit, reuocauit, medietatem uero quam episcopus dedit Assere[2] occupauit Vrso.*b* Set paruo post tempore iusto Dei iudicio rex Willelmus contra fratrem nefandum nimium commotus, fecit eum durissimis uinculis ferreis alligari et usque ad diem obitus sui in arta custodia teneri.[3] Similiter fere omnes periuros huius ecclesie diuina ultio citius ex hac luce miserabiliter extinxit.

175. *c*Iste abbas, licet tot terris priuatus, numerum tamen fratrum et rigorem ordinis solicite auxit. Ipse tamen primo fecit clericum decanum et senescallum iure hereditario de consanguineis suis,[4] priore senescallo amoto.*c* Fecit etiam criptas et ecclesiam superius usque ad nauem,[5] excepta turri quam non perfecit nisi arcus et primas fenestras, maxime de pecunia quam Ageluuinus abbas*d* ad hoc opus reliquerat.[6] Vineam etiam ultra aquam ille primitus fieri fecit. Terra de Hildedun et Penuurtham Hocuuic et piscatio apud Theleuuelle suo tempore reddite sunt huic ecclesie. *e*Libros multos fecit.[7]

---

a-a Wiuleshale . . . Budiford *written over erasure*   *b-b* Hamptun' . . . Vrso *written over an erasure*   *c-c* Iste . . . amoto *written over an erasure*   *d* Ageluuinus abbas *? written over an erasure*   *e-e¹* Libros . . . hereditauerit *written over an erasure*

---

[1] The Roll of Winchester is undoubtedly Domesday Book, which was kept in the treasury at Winchester and which the writer, like Jocelin of Brakelond (see *JB*, p. 42, and for the Latin text, *The Chronicle of Jocelin of Brakelond*, ed. and trans. H. E. Butler (NMT, 1949), p. 46), mistakenly believed to be in the form of a roll, as indeed most Exchequer records were. *DB Worcs.* 11, 2 (176a) says that Urse held Sheriff's Lench (four hides) and also Acton Beauchamp from the bishop of Bayeux. It also states that the bishop had wrongfully taken the four hides in Lench from the church of Evesham and given them to Urse. Two hides of this land had been given, with King William's consent, by Gilbert, son of Thorold, to the church of Evesham for the soul of Earl William, and one monk was accordingly placed in the church of Evesham. The other two hides were acquired by Abbot Æthelwig from King William for 1 gold mark, assigning the land to the church of Evesham for his own soul. Cf. V fos. 10ᵛ–11: 'Lench (Bernardi': inserted). Cotton MS Vesp. B XXIV (V) fos. 6ʳ–7ᵛ is (part of) a Domesday satellite (see 'Evesham A: a Domesday Text', ed. P. Sawyer, *Miscellany*, i (Worcs. Hist. Soc. 1960): it does not, however, include this account, but much the same story is given in V on fos. 10ᵛ–11ʳ. Thomas undoubtedly had access to these texts.

[2] Cousin and chamberlain of Brihtheah, bishop of Worcester from 1033–8; see Hemming. For the restorations to Abbot Walter, see *English Lawsuits*, ed. van Caenegem,

Warren, Witton, Arrow, Exhall, Ragley, Salford, Edstone, Broom, Grafton, the two Chastletons, Cornwell, Quenington, Shipston on Stour, Salford, Dornford, Stoke, Hidcote, Pebworth, Dorsington, the two Milcotes, Acton Beauchamp, Bransford, 'Wileshale', Binton, Bidford, Evenlode, Daylesford, Weston-upon-Avon, and Lench which the family of Urse hold wrongfully, according to Domesday Book.[1] Of these lands Abbot Walter recovered Weston, Hampton, and that part of Bengeworth which Ernegrim held, though Urse seized the part which the bishop gave to Asser.[2] Not long after this, however, King William through the just judgment of God, being greatly provoked by his evil brother, had him clapped in the harshest of iron chains and had him kept in prison under close guard until the day of his own death.[3] Similarly, divine punishment soon brought about the wretched death of almost all those who had borne false witness against this church.

175. Abbot Walter, though deprived of so many lands, took pains to enlarge the number of brethren and to increase the austerity of the Order. He first appointed a secular clerk as dean and made one of his kinsmen hereditary steward, having removed the former steward.[4] He also had the crypts built and the upper church as far as the nave,[5] though this did not include the tower, of which he only completed the arches and the first windows: this work he carried out mostly with the money which Abbot Æthelwig had left for it.[6] He first had the vineyard planted beyond the river. It was during Walter's time that the land of Hillingdon [Middx.], Penwortham, Howick [both Lancs.], and the fishery at Thelwall [Ches.] were returned to this church. He had many books made.[7] It is said,

---

p. 32. Both the writ and the notification are from the Evesham cartulary, V fos. 24^r and 28^r, and may have received some Evesham emendations.

[3] The source for Odo's arrest in 1082 is the *ASC*. The reasons for the arrest were supplied considerably later in three sources of the 1120s when it was suggested that Odo was trying to buy the papacy. For the likely veracity of the story, see Bates, 'Odo', pp. 1–20, at 15–19.

[4] Another relative, his brother Ranulf, was enfeoffed by the abbot in Witley, Kinwarton, Stoke, Morton, Littleton, and Bretforton; see V fo. 11^v, and *DB Worcs.* 10, 13 (175d). On the hereditary steward, see P. Brand, 'The rise and fall of the hereditary steward in English ecclesiastical institutions', in *Warriors and Churchmen in the High Middle Ages: Essays presented to Karl Leyser*, ed. T. Reuter (London and Rio Grande, 1992), pp. 145–62 at 152, 161, for Evesham.

[5] Medieval churches were constructed from the east to the west.

[6] On the building works at Evesham from the abbacy of Abbot Walter to that of Abbot Adam, see Cox, 'Building, destruction and excavation', pp. 125–7.

[7] The sense here is that he had many books copied.

Dicitur tamen quod fere omnes milites huius abbatie hereditauerit.*[1]

176. De operibus abbatis Roberti

Huic substitutus est Robertus monachus de Gimeges[2] cuius tempore
per Randulfum cancellarium regis forum de Stowa fuit adquisitum.[3]
Iste multas terras dicitur distribuisse consanguineis suis, sicut et
predecessor eius.

177. De operibus abbatis Mauricii ualde bonis

Huic successit Mauricius huius ecclesie monachus. Iste fecit capitulum et dormitorium et priuatum locutorium cum capella sancte Marie
Magdalene et multa ornamenta ecclesie adquisiuit, et multa alia bona
fecit.

178. De operibus abbatis Reginaldi summe bonis

Isti substitutus est Reginaldus, monachus Gloucestrie, nepos |
comitis Milonis Herefordie,[4] cuius adiutorio et aliorum consangui-
neorum amouit domos militum de Kinewertun et de Coctun[5] et
aliorum a loco ubi modo est ortus monachorum et crufta sancti
Kenelmi, quibus quasi obsessa fuit abbatia. Totam etiam abbatiam et
cimiterium muro optimo uallauit,[6] et uillam aqua circumdedisset,
sicut apud Quiquewelle[7] patet, nisi salubri consilio predicti comitis

fo. 146rb

---

[1] While this had become the practice by Thomas's time, it would be an early example of
the growing tendency for both lay and ecclesiastical lords to enfeoff in heredity, if it had,
indeed, taken place under Abbot Walter.

[2] Benedictine abbey, dioc. Rouen, Seine-Maritime, Normandy. There are some
problems over the sequence of the abbots between Walter and Reginald Foliot. H. B.
Clarke ('The Early Surveys of Evesham Abbey') has argued, on the basis of Survey O, that
Maurice preceded Robert and was abbot from 1104–c.1121, but if we accept that the
market at Stow was, indeed, granted in 1107 (see next note) in the abbacy of Robert, then
this order is doubtful. Other Evesham sources, Harley MS 229 and Vesp. B XV, also give
the sequence as Robert followed by Maurice (printed *Mon. Angl.*, ii. 26, 37), but both of
them say that Robert died in 1096, which must be wrong, and Maurice in 1122, which is
unlikely. J. C. Jennings's solution to the problem seems the most likely, namely that there
were two abbots Robert, one before Maurice and one after, and that Thomas of
Marlborough missed out the second Robert. Jennings suggested the following chronology:
Walter of Cerisy, May 1077–20 Jan. 1104; Robert of Jumièges, 1104–post 1108; Maurice,
post 1108–c.1121; Robert II c.1121–29; Reginald, 27 Jan. 1130–25 Aug. 1149; 'Prior
Dominic' (B.Litt., 1958), pp. 12–14.

[3] The charter of King Henry I, granting to the abbey of Evesham a market at Stow
every Thursday, on the petition of Ranulf, the chancellor, probably of 1107 c.1 Aug., is
noted in *Regesta*, ii. no. 831. For Ranulf the chancellor, see *Henry, Archdeacon of
Huntingdon: Historia Anglorum*, ed. and trans. Diana Greenway (OMT, 1996), pp. 468–

however, that he gave hereditary tenures to almost all the knights of this abbey.[1]

176. The deeds of Abbot Robert

Robert, a monk of Jumièges,[2] succeeded him, and it was during his time that a market was acquired at Stow-on-the-Wold [Glos.] through Ranulf, the king's chancellor.[3] Robert is said to have distributed many of the abbey's lands to his relatives, as had his predecessor.

177. The excellent deeds of Abbot Maurice

Maurice, a monk of this church, succeeded Robert. He built a chapter house, a dormitory, and a private parlour, with the chapel of St Mary Magdalene; he acquired many treasures for the church, and did many other good things.

178. The excellent deeds of Abbot Reginald

Maurice was succeeded by Reginald, a monk of Gloucester, the nephew of Milo, earl of Hereford.[4] It was with the help of the earl and other of his relatives that he removed the houses of the knights of Kinwarton and Coughton[5] and of others from the place where there is now the monks' garden and St Kenelm's croft. The abbey had been besieged, as it were, by their houses. He enclosed the whole abbey and cemetery with a well-built wall,[6] and he would have surrounded the vill with a moat like the one to be seen at 'Quiquewelle',[7] had he not received some

71; and Judith Green, *The Government of England under Henry I* (Cambridge, 1986), pp. 28, 45, 160, 172, 175.

[4] Reginald Foliot succeeded Maurice in 1130. He was the uncle of Gilbert Foliot, abbot of Gloucester from 1139–48, who later became bishop of Hereford, and then of London. On Milo, created earl of Hereford by the Empress Matilda in 1141, see GEC vi, cols. 451–4.

[5] Evesham owed the service of five knights in 1166; two of these were Ranulf of Coughton and Ranulf of Kinwarton (Warws.): *Liber Niger Scaccarii*, ed. Thomas Hearne, i (London, 1774), 175. *DB Worcs.* records three hides in Kinwarton belonging to Evesham which were held by Ranulf, probably Abbot Walter's brother (for whom see Hemming, i. 80–3, trans. *DB Worcs.*, App. v, H Texts no. 2). The land held in Coughton seems to have come to Ranulf from the gift of William Fitz Corbucion who at the time of Domesday Book held four hides from Turchil, abbot of Abingdon (VCH *Warws.*, i. 325 and iii. 79). Knights had residences in the monasteries they protected: those at Peterborough have survived near the west end.

[6] On the removal of the knights' houses and the building of the boundary wall, see Cox, 'Building, destruction and excavation', p. 133.

[7] The identification of this place is far from certain, but it may be Quevilli (Latin *Quevillium*) near Rouen, in the Seine-Maritime. Roger of Torigni records that Henry II

impediretur, ne forte locus tam munitus a rege occuparetur. Magnam etiam partem murorum nauis ecclesie sicut adhuc distingui potest fecit, et refectorium et regulare locutorium[1] cum capella et aulam hospitum cum camera et magnam coquinam fecit, et duo brachia, scilicet sancti Ecgwini et sancti Osuualdi,[2] et magnum textum,[3] et crucem huius ecclesie pretiosiorem, et culmen feretri sancti Ecgwini in recompensationem feretri quod abbas Mannius fecerat, et tempore suo, instante werra et urgente fame ut dicebant, 'filii Belial'[4] multi monachi huius ecclesie, abbate ignorante inter prandendum, auro et argento et lapidibus spoliauerunt. Duo etiam thurribula et candelabra deaurata fecit. Campanas etiam, Benedictum uidelicet et socium eius fecit, et tintinnabula,[5] scilicet Glucestre et socium eius adquisiuit. Magnum etiam dorsellum[6] et duo sancti Ecgwini de choro fieri fecit. Maiorem etiam nigram capam et multa alia uestimenta, libros etiam et ornamenta, huic ecclesie adquisiuit. Iste etiam tempore pape Innocentii secundi pro libertate ecclesie tuenda contra episcopum Simonem pedetemtim cum eo Romam iuit, et in libertatem uiriliter conclamauit et in parte obtinuit, et super eo priuilegium predicti pape adquisiuit.[7]

179. De sanctis et uirilibus actibus abbatis Willelmi

fo. 146ᵛᵃ Huic successit Willelmus de Andeuilla[8] monachus Christi | ecclesie Cantuarie, ubi iacet sepultus ad capud beati Thome martiris, qui antequam illuc iret causa uisitationis[9] quando ibi a domino est uisitatus, uidit in sompnis, sicut fratribus retulit, quod sol sepultus erat ad pedes eius. Que uisio interpretationem accepit processu temporis, postquam beatus Thomas sepultus est ad pedes eius.

180. Iste audacter Willelmum de Bellocampo[10] et complices suos,

---

restored and improved his grandfather's castles and (fortified) dwelling houses including that at Quevilli; *Chronicle of Robert of Torigni*, ed. R. Howlett, *Chronicles of the Reigns of Stephen, Henry II, and Richard I*, iv (RS lxxxii, 1889), 209.

[1] The use of the adjective *regulare* before parlour here seems to be to accentuate that the refectory and the parlour, with the chapel, were for the monks' use, while the hall, the chamber, and the kitchen were for the use of the guests. *RSB* cap. 53, on the reception of guests, draws attention to the separate kitchen.

[2] On arm reliquaries, see above, 95 n. 2. On Oswald's arm at Evesham, see Cox, 'St Oswald of Worcester at Evesham Abbey', pp. 1–17, at 5–7.

[3] This could be taken to mean a large woven tapestry rather than a gospelbook.

[4] 1 Kgs. (1 Sam.) 2: 12.

[5] *Tintinnabula* suggests smaller bells.

[6] The dorsal is a curtain, placed usually behind an altar.

[7] See below, 329–31 (JL 7999). The privilege of Innocent II was acquired at the time of the Second Lateran Council of 1139.

sensible advice from the earl of Hereford not to do so lest so well
fortified a place be seized by the king. He built the greater part of the
nave walls of the church just as they can be seen today, and he also
built a refectory, a parlour, with a chapel, and a hall for guests, with a
chamber, and a large kitchen.[1] He had two arm [reliquaries] made,
one for the arm of St Ecgwine and the other for St Oswald's,[2] a large
gospelbook,[3] the most valuable cross of this church, and the roof of St
Ecgwine's shrine to make good the shrine which Abbot Mannig had
made, for it was during Reginald's time, when they were threatened
by war and oppressed by famine, so they said, that many monks of
this church—'sons of Belial'[4]—stripped the shrine of its gold, silver,
and precious stones between meal times, without the knowledge of
the abbot. He also had made censers and gilded candlesticks. Then he
had bells made, the 'Benedict' and its companion, and acquired two
bells,[5] the 'Gloucester' and its companion. He also had a large dorsal[6]
made, and two for St Ecgwine in the choir. He acquired for this
church a large black cope and many other vestments as well as books
and treasures. In the time of Pope Innocent II, in order to protect the
exemption of this church from the jurisdiction of Bishop Simon, he
went with him with some trepidation to Rome, and manfully
championed our freedom. He won his case in part and acquired a
privilege concerning it from this pope.[7]

179. *The holy and courageous deeds of Abbot William*
Reginald was succeeded by William de Andeville,[8] a monk of Christ
Church Canterbury, where he lies buried by the head of St Thomas
the Martyr. Before he went there [to Canterbury] on a visit,[9]
William was visited by the Lord here, when he saw in a dream,
so he told the brethren, that the sun had been buried at his feet.
This vision had its fulfilment in process of time after Thomas was
buried at William's feet.
180. This William courageously excommunicated William Beauchamp[10] and his accomplices who had destroyed the walls of the

[8] Abbot from 1149 to 1159, when he was buried in the crypt of Canterbury cathedral
near St Thomas's first resting place after his murder in 1170. His obit was kept at
Canterbury on 3 Jan., see Christ Church obits, BL Cotton MS Nero C IX fo. 3ʳ; printed
by J. Dart, *History and Antiquities of . . . Canterbury* (1726), p. xxxii, and R. Fleming in *The
Culture of Christendom*, ed. M. A. Meyer, p. 130.

[9] The Latin *causa uisitationis* is used below by Thomas to mean a visitation rather than
a visit, but it would not seem to be an appropriate interpretation here.

[10] William (I), son of Walter, d. 1170 (see *Ann. Mon.*, i. 55, ii. 65, iv. 382, 389)
succeeded his father Walter, who d. *c.*1131 (see E. Mason, *St Wulfstan*, p. lviii for a

qui muros cimiterii destruxerant et bona ecclesie tempore werre
rapiebant,[1] in facie inermis armatos excommunicauit, *quare nullus
eorum secundum religionem Christianam et ritum Christianorum
decessit; set et eadem die multi ex eis ab hominibus abbatie occisi
sunt, quorum unus miles, cognomento de Abetot ab eis occisus
apud Almeleiam est sepultus extra cimiterium nec adhuc reconciliatus.*[2] Viriliter etiam castellum quod erat Bengewrthe ad capud
pontis contra eundem Willelmum obtinuit et funditus destruxit, et
cimiterium ibidem consecrari fecit.

181. De paruo Rogero, set factis magnanimo

Huic substitutus est Rogerus monachus sancti Augustini Cantuarie,[3]
qui paruo tempore, uiriliter tamen sicut abbas prior, uixit, et
molendina iuxta pontem de Euesham[b] fecit.

182. De regulari conuersatione Ade abbatis, et bonis operibus et malis tempore eius peractis

Isti successit Adam monachus Cluniacensis de Caritate. Iste ferme
uixit triginta annos,[4] et felicia habuit tempora, et multa bona hic eius
tempore facta sunt, et ipse 'uiriliter egit'[5] et benefacientes adiuauit,[c] et
multos ad benefaciendum ortatus est et coegit. Eius enim tempore
feretrum sancti Ecgwini perfectum est, et aqueductus et lauatorium

---

a–a over an erasure in the text; text extends into the left-hand margin   *b* de Euesham interlined (s. xv)   *c* adiuuit

genealogy, and Green, *Aristocracy*, p. 300). He joined the empress in 1141, following Stephen's grant of the earldom of Worcester to Waleran of Meulan, and the king's insistence that William should become Waleran's vassal. The empress's charter to him, of *c*.25 July–1 Aug. 1141, confirmed the castle of Worcester to him, to be held in chief hereditarily, and the shrievalty of Worcestershire at the same farm as his father had paid (*Regesta*, iii. 68).

[1] It would seem likely that William's destruction of the cemetery walls at Evesham and his plundering of the abbey's property occurred soon after William de Andeville's election as abbot in 1149. The abbey of Evesham seems to have suffered considerably from acquisitive magnates at this time. In a letter of Gilbert Foliot, of *c*.April–May 1150, it is reported that Roger, earl of Hereford, had infringed sanctuary at Evesham by capturing some knights of Ralph of Worcester in the abbey (*Foliot Letters*, pp. 127–9, no. 93); and in another letter, of *c*.July to Aug. 1150, Foliot refers to knights being captured in a cemetery and to sacrilege at Leominster, as well as at Evesham (ibid. no. 96, pp. 133–5). The attack on the walls of the cemetery and the spoiling of church property were conceived as forms of sacrilege by churchmen who at this time were attempting to limit warfare by introducing the idea of the Truce of God, periods when hostilities ceased.

[2] The castle at Elmley is supposed to have been built by Robert le Despenser, brother of Urse d'Abetot, the sheriff. When the castle at Worcester fell into decay it became the chief stronghold of the Beauchamps (VCH *Worcs.* iii. 339). When Urse d'Abetot's son, Roger,

cemetery and plundered the property of the church during time of war,[1] armed as they were while he faced them unarmed. So none of them departed this life with the blessing of the Christian religion or the Christian rite. Indeed, many of them were killed on the same day by the men of the abbey, and one of them, a knight called Abetot who was killed by the abbey men, was buried at Elmley Castle[2] outside the cemetery, and he still remains unreconciled. Furthermore William courageously won possession from William Beauchamp of the castle which was situated at the head of Bengeworth bridge, and he utterly destroyed it. He then had the cemetery there reconsecrated.

181. The deeds of Roger, brief but magnanimous
Roger, a monk of St Augustine's Canterbury, succeeded William.[3] He lived for but a short time but, like the previous abbot, lived courageously. He built mills by the bridge at Evesham.

182. Abbot Adam, his life according to the Rule, his good works, and the evils perpetrated in his time
Adam, a Cluniac monk of La Charité, succeeded Roger. He lived for almost thirty years and enjoyed prosperous times. [4] Many good things were done here in his time: he 'acted with courage',[5] helped those who did good, and urged and compelled many to do good. Indeed, in his time the shrine of St Ecgwine was completed, and a conduit and a washing place were constructed with the help of

had been disgraced and deprived of his lands before 1114, Henry I soon granted the d'Abetot lands and Elmley to Walter de Beauchamp (I), the husband of Urse's daughter; see Mason, pp. xx–xxi, and p. lviii for the Beauchamps of Elmley. It is not clear who this particular d'Abetot was.

[3] Roger was abbot from 1159 to 1160. In May to June 1159 Archbishop Theobald wrote to the convent of Evesham, charging them to proceed to an election in June, with the assistance of the bishops of Coventry and Worcester and of the abbots of Pershore and Winchcombe; The Letters of John of Salisbury, i, ed. W. J. Millor, H. E. Butler, rev. C. N. L. Brooke (OMT, 1986), no. 109. The archbishop's letter, if known to Thomas, might have been taken to support Thomas's claim that the church of Evesham was subject only to the archbishop of Canterbury.

[4] He was abbot from 1161–89 (so he was abbot for almost thirty years and must have lived considerably longer). Originally a monk of the Cluniac priory of La Charité-sur-Loire in the diocese of Auxerre, Nièvre (Cottineau, i, col. 705), he was prior of Bermondsey, dependent on La Charité, from 6 June 1157 until his election as abbot of Evesham on 16 Apr. 1161 (HRH, pp. 47, 115). Early in 1161 Gilbert Foliot, bishop of Hereford, presumably acting as vicar during a vacancy in the see of Worcester, wrote to the prior and convent of La Charité asking them to release Adam from obedience to them; Foliot Letters, pp. 177–8, no. 134.

[5] Cf. Deut. 31:6; Ps. 30: 25 (31: 24); 1 Macc. 2: 64; and 1 Cor. 16: 13.

multorum bonorum uirorum adiutorio facta sunt. Iste fecit duas maximas campanas, et emit magnam nigram casulam de nigris secundo meliorem, et capam rubeam cum auibus aureis et stolam et manipulum suum tintinnabulis et alia uestimenta emit, et multa obedienciarios emere compulit. Quedam redemit et quedam uarie ornauit et bene disposuit. Et Nouum Testamentum et Vetus glosata huic ecclesie adquisiuit.[1] Pistrinum etiam, bracinum et granarium et uetus infirmaria, que nunc est thalamus abbatis, et priuatum dormi-
fo. 146[vb] torium eius tempore facta sunt. Indagi|nem etiam de Vffeham [a]domos et uiuaria et thalamum qui nunc est ad infirmariam et lectricium capituli ipse[a] fecit.[2] Claustrum etiam, quod Mauricius et Reginaldus abbates pro parte fecerant, et nauis ecclesie, cum adiutorio decani de Welles[3] maxime et aliorum bonorum uirorum, eius tempore perfecta sunt. Et ipse multas fenestras uitreas apposuit, et multas apponi fecit. Duas etiam hidas terre in Neuueham pro centum marcis emit ecclesie isti ab illis qui dicuntur de Watteuilla. Calicem etiam aureum in egritudine in qua decessit fieri fecit, quem Rogerus abbas postea distraxit pro redemptione regis Ricardi.[4] Partem etiam illam de Raggeleie que de feodo [b]modo est et Kingleyam, que fuerunt quondam uaccaria huius ecclesie, et postea caducum per exilium Wiberti Trunket, quas de consensu eiusdem post reuersionem eius et ad petitionem domini regis dederat Rogero filio Willelmi, postea ab Henrico filio eiusdem Rogeri redemit. Set predictus successor, eas ne exhiberet, pro eis sex homines tantum in uita eorum, sine consensu conuentus, retento tantum molendino, remisit.[b]

[a–a] ? written over an erasure   [b–b] *written over an erased passage*

[1] On the biblical *Glossa ordinaria* (the standard exposition of the text for teaching purposes), see B. Smalley, *The Study of the Bible in the Middle Ages*, 3rd edn. (Oxford, 1983), pp. 46–66. The glosses to Abbot Adam's bible may have been those of Anselm of Laon and his assistants, and of Gilbert the Universal. By the middle of the 12th cent. all the books of the bible had been covered by various glossators, the chief of whom were the above, and most monasteries acquired glossed bibles for the instruction of their monks in the Holy Scriptures.

[2] This may be the splendid lectern dug up in the grounds of Evesham abbey in 1813 and now in Norton church, see Nikolaus Pevsner, *Worcestershire* (The Buildings of England: Penguin, 1968), p. 226 and pl. 17, who compares it with that at Crowle and a similar piece at Much Wenlock (p. 130). Pevsner inclined to the view that if it is Abbot Adam's lectern it dates from the end of his abbacy, and Neil Stratford has seen in the Crowle lectern similarities with the foliage in the south transept at Wells. Edward Rudge, 'Description of the reading desk of the abbey church of Evesham in Worcestershire', *Archaeologia*, xvii (1814), 278–9, with two plates, on whose grounds the Evesham lectern was found, on not much authority connected it with Thomas of Marlborough's lectern, see below, 521. There is a plate of the Wenlock lectern in *English Romanesque Art 1066–1200*

many good men. He had two large bells made, bought a large black chasuble better than the second-best amongst the black ones, a red cope ornamented with golden birds, a stole and a maniple with little bells, and other vestments, and he compelled the obedientiaries to buy many more. Some of these he got out of pawn, some he ornamented in various ways and put in good order. He also acquired for this church glossed New and Old Testaments.[1] A bakery, brewery, granary, and the old infirmary, which is now the abbot's chamber, and a private bedroom were all built in his time. He also had constructed a park for game at Offenham, houses and fishponds and a chamber, which is now near the infirmary, and he himself made a lectern for the chapter house.[2] The cloister which Abbots Maurice and Reginald had in part built, and the nave of the church, were completed during his time with the help of the dean of Wells[3] in particular and of other good men. He himself put in many glazed windows and had many others put in. He bought for this church two hides of land in Newnham [Northants] from the de Waterville family at a cost of one hundred marks. He had a golden chalice made during the time of the illness from which he died, though Abbot Roger later disposed of it to ransom King Richard.[4] That part of Ragley [Warws.], which is at present held in fee, and Kingley [Warws.], which were once cow farms of this church, were later escheated because of the exile of Wibert Trunket; but after his return, when he was asked by the king to give these lands to Roger fitz William, he did so. Subsequently Adam bought these lands back from Roger's son Henry. But his successor, so that he would not have to give up the lands, conceded for them six men during their lifetime, not including the mill, without the consent of the convent.

(Arts Council, 1984), p. 203, pl. 170, where Zarnecki dates it to *c*.1180, and all three lecterns are illustrated in F. T. S. Houghton, 'The stone lecterns at Abbots Norton, Crowle and Wenlock', *Birmingham and Midland Archaeological Society Transactions*, xxxix (1914), 1–4.

[3] See below, 184. His interest in Ombersley and Badby, as well as the convent of Evesham, suggests that he may have been a local man. Little else is known about him, other than that as dean of Wells he acted on occasion as judge delegate and expressed an interest in the customs at Salisbury; see Greenway, *Fasti*, vii. 8–9, and the references cited there.

[4] In 1193, the emperor Henry VI demanded a ransom of 150,000 marks of silver for the release of King Richard I. The monastic houses were not exempt from the taxation and requisitioning of plate that ensued; see Howden, *Chronica Magistri Rogeri de Houedene*, ed. W. Stubbs (4 vols., RS li, 1868–71), iii. 208–11, and 290, for the replacement of chalices by King Richard I in 1195. The king's begging letter of 1193 to the prior and convent of Christ Church, Canterbury, asking for a loan, and promising compensation 'ad duplum' is in *Ep. Cant.*, pp. 61–2.

183. Hic etiam insignia episcopalia preter anulum primo ecclesie isti adquisiuit, et priuilegium Alexandri pape quod bene operatur ad libertatem.[1] Verum molendinum *a*de Samburna et Hocwike et Farintone et Wrotesleie et Liuinton' ad firmam posuit et uirgatam terre in Euesham Ernaldo Camberlango. In Baddebi fratri prioris manerium, in Salford Waltero Grim quasdam terras male dedit et quasdam amisit ueluti iuxta Oxoniam Goldore et Hildendun quas potuit retinuisse. Hic etiam primo confirmauit officium porte per cartam ecclesie Henrico cum quadam muliere que petiit illud iure hereditario.

184. Viginti etiam libras de Burtona que prius libere pertinebat ad cameram monachorum sibi appropriauit. Eius tamen tempore*a* fuit Ricardus decanus de Welles qui adquisiuit redditum quindecim marcarum de ecclesia de Ambresleia ad opera ecclesie istius et optimas confirmationes earundem,[2] et qui fecit aulam que nunc est abbatis. Iste etiam decanus pensionem ecclesie de Baddebi duarum marcarum*b* et quosdam alios redditus adquisiuit, unde cereus ante magnum altare et corpora sanctorum perhenniter ardens appositus fo. 147ra est. Cuius etiam maxime auxilio | et ecclesia et ornamenta et omnia predicta perfecta sunt. Igitur quamuis predecessores istius abbatis fuerint uiri religiosi et ualde ordinati, iste tamen abbas dicitur pre ceteris ordinem reformasse. Hec uobis fideliter scripsimus sicut cognouimus et uidimus pro parte, pro parte uero a fidelibus relatoribus audiuimus et didiscimus.

185. *De intrusione abbatis Rogeri, et qualiter monachos depresserit tam ecclesie Christi Cantuarie quam ecclesie Eueshamsis*
Huic successit Rogerus, nullius monasterii monachus, quia cum esset quondam monacus ecclesie Christi Cantuarie propter proditionem missus est in carcerem a conuentu, et eo quod*c* reuelasset secreta capituli domino Balduuino Cantuariensi archiepiscopo qui tunc

---

a–a de Samburna . . . Eius tamen tempore *written over an erased passage*   *b* duarum marcarum *inserted in margin (s. xv)*   *c* eo quod ? *written over an erasure*

[1] For the text of the letter of Alexander III, see below, 332–6.
[2] William, bishop of Worcester's charter (V fo. 16ᵛ; H fos. 86ᵛ–7), allowing Evesham 15 marks a year from the church of Ombersley can be very precisely dated to between 1189/90 and 2 or 3 May 1190 when Bishop William died. Master Peter de Leche, archdeacon of Worcester, who witnessed the charter, did not succeed to the archdeaconry until 1189/90. See Greenway, *Fasti*, ii. 100, 105. John (of Coutances), bishop of Worcester (1196–8),

183. Adam was the first to acquire the episcopal insignia for the church, except for the ring, as well as the privilege of Pope Alexander which well defines our liberty.[1] But the mill of Sambourne [Warws.], as well as Howick and Farington [Lancs.], and Wrottesley and Loynton [Staffs.], he farmed out to Ernald Camberlang, as he did a virgate of land in Evesham. In Badby [Northants] he made a poor gift of the manor to the prior's brother, and in Salford [Oxon.] of certain lands to Walter Grim, and lost others, just as he did Goldor near Oxford and Hillingdon [Middx.] which he could have held on to. He first confirmed by a charter of the church the office of porter for Henry, and for a certain woman who claimed it by hereditary right.

184. Adam also appropriated for himself twenty pounds from Bourton-on-the-Water [Glos.] which had previously and freely belonged to the monks' chamber. During his time Richard, dean of Wells, acquired a rent of fifteen marks from the church of Ombersley to undertake building works in this church and excellent documents confirming this money;[2] he also built a hall which now belongs to the abbot. Dean Richard also acquired a pension of two marks from the church of Badby, and certain other revenues which enabled a candle to be kept permanently burning before the high altar and the bodies of the saints. It was with his assistance in particular that the church and its treasures, and all the things mentioned, were completed. Hence, though his predecessors had been devout men who had lived strictly in accordance with their Order, nevertheless it is said that Adam surpassed them in his regeneration of discipline. This record is a faithful account of these deeds as I either learned of them or saw them myself, or as I heard or ascertained them from the trustworthy accounts of others.

185. *The intrusion of Abbot Roger and how he oppressed the monks of both Christ Church Canterbury and the church of Evesham*
Adam was succeeded by Roger, who was not a monk of any monastery. Indeed, he had once been a monk of Christ Church Canterbury, but was imprisoned by the convent as a traitor and because he had revealed the secrets of a chapter-meeting to Baldwin, archbishop of Canterbury, who at that time was in dispute with the

confirmed this (V fo. 17^r; H fo. 87^r). Abbot Adam died on 12 Nov. 1189 and Richard, dean of Wells, was dead by late 1189, so there may have been earlier charters of the bishops of Worcester allowing this, the 'excellent confirmations' referred to. Richard's role seems to have been that of a fund raiser.

temporis aduersabatur monachis, uolens erigere capellam de Hakin-
tune.[1] *a* A quo carcere, iuratoria data cautione de stabilitate,[2] egressus,*a*
nescio per que loca nudus*b* effugit manus eorum et a Cantuariensi
archiepiscopo honorifice est susceptus, qui eum lateri suo quasi
socium indiuiduum iunxit, et postea, inuitis monachis et reclamantibus, priorem ecclesie eiusdem prefecit;[3] set non profecit, quia
nunquam postea uniuersitati reconsiliatus est, quamuis exactissimam
diligentiam et multas expensas ad hoc postea apposuerit, et sic inde
exclusus nullius monasterii monachus remansit.

186. Quem cum monachi nollent recipere ipse intrusit se, et omnes
possessiones monachorum inuadendo sibi usurpauit, et bona eorum
diripuit, et monachis uictum et uestitum subtraxit, et prioratum
eorum per 'filios Belial'[4] ministros suos ne monachi exirent obseruauit, *c* tantum duorum fratrum fugitiuorum fultus auxilio. Duos
etiam fratres ad ipsum archiepiscopum destinatos honoris gratia
statim capi fecit et a se diuisos custodie mancipari. Tandem*c* studuit
archiepiscopus eum alteri preficere ecclesie. De qua prefectura, quasi
spiritu prophetico preuentus, ita scribit Alanus abbas Theokesberie in
libro de demolitione capelle de Hakintona, ubi etiam omnia predicta
de eo plenius scribit:

Interim uero ob reuerentiam archiepiscopi ne uideretur et ipse in
hac parte succubuisse, ipso rege id procurante, uix semel nomi-
nandus set ubique dampnandus Rogerus Norreis, Dei et ecclesie
sue hic et ubique inimicus manifestus, in Eoueshammsem pro-
mouetur abbatem, conuentu illius ecclesie quantum licuit recla-
mante, set aduersus equitatem preualente malicia, hic ille sicut
promeruit 'de mercede iniquitatis agrum possedit'.[5] In huiusmodi

---

a–a A quo carcere . . . egressus *written over an erasure*   *b* nudus *written over an erasure*
c–c tantum duorum fratrum . . . custodie mancipari. Tandem *written over an erasure;
followed by further erasure and overwriting. This is followed by a passage which extends by seven
lines into the lower margin and into two added lines at the top of the right-hand column* (*b*), *being
carefully crafted to fit in with the original text, ending* abbatiam ac si di (di/ceret)* (*p. 192*)

[1] In the dispute between the archbishop and convent, Roger Norreis had sided with
Archbishop Baldwin. On Hackington (1 mile north of the city of Canterbury) and the
proposed chapel and college there, see *Ep. Cant.*, the convent's letter-book, which is largely
devoted to the archiepiscopal plans to build a college with prebends at Hackington, esp.
pp. 2–3, 8–73, 79–80, 339–41, and Gervase, i. 337–8 (its origins) and 498–500 (its
demolition).
[2] The Latin 'stabilitas' meaning steadfastness; to a Benedictine, this implied steadfast-

monks over his wish to build a chapel at Hackington.[1] He was let out
of prison after giving a promise on oath of 'stability',[2] and, having
escaped unclothed from the hands of the monks through certain
places, he received a warm welcome from the archbishop of Canterbury, who accepted him as a confidant and subsequently, despite the
opposition and protests of the monks, made him prior of that very
same church.[3] But he did not profit from this, for he was never after
that reconciled to the whole community no matter how great the
effort he made or how large the expense he subsequently paid out to
achieve this, and so he was excluded from Christ Church, and was no
longer a monk of any monastery.

186. When the monks refused to accept him, he intruded upon them:
there he made an assault upon all their possessions, and appropriated
them for himself. He stole their property, deprived the monks of food
and clothing, and used his servants, those 'sons of Belial',[4] to keep a
watch on the priory so that the monks should not get out, and was
supported with aid from two runaway brethren. He sent the two
brethren to the archbishop himself to receive his commendation, but
then immediately afterwards he arrested them, and, disclaiming
them, had them placed in custody. In the end the archbishop was
keen to put him in charge of another church. Alan of Tewkesbury, as
if inspired by a prophetic spirit, wrote as follows about this
'promotion' in a book concerning the destruction of the chapel of
Hackington in which he also recorded, at greater length, all the
aforesaid deeds of Roger:

> Meanwhile—in fairness to the archbishop, lest it should seem
> that he himself had slipped up in this matter, it was in fact the
> King himself who had procured it—Roger Norreis, to be named
> barely once but to be damned everywhere, an open enemy of
> God and His church here and everywhere, was promoted abbot
> of Evesham, and this was despite the objections of the convent of
> that church being expressed as loudly as was permissible. But
> wrong prevailed against right, and he 'purchased a field bought
> with the proceeds of infamy'.[5] But what sort of end will result

---

ness of purpose and observance of his vow not to leave the cloister without permission of
the abbot; for its use see *RSB* caps. 4, 58, 60 and 61.

[3] In 1189. For Norreis's character, career, and escape down the monastic sewer, see
Gervase, i. 379–82, 404, 460, 481, and 484.

[4] 1 Kgs. (1 Sam.) 2: 12.

[5] Acts 1: 18. A reference to Judas Iscariot.

autem introitu qualis sequetur exitus, ipsum non latet iudicem qui examinator est meritorum, et cetera.[1]

fo. 147rb De hoc sui ipsius ingressu ipse abbas Rogerus | sepe dicere consueuerat, quod dominus rex pro seruitio suo dedit ei hanc abbatiam, ac si diceret, * 'Non per ostium set aliunde ingressus sum in ouile ouium';[2] et reuera a nullo capitulo fuit postulatus, sicut canones fieri precipiunt.[3] Iste abbas magnanimum se exibebat et multis litteris habundare uidebatur, facundus enim erat et eloquencia pollebat. Curialis etiam nimium extitit et dapsilis, et gloriosus in mensa, cibis et potibus habundancius affluens, et quibus et quando uolebat copiose et honorifice hec largiebatur, non ut Christi^a militem ut beatus Sebastianus,[4] set ut exordinationes suas sub absconso clamide tegeret.

187. Erat enim uinolentus et luxuriosus super omnes monachos Anglicanos, quamuis se monachum non confiteretur, et simplicem fornicationem mortale peccatum esse non concederet, et per hoc mulieres seduceret, nisi incestui uel adulterio iungeretur, quamuis ipse nec hiis nec illis parceret, ut dicebatur. Et nos ex parte hec uera esse cognoscimus, stilum tamen temperamus, Deo teste, propter ordinis reuerentiam.

188. Et cum talis esset post paucos annos postquam huc uenerat, quibus satis modeste erga conuentum se habebat, in tantam superbiam elatus est ut quasi pro multis litteris suis et dapsilitate sua uideretur insanire,[5] et ecclesiam, capitulum, claustrum et refectorium, fere penitus cum cura animarum et obseruancia ordinis abiecit. Per multos enim annos ante depositionem suam (septem uel amplius) capitulum non tenuit, in refectorio non comedit, in

---

^a Followed by domini erased

[1] Alan, abbot of Tewkesbury, who had been prior of Christ Church, Canterbury, from 1179–86, collected the letters and wrote a life of St Thomas of Canterbury; Greatrex, Biog. Reg., pp.69–70, and Richard Sharpe, A Handlist of Latin Writers of Great Britain and Ireland before 1540 (Publications of the Journal of Medieval Latin, i, Turnhout, 1997), pp. 33–4. In 1184, as prior of Canterbury, he had been much concerned with the process of electing an archbishop, favouring free election by the chapter. In the course of this dispute, the king declared that the prior wished to be a second pope in England; Gervase, i. 310–25, and esp. 313. The book on the destruction of the chapel at Hackington has unfortunately not survived, but M. Harris's edition of Alan's own letters, written as prior of Canterbury and abbot of Tewkesbury ('Alan of Tewkesbury and his letters, I–II', Studia Monastica, xviii (1976), 77–108, 299–351), includes letters relating to Hackington (nos. 20–3, 26, pp. 308–14, 315) and one which refers to this work (no. 30, p. 319: see also p. 101). The et cetera makes it certain that Thomas had more of the text, and probably all of it, by him.

[2] Cf. John 10: 1.

from such a beginning! for he will not escape the Judge Himself, who will decide our just dues, etc.[1]

Abbot Roger himself would often say of this entry of his into his possessions that the king gave him this abbey in return for his service, as if he were saying 'I have entered the sheepfold not by the door but by some other way'.[2] And indeed, he had not been chosen by any chapter-meeting as the canons decree should be done.[3] As abbot he made himself out to be high-minded, and he seemed to be a well-lettered man, for he was a fluent and eloquent speaker. He was also too much the man of court, and loved feasting; he was boastful at the table, and too fond of food and drink, which he would bestow lavishly, and as a mark of honour, upon anyone he wished, whenever he wished, not with the intention of concealing his being a soldier of Christ, like the blessed Sebastian,[4] but rather to hide his misconduct beneath a cloak of concealment.

187. Roger surpassed all English monks in his winebibbing and lechery, although he did not claim to be a monk, and did not agree that simple fornication was a mortal sin. He would therefore seduce women, provided it did not involve incest or adultery, though it is said he refrained from neither the one nor the other. We know this to be entirely true, though we are restraining our pen out of respect for the Order.

188. Although the abbot was that kind of man, he behaved quite reasonably towards the convent for a few years, but after that he became so puffed up with pride that his great learning and his lavish living seemed to make him mad,[5] and he abandoned the church, the chapter-house, the cloister and the refectory almost entirely, as also the care of souls and the observance of discipline. During the many years before his deposition he did not hold a chapter for seven or more years, he did

---

[3] It is difficult to know what the writer has in mind here: perhaps *Decretum* C 17 q. 2 c. 3 (Friedberg i col. 814), which incorporated *RSB* 64, lines 1–5, or *X*. I 6. 14 (Friedberg ii col. 54), ' ut forma electionis canonice in omnibus conventualibus ecclesiis observetur . . . electores in unum locum', but, if the latter, it means that the comment was written after 1191 which may well be the case. Richard I made a practice of imposing his nominees as abbots, as Alan of Tewkesbury notes, and as after the Constitutions of Clarendon elections took place in the king's chapel, it was not difficult for kings to impose their choice more subtly.

[4] St Sebastian was created a captain of the pretorian guards by the Emperor Diocletian, who did not know he was a Christian. One of the most renowned Roman martyrs, but one for whom there is very little certain evidence, he was believed to have suffered death from arrows and came to be regarded as the model Christian soldier, like St George; see *Acta Sanctorum*, ii (Antwerp, 1643), 20 Jan., pp. 257–96, esp. 258, 265.

[5] Cf. Acts 26: 24.

claustro cum fratribus non sedit, ecclesiam raro introiuit, et tam in ecclesiam quam claustrum capitulum cappatus uenire consueuit, et camisiis et lintheaminibus, ut de ceteris exordinationibus circa uestimenta taceamus, palam utebatur.[1]

189. Monachos etiam tanto contemptui habere cepit, quod non propriis nominibus nec monachos, set caniculos, uassallos et ribaldos nominare consueuerat.[2] Et si aliquando pro defectu ciborum murmurarent, quod sepe non sine causa | contingebat, eos prebendarios suos nominauit,[3] et ideo quod placeret ei ipsis daret; et quasi ad proprii criminis excusationem omnes indifferenter mecos uocauit. Verum quamuis in tanto despectu haberemur, tamen hec fuit in nostro pectore cura minor, set super hoc magis dolebamus quod abbas noster, ut diximus, non tantum alienauit se a nobis, set etiam uictum et uestitum nobis subtraxit, et ea in abyssum suam conuertit,[4] et cameram et sacristariam et alias obediencias in manu sua quantum ei placuit tenuit.[5]

fo. 147ᵛᵃ

190. Aliquando quibusdam falsis fratribus[6] ad firmam tradidit, retinens aliquando sibi et approprians meliorem portionem obedienciarum et aliam tradens falsis fratribus. Aliquando etiam commutauit, nobis inconsultis, bonas portiones cum peioribus, ueluti Burthonam[7] que fuit de camera cum Samburna que est de celeraria. Ita nos spoliauit aliquando camera quod per multa tempora multi fratres, ob defectum frocorum, nec chorum nec capitulum sequi poterant, alii, quod peius erat, ob defectum cucullarum et femoralium nec diuina celebrare nec in conuentum intrare poterant. Per multos etiam dies in solo pane et aqua uiximus, et multis in pane duro et ceruisia parum differente ab aqua sine pitancia[8] fuimus. Ipse uero 'deliciis affluebat'[9] cum quibusdam fratribus, et tum per quartam partem anni, tum amplius, apud Baddebi, et iterum apud Bradeuuelle uel Burctun, in

---

[1] RB cap. 55 has little to say about clothing, other than that it should be suitable to the climate, fit properly, and the cowls and tunics were to be of better quality if the monks had to travel, when they were also to wear drawers. It was obviously supposed to be plain, unattractive, and serviceable. While abbots were allowed garments of better cloth, Norreis's attire was clearly more akin to a wealthy lay person's; see below, 477 and 478, for further comments.

[2] The word 'ribald', meaning a person of low status, a menial of a rascally kind, appears in use in the 12th cent. and came to be used by other clerics of rascally monks.

[3] Diana Greenway has pointed out to us that the term prebendary was used not only for a canon, but also for an estate-labourer of very low grade who lived in the lord's household.

[4] Rev. 20: 3.

[5] This means that he was taking the revenues of these departments, as Abbot Samson did with the cellary at Bury; see JB, pp. 78–9.

[6] Cf. 2 Cor. 11: 26.

not eat in the refectory, did not sit in the cloister with the brethren, and rarely entered the church, but when he did come into it he would do so wearing a cloak, as he did when entering the cloister and the chapter-house; and he would openly wear shirts and linen garments, not to mention other irregular clothing, over his vestments.[1]

189. He began to treat the monks with such contempt that it had become usual for him to call them, not by their proper names or 'monks', but 'puppies', 'vassals', or 'ribalds'.[2] If ever they grumbled about the lack of food, which they often did with good reason, he would call them his prebendaries[3] and so give them what he pleased and, as if to excuse his own crime, he called them adulterers. Yet, though we were held in such contempt, we were less concerned about this in our hearts, for we were more saddened by the fact that our abbot, as we have said, not only alienated from us so much of our property but also deprived us of food and clothing which he diverted to his own bottomless pit,[4] and kept the chamber, the sacristy, and other obediences in his own hands to do as he pleased with them.[5]

190. Sometimes he handed over this property to some false brethren[6] for them to farm, sometimes he kept back and appropriated for himself the better portion belonging to the obediences, handing over the other portion to the false brethren. Sometimes, without consulting us, he finally exchanged the good portions for the inferior, like Barton,[7] which was the property of the chamber, for Sambourne [Warws.], property of the cellary. At last, then, he robbed us of the wardrobe, so that many brethren were often unable to attend either the choir or the chapter because of the lack of garments, while others—which is worse—could not celebrate divine offices or go in to the convent because they had no cowls or breeches. For days on end we lived on bread and water alone, and on many occasions we lived on stale bread and ale that was hardly distinguishable from water, and received no pittance.[8] The abbot himself enjoyed with certain brethren 'an abundance of choice foods'.[9] Then for three months of the year, and for longer later on, he would stay at Badby [Northants.], or again at Broadwell or Bourton-on-the-Water [both Glos.], for in

---

[7] The demesne farm in Evesham.

[8] The monastic pittance was an additional small dish, usually of fish, eggs, or some kind of delicacy, provided in addition to the normal diet on special days or for special reasons, as after blood-letting. The obedientiary concerned was the pittancer, and his department the pittancery, see Barbara Harvey, *Living and Dying in England 1100–1540: The Monastic Experience* (Oxford, 1993), pp. 10–12.

[9] Cf. Isa. 66: 11; S. of S. 8: 5; Eccles. 2: 1 and 25; and Job 22: 26.

quibus maneriis nobilia et quasi regia edificia construxerat, moram faciebat, et uentri et lateri uacabat omni tempore usque ad depositionem suam. Nos uero, teste Deo, apud Eouesham cupiebamus saturari de secundo pane quam famuli eius comedebant, et non erat qui daret nobis.[1]

191. *Prima querela monachorum contra abbatem archiepiscopo tunc legato et assignatione reddituum ad pitanciariam*

fo. 147[vb]   Tandem,[2] inedia urgente, ad nos reuersi, conquesti | sumus super hiis domino Huberto Cantuariensi archiepiscopo tunc temporis tocius Anglie legato. Set abbas ad callida argumenta conuersus, muneribus promissis et datis et quibusdam fratribus corruptis, obedientiis nobis ad tempus restitutis, pacem sibi comparauit, et sic tunc a manu domini legati euasit, assignatis tamen pro bono pacis ex precepto domini legati certis redditibus ad pitanciariam, quia prius uina et medones de celario et carnes de lardario abbatis statutis temporibus ad hoc accipere consueuimus, unde magnum murmur et magni defectus sepe contingebant. Restituta etiam nobis tunc est ecclesia sancti Laurentii per dominum legatum,[3] quam prius abbas dederat, nobis reclamantibus, cuidam clerico suo Gilberto, et sic per istas tribulationes in melius reparati sumus.

192. Legatione autem finita post annum,[4] abbas iterum monachos subpeditauit, et tam redditus pitanciarie quam redditus operis et omnes redditus eorum fere sibi iterum appropriauit et 'infinitam peccuniam sibi congregauit',[5] maxime de hiis que ad monachos pertinebant, per quam pecuniam monachos eum sepe accusantes ab accusatione uiriliter repulit et eos prout uoluit sibi subiugauit. Multos enim magnates regni et maxime iusticiarium[6] per ciborum dapsilitatem et munerum largitionem, que temporibus necessitatis habundantissime effundebat, sibi amicos comparauerat. Monachi uere nichilominus semper insidiabantur ei et uicia eius pro posse suo

---

[1] Cf. Luke 15: 16, 'et nemo illi dabat'.

[2] This was probably in 1197; see below, n. 4.

[3] One of the two chapels within the abbey precinct.

[4] According to Gervase of Canterbury, Hubert's legatine jurisdiction ceased on 8 Jan. 1198, following the death of Pope Celestine III (Gervase, i. 551). He had been appointed on 18 Mar. 1195; *Ep. Cant.*, pp. 368–9. Hubert had been an active papal legate, in 1195 holding a council at York, in which he deposed the abbot of St Mary's, a house with close connections with Evesham; see *C. & S.*, i pt 2, pp. 1042–52, for the accounts of the council and its canons.

[5] Cf. Gen. 47: 14.

these manors he had built noble edifices, like palaces, and he always had time for his belly and 'bed' right up to the day he was deposed! As God is our witness, we at Evesham would have been satisfied to eat the inferior bread which his servants ate, but there was nobody to give it to us.[1]

191. *The first complaints of the monks against the abbot made to the archbishop, at that time papal legate, and the allocation of revenue to the pittancery*

Eventually,[2] compelled by hunger, we came to our senses and complained of our ill-treatment to Hubert, archbishop of Canterbury, who was then papal legate. The abbot resorted to cunning argument and corrupted some brethren with gifts or promises of them. He restored the departments to us for a while, won himself a reprieve, and so escaped being punished by the legate. Nevertheless, to keep the peace, fixed revenues were assigned to the pittancery by command of the legate, for previously we used to receive at appointed times wine and mead from the cellarer instead, and meat from the abbot's larder, which often resulted in much grumbling and numerous deficiencies. The church of St Laurence was also restored to us at this time by the legate.[3] The abbot had previously given this church, despite our objections, to his clerk Gilbert, so out of our troubles our fortunes were restored.

192. A year later, when the legate's jurisdiction ceased,[4] the abbot again began his oppression of the monks: he once again appropriated for himself the revenues of the pittancery and the income of the building fund; in fact, virtually all of their revenues. He 'accumulated endless sums of money'[5] for himself, especially from sources which belonged to the monks. He used this money to fend off with vigour the accusations frequently made against him by the monks, and he made them subject to his own will. In fact, the abbot had secured the friendship of many magnates of the realm, and particularly that of the justiciar,[6] because of the extravagant banquets and generous gifts that he bountifully lavished upon them during times of want. Nevertheless, the monks were always setting traps for him and attacking his

[6] Geoffrey Fitz Peter, earl of Essex from 1199, succeeded Hubert Walter as justiciar in 1198 and remained in the office until his death in 1213. As justiciar, the chief executive, regent when the king was abroad, and presiding over the Exchequer and the court of King's Bench, he was the most powerful person in the land after the king; see GEC, v, cols. 122–5, and F. West, *The Justiciarship in England 1066–1232* (Cambridge, 1966), pp. 102–77.

impugnabant. Ipse uero eos paruipendens et conatus eorum, ipsos persequebatur et odio habebat, et quosdam a domo postea eiecit. In quosdam uero in thalamo suo missos a conuentu manus uiolentas inici fecit, in alios precepit inici. Set tamen, Deo adiutore, semper manus eius uiui effugimus, quamuis dicatur quod quidam ob defectum necessariorum perierunt.

193. *Secunda querela conuentus archiepiscopo non tunc legato, et commutatione Samburne pro Tetlestrop, et turris constructione*

Iterum miseria et inedia compulsi hec ferre non potentes domino
fo. 148ʳᵃ Cantuariensi, | ut suo speciali legato quamuis iam non generali, in transmarinis agenti,[1] unde abbas seuiendi assumpserat audatiam, scripserunt monachi suas afflictiones et abbatis tirannidem et exordinationes; qui postquam rediit ualde commotus uenit Eueshamiam, et ibi de hiis que audierat diligentem fecit inquisitionem. Set abbas et tunc etiam ad nota subsidia confugiens, fratribus corruptis sicut prius per munera et amicos suos, obedienciis nobis restitutis, pacem sibi comparauit. Recepit tamen ea uice pro bono pacis Samburne iterum, et dedit nobis Thatlestrope ad cameram loco Burtune, et sic semper tribulatio profuit. Set adhuc pax paruo tempore durauit; nam iterum, paruo post occupato archiepiscopo pro causa de Lameithe,ᵃ[2] peius quam unquam prius nos flagellauit, et omnia nostra sibi appropriauit et 'facta sunt nouissima nostra peiora prioribus';[3] et sic sepe habuimus redditus ad nos pertinentes et sepe eis spoliati eramus. Et quamuis tot aduersa sustineremus, tamen per quendam magnanimum et magni consilii uirum et bonum monachum, magistrum uidelicet Thomam de Northuuic,[4] qui per sapientiam suam et maxime fisicam qua pollebat magnam gratiam tocius patrie sibi comparauerat, turrim ecclesie ereximus conuertentes redditus pitanciarie quandocunque

---

ᵃ Lameit[he]; he *interlined* (s. xv)

[1] After ceasing to be legate, Hubert Walter is not recorded as being abroad again until Sept. 1198 (with only one possible short return in the middle of the month), staying abroad until Apr. 1199. He then returned to Normandy in June and was there until almost the end of the year. He may have come to Evesham in the spring of 1200: he is recorded as at Worcester on 10–11 Apr. See *EEA, 3: Canterbury 1193–1205*, ed. C. R. Cheney and Eric John (1986), pp. 311–12.

[2] After the plan for the college at Hackington failed, the archbishops did not give up their idea of a secular college to provide for their clerks, but transferred the project to Lambeth, where they now owned the manor. Innocent III's decision of 20 Nov. 1198, ordering destruction of the chapel, did not reach Hubert until 2 Jan. 1199, when he was in

vices whenever they could. He himself scorned them and their efforts, and he persecuted and hated them; some he later expelled from the house. Some of those whom he had expelled he physically assaulted in his own chamber, and gave orders for the same to be done to others. Yet, with God's help, we always escaped from his hands with our lives, though it must be said, some died because of the lack of life's necessities.

193. *The convent's second complaint to the archbishop, who was no longer legate; the exchange of Sambourne for Adlestrop; and the building of a tower*

Again, forced by wretchedness and need, and unable to endure this ill-treatment, the monks wrote of their troubles and of the abbot's tyranny and outrageous behaviour to the archbishop of Canterbury as their special legate, though no longer general legate. He was busy abroad,[1] so the abbot had resumed his bold attacks upon us. When the archbishop returned he was very concerned about our complaint and came to Evesham. There he conducted a careful inquiry into the reports he had heard, However, the abbot took refuge among his well-known helpers—brethren whom he had bribed with gifts and his own friends—and, restoring the departments to us, he secured a reprieve for himself. At that time he took Sambourne [Warws.] back again to maintain the peace, and gave us Adlestrop [Glos.] for the chamber in place of Bourton-on-the-Water [Glos.]: so our constant trouble eventually benefited us. Yet peace lasted for but a short time, for soon after this the archbishop's time was taken up with the Lambeth affair,[2] and once again the abbot scourged us worse than before. He appropriated everything belonging to us, and 'our last state was worse than our first'.[3] So, whenever we had revenues belonging to us we were robbed of them. Yet we endured all those adversities with the help of a good monk, Master Thomas de Northwich, who was a man of good sense.[4] He had won a considerable reputation throughout the land for his wisdom and especially for his knowledge of medicine in which he had shown great skill. With his help we built a tower for the church, using the revenues of the pittancery whenever we possessed

Normandy. Hubert, however, kept up the struggle over the Lambeth college until an arbitrated award was accepted on 6 Nov. 1200, and ratified by the pope in the following May; see *Ep. Cant.*, pp. 459–68, and 512–14; and Gervase, i. 483, 534–59, 562–5, 576–87.
[3] Cf. Matt. 12: 45.
[4] He does not appear in *BRUO* or *BRUC*, but see below, **268**.

eos habuimus et omnia alia quecumque nobis subtrahere potuimus in opus illud.

194. Hactenus de hiis; ueniam autem nunc ad ea que pro libertate ecclesie passi sumus in labore et erumpna, in fame et siti, in frigore et nuditate, 'in itineribus sepe, periculis fluminum, periculis latronum, periculis in ciuitate' Romana, 'periculis in solitudine, periculis in mari, periculis in falsis fratribus', ut 'minus sapiens dico',[1] plus omnibus passus sum ego. 'Deus et pater Domini nostri Iesu Christi scit, qui est benedictus in secula, quod non mentior.'[2]

---

[1] 2 Cor. 11: 23.
[2] 2 Cor. 11: 26–31. The passage is closely related to the Pauline epistle. Whole phrases

them, and every other source of revenue which we could secure for that work.

194. This is the story so far. I shall now come to what we endured to secure the liberty of our church through toil and hardship, in hunger and thirst, in cold and nakedness, 'in being constantly on the road, in danger from rivers, danger from robbers, danger in the city' of Rome, 'danger in the wilderness, danger on the sea, danger from false brethren', and—as 'I am speaking like a fool'[1]—I suffered more than all my brethren. 'The God and Father of our Lord Jesus Christ, who is blessed for evermore, knows that I do not lie.'[2]

have been taken over by Thomas, and reworked, changing the order slightly. To danger in the city, he has added 'of Rome'.

195. *Incipit particula secunda qualiter episcopus mandauerat se uenturum causa uisitationis et ⟨de⟩ fatuo responso abbatis*

fo. 148rb In diebus illis erat dominus Malgerius episcopus | Wigornie, 'uir iustus et timens Deum'.[1] Iste abbatis exordinationibus condolens et nostre miserie compatiens, zelo bono ductus,[2] indulgentiam[3] a domino papa maxime propter correctionem status nostri, ut ipse sepe dicebat, impetrauit, uidelicet ut liceret sibi ecclesias diocesana lege sibi subiectas, appellatione remota, uisitare. Et scripsit abbati sub hac forma: 'Noueritis quod tali die ueniemus ad uos, causa uisitationis eadem die uobiscum moram facturi.' Abbas uero uisis litteris post cibum in die assumptionis beate Marie,[4] iuris tam ciuilis quam canonici ignarus, nullius communicato consilio, respondit, 'Bene uenerit', pro paruo reputans, ut erat dapsilis, quod episcopus cum eo hospitaretur, non capiens intellectum litterarum.

196. Recedente itaque nuncio cum tali responso, facta est contentio inter discipulos abbatis quidnam sibi uellet tale mandatum, et quia iuris peritus eram uocatus sum ego qui eram in claustro.[5] Quibusdam dicentibus quod episcopus uenit uidere abbatem ut amicus, aliis non, set ut abbatem deponeret quia odio eum habebat. Ego uero dicebam quia si eum causa uisitationis admitteret, ex ui uerbi huius 'causa uisitationis' et ratione predicte indulgentie quam apud Gloucestriam, ubi uisitacionem inceperat,[6] iam exhibuerat, quod episcopus potestatem habebat tam in capite quam in menbris[7] errata usque ad depositionem et degradationem corrigere; et quod nichil libertatis amodo ecclesie nostre relinqueretur si eum ut diocesana lege subiecti

---

[1] Acts 10: 22. Mauger was consecrated bishop on 4 June 1200 and died on 1 July 1212; and see below, n. 4 (p. 204). All the dating for this section depends on proceeding back from the secure date of the pope's mandate of 22 May 1203, see below, 247.

[2] For 'zelus bonus' cf. *RSB* cap. 72.

[3] The Latin *indulgentia* is not easy to translate into English. The literal translation 'indulgence', meaning the papal letter that remitted enjoined penance, is not appropriate here. The papal letter in question, where 'indulgemus' was used, was obtained on 24 Apr. 1202. It is printed in *Reg. Inn. III*, v (1993), no. 23 (24), and calendared in Cheney, *Letters*, no. 407: it empowered the bishop to visit churches subject to him under diocesan law, forbidding appeal. Mauger clearly knew that he was treading on glass here: for example, 1 *Comp.* III. 25. 4 (Alexander III to the archbishop of Canterbury) makes it quite clear that diocesan rights of visitation were clearly circumscribed when monasteries were 'the special sons of the Roman church', in which case visitation could only be by the pope or his representative.

[4] 15 Aug.

PART TWO

195. *Here begins the second part concerning the bishop's instruction that he would be arriving to undertake a visitation, and the foolish reply of the abbot*

At that time [1202] Mauger, 'a just, godfearing man', was bishop of Worcester.[1] Commiserating with us over the abbot's irregularities, and sympathizing with our suffering, he was led by a great zeal[2] to petition the pope for an empowerment[3] especially to bring us back into a proper state—as he himself often said—so that he might visit the churches which were subject to him by diocesan law without the possibility of appeal. He wrote to the abbot in these terms: 'Know that we shall be coming to you on a particular day for a visitation with the intention of staying with you from that day.' The abbot read the letter after dinner on the feast of the Assumption of the Blessed Mary,[4] but ignorant of both civil and canon law and taking no one's advice, he told the bishop, in reply, that he would be welcome, and as he was an extravagant man he thought little of it that the bishop would be lodging with him, for he did not perceive the significance of the letter.

196. When the messenger had left with the abbot's reply, a disagreement occurred amongst the abbot's monks over what the bishop's instruction meant, and as I had legal knowledge I was summoned, for I was a cloister monk.[5] Some monks were saying that the bishop was coming to see the abbot as a friend, but others disagreed, saying that he was coming to depose the abbot because he disliked him. I said that if he admitted him for a visitation then because of the force of the words 'for a visitation', and in consideration of the previously mentioned empowerment which he had already shown at Gloucester when he had undertaken a visitation there,[6] the bishop had complete power as much over the head as over the limbs[7] to punish wrongs even to deposition from office or by deprivation of orders; and that no freedom would remain to our church if we admitted him as we were

---

[5] The cloister monks were the learned monks employed primarily in some scholarly pursuit. [6] No record survives of this visitation.

[7] *Caput* and *membra* are used by Thomas in conjunction to signify the head, the mother church or monastery, and the limbs, the chapels; see below, **204, 215, 229, 283**. Its origin is in the idea of the Roman church as the *caput*, and all other subject churches as the limbs; see Gratian, *Decretum*, D 12. 1; D 34. 6; C 1 qu. 1 c. 63 (Friedberg i cols. 27, 127, 381). In this instance, however, it might mean the abbot (*caput*) and the monks (*membra*).

admitteremus. Quare statim dissuasi, immo ex parte conuentus prohibui, ne eum sub tali forma admitteret.

197. *De controuersia et dissentione conuentus de admittendo uel non admittendo episcopo*

Mane autem facto[1] conuenimus cum abbate nostro ut de admittendo episcopo uel non admittendo sufficiencius tractaremus. Et facta est inter nos magna dissencio et multi parietes[2] facti sunt. Quibusdam[3] |

enim fautoribus abbatis bene erat, qui cum ipso in stercore suo quasi sus in uolutabro computruerant; isti semper ita uiuere uellent ut cotidie cum abbate suo splendide epularentur. Hii litem nolebant, scientes quia lites magnas expensas requirunt. Alii autem ualitudinarii, alii uero senes, alii hic nutriti quibus alia loca erant incognita, propter nimias litis expensas timentes maiorem inediam, et etiam, si ita res urgeret, fratrum dispersionem: querebant ut pax fieret in diebus suis, qui, licet in aliis non fauerent abbati, in hoc tamen casu communiter cum eo steterunt.

198. Isti omnes cum abbate dicebant quia res de qua agebatur ualde ardua erat et supra uires ecclesie et nostras, dicentes totam abbaciam etiam si monachi nichil ex ea perciperent tantis sumptibus non sufficere. Non tacentes quod episcopus ualde fauorabilis erat utpote uir sanctus et in scientiis profundi pectoris ecclesie Romane cardinalis. Et a domino papa speciali quadam dispensatione propter magnas uirtutes quibus pollebat in episcopum consecratus, et pre ceteris episcopis, ut dicebatur, dilectus.[4] Quod ex multis argumentis comprobabant, addentes quod multi abbates et monachi ante nos fuerunt qui nos sciencia, moribus, sanctitate et seculari prudencia precellebant et nobis prefulgebant, et illi tam ardua non attemptauerunt, et

---

[1] Of 16 Aug.

[2] The MS clearly has *parietes* and although there do not appear to be other examples of its use in the sense of 'factions', this reading is supported by the unambiguous masc. pl. endings for *facti* and *multi*, so that there is no strong case for emending the text to *multe partes facte sunt*.

[3] At the bottom of this fo. has been transcribed, in a fine charter hand of the early 13th cent., a letter from Abbot Reginald Foliot to his nephew Abbot Gilbert Foliot of Gloucester, concerning Evesham's relationship with the bishops of Worcester, which can be dated 1139×1148. It was doubtless placed here with some care. The text is printed below in App. III.

[4] Mauger, formerly archdeacon of Évreux, royal clerk, and physician, was elected bishop of Worcester before 8 Apr. 1199. On account of Mauger's illegitimate birth, the election was quashed by Pope Innocent III; see Greenway, *Fasti*, ii. 100. In Feb. 1200, however, probably immediately after declaring the election void, the pope wrote allowing

subject to diocesan law. I therefore urged him at once not to admit the bishop under such a formula—in fact on behalf of the convent I forbade him to do so.

197. *The dispute and disagreement within the convent over the admittance or non-admittance of the bishop*
In the morning[1] we met our abbot to discuss more fully whether to admit the bishop or not. There was considerable disagreement amongst us and many factions[2] were formed.[3] Some supporters of the abbot who had been wallowing with him in their own dung like swine in a hog-pool were happy with his decision; they would want to go on living evermore as they were doing every day, feasting splendidly with their abbot. They did not want litigation, knowing that lawsuits incur heavy expenses. There were some who were infirm, some old, others who had grown up here and, knowing nothing of other places, were afraid of greater privation because of the heavy expenses of litigation, and feared even the dispersal of the brethren if circumstances forced it: these men were for peace being made in their time, and though they did not support the abbot in other matters, they stood together with him in this emergency.

198. All of them said, as did the abbot, that the point of the dispute was a very difficult one and beyond our strength or that of our church, and that even if the monks could understand nothing of this the whole abbey was unable to bear the cost of such expenses. They voiced their opinion that the bishop was highly respected as a holy man and as a man with the depth of understanding of a cardinal of the Roman church. He had been consecrated bishop by the lord pope by a special dispensation because of the great virtues in which he excelled, and, so men said, was beloved above other bishops.[4] They tried to prove this by many arguments, adding that there were many abbots and monks before us who surpassed and outshone us in knowledge, behaviour, holiness, and worldly wisdom, but they had not attempted the chapter to postulate Mauger, so that he might then dispense him and confirm the election. This letter (printed *SLI*, no. 6) was seen by the decretal collectors as a significant pronouncement, as it outlined both the pope's power over the control of elections and the position of illegitimates promoted to high orders. It was included in the contemporary collections of Rainer, Gilbert, and Bernard, and Innocent's first official collection, 3 *Comp.* I. 6. 5, and thence *X*. I. 6. 20 (Friedberg ii cols. 61–3). Macray (p. xxiii n. 1) understood Thomas to mean that Mauger was a cardinal, but there is no other evidence that Mauger was a cardinal and it is highly unlikely. Knowles answered the problem by changing *cardinalis* to *cardinalibus*; then the sentence might read that Mauger was well-regarded by the cardinals (*M. O.*, p. 335 n. 1), but the sense of *utpote* can be 'as'.

tamen pie et sancte et iuste uixerunt in hoc seculo, et diuitiis et honoribus gauisi sunt;[1] nos uero propter exordinationes nostras Deo et hominibus minus fauorabiles, immo quasi contemptibiles habebamur et pauperes. Ius etiam nostrum ualde exile et infirmum dicebant, maxime eo quod a ducentis uel trescentis annis retro episcopi Wigornenses omnes fuissent sollempniter cum processione sollemni ad diuinorum celebrationem et procurationem sufficientem in ecclesia nostra admissi.[2] Et abbates nostri supra memoriam hominum | ab episcopis Wigornie benedictionem acceperunt et eis professionem fecerunt, et crisma et oleum et ordines ab eisdem monachi susceperunt.[3] Et ideo presumptuosum et supersticiosum uideri tam longam consuetudinem et tantorum uirorum 'sequi uestigia'[4] nolle, et tam sanctorum magnorum et prudentum predecessorum nostrorum metas et uite fines uelle transgredi. Et etiam si quod ius ad proclamandum in libertatem haberemus, per tantum et tam longum abusum, immo contrarium usum, uideatur penitus abolitum et abrogatum.[5] Obiciebant etiam nobis quod nos iuuenes querebamus litem causa euagandi, scientes quia nos qui liti insisteremus semper bonis habundaremus sicut tanta causa exigebat, illi uero domi inedia perirent.

fo. 148[vb]

199. Et illi qui hec dicebant erant 'de senioribus populi',[6] qui quasi uidebantur regere ecclesiam nostram, et reuera de filiis prudentioribus lucis huius erant in generatione sua,[7] et si aliqui illorum zelum bonum[8] habebant tamen non secundum scientiam.[9] Alii nec zelum habentes bonum, querebant que sua erant non que Iesu Christi.[10] Set fauorem et pacem captantes multos fratres seduxerunt qui cum non essent ex nobis a nobis exierunt,[11] et usque ad diem sententie pro nobis late nobiscum amplius non ambulauerunt.[12] Et adhuc ex corde quidam nobiscum non ambulant quamuis nobiscum de libertate participentur et gaudeant.

---

[1] This may be a quotation, but we have not been able to identify it.

[2] See X. III. 39. 6 (Friedberg, ii cols. 623–4), clause 3 of the Third Lateran Council: on such occasions demands were not to be excessive. For a useful survey of *procuratio canonica*, the proper reception of a bishop, receiving him in a solemn procession and entertaining him and his retinue, see C. Bruhl, 'Zur Geschichte der Procuratio canonica vornehmlich im 11. und 12. Jahrhundert', in *Aus Mittelalter und Diplomatik*, i (Hildesheim, Munich, and Zurich, 1989), pp. 323–35.

[3] Only a bishop could confer the holy orders of deacon, priest etc., and bless the oils used in consecration and anointing.

[4] Cf. 1 Pet. 2: 21.

[5] On rights that were abused or fell into disuse, see *Decretum*, D 74. 7 (Friedberg, i col. 263); and for a full discussion, see below, **354** and n.

so difficult a task and yet had lived in this world with piety, holiness, and righteousness, and had rejoiced in riches and honours;[1] indeed, because of our breaches of the Rule we experienced less favour with God and men, and were in fact considered contemptible and poor. They even said that there was scant or weak justice in our cause, and made the particular point that for the past two or three hundred years all the bishops of Worcester had been duly admitted into our church in solemn procession for the celebration of divine service and had been properly entertained.[2] Our abbots had, as far back as could be remembered, been blessed by the bishops of Worcester and made profession to them, and the monks had accepted chrism, oil, and orders from those same bishops.[3] For these reasons it seemed to them presumptuous and pretentious to be unwilling to maintain their long-standing custom, to refuse to 'follow in the footsteps'[4] of such great men, and so prefer to cross the 'metes and bounds' of life set by our great saints and wise predecessors. Even if we had any right to freedom, that right would appear to have been completely destroyed and abrogated by long and considerable abuse of it,[5] or rather by our total disregard of it. They also accused us of being young men who wanted to go to law so that we might roam about, on the grounds that they knew that we who were insisting on litigation would always have more than enough personal wealth if this lengthy case demanded it, while they would perish at home from starvation.

199. Those who were expressing these views were from among 'the older members of our people'[6] who seemed, as it were, to rule our monastery and, in fact, belonged to the 'children of light' who are wiser in their generation,[7] and if any of them possessed great zeal[8] it was not according to knowledge.[9] Some who did not have great zeal were seeking their own interests not the interests of Jesus Christ.[10] In courting favour and peace they misled many brethren who, although they were not of their number, deserted us,[11] and until the day when judgment was pronounced in our favour no longer walked with us.[12] Indeed, some of these still do not walk with us in their hearts even though they share with us, and rejoice in, our liberty.

---

[6] Cf. e.g. Matt. 26: 47.
[8] Cf. *RSB* cap. 72.
[10] 1 Cor. 10: 24.
[12] Cf. John 6: 66.

[7] Cf. Luke 16: 8.
[9] Romans 10: 2.
[11] Cf. 1 John 2: 19.

200. Erant ibidem tunc et alii fratres habentes zelum Dei secundum scientiam,[1] zelantes libertatem sicut legem Finees,[2] scientes quod libertas rei est inestimabilis. Qui propter ea que audierant quasi furore accensi, cum sanioris consilii fratribus, sicut quondam Mathathias cum filiis suis et amicis, firmantes facies suas steterunt ex aduerso, opponentes se murum pro domo Domini.[3] Eligentes mori in curia Romana ad quam reuersio nostra et ecclesie nostre est et erat, fo. 149ra quam subire plenam subiectionem et seruitutem | et libertatis ecclesie sue perpetuam subuersionem.

201. Et dixerunt, 'Quare detraxistis sermonibus ueritatis?[4] Ad detrahendum uerba componitis et nitimini subuertere libertatem ecclesie uestre. Non timeatis paupertatem uestram uel litis expensas, quia si maneria nostra impignorare uoluerimus uel si pecuniam a Iudeis sub usuris uoluerimus uel in curia Romana a Romanis sub penis statutis, inueniemus qui usque ad mille marcas uel amplius quantum uoluerimus accommodabunt nobis, sub testimonio sigilli capituli nostri, quia conuentus quasi immortalis est.[5] Et nos in longa tempora soluendam peccuniam accipiemus et non dispergemur. Episcopus autem non inueniet qui aliquod manerium eius loco pignoris accipiat, nec qui pecuniam ei mutuo det nisi in modica summa, quia si episcopus moreretur statim pignus liberaretur, et nisi creditor probaret demonstratiue quod in necessarios usus ecclesie pecunia esset expensa, successor debitum soluere non teneretur. Quare nos in expensis magis possumus quam episcopus. Quod dicitis episcopum esse fauorabilem tam aput Romanos quam alios, hoc non timeatis, quia causa sua ecclesie Romane odiosa est,[6] ueluti que contra eam est instituta; et causa nostra, que libertatis est, inter omnes causas magis fauorabilis est, et maxime apud ecclesiam Romanam, cui uolumus, sicut debemus, nullo mediante[7] subici, que etiam diligit exemptiones. Et apud dominum Cantuariensem fauorabiles sumus, cui cura animarum nostrarum et correctio status huius ecclesie a domino papa specialiter sunt commissa. Quod dicitis ante nos fuisse et maiores et sanctiores uiros, uerum est, et in hoc

---

[1] Romans 10: 2.

[2] 1 Macc. 2: 26; Num. 25: 11. Phineas' zeal for the law was shown by his slaying of an Israelite who had dared to have intercourse with a Midianite woman, Num. 25: 6–8.

[3] Ezek. 13: 5.

[4] Job 6: 25.

[5] This comment reflects the Roman law notion of the undying corporation.

[6] Thomas's use of the word 'odious' here perhaps stems from 'prescription is odious (or hated)', for which see below, 370, 382.

[7] The claim of being directly subject to the Roman pontiff 'nullo mediante', without

200. There were also other brethren in the monastery at that time who had a zeal for God based upon knowledge[1] and a zeal for liberty of the sort Phineas had for the law,[2] knowing that liberty is a precious possession. These brethren were enraged by what they had heard and, with brethren of sound judgment, set their faces against them, and set themselves as a wall for the house of the Lord, as Mattathias once did with his sons and friends.[3] They preferred to die in the Roman curia upon which depends and depended our recovery and that of our church, rather than to suffer complete subjection, subservience, and the perpetual loss of their church's liberty.

201. This was what they said: 'Why have you despised the words of truth?[4] You compose speeches to despise it, and strive to deprive your church of its liberty. You should not be fearful for your own poverty or for the expenses of a lawsuit, for if we are willing to mortgage our manors or borrow money from Jews at interest or from Romans in the Roman curia under a binding legal contract, we shall find those who will accommodate us up to a thousand marks or to an even greater sum if we wish under the authority of our chapter seal, for a convent is virtually immortal.[5] We shall receive money to be repaid over a long period of time and we shall not be broken by this. But the bishop will not find anyone to accept any manor of his as a security, and no one to lend him money except a paltry sum, because should the bishop die the security would immediately disappear, and unless his creditor could prove conclusively that money had been spent for the necessary use of the church, a successor would not be compelled to pay the debt. So then, we are more able to face expenses than the bishop. You should not fear, as you say, that the bishop is in favour both with the Romans and with others, for his cause is odious[6] to the Roman Church as it is directed against that Church; whereas our cause, that of liberty, is the most approved amongst causes, and especially in the Roman Church to which we are willing, as we ought, to be subject without any intermediary,[7] which Church also looks kindly upon exemptions. Further, we enjoy the favour of the archbishop of Canterbury to whom the care of our souls and the power of correction of this church has been specially entrusted by the pope. Your statement that our predecessors were great and holy men is true,

---

any intermediary, was the hallmark of exemption. Privileges using this phrase are found for St Albans from the 1180s, Lucius III and Clement III, for Malmesbury granted by Celestine III in the 1190s. For Evesham, 'nullo mediante' appears for the first time in the indult of Clement III, see below, 337–8.

bene patet quod nunquam illi pleno iure et diocesano subiecti erant Wigornensi episcopo. Si uero nos episcopum causa uisitationis admiserimus, quod antecessores nostri nunquam fecerunt, nichil | libertatis ecclesie isti remanebit. Si exordinati sumus, ecce tribulatio, pena peccati et exordinationis nostre; qua tribulatione correpti, patienter sustineamus et emendemus in melius quod negligenter peccauimus, et non rememorabuntur omnes iniquitates nostre nec coram Deo nec coram hominibus.[a][1]

fo. 149[rb]

202. 'Quod autem dicitis predecessores nostros admisisse episcopos sollempniter, et abbates fecisse eis professionem, et benedictionem et crisma et oleum et ordinationes ab eis recepisse, uerum est, et male factum est illud, et periculum imminet nobis.[b][2] Set, benedictus Deus! semper cum protestatione libertatis et cum reclamatione facta sunt ista, quare prescriptionem[3] non timemus, et de iure nostro, per gratiam Dei conseruantis nobis priuilegia nostra, certissimi sumus, nisi prescriptio obsit, cuius interruptio facillime probatur. Et si in iudicio possessorio succubuerimus,[c] que cura? Cum quasi certi simus quod in petitorio obtinebimus.[d][4] Et quia ambigua sunt fata causarum,[e] miser est qui sponte se offert seruituti dum stare potest in libertate, maxime cum nil peius possit ei contingere quam ut seruus efficiatur. Et absit a nobis quod bonis ecclesie in deliciis abutamur, et illa que libera creata est ancilletur eternaliter, quod nec etiam amodo locus sit ei in libertatem proclamandi, et sic iniuste pereat, et non sit qui condoleat, cum satis habunde habeat unde defendatur.

203. 'Ergo state nobiscum si uultis, quia nos neque pro uita neque pro morte a libertate recedemus, nisi per sententiam domini pape. Quod nunquam continget, quod dominus papa uidelicet contra se ipsum et ecclesiam Romanam et tot priuilegia Romanorum pontificum sententiam det.[f] Nos uero parati sumus omne pondus litis in nos suscipere, et adire curiam Romanam, et stare ibi pro libertate, non ut euagemus ut uos dicitis, set ut ibi moriamur si forte transierint dies nostri; et sicut fuerit | uoluntas in celo sic fiat.'[5] Hec nos sanioris consilii fratres cum fletu dicebamus.[6]

fo. 149[va]

---

[a] Romana papa (?s. xiv²) add. in marg.   [b] ?Romana ecclesia (?s. xiv²) add. in marg.
[c] marg. iudicium possessorium (?s. xiv²)   [d] marg. iudicium petitorium (?s. xiv²)
[e] marg. nota optime (?s. xiv²)   [f] marg. nota constanciam (?s. xiv²)

---

[1] Cf. Isa. 43: 25.
[2] This may be a quotation (cf. below, 266) but it has not been traced.
[3] Rights that had been held for a considerable time and gone unchallenged. See below, 302–5, 359.

and in this respect it is quite clear that they were never fully subject to the bishop of Worcester as their diocesan. But if we admit the bishop for a visitation, something our predecessors never did, no liberty will remain for this church. If we cause a breach of the Rule then expect tribulation and punishment for our sin and for our transgression; but when chastened by this suffering let us endure it patiently and do our best to correct our thoughtless sins, and not all our iniquities will be remembered before God or before men.[1]

202. 'Your statement that our predecessors formally admitted bishops, that abbots made profession to them, received the blessing, chrism, oil and orders from them, is true, but it was a mistake to have done so and perilously threatens us now.[2] But blessed be God, those things were always done with a declaration of freedom and a protest, so we do not fear prescription,[3] and (through the grace of God who preserves our privileges for us) we are very sure of our rights, but if prescription goes against us, we can easily show interruption. Even if we are not successful in a possessory judgment, why worry? For we can be virtually certain of being successful in the petitory judgment.[4] And because the outcome of lawsuits is doubtful, he is a miserable man who voluntarily consigns himself to servitude when he can make a stand for liberty, especially when nothing worse could happen to him than to become a slave. God forbid that we should waste the church's possessions in pleasure-seeking and that that which has been created free should be enslaved for ever; or that henceforth there should be no chance for it to champion its liberty, but simply to perish unjustly with no one to grieve over it, when it has abundant resouces with which to defend itself.

203. 'Therefore stand with us if you will, for we shall not give up our liberty either for life or death unless through the pope's sentence. But that will never happen, for in truth the pope would never pass a sentence against himself, the Roman church, and the many privileges of the Roman pontiffs. We are certainly prepared to shoulder the whole burden of a lawsuit, to go to the Roman curia and to make a stand there for liberty, not to roam about abroad as you say, but to die there if perchance our time has come; and may God's will be done as it is in heaven.'[5] Such were the words that we brethren of sounder judgement spoke tearfully.[6]

---

[4] The petitory action was the action concerning the right of ownership, while the possessory action concerned the actual possession at the time.   [5] Luke 11: 2.

[6] On the brethren of sounder judgement or wiser counsel, see *RSB* cap. 64. *RSB* cap. 3

204. Abbas uero, constantiam nostram uidens, considerabat omnia uerba hec, conferens in corde suo.[1] Et communicato consilio missi sumus tres monachi in crastino[2] ad episcopum, qui libertatem et ius ecclesie nostre protestaremur et quod nequaquam eum causa uisitationis admitteremus, et pro iure ecclesie et contra omnia grauamina que propter hoc nobis contingere possent appellaremus. Quod et factum est.[a] Episcopus uero se nichilominus uenturum et secundum indulgentiam domini pape, appellatione remota, iure diocesano, corrigenda tam in capite quam in menbris se correcturum asserebat.[3]

205. *De dolo abbatis ut accepta securitate status sui episcopum admitteret et nos ei dolo traderet*

Quod cum abbati retulissemus, ad callida argumenta et assueta presidia se conuertit. Et per quosdam familiares suos sollicitauit episcopum si quo modo posset ad hoc inducere eum, ut accepta securitate status sui, uidelicet quod in personam suam non animaduerteret, eum admitteret. Hoc enim prius fecerat cuidam episcopo Wigornensi, Iohanni uidelicet de Constantiis, quem ad capitulum admisit et statuta eius et decreta scripta et lecta, reclamantibus fratribus, ibidem custodienda suscepit. Set dedit ei sexaginta marcas et renunciauit usui mitre, tunice, dalmatice et sandaliorum omnibus diebus uite illius episcopi ne in personam suam animaduerteret. Set iste episcopus nichil simoniace facere uoluit, set tamen distulit diem aduentus sui in alium diem.[4]

206. *De fuga abbatis et repulsione episcopi*

Veniente igitur die abbas summo mane recessit Bradeuuellam.[5] Et relictis ouibus mercennarius fugit quia non pertinebat ad eum de

---

[a] *marg.* nota appellacionem contra episcopum. (?s. *xiv*[2])

---

requires the abbot to consider the important business of the house in council and exhorts the abbot to listen to advice. However, it leaves no doubt that the abbot is the final arbiter. Those of sounder judgement neither implied necessarily a majority nor the older monks. See below, **293, 402, 502,** for further references.

[1] Cf. Luke 2: 19.

[2] 17 Aug.

[3] See above, **196** at n. 7.

[4] Bishop John of Coutances, Mauger's predecessor, was elected probably in Jan. 1196, consecrated on 20 Oct. and died on 24 Sept. 1198. The visitation would not have taken place until after consecration. The account suggests that no formal visitation did, indeed, take place, so probably no statutes or decrees were ever issued. At any rate no trace of them has survived. The use of the mitre, tunic, dalmatic, and sandals, in addition to the gloves and the ring, had been granted to Abbot Adam by Pope Clement III on 10 July 1189

204. The abbot, seeing our determination, thought over all that we had said and pondered it in his heart.[1] After there had been a discussion, three of us monks were sent the following day[2] to the bishop to affirm the liberty and rights of our church, to say that we had no intention whatsoever of admitting him for a visitation, and that we should be making an appeal regarding the rights of the church in spite of all the trouble which might afflict us because of this. And that was what happened. The bishop declared that he would still come and, in accordance with the pope's empowerment, forbidding an appeal, would by diocesan right correct everything that needed correcting both in the head and in the limbs.[3]

205. *The abbot's deceitful plan to admit the bishop provided his own status was maintained, and to sacrifice us to that plan*

When we reported this to the abbot, he resorted to cunning arguments and to ensuring that he had his customary protection. Using some members of his household he made an approach to the bishop saying that, provided he could persuade the bishop to maintain his status and not proceed against him personally, he would admit him. He had in fact proposed this before to a bishop of Worcester, namely John of Coutances, whom he admitted into the chapter-house and, despite the objections of the brethren, agreed to observe both his statutes and decrees written down and read out. In fact he gave the bishop sixty marks and renounced the use of the mitre, the tunic, dalmatic, and sandals for the rest of that bishop's lifetime so that the bishop should not proceed against him personally. But that bishop had refused to commit simony and postponed his visit to another time.[4]

206. *The flight of the abbot, and the rebuff of the bishop*

Early the next morning the abbot withdrew to Broadwell.[5] The hireling abandoned the sheep and fled because he neither cared for

---

(below, 337–8; JL 16426): they were confirmed to Abbot Norreis by the same pope on 25 Jan. 1191 (H fo. 98ʳ; V fo. 79ʳ, printed *PUE* i, no. 269; JL 16664; not in R) and then reissued to Roger Norreis by Pope Celestine III on 13 Jan. 1192 (339–41). Simony was the sin of Simon Magus (Acts 8: 18–20), trying to obtain spiritual powers for money, widely condemned by this time, of which the bishop might well have been accused had he proceeded with the visitation.

[5] On 18 Aug. There was a manor house of the abbot at Broadwell, near Stow-on-the-Wold (Glos.). VCH *Glos.*, vi (1965), 51, says that Norreis built a house there about 1200, from this evidence.

ouibus, quia non est ingressus per ostium in ouile ouium,[1] sicut prius dictum est. Nos uero ut acefali magis de recessu abbatis quam de aduentu episcopi consternati. Timentes eum 'inuenisse gratiam in oculis' episcopi,[2] uidentes etiam quod pro anima nobis res erat, accinximus | nos, et inuocantes adiutorium Dei uiriliter stetimus ex aduerso.[3] Et summo mane, anticipantes horam canonicam,[4] celebrauimus capitulum nostrum multis ex causis, scilicet ut cum episcopo iterum non ingrederemur pretorium, et ut longo tractatu quid facto opus esset deliberaremus.

fo. 149vb

207. Veniente itaque episcopo,[5] de communi consilio obserata sunt hostia tam celle hospitum quam stabuli et coquine, et omnia suppellectilia episcopi et equi et falere equorum posita sunt sub diuo, quia 'non erat eius locus in diuersorio'.[6] Porte uero et hostia ecclesie, qua omnes Cristiani ingrediuntur, aperta erant. Et ingrediens episcopus per claustrum recepit se in ecclesiam. Et facta oratione, cum sedisset iuxta maius altare, uocati sunt abbas et conuentus noster uoce preconia. Et aliis sedentibus in claustro, comparuimus coram eo duodecim ad hoc electi ut iudicem responsis aggrederemur. Et episcopus, demisso uultu et simpliciter ut erat uir sanctus, dixit: 'Deo teste, compassus^a miserie uestre et desolationi huius ecclesie, ueni huc propter uos ut statum uestrum et ecclesie uestre in melius reformem. Igitur conuenite omnes in capitulo, et audite mandatum domini pape, et obedite michi ut episcopo uestro sicut faciunt ceteri monachi uicini uestri, et bene erit uobis.'[7]

208. Et ego, in cuius ore posuerunt uerba sua quia iurisperitus eram, licet minor essem omnibus fratribus meis,[8] sic respondi: 'Domine episcope, de bona uoluntate uestra gratias agimus uobis, et bonum zelum uestrum retribuat uobis dominus.[9] Verum quia ea que dicitis sine perpetua subuersione libertatis ecclesie nostre et detrimento honoris nostri et periculo animarum nostrarum, immo perpetua dampnatione earum, facere non possumus: eligimus magis

---

^a sum *erased*

[1] John 10: 1 and 13.
[2] Cf. Gen. 18: 3.
[3] Cf. Eph. 6: 11.
[4] This probably means that the chapter was held before Prime.
[5] The chronology is not clear here as to when exactly the bishop came. Abbot Roger had retired to Broadwell on Sunday 18 Aug. and the bishop excommunicated the monks on the following Friday, 23 Aug.
[6] Luke 2: 7.

the sheep nor 'entered through the door into the sheepfold',[1] as has been said before. So, being headless, we were more perturbed by the abbot's departure than by the arrival of the bishop. Since we feared that he had found favour in the bishop's sight[2] and saw also that the matter concerned our souls, we prepared for action, called upon the help of God and took up a firm 'stand against him'.[3] At dawn, before the canonical hour,[4] we celebrated our chapter for several reasons, but especially that we might not enter into the chapter-house with the bishop again, and also to engage in a long discussion as to what needed to be done.

207. Accordingly, when the bishop came[5] the doors were by common consent locked, not only the doors of the guest chambers but also of the stables and kitchen; then all the bishop's belongings, horses, and harnesses were put out in the open because there was 'no place for him in the inn'.[6] The gates and entrances of the church where all Christians enter were open. So the bishop entered and made his way through the cloister into the church. After he had delivered a speech and had sat down by the high altar the abbot and our community were publicly summoned. While other monks sat in the cloister twelve of us, selected for this purpose, appeared before him to put our case to our judge. The bishop with downcast looks spoke to us in plain language, being the holy man he was: 'As God is my witness, it is out of compassion for your suffering and because of the desolation of this church that I have come here on your account, so that I may re-establish for the better your status and that of your church. Assemble then all of you in the chapter-house, hear the mandate of the pope, and obey me as your bishop as other neighbouring monks do, and it shall be well with you.'[7]

208. I was given the task of speaking on the others' behalf because I had legal knowledge, though I was the least of all my brethren.[8] This was my reply: 'Lord bishop, we thank you for your good will, and may the Lord reward you for your great zeal.[9] However, we cannot comply with your wishes without for ever surrendering our church's liberty, without losing our honour or endangering our souls, indeed, without damning them eternally: we prefer instead to suffer earthly

---

[7] Cf. Deut. 5: 33 'et bene sit uobis'.

[8] Matt. 25: 40. This is a common form of expressing humility, but here it may also be a reference to the date of Thomas's entry into the community (1199–1200) and late profession, i.e. he was the most recently professed of the monks, having studied at Paris and taught at Oxford; see Introduction.

[9] Cf. *RSB* cap. 72.

temporaliter hic flagellari et temporalium sustinere defectum donec
a domino papa per legatum suum uisitemur,[1] quam a non | nostro
pastore correctionem momentaneam accipientes, ecclesiam nostram
que libera est ancillando, in perpetuam, a qua resurgere non
possimus, retrudere seruitutem.'

209. Et intrante conuentu ad horam terciam, dixi episcopo, 'Surge
uelociter[2] et recede hinc cito; et exi a nobis. Ecce enim conuentus
adest ad opus Dei.' Et episcopus, 'Num mine?' Et ego,'Vtique; stulte
enim uenistis.' Et episcopus exiens ab ecclesia secessit in capitulum
cum abbatibus, prioribus, et multis clericis; et iterum et secundo et
tertio preconia uoce uocati sumus. Et qualibet uice nos duodecim
coram eo comparuimus probris et conuiciis inuicem affecti et nos
afficiendo, et comminantes episcopo ut recederet, semper predicta
repetendo et apellationem innouando.

210. *Qualiter episcopus excommunicauerit conuentum excepto abbate*
Tandem circa horam diei nonam cum ingredi deberemus ad sumen-
dum cibum, erat enim uigilia sancti Bartholomei,[3] per priorem de
Gloucestria et quosdam alios nuntiauit nobis quod nos et ecclesiam
nostram a diuinorum celebratione propter contumaciam suspendit,[4]
excepto abbate. Et sic nec petita nec data benedictione a nobis
recessit.[a]

211. Nos uero appellationi nostre innitentes solempnius quam prius,
si fieri potuit, diuina celebrauimus. Et statim post cibum duos
monacos suos, qui hic propter combustionem ecclesie Wigornensis
morabantur,[5] mandantes quod illos tantum ut sibi subiectos suspen-
derat et ideo eos a nobis emisimus illi transmisimus.

212. In crastino uero misit hic abbatem de Alincestre[6] et quosdam
clericos, quibus cum nusquam ad nos pateret ingressus, sicut
precauimus, scientes ea que futura erant, illi accensis candelis et
fixis in porta cymiterii. Sollempniter auctoritate episcopi nos

---

^a *marg.* episcopus cum rubore recessit (*s. xiv*²)

[1] The claim that only a pope or his legate could visit was made by exempt houses. Pope
Alexander III granted this exemption to Bury St Edmunds in 1175, and in 1196 Pope
Celestine III warned Archbishop Hubert Walter to keep away from exempt houses; see
PUE iii. nos. 217 and 477. Evesham had not as yet acquired any such right.

[2] Acts 12: 7.

[3] 23 Aug.

[4] Contumacy was the refusal to appear before an ecclesiastical tribunal or gathering to
give answer, the citation or summons having been made three times, as stated above.

scourging and endure earthly loss until we receive a visit from the pope through his legate,[1] rather than to accept temporary correction from one who is not our shepherd and, by handing over our church, which is free of servitude, force upon it perpetual enslavement from which we could not recover.'

209. When the community came in [to the church] at nine o'clock in the morning I said to the bishop, 'Rise quickly[2] and leave this place at once; depart from us! See, the community is here to undertake the work of God.' The bishop replied, 'Surely these are not threats?' I said, 'They are indeed, for you came on a foolish errand.' So the bishop left the church and retired to the chapter-house with abbots, priors, and many clerks; a second and a third time we were publicly summoned. Whenever we twelve appeared before him we were each time assailed by reproaches and noisy abuse, but we retaliated and demanded that the bishop should withdraw, constantly repeating what we had said before and renewing our appeal.

210. *The bishop excommunicates the convent except for the abbot*
Eventually about three o'clock in the afternoon, when we should have been going in to eat, for it was the vigil of St Bartholomew,[3] he informed us through the prior of Gloucester and some others that because of our contumacy[4] he was suspending us and our monastery, except for the abbot, from the celebration of divine service. He left us without a blessing being asked for or given.

211. Setting our sights now upon our appeal we celebrated divine service with greater solemnity, if such were possible, than before. Straightway after our meal we sent back to the bishop two of his monks, who were staying with us because of a fire in the church of Worcester,[5] telling them that the bishop had suspended only those that were subject to him and that we were therefore sending them away from us.

212. The next day he sent here the abbot of Alcester[6] and some clerks, but as there was no entry for them anywhere by which they could reach us—for we had kept a careful watch in anticipation of what might happen—they lit candles and fastened them on to the gate of the cemetery. Then on the authority of the bishop they solemnly

---

[5] The fire at Worcester had occurred on 17 Apr. 1202 and was very devastating; see 'Annales Prioratus de Wigornia', *Ann. Mon.* iv, ed. H. R. Luard (1869), p. 391.
[6] 24 Aug. It is impossible to identify the abbot of this Benedictine house in Warwickshire; see *HRH*, p. 26.

excommunicauerunt, excepto abbate.*ᵃ* Et hec non fuit in nostro pectore cura minor quod abbas noster a nobis semper separabatur, set maxima causa timoris ne cum episcopo collusisset, nec stetit per abbatem quin ita fieret. Nos uero nichilominus semper diuina sollempniter celebra | uimus.

fo. 150ʳᵇ

213. *Qualiter abbas noluit communicare magistro Thome de Merlebergia monacho propter sentenciam episcopi*
Eadem die missus sum a conuentu ut nuntiarem hec domino abbati, quamuis a suis omnia ei prius nuntiarentur et, quicquid abbas diceret, iniunctum est michi ut ad dominum Cantuariensem procederem et sententie episcopi peterem infirmationem.

214. Qui cum uenissem Bradeuuelle ad abbatem, stans deforis et querens loqui ei, responsum est michi ex parte abbatis quod recederem et quod abbas non loqueretur michi quia excomunicatus eram. Ego uero recessi apud Suellam, manerium de camera,¹ et pernoctaui ibi, cogitans quia nox haberet consilium.² Et putans quod abbas ebrius esset, sicut cotidie esse consueuit et sepe bis una die, uel quod tunc haberet ibi aliquam de concubinis suis, propter quas sepe nos consueuerat excludere a thalamis suis, quamuis concubinas suas nobis uidentibus in thalamis suis passim consueuerit habere. Summo itaque mane ueni iterum Bradeuuellam,³ et non patebat michi ingressus, nec in melius mutatum est consilium. Set idem responsum recepi quod prius; nondum enim spem amiserat quin episcopum adhuc aliquo modo corrumperet et nos ei dolo traderet. Set episcopus filius ueritatis iniquitati eius non consensit.⁴

215. *Qualiter archiepiscopus Hubertus ad monachos contra episcopum sit conuersus, et de potestate archiepiscopi in ecclesia Euesha⟨m⟩ensi*
Et ego recessi, et tercia die⁵ occurri domino Cantuariensi in itinere per tria miliaria ultra Londonias.⁶ Et eo cum fletu et eiulatu magno ex parte fratrum salutato, tamen satis rhetorice ex ordine narraui ei omnia que facta erant, et instanter petii sentencie episcopi relaxationem,

---

ᵃ marg. nota qualiter conuentus est excommunicatus (*s. xiv²*)

¹ Swell, about two miles from Broadwell, belonged to the chamberlain, the obedientiary in charge of providing the monks' clothing.
² This would appear to be a classical quotation, but we have been unable to trace the author. It is included in a series of Latin proverbs in Bodleian Library, MS Bodley Auct. F. 16, p. 54a l. 23, a 15th-cent. MS from Worcester priory.
³ 25 Aug.

excommunicated us, except for the abbot. We felt deeply concerned that the abbot was always separated from us, but it was a particular cause for anxiety that he might have conspired with the bishop, and it was no fault of the abbot that this did not happen! We nevertheless continued to celebrate divine service with full solemnity.

213. *The abbot refuses to associate with the monk, Master Thomas of Marlborough, because of the bishop's sentence*
The same day [24 Aug.] I was sent by the community to inform the abbot [at Broadwell] of these matters, though he received prior information of everything from his own men, and I was commanded, no matter what the abbot might say, to proceed to the archbishop of Canterbury to seek annulment of the bishop's sentence.

214. When I came to the abbot at Broadwell, I stood outside [the manor house] and asked to speak to him. The reply I received on behalf of the abbot was that I should return home as the abbot would not speak to me because I had been excommunicated. I left for Swell, a manor belonging to the chamber,[1] and I spent the night there, thinking that the night has its counsel.[2] I thought that the abbot might have been drunk, as he usually was every day, often twice a day, or that on this occasion he had one of his concubines there, for he had often kept us out of his apartments because of them, despite the fact that he used to have his concubines wherever he had bed-chambers and that we saw what was going on. So very early next morning I went again to Broadwell,[3] but I was not let in and there was no change for the better in the abbot's intentions. Indeed, I received the same reply as before, for he had not lost the hope yet of corrupting the bishop in some way and of delivering us up treacherously to him. But the bishop, a child of truth, did not consent to his wickedness.[4]

215. *Archbishop Hubert is won over to the side of the monks against the bishop: the archbishop's powers over the monastery of Evesham*
So I left, and three days later[5] I met with the archbishop of Canterbury on my journey, three miles from London.[6] I greeted him on behalf of the brethren with bitter tears and groans, but then I told him in very persuasive terms in detail all that had happened and immediately requested release from the bishop's sentence, adding in

---

[4] Cf. 1 Cor. 13: 6.   [5] ?27/28 Aug.
[6] Broadwell, just outside Stow, to London, is a distance of about 80 miles.

aditiens in fine, 'Pater sancte, res uestra magis agitur[1] quam nostra et causa uestra est pro qua stamus. In priuilegiis enim nostris continetur, quod cura animarum ecclesie nostre a domino papa uobis commissa est et si quid sinistre partis inibi compertum fuerit oriri, potius auribus uestris deferatur quam per alicuius occultam sententiam locus sanctus deprauetur iniuste. Et uos anno preterito, si ad memoriam reducitis, hoc priuilegio et iure nostro usi estis, et, episcopo presente et non |

fo. 150[va] contradicente, que erant corrigenda in domo nostra.[2] Et nobis omnibus presentibus etiam scriptis nostris tam in capite quam in membris correxistis, et sic in possessione iuris uestri et nostri constituti estis. Ergo, domine, defendite partes uestras et oues uestras.'

216. Et archiepiscopus, 'Bene meminimus omnium horum, et nolumus quod omnibus palam dicatis set dissimuletis, quia per beatum Iulianum[3] nec ius nostrum nec possessionem quamdiu uixerimus, Deo dante, amittemus'.[a] Igitur tam in diuinis offitiis quam in mensa iunxit me lateri suo per tres dies,[4] 'et cum accepissem cibum cum eo confortatus sum'.[5]

217. Tercia uero die[6] obuiauit nobis apud Haueringedune[7] magister Iohannes de Cerneia,[8] clericus episcopi Wigornensis, uir in iure canonico ualde profundi pectoris.[b] Et narrauit domino Cantuariensi modo suo ea que facta fuerant, petens confirmationem sententie episcopi instanter, et ego in multis contradicens ei petii constantissime infirmationem eiusdem.[c] Et archiepiscopus, 'Magister Iohannes, quedam ita sunt ut dicitis, quedam non. Set bene scimus quod episcopus uester non de consilio uestro ut credimus, set potius

---

[a] *marg.* nota constanciam archiepiscopi pro priuilegiis (*?s. xiv²*)   [b] *marg.* altercacio episcopi Wig' contra nos (*?s. xiv²*)   [c] *marg.* ?Responsio

---

[1] Cf. Horace, *Ars Poetica*, 179.

[2] This was perhaps in Feb. or March 1201, when Hubert was in the vicinity at Worcester; *EEA 3: Canterbury, 1193–1205*, p. 313.

[3] This oath of Hubert Walter's, reported again later, **231**, perhaps proceeds from the popularity of St Julian of Le Mans under King Henry II, for the king was born in Le Mans and baptized in the church of St Julian, where the saint's relics were venerated. It is said that at his baptism Henry was placed under the protection of St Julian, the Empress offered a pall in gratitude, and his grandfather gave an annual rent in England; see M. Chibnall, *The Empress Matilda* (Oxford, 1991, Cambridge, Mass., 1992), pp. 60–1. St Julian was reputedly the first bishop of Le Mans and the apostle of the neighbourhood, with many churches dedicated to him there, and a few in England. Hubert Walter had early connections with the royal court of Henry II through his uncle Ranulph Glanville, the justiciar; see C. R. Cheney, *Hubert Walter* (London, 1967), pp. 17–19. Perhaps the king himself used the oath.

[4] To ?30/31 Aug. Hubert Walter was on his way to Worcester, this time in connection with the canonization of Wulfstan. Worcester is some 75 miles from West Wycombe (see

conclusion, 'Holy father, this case concerns your interests[1] even more than ours, and it is your cause for which we stand. For contained in our privileges is the fact that the care for the souls of our church has been entrusted by the pope to you, and that if anything of an evil nature is found to have occurred there it should be brought to your notice to prevent that holy place being unjustly slandered by anyone's secret sentence. Last year, if you recall, you had recourse to this privilege and our rights, and in the presence of the bishop, who did not contradict you, you completely amended what needed amending in our house.[2] You corrected both the head and the limbs, in the presence of us all, even putting it in writing, and by doing this you were established as the possessor of what was your right and ours. Therefore, my lord, protect your own interests and your sheep.'

216. The archbishop replied, 'We well remember all these things, but we do not wish you to make this common knowledge but to keep it to yourselves for, by the blessed Julian,[3] we shall not relinquish either our right or possession as long as we live, God allowing it.' He then took me for three days[4] as his companion not only during divine office but also at his table, 'and when I had dined with him I was reassured'.[5]

217. On the third day[6] we were met at 'Haveringedune' [in West Wycombe][7] by a clerk of the bishop of Worcester, Master John de Cerneia,[8] who had a profound understanding of canon law. He informed the archbishop of Canterbury in his own manner of the things which had occurred, and asked earnestly for confirmation of the bishop's sentence, but I opposed him on many points and resolutely attacked the weakness of his arguments. The archbishop replied, 'Master John, some points are as you say, some are not. But we are well aware that your bishop has, in our opinion, been hasty in passing such a sentence against such an important convent, and done

below, n. 7), but he arrived in Worcester on 1 Sept.; see *Ann. Mon.* iv. 391, and *EEA 3: Canterbury*, p. 314 (for Hubert's itinerary).

[5] Acts 9: 19.

[6] ?30/31 Aug.

[7] West Wycombe (Bucks.) was on the usual route between Oxford and London for travellers from Worcester and Evesham; see *William of Malmesbury's Saints' Lives*, ed. R. Thomson and M. Winterbottom (OMT, 2002), pp. 76–7 and n. 3.

[8] Master John de Cerneia was probably an Oxford master, as he occurs *c.*1184–1200 witnessing charters in the Oxford area (mainly included in the Oseney Cart.). *BRUO*, p. 378. See also *Charters and Documents . . . of Salisbury*, selected by W. Rich Jones and ed. W. D. Macray (RS xcvii, 1891), p. 50, where he witnesses a Salisbury charter of 1191 in company with Azo, archdeacon of Salisbury. He may be the Master J., rector of Cerney (Glos.), who occurs in the Cirencester formulary; see Sayers, *PJD*, p. 50.

magistri Willelmi de Verdun[1] talem precipitauit sententiam, non deferens appellationi, in tantum conuentum, nobis inconsultis.' Et reuera de consilio Willelmi fuit, sicut prius archiepiscopo suggesseram. 'Ite', inquit archiepiscopus, 'et quinta die post hanc compareatis coram nobis apud Wigorniam,[2] et ibi quod iustum fuerit statuemus.' Et accepta benedictione recessimus. Et cum uenissem domum nuntiaui fratribus que facta fuerant, qui, 'gauisi gaudio magno',[3] cantabant et flebant.

218. *De arreptione itineris abbatis ad curiam Romanam et reuocatione eiusdem, et pace reformata inter eum et conuentum*

Abbas uero noster secesserat apud Baddebi,[4] et preparauit se ad iter ut Romam iret, iam enim plene spem amiserat de corrumpendo episcopo. Veniente igitur die comparuimus coram archiepiscopo, episcopo cum aduocatis suis et multis allegationibus petente[a] sententie sue confirmationem, et similiter nobis petentibus e contrario infirmationem. Et non profecimus, set | datus est nobis alius dies apud Lincolniam.[5]

fo. 150[vb]

219. Veniens autem domum, ex precepto fratrum secutus sum abbatem nostrum ut eum ab errore uie sue reuocarem.[6] Iam enim iter arripuerat et habitum mutauerat, ut quibusdam fratribus nuntiauerat, non enim conuentui hec mandauerat. Ego uero procedens inueni eum apud Neweburi uersus mare in habitu seculari.[7] Et narrans ei que facta fuerant et qualiter dominus archiepiscopus Cantuariensis communicauit nobis, consolans etiam eum per uerba archiepiscopi que dixerat michi, et qualiter spem concepimus de infirmanda sententia episcopi, promisi etiam ei in uerbo Domini quod si episcopus obtineret contra nos in possessorio iudicio,[8] quod maxime timebamus, qui 'timor postea euenit nobis',[9] quod nos

---

[a] petende R

---

[1] Clerk of Bishop John of Coutances and archdeacon of Gloucester from 1200 to 1210, when he died (obit 7 May); see *Ann. Mon.* iv. 390 and *The Cartulary of Worcester Priory*, ed. R. R. Darlington (PRS lxxvi, n.s. xxxviii (1968)), p. lxvi; as witness, nos. 175, 370 (pp. 95, 195); and as papal judge delegate in 1200×1203 in a case between the priory of Worcester and Richard of Peopleton over tithes in Harvington, no. 384 (p. 201). He does not appear in *BRUO* and was probably not an Oxford master. He was also a canon of Rouen and probably a relative of the baron Bertram de Verdun; Greenway, *Fasti*, ii. 108. See also below, 257 at n. 3.

[2] On ?4/5 Sept.

[3] Matt. 2: 10.

it not on your advice, we believe, but rather on that of Master William de Verdun;[1] he has disregarded the appeal and failed to consult us.' It was indeed on the advice of William [de Verdun] as I had previously intimated to the archbishop. 'Go now,' said the archbishop, 'and appear before us in five days' time at Worcester,[2] and there we shall decide what is right.' After receiving his blessing we left. On arriving home I told the brethren what had occurred and they, 'rejoicing with great joy',[3] sang and wept.

218. *The abbot undertakes a journey to the Roman curia; he is recalled and peace is restored between him and the convent*

Our abbot had retired to Badby[4] and prepared himself for a journey to Rome, for he had completely lost hope of corrupting the bishop. On the appointed day we appeared before the archbishop, as did the bishop with his advocates pleading confirmation of his sentence with many arguments, while we for our part were pleading its annulment. We did not complete the proceedings, so another date was given to us at Lincoln.[5]

219. I arrived home, but on instructions from the brethren I went off to find our abbot to recall him from the error of his ways.[6] He had already begun his journey and had taken off his habit, as he informed some brethren, though he had not sent word of this to the convent. On the journey I found him at Newbury on his way to the coast clothed in secular dress.[7] I informed him of events and of the manner in which the archbishop of Canterbury received us. Cheering him by repeating the words the archbishop had spoken to me, and telling him how we entertained the hope that the bishop's sentence would be annulled, I also promised him in the name of the Lord that, if the bishop was successful against us in the possessory judgment,[8] which we very much feared ('a fearful thing that later came about'),[9] we

---

[4] Badby (Northants.) belonged to Evesham, and the abbot had a house there, see above, 190.

[5] Cheney in *EEA 3: Canterbury, 1193–1205*, p. 314, puts this as early Oct., but it could just as well be late Sept.: all we know for certain is that it was before 19 Oct.

[6] Jas. 5: 20.

[7] Newbury (Berks.). He was presumably on his way to Southampton. While abbots may have been allowed more freedom in their dress than monks, and while monks, too, appear to have been permitted warmer and more practical clothing when travelling, Thomas seems to have regarded Norreis's attire as constituting, in intention at least, a definite breach of the Rule (*RSB*, cap. 55), though there does not appear to have been legislation on the matter at this date.

[8] A temporary order for possession, while the case was heard prior to a final judgment.

[9] Cf. Job 3: 25.

nunquam coram episcopo aliquid quod faceret ad eius depositionem ei obiceremus, set fideliter cum eo contra episcopum pro statu persone sue staremus, si reuerteretur et staret nobiscum in causa ecclesie.

220. Quam promissionem meam fratres mei, cum postea Rome essem, tempore restitutionis episcopi uiriliter compleuerunt, stantes cum eo usque ad habitus sui deiectionem, cum episcopus circa personam suam uellet facere inquisitionem. Et fratres ei nichil dicere uellent, episcopo sub pena excommunicationis precipiente. Ille uero tali accepta securitate reuersus est Eueshamiam, et facti sunt amici eadem die abbas et conuentus, quia 'antea erant inimici ad inuicem'.[1]

221. *De auxilio conuentus ad litis expensas*
Tunc etiam prouisum est quod omnia ea que prius nobis inuitis abstulerat,[2] uidelicet redditus pitantiarie[3] qui pertinebant ad potum, saluis paucis nobis caritatibus[4] uini, et fabrice ecclesie, et duo pulmenta, scilicet frumenti et fabe,[5] et uuastelli,[6] et caritates de cellario exceptis quibusdam certis diebus, et coopertoria, cederent in usus suos, ad sustentationem litis quamdiu lis duraret. Et quamuis prius hospitalitas apud nos deperiisset et, resecante abbate tam fo. 151ra hospitibus quam seruientibus abbatie pro | uoluntate sua liberationes, multi fame periissent, tamen modo concessimus quod hec omnia cederent in usus abbatis ad litem, et nos nunquam super hiis quamdiu de uoluntate nostra subtraherentur eum accusaremus. Nos uero, sicut prius nolentes ita modo uolentes, per multos annos postea nudis et puris oleribus pro pulmento usi sumus, et elemosinarius pascebat seruientes nostros; et facta est tranquillitas[7] in mari nostro.

222. *Qualiter archiepiscopus nos pro non excommunicatis habuerit, sentenciam episcopi nec confirmando nec infirmando*
Igitur pace inter nos sic reformata, abbas noster, quasi tiro ut erat magnanimus, uiriliter preparauit se ad litem aput Lyncolniam^a ubi

---

^a Lyncolnuiam *the* yn *written over* (s. xv)

[1] Luke 23: 12.
[2] See above, 189–90, 191–2, 193.
[3] The pittancer was the monastic official who distributed 'pittances'. Pittances were small dishes of food, usually fish, eggs, or delicacies of some kind, in addition to the normal diet, given on special days, and for particular reasons: they were thus the first target if economies had to be made. See *M.O.*, pp. 463–4; *JB*, p. 126 n. 7, and cf. p. 97.

would never accuse him before the bishop of anything that he had done which would cause him to be deposed, but would stand by him loyally against the bishop in order to maintain the status of his person, provided that he returned and stood by us in the cause of the church. **220.** My brethren manfully fulfilled my promise when I was later in Rome during the time of the bishop's restitution. They stood by him even over his abandonment of his habit, when the bishop wanted to hold an inquiry into his character and behaviour. The brethren refused to say anything, despite the bishop's command to do so under pain of excommunication. On receiving such an assurance he returned to Evesham, and that same day the abbot and the convent, 'previously mutual enemies, became friends'.[1]

221. *The help given by the convent towards the expenses of the lawsuit*
Then agreement was reached that all those things which the abbot had previously taken away from us against our will[2] should be given up for the abbot's use in sustaining the lawsuit as long as it lasted; these were the revenues of the pittancery[3] for drink (except for a few *caritates*[4] of wine being granted to us), for the church fabric, for the two dishes, namely of cereal and beans,[5] for wastel-bread,[6] for the *caritates* from the cellary (except on certain agreed days), and for outer garments. Even though hospitality had previously perished amongst us and, during the time that the abbot was dividing up the allowances as he wished—both amongst the guests and amongst the servants of the abbey—many had perished through hunger, yet we now agreed that all these things should be surrendered to the abbot to use for the lawsuit, and we never made any accusations against him over these sacrifices as long as they were made with our consent. Just as we had previously refused, so we now agreed, and for many years after this we used only plain and simple vegetables in place of pulses, and the almoner fed our servants; and tranquillity reigned[7] in our sea.

222. *The archbishop treats us as though we have not been excommunicated though he does not confirm or annul the bishop's sentence*
So, when peace had in this way been re-established between us, our abbot, like a confident young blood, prepared himself manfully for the

---

[4] Also extra allowances, especially of drink, made on feast days and on the commemoration of benefactors.   [5] See below, **405**.
[6] Bread made with the finest flour; see below, **425**.
[7] Cf. Matt. 8: 26; Mark 4: 39; and Luke 8: 24.

honorifice ab archiepiscopo susceptus est et confortatus. Et ibi pondus litus uersum est super me, in tantum quod propter elegantes allegationes meas abbas meus, ut ipse sepe fatebatur, in specialem dilectionem recepit me; ipse enim iam audierat ex ore meo.[1] Set aliud erat in ore suo, aliud in corde. Hec et alia de me ipso,[a] Deo teste, ideo uobis dico ut memoriam mei in orationibus uestris habeatis qui de hac libertate gauisuri estis, quia plus omnibus pro ea laboraui.

223. Set nec tunc apud Lincolniam ad plenum profecimus, licet ibi certitudinem de non confirmanda sententia episcopi receperimus et de adiutorio archiepiscopi. Set datus est nobis alius dies apud Londonias in crastino sancti Luce euangeliste.[2] Et illuc processimus copiose muniti aduocatis, episcopus uero constipatus non solum aduocatis set etiam fere omnibus episcopis huius prouincie, et precipue astantibus ei Eliensi, tante auctoritatis uiro,[3] et Here-fordensi.[4]

224. Tandem post multas et uarias allegationes utrimque propositas, archiepiscopus taliter exorsus est: 'Sententiam episcopi licet post appellationem latam[5] nec confirmabimus nec infirmabimus, ideo precipue quia causa pro qua lata est commissa est iudicibus delegatis a domino papa. Et tu, domine abbas, sequere litteras tuas et iudices tuos.'

225. Et recessimus gaudentes, et prosecuti sumus causam nostram coram iudicibus nostris. Iam pridem enim me procurante omnibus uiribus meis ut questio status | moueretur inter nos et episcopum et crebro me predicante quod in breui moueretur, perquisiuimus litteras domini pape, uidelicet quod episcopus contra priuilegia Romanorum pontificum nobis iniuriosus existeret.[6] Et per has litteras fecimus uocari episcopum in prima die litis nostre ante archiepiscopum apud Wigorniam.

fo. 151rb

---

[a] Nota (s. xiii)

[1] Luke 22: 71.
[2] 19 Oct.
[3] Eustace, bishop of Ely from 1198 to 1215, had been treasurer of York and dean of Salisbury before his promotion to the episcopacy; Greenway, *Fasti*, ii. 45. He was a much respected judge, who was noted for his interest in the canon law and for his attention to its implementation; see Sayers, *PJD*, pp. 125, 180, 242, and *SLI*, no. 22 for Innocent III's decretal letter 'Pastoralis' which was addressed to him.

case at Lincoln where he was honourably received and encouraged by the archbishop. There the heavy responsibility of the case devolved upon me to such an extent that, as a result of my eloquent arguments, the abbot conceived a special affection for me, as he often admitted; he had himself now heard the case from my own mouth.[1] But he used to say one thing and mean another. I am telling you of these things and others about myself, as God is my witness, so that you who will rejoice in this liberty may remember me in your prayers, for I laboured more than any to secure it.

223. However, we were not then wholly successful at Lincoln, though we received a definite assurance that the bishop's sentence would not be confirmed, and that the archbishop would support us. Another date was fixed for us at London on the morrow of the feast of St Luke the Evangelist.[2] We proceeded there fortified by an abundance of advocates, though the bishop was surrounded not only by advocates but also by nearly all the bishops of this province, especially by his supporters, the bishop of Ely, who was a man of great authority,[3] and the bishop of Hereford.[4]

224. At length, after both sides had made many various allegations, the archbishop began his reply: 'We shall neither confirm the bishop's sentence nor annul it, though given after appeal,[5] and this is particularly because the case which it concerns has been entrusted to judges delegated by the pope. You, my lord abbot, obey your letters and your judges.'

225. We left rejoicing, and proceeded with our case before our judges. For some time past I had been vigorously insisting that an inquiry into the status between the bishop and ourselves should be instituted and frequently predicted that this would soon happen, when we secured a letter from the pope stating that the bishop was acting unlawfully and contrary to the privileges granted to us by Roman pontiffs.[6] Using this letter we succeeded in having the bishop summoned on the first day of our case before the archbishop at Worcester.

---

[4] Giles de Braose, elected before 19 Sept., cons. 24 Sept. 1200, d. 17 Nov. 1215, was the son of one of King John's closest followers. His career prior to his election is completely unknown, but, as bishop of Hereford, he, too, was a frequent judge delegate; see *EEA 7: Hereford, 1079–1234*, ed. J. Barrow (1993), pp. xlv–vi.

[5] It was strictly illegal to proceed after appeal, though, as here, this was not always observed; see Sayers, *PJD*, p. 96.

[6] The letter has not survived.

226. *De primo itinere episcopi et nostro Romam pro hac causa*

Erant autem iudices nostri de Malbesburia,[1] Abbendonia[2] et de Eignesham[3] abbates. Coram quibus cum episcopus aliquotiens comparuisset, tandem ab eis ut sibi suspectis appellauit,[4] et in propria persona appellationem est prosecutus. Nos uero misimus contra eum quendam monachum Ermefredum nomine,[5] uirum discretum bene litteratum et optimum notarium, qui in curia Romana diem clausit extremum, et quendam cursorem, collateralem abbatis, qui litterarum nostrarum portitor fuit. Qui similiter postea rediens a curia labore consumptus obiit. Hic enim mos semper erat noster quod nos mittebamus unum quasi ex latere nostro, et abbas alium quasi ex latere suo, non enim unquam credebamus nos nobis ad inuicem. Iudicibus uero nostris non deferentibus appellationi, datis magnis indiciis et diffusis dilationibus episcopo, causam quasi lento pede prosecuti sumus, expectantes quidnam episcopus impetraret.

227. *De iterata depressione conuentus ab abbate et dilapidatione immobilium*

Abbas autem noster, quasi canis ad uomitum conuertens,[6] ut semper consueuerat deprimi in aduersis et eleuari in prosperis. Videns quia in longa tempora restitutio episcopi, si quando tamen futura erat, dilata fuit, confisus etiam de eo quod nos uix uel nunquam durante lite inter nos et episcopum contra eum actionem institueremus, quasi securus factus, non hiis que nos ei concesseramus ad litem sustinendam contentus, cepit in nos durius grassari quasi expectans ut adhuc Iordanis efflueret in os eius.*[7] Et sacristariam, thalamum et omnes obedientias nostras amplius et durius quam unquam prius sibi appropriauit, et nos fame, frigore et inedia durius quam prediximus

---

a marg. nota (*s. xiv²*, *probably referring to the next sentence, and below to the right of* nota) cameram (*s. xiii'*)

---

[1] The abbot at the time was Robert of Melun, a royal clerk and justice; *HRH*, p. 56. Malmesbury in Wiltshire was a Benedictine house that also claimed exemption from the diocesan; see D. Knowles, 'Essays in Monastic History. IV. The Growth of Exemption', *Downside Review*, l (1932), 201–31, and 396–436, at pp. 225–31.

[2] Hugh, abbot of Abingdon (Benedictine, Berks.), was a friend of Roger Norreis; see Cheney, *Innocent III*, p. 197 n. 73, citing Gerald of Wales, iv. 192.

[3] Benedictine, Oxon. Robert, abbot of Eynsham, was a former sub-prior of Christ Church, Canterbury (before 1193), and prior of Dover *c.*1194–7, *HRH*, pp. 49 and 88. He was known to Roger Norreis, being reappointed by the archbishop as sacrist of Christ Church in 1187 when Norreis was chosen as cellarer. Both appointments were unacceptable to the convent. Unlike Norreis, however, he had spoken out against the archbishop's treatment of the monastic chapter, and became, indeed, a proponent of the

226. *The first journey of the bishop and ourselves to Rome in connection with this case*

Our judges were the abbots of Malmesbury,[1] Abingdon,[2] and Eynsham.[3] After the bishop had appeared before them on several occasions, he eventually appealed from them [to Rome], as he doubted their impartiality,[4] and prosecuted his appeal in person. To oppose him we sent a monk called Ermefred,[5] a man of good sense, well-educated and a very good notary, who died at the Roman curia, and a courier, an associate of the abbot, who was the carrier of our documents. Later he likewise died returning from the curia, worn out by hard work. It was always our custom to send one of our men to represent us, and for the abbot to send one of his men to represent him, as we had a mutual distrust of each other. Our judges did not pay any regard to the appeal, but allowed lengthy adjournments and caused extended delays for the bishop, with the result that we prosecuted a case which proceeded at a snail's pace, while we waited to see what response the bishop would obtain.

227. *The abbot's oppression of the convent once again, and his squandering of its property*

Our abbot, however, who had always had a tendency to experience depression in adversity and elation in prosperity, now changed his attitude again, like a dog returning to his vomit.[6] Seeing that the restitution of the bishop's powers was likely to be delayed, if in fact it ever occurred, and confident that we would be very unlikely to bring an action against him if the lawsuit between us and the bishop went on for any length of time, he became virtually fearless, and began to prey upon us more harshly, not content with the concessions we had already made to him to help him sustain the suit, expecting Jordan to continue flowing, as it were, into his mouth.[7] He appropriated for himself a larger and more injurious share of the sacristy, of the chamber, and all our obedientiaries' offices than ever before, and inflicted upon us hunger, cold, and privation more grievously than we

---

convent against the archbishop; Greatrex, *Biog. Reg.*, pp. 265–6, citing Gervase, and *Ep. Cant.*, and *HRH*, pp. 49, 88.

[4] See L. Fowler, '*Recusatio iudicis* in civilian and canonist thought', in *Post Scripta: Essays in Medieval Law . . . in honor of Gaines Post*, ed. J. R. Strayer and D. E. Queller (Studia Gratiana, xv, 1972), pp. 717–85, esp. 777–8 and the references cited there.

[5] See below, **245**, **358**, **432**.

[6] Cf. Prov. 26: 11; 2 Peter 2: 22.

[7] Job 40: 18.

fo. 151va affecit. Nec hoc ei ad cumulum dampnationis sue suf | fecit, set quasi sciens que super eum uentura erant, antequam deponeretur, ut ipse sepe dicebat, quod talem redderet abbatiam quod nunquam aliquis post eum ea gauderet. Cepit possessiones ecclesie dilapidare,[a] consanguineos suos ditare, dans nepoti suo Rogero assarta de Ambresleia ad ualentiam centum solidorum annuorum et amplius; et colludendo cum aduersariis nostris, possessiones ecclesie pro pecunia in curia domini regis eis concedens:[1] ueluti Waltero le Poer[2] in eadem uilla de Ambresleia terram que fuit Hardingi, caducum ecclesie, ad congregandam sibi 'mammonam iniquitatis'.[3] Et aliis multas alias: scilicet sex uirgatas in Tatelestrop,[4] et duas in Neuham scilicet Iohanni et Hugoni,[5] et ut quasi tales, deposita uillicatione, reciperent eum in domos suas.

228. *De diligencia conuentus et tribulatione eorum circa reuocat⟨i⟩onem alienatorum*

Set nos non ferentes tantam iniquitatem, licet circumdedissent nos undique angustie, quoddam assartum quod dederat senescallo nostro ad tuitionem aliorum, quod ipse seminauerat, non ueriti sumus metere. Pro quo facto et regis iram contra nos excitauimus et indignationem archiepiscopi incurrimus. Quantum tunc abbas noster subleuatus et elatus fuerit supersedeo dicere quia non possem edicere.

229. Itaque missus sum ego et tunc ut animos regis et archiepiscopi quocumque modo mitigarem et nos in facto isto excusarem. Et ueniens ad curiam regis non potui loqui ei, set minas et opprobria ibi recepi. Veniens ad archiepiscopum prius ab eo conuicia et asperas increpationes sustinui.[b] Tandem post multas excusationes ita conclusi: 'Pater sancte, nostis quia periculosa est desperatio. Obseruatio ordinis periit apud nos quia nos fame et inedia perimus.[c] Possessiones ecclesie nostre dilapidantur, edificia nostra diruuntur. Nichil ergo

---

[a] *marg.* nota dilapidationes Rogeri (*s. xiv*^{2})   [b] *marg.* nota conuicia (*s. xiv*^{2})
[c] *marg.* Super (or Si?) i.c. secunda querela. Iterum ii. c. diterata?? {et omnibus rf. pro eodem questione {otia est (?) *or* onera est. (*This is in the same hand that guides for rubrics.*) *Underneath* Responsio (*?s. xiv*^{2})

---

[1] The most common way of conveying land by this time was by the fine, which was drawn up under the superintendence of the king's court and from 1195 preserved in its records, being drawn up in the form of a tripartite indenture, the third part, or foot, remaining with the royal court; see A. W. B. Simpson, *An Introduction to the History of the Land Law* (Oxford, 1961), pp. 115–17. The Curia Regis rolls record no suits concerning these grants at the time in question.

had expected. But he did not do this to add to the weight of his guilt, but as if he knowing what was to come to him, before he was deposed, as he himself had often said, to reduce the abbey to such a state that no one should ever after him have joy in it. He began to squander the possessions of the church and to enrich his own relatives: to his nephew Roger he gave assarts at Ombersley which had an annual value of 100 shillings or more; he colluded with our adversaries, granting them in the king's court[1] possessions of the church for money: to Walter le Poer[2] he granted land in the same vill of Ombersley, land which belonged to Harding, an escheat of the church, to gather for himself 'the mammon of unrighteousness'.[3] He also granted many other possessions to other people: six virgates of land in Adlestrop[4] and two in Newnham to John and Hugh,[5] so as to ensure that these people would receive him in their homes once he had laid down his stewardship.

228. *The efforts of the convent, and its ordeal over the recovery of alienated land*
Indignant at such ill-treatment, though difficulties hemmed us in on every side, we were not afraid to gather in the harvest on an assart which the abbot had given to our steward in return for overseeing other lands and in which he had himself sown the seed. Our action stirred the king's anger against us, and we incurred the displeasure of the archbishop. I refrain from mentioning how delighted and elated our abbot was as I could not adequately describe it.
229. I was therefore sent to allay the animosity of the king and archbishop in any way I could, and to offer explanations for what we had done. When I came to the king's court I was not able to speak to him, but received threats and insults there. On coming to the archbishop I at first sustained reproach and sharp rebuke. But eventually after lengthy explanation I concluded with these words, 'Holy father, you know that despair is dangerous. Maintenance of discipline has perished amongst us because we are perishing of hunger and privation. The possessions of our church are being squandered and our buildings destroyed. There is nothing left for

---

[2] See *Curia Regis Rolls of the Reigns of Richard I and John, 1207–9*, v (HMSO, 1931), p. 238. The le Poers held land from Evesham also at Newnham in Northants.
[3] Luke 16: 9.   [4] In Glos.
[5] Feet of Fines searched from 1182–99 in PRS, vols. xvii, xx, xxiii, and xxiv, reveal only a fine between the Abbot and Roger Huberti of 20 Jan. 1199 for land in Newnham, Northants. (PRS xxiv, no. 219).

superest, nisi ut nos a loco discedamus. Set quia turpe est monacho furtim recedere, et inhonestum sine cause connitione habitum relinquere, | ex certa scientia[1] hec fecimus,[a] scientes quia contra iura regni fecimus, quamuis de iure ciuili[2] recte fecerimus quia quicquid plantatur, seritur uel inedificatur, omne solo cedit, radices si tamen egit; et solum nostrum esse constat, nec sine consensu nostro potest alienari; ergo recte messi sumus quod ille seminauerat in solo nostro. Cum igitur domino regi conquesti fuerimus et ibi auxilium non inuenerimus, et cum pluries uocauerimus uos litteratorie et uiua uoce ut perpetuum legatum nobis a domino papa datum et nolletis uenire, communicato consilio tale quid fecimus. Et nisi modo ueneritis, peiora faciemus, propter que oportebit uos uenire et tam in capite quam in membris corrigenda corrigere. Sin autem ut requiratur sanguis noster de manibus uestris,[3] non in occulto set palam relinquemus habitus nostros ad pedes uestros ut "ante tribunal domini nostri Iesu Christi reddatis rationem pro animabus nostris";[4] quamuis coram domino papa sitis inexcusabiles nisi corrigenda apud nos correxeritis, sicut in priuilegiis nostris continetur, ad quem nos contra uos et abbatem nostrum appellauimus, nisi ad uos ueneritis, et sic poteritis amittere curam quam habetis de nobis.'

fo. 151[vb]

230. Et cum audisset hunc sermonem motus est archiepiscopus. Immo et magistri mei in scolis, clerici archiepiscopi, uidelicet I. de Tinemue[5] et S. de Suuelle[6] et Honorius,[7] exclamauerunt dicentes

---

[a] hec fecimus *interlined* (s. xiii[r])

[1] For the origin and the history of the phrase, see J. Krynen, ' "De nostre certaine science": remarques sur l'absolutisme législatif de la monarchie médiévale française', in *Renaissance du pouvoir législatif et genèse de l'état moderne*, ed. A. Gouron and A. Rigaudière (Montpellier, 1988), pp. 131–44; and *L'empire du roi: idées et croyances politiques en France, xiiie–xve siècle* (Paris, 1993), pp. 395–402, noted by Boureau, 'How Law came to the monks', pp. 53–7. Krynen traces the notion of 'certain knowledge', (i.e. what is generally known to be the case), back to late-12th cent. Bologna and the school of Bulgarus in their considerations of the place of custom. See also O. Hageneder, 'Probleme des päpstlichen Kirchenregiments im hohen Mittelalter (Ex certa scientia, non obstante, Registerführung)', in *Lectiones Eruditorum Extraneorum in Facultate Philosophica Universitatis Carolinae Pragensis Factae*, fasc. iv (Prague, 1995), pp. 49–77, at 71–7. Familiarity with its use may have been imparted to Thomas through works available to him before he reached Bologna, see next note, and for further example of its use by Thomas, see below, 264.

[2] i.e. Roman Law. This is a paraphrase of Justinian's *Institutes* 2. 1. 31–2. Cf. F. de Zulueta and P. Stein, *The Teaching of the Roman Law in England around 1200* (Selden Soc. Supplementary ser. viii: London, 1990) for the text of a *Lectura* on the Institutes produced for English students in c.1200, and p. 33, for the particular reference. The MS (BL Royal MS 4 B IV) belonged to Worcester priory in the 14th cent. We do not know the author of the Lecture, but it is likely to have been a pupil of Vacarius who was also influenced by Johannes Bassianus, of whom Simon of Sywell (Thomas's own master) was probably a

us but to abandon the place. But because it is a disgrace for a monk to leave secretly and dishonourable for him to renounce his habit without examination of the case, we have done these things in the certain knowledge[1] that our actions have been contrary to the laws of the kingdom but in accordance with the civil law[2] which states that whatever is planted, sown, or built becomes altogether the possession of the soil if it takes root there; and it is undisputed that it is our soil, and cannot be alienated without our consent. Therefore we were right to reap what he had sown in our soil. We complained to the king but found no help there, and we appealed to you as the permanent legate given to us by the pope on many occasions both by letter and orally, but you declined to come, so, after taking advice, which we have done, unless you come now we shall do worse things and you will have to come and rectify whatever needs rectifying not only in the head but also in the limbs. But if our blood be required at your hands,[3] we shall abandon our habits at your feet, not secretly but openly, that you may "render account for our souls before the judgment seat"[4] of our Lord Jesus Christ. However, you will be utterly without excuse before the pope unless you rectify what needs rectifying amongst us, as is contained in our privileges. We have appealed to the pope against you and our abbot in case you do not come to us, and you will thus be able to give up the responsibility which you have for us.'

230. The archbishop was perturbed when he heard what I said. Indeed, my masters in the schools, clerks of the archbishop [Hubert Walter], namely J[ohn] of Tynemouth,[5] S[imon] of Sywell,[6] and Honorius [of Richmond][7] spoke out, saying that what I said was just,

student; pp. xliv n. 1, l–li. Thomas, therefore, could have become acquainted with it in Oxford and it is certainly possible that the author was Simon of Sywell. The 'laws of the kingdom' are those of the feudal law.   [3] Cf. Ezek. 3: 18, 20 et al.

[4] Cf. Matt. 12: 36; Luke 16: 2; Rom. 14: 12; 1 Pet. 4: 5.

[5] A noted canonist, some of whose glosses, like those of Simon of Sywell (see next note), survive in a student's lecture notes. Both were teaching at Oxford before 1199: this dating comes from their having taught Thomas of Marlborough before his profession at Evesham. In general see Boyle,'Canon law before 1380', in History of the University of Oxford, i. The Early Schools, ed. J. I. Catto (Oxford, 1984), pp. 531–2; the seminal article of E. Rathbone and S. Kuttner, ANC, pp. 317, 325; and BRUO, p. 1923. There is evidence for John of Tynemouth in Oxford as early as 1188. Probably in or before 1198 he became a member of Archbishop Hubert Walter's household, then a canon of Lincoln, and finally archdeacon of Oxford.

[6] Also in the archiepiscopal household, he was entrusted with the archbishop's counterseal in 1202 when Hubert Walter was abroad (the archbishop returned in May); EEA 2: Canterbury, 1162–90, ed. C. R. Cheney and B. E. A. Jones (1986), p. xxvii; and EEA 3: Canterbury, 1193–1205, ed. C. R. Cheney and E. John (1986),p. 313. He became a

[See p. 234 for n. 6 cont. and n. 7]

quia recte locutus sum,[a] murmurantes contra archiepiscopum; propter uerbum quod subieci, 'Domine pater, consulite fame uestre quia abbas noster aperto ore clamat cotidie se non timere quamdiu uos et iusticiarius[1] uixeritis, exprimens causam uos diffamando quod uidelicet uobis tantum seruierit quod securus sit de uobis.'

231. Et archiepiscopus, 'Vt sciat mundus quia manus mee munde sunt in hac parte, non erit hoc prouerbium amodo in Israel,[2] per beatum Iulianum[3] nos ueniemus et ita corrigenda corrigemus quod secundo opus non erit.' Et facto | dictum compensasset nisi morte preoccupatus fuisset.[4]

fo. 152[ra]

232. *Qualiter Thomas monachus captus fuerit ab abbate et liberatus per archiepiscopum et clericos eius*

Igitur de consilio archiepiscopi secessi Wigorniam ut possessionem nostram de assarto contra abbatem et senescallum defenderem, qui illuc conuenerant in manu forti ut possessionem assarti recuperarent et factum abbatis saluarent. Ad hoc enim semper nitebatur abbas ut de ecclesiis et possessionibus ecclesie sine consilio nostro pro uoluntate sua posset disponere.[5] Et cum audisset abbas que feceram, excommunicauit me et cum cognouisset quod essem Wigornie gauisus est. Et obseruauit portas ciuitatis ut me comprehenderet. Set ego non ueneram ut fugerem set ut ex aduerso starem,[6] et cum stetissem coram iusticiariis, et abbas ex aduerso cum senescallo obiciens michi quod eram excommunicatus. Orta est dissentio inter iusticiarios utrum deberem admitti contra abbatem, et nobis recedentibus ut super hoc interlocutionem reciperemus, data est interlocutio contra

---

[a] *marg.* ?Responsio ?optima (*?s. xiv²*)

---

canon of Lincoln, like John of Tynemouth, and treasurer of Lichfield. He had taught at Bologna before his spell in Oxford (Boyle, p. 532; *BRUO*, p. 1704; *ANC*, pp. 326–7).

[7] The third of the trio in the archiepiscopal household, who had taught Thomas, had studied in Paris. He wrote a very successful textbook of canon law, the *Summa decretalium questionum* (not as yet edited), and was probably teaching in Oxford from (?) 1192, when he occurs as a witness to a judge-delegate case. In 1195 he became chief legal officer to the archbishop of York (*BRUO*, pp. 956–7; Southern, in *History of the University of Oxford*, i, p. 19; *ANC*, pp. 296, 304). Archbishop Hubert Walter presented him to the churches of Tarring and Patching (in the archiepiscopal peculiar of Tarring in Sussex) between 25 Sept. 1198 and ? Nov. 1200, and it is at this time that he must have joined the archiepiscopal household (Cheney thought not much before 1200, *EEA 3* no. 384 n.). He went to Rome and established his claim to the archdeaconry of Richmond in the curia (20 Dec. 1200), returned to England in 1201, but was in Rome again in 1202, and back in England by late 1203, as appears from an archiepiscopal charter which he witnessed with Simon of Sywell and John of Tynemouth, dated ?late 1203×April 1204 (*EEA 3* no. 536). This meeting, however, suggests that he may have returned to England earlier.

and they expressed their disapproval of the archbishop because of what I went on to say: 'Father, consider your reputation, for our abbot openly declares every day that he is not afraid so long as you and the justiciar [Geoffrey fitz Peter][1] are alive, giving as his reason (and so slandering you) that he obeys you only because he owes his safety to you.'

231. The archbishop replied, 'So that the world may know that my hands are clean in this connection, henceforth this proverb will cease in Israel,[2] by the blessed Julian,[3] we shall come and thus amend what needs amending, and it will not need to be done again.' And he would have matched the word with the deed had he not been overtaken by death.[4]

232. *The monk Thomas is arrested by the abbot and freed by the archbishop and his clerks*

After my discussion with the archbishop I left for Worcester to defend our possession of the assart against the abbot and his steward, but they had met in strong force there to recover possession of the assart and vindicate the abbot's action. Moreover, the abbot was for ever trying to dispose of the churches and of the possessions of the church as suited him without consulting us.[5] When he heard what I had done he excommunicated me, and was delighted when he heard that I was in Worcester. He kept a watch on the gates of the city with the intention of seizing me. But I had not come with the intention of fleeing but of 'making a stand against him',[6] and when I took my place before the justices, the abbot opposing me with his steward objected to my presence on the grounds that I had been excommunicated. A dispute therefore broke out amongst the justices as to whether I should be allowed to oppose the abbot, so we withdrew in order that a decision might be given us on this matter. This was given against me

[1] Geoffrey Fitz Peter, created earl of Essex in 1199, was appointed justiciar on 11 July 1198 and remained in office until his death on 14 Oct. 1213; F. West, *The Justiciarship in England, 1066-1232* (Cambridge, 1966), pp. 97-177, and *HBC*, pp. 71-2.

[2] Cf. Matt. 27: 24, for Pilate washing his hands, and Ezek. 12: 23 for the proverb in the land of Israel which said that the days were prolonged and every vision failed.

[3] See above, 216 and n.

[4] Hubert Walter died at Teynham on 13 July 1205.

[5] *RSB* cap. 3 envisaged two councils, one of all the brethren called by the abbot only for important affairs, and a council of elders for routine affairs. See A. de Vogüé, *Community and Abbot in the Rule of St Benedict*, trans. C. Philippi (Cistercian Studies Series, v.1:Kalamazoo, 1979), pp. 162-3.

[6] Cf. Eph. 6: 11.

me, uidelicet me non habere personam standi in iudicio quia excommunicatus eram.[a][1]

233. Et tunc comprehendit me abbas meus ut mitteret me in carcerem apud Ambresleiam et occideret me, ut credebam. Idem enim fecerat monachis Cantuariensibus et cuidam homini nostro Augustino de Salford quem duris cruciatibus occidit, et ideo magis timui cognoscens eius tirannidem. Et cum iter agerem cum hiis qui ducebant me, ecce subito apparuerunt michi tres predicti uiri, magistri mei,[2] 'in uia qua ambulabam',[3] et statim circumdederunt me et liberauerunt me de manibus eorum denunciantes eos excommunicatos.[b] Quorum tres morte subita perierunt,[c] uidelicet Simon frater senescalli, qui occisus est a latronibus extra Wigorniam; Mattheus Dolfinus, cognatus abbatis, qui proprie sagitte incumbens obiter mortuus est;[d] Dauid Pugio a Willelmo de Arderne pede percussus in pectore ab equo cecidit et membris confrac|tis mortuus est. Quartus uero Ricardus de Kent, camerarius abbatis, rogante abbate cum essemus in curia Romana ut iniuriam ei remitterem ad peticionem meam a penitenciario domini pape absolutus est.[4]

fo. 152rb

234. Hec ideo scripsi 'ut timeant subditi obedire dominis'[5] in atrocioribus contra canones sicut illi fecerunt.[6]

235. Ductus itaque sum a predictis magistris meis ad dominum Cantuariensem qui et ipse uenit Wigorniam eadem die.[7] Qui cum collocasset me a latere eius dum sumeremus cibum, uenerunt ex parte abbatis clerici eius magistri Robertus de Vulfeia[8] et Germanus. Offerentes ei palefridum et cuppam argenteam cum litteris abbatis in quibus petebat quod redderet me, excommunicatum suum, secundum regulam beati Benedicti puniendum et tractandum.[9] Et

---

[a] *marg.* utrum monacus excommunicatus potest admitti in iudicio contra abbatem (?s. xiv²)   [b] *marg.* quomodo (or ?quando) liberata est(?) .. incarceretur(?) (s. xiv²) [c] *marg.* vindicta Dei (?s. xiv²)   [d] *marg.* nota optime. *Passage bracketed down to* Germanus (235)

---

[1] It was a common principle in both royal and ecclesiastical courts that anyone excommunicated might not take part in the proceedings.

[2] John of Tynemouth, Simon of Sywell, and Honorius of Richmond.

[3] Isa. 48: 17.

[4] By the 14th cent. the office of the papal penitentiary operated under a cardinal penitentiary who had under him minor penitentiaries, native speakers from the various countries of Christendom, and at this time the English penitentiaries recorded were almost entirely Benedictines; see M. Harvey, *The English in Rome 1362–1420* (Cambridge, 1999), p. 154. The papal penitentiary in question may have been an unnamed Cistercian monk mentioned by Gerald of Wales (iii. 288) in 1203. John of Salerno acted as cardinal penitentiary in 1207; Cheney, *Letters*, no. 741, but he is less likely because the absolution probably took place in 1204–5, i.e. when both Thomas and Richard were in Rome.

on the grounds that I had no right to appear in court because of my excommunication.[1]

233. My abbot then seized me in order to send me to prison in Ombersley, and put me to death, as I believed. Indeed, he had done this to monks of Canterbury and to one of our men called Augustine de Salford whom he murdered by cruel tortures, so I had all the more reason to fear this, knowing of his tyranny. However, while I was journeying with the men who were taking me to prison, the three men, whom I have mentioned previously as my masters,[2] suddenly appeared 'on the road along which I was walking':[3] they immediately surrounded me and freed me from the hands of my captors, declaring them excommunicated. Three of them perished by sudden death: Simon, brother of the steward, was killed by robbers outside Worcester; Matthew Dolfin, a relative of the abbot, died incidentally by falling on his own arrow; and David Pugio, being kicked in the chest by William de Arderne, fell from his horse and died of fractured limbs. There was a fourth man, Richard of Kent, the abbot's chamberlain: when we were in the Roman curia the abbot asked me to forgive that man's ill-treatment of me, and he was absolved by the papal penitentiary on my petition.[4]

234. I have recorded this in the hope that 'subordinates may be afraid to obey their masters',[5] as these men did, in cruel acts which are contrary to the canons.[6]

235. I was accordingly taken by these masters of mine to the archbishop of Canterbury who also came himself to Worcester on the same day.[7] He gave me a place by his side while we dined, when clerks from the abbot's party arrived, Master Robert de Wolvey[8] and Master German. They offered the archbishop a palfrey and a silver cup along with a letter from the abbot in which he requested that the archbishop return me, his excommunicant, to be punished and dealt with according to the Rule of the blessed Benedict.[9] My response to

---

[5] I Pet. 2: 18, 'servants obey your masters', the opposite command, has clearly influenced Thomas's choice of words here.

[6] This is clearly a reference to 'Si quis suadente diabolo', requiring those who committed violent acts against the clergy to go to the pope for absolution, *Decretum* C 17 q. 4 c. 29 (Friedberg i cols. 822–3); c. 15 of the second Lateran Council). On the point, see E. Vodola, *Excommunication in the Middle Ages* (University of California Press: Berkeley, Los Angeles, London, 1986), pp. 28–9, 139.

[7] 1203 ? spring. The date depends on arguing back from the mandate in **247** for the sequence of events.

[8] Warws.: for him see below, App. II A.

[9] According to the Rule, the abbot had general corrective powers over his monks.

ego, 'Pater sancte, ante sententiam appellaui et in prosecutione appellationis mee sum: et ideo nulla est sententia abbatis. Cum igitur uestrum sit tueri appellantes,[1] etsi oportuerit me mori uobiscum non recedam a uobis.'

236. Et archiepiscopus nuntiis, 'Ite cum exeniis uestris ad abbatem ut seruet ea usque dum mittamus pro eis, quia nos in breui ueniemus Eueshamiam et secundum posse nostrum pacem inter abbatem et conuentum et monacum istum, Deo donante, reformabimus.' Hec omnia dicebat, ut erat uir summe prudentie, ne abbatem terreret et ut sine appellatione iudicium eius subiret. In crastino uero missi sunt ad me priores Iohannes et Petrus[2] cum clericis predictis ex parte abbatis et conuentus ut uenirem domum, quia paratus erat pacem pro uoluntate conuentus reformare. Quod cum nunciassem archiepiscopo, submurmurans dixit quod ad colludendum recessi, et ego, quod non. Tandem dixit,'Vade, et per beatum Iulianum,[3] si ab accusatione quam instituisti coram nobis recesseris, animaduertemus in te durius quam in abbatem si | uictus esset.'

fo. 152va

237. Et accepta benedictione recessi cum prioribus meis, et ueniens domum multos 'falsos fratres'[4] inueni querentes occasionem aduersum me, qui dixerunt me nuntiasse domino Cantuariensi exordinationes domus nostre. Et uerum fuit, quia aliter non potui expedire negotium; quia scriptum est, 'Iustus in principio accusator sui est.'[5] Ego uero rem tacitus considerabam cum quibusdam fratribus fidelibus, quibus uerba archiepiscopi reuelaui, et reformationem pacis impediui.

238. *De exilio quatuor monachorum pro assarto et de compromissione in archiepiscopum et coarbitros suos, et de prima scriptura consuetudinum et reddituum conuentus*

Quarta autem die uenit ad nos archiepiscopus.[6] Et ingressus capitulum blande leniterque locutus est abbati, nobis uero durius, obiurgans nos et increpans tam pro assarto quam pro aliis exordinationibus nostris. Tandem proposuit ea que ego dixeram ei, requirens an uera

---

[1] This is a reference to the archbishop's right and obligation of tuitorial appeal, by which he might protect the person and property of the appellant pending litigation; see Sayers, *PJD*, pp. 96–9.

[2] In the larger Benedictine convents, the prior was often assisted in his duties by a subprior and a third prior.

[3] See above, 216 n. 3.

[4] Gal. 2: 4.

this was, 'Holy father, I appealed before the sentence, and am in process of prosecuting my appeal: the abbot's sentence therefore has no validity. Since it is your duty to protect appellants,[1] I will not leave you even if I have to die in your presence.'

236. The archbishop's reply to the messengers was, 'Go with your gifts to the abbot that he may keep them until we send for them, for we shall shortly be coming to Evesham, and if God grants it, we shall use every means in our power to restore peace between the abbot and the convent, including this monk.' Being a man of great ingenuity he said all this so that he should not frighten the abbot, and so that he would submit to judgment without an appeal being made. The next day Priors John and Peter[2] were sent to me, with the previously mentioned clerks, on behalf of the abbot and the convent telling me to come home, as the abbot was prepared to restore peace in accordance with the convent's wishes. When I informed the archbishop of this he grumbled a little, saying that I left to make terms with the abbot against him, but I denied this. At last he said, 'Go, and by the blessed Julian,[3] if you withdraw the accusation which you have made before us, we shall punish you more severely than we shall the abbot if he is defeated.'

237. After receiving his blessing I left with my priors, and on arriving home I found many 'false brethren'[4] looking for an opportunity to attack me, who said that I had informed the archbishop of Canterbury of the breaches of the Rule in our house. This was the truth, for I could not speed the business in any other way; as it is written, 'the first to present his case seems to be the one in the right.'[5] I secretly considered the matter with some of the brethren I trusted, informed them of what the archbishop had said, and hindered the restoration of peace.

238. *The exile of four monks over the assart, the agreement to submit to the arbitration of the archbishop and his fellow arbiters, and the first written record of the customs and revenues of the convent*
Four days later the archbishop came to us.[6] He entered the chapter-house and spoke in a friendly, amiable manner to the abbot, but more sternly to us, reproaching and upbraiding us as much over the matter of the assart as about our other breaches of the Rule. Finally he laid before us the facts which I had told him, asking whether they were

[5] Prov. 18: 17.
[6] The visit was probably in the spring of 1203, see above, 235 n. 7.

essent. Et paucis respondentibus quia sic, abbate uero quod non, et multa contra conuentum proponente. Archiepiscopus lite sic contestata excommunicauit omnes qui falsa ei dicerent de statu domus, tam de capite quam de membris, uel uera celarent. Et facta singulari inquisitione, tam per se quam per clericos suos et uiros religiosos. Tandem, communicato consilio, ita exorsus est archiepiscopus, 'Quamuis solus possem corrigere que corrigenda sunt, tamen quia debemus omnia facere cum consilio, consulimus si uultis quod abbas eligat unum bonum uirum, et conuentus alterum, in quos simul et in nos compromittatis quod appellatione remota arbitrio nostro[1] stabitis quicquid circa statum ecclesie huius uel personarum uestrarum arbitrando dictauerimus, uel modo statim iudicium recipiatis'.

239. Ego uero sciens quod abbas a sententia archiepiscopi posset appellare, consului conuentui ut arbitros eligeremus. Abbas uero de facili consensit, timens sibi, et sciens quia reis et fugientibus prosunt dilationes, et quod nox habet consilium;[2] hic enim semper mos eius fuit quod omnia negotia in diem futurum prorogauit. Et abbas elegit Clementem abbatem de Certesia,[3] nos | uero Eustachium episcopum Eliensem:[4] et firmata est hec compromissio per iuramentum utrarumque partium[a] in uerbo Domini, et per cartam sigillo abbatis et conuentus munitam. Conditionem etiam nostram quantum causa nostra permisit correxit tunc archiepiscopus et abbatem coartauit. Et tunc primo consuetudines nostras scribi iussit, set non confirmauit. Set, ut domino regi satisfaceret, qui motus erat pro assarto, quatuor ex fratribus relegauit, quorum ego unus eram, set post quindecim dies ut causam nostram contra episcopum agerem reuocatus sum.

240. Quamuis hoc bellum quasi intestinum cum abbate nostro haberemus, nichilominus tamen causam contra episcopum egimus et defendimus tam uiriliter et diligenter, sicut rei exitus comprobauit, quod ipse archiepiscopus et alii terre magnates admirati sunt, dicentes quod nunquam tales monacos uiderunt.

fo. 152vb (margin, beside 'Clementem abbatem')

---

[a] partium *corr. and followed by* trium *del*

[1] For arbitration, see Sayers, *PJD*, pp. 104–8. In theory (at least) there was no appeal from arbiters as they were freely chosen and submitted to.
[2] See above, 214 n. 2.
[3] *HRH*, p. 39, has no Clement, but a Master Martin as abbot from 1197 to 1206.

true. A few replied that they were, but the abbot said they were not, and made many charges against the convent. So, since the case was contested, the archbishop pronounced excommunicate all who should make false statements to him about the state of the house, both the mother house and the dependencies, or conceal the truth. He then examined them one by one, not on his own but with his clerks and other religious. Finally, having taken advice, he communicated his decision in these words, 'Although I have the power alone to rectify what needs rectifying yet, because we ought to do everything with advice, we are asking you either to be willing for the abbot to choose one good man, and the convent another, and to submit to their and our arbitration[1] without appeal, whatever the results of our arbitration may be concerning the state of this church and your persons, or to receive judgment here and now.'

239. Knowing that the abbot could appeal against a judgment made by the archbishop, I advised the convent to choose arbitration. The abbot readily agreed out of fear for himself, knowing that delays always benefit the defendants and fugitives, and that 'night has its counsel';[2] it was always his way to procrastinate in all matters of business. The abbot chose Clement, abbot of Chertsey,[3] and we chose Eustace, bishop of Ely:[4] the compact was ratified by both parties swearing an oath in the name of the Lord, and in a charter sealed with the seal of the abbot and convent. The archbishop then revised our position so far as our case allowed, and restricted the powers of the abbot. He also gave orders for our Customs to be put into writing then for the first time, but he did not confirm them. However, in order to placate the king, who had been perturbed over the matter of the assart, he banished four of the brethren, of whom I was one, though I was recalled a fortnight later to plead our case against the bishop.

240. Although we were having this internal battle, as it were, with our abbot, we nevertheless conducted our case against the bishop, and we were so forceful and energetic in our defence, as the outcome of the suit proved, that the archbishop himself and other leading magnates in the land were amazed, saying that they had never before seen such monks.

Clement, abbot of the Cistercian house of Neath, who died in 1218 and may have been abbot at this date (p. 138) seems the only possible recorded candidate.

[4] See above, **223** n. 3.

241. *Qualiter causam libertatis coram iudicibus communibus egerimus*
Episcopus enim iam pridem redierat a curia et litteras de consensu
nunciorum nostrorum predictorum impetratas apportauerat[1] directas
episcopo[2] et priori[3] de Couentre et archidiacono Norhamptonie,[4] in
quibus continebatur quod ipsi causam super exemptione ac subiectione tam monasterii quam ecclesiarum Vallis audirent, et in
iudicio possessorio sentenciarent,[5] super proprietate uero causam
diligentissime examinatam ad dominum papam diffiniendam trans-
mitterent, certum partibus terminum prefigentes, quo cum ipsis
instrumentis autenticis, quod ualde periculosum fuit nobis, et attestationibus domino pape se presentarent, sententiam recepture.

242. In cuius cause actione[6] summa cautela fuit hec, quam nemo
nouit preter me solum usque ad publicationem attestationum. Cum
enim dominus papa distinxisset, ut audistis,[7] quod iudices in
possessorio cognoscerent et sentenciarent, in petitorio uero tantum
cognoscerent et non sententiarent, aduersarii nostri a Domino
infatuati[8] nobiscum sine distinctione simul et semel in utroque
iudicio litem contestati sunt, gaudentes propter litis contestationem
et cupientes quocumque modo, ut moris est actorum, peruenire ad
fo. 153ʳᵃ eam. Quare | indifferenter testes et mixtim tam super proprietate
quam possessione admissi sunt, et sic, Deo disponente, causa
proprietatis cum causa possessionis citissime sine omni dilatione
et difficultate examinata est. Hec ideo uobis dixerim quia si
aduersarius noster usus fuisset consilio legis, prius egisset causam
possessionis, et nactus possessionem compulisset nos ad onera
probationum in causa proprietatis. Et sic in longa tempora

---

[1] The messengers (perhaps more fittingly described as the convent's representatives)
were Ermefred and Richard, see **226** above and **245** below. For the text of the letters,
which were dated 22 May 1203, see below, **245–7**; see also Cheney, *Letters*, no. 478.
Mandates were usually addressed to offices rather than to their holders, as in this case.

[2] Geoffrey Muschamp, cons. 21 June 1198, d. 6 Oct. 1208; previously archdeacon of
Cleveland; see *EEA 17: Coventry and Lichfield, 1183–1208*, ed. M. Franklin (Oxford,
1998), pp. xlvii–xlix, and *HBC*, p. 253.

[3] Master Jorbert (?Josbert), 1198–1216, formerly a monk of La Charité, was also prior of
Much Wenlock, which he retained with Coventry. According to Roger of Wendover
(*Chronica sive flores historiarum*, ed. H. O. Coxe (4 vols., English Historical Soc.: London,
1841–2), iii. 128, and *Matthaei Parisiensis chronica majora*, ed. H. R. Luard (7 vols., RS lvii,
1872–83), ii. 445–6, s.a. 1198) he was furthermore prior of Daventry and of Bermondsey,
both, like Much Wenlock, Cluniac houses dependent on La Charité; see *HRH*, pp. 41,
116, 117, 123. He was a likely choice of judge for the convent of Evesham. The monks of
Coventry elected him bishop in 1208 or 1209, but the king for his part was trying to get the
canons of Lichfield to elect his nominee, the royal chancellor, Walter de Grey. The legate
Pandulf is said to have quashed both elections; *SLI*, p. 125 n. 3.

241. *We conduct the case for liberty before the accepted judges*

The bishop had now been back from the curia for some time and had brought letters—which had been impetrated with the consent of our previously mentioned messengers[1]—addressed to the bishop,[2] to the prior of Coventry,[3] and to the archdeacon of Northampton.[4] The contents of these letters were that these men should themselves hear the case regarding the exemption or subjection of both the monastery and the churches of the Vale, and should give a judgment as to possession,[5] and after careful investigation, should submit their findings about the ownership to the pope for him to make a decision. They were to arrange a particular day for the parties to present themselves before the pope with the authentic documents (a most perilous situation for us!) and with their evidence, to receive judgment on the case.

242. In the proceedings of this case[6] there was this very important safeguard which nobody knew but me until the publication of the witnesses' evidence. This was that when the pope made this distinction, as you have heard,[7] that the judges should listen to testimony and pass judgment in the possessory case, but should only listen to testimony and not pass judgment in the petitory case, our opponents were frustrated by the Lord,[8] for they contested both cases at one and the same time without distinction. They had been glad to join issue and eager to start the contest in any way they could, as is often the case with plaintiffs. So they admitted testimony without distinction or discrimination concerning both 'ownership' and 'possession', and by divine providence the case concerning 'ownership' was very quickly heard along with that concerning 'possession' without any delay or difficulty. I have told you this to point out that if our opponent had followed the counsel of the law before he had argued the case for possession and so had won possession, he would have forced us to shoulder the burden of proof in the case about ownership. Then the examination of the

---

[4] This R. (see below, 245 n. 3) was probably Master Robert de Manecestre, but it might be Master Richard of Kent; Greenway, *Fasti*, iii. 31.

[5] i.e. a judgment as to immediate possession as distinct from a judgment as to the main case of ownership. The churches (or chapels) of the Vale were six in number: St Lawrence Evesham, All Saints Evesham, Lenchwick, Norton, Abbot's Morton, and Offenham. Nine extra churches were also claimed: Church Lench, Kinwarton, Weston, Ombersley, Willersey, Broadwell, Stow, Bourton, and Swell; see below, 433–4.

[6] For the procedure before the church courts, see Sayers, *PJD*, ch. 2, esp. pp. 70–95.

[7] See above, 241.

[8] This may be a quotation, but we have been unable to identify it.

differetur examinatio cause proprietatis, et episcopus diutius, immo forte usque in hodiernum diem, gauisus esset possessione, sicut nos gaudemus de possessione iurisdictionis Vallis, predicte legis usi consilio.

243. Igitur cum uentum esset ad publicationem attestationum, tunc primo recordati sunt aduersarii nostri quod stulte egerint, et querentes quod iudices publicarent tantum attestationes de possessione, illas uero de proprietate tegerent, nobis reclamantibus ne hoc fieret, immo omnibus publicatis simul utraque lis marte suo discerneretur.*a* Allegantibus etiam nobis hec fieri non posse, quia ita commixte erant attestationes quod nequaquam sine preiuditio et discrimine partis nostre quin alique publicande tegerentur et tegende publicarentur poterant separari. Quasi impossibilitate separandi constricti, omnes publicauerunt. Et sic utraque causa simul examinata est et adiudicata est episcopo restitutio plene iurisdictionis in nos et monasterium nostrum. Nobis uero possessio plene iurisdictionis Vallis totius reseruata est et absoluti sumus ab impetitione episcopi in possessorio iudicio de iurisdictione ecclesiarum Vallis. Et missus est episcopus in plenam possessionem iurisdictionis quo ad monasterium et monachos anno secundo ex quo lis inceperat, dominica qua cantatur Misericordia Domini.[1] Et causa instructa cum attestationibus tradita est utrique parti: et nobis priuilegia, episcopo uero eorum transcripta signata, tradita sunt, deferenda ad dominum papam statuto termino, in octabis uidelicet sancti Martini fo. 153rb proximo sequente,[2] | quo cum his omnibus coram domino papa compareremus sententiam recepturi.

244. *Litere domini pape per quas causa ista actitata fuit et sententia in possessorio iudicio pro episcopo lata*
Hic litteras domini pape per quas hec causa actitata*b* est, necnon et sententiam in possessorio iudicio de monasterio nostro contra nos latam, et grauem satisfactionem nostram, simul et in eodem iudicio de ecclesiis Vallis pro nobis sententiam latam, cum ipsa relatione ad dominum papam facta, huic operi interserenda dignum duxi.

---

a sua *for* suo *and marg.* discereret   *b* actitata: *final* -ta *interlined*

[1] 24 Apr. 1205.
[2] The octave is the eighth day after the feast, including the day of the actual feast in the reckoning, so in this case between 18 Nov. (St Martin's day) and 25 November.

case for ownership would have been prolonged and the bishop would have enjoyed possession for a longer time, indeed, very probably until the present time, just as we rejoice in our possession of the jurisdiction of the Vale, because we followed the counsel of the afore-mentioned law.

243. Accordingly, when it came to the publication of the evidence of the witnesses, our opponents then for the first time realized the foolishness of what they had done, and requested that the judges should publish only the evidence relating to possession and withhold that relating to ownership. We objected to this being done, demanding instead that, since all the testimony had been published at the same time, each of the two cases should be decided in its own context. We also argued that our opponents were asking for the impossible, for the evidence had been so intermingled that it could in no way be separated without prejudice or discrimination against our case, and some evidence which should be published might be withheld while other evidence which should be withheld might be published. Forced by the virtual impossibility of separating the evidence, they published all of it. So both cases were tried at the same time and the judgment given was that the bishop should have restored to him full jurisdiction over us and our monastery. We were to keep possession of full jurisdiction over the whole of the Vale and were absolved from the bishop's claim to possession of jurisdiction over the churches of the Vale. The bishop entered into full possession of jurisdiction over the monastery and its monks two years after the instigation of the lawsuit, on the Sunday when Misericordia Domini is sung.[1] The case which had been drawn up, with the evidence of the witnesses, was handed over to each party: we received our privileges, the bishop received sealed transcripts of them, to take to the pope on an appointed date; this was in the octave of the next feast of St Martin,[2] when we were to appear before the pope with all these things to receive sentence.

244. *The papal letter which commenced the case, and the possessory judgment given in favour of the bishop*
At this point I have thought it worth including in this work the letter of the pope through which the case was initiated, the sentence given against us in the possessory judgment relating to our monastery, our heavy penance, and the sentence given simultaneously in our favour in the same judgment relating to the churches of the Vale, together with the report made to the pope.

245. 'Omnibus sancte matris ecclesie filiis tam presentibus quam futuris, G. Dei gratia episcopus,[1] et I. prior Couentren',[2] et R. archidiaconus de Norhamton',[3] eternam in Domino salutem. Litteras domini pape Innocentii tercii in hec uerba suscepimus: "Innocentius episcopus, seruus seruorum Dei, uenerabili fratri episcopo et dilectis filiis priori Couentr' et archidiacono de Norhampton' Lincoln' diocesis, salutem et apostolicam benedictionem. Constitutis in presentia nostra uenerabili fratre nostro Wigorn' episcopo et dilectis filiis E. et R. nuntiis abbatis et monachorum Euesham', cum super subiectione ac exemptione ipsius monasterii uellent adinuicem litigare, dilectum filium B. tituli sancte Susanne presbiterum cardinalem eis concessimus auditorem.[4] In cuius presentia proposuit episcopus memoratus quod cum abbas et monachi de Euesham hactenus ecclesie Wigorn' diocesana extiterint lege subiecti, et predicti loci abbates ab episcopo Wigorn' benedictionis munus suscipere, sibique per libellum professionis canonicam obedientiam exibere, ad sinodum Wigornie uocati accedere, consueuerunt. Et ipsos episcopos ad eorum monasterium accedentes cum processione recipere, ac in multis aliis ipsis quasi deuoti filii obedire, et omnia spiritualia ab ecclesia Wigornie percipere; nunc in spiritu contumaci debitam eidem episcopo reuerentiam et obedientiam subtrahere moliuntur. Cum enim nuper idem episcopus una cum dilectis filiis abbate Winchelc',[5] priore Gloecestrie, clericis pluribus et iurisperitis, certo die prefixo et ab eis recepto ad eorum monasterium causa uisitationis accederet, ipsum re*a*|cipere noluerunt, set contumaciter resistentes eidem, neque iure uti communi[6] nec speciale priuilegium per quod essent exempti ostendere uoluerunt. Set nec etiam indulgentiam eidem episcopo a nobis concessam, cuius auctoritate de intrinseca et extrinseca religiosarum domorum administratione que ipsi diocesana sunt lege subiecte, appellatione remota, potest cognoscere, curauerunt

fo. 153va

---

a *bottom right-hand corner of fo. 153^r* uastium (?nascium) accedentes (?s. xiv)

[1] See above, 241.
[2] See above, 241.
[3] See above, 241.
[4] See Maleczek, pp. 134–6. Benedict had been promoted cardinal priest of S. Susanna in 1201. He had been previously cardinal deacon of S. Maria in Domnica, and was to become cardinal bishop of Porto and S. Rufina from 1213 to 1216. He was sent on legation to the Latin kingdom (Constantinople) from 1205 to 1207, and had links with the Greek Church. On auditors who might be appointed to examine cases in Rome, see Sayers, *PJD*, pp. 14–25.
[5] Master Robert of Hasleton, 1196–1221; *HRH*, p. 79. Not in *BRUO* or in *BRUC*.

245. 'To all the sons of holy mother church, both present and future, G[eoffrey Muschamp], by the grace of God, bishop [of Coventry],[1] and J[orbertus], prior of Coventry,[2] and R[obert], archdeacon of Northampton,[3] everlasting salvation in the Lord be yours. We have received a letter of Pope Innocent III in these words: "Innocent, bishop, servant of the servants of God, to his venerable brother bishop and his beloved sons, the prior of Coventry and the archdeacon of Northampton, of the diocese of Lincoln, greetings and apostolic benediction. Since we have before us our venerable brother, the bishop of Worcester, and the beloved sons E[rmefred] and R[ichard], the representatives of the abbot and monks of Evesham, who wish on each of their parts to contest in law the issue of the subjection or exemption of the same monastery, we have appointed our beloved son B[enedict], cardinal priest of St Susanna, as auditor.[4] In his presence the said bishop has submitted that the abbot and monks of Evesham have until now been subject to the church of Worcester under diocesan law, that abbots of the said place have received the grace of benediction from the bishop of Worcester, have been accustomed to show canonical obedience to him through a deed of profession, and to attend the synod at Worcester when summoned. Furthermore he submits that when bishops of Worcester have come to their monastery it has been their custom to receive them with a procession, to obey them in many other respects also as devoted sons, and to accept all spiritual benefits from the church of Worcester; but that now, in a contumacious spirit, they are endeavouring to abandon the reverence and obedience owed to that same bishop. Recently, when the same bishop with his beloved sons, the abbot of Winchcombe,[5] the prior of Gloucester, several clerks and men experienced in the law, came to their monastery on a day previously arranged and agreed by them in order to undertake a visitation, they refused to receive him, and contumaciously opposing him, were unwilling either to refer to anything in the *ius commune*[6] or produce any special privilege by which they had acquired exemption. Furthermore, they have not bothered to give heed to the empowerment granted by us to the same bishop, by the authority of which he can exercise, without appeal, jurisdiction over the internal and external administration of religious houses which are subject to him under diocesan law, even

---

[6] The *ius commune* was an amalgamation of Roman law and of canon law. It should not be confused with English common law. For further citations, see below, **302, 303, 357, 381** and **382** (twice).

audire multociens requisiti. Episcopus uero, communicato predictorum uirorum et iurisperitorum consilio, tam manifestam
ipsorum contumatiam et inobedientiam canonica pena percellens,
ipsos et eorum monasterium et capellas pertinentes ad ipsos a
diuinorum celebratione suspendit. Set ipsi, contumatie contumatiam
adiungentes, illam sententiam contempserunt et officium exequi
minime formidarunt; Wigornensem ecclesiam ac episcopum memo-
ratum iurisdictione atque obedientia in eos hactenus habita et obtenta
pacifice, pretermisso iuris ordine, spoliantes. Preterea in ecclesiis et
capellis Vallis Eueshamie cum uacant, personas et uicarios instituere,
causas matrimoniales et sacrilegii tractare,[1] licet nullum super hiis
priuilegium habeant uel ostendant, presumunt et iniungere peniten-
tias publicas et sollempnes.

246. "Nuntii uero prefati abbatis et monachorum ex aduerso propo-
nere curauerunt *quod, cum monasterium de Euesham ad Romanam
ecclesiam nullo pertineat mediante, sicut in priuilegio felicis memorie* Constantini *pape tercii*[b][2] et aliorum predecessorum nostrorum
noscitur contineri, predictus episcopus contra libertatem *ab apostolica sede optentam* et iam per quingentos annos in pace possessam
presumit contra iusticiam molestare. Illud cum omnibus ad idem in
diocesi sua pertinentibus, post appellationem ad nos legittime interpositam et coram officialibus uenerabilis fratris nostri Cantuar'
archiepiscopi et ipso episcopo sepius innouatam, ecclesiastico interdicto et excomunicationi supponens. Pensiones insuper prohibuit eis
fo. 153vb   reddi, et multa | alia grauamina eis non cessat pro sue uoluntatis
arbitrio irrogare.

247. "Volentes igitur tam episcopi predicti quam memorati monasterii iura integre conseruari, discretioni uestre per apostolica scripta
mandamus, quatinus episcopo, si de spoliatione constiterit, sicut
iustum fuerit appellatione postposita restituto, reuocantes in irritum
si quid post appellationem ad nos legittime interpositam temere fuerit

---

a–a quod . . . memorie *struck through*   *b–b* pape tercii *erased*   *c–c* ab . . . optentam
erased

---

[1] On sacrilege, the violation or profanation of any person, place, or thing belonging to
the Church, see *Dictionnaire de Droit Canonique*, vii, cols. 830–4.

[2] The mistake here is obvious: for it was Pope Clement III who had first incorporated
the phrase 'nullo mediante' in a letter for the convent of Evesham. The mistake was
perhaps one of a brainwashed copyist who had drunk deeply of Evesham myth. No Pope
Constantine III is recorded. Pope Constantine I was crowned on 25 Mar. 708 and died on
9 Apr. 715; Pope Constantine II, elected on 28 June 767 and crowned on 5 July, was
deposed on 6 Aug. 768. To accord with the story of Ecgwine, Pope Constantine I must

though they have been many times required to do so. After consulting with the said persons and men experienced in the law, the bishop inflicted canonical punishment for such wilful disobedience and contumacy, and suspended the monks and their monastery and dependent chapels from the celebration of divine services. The monks, however, compounded their wilful behaviour with further contumacy. They scorned that sentence and celebrated divine service without any fear. By so doing they ignored the rule of law and robbed the church of Worcester and the said bishop of jurisdiction and of their obedience to them which had been peaceably held and maintained till the present day. Moreover, when the churches and chapels of the Vale of Evesham become vacant, they take it upon themselves to institute parsons and vicars in them, to decide matrimonial disputes and cases of sacrilege,[1] though they neither have nor produce any privilege to do these things, and they also presume to impose solemn and public penance.

246. "The said representatives of the abbot and the monks on their part have thought fit to submit that, since the monastery of Evesham belongs to the Roman church with no intermediary, as is known to be stated in a privilege of Pope Constantine III[2] of happy memory and of others of our predecessors, the said bishop presumes to act contrary to the liberty obtained from the apostolic see and possessed peaceably for five hundred years and to cause the monastery trouble unjustly. He [the bishop] has pronounced an ecclesiastical interdict and sentence of excommunication upon it and upon all belonging to it in his diocese, after an appeal has been lawfully made to us and often reiterated in the presence of officials of our venerable brother, the archbishop of Canterbury, and made to the bishop himself. Furthermore, he has forbidden pensions to be paid to the monks, and continues to impose many other burdens upon them in order to achieve his purpose.

247. "Since therefore we desire that the rights of the said bishop and the said monastery be wholly preserved, we command you, by this apostolic letter, to see that the bishop is restored, if he ceases his spoliation, as he should do while an appeal is pending, and to reject as invalid any imprudent action attempted after an appeal which has been lawfully made to us. You are to see that the sentence of the said

have been intended, but as the papal chancery at this stage was not investigating the early sources, and no mention is made of the story of Ecgwine here, the original mandate is likely to have read 'felicis memorie Clementi pape tercii'.

attemptatum; et facientes predicti interdicti sententiam si rationabiliter lata est usque ad satisfactionem debitam inuiolabiliter obseruari.
Audiatis que adinuicem duxerint proponenda, et omnia redigentes in
scriptis, eadem sigillis uestris inclusa et originalia etiam, si qua
habent, nobis mittere procuretis: prefigentes partibus terminum
competentem quo cum ipsis sententiam, auctore Domino, recepture
nostro se conspectui representent. Testes autem qui fuerint nominati
si se gratia, odio uel timore subtraxerint, per censuram ecclesiasticam
cessante appellatione cogatis ueritati testimonium perhibere, nullis
litteris obstantibus, si que apparuerint harum mentione non habita a
sede apostolica impetrate. Quod si non omnes hiis exequendis
interesse potueritis, tu, frater episcope, cum altero eorum ea nichilominus exequaris. Datum[1] Ferent' xi kal. Iunii pontificatus nostri
anno sexto." [2]

248. Huius igitur auctoritate mandati cum partes in presentia nostra
die ad hoc prefixo consisterent, dictus episcopus intentionem suam
iuxta narrationem in litteris summi pontificis comprehensam con-
cipiens. R. abbatem et monachos de Euesham obedientiam et
subiectionem quam ipsi predecessoribus suis episcopis exhibere
consueuerant, ipsi preter iuris ordinem subtraxisse asseruit. Sibique
tanquam iniuste spoliato restitutionem fieri, et sententiam suspensionis, quam in monasterium et abbatem et monachos Eueshamie ob
fo. 154ra contumatiam eorum tulerat, confirmari postulauit. | Pars uero abbatis
et monachorum intentionem episcopi expressius infitians, ea que
domino pape ex parte eorum suggesta erant et que in litteris ipsius
domini pape comprehensa sunt, se probaturam proposuit.

249. Itaque super predictis admissis ex utraque parte sufficienter ad
probationem testibus diligenterque examinatis, tandem tempore suo
attestationes pupplicauimus. Cumque ex[a] attestationibus et disputatione super eis copiose habita, aliisque documentis indubitatum
redderetur, R. abbatem a Willelmo bone memorie Wigornensi
episcopo[3] benedictionis munus recepisse; et tam ipsi quam Wigorn'
ecclesie professionem in libello sollempniter fecisse;[4] procurationem

---

[a] ex *ins. in marg.* (s. *xiii'*)

[1] There are certain problems with the meaning of *Dat'* (whether it means given, i.e.
issued or dated) as opposed to *Actum*, used rarely in papal documents, but presumably
then signifying given or enacted, rather than dated.

[2] Cheney, *Letters*, no. 478 (PRO E 135/21/60).

[3] Master William of Northolt, elected *c*.25 May, cons. 21 Sept. 1186, d. 2 or 3 May
1190. He had been archdeacon of Gloucester and a prebendary of London, and before that
clerk to archbishops Theobald and Richard of Canterbury; Greenway, *Fasti*, ii. 100, 107.

interdict is inviolably observed, if it has been reasonably imposed, until there is due satisfaction. You are to hear the submissions of both parties and, after making a copy of all of these, you are to send them to us under your seals, and also the originals, if they have any: arrange a day convenient for both parties to present themselves before us on which they shall in person receive sentence in the name of the Lord. If any witnesses who have been named withdraw through favour, hostility, or fear, you are, disallowing appeal, to compel them under threat of ecclesiastical censure to give evidence to the truth, notwithstanding any letters that appear to have been impetrated from the apostolic see which do not make mention of these matters. But if all three of you are not able to be present in the execution of these duties then you, brother bishop, are to carry them out nevertheless with one of the two other commissioners. Dated at[1] Ferentino the 22nd of May in the sixth year of our pontificate [1203]".[2]

248. When the parties had assembled before us on the day previously arranged in compliance with the pope's mandate, the said bishop imagined that his claim was as set out in the account included in the pope's letter. He therefore declared that abbot R[oger] and the monks of Evesham had contrary to the rule of law withdrawn the obedience and submission which it had been their practice to show to previous bishops. He demanded that, since he had been, as it were, robbed unjustly of these things, they should now be restored to him, and that the sentence of suspension for contumacy, which he had passed on the monastery and on the abbot and monks of Evesham, should be confirmed. The abbot and monks for their part expressly rejected the claim of the bishop and declared that they would prove the arguments laid before the pope on their behalf and contained in the pope's letter.

249. Therefore, when the said witnesses for both parties had been admitted and had been thoroughly examined sufficiently to establish proof, we finally published the attestations at an appropriate time. When the truth was clearly established from the attestations and detailed discussion of it had been undertaken, as well as from other documentary evidence, the following facts clearly emerged. Abbot R[oger] had received the grace of blessing from William of blessed memory, bishop of Worcester;[3] he had made solemn profession in writing both to him and to the church of Worcester;[4] he had provided

[4] M. Richter, ed., *Canterbury Professions* (Canterbury and York Soc. lxvii: London, 1973), p. 111, prints a form of a profession by an abbot.

conuentui Wigornensis ecclesie die impense benedictionis, ut abbatum lege diocesana subditorum et benedictorum moris est, ministrasse; installationemque ab eodem episcopo per personas ad hoc ab eo delegatas ei factam esse. Item, cum liquido innotesceret felicis recordationis episcopum Iohannem[1] uisitationis officium apud Euesham explentem et quedam statuta in capitulo promulgantem, ab abbate et monachis fuisse benigne admissum, necnon abbatem predictum sinodo quam idem episcopus apud Wigorniam celebrauit tanquam quemlibet ex subiectis abbatibus interfuisse, adeo quod et primum in sinodo locum post episcopum sibi uendicaret. Preterea, cum luce clarius constaret prescriptos abbatem et monachos oleum, crisma et ordines ab antiquis retro temporibus ab episcopis Wigornie percepisse, et omnes in primo aduentu suo apud Euesham cum processione, procuratione et debita reuerentia, de antiqua consuetudine,[2] ab abbate et monachis fuisse receptos, et eos in memoratis abbate et monachis et monasterio quedam alia que iuris ordinarii sunt plerumque exercuisse.

250. Nos, uirorum prudentum consilio freti, supradictum episcopum, tanquam indebite iurisdictionis | sua spoliatum, restituendum decreuimus, et ei ecclesieque sue possessionem iurisdictionis in sepedictis abbate et monachis et eorum monasterio tanquam sibi lege diocesana subditis, salua secundum tenorem mandati apostolici proprietatis causa, sententialiter adiudicamus. Insuper etiam sentenciam suspensionis quam idem episcopus in monasterium de Euesham et monachos ob eorum contumatiam tulerat usque ad condignam satisfactionem confirmauimus. Que quidem satisfactio secundum dispositionem nostram exhibita est, sicut idem episcopus postea coram nobis in iure confessus est. Vt igitur sentencia nostra firmitatis uigorem optineat in posterum, eam presenti scripto et sigillorum nostrorum appositione roborauimus.'

fo. 154rb

251. *Forma satisfactionis contumacie conuentus*
Est autem forma satisfactionis huiusmodi: 'G. Dei gratia episcopus et I. prior Couentr' et R. archiadiaconus Norhamtonie, R. Dei gratia abbati et conuentui Eueshamie, salutem in Domino. Nouerit uniuersitas uestra nos auctoritate nobis a domino papa commissa obseruato iuris ordine confirmasse sentenciam suspensionis quam dominus Wigorn'

---

[1] Master John of Coutances, el. ?Jan., cons. 20 Oct. 1196, d. 24 or 25 Sept. 1198. He had been previously dean of Rouen and archdeacon of Oxford; Greenway, *Fasti*, ii. 100.
[2] See above, 198 and n.

hospitality for the representatives of the church of Worcester on the day the benediction was bestowed, as abbots who are subject to diocesan law are accustomed to do when they receive blessing; and his installation in office had been undertaken by the same bishop through the agency of priests chosen by him for this purpose. It was also well known that bishop John[1] of happy memory had been kindly admitted by the abbot and monks, when carrying out the duty of a visitation at Evesham and promulgating certain statutes in the chapter. The said abbot had also been present at a synod, which the same bishop celebrated at Worcester, like any other subject abbot, and indeed to the extent that he claimed his position next to the bishop in the synod. Moreover, it has been made manifestly clear that the said abbot and monks have received oil, chrism, and orders from the bishops of Worcester since the earliest times and that all the bishops on their first coming to Evesham were received by abbot and monks according to ancient tradition with a procession, hospitality and due reverence;[2] and that the bishops had generally exercised other rights possessed by the ordinary over the said abbot, monks and monastery. 250. We, therefore, relying on the counsel of wise men, have decided to make restoration to the said bishop on the grounds that he has been unjustly robbed of his jurisdiction, and we give formal judgment that he possess jurisdiction over the said abbot, monks and monastery on the grounds that they are subject to him under diocesan law, without prejudice, as is said in the papal mandate, to the case of ownership. Furthermore, we have confirmed the sentence of suspension that the same bishop passed on the monastery and monks of Evesham for contumacy, until the appropriate penance has been done. This penance has been specified to accord with our requirements, as the bishop himself later lawfully accepted in our presence. In order that our judgment should possess permanent validity, we have ratified it in the present document by affixing our seals to it.'

251. *The terms of the convent's atonement for contumacy*
The terms of the atonement are as follows: 'G[eoffrey] by the grace of God bishop, and J[orbertus] prior of Coventry, and R[?Robert] archdeacon of Northampton, to R[oger], by the grace of God abbot, and the convent of Evesham, greetings in the Lord. Let it be known that, by the authority entrusted to us by the pope, having duly observed the rule of law, we have confirmed the sentence of suspension which the bishop of Worcester promulgated against you

episcopus in uos et monasterium uestrum propter inobedienciam uestram promulgauit. Que iuxta tenorem mandati domini pape usque ad condignam satisfactionem est obseruanda. Licet autem in uos pro delicti uestri qualitate durius forsan esset animaduertendum, mitius tamen uobiscum agere uolentes, modum satisfactionis sub hac forma temperauimus, uidelicet ut monasterium uestrum et tota congregatio uestra ab illa hora qua dominus Wigorn' satisfactionem de delicto uestro recepturus ad monasterium uestrum accesserit ab omni cesset offitio diuino et campanarum pulsatione per triduum continuum. Quo expleto, assumantur de congregatione uestra tresdecim monachi qui diuina celebrent in ecclesia uestra per tres septimanas continuas ad maius altare, dumtaxat aliis omnibus preter predictos | tresdecim toto illo tempore ab omni diuino offitio cessantibus. Completis uero illis tribus septimanis, predicti tresdecim per tres alias septimanas ab omni diuino offitio cessabunt, ceteris omnibus qui prius cessauerant ad officium diuinum restitutis.

fo. 154va

252. Decreuimus etiam ut in aduentu domini Wigornensis ei ad ianuam maiorem abbatie uestre nudis pedibus omnes occurratis ibique, coram eo prostrati, de commisso uestro ueniam humiliter postuletis, presentibus et astantibus cum eo quot et quibus uoluerit uiris religiosis presbiteris et clericis et seruientibus. Deinde capitulum uestrum una cum eodem capitulo ingressi cum uiris religiosis quotquot episcopus secum ducere uoluerit, singuli singulas ab eodem recipiatis disciplinas. Hunc autem satisfactionis modum procuratori uestro sentencialiter iniunximus, et uniuersitati uestre benigne suspiciendum et humiliter obseruandum mandamus. Valete.'

253. *Sentencia pro ecclesia Eueshamensi lata in possessorio iuditio de iurisdictione Vallis*

Forma autem sentencie pro nobis late est huiusmodi: 'Omnibus sancte matris ecclesie filiis, illi qui prius, salutem. Litteras domini pape Innocentii tercii in hec uerba suscepimus: "Innocentius et cetera, ut prius". Harum igitur auctoritate cum partibus presentibus causa prenominata in nostra uentilaretur presentia. Dominus episcopus inter cetera proposuit quod episcopi Wigorn' et eorum officiales causas matrimoniales et sacrilegii de parrochianis monachorum in Valle consistentibus, tractare et diffinire solebant, quibus cognitionibus monachi preter iuris ordinem ipsum spoliauerunt.

and your monastery because of your disobedience. This must be observed in accordance with the terms of the pope's mandate until amends have been made. Although a harsher punishment should perhaps have been meted out to you in view of the nature of your sin, nevertheless, wishing to deal gently with you, we have moderated the atonement in the following terms. From the moment that the bishop of Worcester arrives at your monastery to receive penance for your sin, your monastery and your whole congregation is to cease all divine services and the ringing of the bells for three whole days. When this time has passed, thirteen monks are to be taken from your congregation to celebrate divine office in your church at the high altar for three successive weeks, while all the other monks except these thirteen are to take no part in any divine service for the whole of that time. When the three weeks are over, those thirteen monks will for three further weeks take no part in any divine services, while those who have abstained previously will resume divine services.

252. We have also decided that on the bishop of Worcester's arrival you are all to meet him at the great gate of your abbey barefooted, and there, after prostrating yourselves before him, are with humility to ask his pardon for your wrongdoing, and you are to do this in the presence of whichever and however many religious, priests, clerks and servants as the bishop chooses to witness the event. Then you are to enter your chapter-house together with the bishop and with as many religious as he chooses to take with him, and are one by one to receive chastisement from him. We have instructed your proctor on the manner of your atonement in the terms of the sentence, and we command your whole community to undergo it in good heart, and observe it with humility. Farewell.'

253. *The sentence in the possessory case in favour of the church of Evesham concerning jurisdiction over the Vale*
The terms of the sentence given in our favour are as follows. 'To all the sons of holy mother church, as before, greetings. We have received letters of Pope Innocent III, in these words: "Innocent, etc. (as before)". This case was heard in our presence on the authority of these letters, with both parties in attendance. The bishop submitted, amongst other things, that the bishops of Worcester and their officials had been accustomed to hearing and deciding matrimonial disputes and cases of sacrilege amongst the monks' parishioners living in the Vale, and that knowing this the monks have, contrary to the rule of

Ideoque restitutionem sibi fieri postulauit. Admissis igitur super hiis, prout ordo iuris exigebat, testibus, cum episcopus prenotata que intendebat non probasset, in illo possessorio monachos ab impetitione episcopi, salua proprietatis causa, auctoritate iudiciali absoluimus.'

254. *Relatio iudicum ad dominum papam*

Est autem forma relationis huiusmodi: 'Sanctissimo domino et patri fo. 154vb in Christo karissimo I. | Dei gratia sancte Romane sedis summo pontifici, G. diuina permissione dictus episcopus et I. prior Couentreie et R. archidiaconus Norhampton' salutem, et promptum in omnibus cum humillima subiectione et debita reuerentia famulatum. Receptis sanctitatis uestre litteris in causa que inter dominum Wigorn' et abbatem et monachos de Euesham super statu eorundem monachorum et monasterii sui uertebatur. Eam que ex eisdem litteris consequebatur negotii prosecutionem cum summa diligentia pro modulo discretionis nostre adhibuimus. Ea siquidem quorum tam cognitio quam decisio nobis fuit commissa, licet non sine multo labore et tedio plene, expediuimus. Illa uero quorum inquisitio nobis fuit demandata, diffinitio uero excellentie uestre reseruata, utpote de statu Vallis et de exemptione monasterii de Euesham negotium, in presentia nostra diu et diligenter uentilari fecimus. Et iuxta tenorem commissionis uestre tandem causam ipsam instructam paternitati uestre transmittimus, terminum partibus quo coram uobis sententiam recepture compareant, scilicet diem octabarum beati Martini,[1] prefigentes. Nequid etiam necessarie instructionis desit, transcriptum uestre commissionis cum attestationibus et partium disputationibus sub sigillis nostris, priuilegia quoque originalia ipsorum monachorum, sanctitati uestre transmittimus; in rite actis a nobis dominationi uestre debitum exsoluentes, in secus gestis uel per incuriam omissis insufficientiam qua laborauimus humiliter recognoscentes. Hoc autem ad instantiam partium adicimus quod neutra pars allegationibus in presentia uestra, si placuerit, proponendis renuntiauit. Item et illud exprimendum duximus, quod priuilegia ipsa monachis de Euesham, transcripta uero domino Wigorn', uobis presentanda de utriusque partis

---

[1] 25 Nov. 1205. The year is determined by the passage in 243, above, at n. 1 (p. 244).

law, robbed him of this right. He has accordingly demanded restitution of this right to himself. Witnesses were admitted in this connection as the procedural law demanded, but since the bishop did not prove the case which he brought, we have by our judicial authority acquitted the monks of the bishop's charge concerning possession, save for the case of ownership.'

254. *The report of the judges to the pope*
The terms of the report are as follows: 'To the most holy lord and beloved father in Christ I[nnocent], by the grace of God high pontiff of the holy Roman see, G[eoffrey], by divine permission, bishop, J[orbertus] prior of Coventry and R[?Robert] archdeacon of Northampton, greetings; we are ready to serve you in all things in humble obedience and with due reverence. The letters of your holiness have been received in the case between the bishop of Worcester and the abbot and monks of Evesham concerning the status of these monks and their monastery. We have undertaken the prosecution of the matters which these letters demand with the greatest care as far as our ability allows. Indeed, we have dealt fully with the matters entrusted to us that required both investigation and decision, but not without considerable exertion and fatigue. We have long and diligently examined in court the matters that we were required to investigate, but upon which the decision was to be left to your excellency, namely the status of the Vale and the exemption of the monastery of Evesham. In accordance with the terms of your commission we are now at last despatching to you, father, the case itself fully documented, and have fixed the octave of the blessed Martin[1] as the day for the parties to appear before you to receive sentence. So that no essential documentation should be lacking, we are despatching to your holiness a copy of your commission with the testimony and arguments of the parties under our seals, and also the original privileges of the monks themselves. In due performance of our task we thus discharge our duty to your lordship; where we have fallen short or overlooked anything through negligence we humbly acknowledge the shortcomings of our labours. We add this, at the request of the parties, that neither side has renounced its right to submit its case in your presence, if it chooses. We have also thought it right to point out that, on the agreement of both parties, we have handed over the privileges themselves to the monks of Evesham, with transcripts to the bishop of Worcester, to be presented to you.

fo. 155ʳᵃ consensu tradidimus. Presit | diu et semper prosit uniuersali ecclesie sanctitas uestra.'

255. *De iterata controuersia et dissensione conuentus de subiciendo se iurisdictioni episcopi uel non subiciendo*

Episcopus uero quamuis non posset impedire quominus relatio fieret et causa super proprietate finem sortiretur legittimum, tamen cogitabat monachos seducere, ne uidelicet instarent quod in petitorio iudicio cito sententiaretur, et eos benigne tractauit. Et omnes consuetudines domus eis habere fecit, et statum illorum in melius reformauit, et quoscumque habere potuit ad sumendum cibum secum apud Fladeburie¹ deduxit, et multos seduxit in tantum quod multi dicerent quod bonum erat subici episcopo per quem tam cito talem et tantam status sui consecuti erant reformationem et correctionem; eligentes cum populo quondam Israelitico permanere in seruitute, sicut illi concupierunt sedere in Egipto super ollas carneas,² magis quam tot et tantis laboribus et inediis et forte in uanum tolleratis ad loci sancti et sui ipsius libertatem elaborare. Non attendebant miseri quia ecclesiam liberam immo ingenuam natam ancillare et in seruitutem retrudere est locum sanctum prophanare, quia prophani inhabitatores hec sustinerent dum mortaliter peccando gauderent et epularentur de bonis ecclesie, quibus ipsa defendi deberet ne in seruitutem detruderetur. Nescientes etiamᵃ onera episcopalia: quod,ᵇ uidelicet, non tantum semel in anno, set quotiens opus fuerit secundum canones³ uisitabit episcopus monasteria sibi subiecta, et procuratio uisitationem semper comitatur, et non tantum episcopi set etiam archidiaconi, officiales et ministri eorum in magnum grauamen monasteriorum admittuntur, et equi eorum ad perhendinandum donec per moram ibi meliorentur.⁴ Et etiam redditus monasteriorum clericis episcoporum et archidiaconorum conferri solent, et alia dona importabilia que ᶜnos omnia aliquando sustinuimus, et uicini nostri fo. 155ʳᵇ grauius. Nec intelligentesᶜ quod | episcopi ab abbatibus ut monachos

---

ᵃ *H substitutes* Item *for* Nescientes etiam   ᵇ *H substitutes* in locis non exemptis sicut ualde onerosa quia *for* quod   ᶜ⁻ᶜ exempti grauiter sustinet et *H*

---

¹ The bishops of Worcester had a manor house at Fladbury.
² Exod. 16: 3.
³ Visitation annually was customary, but the canons were vague on this matter, see *Decretum* C 18 qu. 2 c. 29 (Friedberg, i cols. 837–8). By the 13th cent., many bishops were seeking to make their inspections more frequently. In the case of exempt monasteries, the archbishop had the right of visitation. Mauger's seeking an empower-

Long may your holiness reign and always be a blessing to the universal church.'

255. *The dispute renewed and disagreement in the convent over its subjection or non-subjection to the bishop's jurisdiction*

Although the bishop could not prevent the report being made and the case about ownership being decided at law, he nevertheless contemplated winning the monks over to his point of view. His purpose was to prevent their insistence that sentence be passed quickly in the petitory matter, so his treatment of them was kindly. He allowed them to retain all the customs of the house, he improved their status, and he invited those monks he could to dine with him at Fladbury;[1] he thus succeeded in winning many of them over to his point of view. Indeed, he seduced many to such extent that they said that it was a blessing to be subjected to a bishop through whom one could so swiftly obtain so great an improvement and amendment of their status. Like the people of Israel in the past, they were choosing to remain in servitude, just as the Israelites desired to sit by the fleshpots in Egypt,[2] rather than strive for their freedom and that of the holy place by enduring the many great labours and the deprivation to be suffered, perhaps in vain. These wretches did not give heed to the fact that to enslave a church which is free and of noble foundation is to desecrate a sacred place, in that irreverent men dwelling here might maintain this place, while rejoicing in acts of mortal sin and squandering the possessions of the church, with which the church ought to be being protected, not thrust into slavery. They are unaware of the burdens that episcopal authority brings: the bishop will visit the monasteries subject to him not just once a year, but as often as there is need in accordance with the canons,[3] and a visitation always requires hospitality, for not only are bishops admitted but also archdeacons, officials, and their servants, to the considerable inconvenience of the monasteries; then their horses have to be stabled until they are rested by their stay there.[4] Furthermore, it is usual for even the revenue of monasteries to be given to the clerks of bishops and archdeacons, as well as other gifts we cannot afford, which we have had to put up with at times and which our neighbours have suffered from still more seriously. Nor do these monks realize that bishops are

ment (*indulgentia*) to visit Evesham suggests that he had some qualms about the legitimacy of his action.

[4] See above, 198 and n. 2 (p. 206)

deprimerent facillime solent corrumpi, *quod nos aliquando experti sumus. Non intellexerunt etiam* quante* expense sint necessarie ad sequendum conuenticula et uocationes oues* episcoporum, *nec scire uolebant quod* mortaliter peccarent *si scientes et uolentes ecclesie sue adulterum superinducerent cum habeat sponsum, dominum uidelicet Cantuariensem, ecclesie nostre tutorem et nobis perpetuum legatum,[1] cui cura animarum nostrarum a domino papa est commissa, et siquid sinistre partis apud nos compertum fuerit oriri potius eius auribus deferatur quam per alicuius occultam sententiam locus sanctus deprauetur iniuste, ut per eius corrigatur cautelam et industriam. Et qui talem habebant absque onere correctionem qui corrumpi non potest, quasi relinquentes Iesum petierunt Barraban.*[2]

256. Et omnibus diebus uite mee quandocumque ab abbate deprimebamur magis uolebant quidam falsi fratres a non suo iudice episcopo Wigornensi habere correctionem cum predictis oneribus quam a patre suo Cantuariensi archiepiscopo sine omni onere,* cum idem archiepiscopus nostram habeat unicam ecclesiam in Anglia sibi commendatam et ideo specialissimam post Cantuariensem sibi intitulatam. Quare nequaquam omittere poterit quin ad uocationem nostram ad nos ueniat et corrigenda ita corrigat, quod ob defectum eius ad dominum papam recurrere nos non oporteat.

257. Set nec hoc eos terruit, quod ego maxime uerebar, ne si episcopus in nos et monasterium nostrum plenam haberet iurisdictionem ad hoc omnimodis operam daret—sicut magister Willelmus de Verdun[3] summus consiliarius eius sepe dicebat—quod episcopus abbas noster efficeretur, sicut fuit beatus Ecgwinus predecessor eius, fo. 155ᵛᵃ sicut fecerunt episcopi Saresburiensis et Bathoniensis | contra Malbesburiam et Glastoniam, et maximos redditus earundem abbatiarum sibi appropriauerunt.[4]

ᵃ⁻ᵃ *om.* H   ᵇ *et follows in* H   ᶜ *om.* H   ᵈ⁻ᵈ miseri igitur essent et H   ᵉ H *fo. 116ᵛ, which ends here, adds* qui ecclesiam que libera est ancillari permitterent   ᶠ *marg.* Nota optime . . . (*two to three words*) pro archiepiscopo   ᵍ *marg. in scored hand* (*pencil*) Super quondam querel'. Iterum

---

[1] This appears to refer to the activities of Hubert Walter, archbishop of Canterbury, in particular as the 'tutor' (protector) and as legate, in connection with the appeal. Perhaps Thomas also had in mind the original protection for Evesham granted by Pope Constantine and addressed to Archbishop Berhtwald of Canterbury; see below, 318–28, esp. 321, 324.

[2] Cf. Matt. 27: 20.

[3] See above, 217 and n. 1 (p. 222).

[4] Malmesbury was challenged c.1174 by the bishop of Salisbury over the consecration of its abbot: the abbot and convent resisted the challenge and in 1191 acquired the right of

usually very easily bribed by abbots to oppress their monks, something we have ourselves at times experienced. They have also failed to
realize the magnitude of the expenses inevitably incurred in attending
the assemblies and summonses of bishops. They did not want to
know that they were committing mortal sin if knowingly and willingly
they were introducing an adulterer into their church when it is
betrothed already to the archbishop of Canterbury, the protector of
our church and our permanent legate.[1] It is to him that the pope has
entrusted the care of our souls, and if anything wrong is found to have
occurred in our midst it is to his attention that this can be brought,
and this is better than allowing a holy place to be unjustly damaged by
a secret sentence of someone else. The wrong can then be put right
through his prudent and painstaking effort. These men already had a
man who cannot be corrupted to put right what was wrong without
any burden to them, but they are like the men who abandoned Jesus
for Barabbas.[2]

256. Whenever during my time here we were being harassed by the
abbot, certain false brethren wanted to accept correction from the
bishop of Worcester, who was not their judge, with the difficulties I
have mentioned, rather than from their father, the archbishop of
Canterbury, which involved no disadvantage at all. Our monastery is
the only church in England which has been entrusted to the
archbishop, and so it has a special claim upon him after Canterbury.
It follows then that he cannot refuse to come to us at our request and
amend what requires amending, for it would not be right for us to
refer a matter to the pope through any default of the archbishop.

257. However, these brethren were not alarmed by what I particularly feared, that if the bishop were to possess full jurisdiction over us
and our monastery, he would exert himself in every way to achieve
one thing (as Master William de Verdun, his chief adviser, has often
said)[3] that as bishop he might become our abbot, as the blessed
Ecgwine his predecessor was, and as the bishops of Salisbury and
Bath became by their actions against Malmesbury and Glastonbury,
appropriating for themselves the very large revenues of those abbeys.[4]

visitation only by a *legate a latere*; Peter of Blois, *Epp.*, ed. Giles, no. 68 (*PL* ccvii, cols.
1456–9); and *Reg. Malmesbury*, i. 370–1. In 1190 the bishop of Salisbury renewed his
claims, not only for the abbot's profession of obedience. He summoned the abbot of
Malmesbury 'to lay aside the very name and staff of a pastor' (*sed de ipso nomine pastoris
ponendo simul et baculo*); *The Chronicle of Richard of Devizes of the Time of King Richard the
First*, ed. J. T. Appleby (NMT, 1963), p. 14. But the popes came to Malmesbury's rescue,
Celestine III exempting them from the bishop's jurisdiction in 1191 (JL 16748). Savaric,

258. Nec propter periculum amissionis iurisdictionis Vallis moti sunt, nescientes quia impossibile est monasterium subiectum esse episcopo et Vallem exemptam, que tantundem ualet quantum residuum abbatie. Sola enim correctio per censuram ecclesiasticam quam habemus in malefactores nostros, quam alii monachi non habent, inestimabilis est, quam nos habere non possemus nisi curam animarum et libertatem Vallis optineremus. Prudentiores uero hec uidebant, et ideo episcopo non consentiebant.

bishop of Bath, a poor see, had engineered an arrangement whereby the abbot of Glastonbury, Henry de Soilli, was given the bishopric of Worcester in 1193, so allowing Savaric to set up a see in the rich abbey of Glastonbury, which he did in 1197, becoming its abbot as well; see *Adami de Domerham, Historia de rebus gestis Glastoniensibus*, ed. T. Hearne, 2 vols. (London, 1727), ii. 352–88, and Cheney, *Innocent III*, pp. 220–5.

258. These brethren were not perturbed by the danger of losing jurisdiction over the Vale. They did not know that it is impossible for the monastery to be subject to the bishop and for the Vale to be exempt from his jurisdiction, for it can only remain intact in so far as the abbey remains so. There is one sole right which we possess, that of correction with ecclesiastical censure against those who would harm us, which other monks do not have, and this is a priceless possession, but we could not have this if we did not possess the care of souls and the liberty of the Vale. The more prudent monks perceived this and accordingly did not agree with the bishop.

259. *Incipit particula tercia de itinere abbatis et Thome monachi et causis itineris eorundem ad curiam Romanam*

Verumptamen tempore restitutionis episcopi dominus abbas et ego absentes fuimus. Publicatis enim attestationibus, quasi certificati eramus de restitutione episcopi quoad iurisdictionem in monasterio nostro. Abbas uero timens ne episcopo restituto eum coram ipso accusaremus, quamuis hoc eum timere non oporteret propter predictam promissionem nostram, sicut ex post facto claruit, et nos tunc ei sepius hoc expressimus. Tamen preparauit se ut curiam Romanam adiret, per hoc et communem ecclesie utilitatem ueram causam itineris sui occultans. Timuit enim maxime compromissionem quam feceramus in dominum archiepiscopum et coarbitros suos, coram quibus parati eramus, immo instanter petiuimus, eum accusare usque ad depositionem. Quam compromissionem effugere uolens et contra eam aliquid impetrare, cupiens ut se a manibus nostris liberaret, nequaquam se ab itinere desiturum predixit.

260. Conuentus uero eius malitiam non ignorans nequaquam se et causam ecclesie sue ei committebat. Set abbatem ad hoc induxit, licet uix, quod me, quia iurisperitus eram et merita cause nostre noueram, de communi assensu procuratorem totius cause coram domino papa constituerunt.

fo. 155vb **261.** Set nec abbas se michi committebat, set socium | itineris quendam clericum suum Thomam de Warrewike michi dedit, ipse uero lento pede subsequebatur. Et antequam iter arriperemus, dominus abbas et ego et predictus clericus iurauimus adinuicem quod in causis ecclesie tam realibus quam personalibus quilibet nostrum alteri in hoc itinere fideliter se haberet, quod nequaquam illi michi obseruauerunt, sicut ex post facto plenius uobis patebit.

262. Fratres uero Deo et beate Marie et beato Ecgwino et aliis patronis huius ecclesie et michi causam suam et ecclesie sue cum summa deuotione et fletu committebant. Ego uero de misericordia Dei et beate Marie et predictorum patronorum nostrorum meritis et

PART THREE

259. *The journey of the abbot and the monk Thomas, and the reasons for their journey to the Roman curia*

To resume: at the time the bishop's rights were restored, the abbot and I were away. The evidence had been published, and we had been informed of the restoration of the bishop so far as jurisdiction over our monastery was concerned. So the abbot, now that the bishop was restored, was fearful that we might make accusations against him before the bishop, though he should not have feared this because we had previously promised not to do so. Later events revealed that his fears were groundless, but we had often to reassure him of this. Nevertheless he prepared for his journey to the Roman curia, concealing the true reason for his journey both because of this fear and for the common good of the church. In particular he feared the agreement which we had made with the archbishop and his arbitrators in whose presence we had been prepared—in fact had urgently requested permission—to make accusations against him to secure his deposition. It was because he wished to escape the effects of this agreement and to gain some advantage against it, and because he desired to extricate himself from our clutches, that he declared that he had no intention whatsoever of giving up the journey.

260. The convent, well aware of the abbot's ill will, had no intentions of entrusting themselves and the cause of their church to him. They therefore persuaded him, though with some difficulty, to make me, by common consent, proctor in the whole case before the pope because of my experience in the law and knowledge of the merits of our case.

261. However, the abbot distrusted me, so he gave me one of his clerks, Thomas of Warwick, to accompany me on the journey, while he himself was to follow behind at a slower pace. Before we set off the abbot, the clerk, and I swore a mutual oath to be loyal to each other on the journey, in the cases of the church both about immoveable and moveable property, but they completely failed to observe this oath in their behaviour towards me, as later events will reveal to you.

262. The brethren tearfully committed their cause and that of their church in heartfelt prayer to God, the blessed Mary, the blessed Ecgwine, the other patrons of the church, and to me. As for myself, I put my trust in the mercy of God, in the merits of blessed Mary and

fratrum orationibus confisus iter michi iniunctum deuotissime obediendo suscepi, cum lacrimis et eiulatu, adiungens quod nisi in causa proprietatis obtinerem irrediturus irem, et nunquam nisi in regno celorum eorum faties uiderem. Proposueram enim si uictus fuissem me apud aliquem locum religiosum in urbe tantum dampnum ecclesie nostre per me illatum deflendo diem clausurum extremum. Tota enim fere patria, de uictoria nostra desperans, per presumptionem meam et superbiam tantam causam et tam arduam supra uires nostras nos fuisse aggressos asserebat.

263. *De primo aduentu Thome monachi et socii eius ad curiam, et quid tunc ibi egerint*

Accepta itaque benedictione, ualedicens fratribus, in die sancti Michaelis[1] cum predicto clerico et duobus seruientibus in duobus equis iter arripui. Et quadragesimo die[2] recessus nostri per gratiam Dei ego et clericus cum equo nostro, quia ipse iam tres mutauerat, urbem sumus ingressi.

264. Et cum ad hoc laboraremus ut litteras ad hoc reuocatorias obtineremus quod iudicium possessorium in Anglia suspenderetur, et super eodem, quia illud maxime timebamus, cum iudicio petitorio ad dominum papam fieret relatio. Quadam | die, cum ad hoc multas induxissem rationes, dominus papa super eo reuocatorias michi benigne concessit. Ego autem super hoc letus effectus optuli domino pape cuppam argenteam sex marcarum. Et cum quadam die sollicitarem illum super litteris illis, dixit, 'Audiuimus quod abbas uester detentus sit in itinere. Vade et inquire ubi et a quo. Et liberabimus eum, et tunc habebis litteras tuas.' Et cum adhuc instarem proterue, dicens quia littere episcopi non fatiebant mentionem de nostris prioribus et ideo debui habere reuocatorias. Dominus papa iratus respondit michi, 'Ex certa scientia[3] dedimus tales litteras episcopo, et ideo nolimus eas reuocare'; et adiecit, 'Est modo responsum tibi.' Et ego, 'Vtique, domine, responsum est, sed de potestate.' Et dominus papa, 'Et non est de iure responsum?' Et ego, 'Domine, nescio.' Et dominus papa commotus precepit ut tacerem et recederem.

fo. 156ra

---

[1] 29 Sept. 1204. The year is determined by working back from the date of the pope's sentence on 24 Dec. 1205.

[2] ? 7 Nov., but the reference is biblical.

[3] Cf. Krynen, *L'empire du roi*, pp. 398–9, who sees its use here in a papal/monarchical context, as, indeed, part of the 'plenitudo potestatis'. See above, 229 and n. 1 (p. 232).

these patrons of ours, and in the prayers of the brethren; and I undertook the journey that I had been instructed to make in loyal obedience, with tears and lamentation. I added these words: that I was setting off never to return, never to see their faces again till we met in the kingdom of heaven, unless I was successful in the case over ownership. It was my intention, should I be defeated, to end my days at some religious house in Rome, mourning the great injury that I had inflicted upon our church. Indeed, virtually the whole locality, despairing of our victory, was asserting that it was through my presumption and pride that we had taken on a great and difficult contest beyond our strength to sustain.

263. *The first visit of the monk Thomas and his companion to the curia, and their actions there at that time*
Having received a blessing and said goodbye to the brethren, I set out on Michaelmas day[1] with the clerk I have mentioned and two servants on two horses. Forty days after we set out for Rome,[2] the clerk and I, by God's grace, entered Rome with our horse, the clerk having changed horses three times by then.

264. We now made efforts to obtain a letter of revocation to have the possessory judgment in England suspended and—we were particularly anxious about this—to have it referred to the pope along with the petitory judgment. Since I had produced many arguments for this to be done, one day the pope kindly granted me a revocatory letter allowing this. Overjoyed at this I made a gift to the pope of a silver cup worth six marks. However, when one day I pressed him for that letter, he replied, 'We have heard that your abbot has been detained on the journey. Go and find out where he is and by whom he has been arrested. We shall free him and you will then have your letter.' I still insisted somewhat boldly on having it, saying that the bishop's letter made no mention of our former judges and that I therefore ought to have the letter of revocation. The pope replied angrily to me, 'It was from certain knowledge[3] that we gave such a letter to the bishop, and we should not therefore wish to revoke it;' and he added, 'You now have my reply.' I retorted, 'A reply has certainly been given, my lord, but from a position of power!' To this the pope replied, 'And is that not a just reply?' I said, 'I do not know, my lord.' The pope, offended by this remark, told me to hold my tongue and leave him.

265. *De recessu eorundem a curia ut liberarent abbatem captum in Francia, et de dolo abbatis contra Thomam monachum et aduentu abbatis ad curiam Romanam*

Et recessimus in octabis sancti Hyllarii,[1] et cum uenissemus Placentiam[2] audiuimus quod abbas noster captus fuerat aput[a] Cabilonem.[3] Taceo causam captionis sue quia de ea certus non sum, cum ibi tunc presens non fuerim. Timeo etenim uerenda patris mei detegere, ubi nulla utilitas sequitur ex reuelatione, nec graue animarum uel ecclesie dispendium prouenit ex[b] taciturnitate. Tunc mansimus ibi per tres dies ut pleniores de abbate audiremus rumores, quia ciuitas illa in biuio posita est.[4] Tertia die audiuimus quod liberatus erat, licet cum magna rerum suarum et pecunie iactura, et quod iam Lumbardiam fuerat ingressus. Tunc communicato consilio ego et socius meus diuisi sumus abinuicem, utrique nostrum ab altero fide data quod quicumque nostrum prius abbati obuiaret alteri nuntiaret. Et ego recessi Papiam, ille uero recessit Vercellum, et obuiauit abbati nec fo. 156rb renuntiauit michi. Abbas | uero ut a me declinaret, per Mediolanum deuiando iter fatiens, per aliquot dies ibidem moram fecit, et post Diem Cinerum Romam recessit.[5]

266. *De secundo aduentu Thome monachi ad curiam et de insidiis abbatis ut eum occideret et de litteris quas abbas contra eum et conuentum impetrauit*

Quod cum michi uigilanti, quia res pro anima michi erat, innotesceret, magis timui, et quamuis periculum michi immineret[6] et 'angustie michi essent undique',[7] tamen indui mente uirum et,[8] accinctis renibus, accepto baculo in manibus, confisus in Domino lento pede secutus sum eum. Et quinto die post eum ingressus sum ciuitatem, occulte tamen, uestibus diuaricatis, et tamen in ipso ingressu porte ciuitatis a quibusdam ex familia abbatis cognitus sum. Ego uero, quia ualde contremuit eum anima mea, dedi quandam summam pecunie cuidam aduocato curie quem prius noueram, qui si abbas me comprehenderet dedit michi fidem quod me liberaret.

267. Et sic securior factus accessi ad abbatem, et inueni eum

---

[a] aput *added in margin* (s. xiii[i])   [b] ex *interlined* (s. xiii[i])

[1] 20 Jan. 1205.
[2] Piacenza was at the cross roads of Lombardy. Roads from it led eastwards to Bologna and southwards, via Lucca and Siena, to Viterbo and Rome.
[3] Chalon-sur-Saône on the main route south to the Alpine passes and northern Italy.
[4] See n. 2 above.

265. *Their departure from the curia to free the abbot who had been arrested in France; the abbot's treachery against the monk Thomas, and the abbot's arrival at the Roman curia*

We left on the octave of St Hilary,[1] and on arriving at Piacenza[2] we heard that our abbot had been arrested at Chalon.[3] I do not mention the reason for his arrest because I am not sure why it occurred, not having been there at the time. I am fearful of disclosing the 'holy acts' of my father when no benefit accrues from the revelation, and no serious harm to souls or to the church follows from remaining silent. We stayed there for three days so that we could hear more detailed reports of what had happened to the abbot, for that city is situated where two roads meet.[4] On the third day we heard that he had been freed, though at great cost to his personal possessions and money, and that he had now entered Lombardy. Then after discussion, my companion and I went our separate ways, each of us promising the other that whoever met up with the abbot first would inform the other. I left for Pavia, he for Vercelli: there he met the abbot, but he did not inform me. To avoid meeting me the abbot turned aside and travelled by way of Milan. He stayed there for several days and after Ash Wednesday left for Rome.[5]

266. *The second visit of the monk Thomas to the curia; the abbot's plot to kill him, and the letters that the abbot obtained against him and the convent*

As this was a matter that concerned my soul, I kept alert and so learnt what had happened. I was accordingly more anxious, but though danger and difficulties threatened me,[6] and 'there were troubles on all sides',[7] I adopted the spirit of a man[8] and, preparing myself for action, took my staff in my hand, trusted in the Lord, and followed the abbot cautiously. I entered Rome five days after he had arrived there, but secretly and in disguise, yet the moment I entered the city gate I was recognized by some of the abbot's household. I was at heart very afraid of him so I gave a sum of money to one of the advocates at the curia whom I had got to know previously, and he promised to bail me out if the abbot arrested me.

267. So it was with more confidence that I visited the abbot, but I

---

[5] 23 Feb. 1205.
[6] This may be a quotation (cf. above, **202**), but it has not been traced.
[7] Cf. Dan. 13: 22 (Sus. 22).
[8] This is probably a quotation, but we have not been able to identify it.

iacentem in lecto (minuerat enim sibi). Et eo salutato non respondit
michi uerbum. Et dixerunt michi famuli eius ut recederem ne
molestus essem domino suo; et recessi. In crastino uero, iterum
assumpto mecum aduocato meo cum quibusdam testibus et relictis
eis eminus extra domum ut uiderent me ingredientem et quererent
me si non egrederer; accessi ad abbatem; petita tamen tunc licentia, et
eo salutato non respondit, et adieci, 'Domine, si ita diuisi fuerimus
cum sim procurator cause nostre et expensas magnas fecero, et uos,
sicut decet, maiores, male erit ecclesie nostre. Quare melius est si
placet uobis quod moram fatiam uobiscum sicut unus de seruientibus
uestris.'

268. Ipse uero tumidas exarsit in iras, et dixit, 'Cum odio me habeas
et inimicus meus sis et proditor pessimus, admitterem ego te in
domum meam ut me occideres?' Et contumelias et probra et
fo. 156ᵛᵃ obprobria | multa dixit michi. Et ego blande et leniter dixi,
'Domine, non sum proditor, nec hic timere me debetis, cum
iurauerim uobis ante recessum meum ab Anglia me uobis fidelem
fore in itinere isto.' Ille uero post multas altercationes, quasi ueneno
effuso mitigatus, dixit, 'Si fidelis es, sta nobiscum; si infidelis,
recede.' Et ego dixi, 'Quia fidelis sum, maneo uobiscum.' Et mansi
ibi per quindecim dies manducans et bibens, set abbas non erat
michi loquens. Verumptamen prima die peruenit ad me edictum
abbatis ne egrederer ostium tabernaculi,¹ nec curiam ingrederer nisi
cum eo. Hoc ideo fecit ne audientiis interessem et aliquibus litteris
eius contradicerem.² Perquisiuit enim interim indulgentiam quod
liceret ei appellatione remota corrigere irregulares excessus monachorum suorum, et aliam quod liceret ei expellere a domo sua
appellatione remota duos pacis perturbatores, unum medicum et
alium iurisperitum, bone memorie magistrum Thomam de North-
wich³ et me uolens ab hac domo eicere.

---

¹ Cf. Exod. 33: 10; a somewhat ironic comment.
² A reference to the courts of the 'audientia publica' and of the 'audientia litterarum
contradictarum'. In the public audience, mandates were read out, enabling the proctors to
make an objection if they thought their clients would be adversely affected. The auditor
then transferred the proceedings to the auditor of contradicted letters, who, if he accepted
the objection, drew up *cautiones*, letters stating that the recipients were exempt from any
adverse effects from the letters in question. The auditor of contradicted letters was also the
papal functionary who supervised the arrangements for the appointment of judges
delegate. The procedure was for each party to choose a judge and for the auditor to
provide the third, getting the parties to agree on the place of the hearing. For further
details and examples of the practice, see J. Sayers, 'Canterbury proctors at the court of

found him lying in bed for he had been letting blood. I greeted him but he made me no reply. His servants told me to leave in case I upset their master, so I did so. Again the next day I took my advocate with me and some men to witness what happened. I left them at some distance from the house so that they might see me entering and then come asking for me if I did not come out again. This time I asked permission before visiting the abbot, but when I greeted him he made no reply, so I added, 'My lord, if you and I stay apart, I as proctor in this case will incur considerable expenses, and you, as befits your position, even greater, and this will ill serve our church. It would be better then, if you agree, for me to stay with you as one of your servants.'

268. The abbot, ablaze with growing anger, replied 'Since you regard me with hatred and are my foe and a most evil traitor, am I to admit you into my house for you to murder me?' And he hurled copious insults, abuse, and reproach at me. My reply was amicable and conciliatory: 'My lord, I am not a traitor, and you ought not to fear me in this place for I swore to you before my departure from England that I would be loyal to you on this journey.' At first he argued a good deal, but then, calming down as if the poison had left him, he said, 'If you are loyal, stay with me; if not, then depart.' I replied, 'I am loyal, so I will stay with you.' I remained there for fifteen days, boarding, but the abbot avoided speaking to me. However, on my first day there I received a command from the abbot not to go out of the door of the lodgings,[1] and not to go into the curia unless it was with him. His intention was to prevent me from attending the audiences and objecting to any of his letters.[2] For he was seeking an empowerment in the mean time to correct the unlawful excesses of his monks, without any appeal being allowed, and a further permission to expel from his house, without appeal, two disturbers of the peace; one of these was a doctor, the other a man experienced in the law, for it was Master Thomas de Northwich of blessed memory,[3] and me, whom he wished to banish from his house.

Audientia Litterarum Contradictarum', *Traditio*, xxii (1966), 311–45 (repr. in *Law and Records in Medieval England* (Variorum: London, 1988), ch. iii, with addenda); and ead., 'The court of *Audientia Litterarum Contradictarum* revisited', in *Forschungen zur Reichs-, Papst-und Landesgeschichte: Peter Herde zum 65. Geburtstag*, ed. K. Borchardt and E. Bünz (Stuttgart, 1998), pp. 411–27. For the formularies of the court, see P. Herde, *Audientia Litterarum Contradictarum* (2 vols., Bibliothek des Deutschen Historischen Instituts in Rom, xxxi–ii: Tübingen, 1970).
[3] Not in *BRUO*, or *BRUC*. See above, **193**, and below, **395**, **436**, and **446**.

269. *Qualiter Thomas monachus reconciliatus sit abbati in curia et quid postea ibi egerint et impetrauerint*

Erat autem ibi tunc quidam capellanus abbatis Henricus de Coleham monachus, cuius memoria in benedictione sit pro eo quod animam meam ibi saluauerit. Qui cum audiret abbatem insidiantem uite mee, quadam nocte cum simul iaceremus, sicut semper consueuimus in itinere illo, non enim de die ausus fuit loqui michi, flens et eiulans dixit michi, 'Doleo super te, frater mi; quere diffugium si potes, quia abbas "querit animam tuam".'[1] Contra multas insidias abbatis me premuniens, et contra modos insidiarum me reddens cautiorem, tunc tradidi ei quadraginta solidos sterlingorum,[2] ne ab*[a]* abbate eis spoliarer si forte manus in me iniceret.

fo. 156vb

270. In crastino post meridiem allocutus est me | abbas sub hac forma, 'Pessime proditor, nondum completa est malitia tua? Quousque durabis in impietate tua? Ecce nichil possumus impetrare in curia ista te impediente. Per reginam angelorum uindicabor in te.' Et ego paratus fui cum cultello quem accinxeram lateri meo si manus michi iniecisset defendere me.

271. Et premunitus et premeditatus securius respondi, 'Domine pater, utinam amouissetis omnes proditores a latere uestro, qui suam imperitiam et insuffitientiam ad negotia complenda per proditionem quam michi imponunt excusant; et utinam nossetis fidelitatem meam et diligentiam in negotiis agendis.' Et ille quasi mitigatus respondit, 'Si fidelis es et sapiens, ut dicis, dic quid facto opus sit in curia ista.' Et cum petissem super hoc deliberationem, suscepit me in ampliorem gratiam. Et tunc in breui impetrauimus confirmationem omnium priuilegiorum in preiuditium aliorum conceptorum quibus usi eramus, et etiam usum illorum que in preiudicium aliorum non sunt concepta. Vnde abbas ibi mitra et aliis insigniis episcopalibus coram domino papa pluries usus est.[3] Impetrauimus etiam optimam indulgentiam appellandi a quolibet grauamine, in qua plura specialia continentur.

272. Set contra episcopum, quia iam significauerat episcopus domino pape quod pro eo lata fuit sentencia in iudicio possessorio, pendente

---

[a] ab *interlined (s. xiii¹)*

[1] 2 Kgs. 16: 11 (2 Sam. 16: 11).
[2] These were probably shillings sterling. For the sterling money of England, and its rates in other currencies before 1300 (including the *denari provisini* of Rome), see P. Spufford, *Handbook of Medieval Exchange* (Royal Historical Society, Guides and Handbooks, xiii: London, 1986), pp. 198, 208–10.

269. *Thomas the monk is reconciled to the abbot in the curia; their actions and petitions there*

At this time one of the abbot's chaplains was in Rome, the monk Henry de Coleham—may his memory be blessed for he saved my life there. He had heard that the abbot was plotting against my life, so one night when we were all in bed (for we both shared a bed as we always did on that journey) he spoke to me sadly and in tears, for he had not dared to talk to me during the day: 'I am sorry for you, my brother; make your escape if you can, for the abbot is "planning to kill you".'[1] He forewarned me against many plots of the abbot, and helped me to be on my guard against the kinds of plot planned. I then entrusted him with forty shillings of silver coin[2] to prevent my being robbed of them if I happened to fall into the abbot's hands.

270. The next afternoon the abbot spoke to me in these terms: 'You most evil traitor, is there no end to your ill-will? How long will you persist in your wickedness? Don't you see, we shall fail to achieve anything in that court while you obstruct proceedings! I swear by the Queen of the Angels that I will punish you.' I was ready to defend myself with the knife which I had belted to my side if he laid hands on me.

271. Forewarned and prepared in mind, I replied with confidence, 'My father, I only wish you had removed from your presence all the traitors who excuse their own inexperience and inability to fulfil the business by accusing me of betrayal; if only you would recognize my loyalty and ability to handle this business.' The abbot, somewhat pacified, answered, 'If you are loyal and knowledgeable, as you say, tell me what must be done in this court.' When I asked for freedom to act in this business he was more friendly towards me. It was not long before we petitioned for confirmation of all the privileges we had used which were perceived as prejudicial to other privileges, and also for the use of those which were not thought to be prejudicial to the other privileges. After this the abbot often wore the mitre as well as other episcopal insignia in the presence of the pope.[3] We also sought the best empowerment for appealing against any hardship suffered, and many detailed provisions were contained in that concession.

272. However, we were not able to impetrate anything against the bishop because he had already indicated to the pope that sentence had been given in his favour in the possessory judgment, while the case

---

[3] One of these privileges was doubtless the right of the abbot to wear the mitre, etc., granted by Pope Celestine III; see below, **339–41**, for the text.

relatione super proprietate, nichil potuimus impetrare, nec contra compromissionem pro qua uenerat, quia iuramento firmata fuit.*

273. Acceptis etiam mutuo quadringentis marcis, uisitauimus dominum papam in ualentia centum librarum sterlingorum, et cardinales et curiam in ualentia centum marcarum,[1] qui hec noluerunt accipere donec multis ex eis constaret quod causam non haberemus in curia.

274. *De recessu abbatis a curia, et mora Thome monachi apud Bononiam*
Cum itaque intemperies aeris instaret et moram fecissemus per sex ebdomadas, in crastino octabarum Pasce cum licentia et benedictione | domini pape recessimus ab urbe. Ex consilio etiam domini pape et domini Hugulini cardinalis, postmodum episcopi Hostiensis,[2] quem prius elegeram (quia iurisperitus erat) ecclesie nostre et cause nostre tutorem et protectorem, relictus sum ego Bolonie cum benedictione abbatis donec relatio ueniret. Et ut ibi plenius de causa nostra instruerer, et moram ibi faciens per dimidium annum reuera multum ibi profeci, audiens cotidie leges et canones.[3]

fo. 157ra

275. *De crudelitate et proditione abbatis circa magistrum Adam Sortes monachum et miseria et laboribus eiusdem Ade in itinere*
Abbas uero uersus Angliam properauit. Et cum ueniret Vercellum occurrit ei magister Adam Sortes monacus noster. In litteratura adprime eruditus, qui antequam esset monacus rexerat scolas artium liberalium per multos annos.[4] Qui missus fuerat a conuentu ad prosequendam appellationem quam fecerant contra sententiam iudicum in Anglia quam tulerant in possessorio iuditio super iurisdictione monasterii pro episcopo. Abbas autem cum cognouisset causam aduentus sui, sciens quod dominus papa in nulla parte reuocaret iurisdictionem iudicum, dixit ei ut reuerteretur cum eo. Ille uero, ut erat simplex et iustus, sciens quia omnia speranda sunt a patre monasterii, uolens regulariter uiuere,[5] tres marcas argenti tradidit

---

ᵃ firmata fuit *erased, written over, and* fuit *extended into the margin (s. xv)*

[1] See above, **269** n. 2. The mark sterling equalled 160 pence or 13s. 4d.; see Spufford, *Medieval Exchange,* p. 198.
[2] A relative of Pope Innocent III, and later elected pope as Gregory IX; see Maleczek, pp. 126–33. He signs as bishop of Ostia by 8 June 1206.
[3] On the law school and teaching at Bologna, see C. Calcaterra, *Alma Mater Studiorum: L'Università di Bologna nella storia della cultura e della civiltà* (Bologna,1948), pp. 21–45, and *Lexicon des Mittelalters,* ii (Munich and Zurich, 1983), pp. 370–87, esp. 374–87.
[4] Abbot Norreis deprived him of the office of sacrist in 1207, and in that year he became prior of Evesham's dependency of Penwortham, remaining there until 1213, when he

for ownership was awaiting decision; nor were we able to petition for anything against the compromise of the arbiters for which the bishop had come, for this had been confirmed under oath.

273. Having acquired a loan of four hundred marks, we visited the pope with a gift worth a hundred pounds of silver coin, and the cardinals and curia with gifts worth a hundred marks,[1] but they refused to accept them until most of them were convinced that we had no case pending in the curia.

274. *The abbot leaves the curia, and Thomas the monk stays at Bologna*

As bad weather persisted, we remained in Rome for six weeks, but the day after the octave of Easter [18 April 1205] we left Rome with the pope's permission and his blessing. After discussion with the pope and Cardinal Hugolinus, later bishop of Ostia,[2] whom I had previously chosen, because of his experience in the law, to be the guardian and protector of our church and our cause, I was left at Bologna with the abbot's blessing until the report should arrive. This was so that I should receive fuller instruction on our case, and, remaining there for six months, I in fact gained much from doing so, for I attended lectures every day on civil and canon law.[3]

275. *The abbot's cruel treatment and betrayal of the monk, Master Adam Sortes, and Adam's suffering and troubles on the journey*

The abbot hurried home to England. On arriving at Vercelli he was met there by one of our monks, Master Adam Sortes. He was extremely learned in literary pursuits and, before he became a monk, had for many years ruled a school of liberal arts.[4] He had been sent by the convent to prosecute the appeal that they had made against the sentence of the judges [delegate] in England passed in favour of the bishop in the possessory judgment concerning jurisdiction over the monastery. The abbot, discovering the reason for Adam's arrival, and believing that the pope would not revoke the jurisdiction of the judges in any respect, told him to return with him. Adam, a guileless and just man, believing that one could completely trust the father of a monastery and desiring to live according to the Rule,[5] handed over to the abbot the three marks of silver which he

presumably died; *HRH*, p. 94. His previous career as a scholar and teacher before he became a monk of Evesham is not known, but he was probably an Oxford master; see *BRUO*, iii. 1730. For further mentions of him, see below, 316, 371, 384, 386, 435, 436, 446, 499, and 525.

[5] i.e. obeying the abbot unquestioningly, *RSB* cap. 5.

abbati suo quas secum habuit. Et cum esset pedes, defecerat enim ei equus eius, prima die precepit abbas ut equus ei conduceretur, set non ad finem diete, et compleuit pedes quod non potuit eques. Simili modo actum est cum eo in crastino, et non apposuit amplius abbas conducere ei equum, et cum non haberet uiaticum usque ad unum denarium necesse habuit sequi abbatem propter uictus necessaria. Et sequebatur pedes abbatem per abrupta montium. Quidam uero de familia abbatis miserti illius, tum per unum miliare tum per duo uel tria fecerunt eum

fo. 157rb ascendere equos suos, ut misera eius membra | refocillaret et compages membrorum quocumque solamine consolidaret. Quod cum abbas comperiisset uel expresse prohibendo uel submurmurando fecit quominus famuli eius hanc gratiam ei amplius impenderent.^a

276. Tunc ualde coartatus amplius eum pedetentim sequi non potuit, set quia res pro anima ei erat, eum lento pede sequens semper ad finem diete peruenit, licet tarde, et semper cum abbate pernoctauit. Ita quod abbas super eo admiraretur non tamen misereretur. Set ad complendam malitiam suam in eo, sepe duplomate uel fere utebatur, ut sic eum sequentem uel labore frangeret, uel non potentem sequi post tergum relinquens fame et inedia perimeret. Inuidebat enim ei propter scientiam suam, et odio habebat eum propter ueritatem suam. Inter hec omnia, cum idem frater esset magister in Israel[1] et sacerdos Dei altissimi[2] et ut scurra uagus[3] haberetur in domo abbatis, abbas ei sepe conuiciabatur et probris et contumeliis eum afficiebat.

277. Tandem cum uideret nec laboribus eum posse frangi nec obprobriis uinci, et uenissent Masconam,[4] abbas dixit ei expresse, 'Recede a me, societatem enim tuam nolo, et recto itinere uade in Angliam; quia ego per aliam uiam circuibo loca sanctorum',[5] et dedit ei unam marcam ad uiaticum; et tamen adhuc secutus est eum, et tercia die nesciebat quo diuerteret abbas.

278. *De aduentu abbatis in Angliam, et qualiter episcopus eum excommunicauerit, et qualiter conuentus fideliter secundum quod prius promiserant cum eo steterint*

Tandem uenit in Angliam et abbas similiter, set non tam cito. Quo cum ueniret et episcopus iam pridem in absentia sua adeptus esset

---

^a *preceded by* non *struck through*

[1] John 3: 10.   [2] Heb. 7: 1.   [3] Horace, *Epist.* i: 15.
[4] Midway between Lyon and Chalon-sur-Saône on the route north.
[5] They were in fact close to Cluny, or perhaps Abbot Norreis had some of the shrines of Auvergne in mind.

had with him. He was travelling on foot as his horse had let him down. On the first day the abbot told him to hire a horse for himself, but not for the whole day, so he finished on foot what he could not do on horseback. The same was done the next day, the abbot spending no more on the hire of a horse for him, and since he had less than one silver penny left for the journey, he had to follow the abbot because he needed food. So he followed the abbot on foot over the precipitous mountains. Some of the servants of this compassionate abbot made him ride their horses, first for one mile, then for two or three miles, so as to refresh his poor limbs and strengthen the joints of his limbs with whatever relief he could get. When the abbot learnt of this he expressly forbade them to do this, and grumbling about it, made sure that his servants did not do him this favour any more.

276. Considerably disabled, therefore, Adam was no longer able to keep up with the abbot on foot, but because it was a matter of life or death for him, he followed him at a slower pace, always catching up with him by the end of the day. Though it was late when he arrived, he always spent the night with the abbot. The abbot was amazed at him on this account, but he never pitied him. Indeed, to satisfy his ill will towards Adam, he would often, or quite frequently, travel with the utmost haste in order to exhaust him with the effort of keeping up with him; or, if he could not keep up, the abbot would leave him behind to die of starvation and want. The reason was that he envied him his knowledge, and hated him for his integrity. While undergoing all this suffering, this same brother was a master in Israel,[1] and a priest of the most high God[2] but, so that he should be regarded as a homeless buffoon[3] in his house, the abbot reviled, abused, and insulted him.

277. At last the abbot saw that Adam could not be broken by his exertions, nor defeated by insults, so when they came to Macon[4] the abbot told him explicitly, 'Leave me, for I do not want your company, and go directly to England; I shall be travelling by another route around the holy places',[5] and he gave him one mark for travelling expenses. However, Adam continued to follow the abbot, but after three days he lost track of him.

278. *The arrival of the abbot in England; the bishop excommunicates him, and the convent stand loyally by him because they had previously promised to do so*

At last Adam arrived in England, as did the abbot, though not as quickly as Adam. On his arrival the bishop, who had during the

possessionem iurisdictionis monasterii, scripsit ei episcopus ut eum reciperet cum fratribus. Abbas uero, clausis ianuis, episcopum exclusit et eum admittere renuit, appellans auctoritate noue indulgentie nostre. Set episcopus non deferens appellationi eum excom-
fo. 157va municauit, et cum | nullus in partibus istis ausus esset ei communicare secessit Lennam,[1] et ibi morabatur per multum tempus.

279. Interim episcopus accessit ad abbatiam et admissus est a fratribus. Et uoluit facere singularem inquisitionem de persona abbatis. Et cum fratres non immemores promissionis sue hoc renuerent et episcopus eos propter hoc uellet excommunicare. Monachi proiecerunt cucullas suas ad pedes episcopi[2] et dixerunt quod recederent a domo ista donec causa principalis finem sortiretur legittimum. Episcopus uero pietate motus inquisitionem distulit, et sic abbas tunc per conuentum euasit manus episcopi.

280. *De tercio aduentu Thome monachi et aduersariorum eius ad curiam et relatione iudicum, et qualiter primo coram domino papa comparuerunt*
Ego uero, interim de causa nostra bene instructus Bolonie, post festum sancti Michaelis recessi Romam.[3] Et in predictis octabis sancti Martini uenit ad me relatio[4] per predictum clericum abbatis, set et aduersarii nostri uenerunt, magister uidelicet Robertus de Clipstonia[5] et R. persona de Rippel et magister Ernaldus de Bathonia,[6] qui plusquam per quartam partem anni steterat in curia prius pro episcopo contra nos, ne aliquid ibi contra eum impetraremus. Et cum esset episcopus in possessione iurisdictionis monasterii nostri, et debuissent aduersarii nostri si prudenter egissent, ut moris est possidentium, subterfugere sententiam. Miro modo a Domino infatuati, statim optulerunt se liti, et relationem cum transcriptis priuilegiorum nostrorum sigillis iudicum signatis domino pape obtulerunt. Ego uero ultra quam credi possit de eorum stulticia pre gaudio admirans gratias egi Deo, cogitans quod manus eius nobiscum operaretur. Et uocatus nomine procuratoris Eueshamensis, sicut

---

[1] Presumably King's Lynn (Norf.): it is not clear why Abbot Norreis should have gone there.   [2] A symbolic gesture signifying renunciation of obedience.
[3] 29 Sept. 1205.   [4] Between 18 Nov. and 25 Nov. See above, 254, for the report.
[5] Master Robert de Clipstone (?Clipston, place unidentified) seems certainly to have been an Oxford master. He witnesses charters connected with the city and its religious houses between 1197 and 1201. An active judge delegate at this time, arbiter, and delegate of the legate Guala, he was official of the bishop of Worcester by 1211 and remained such until at least 1223–4; see Sayers, *PJD*, pp. 49–51, and 126; *BRUO*, i. 443. The Cirencester

abbot's absence now gained possession of the jurisdiction over the monastery, wrote to him and told him to receive him with the brethren. But the abbot closed the doors, shut the bishop out, and refused to admit him, appealing to the authority of our new 'empowerment'. However, the bishop, ignoring the appeal, excommunicated him, and when nobody in those parts of the country dared to give him communion, he left for *Lenna*,[1] and remained there for some considerable time.

279. In the mean time the bishop came to the abbey and was admitted by the brethren. He wanted to conduct a special inquiry into the character and behaviour of the abbot. When the brethren, remembering their promise, refused to participate in this, the bishop wished accordingly to excommunicate them. However, the monks threw their cowls at his feet[2] and said that they would leave that house until the principal lawsuit was legally settled. The bishop, moved by their loyalty, postponed the inquiry and, as a result, the abbot at that time because of the convent escaped the hands of the bishop.

280. *The third visit of Thomas the monk and his opponents to the curia, and the report of the judges [delegate]; their first appearance before the pope*

After receiving excellent instruction at Bologna on our case, I returned to Rome after Michaelmas.[3] The report arrived in the octave of St Martin[4] by way of the abbot's clerk, but our opponents also arrived, Master Robert de Clipstone,[5] R. parson of Ripple, and Master Ernald of Bath[6] who had previously acted in the curia against us for three months on the bishop's behalf, in case we should petition there for anything to his prejudice. When the bishop was in possession of the jurisdiction over our monastery, our opponents, if they were going to act wisely as those in possession usually do, ought quietly to have avoided forcing sentence. However, in a marvellous way the Lord befuddled their minds, for they immediately initiated litigation, and presented the report to the pope with copies of our privileges impressed with the seals of the judges. I was amazed and delighted, for their foolishness was beyond belief, and I gave thanks to God, convinced that His hand was with us in our task. On being summoned in my capacity as the Evesham proctor—a title by which I

formulary (Oxford, MS Bodley Laud lat. 17, fo. 224vb) suggests that he was a clerk to the canonist John of Tynemouth, as archdeacon of Oxford 1215–21; see *ANC*, p. 325 and n. 39.

[6] No more is known of either R. parson of Ripple (Worcs.) or Master Ernald of Bath.

quamdiu steti ibi semper a domino papa et omni curia nominatus
sum, comparui, et precepit dominus papa quod in tercium diem
parati essemus ad litigandum.

281. Ego uero cogitans si Dominus ita prouidisset, sicut per gratiam
Dei postea factum est, quod causa super iurisdictione monasterii qua
fo. 157ᵛᵇ destituti eramus | procederet, illa uero super iurisdictione Vallis
cuius possessione gaudebamus semper uel in longa tempora differetur. Dixi, 'Pater sancte, nondum plene peruenerunt ad me
priuilegia nostra quibus causam libertatis et exemptionis ecclesiarum
Vallis defendam, nisi tantum ea que ad consequendam libertatem et
exemptionem monasterii nostri pertinent.' Et reuera tantum unum
Constantini, et aliud Innocentii secundi, et indulgentie Clementis et
Celestini ad me uenerant cum attestationibus et transcriptis omnium
priuilegiorum.[1] Aliud uero Constantini et illud Alexandri attulit
michi post sententiam latam magister Adam Sortes.[2]

282. Et dominus papa dixit, 'Sufficit: uolumus enim ut tantum
causam super libertate monasterii agatis; super libertate autem
Vallis postea agetis'. Et gauisus sum de diuisione causarum; et cum
multum cogitarem quenam esset stulticia aduersariorum nostrorum
quod tam instanter sententiam in causa proprietatis super iurisdictione monasterii quererent, in cuius possessione erant constituti, cito
comperi quod timebant ne morerentur si in ciuitate morarentur,
magis querentes uitam propriam saluam facere quam causam domini
sui lucrifacere. Set ego habens preciosiorem causam meam quam
animam meam, quia, ut sepe dixi uobis, pro anima michi res erat, non
que mea erant querebam,[3] set que Iesu Christi et ecclesie mee. Nec
moram nec mortem timui, cupiens si opus esset animam meam pro
causa libertatis ecclesie mee ponere. Hoc ideo uobis scripsi ut sciatis
omnes homines esse quasi mercennarios[4] in negociis ecclesie nostre
preter solos monachos, et ut nunquam negotia ecclesie nostre alicui
sine monacho commitatis.

283. *De secunda apparitione coram domino papa et allegationibus
magistri Roberti*
Igitur die a domino papa nobis constituta coram eo comparuimus,
et dixit dominus papa, 'Tantum de causa principali et de capite

---

[1] For the text of these documents, see below, 318–31, 337–41.
[2] The sentence is 'Ex ore sedentis' of 18 Jan. 1206, 342–55. For the text of the
documents that came after that, see below, 318–31, 332–6.
[3] 1 Cor. 10: 24.   [4] Cf. John 10: 12.

was always known by the pope and the whole curia as long as I acted in that court—I appeared, and the pope instructed me to be ready to start proceedings in three days.

281. I now believed that, if the Lord so provided, as by God's grace it later proved he did, the case for jurisdiction over the monastery, of which we had been deprived, would proceed, and the case for jurisdiction over the Vale, of which we were in joyful possession, would be deferred either for ever or at least for a considerable period of time. I thus addressed the pope: 'Holy father, I have not yet received our privileges in full upon which I shall base my defence of the liberty and exemption of the churches of the Vale, but only those which support our case for the liberty and exemption of our monastery.' In fact I had received only one of Constantine, another of Innocent II, and indults of Clement [III] and Celestine [III], along with the written evidence and copies of all the privileges.[1] Master Adam Sortes brought me the other of Constantine and that of Alexander [III] after sentence had been passed.[2]

282. The pope replied, 'That is sufficient, for we want you to conduct only the case for the liberty of the monastery; the case for the liberty of the Vale you will conduct later.' I was delighted about the separation of the cases, and pondered over the foolishness of our opponents in seeking an immediate sentence in the case of 'ownership' of the jurisdiction over the monastery when 'possession' had already been decided in their favour. I soon discovered that they were afraid that they might die if they remained in the city, being more concerned to preserve their own lives than winning their master's case. But I considered my case more precious than my own life for, as I have often remarked to you, the issue concerned the good of my soul, and I was seeking not my own things[3] but those of Jesus Christ and my church. I feared neither delay nor death, and was willing, if necessary, to lay down my life for the cause of my church's liberty. I have written this for you, first that you may know that all men, except for the monks, are working in the affairs of our church like hirelings,[4] and secondly that you may never entrust the affairs of our church to anyone but a monk.

283. *The second appearance before the pope, and the arguments of Master Robert*

Accordingly, on the day appointed for us by the pope we appeared before him, and his words to us were, 'You are to confine your speech

dicatis, non de menbris.'[1] Et magister Robertus de Clipston' procurator episcopi, cum esset reus a re, quia in possessione fo. 158ʳᵃ iurisdictionis monasterii | erat constitutus, immo et a reatu, sicut per sententiam contra eum postea latam est declaratum, actor effectus est. Ego uero gratias agens Deo, cogitabam quia digitus Domini esset[2] qui mecum operabatur. Et ut uir facundissimus et in utroque iure, ciuili uidelicet et aᵃ canonico, adprime eruditus. Quoddam proemium multis et magnis sententiis inuolutum et profundis misteriis implicatum premisit, nesciens modum curie, quia dominus papa ueluti seriis occupatus talia fastidiret. Et cum in longum protraheret sermonem, dominus papa tedio affectus aliquantum toruo oculo illum respitiens, dixit, 'Nolumus tantum proemium; ad ea que res desiderat accede.' Et ipse propter sermonis sui interruptionem, ut michi uidebatur, perturbatus, ad iudicium possessorium se conuertit. Et omnem intentionem suam super eo fundauit, et elegantissime allegans profundis et optimis rationibus nitebatur ostendere sententiam in iudicio possessorio in Anglia pro episcopo rite fuisse latam et esse legittimam, quare eiusdem a domino papa petiit instanter confirmationem. Et cum dominus papa adhuc ei diceret ut breuiloquio uteretur, tandem completis allegationibus super predicta sententia lata pro episcopo in iudicio possessorio, intacta causa proprietatis,ᵇ subticuit.

284. *De responsione Thome monachi et allegationibus magistri Roberti*
Tum ego dixi, 'Pater sancte, cum ad recipiendam sentenciam in causa proprietatis super subiectione et exemptione monasterii nostri ad pedes sanctitatis uestre uenerimus, numᶜ placet uobis quod hiis que super possessione ab aduersario nostro dicta sunt respondeam cum per gratiam Dei et uestram quasi momentanea sit illa possessio episcopi?' Et dominus papa, 'Non loquamini', inquid, 'amodo de illa possessione, set tantum de subiectione et exemtione monasterii, et tantum procuratores loquantur ut per eos de facto certificemur, quia fo. 158ʳᵇ uterque uestrumᵈ iurisperitus est. Et cum opus fuerit aduo|cati respondeant nobis de iure.'
285. Stetimus enim uallati aduocatis nostris (conduxeramus enim

---

ᵃ *expunged* R   ᵇ proietatis R   ᶜ *erasure of* ?unum *before* num (*scribe may have written* unum)   ᵈ uestrum *add.* R

---

[1] The words *caput* and *membra* are used to signify the abbey of Evesham, on the one hand, and the dependent parishes, on the other.
[2] Cf. Exod. 8: 19.

to the principal case only, and to the monastery, not to the dependent parishes.'[1] The bishop's proctor, Master Robert de Clipstone, although he was in a position of defence because his party was already in possession of the jurisdiction over the monastery and also because he was in actual fact the defendant—as the sentence passed against him later showed—was in effect the plaintiff. I gave thanks to God, for I believed it was the hand of the Lord[2] that was working with me, even as that very eloquent man [Robert], especially erudite in both civil and canon law, began a prologue complicated by many and long legal opinions and interlaced with profound mysteries, not knowing the ways of the curia, for the pope, a man occupied in serious matters, is disdainful of such things. As his speech went on and on, the pope became bored stiff, and finally, glaring at him, said, 'We don't want all this introduction; get to the point of your argument!' Robert, in my view, was put off by this interruption of his speech, and turned to the subject of the possessory judgment. He based his whole case upon this and, making a very eloquent submission, he endeavoured to show by some profound and well-argued points that the sentence in the possessory judgment in England had been rightly and legitimately made in favour of the bishop, and that he was therefore requesting that this judgment should be confirmed immediately by the pope. When the pope insisted that he should be brief, he concluded his arguments on the sentence made in the possessory judgment in the bishop's favour and brought his speech to an end without touching upon the case of ownership.

284. *The response of Thomas the monk to the arguments of Master Robert*
I then said, 'Holy father, since we have come before your Holiness to receive sentence in the case of "ownership" which concerns the subjection and exemption of our monastery, I take it you do not want me to reply to what our opponents have said about "possession", since, by God's grace and your own, the bishop's possession is, as it were, temporary?' The pope replied, 'Do not talk now about possession, but only about the subjection or exemption of the monastery, and let only the proctors speak so that we may be apprised by them of the actual situation, because both of you are experienced in the law. And when there is need the advocates may reply to us on the rights of the case.'
285. Indeed, we stood there hemmed in by our advocates, for we had

nobis optimos aduocatos): ego quatuor et^a aduersarius quatuor, set ego meliores. Preueneram enim aduersarium, et elegeram michi de tocius mundi partibus meliores: magistrum uidelicet Merandum Hispanum, quem postea tempore consilii[1] uidi episcopum, qui nulli mortali simul in utroque iure tunc temporis habebatur secundus.[2] Hunc cum regeret scolas Bononie dominus Winton' Romam adduxerat, et stetit ibi pro domino rege et episcopis Anglie contra monachos Cantuarienses super iure eligendi Cantuar' archiepiscopum.[3] Et alium, quendam^b uidelicet militem Papiensem, Bertrandum nomine, dominum legum, qui nulli totius Lumbardie post dominum Assonem in iure ciuili habebatur secundus.[4] Hunc monachi Cantuarie adduxerant, et stetit pro eis in predicta causa contra dominum regem et episcopos Anglie. Et cum hiis duobus locutus fui Bononie antequam Romam uenirent. Habui etiam magistrum Petrum Beneuentanum, capellanum domini pape, postea cardinalem et episcopum Portuensem, qui primus habebatur inter aduocatos curie;[5] set et magistrum Willelmum prouintialem clericum domini cancellarii:[6] hac usus cautela ut per istos duos aliqua secreta curie discerem, quod et ita factum est. Et dedi primo qualibet die consistorii quinquaginta solidos Proueniensium,[7] secundo et tercio quadraginta,

---

^{a} et interlined; contemporary or same hand ^{b} quendam corrected from quendand'

[1] The Fourth Lateran Council of 1215.

[2] Merandus (also occurs as Melendus) of Spain was a famous canonist and teacher at Bologna, the senior colleague of his compatriot, Bernard of Compostella. He was teaching at Vicenza c.1209. He glossed the Decretum (before 1188) and the Compilatio Prima (of Bernard of Pavia) and produced some Questiones, which survive. He became bishop of Osma (Spain) in c.1210. The identification was made by S. G. Kuttner, 'Bernardus Compostellanus Antiquus. A study in the glossators of the canon law', Traditio, i (1943), 277–340, at pp. 301–2, 327; repr. in Gratian and the Schools of Law 1140–1234 (Variorum: London, 1983), article vii.

[3] On the death of Hubert Walter on 13 July 1205, a dispute over the right to elect the archbishop of Canterbury broke out between the monks of the cathedral priory of Christ Church, Canterbury, and the suffragans of the see. The bishop of Winchester in question was Peter des Roches who was in Rome in 1205 to secure his own election to that see (Cheney, Letters, no. 631, and Ann. Wint., p. 79), and it was apparently at this time that he hired Merandus to act for the king and the suffragans (of whom he was one) in the matter of the Canterbury election. Thomas is the only source for this.

[4] No more is known of the civilian, Bertrand of Pavia. C. R. Cheney (in his index under Pavia in Innocent III) calls him Bernard bishop of Pavia, but there is nothing to substantiate that statement. Pavia was a notable Lombard and Roman law school from the beginning of the 11th cent. and probably the main centre for legal studies before the rise of the schools at Bologna; see C. Radding, The Origins of Medieval Jurisprudence: Pavia and Bologna 850–1150 (New Haven, 1988), pp. 171–4, and F. Calasso, Medio Evo del diritto, i, Le Fonti (Milan, 1954), pp. 305–15. On Azo see below, note to 313.

hired for ourselves the very best: I had hired four and my opponent four, though mine were better. In fact, I had forestalled my opponent by choosing the best advocates in the whole world: they were Master Merandus Hispanus whom I later saw, at the time of the Council[1] as a bishop, and he was considered second to none at that time in both branches of the law.[2] The bishop of Winchester had taken him to Rome when he lectured in the schools at Bologna, and he there represented the king and the bishops of England against the monks of Canterbury over the right to elect the archbishop of Canterbury.[3] The second was a knight from Pavia called Bertrand, a law teacher, who was considered second to none in the whole of Lombardy after Azo in civil law.[4] The monks of Canterbury had brought him to Rome, and he represented them in the above-mentioned case against the king and bishops of England. I had spoken to these two men at Bologna before they came to Rome. Thirdly, I had Master Peter of Benevento, papal chaplain, and afterwards cardinal bishop of Porto, who was considered the best of the advocates in the curia;[5] and my fourth was Master William, 'provincial' clerk of the chancellor:[6] I contrived to engage these two men in order to learn some of the secrets of the curia, and I succeeded in this. And I gave to the first on each day of the consistory fifty shillings of Provins,[7] to the second and third forty

[5] Master Peter (Collivaccinus) of Benevento, papal notary and subdeacon, and compiler of Innocent III's official canon law collection, *Compilatio Tertia*, was created cardinal deacon of S. Maria in Aquiro in 1212, cardinal priest of S. Lorenzo in Damaso in 1216, and cardinal bishop of Sabina, not Porto as Thomas states, in 1217; Maleczek, pp. 172–4 and 293.

[6] He is possibly the notary who dated *per manum* only a few weeks after Pope Honorius III's election and who became his vice-chancellor from 1220 to 1222 (cf. P. M. Baumgarten, *Von der apostolischen Kanzlei* (Cologne, 1908), pp. 72–3. The reference, however, to a notary of Innocent III called William, with whom this person had been tentatively identified, acting as datary on 25 Feb. 1211 (see H. Bresslau, *Handbuch der Urkundenlehre für Deutschland und Italien*, 2nd edn., i (Leipzig, 1912), p. 248), was shown by R. von Heckel to be incorrect (*Historisches Jahrbuch*, lvii (1937), 278–9). S. G. Kuttner (in *Traditio*, vii (1949–51), 279–358, at p. 301 n. 54) and J. E. Sayers (*Papal Government and England during the Pontificate of Honorius III (1216–1227)* (Cambridge, 1984), p. 30) wrongly followed Bresslau. Master was a courtesy title for papal officers, and the 'provincial' clerk may have been the clerk who dealt with the *Provinciale*, or list of dioceses of the western Church; see Gerald of Wales, iii. 165. According to C. R. Cheney, 'The office and title of papal chancellor 1187–1216', *Archivum Historiae Pontificiae*, xxii (1984), 369–76, at p. 373, the pope did not appoint an officer with the title of chancellor, until John, cardinal deacon of S. Maria in Cosmedin, in Dec. 1205, and the action we are concerned with was presumably still in Nov. 1205.

[7] For shillings of Provins, see Spufford, *Handbook of Medieval Exchange*, pp. 164–7, esp. 164 and 167. The denier of Provins travelled from the great fair-town of Champagne along all the major trade routes. By the 1170s the *denarius provisinus* was the dominant currency of central Italy. The senate of Rome, with the agreement of the pope, began to

quarto uiginti. Et cum conqueretur aduersarius noster quod subtraxissem ei copiam aduocatorum, respondit dominus papa subridendo, 'Nunquam defuit alicui copia aduocatorum in curia Romana', et precepit ut dicerem.

286. *De primis allegationibus Thome monachi pro exemptione Eueshamensis cenobii*

Tunc ego, iam pridem cognoscens quia curia breuiloquio gaudebat, flens et eiulans dixi, 'Pater sancte, postpositis philosophorum figuris, dialeticorum enigmatibus | et retorum coloribus, lingua pre timore balbutiente, sermone licet incomposito ad ea que res de qua agitur desiderat accedo. Igitur, pater sancte, monasterium nostrum, immo uestrum, a tempore fundationis sue liberum extitit et exemptum. Immo, quod maius est, quasi ingenuum natum quia liberum fundatum, et ad hoc probandum habemus priuilegia Romanorum pontificum. Dicit enim Constantinus papa quod duo reges Anglie Kenredus et Offa, cum quibus beatus Ecgwinus ad limina apostolorum uenit, in loco ostense uisionis plurima de suis beneficiis in presentia sua regia libertate donata et apostolica auctoritate confirmata contulerunt. Pater sancte, non dicitur quod contulerint plurima loco, set plurima in loco, hoc est de loco, et dicitur plurima de suis beneficiis, non omnia.*ᵃ* Non enim totum locum qui uocatur Vallis Gloecestrie contulerunt set quedam beneficia in Valle Gloecestrie. Nec dicitur cui contulerint illa beneficia; unde necesse est intelligere quod domino pape et ecclesie Romane contulerint ea, cum omnia sint principis et maxime ea que non determinantur in cuius bonis sint, et cum eo presente et confirmante hec donata sint.

287. 'Et quod clausula illa ita debeat intelligi, expresse per subsequentia capitula *ᵇ*in eodem priuilegio contenta et in sequenti declaratur; dicit enim idem Constantinus*ᵇ* in eodem priuilegio Britwaldo Brittanniarum primati, "Constitue ouile Christo diuinitus ostensum, apostolica auctoritate fultum, regia libertate donatum",[1] nec dicit cui. Et cum non consueuerit summus pontifex precipere quod aliquod monasterium fundetur nisi quod in solo sibi donato

fo. 158ᵛᵃ

ᵃ marg. Nota optime hic ad ?animandum dominum papam contra adversarios nostros (s. xv)   *ᵇ⁻ᵇ inserted in the margin* (s. xiiiᶦ)

---

mint *provisini*. *Provisini* became the standard money of Rome (lire, soldi, and denari), Innocent III himself, in 1208, fixing an official rate of exchange between senatorial and French *provisini*; by this time the number of French coins in circulation was dwindling.

shillings, and to the fourth twenty shillings. When our opponent complained that I had deprived him of the supply of advocates, the pope replied with a smile, 'No one has ever lacked a supply of advocates in the Roman curia!', and he then instructed me to speak.

286. *The first arguments of Thomas the monk in favour of the exemption of Evesham monastery*

Aware now for some time that the curia rejoiced in brevity, I spoke as follows, with much emotion: 'Holy father, I am abandoning all philosophical concepts, dialectical puzzles and rhetorical embellishments. Instead, it is with a hesitant tongue, from fear, and with simple language that I come to the essential points of this case. Holy father, our monastery, or rather, your monastery, has been free and exempt from the time of its foundation. What is more, it is as if it were of noble birth because it was founded free, and we have the privileges of the Roman pontiffs to prove it. Pope Constantine says that in his presence two kings of England, Cenred and Offa, with whom the blessed Ecgwine came to the threshold of the apostles, granted very many gifts in the place where the vision was revealed, and these were donated as a royal liberty and confirmed by apostolic authority. Holy father, it does not say that they granted very many things to the place, but very many things in the place; that is, relating to the place, and it says very many of their gifts, not all. For they did not bestow the whole place which is called the Vale of Gloucester, but certain estates in the Vale of Gloucester. It does not say to whom they granted those gifts: hence, it is necessary to understand that they granted them to the pope and the Roman church, since all things belong to the head, especially those things which are not specified as belonging to anyone in particular, and especially when they are granted in the pope's presence and with his confirmation.

287. 'In order that that clause should thus be understood, it is expressly contained in the subsequent clauses of the same privilege, and affirmed in the same privilege, for Constantine tells Berhtwald, primate of Britain, in the same privilege, "Establish for Christ a flock which has been divinely revealed, supported by apostolic authority, and endowed with royal liberty",[1] but he does not say for whom. But since the pope did not usually give instructions for any monastery to be founded unless it was to be founded on soil that had been given to

---

[1] See below, 320.

fuerit fundandum, relinquitur quod reges locum illum summo pontifici et ecclesie Romane contulerint, et illud ouile "diuinitus ostensum", apostolica auctoritate fultum, regia libertate donatum, fuisse collatum summo pontifici et ecclesie Romane, et ideo, excepto fo. 158vb apostolico, ut suum et in suo solo | constitutum nulli est subiectum. Ad hoc etiam benefacit quod in eodem priuilegio Constantinus statim subiungit, loquens Brituualdo, "Tibi autem et successoribus tuis, memorato episcopo Ecguuino assentiente, curam animarum eiusdem ecclesie precipue iniungimus."[1] Non enim auferret summus pontifex alicui diocesano episcopo curam animarum alicuius ecclesie sicut isti fecit, quod ex eo patet quod eo consentiente alii, ut suo uicario, curam animarum tradidit, non enim requiritur consensus alicuius nisi in his que in eius fiunt lesionem, nisi ecclesie specialiter sue et auctoritate sua fundate. Quod expresse in secundo priuilegio Constantini continetur, ubi denuntiat Brituualdo, "quatinus ecclesias Dei per Brittanniam dispositas tua ipsius^a et sanctorum apostolorum auctoritate protegas ne quis peruasor cuiuscumque ordinis a Deo et nobis constituta priuilegia subruat. Inter quas^b eam que nuperrime a uenerabili uiro Ecguuino nostra et regia auctoritate constituta est, precipue tue ditioni submittimus."[2]

288. 'Ecce quod auctoritate summi pontificis est ecclesia nostra constituta et Brittanniarum primati ut suo legato commissa. Cum ergo suffitienter probauerim, ut michi uidetur, quod monasterium nostrum a tempore fundationis sue fuerit summo pontifici donatum et eius auctoritate fundatum, sequitur necessario quod illi soli et ecclesie Romane sit subiectum: quia nephas esset dicere quod aliquis ordinariam potestatem in rebus et bonis summi ordinarii haberet;[3] nam et hoc in inferioribus ecclesiis uideo. Non enim aliquis diocesanus episcopus in possessionibus metropolitani sui quamuis infra limites diocesis sue sitis ordinariam exercet iurisdictionem, multo fortius nec in possessionibus summi pontificis.

---

^a tua ipsius *struck through*   ^b *interlined*

[1] See below, 321.
[2] On interpretation of the early texts and the ambivalence of the words used, particularly *ditio* (rule, authority) in relation to Evesham, see M. Rathsack, *Die Fuldaer Fälschungen: Eine rechtshistorische Analyse der päpstlichen Privilegien des Klosters Fulda von 751 bis ca. 1158* (2 vols., Päpste und Papsttum, xxiv (I–II): Stuttgart, 1989), i. 74–6. On the early privileges for Fulda, cf. the views of H. Jakobs, 'Zu neuen Thesen über der Fuldaer Papsturkunden', *Deutsches Archiv*, xxxvii (1981), 792–5, and id., 'Zu den Fuldaer Papsturkunden des Frühmittelalters', *Blätter für deutsche Landesgeschichte*, cxxviii (1992), 31–84.

him, it follows, first, that the kings had granted that place to the pope and the Roman church, secondly, that the flock which had been "divinely revealed", supported by apostolic authority, and endowed with royal liberty had been granted to the pope and the Roman church, and thirdly, therefore, as it is the pope's flock, established on his soil, it was subject to no authority except the apostolic one. Moreover, there is an additional benefit in that in the same privilege Constantine straightway commands Berhtwald, "Especially do we lay upon you and your successors, with Bishop Ecgwine's consent, the care of souls in that same church."[1] Now the pope will not deprive any diocesan bishop of the care of souls of any church, as he did to Ecgwine, unless the church has been specifically founded as his own and by his authority—it is clear from this that it was with the bishop's consent, as his vicar, that he handed over to another the care of souls, for consent is not required of anyone except in those cases in which someone suffers loss. This is clearly contained in the second privilege of Constantine in which he declares to Berhtwald, "We command you to protect the churches of God scattered throughout Britain by your own authority and that of the holy apostles, so that no assailant of any rank may undermine the privileges instituted by God and us. Amongst those we especially place under your rule that church most recently founded by the venerable Ecgwine with our authority and that of the king."[2]

288. 'Notice then that our church was established by the authority of the pope, and was entrusted to the primate of Britain as the pope's legate. Since in my view I have given sufficient proof that our monastery was from the time of its foundation presented to the pope and founded on his authority, it of necessity follows that it is subject to him alone and to the Roman church. It would be wrong to say that anyone might have the power of the ordinary in matters or property belonging to the highest ordinary;[3] I see that this is also the case in churches of less importance. No diocesan bishop exercises jurisdiction as ordinary over the possessions of his metropolitan even if these are situated within the boundaries of his diocese, and much stronger are the arguments against his doing so over the possessions of the supreme pontiff.

---

[3] This is the classic argument concerning exemption. The ordinary, the diocesan bishop, had no jurisdiction if the monastery was directly under the pope. The reference in the next sentence is to peculiars, areas within a diocese, subject to a superior who was not the bishop of the diocese.

289. 'Si uero alicui hec ad plenam libertatem ecclesie nostre minime |

sufficere uidentur, habemus ex eisdem priuilegiis et aliis expressam exemptionem. Dicit enim Constantinus in primo priuilegio, "Ipsum ergo locum quem regia potestas regie libertati donauit, et nos auctoritate Dei et sanctorum apostolorum et nostra donamus."[1] Cum itaque reges dederint locum illum regie libertati, hoc est seculari et temporali, et summus pontifex Romane et ecclesiastice libertati donauit. Cum enim summus pontifex indeterminate locum dedit libertati, quia beneficia imperatoris[2] amplissime sunt interpretanda, omnimode et summe, id est, Romane, libertati donasse intelligitur. Nam cum serui manumittuntur, Romane libertati donantur, et sicut reges donarunt eum libertati quoad temporalia sic et summus pontifex quoad spiritualia libertati donauit.

290. 'Quod autem priuilegium hoc ita debeat intelligi expresse in indulgentiis Clementis et Celestini innuitur, ubi dicitur, "Largitione nostri muneris et gratie eos duximus decorandos quos fidei meritum ac deuotionis constantia nobis reddunt acceptos, et qui nullo mediante ad iurisdictionem beati Petri et nostram specialiter pertinere noscuntur. Hac itaque ratione inducti et deuotionis et fidei uestre intuitu prouocati, tibi, fili*a* abbas, et successoribus tuis usum mitre, anuli, cirotecarum et dalmatice, tunice et sandaliorum, necnon et sacerdotalia uestimenta benedicendi de consueta clementia et de benignitate sedis apostolice duximus concedendum."[3]

291. 'Ecce constat locum nostrum Romane libertati a Constantino esse donatum cum per istos constet eum soli Romano pontifici et ecclesie Romane esse subiectum. In secundo uero priuilegio Constantini dicitur, "Constituimus ergo in nomine Domini ut isdem locus sub monarchia proprii abbatis sit liber." Cum igitur monarchia interpretetur "unicus principatus", constat quod solus abbas ibi

principalem potestatem | et iurisdictionem debet exercere, et sic episcopus excluditur. Et quod hoc priuilegium ita debeat intelligi, expresse continetur in priuilegio Innocentii pape secundi, ubi dicitur, "Statuimus insuper ac, predecessoris nostri felicis memorie Constantini pape uestigiis inherentes, decreuimus, ut solummodo penes

---

a filii *R*

---

[1] See below, 322.
[2] For the *beneficium imperatoris*, see *Digest* 1. 4. 3. And for the use of the maxim by Innocent III himself, see 3 *Comp.* 1. 2. 6 (*X.* 5. 40. 16, Friedberg ii col. 916) and 3. 18. 3 (*X.* 3. 24. 6, Friedberg ii cols. 534–5), cited by K. Pennington, *Pope and Bishops: The Papal Monarchy in the Twelfth and Thirteenth Centuries* (Philadelphia, 1984), p. 170 n. 64.

289. 'Should these arguments seem to anyone not sufficiently convincing to justify the complete liberty of our church, we have exemption categorically declared in those same privileges, and in others. In the first privilege Constantine says, "the very place which royal power has given as a royal liberty, we also give by the authority of God and the holy apostles, and by our own authority."[1] Although then kings have given that place royal liberty, that is, a worldly and temporal liberty, the supreme pontiff has given it Roman and ecclesiastical liberty. But since the supreme pontiff has given the place indefinite liberty—and the gifts of the emperor[2] must be interpreted in the fullest sense—then he is understood to have granted a liberty which embraces the highest and the most comprehensive liberty, that is, Roman liberty. When slaves are set free they are given Roman liberty, and when kings have given a place liberty so far as temporal things are concerned, so the pope has given it liberty so far as spiritual things are concerned.

290. 'In order that this privilege should be understood, it is made perfectly clear in the indults of Clement and Celestine when it is stated, "We have decided that those men, whose faithfulness and undying devotion render them acceptable to us, and are known to belong especially to the jurisdiction of the blessed Peter and ourself without any intermediary, should be honoured with the generosity of our grace and favour. Motivated by this principle and stirred by an awareness of your devotion and faith, we have decided to bestow upon you, my son abbot, and your successors, through the grace and favour of the apostolic see, the right to use the mitre, ring, gloves, dalmatic, tunic and sandals, as well as to bless priestly vestments."[3]

291. 'Notice then, it is established that our place has been given Roman liberty by Constantine, since it is established by those privileges that it is subject to the pope alone and the Roman church. In the second privilege of Constantine it is stated, "We therefore decree in the name of the Lord that the same place be free under the sole rule of its own abbot." Since then sole rule is to be interpreted as "the leadership of one only", it is established that the abbot alone ought to exercise principal power and jurisdiction, and the bishop is thus excluded. In order that this privilege should be understood in this way, it is expressly stated in a privilege of Pope Innocent II, where it says, "Following in the steps of our predecessor, Pope Constantine of happy memory, we further command and decree

[3] See below, 337–41.

te et successores tuos tocius domus et ecclesie tue et aliorum locorum ad eandem ecclesiam pertinentium pastoralis cura consistat, et eorundem ordinatio in tua et successorum tantum tuorum potestate permaneat, sicut est hactenus obseruatum, salua per omnia sedis apostolice auctoritate."[1] Non dicitur quod aliqua ibi sit salua episcopi auctoritas, set tantum abbatis ibi exerceatur potestas. Ecce manifeste probatur quod solus abbas noster ibi ordinariam habeat dispositionem et iurisdictionem. Si cui uero, quod tamen non credo, adhuc in dubium uenit quin ecclesia nostra ab ipsa fundatione sit libera, ueniamus ad iura episcopalia que habent episcopi in monasteriis non*a* exemptis, et uideamus si contra hec muniti simus per Romanorum pontificum priuilegia.

292. 'Igitur episcopi ab abbatibus non exemptis professionem et obedientiam cum eis benedicunt exigunt et accipiunt, nec ab aliis possunt benedici quam ab episcopo diocesano. Abbas uero noster ab episcopo Wigornensi nec benedictionem accipere nec professionem nec obedientiam ei facere tenetur.[2] Dicit enim Constantinus in secundo priuilegio, "Defuncto autem abbate, secundum canonicam auctoritatem uel de ipso monasterio uel de parrochia Wictiorum[3] abbas a fratribus eiusdem loci eligatur. Qui in eadem ecclesia libere et canonice sine aliqua exactione consecratus ob reuerentiam uenerabilis Ecgwini anulo in celebratione missarum utatur."[4] Ex uerbis huius priuilegii habere potestis quod a quocumque maluerit episcopo possit abbas noster benedici cum in propria ecclesia debeat benedici.

fo. 159ᵛᵃ Absurdum enim esset | quod episcopus, si abbas ei subiceretur, ab abbate nostro uocaretur ut ei in propria ecclesia benediceret, cum abbas subiectus ad episcopum uenire debeat propter benedictionem, et subiectus a superiore debeat uocari, et non e conuerso. Et cum absque omni exactione debeat benedici, patet quod nec professio nec obedientia ab eo debet exigi.

293. 'Quod autem hoc priuilegium ita debeat intelligi expresse continetur in priuilegio Innocentii secundi; dicit enim, "Obeunte

_____

a non *interlined s. xiii*ᵗ

[1] See below, 325, 330. Thomas is clearly interpreting the silence of the Constantinian privilege on the rights of the diocesan in the light of what Innocent II had granted.

[2] A sign of exemption was that an abbot might be blessed by any bishop of his choice: he might therefore escape professing obedience to the diocesan. Papal privileges to exempt houses specified this; see *PUE* iii. no. 187 (JL 12148) Alexander III for Bury St Edmunds, dated 7 Apr. 1172. Thomas is clearly amplifying the Constantinian text here in the light of Innocent II's privilege. The failure to mention the diocesan specifically cannot be taken as the grant of free choice of bishop. Cf. Rathsack, *Die Fuldaer Fälschungen*, who analyses the

that the pastoral care of your entire house, church, and other places belonging to the same church should rest solely with you and your successors, and that the ordering of those places remain your prerogative alone and that of your successors, as has been observed hitherto, saving the authority of the apostolic see in all things."[1] Nothing is said in the privilege about the bishop having any authority in the monastery, only that the power of the abbot be exercised there. There is clear proof then that our abbot alone has the authority and jurisdiction of the ordinary. But should anyone remain in doubt— though I cannot believe this—that our house has enjoyed freedom from its very foundation, let us come to the episcopal rights which bishops have in those monasteries which are not exempt, and see whether we have been protected against these through the privileges of the Roman pontiffs.

292. 'Bishops demand and receive profession and obedience from abbots not enjoying exemption when they give them blessing, and such abbots cannot receive blessing from any other than their diocesan bishop. But our abbot is not bound to receive blessing from the bishop of Worcester, nor to make profession or promise obedience to him.[2] For Constantine says in the second privilege, "When the abbot dies, his successor is to be chosen by the brethren of that place, in accordance with canonical authority, either from the monastery itself or from the diocese of the Hwicce.[3] He is then to be consecrated in that church freely and canonically without any exactions and, out of reverence for the venerable Ecgwine, is to use the ring in the celebration of mass." [4] From the words of this privilege you can gather that our abbot can receive blessing from any bishop he chooses, though he should receive blessing in his own church. It would be absurd for a bishop to be invited by our abbot to give him blessing in his own church if the abbot were subject to him, for a subject abbot must come to the bishop for blessing, as a subject must be invited by his superior, not vice versa. Further, since he must receive blessing without any exaction, it is clear that neither profession nor obedience must be demanded of him.

293. 'This privilege ought to be understood, for it is expressly stated in the privilege of Innocent II, "When you, the present abbot of this

---

papal privileges for Fulda from 751 to c.1158, on the imprecision and nebulousness of the texts where exemption is concerned.

[3] i.e. the diocese of Worcester.

[4] See below, 326.

uero te nunc eiusdem loci abbate uel tuorum quolibet successorum, nullus ibi qualibet subreptionis astutia seu uiolentia proponatur nisi quem fratres eiusdem loci communi assensu uel fratrum pars consilii sanioris elegerit.ᵃ¹ Qui in eadem ecclesia absque omni exactione a quocumque maluerit benedicatur episcopo, dum tamen catholicus sit et gratiam sedis apostolice habeat et communionem."² Ecce manifeste ostensum est abbatem nostrum ab episcopo Wigornensi nec benedictionem debere suscipere nec professionem nec obedientiam ei debere facere.

294. 'Habent etiam episcopi diocesani monasteria sibi subiecta tueri et uisitare et in eis errata corrigere, quorum nullum habet episcopus Wigorn' in monasterio nostro. Scribit enim Constantinus Brittanniarum primati in primo priuilegio, dicens, "Tibi autem, et successoribus tuis, memorato Egwino episcopo assentiente, curam animarum eiusdem ecclesie precipue iniungimus, ut si, quod absit, aliquo diaboli impulsu quisquam peruasor aut tirannus sanctum locum minuere aut impugnare presumpserit, tibi a Deo concesse potestatis sententia et anathematis percussus uerbere, complere non audeat."³

295. 'Ecce expresse patet quod, cum cura animarum nostrarum, tutela tociusᵇ ecclesie nostre Cantuar' archiepiscopo sit commissa. Et quod cum tuitione etiam errata nostra habeat corrigere, ut tam tuitio quam correctio ei committatur, expresse subiungitur in eodem priuilegio, ubi dicitur, "Si quid uero sinistre partis inibi compertum fuerit oriri, auribus summi pontificis patrie potius deferatur quam per alicuius occultam sententiam sanctus locus iniuste deprauetur."⁴

296. 'Cum igitur onera tuitionis et correctionis sequantur honores et commoda uisitationis et procurationis, merito illi cui onera non imponuntur honores et emolumenta subtrauntur. Ex hoc igitur priuilegio patet nullum ab ecclesia nostra predictorum deberi Wigorn' episcopo, cum a domino papa Cant' archiepiscopo ut suo legato uel uicario hec sint commissa. Et de consensu Ecgwini episcopi Wigorn', cuius consensus non requirereturᶜ nisi in eius preiudicium fo. 159ᵛᵇ aliquid statueretur, quamuis dominus papa | qui uocatus est in

---

ᵃ elegerint *in the privilege below*   ᵇ tocius *interlined (s. xiii')*   ᶜ requiretur R

---

¹ See the charges against the election of Abbot Norreis, above, 186 and n. 3 (p. 193). For election by the wiser part, the *sanior pars*, see *RSB* cap. 64: 'siue etiam pars quamuis parua congregationis saniore consilio elegerit', and *The Monastic Constitutions of Lanfranc*, ed. and trans. D. Knowles, rev. C. N. L. Brooke (OMT, Oxford, 2002), pp. 108–9 and n. 293.
² See below, 329–30   ³ See below, 321.   ⁴ See below, 321.

place, or any of your successors, die, let no successor be appointed there through any kind of underhand chicanery or force, but only a man chosen by the brethren of the monastery by common consent, or by that part of the brethren of wiser counsel.[1] Then let him receive blessing in that church from any bishop he chooses without any payment provided that he is catholic and enjoys the grace and communion of the apostolic see."[2] There is clear evidence then that our abbot is not bound to receive blessing from the bishop of Worcester, nor bound to make profession or vows of obedience to him.

294. 'Diocesan bishops have to protect and visit monasteries which are subject to them, and to correct what is wrong in them, but the bishop of Worcester has to do none of these things in our monastery. Indeed, in his first privilege Constantine writes to the primate of Britain in these words, "We especially lay upon you and your successors, with Bishop Ecgwine's assent, the care of souls in that same church so that, if any trespasser or tyrant, God forbid, should presume through any devilish impulse to impair or impugn this holy place, he may be alarmed by the condemnation which God has empowered you to pronounce and by the shock of an anathema, and so not dare to carry out his intention."[3]

295. 'There is clear evidence that, along with the care of our souls, the protection of the whole of our church has been entrusted to the archbishop of Canterbury. Also, it is expressly decreed in the same privilege that along with protection the archbishop has to correct our errors, so not only protection but also correction is entrusted to him: "Should anything of an evil nature be found to have occurred there, let it be brought to the notice of the archbishop of the country rather than that holy place should be unjustly brought into ill-repute by someone else's underhand condemnation."[4]

296. 'Since therefore the responsibilities of protection and correction go with the honours and advantages of visitation and procuration, it is right that the one who is not burdened with these responsibilities should be deprived of the honours and rewards. It is clear from this privilege that our church owes none of these latter to the bishop of Worcester, since the pope has entrusted these things to the arch-bishop of Canterbury as his legate or vicar. He did this with the consent of Ecgwine, bishop of Worcester, though his consent would not be required unless something were decided to his prejudice, for the lord pope who is called to the plenitude of power can do all these

plenitudinem potestatis[1] hec omnia auctoritate sibi a Deo commissa ex propria potestate facere possit, nullius requisito consensu uel fauore. Et tamen sine ratione talia facere non consueuit. Et cum possint episcopi infra diocesim suam in qua maluerint ecclesia non priuilegiata sinodum, capitula, ordinationes et missas publicas celebrare, hec Wigorn' episcopo in ecclesiis nostris facere ab Innocentio prohibetur ubi dicitur, "Sanximus etiam ut in abbatia uestra aut in capellis uestris aliquis episcopus sinodum uel capitula aut ordinationes aut missas publicas, nisi inuitatus ab abbate illius loci uel a fratribus, celebrare non presumat."[2] Cum etiam non liceat non exemptis sacramenta ecclesiastica nisi a suo episcopo diocesano accipere, ut nichil nobis desit ad plenitudinem libertatis conceditur nobis ab Alexandro papa tercio ut ea a quo maluerimus accipiamus episcopo, ubi dicitur, "Crisma uero, oleum sanctum, dedicationes ecclesiarum,[a] consecrationes altarium, ordinationes clericorum qui ad sacros ordines fuerint promouendi, a quocumque malueritis succipiatis episcopo."[3]

297. 'Ecce, pater sancte, ut michi uidetur, sufficienter ostendi monasterium nostrum esse liberum et ab omni iurisdictione episcopali prorsus exemptum, et contra omnia iura episcopalia per predictorum priuilegiorum dicta capitula plene esse munitum. Si uero alia sunt iura episcopalia contra que per priuilegia Romanorum pontificum non simus muniti, petimus ut uos uestigia predecessorum uestrorum sequentes de consueta clementia et benignitate sedis apostolice suppleatis, ne ecclesia nostra, immo uestra, a sui fundatione libera pro modico episcopo seruiat. Sin autem necesse est ut pro hiis episcopo satisfaciamus'. Et hec cum magno fletu et eiulatu dixi.

298. Et dominus papa conuersus ad cardinales, subridendo, uulgariter loquens, dixit, 'Iste omnia aufert episcopo, et postea dicit, habeat episcopus residuum.' Et conuertens se | ad aduersarium nostrum dixit, 'Responde hiis.'

fo. 160ra

299. *De responsione magistri Roberti et[b] allegationibus Th[ome] monachi, et qualiter priuilegia falsa[c] fuerunt a magistro R. accusata, set a domino papa ut uera approbata*
Et ille: 'Pater sancte, bene dixisset aduersarius noster si priuilegia, in quibus omnem uim et potestatem allegationum suarum fecit et

---

[a] dedicationes ecclesiarum *om. in the privilege recited below*   [b] *interlined*
[c] *corrected from* falsi

---

[1] On the plenitude of power, see K. Pennington, *Pope and Bishops*, pp. 43–74.

things in his own power by the authority entrusted to him by God, and requires the consent or favour of no one.[1] But it was not his habit to act in this way without reason. Although bishops are able to celebrate a synod, chapters, ordinations, and public masses within their own diocese in whatever church they choose that is not privileged, the bishop of Worcester is forbidden by Innocent [II] to do so in our churches when it is stated, "We also decree that no bishop should presume to celebrate a synod, chapters, ordinations, or public masses in your abbey or in your chapels unless invited to do so by the abbot of the monastery or by the brethren."[2] Now churches which do not enjoy exemption would only be allowed to receive the sacraments of the church from their own diocesan bishop, but in order that we should enjoy full exemption, Pope Alexander III permits us to receive the sacraments from any bishop we choose when he states, "You may receive chrism, holy oil, the dedication of churches, the consecration of altars, the ordination of clerks who are to be promoted to holy orders, from any bishop of your choice."[3]

297. 'So then, holy father, I believe I have given sufficient reason to establish that our monastery is free and absolutely exempt from all episcopal jurisdiction, and that it is fully protected against all episcopal rights over it, in the said sections of the privileges I have quoted. Should there be other episcopal rights against which we are not protected by the privileges of the Roman pontiffs, we petition you to follow the examples of your predecessors, and act with the customary clemency and kindness of the apostolic see to prevent our church, or rather, your church, which has been free from its foundation, from being subject, even for a short time, to a bishop. If you cannot do this, then we would have to meet the bishop's demands.' I delivered this speech with expressions of deep emotion.

298. The pope turned to the cardinals with a smile and in his native language said, 'This fellow takes everything away from the bishop and then says "let the bishop have the leftovers!"' He then turned to our opponent and said, 'Make your reply to these arguments!'

299. *The reply of Master Robert to the arguments of Thomas the monk. He impugns the genuineness of the privileges; but the pope accepts them as genuine*

Master Robert began, 'Holy father, our opponent's speech would have been valid if the privileges, upon which he has based all the force

---

[2] See below, 329.   [3] See below, 334.

fundamentum totius cause sue posuit, uera essent, cum sint falsa. Nam carta[1] et stilus, filum et bulla, priuilegiorum Constantini penitus in terra nostra ignota sunt. Portitor uero indulgentiarum Clementis et Celestini fuit publicus falsarius, Nicholaus de Wareuuich, et ideo eas falsas credimus, et hoc idem de aliis dicimus.'[2]

300. Et dominus papa precepit ut exhiberem ea, et exhibui. Et dominus papa propriis manibus tractauit ea, et traxit per bullam et cartam si forte posset bullam a filo amouere.[3] Et diligentissime intuens ea tradidit cardinalibus intuenda; et cum per girum uenissent iterum ad dominum papam, ostendens priuilegium Constantini dixit, 'Huiusmodi priuilegia que uobis ignota sunt, nobis sunt notissima, nec possent falsari', et ostendens indulgentias dixit, 'Iste uere sunt', et restituit michi omnia. Set qualiter michi et ecclesie et cause nostre timuerim cum per girum uiderent priuilegia cardinales et cum dominus papa ita dure ea tractauit, supersedeo dicere quia non possem uobis edicere. Quamuis nichil michi conscius essem, tamen sciui quod ille qui habebatur pro falsario, forte quia publicus cursor fuit curie, indulgentiarum portitor fuit; et circa priuilegia Constantini omnia michi ignota erant. Set cum approbata fuerunt, inestimabili gaudio repletus sum. Et hec fuit secunda interlocutio[4] pro nobis data. Prima enim fuit cum primo fui Rome pro reuocanda iurisdictione iudicum, ne in iudicio possessorio[5] sententiarent, quam interlocutionem propriam ipse papa postea reuocauit.

301. Et cum iam esset hora prandendi precepit dominus papa quod recederemus, et quod aduersarius noster aliter responderet cum alias uocati essemus. Et post triduum iterum uocati fuimus, et respondit tunc aduersarius noster.

---

[1] *Carta* can mean a sheet of writing material (hence possibly papyrus); see A. Giry, *Manuel de Diplomatique* (Paris, 1894), p. 495, and esp. n. 3, and it makes much better sense here if taken to mean the material of the document. It is just possible that what was shown to Innocent was a papyrus document, for he had seen such whereas Master Robert had obviously not. R. L. Poole (*Lectures on the History of the Papal Chancery*, (Cambridge, 1915), p. 148) assumed it to be parchment, following Bresslau (i.[2] p. 19), and see M. Spaethen, 'Giraldus Cambrensis und Thomas von Evesham über die von ihnen an der Kurie gefürhten Prozesse', *Neues Archiv*, xxi (1906), 595–649, at p. 639.

[2] For Innocent's decretals on forgery, see *X*. V. 20 cc. 4–9 (Friedberg, ii cols. 817–

and import of his arguments and rested the foundation of his whole case, were genuine, but they are forgeries. Indeed, the writing material,[1] the style, the thread, and the bulla of Constantine's privileges are completely unknown in our land. What is more, the bearer of the indults of Clement and Celestine was a known forger named Nicholas of Warwick, and we therefore believe them to be false, and say the same about the others.'[2]

300. The pope instructed me to produce them, and I did so. He took them in his own hands and pulled between the bulla and the document to see if he could separate the bulla from the cord.[3] Scrutinizing them very carefully, he then handed them to the cardinals for them to scrutinize, and when they had gone the rounds of them all they came back to the pope. Holding up the privilege of Constantine, he said 'Privileges of this kind which are unknown to you are very well known to us, and could not be forged'; then holding up the letters, he said, 'These are genuine', and he returned them all to me. I am not going to tell you how fearful I was for myself, our church and our case, when the cardinals looked in turn at the privileges and when the pope handled them so roughly, for I could not describe it to you. Although I personally had nothing to be guilty about, I knew that the man who was the bearer of the letters, and happened to be an official messenger of the curia, was considered a forger; and about the privileges of Constantine, I was entirely ignorant. But when they were accepted as genuine I was overjoyed. This was the second interlocutory[4] judgment given in our favour. The first was when I was originally at Rome acting for the revocation of the jurisdiction of the judges [delegate] to prevent a possessory judgment[5] being given, though this interlocutory sentence the pope later revoked.

301. Since it was now time for dinner, the pope commanded that we should adjourn, and that our opponent should make his reply in opposition when we were summoned again. Three days later we were again summoned, and our opponent continued his speech in reply.

22). He was particularly concerned about the probity of the messengers who delivered letters. Unfortunately no more is known of Nicholas of Warwick.

[3] *X*. V. 20 c. 5 (Friedberg, ii cols. 818–19), provides nine tests for forgeries, drawing attention to a close examination of how the *bulla* was attached to the cords. Expert forgers might attach an authentic *bulla* to a forgery.

[4] An interim sentence, dealing only with part of the matter in dispute.

[5] A sentence giving possession.

302. *De secundo consistorio et de obiectione prescriptionis*[a] *contra priuilegia*

'Pater sancte, si priuilegia uera sunt et uideantur operari pro eis, ad fo. 160rb liber|tatem tamen nichil prosunt illis, quia eis usi non sunt. Immo episcopi Wigornenses e contrario in monachos et monasterium eorum iure communi[1] tanto tempore usi sunt quod contra eos et priuilegia eorum ius episcopale prescripsisse uidentur, sicut per depositiones testium sanctitati uestre plenissime patebit.'

303. Et incipiens a capite allegationum mearum probauit per dicta testium omni exceptione maiorum quod episcopi contra omnia capitula priuilegiorum nostrorum iure communi in monasterio nostro usi erant, sicut in aliis diocesana lege sibi subiectis. Probauit enim per testes quod episcopi abbatibus nostris benedixerant, et quod abbates professionem eis fecerant, et quod episcopi in ecclesia nostra sollempniter cum processione admissi fuerant, et quod missas publicas et sollempnes in ecclesia nostra celebrauerant, et quod decreta eorum et statuta ibi admissa fuerant, et quod ab eis crisma et oleum et ordinationes receperimus, et quod abbas noster ad sinodum episcopi uenerat. Tunc conuersus ad me dominus papa dixit, 'Procurator, responde.' Prohibuerat enim ne aduocati loquerentur de facto, nisi de iure tantum et cum opus esset, quia dixit procuratores nosse factum et iura. Ego sciens quod hec omnia uentura erant super me,[2] bene premeditatus respondi.

304. *De responsione Thome monachi contra obiectionem prescriptionis*[b]

'Pater sancte, nequaquam ita est ut dicit aduersarius noster. In nullo enim priuilegiis nostris abusi sumus, immo legittime et plenissime eis usi sumus, ita etiam quod prescriptione contra omnia iura episcopalia optime muniti sumus. Et si aliquando episcopi contra priuilegia nostra nitebantur uenire, per optimas contradictiones et iuris nostri et priuilegiorum nostrorum protestationes eorum malicie obuiauimus. Ita quod contra ecclesiam nostram numquam aliqua currere potuit prescriptio, sicut ex ipsis attestationibus sanctitas uestra liquido perpendet. Quod enim dicit episcopos Wigorn' abbatibus nostris fo. 160va benedixisse et abbates eis professionem fecisse uerum est, | sed

---

[a] prescriptoris *R*   [b] prescriptoris *R*

---

[1] See above, **245**, and below, **303, 357, 381, 382**.
[2] John 18: 4.

302. *The second consistory and the charge of prescription made against the privileges*

'Holy father, even if the privileges are genuine and were to appear to operate in their favour, yet they are of no advantage to them so far as liberty is concerned, for they have not made use of them. On the contrary, bishops of Worcester have for so long a time used the *ius commune*[1] against the monks and their monastery that they appear to have asserted episcopal right by prescription against them and their privileges, as will be abundantly clear to your holiness in the depositions of witnesses.'

303. Beginning with the chief of my arguments he proved through the statements of witnesses, using every extract of the more important of them, that bishops, contrary to the clauses of our privileges, had used the *ius commune* in the case of our monastery as in that of other monasteries subject to them under diocesan law. Through the statements of witnesses he proved that bishops had given blessing to our abbots, that abbots had made profession to them, that bishops had been formally admitted into our church in procession, that they had celebrated solemn masses publicly in our church, that their decrees and statutes had been accepted there, that we had received chrism, oil, and ordinations from them, and that our abbot had attended the bishop's synod. Turning to me, the pope said, 'Proctor, make your reply.' He had forbidden the advocates to speak about the facts of the case, unless they concerned the law, and then only when necessary, because he said proctors know the facts and the rights. Knowing that I would be faced with all these matters,[2] and so having thought about them beforehand, I made my reply.

304. *The reply of Thomas the monk to the argument of prescription*

'Holy father, it is not at all as our opponent says. In no respect have we failed to use our privileges, rather have we made the fullest legitimate use of them as to have been very well protected by prescription against all episcopal rights. If bishops endeavoured at any time to oppose our privileges we met their ill intent with the excellent counter-arguments of our rights and the counter-evidence of our privileges. The result was that no prescription was ever able to operate against our church, as your holiness will clearly judge from the written statements of the witnesses themselves. Our opponent's statement that bishops of Worcester gave blessing to our abbots, and that abbots made profession to them is true, but these things were

capitulo Eueshamensi contradicente hec facta sunt et abbatibus
protestantibus quod saluis priuilegiis suis hec fecerunt sicut per
tales testes probatur.ᵃ Quod autem dicit episcopos Wigornie cum
sollempni processione fuisse a nobis admissos uerum est, set cum
protestatione priuilegiorum et caritatiue et pro ecclesiis que non
probantur exempte hec fecimusᵇ sicut illi testes probant. Ad missas
etiam sollempnes eos admisimusᶜ set uocatos sicut in priuilegio
Innocentii pape continetur et sicut tales testes probant. Quod
autem dicit statuta episcoporum fuisse a nobis admissa falsum est.
Immo statuta Henrici episcopi¹ ab abbate nostro penitus fuerunt apud
Fladeburiam refutata et reiecta post traditionem. Et decreta eciam
episcopi Iohannis² postquam lecta fuerunt in capitulo omnino a
saniori parte capituli contradicta et refutata fuerunt sicut plenissime
per hos et illos testes probatur. Quod uero sacramenta ecclesiastica ab
eis recepimus, hoc nobis non nocet quia secundum priuilegium
Alexandri pape hoc nobis licet a quo maluerimus episcopo facere,³
et cum protestatione talis libertatis et auctoritate priuilegii illius hoc
fecimus. Et caritatiue petiuimus et accepimus sicut per tales testes
probatur. Quod autem abbas noster ad sinodum uenit non nocet, quia
pro membris que non probantur exempta hoc fecit, et hoc ibi publice
protestatus est sicut illi testes probant.

305. *De disputatione aduocatorum circa usum et abusum priuilegiorum et
prescriptionem et interruptionem per tres audientias*
Tunc dominus papa conuersus ad aduocatos dixit, 'Ecce instructi
sumus de facto per procuratores. Nunc autem instruatis nos de iure
circa usum et abusum priuilegiorum et circa prescriptionem et
interruptionem, et cum deliberatione cum uocati fueritis.'
306. Et recessimus. Et post aliquot dies uocati sumus. Tunc
aduocati nostri tam illa die quam iterum post aliquot dies per duas
uidelicet audientias quam egregie et subtiliter fere omnes utriusque
fo. 160ᵛᵇ   iuris, canonici uidelicet | et ciuilis, apices et difficultates in
allegationibus circa usum et abusum priuilegiorum et prescriptionem

---

ᵃ *marg.* Nota quod nullus prior celle nostre (*ins.*) nec aliquis eiusdem debet facere
obedienciam episcopo. Et conpulsus debet dicere saluis priuilegiis monasterii nostri (*s. xvᵃ*)
ᵇ *two to three words erased after* fecimus *and before* sicut   ᶜ *one to two words erased after*
admisimus *and before* set

---

¹ el. 4 Dec., cons. 12 Dec. 1193, d. 24 or 25 Oct. 1195; *HBC*, p. 279. The statutes in
question are not known to have survived.
² el. *Jan.*, cons. 20 Oct. 1196, d. 24 Sept. 1198; ibid.
³ For Alexander III's privilege, see below, 332–6.

done despite the opposition of the Evesham chapter, and with the protestation of the abbots that they did these things saving their privileges, and the witnesses' evidence proves this. His contention that we admitted bishops of Worcester in a solemn procession is true, but we did so saving our privileges and in a spirit of love, and only for the churches that do not have proof of exemption, as the witnesses' evidence proves. We admitted bishops even to solemn masses, but they were invited, as the privilege of Pope Innocent provides, and the evidence of the witnesses proves. His statement that the statutes of bishops were accepted by us, however, is false. Indeed, the statutes of Bishop Henry [de Soilli][1] were utterly refuted and rejected by our abbot at Fladbury after they were handed over. When the decrees of Bishop John [of Coutances][2] had been read in chapter they were completely opposed and rejected by the wiser section of the chapter, and this is fully proved by the various witnesses. It is not prejudicial to our case that we received church sacraments from bishops because, according to the privilege of Pope Alexander [III], we are allowed to receive them from any bishop of our choosing,[3] and we have done this still affirming the liberty to do so and on the authority of that privilege. We have asked for, and received, this service in a spirit of love, as is proved by the appropriate witnesses' evidence. Again, it is not prejudicial to our case that our abbot went to a synod, because he did this on behalf of those dependencies which have no proof of exemption, and this was publicly proclaimed there, as the witnesses' evidence proves.'

305. *The disagreement of the advocates in the three hearings over the use and lack of use of the privileges, and over prescription and interruption in the exercise of prescriptive rights*
Then the pope turned to the advocates and said, 'We have been instructed by the proctors upon the facts. You must now instruct us upon the law relating to the use and lack of use of privileges, and relating to prescription and interruption, and must do so with deliberation, since you have been summoned.'
306. We withdrew. Then several days later we were summoned. That day, and again on an occasion several days later, our advocates cleverly and subtly exhausted in the two hearings almost all the finer points and difficulties of both branches of the law, canon and civil, relating to the arguments about the use and lack of use of privileges

et interruptionem exhauserint. Supersedeo dicere quia non possem uobis edicere.

307. In secundo uero consistorio dixit dominus papa, 'Sufficit usque huc dixisse de hiis. Nunc autem, procuratores, redite ad priuilegia et per ea de iure ecclesiarum uestrarum sufficientius nos instruite quando uocati fueritis'. Et exiuimus. Post aliquot dies uocati comparuimus et dixit magister Robertus.

308. *De quinto consistorio et de allegationibus magistri Rodberti super interpretatione priuilegiorum*

'Pater sancte, prima die proposuit aduersarius noster quedam capitula priuilegiorum suorum per que nitebatur ostendere monasterium suum esse liberum et exemptum. Set ego uideo quedam capitula in eisdem priuilegiis predictis sibi repugnantia. Vnde michi uidetur quod cum priuilegia sibi adinuicem sint contraria*a* nullius sunt momenti, uel saltem ad plenam libertatem insufficientia cum per ipsa priuilegia quedam iura episcopalia in monasterio illo episcopo nostro reseruentur. Dicit enim Constantinus quod abbas eiusdem loci primum locum post Wictiorum presulem[1] sua auctoritate iugiter optineat. Set cum locum illum nec in generali consilio nec prouinciali possit optinere, quia hoc alii episcopi inferiores nostro non permitterent, restat ut ad sinodum episcopalem ueniat, et ibi locum illum optineat et sic episcopo subitiatur. In priuilegio uero Alexandri continetur quod Wigornenses episcopi aliquid iniuste ab eis non exigant set hiis tantum contenti sint que antecessores eorum*b* antecessoribus suis constat rationabiliter exhibuisse. Ergo constat antecessores eorum aliquid antecessoribus episcoporum rationabiliter impendisse. Ergo episcopi aliquid petere possunt et ipsi hoc eis exhibere tenentur. Ergo episcopo in aliquo subitiuntur; ergo non sunt plene exempti, uel potius, cum nullus possit esse in parte liber et in parte seruus,[2] nullo modo sunt exempti'.

---

a quod *add*   *b* *followed by* aliquid *struck through*

---

[1] See *X.* V. 33. 17 (Friedberg, ii cols. 862–4). In 1219, Abbot Randulf appealed that, although mitred, he was not given the place after the bishop at the synod called by Bishop William of Blois; see 'Annales de Wigornia', *Ann. Mon.*, iv. 411.

and about prescription and interruption. I refrain from telling you what they said for I could not repeat it.

307. In the second consistory the pope said, 'Enough has now been said on these subjects. Return now to the privileges, proctors, and instruct us more fully upon the rights of your churches when you are summoned.' We departed. On being summoned several days later we made our appearance. Then Master Robert spoke.

308. *The fifth consistory, and the arguments of Master Robert about the interpretation of the privileges*

'Holy father, on the first day our opponent laid before us certain sections of his privileges by means of which he was endeavouring to show that his monastery was free and exempt. However, I see some sections in those same privileges that contradict one another. Hence, it seems to me that, because there are privileges that oppose one another, then they are of no importance, or at least of insufficient competence to allow full liberty because in those same privileges certain episcopal rights are reserved in that monastery for our bishop. For Constantine states that the abbot of the same place should on his own authority always hold the first place after the bishop of the Hwicce.[1] But as he could not hold that position either in a general council or in a provincial council, because the other bishops, though less important, would not allow this, it remains for him to come to the episcopal synod and to hold that place there and so be subject to the bishop. In the privilege of Alexander [III] it is stated that bishops of Worcester should not make any unjust demands upon the abbots but be content with those things alone which it is agreed the abbots' predecessors had reasonably rendered to the bishops' predecessors. It is agreed therefore that the abbots' predecessors had reasonably rendered some things to the bishops' predecessors. Therefore bishops can make some demands of them, and the abbots are bound to meet them. The abbots are therefore subject to the bishops in some measure; they are not therefore fully exempt, or rather, since no one can be partly free and partly a slave,[2] abbots are in no respect exempt.'

---

[2] 'Cum nullus possit esse in parte liber, etc.' is probably a comment on *Institutes* 1.3 pr. 'Omnes homines aut liberi sunt aut serui', deliberately echoing *Institutes* 2. 14. 5. Cf. de Zulueta and Stein, *Teaching of Roman Law in England*, pp. 12, 49, and lxi.

fo. 161ra **309.** | *De subtilissima responsione Thome monachi et aduocatorum eius circa interpretationem priuilegiorum* ^a

Et cum perorasset respondi ego dicens, 'Mirum michi uidetur qualiter aduersarius noster ponere os in celum ausus sit,[1] dicens priuilegia Romani pontificis nullius esse momenti cum etiam instar sit sacrilegii de sententia eius disputare.[2] Cum enim dicta testium secundum leges ita sint interpretanda ut sibi adinuicem non sint contraria, ne testes periurii arguantur, multo fortius priuilegia summi pontificis benigne sunt interpretanda, ut sicut nunquam possunt esse inania ita nec sibi unquam sint contraria.'^b

310. Et post hec responderunt aduocati nostri quod absque preiudicio libertatis ecclesie nostre poterat abbas ad sinodum episcopi uenire et ibi locum primum optinere, set non pro capite set pro membris que non probantur exempta. Et statuta episcoporum que illa membra contingunt recipere et seruare absque libertatis nostre lesione. Sic enim necesse est et nos aliorum episcoporum in quorum episcopatibus beneficia ecclesiastica habemus, si uocati fuerimus, sinodos adire, et quoad illa beneficia eorum statuta seruare, non tamen ipsi in monasterio nostro uel in nobis aliquam possunt exercere iurisdictionem. Simili modo dixerunt illud Alexandri intelligendum, uidelicet quod aliquid tenebamur exhibere episcopis pro membris que nondum probantur exempta, sicut et aliis episcopis pro beneficiis que habemus in eorum episcopatibus. Et subticuerunt aduocati.^c

311. Dominus uero papa conuersus ad me dixit, 'Procurator, uisne aliter respondere hiis, ut si forte capitula ista non possint intelligi de membris, quod illis de capite intellectis monasterium uestrum conseruetur illesum, liberum et exemptum?' Ego uero, qui ab initio cause hec duo capitula fere usque ad mortem timueram, uidens quod timor quem timueram iam euenit michi. Quia iacula que preuidentur minus feriunt, bene premeditatus, dixi,^d 'Pater sancte, ego hec de capite bene expono, et ne libertatem nostram in fo. 161rb aliquo ledant eis multipliciter respondeo.' | Et dominus papa dixit, 'Non credimus.' Et dixi, 'Deo propitio, faciam.' Et respondi, 'Bene

---

^a *The heading is incorrectly indicated to be placed after* sint contraria *at the end of the paragraph* ^b *marg.* priuilegia Romani pontificis benigne sunt interpretanda (?s. xv) ^c *marg.* Responsio procuratoris nostri (s. xv) ^d *marg.* Responsio (s. xv)

[1] Cf. Ps. 72: 9 (73: 9).
[2] The origin of this idea is in the Roman law, *Code* 9. 29. 2, whence Gratian, *Decretum* C 17 q. 4 p. c. 29 §1. 2 (Friedberg, i cols. 822–3). It is found in a letter of Innocent III of 1203 (*Reg. Inn. III*, vi no. 75 (P 1925) p.114 and n. 101), 'quod . . . legitime non fuisset, cum instar sacrilegii sit de statutis principum iudicare'.

309. *The astute reply of Thomas the monk and his advocates on the interpretation of the privileges*

When he had finished his speech, I replied in these words: 'I consider it amazing that our opponent should set his mouth against the heavens[1] and say that the privileges of the Roman pontiff are of no importance, for it is tantamount to sacrilege to question the pope's judgment.[2] Just as the statements of witnesses made in accordance with the law must be so interpreted as not to conflict with one another, lest witnesses be accused of perjury, much more important is it that the privileges of the high pontiff be generously interpreted so that, as they can never be foolish, they may never conflict with one another.'

310. After this our advocates replied that the abbot could go to the episcopal synod and hold first position there without prejudice to the liberty of our church, but not on behalf of the mother church, only on behalf of the dependencies which do not have proof of exemption. They said that he could receive and observe decrees of bishops which concern those dependencies without detriment to our liberty. Indeed, it is necessary for us not only to go, if summoned, to the synods of other bishops in whose dioceses we have ecclesiastical benefices, but also to observe their decrees while we hold those benefices, but they have no power to exercise any jurisdiction in our monastery or over us. In similar terms the advocates said that Alexander's privilege must be understood to mean that we were bound to render something to the bishops on behalf of the dependencies which do not yet have proof of exemption, just as we do to other bishops for the benefices we hold in their dioceses. The advocates said no more.

311. The pope turned to me and said, 'Proctor, do you wish to refute these arguments, on the grounds that even if those sections of the privileges perhaps cannot be understood to apply to the dependencies, being understood to apply to the mother church, your monastery will be preserved unharmed, free and exempt?' Indeed, I had been frightened almost to death from the outset of the suit by these two articles, and saw that the fear which I had experienced was now being realized. However, just as darts which are foreseen have less impact, I was well prepared in mind and said, 'Holy father, I am going to give a full explanation of these arguments that concern the mother church and make various assertions in my reply to them to prevent them harming our liberty in any respect.' The pope replied, 'We do not believe this possible.' My response was, 'With God's help

concedo quod abbas noster in sinodo episcopali primum locum post episcopum obtineat, set non ratione abbatie uel menbrorum set ut nuncius uester et minister.ᵃ Sic enim dicit Constantinus, ut "locum primum post Wicciorum presulem auctoritate nostra iugiter obtineat"; non dicit quod auctoritate propria ut abbas uel ut persona alicuius ecclesie set ut missus uester. Si queritis ad quid missus, dico ad hoc, ut uideat ne episcopus aliquid contra priuilegia Romani pontificis statuta, et ne ecclesiam domini pape, uidelicet Eueshamensem, in aliquo ledat. Et hoc dico ad similitudinem illius quod idem papa Constantinus Britwaldo Brittanniarum primati in eodem priuilegio precipit, dicens, "Tue fraternitati denuntiamus quatinus ecclesias Dei per Brittanniam dispositas, tua ipsius et sanctorum apostolorum auctoritate protegas, ne quis peruasor cuiuscumque ordinis a Deo et nobis constituta priuilegia subruat. Inter quas eam que nuperrime a uenerabili uiro Ecguuino nostra et regia auctoritate constituta est tue ditioni precipue submittimus, ut tibi et posteris tuis potestate diuinitus concessa ab omni eam aduersariorum impugnatione liberam in perpetuum reddas."¹ Cum igitur gratia uestri et in priuilegio nostro domino Cantuariensi precipitur ut priuilegia nostra et ecclesiam nostram protegat et defendat, quis dixerit hoc abbati nostro pro propria ecclesia ᵇ et in proprio priuilegio non esse iniunctum,ᶜ maxime cum absurdum esset archiepiscopum qui nos tueri tenetur, propter hoc ad sinodum episcopi uenire. Relinquitur ergo abbati faciendum, quod facere ᵈ non potest archiepiscopus, ut uidelicet abbas intersit synodo episcopi ad tuitionem priuilegiorum nostrorum. Et hoc auctoritate domini pape non aliqua sua propria necessitate.

fo. 161ᵛᵃ   **312.** 'Quod autem | ᵉ dicit Alexander quod Wigornenses episcopi hiis contenti sint que antecessores nostros antecessoribus suis constat rationabiliter ᶠ exhibuisse. Cum non constet antecessores nostros antecessoribus suis aliquid rationabiliter exhibuisse et iam productionibus testium sit renuntiatum, et non probauerunt aliquid fuisse eis rationabiliter a predecessoribus nostris exhibitum. Constat nos nichil debere eis exhibere.ᵍ Non enim hoc nomen que hic aliquid implicat

---

ᵃ *marg.* Nota optime quod abbas debet interesse sinodo episcopi non ratione abbatie uel membrorum set ut nuncius [pape] (*s. xv*)   ᵇ *followed by* et in propria ecclesia *expunged*   ᶜ *marg.* Nota hiis(?) bene (*s. xv*)   ᵈ *followed by* non facere *struck through*   ᵉ *Top of fo. left margin* R' penbrok (*s. xv*). (*Richard Pembroke was elected abbot in 1460*)   ᶠ constat *expunged*   ᵍ *marg.* Nota quod abbas non debet facere episcopo Wyg' non sub conditione aliquod(?) obsequen(?) ad [pape?] non expressat' in bull' (?*s. xv*)

I shall succeed.' I went on, 'I readily admit that our abbot may hold first place after the bishop in the episcopal synod, but this is not in respect of the abbey or the dependencies, but because he is your messenger and minister. For Constantine puts it like this, "Let him hold for ever the first place after the bishop of the Hwicce on our authority"; he does not say that he should hold it on his own authority as abbot or as parson of any church, but as your representative. If you ask "representative for what?", I say for this, that he may see that the bishop does not make any decree against the privileges of the Roman pontiff, and does not in any way harm the pope's church at Evesham. I say this to comply with the command which the same Pope Constantine gave to Berhtwald, primate of Britain, in the same privilege when he said, "We command you, brother, to protect the churches of God scattered throughout Britain, by your own authority and that of the holy apostles, so that no assailant of any rank may undermine the privileges instituted by God and us. Amongst these churches we especially place under your authority that church most recently founded by the venerable Ecgwine under our authority and that of the king, to ensure that by the power divinely granted to you and your successors you keep it for ever free from all assaults of its enemies."[1] Since therefore it is by your favour and in our privilege that the archbishop of Canterbury is commanded to protect and defend our privileges and our church, who could say that this command has not been given to our abbot on behalf of his own church and in respect of his own privilege, especially since it would be absurd for the archbishop himself, who is bound to protect us, to come to the bishop's synod for this purpose? It remains to say therefore that the abbot must do what the archbishop cannot do, attend the bishop's synod to protect our privileges: he does this on the authority of the pope, not because he needs to do so on his own account.

312. 'Pope Alexander says that the bishops of Worcester should be content with those things which it is agreed our predecessors regularly rendered to their predecessors. Since, however, it is not agreed that our predecessors regularly rendered anything to their predecessors and any suggestion that they did has been repudiated by the evidence submitted by witnesses, our opponents have not proved that anything was regularly rendered to them by our predecessors. It is established therefore that we are under no obligation to render

[1] See below, 324.

nec implicite ponitur. Set magis quasi sub conditione dicitur,ᵃ ut is sit sensus, quod Wigornenses episcopi hiis contenti sint que, id est, si que, antecessores nostros antecessoribus suis constat rationabiliter exhibuisse.ᵇ Si enim domino pape constitisset quod antecessores nostri antecessoribus episcopi aliquid impendissent, illud expressisset. Set quia de nullo exhibito uel exhibendo ei constitit, ideo sub conditione dixit et probandum quod esset exhibendum episcopo reliquit. Ergo cum nichil probauit exhibitum, nichil est exhibendum.'ᶜ

313. Et ad hanc interpretationem confirmandam quasdam leges quas a domino Assone,ᵈ tunc temporis legum dominorum domino Bononie,¹ non sine precio didiceram, induxi. Cum igitur conclusissem, et placuisset ei simulque assidentibus, ut michi uidebatur, dixit michi dominus papa, 'Visne amplius allegare?' Et ego, 'Pater sancte, sufficit michi: peto sententiam nisi aduersarius noster aliud dixerit.' Et respiciens ad aduersarium nostrum, dixit, 'Renuntias tu allegationibus?' Et ille, 'Renuntio.' Et dominus papa, 'Discedite, et scribite nobis summatim allegationes uestras et detis nobis hac die. Et confidite in Domino et per gratiam Dei in breui habebitis sententiam.' Et recedentes uterque nostrum seorsum suas scripsit allegationes. Nos uero breuius, quam hic sint scripte et subtilius et melius. Et tradidimus eas domino pape in uespera.

314. De ieiunio,ᵉ orationibus et elemosinis Thome monachi postquam in causa fuit conclusum et allegationibus renuntiatum

Tunc bene sciens ego quod iam ad humanas rationes nullus erat
fo. 161ᵛᵇ recursus, | ad diuina presidia, sanctorum uidelicet suffragia, elemosinas, orationes et ieiunia sum conuersus. Erat autem feria quinta, dies scilicet Iouis ante natiuitatem Domini² que instante die Dominica erat celebranda, et circumiui loca sanctorum commendans eis me et causam ecclesie mee. Et cuilibet egeno tam petenti quam non petenti de bonis ecclesie conferens, in continua oratione ieiunus permansi usque ad sabbatum postquam lata fuit pro nobis sentencia.³ Sabbato

---

ᵃ marg. Nota sub conditione fit quicquid fit episcopo Wig' (?s. xv)   ᵇ marg. Nota optime (?s. xv)   ᶜ marg. Nota sententiam (?s. xv)   ᵈ marg. Nota sententiam doct[oris] Assonis Bononie (?s. xv)   ᵉ ieunio R

¹ Azo was the leading glossator at the time, see H. Lange, *Römisches Recht im Mittelalter*, i: *Die Glossatoren* (Munich, 1997), pp. 257–71, for his influence and writings, and 'Azzone' in *Dizionario Biografico degli Italiani*, iv. 774–81. It was said that he who did not have Azo's *Summa* 'should not go to court', cited P. Stein, *Roman Law in Medieval History* (Cambridge, 1999), p. 48.

anything to them. Indeed, this expression "which things" does not imply, nor implicitly specify, any actual thing. Rather it is a hypothetical statement, so that the sense is that the bishops of Worcester should be content with those things, that is, *if there are any things*, which it is agreed our predecessors regularly rendered to their predecessors. Indeed, if the pope had been convinced that our predecessors had paid anything to the predecessors of the bishop he would have said so. But because he was not convinced that anything was rendered or ought to be rendered, he spoke hypothetically, and left it to be proved that some service was rendered to the bishop. Since no proof has been forthcoming that anything was rendered, there is no obligation for anything to be rendered now.'

313. In order to corroborate this interpretation I referred to certain laws which I had learned—not without expense—from Azo, at that time the leading lawyer at Bologna.[1] When I had concluded my speech, and the pope and the judges sitting with him were satisfied, as it seemed to me, the pope said to me, 'Do you wish to put forward any further arguments?' I said, 'No, holy father, I am satisfied: I ask for sentence, unless our opponent has anything else to say.' Looking at our opponent he said, 'Do you reject their arguments?' And he replied, 'I do.' So the pope then said, 'Go and make written summaries of your arguments and give them to us today. Then put your trust in the Lord, and by God's grace you will soon receive sentence.' Each of us went off to our separate quarters and wrote out our arguments. I did it more concisely than is recorded here, and better and more subtly. We then handed them over to the pope that evening.

314. *The fasting, praying, and almsgiving of Thomas the monk after the conclusion of the case and the rejection of the charges*

Well aware then that I had no recourse to human solutions, I turned to divine protection, that is to the intercession of the saints, to almsgiving, prayer, and fasting. It was the Thursday before Christmas,[2] which was to be celebrated this year on a Sunday, so I travelled around the holy places commending myself and the cause of my church to the saints. I bestowed alms from the church upon any needy person I met who asked for them as well as upon those who did not ask for them, and I persisted in prayer and fasting until the Saturday after the sentence was given in our favour.[3] Very early on

---

[2] 22 Dec. 1205.   [3] 31 Dec.

uero summo mane[1] accessi ad curiam et, cuiuslibet cardinalis ingredientis pedes[a] tenens, magis lacrimis quam uerbis motum animi mei indicaui, ut scilicet seruorum suorum et ecclesie sue misererentur. Supplicaui et tam miserabiliter quod non solum cardinales set etiam aduersarii mei et omnes qui me uiderunt mei miserebantur. Tandem perseuerante me in oratione, circa horam diei nonam exiuit de thalamo dominus papa cum cardinalibus. Et cum sedisset uocati sumus procuratores Eueshamie et Wigornie. Et confortatus[b] sum eo quod preponerent me aduersario meo in casu illo, quamuis fere semper ita consueuerant apparitores, multociens enim benefeceram eis ut liberiorem haberem ingressum; idem enim ibi sunt apparitores et hostiarii. Et cum staremus sicut consueuimus ex aduerso ad inuicem, dixit dominus papa, 'State simul in medio, iam enim non est lis inter uos[c] quia pacificata sunt omnia'. Et non intellexi primum quid loqueretur, set postquam spiritus sanctus datus est nobis[2] per sententiam domini pape, omnia nuda et aperta erant oculis meis.[3] Et cum coniungeremur, dixit dominus papa.

315. *De sententia domini [pape] et aduentu magistri Ade monachi ad curiam*

'Causam que uertebatur inter uenerabilem fratrem[d] nostrum Wigornensem episcopum et dilectos filios nostros abbatem et conuentum Eueshamie super subieccione et exemptione cenobii Eueshamensis fo. 162[ra] diligentissi|me examinauimus. Et inspectis priuilegiis et attestationibus et perspicaciter intellectis, eam sentencialiter determinauimus.[e] Et in scriptum[f] redigi fecimus et preter consuetudinem nostram per scripturam eam recitari uolumus'.

316. Et surgens magister Philippus primus notariorum, postea Troianus episcopus,[4] dixit, 'Abbati et fratribus Eueshamensis cenobii, et cetera'. Et cum audissem quod scriberet nobis, reuixit spiritus

---

[a] *marg.* Nota bene (*s. xv*)   [b] *marg.* Nota processu(?m) gau.. (*s. xv*)   [c] nos R
[d] *marg.* Nota sententiam pape   [e] decreuimus *written above in the hand of the scribe of the marginal note*   [f] *marg.* sententia lata

---

[1] 24 Dec.
[2] Cf. John 15: 26.
[3] Cf. Gen. 3: 7.
[4] This is probably the papal official who acted as tax collector in England, arriving before 24 Apr. 1200. He presumably did not stay long, as he was on legation in Germany in 1201–2, but as C. R. Cheney states ('Master Philip the notary and the fortieth of 1199', *EHR* lxiii (1948), 342–50), there were two notaries called Master Philip, so the identification is not certain. He became bishop of Troja (Foggia, prov. Apulia) in 1212

the Saturday morning,[1] I went to the curia and, grasping the feet of any cardinal who was entering, I showed my feelings more by my tears than by my words to gain their pity for their servants and their church. So pitiable was my supplication that not only the cardinals but also my opponents and all who saw me pitied me. At last, while I was still at my prayers, at three o'clock in the afternoon the pope came out of his chamber with the cardinals. When he had sat down the proctors of Evesham and Worcester were summoned. I was encouraged by the fact that they placed me in front of my opponent on that occasion, though the ushers had almost always done this, for I had on many occasions rewarded them so that I might get in more easily (the summoners there are the same as the doorkeepers). When we stood, as we were accustomed to do, facing each other, the pope said, 'Stand together before me, for there is no lawsuit between you now, as everything has been settled.' At first I did not understand what he meant, but after the Holy Spirit was given to us[2] through the sentence of the pope, everything was unveiled and my eyes were opened.[3] When we were standing side by side the pope spoke.

315. *The sentence of the pope and the arrival of the monk, Master Adam [Sortes], at the curia*
'We have most carefully examined the case which has been argued between our reverend brother, the bishop of Worcester, and our beloved sons, the abbot and convent of Evesham, about the subjection or exemption of the monastery of Evesham. The privileges and the testimony of witnesses have been examined and clearly understood, and we have come to a decision on the sentence. We have had this put in writing and, in accordance with our custom, we wish the sentence to be read out from the document.'

316. Master Philip, the senior notary and afterwards bishop of Troja,[4] rose and said, 'To the abbot and brethren of Evesham monastery, etc.' When I heard that the document was addressed to

(P. B. Gams, *Series episcoporum ecclesiae catholicae a beato Petro apostolo* (Leipzig, 1931), p. 937). On the *primicerius notariorum*, the senior notary, cf. M. Tangl, *Die päpstlichen Kanzleiordnungen von 1200–1500* (Innsbruck, 1894), pp. 62 n. 5, 63 nn. 20, 21, and 65 n. 6. There is little on the curial notaries as early as this, but see P. Herde, 'Öffentliche Notare an der päpstlichen Kurie im dreizehnten und beginnenden vierzehnten Jahrhundert', *Studien zur Geschichte des Mittelalters: Jürgen Petersohn zum 65. Geburtstag*, ed. M. Thumser, A Wenz-Haubfleisch, and P. Wiegand (Stuttgart, 2000), pp. 239–59, at 239–40.

meus. Noui enim modum scribendi domini pape per moram quam feceram in curia, quod multum profuit cause nostre, quia non scriberet nisi uictori. Vnde cum episcopus habeat eandem sententiam quam et nos procurator eius non potuit impetrare ut in sententia episcopi scriberet episcopo set nobis sicut et in nostra. Et cum legisset sententiam latam pro nobis, iuimus ad pedes domini pape tam uictus quam uictor, ut mos est, gratias agentes. Et cum inclinarem me ad osculandum pedes domini pape, tum pre gaudio tum pre ieiunio defecit spiritus meus et factus sum fere exanimatus, ita quod non potui surgere et *a* precepit dominus papa ut subleuarer. Et cum iam quasi a graui sompno euigilassem, dixit dominus papa ut acciperem notam et diligenter inspicerem si forte quid esset corrigendum et nuntiarem ei. Et, accepta benedictione, cum nota recessi gaudens. Et cum uenissem ad hostium, inueni magistrum Adam Sortem *b* stantem; qui uenerat tunc ab Anglia cum quibusdam instrumentis. Et suscepto eo in osculo pacis, cum simul cibum sumpsissemus, confortati sumus, gratias agentes Deo pro omnibus benefitiis suis, qui fecit nobiscum secundum magnam misericordiam suam,[1] qui uiuit et regnat per omnia secula seculorum. Amen.[2]

317. *Transcripta priuilegiorum quorum auctoritate sententia lata fuit pro exemptione Eueshamensis ecclesie*
In hoc loco tam ipsa priuilegia quorum auctoritate sententia pro nobis lata est quam ipsam sententiam per quam quasi ab Egyptiaca seruitute liberati sumus, huic scripto interserenda bonum et utile putaui.

318. *Primum priuilegium Constantini pape* *c*

fo. 162*rb* | Constantinus*d* episcopus seruus seruorum Dei Brithwaldo*e* *f*ecclesiarum*g* Brittanniarum*f* primati salutem et apostolicam benedictionem. Venerabilem uirum Ecgwinum episcopum quem bis tua fraternitas ad apostolicam sedem misit, etiam nunc secundo manipulis iustitie refertum tibi remittimus, monentes quatinus sic suos effectus adiuuando prosequaris sicuti illum a Deo incepisse et in uia Dei cucurrisse cognouisti.

319. Porro de uisione illa, immo aperta ostensione qua se beata uirgo

---

a *interlined*   *b* *marg.* Adam magister et monachus   *c* *The text appears also in H and V: variants from R are reported below*   *d* C V   *e* Brihtwaldo H
f-f Britanniarum ecclesie *H*; Brittaniarum ecclesie *V*   *g* ecclesiarum *struck through*

[1] 1 Pet. 1: 3; Titus 3: 5, *et al.*

us, my spirit revived. During my stay in the curia I had learned of the pope's manner of writing (which was of considerable benefit to our cause) that he addressed only the victorious party in writing. Now since the bishop has the same sentence as we do, his proctor could not demand that in the bishop's [copy of the] sentence the pope should address it to the bishop in writing, for it had to be addressed to us, as in our [copy of the] sentence. When he had read the sentence which had been given in our favour, we both approached the pope's feet as vanquished and victor and expressed our thanks as was the custom. I then bent to kiss the pope's feet, but my spirit failed me because of my joy, and my weakness through fasting, and I all but fainted. As I could not get up the pope gave instructions that I should be helped up. When I came to my senses as if after a deep sleep, the pope said that I would receive a draft and that I should examine it carefully to see if anything in it required correcting and bring it to his attention. Then after receiving his blessing, I left overjoyed with the draft. When I reached the door I found Master Adam Sortes standing there; he had just arrived from England with some documents. After greeting each other with a kiss of peace, we had a meal together, and then, being in good heart, we gave thanks to God for all his benefits who had dealt with us according to his great mercy,[1] who lives and reigns for ever and ever, Amen.[2]

317. *Transcripts of the privileges on whose authority the sentence was given in favour of the exemption of the church of Evesham*
At this point I have thought it right and beneficial to insert in this written account not only the actual privileges on whose authority the sentence was given in our favour, but also the sentence itself by which we were freed, as it were, from slavery in Egypt.

318. *The first privilege of Pope Constantine*
Constantine, bishop, servant of the servants of God, to Berhtwald, primate of the churches of Britain, greeting and apostolic benediction. We are now sending back to you a second time, with his hands filled with justice, the venerable bishop Ecgwine, whom you have twice sent to the apostolic see. We advise you to assist and promote his accomplishments, knowing that he has begun the course with God and is continuing in the way of God.

319. Concerning the vision, or indeed this open manifestation by

---

[2] A common ending to a collect.

Maria ei manifestauit, eque ita certum esse teneamus quemadmodum de uiri bonitate non dubitamus.[a] Denique uigilantiam tuam admonemus quatinus illis in partibus in quibus manifestatio habita fuisse refertur concilium[b] tocius Anglie cogas, episcopos sacrique[c] ordinis religiosas personas illuc conuenire facias, optimatesque regni cum proceribus suis adesse precipias.

320. Quibus in nomine Domini congregatis denuntiamus quod duo reges Anglie, Kenredus et Offa,[d] cum quibus iamdictus episcopus ad limina apostolorum uenit, in loco ostense uisionis plurima de suis beneficiis in presentia nostra regia libertate donata et apostolica auctoritate confirmata contulerunt, quatinus ibidem congregatio monachorum secundum regulam memorandi patris Benedicti, que minus in illis partibus adhuc habetur, possit instaurari et indesinenter Christo famulari. Ipsas autem donationes et beneficia prefati reges in ipsorum priuilegio nominatim determinauerunt et a nobis corroborari fecerunt.[e] Igitur, frater dilecte, quoquomodo Christus annuntietur lucrum Christi inquire,[f] opus Christi exerce, promulgatisque in concilio undique[g] sententiis tum a Deo ostense uisionis, tum apostolice auctoritatis, tum regie libertatis et donationis, tum tui ipsius clerique et populi assensus | et fauoris, constitue ouile Christo, diuinitus ostensum, apostolica auctoritate fultum, regia libertate donatum, cleri et populi benedictione sancitum.

fo. 162va

321. Tibi autem et successoribus tuis, memorato episcopo Ecgwino[h] assentiente, curam animarum eiusdem ecclesie precipue iniungimus ut si, quod absit, aliquo diaboli impulsu quisquam peruasor aut tirannus sacrum locum minuere aut impugnare presumpserit,[i] tibi a Deo concesse potestatis sententia et anathematis percussus uerbere, complere non audeat. Si quid uero sinistre partis inibi compertum fuerit oriri, auribus summi pontificis patrie potius deferatur quam per alicuius occultam sententiam sanctus locus deprauetur iniuste.[j]

322. Ipsum ergo locum quem regia potestas regie libertati donauit et nos auctoritate Dei et sanctorum apostolorum et nostra donamus ut nullus cuiuscumque ordinis homo hoc quod constituimus deprauare aut minuere[k] presumat. Qui hoc destruxerit aut male contaminauerit sit ille maledictus. Qui uero conseruauerit[l] et adauxerit benedictionibus repleatur.

---

[a] marg. Visio beate Virginis beato Egwino est auctorizata ab ecclesia (s. xv) [b] concilitium V   [c] que om. H   [d] marg. reges Kenredus Offa (s. xv) [e] marg. nota exortationes [? pape erased]   [f] require V   [g] concilio and undique om. V [h] Egwino episcopo H V   [i] marg. contra peruasores ecclesie nostre sententia excommunicationis (s. xv)   [j] iniuste deprauetur H V   [k] diminuere H

which the blessed Virgin Mary showed herself, we hold it to be just as certain as we do not doubt the man's goodness. Finally we advise you to be watchful and to call a council of all England in those parts in which the manifestation is said to have occurred, to have the bishops and religious of a holy order assemble there, and to instruct the magnates to attend together with their followers.

320. We proclaim to those who are gathered in the name of the Lord that two kings of England, Cenred and Offa, with whom the said bishop came to the threshold of the apostles, have in our presence granted very many of their beneficences in the place where the vision was revealed, and these were given with royal liberty and confirmed by apostolic authority. This is so that in that place a congregation of monks can be installed and for ever serve Christ in accordance with the Rule of the memorable father Benedict which is as yet little observed in those parts. The aforesaid kings have named those gifts and beneficences in their privilege, and have had them ratified by us. Therefore, beloved brother, seek the good of Christ in whatever way it may redound to Christ's glory; carry out Christ's work; and having set out in council overall the opinions both of the vision shewn by God, of apostolic authority, of royal endowment and liberty, and of the consent of your own clergy and people, establish for Christ a flock which has been divinely revealed, supported by apostolic authority, granted the royal liberty, and ratified by the blessing of the clergy and the people.

321. Especially do we lay upon you and your successors, with Bishop Ecgwine's consent, the care of souls in that same church, so that if any assailant or tyrant, God forbid, presume through any devilish impulse to impair or impugn this holy place, he may be alarmed by the condemnation which God has empowered you to pronounce and by the shock of an anathema, and so not dare to carry out his intention. Should anything of an evil nature be found to have occurred there, let it be brought to the notice of the high pontiff [archbishop] of the country rather than that holy place be unjustly brought into ill-repute by someone else's underhand condemnation.

322. Therefore, let no man of any rank dare to bring in to ill-repute or to impair the very place to which royal power has granted the royal liberty, and to which we also grant liberty by the authority of God and the holy apostles, and by our own authority. Let any man who destroys or maliciously pollutes it be accursed. But let the man who preserves or increases it be showered with blessings.

¹ seruauerit *H V*

323. Scripta est*[a]* hec epistola anno dominice incarnationis *[b]*septingentesimo nono*[b]* in ecclesia saluatoris Lateranensi,*[c]* precipiente et confirmante Constantino*[d]* apostolice sedis antistite,*[e]* astantibus et confirmantibus regibus Anglie Kenredo et Offa,[1] rogante uenerabili uiro Ecgwino episcopo coram archiepiscopis*[f]* et episcopis et principalibus*[g]* et nobilibus diuersarum prouinciarum, cunctis clamantibus et dicentibus, 'Quicquid in hac constitutione uestra sanctitas exercet laudamus, concedimus et confirmamus.'

+ Ego Constantinus Romane sedis episcopus per signum sancte crucis has donationes et libertatem*[h]* confirmaui.

+ Ego Ecgwinus humilis episcopus confirmaui.

+ Ego rex Kenredus*[i]* corroboraui.

+ Ego rex Offa consensi.

fo. 162[vb]   **324.** | *Secundum priuilegium Constantini*
Constantinus*[j]* episcopus seruus seruorum Dei Britwaldo*[k]* Brittanniarum*[l]* primati salutem et apostolicam benedictionem. Diuina dispensatione ad hoc promoti ut apostolica auctoritate paci ecclesiarum insistamus, tue fraternitati denuntiamus quatinus ecclesias Dei per Brittanniam dispositas tua ipsius et sanctorum apostolorum auctoritate protegas, ne quis peruasor cuiuscumque ordinis a Deo et nobis constituta priuilegia subruat. Inter quas eam*[m]* que nuperrime a uenerabili uiro Ecgwino nostra et regia auctoritate constituta est tue ditioni precipue*[n]* summittimus ut tibi et posteris tuis potestate diuinitus concessa ab omni eam aduersariorum impugnatione liberam in perpetuum reddas.

325. Iustum enim nobis uidetur ut, *[o]*quoniam isdem*[o]* uenerabilis Ecgwinus, exemplum Domini secutus,*[p]* se humiliando inibi effectus est abbas, iccirco hec ecclesia secundum quod per legatum suum Ethelwoldum*[q]*[2] expetiit, ampliorem dignitatem a nostra sede sui merito optineat. Constituimus ergo in nomine Domini ut isdem

---

[a] om. V   *[b-b]* d. cc° ix ° H V   *[c]* Lateran' V; scripta anno 709 in ecclesia saluat' marg. R (s. xv)   *[d]* C V   *[e]* antiste V   *[f]* pluribus archiepiscopis H V   *[g]* principibus H V   *[h]* libertates H   *[i]* Kenredus rex V   *[j]* C. V   *[k]* Brithwaldo H V   *[l]* Britanniarum H; Brithanniarum V   *[m]* etiam eam V   *[n]* om. V   *[o-o]* quem idem H   *[p]* om. V   *[q]* Ethelwaldum H V

---

[1] Early papal privileges were dated by the year of the emperor, the eastern emperor until 781 under Pope Adrian I. From Pope Leo IX (798) the regnal year of the western emperor was substituted. The year of grace was not used before the late 10th cent., even possibly not until the mid-11th cent.; see R. L. Poole, *Studies in Chronology and History*,

323. This letter has been written in the seven hundred and ninth year of our Lord's incarnation in the Lateran church of the Saviour, by the command and with the confirmation of Constantine, bishop of the apostolic see, in the presence, and with the confirmation, of the kings of England Cenred and Offa,[1] at the request of the venerable bishop Ecgwine, in the presence of archbishops, bishops, chief men, and nobles of various provinces, all crying out and saying, 'Whatever your holiness is executing in this statute, we approve, allow and confirm.'

+ I Constantine, bishop of the Roman see, have confirmed these gifts and liberty, with the sign of the holy cross.

+ I, the humble bishop Ecgwine, have confirmed these.

+ I King Cenred have ratified these.

+ I King Offa have given my assent.

324. *The second privilege of Constantine*

Constantine, bishop, servant of the servants of God, to Berhtwald, primate of Britain, greetings and apostolic benediction. Appointed by divine dispensation so that with apostolic authority we might preserve the peace of churches, we command you to protect the churches of God scattered throughout Britain by your own authority and that of the holy apostles so that no assailant of any rank may undermine the privileges instituted by God and us. Among these churches we especially place under your rule that church most recently founded by the venerable Ecgwine with our authority and that of the king, to ensure that by the power divinely granted to you and your successors you keep it for ever free from any assault of its enemies.

325. It seems right to us that, since the same venerable Ecgwine, following the example of the Lord, humbled himself and was made abbot in that place, this church should therefore obtain greater honour from our See through the merits of its lord, as it has requested through its legate Æthelwold.[2] We therefore decree, in the name of

ed. A. L. Poole (Oxford, 1934), pp. 172–9, esp. 178–9 and notes. The ratification by the kings is also unacceptable.

[2] Bishop Æthelwold was responsible for the removal of the canons and the return of the monks in the early 970s (see above, 133). It is, of course, impossible that he had acted on behalf of the community at Evesham in the days of Pope Constantine. Among other peculiarities, the unusual sanction clause forbidding the substitution of canons for monks, together with the reference to Æthelwold, dispels the possibility that this privilege dates from 713. Most likely this redaction dates from the 1120s, see Sayers, '"Original", Cartulary and Chronicle', pl. I, and pp. 375–7. If Æthelwold were a misreading for Æthelred, king of the Mercians (675–704), and Evesham's patron, though it is clear in all the sources, it is no more illuminating. Forgers were clearly at work.

locus sub monarchia proprii abbatis sit liber ab omni tirannica exactione, et nullus cuiuscumque ordinis homo aliquod grauamen ibi inferre audeat.

326. Defuncto autem abbate, secundum canonicam auctoritatem uel de ipso monasterio uel de parrochia Wictiorum abbas a fratribus eiusdem loci eligatur. Qui in eadem ecclesia libere et canonice sine aliqua exactione consecratus, ob reuerentiam uenerabilis Ecgwini anulo in celebratione missarum solummodo utatur, primumque locum post Wictiorum presulem nostra auctoritate iugiter obtineat.

327. Si quis igitur hoc priuilegium infringere uoluerit siue in loco monachorum clericos immittere temptauerit, coram Deo et angelis eius in perpetuum sit anathema. Si quis uero hanc nostram auctoritatem seruauerit, conseruet eum Deus in eternum.

328. Scripta est hec epistola anno Dominice incarnationis septingentesimo tercio*a* | decimo,*b* presidente apostolice sedi papa Constantino*c* et +*d* hoc signum sancte crucis*e* propria manu faciente.

fo. 163ra

329. *Priuilegium Innocentii secundi*

Innocentius episcopus, seruus seruorum Dei, dilecto filio Reginaldo*f* abbati Eueshamensis monasterii eius*g* que successoribus canonice substituendis in perpetuum. Sicut iniusta poscentibus*h* nullus est tribuendus effectus, ita legittima desiderantium non est*i* differenda petitio. Hoc nimirum intuitu, dilecte in domino fili Reginalde abbas, tuis iustis postulationibus impertimur assensum, et monasterium Eueshamie cui, Deo auctore, presides, quod a tempore fundationis sue sedes apostolica specialibus decreuit priuilegiis*j* honorandum, sub beati Petri et nostra protectione suscipimus et presentis scripti priuilegio communimus. Statuentes ut quascumque possessiones, quecumque bona, idem locus inpresentiarum iuste et canonice possidet aut in futurum concessione pontificum, largitione regum uel principum, oblatione fidelium, seu aliis iustis modis poterit adipisci, firma tibi tuisque successoribus*k* et illibata permaneant. Sepulturam quoque eiusdem loci liberam esse omnino decreuimus, ut eorum*l* qui se ibi*m* sepeliri deliberauerint deuotioni et extreme uoluntati nullus obsistat. Sanctimus*n* etiam ne in uestra abbatia aut in

---

a tercio *written over an erasure*   *b* dec° xiii° *H V*   *c* Constantino papa *V*   *d* +
om. V   *e* + *V*   *f* Reinaldo *V*   *g* eiusdem *H*   *h* petentibus *H*   *i* *om. V*
j priuilegiis decreuit *V*   *k* successoribus que tuis *H*   *l* illi *H*   *m* illic *H*
n Statuimus *H*

the Lord, that the same place should be free of the demands of all tyrants and be under the sole rule of its own abbot, and that no man of any rank whatsoever should dare to inflict any trouble upon it there.

326. When the abbot dies his successor is to be chosen by the brethren of that place, in accordance with canonical authority, either from the monastery itself or from the diocese of Hwicce. He is then to be consecrated in that church freely and canonically without any charge and, out of reverence for the venerable Ecgwine, is to use the ring only in the celebration of mass, and on our authority always to hold the first place after the bishop of the Hwicce.

327. Should anyone want to violate this privilege or to attempt to introduce clerks in the place of monks, let him be forever accursed before God and his angels. But may God preserve him who protects our authority unto eternal life.

328. This letter has been written in the seven hundred and thirteenth year of our Lord's incarnation when Pope Constantine was occupying the apostolic see, and we make this sign of the cross with our own hand.

329. *The privilege of Innocent II*

Innocent, bishop, servant of the servants of God, to the beloved son Reginald, abbot of Evesham monastery and to his canonically appointed successors in perpetuity. Just as those who make unjust demands should not be granted fulfilment of their desires, so those who make legitimate requests for things they desire should not be kept waiting. It is no wonder then, abbot Reginald, beloved son in the Lord, that, thus motivated we assent to your just demands, and receive the monastery of Evesham, over which you preside with God's permission, and which from the time of its foundation the apostolic see has decreed should be honoured with special privileges, under the protection of the blessed Peter and of ourselves, and we confirm this by the privilege of this present document. We decree that whatever possessions and whatever goods this same monastery at present holds justly and canonically, or is able to obtain in future from the grant of popes, or from the gifts of kings or princes, from the offerings of the faithful or by other lawful means, these are to remain secure and unimpaired for you and your successors. We also decree that burial in the same place be entirely free, so that no man may obstruct the prayers or last wishes of those who have entrusted their bodies to be buried there. We also decree that no bishop should

capellis uestris aliquis episcopus sinodum^a uel capitula aut ordinationes aut missas publicas nisi inuitatus ab abbate illius loci uel a^b
fratribus celebrare presumat. Oblationes etiam que in eadem abbatia
uel in ceteris ecclesiis uestris ad manum pontificis uel cuiuslibet ibi^c
missam celebrantis offeruntur uestris usibus cedant, nec eisdem
personis eas sibi retinere aut clericis uel laicis distribuere liceat.
Decimas insuper quas hucusque canonice optinuistis in refectiones
fo. 163rb pauperum uel in edificia et ornamenta | ecclesiarum, distribuendi
iuxta consuetudinem apud uos hactenus habitam liberam uobis
concedimus facultatem.[1] Liceat quoque uobis clericos uel laicos e
seculo fugientes, nisi forte certis ex causis excommunicati sint, absque
alicuius contradiccione ad conuersionem suscipere, et ea que de iure
suo legittime secum attulerint usibus monasterii cedant. Prohibemus
sane ne altaria, cimiteria, decime et quecumque alia eiusdem mo-
nasterii iuris existunt, a quolibet auferantur uel minuantur. ^dNec pro^d
communi terre interdicto uestrum monasterium a diuinis uacet officiis,
set clausis ianuis, exclusis excommunicatis uel interdictis, diuina
^eliceat uobis officia^e summissa uoce celebrare et debita sepulture tam
uobis quam famulis uestris impendere. Obeunte uero te nunc eiusdem
loci abbate uel tuorum quolibet successorum, nullus ibi qualibet
subreptionis astutia seu uiolentia preponatur nisi quem fratres eius-
dem^f loci communi assensu uel fratrum pars consilii sanioris elegerint.
330. Qui in eadem ecclesia absque omni exactione a quocunque
maluerit benedicatur episcopo, ^gdum tamen^g catholicus sit et gratiam
^hsedis apostolice^h ⁱhabeat et communionem.ⁱ Sane dignitates et
libertates omnes sancto Ecgwino episcopo ipsius^j loci fundatori ac
postmodum abbati ab apostolica sede concessas et scripto confirmatas,
consuetudines etiam quas peculiares eius merito hucusque tenuistis in
parrochiis, in^k processionibus, in ordinationibus, inconuulsas uobis
manere sancimus. In crismate ab episcopo accipiendo et per ecclesias
uestras gratis distribuendo sicut hucusque consueuistis teneatis.
Statuimus insuper ac, predecessoris nostri felicis memorie Constantini pape uestigiis inherentes, decreuimus^l ut solummodo penes te et
fo. 163va successores tuos tocius domus et ecclesie | tue et aliorum locorum ad
eandem ecclesiam pertinentium pastoralis cura consistat et eorundem

---

^a V; om. R   ^b om. H   ^c ibidem H   ^{d-d} nisi H   ^{e-e} uobis officia liceat V
^f eius V   ^{g-g} dummodo V   ^{h-h} Romane sedis V   ⁱ⁻ⁱ et communionem habeat V
^j eiusdem V   ^k et H   ^l decernimus V

---

[1] On monastic possession of tithes, see G. Constable, *Monastic Tithes from their Origins
to the Twelfth Century* (Cambridge, 1964), pp. 82–3, 99–136.

presume to celebrate in your abbey or in your chapels, a synod, chapters, ordinations, or public masses, unless invited to do so by the abbot of that place or by the brethren. Let the oblations in that abbey or in your other churches which are handed to the bishop or other celebrant of mass there, be given up for your use, and not be kept by those persons for themselves or distributed to the clerks or laity. As for the tithes which you have canonically possessed up till now for the relief of the poor or [to be used] for the buildings and ornaments of the churches, we grant you free licence to distribute these in accordance with the custom hitherto practised among you.[1] You are also to be permitted to receive into the religious life, without hindrance from anyone, clerks or lay persons abandoning the world, unless they have for particular reasons been excommunicated, and they are to surrender for the use of the monastery the things they have lawfully brought with them which are rightfully theirs. We forbid anyone to remove or impair the altars, cemeteries, tithes, or any other things which rightfully belong to that monastery. Your monastery is not to be without divine services because of a general interdict placed upon the land, but after closing your doors and excluding those who are under sentence of excommunication or interdict, you may celebrate divine services with subdued voices, and you may carry out the obligations of burial both for yourselves and your servants. When you, the present abbot of the monastery, die, or any of your successors, let no successor here be proposed through any kind of underhand chicanery or force, but only a man chosen by the brethren of the same place by common consent, or by a company of brethren of wiser counsel.

330. The abbot may be blessed in that church by any bishop of his choice, provided that that bishop is catholic and has the favour of, and is in communion with, the apostolic see. Furthermore, we decree that you should continue to enjoy undisturbed all the honours and liberties granted by the apostolic see to St Ecgwine, bishop and founder of that place and later abbot, and confirmed in writing, as well as the special customs in his honour which you have hitherto maintained in the parishes in processions and ordinations. You are to continue to receive chrism from the bishop and to distribute it free around your churches just as you have hitherto been accustomed to do. Following the example of our predecessor Pope Constantine of happy memory, we further command and decree that the pastoral care of your entire house, church and other places belonging to the

ordinatio, sicut hactenus est obseruatum,*a* in tua et successorum tantum*b* tuorum potestate permaneat, salua per omnia sedis auctoritate apostolice.*c*

331. Si quis sane in posterum hanc nostram constitutionem sciens contra eam temere uenire temptauerit potestatis honorisque sui periculum patiatur et a sacratissimo corpore et sanguine domini nostri Iesu Christi alienus fiat atque in extremo examine districte ultioni subiaceat. Conseruantes autem hec, omnipotentis Dei et beati Petri ac*d* Pauli apostolorum eius gratiam consequantur. Amen. Amen. Amen.*e*

Ego*f* Innocentius catholice ecclesie episcopus subscribo.

Ego Lucas presbiter cardinalis tituli sanctorum Iohannis et Pauli subscribo.*g* 1

Datum Laterani per manum Almerici sancte Romane ecclesie diaconi cardinalis et cancellarii[2] sexto decimo kalendas Maii, indictione secunda, incarnationis dominice anno millesimo centesimo tricesimo octauo, pontificatus domini Innocentii pape*h* secundi anno decimo.

332. *Priuilegium Alexandri tercii*

Alexander episcopus, seruus seruorum Dei, *i*dilectis filiis*i* Ade abbati monasterii Euesh' eiusque fratribus tam presentibus quam futuris regularem uitam professis in perpetuum. Pie postulatio uoluntatis effectu debet prosequente compleri ut et deuotionis sinceritas laudabiliter enitescat et utilitas postulata uires indubitanter assumat. Quocirca, dilecti in Domino filii, uestris iustis postulationibus clementer annuimus, et prefatum monasterium in quo diuino mancipati estis obsequio, et predecessoris nostri felicis memorie Innocentii pape uestigiis inherentes sub beati Petri et nostra protectione suscipimus, et presentis scripti priuilegio communimus, statuentes ut quascumque possessi|ones, quecumque bona, idem monasterium inpresentiarum iuste et canonice possidet, aut in futurum concessione pontificum, largitione regum uel principum, oblatione fidelium, seu aliis iustis modis, prestante Domino, poterit adipisci, firma uobis

fo. 163*vb*

---

a oberuatam (*sic*) est *V*   *b* om. *H*   *c* apostolice auctoritate *V fo. 79*   *d* et *H*
e *Single* Amen *V*   *f* *V adds* +   *g* *V adds* +   *h* om. *H*   *i–i* om. *H*

---

1 French in origin, and a papal scribe, he assisted the chancellor in 1137/8 (see next note), and was created cardinal priest of SS. John and Paul in 1132. He subscribed (i.e. witnessed papal documents with his autograph signature) from 1132 to 1140. He died in

same church, rest solely with you and your successors, and that the ordering of those places remain your prerogative alone and that of your successors, as has been observed hitherto, saving the authority of the apostolic see in all things.

331. If in future anyone knowing our decree should dare to try to set aside its provisions, let his position of power and honour be endangered and he be deprived of the most sacred body and blood of our Lord Jesus Christ, and at the last Judgment may he endure the severest punishment. Let those who preserve these decrees receive the grace of Almighty God and his apostles, blessed Peter and Paul, Amen, Amen, Amen.

I Innocent, bishop of the catholic church, subscribe.

I Luke, cardinal priest of the title of St John and St Paul, subscribe.[1]

Dated at the Lateran by the hand of Almeric, cardinal deacon of the holy Roman church, and chancellor,[2] on the sixteenth day of April, the second Indiction, in the year of our Lord's incarnation 1138 [recte 1139], in the tenth year of the pontificate of Pope Innocent II.

332. The privilege of Alexander III

Alexander, bishop, servant of the servants of God, to the beloved sons Adam, abbot of the monastery of Evesham, and his brethren professing the religious life both now and in future, in perpetuity. The demands of a pious request should meet with a swift response so that the purity of devotion may laudably shine forth and the benefit demanded take sure strength from this response. Therefore, beloved sons in the Lord, we are pleased to consent to your just demands and we receive into our protection and that of the blessed Peter the aforesaid monastery in which you are bound by divine service; in doing so we are following the example of our predecessor Pope Innocent of happy memory. We confirm this by the privilege of this present document. Hence, we decree that whatever possessions and whatever goods this monastery at present holds justly and canonically, or is able to obtain in future from the grant of popes, or from gifts of kings or princes, from the offerings of the faithful or by other lawful means, by the Lord's providence, these are to remain secure

---

[1] 1140/1; see B. Zenker, *Die Mitglieder des Kardinalkollegiums von 1130 bis 1159* (Würzburg, 1964), p. 136.

[2] Papal chancellor and cardinal priest of S. Maria Nuova from 1123 to his death in 1141; Zenker, *Kardinalkollegium*, pp. 142–4.

uestrisque successoribus et illibata permaneant. Decimas fructuum uestrorum a quadraginta*a* annis ab ecclesia uestra canonice et inconcusse possessas, in refectiones pauperum uel in edificia et ornamenta ecclesiarum, distribuendi, iuxta rationabilem consuetudinem apud uos hactenus habitam, liberam uobis concedimus facultatem. Liceat *b*uobis insuper*b* clericos uel laicos liberos et absolutos e seculo fugientes, absque alicuius contradictione ad conuersionem suscipere, et ea que de iure suo legittime secum attulerint usibus monasterii cedant. Prohibemus sane ne altaria, cimeteria, decime et quecumque alia eiusdem monasterii iuris existunt a quolibet auferantur uel minuantur. Sepulturam quoque ipsius loci liberam esse concedimus ut eorum deuotioni et extreme uoluntati qui se illic sepeliri deliberauerint, nisi forte excommunicati uel interdicti sint, nullus obsistat salua tamen canonica iusticia *c*ecclesiarum illarum*c* a quibus mortuorum corpora assumuntur.[1] Cum autem commune interdictum terre*d* fuerit, liceat uobis clausis ianuis, non pulsatis tintinnabulis, exclusis excommunicatis et interdictis, suppressa uoce diuina offitia celebrare.

333. Obeunte uero te nunc eiusdem loci abbate uel tuorum quolibet successorum, nullus ibi qualibet surreptionis astutia seu uiolentia preponatur nisi quem fratres communi assensu uel fratrum pars consilii sanioris, secundum Dei timorem et beati Benedicti regulam,

fo. 164*ra* prouiderint | eligendum.

334. Sane dignitates et libertates omnes sancto Ecgwino episcopo eiusdem*e* loci fundatori ac postmodum abbati ab apostolica sede concessas et scripto confirmatas, consuetudines etiam quas peculiares eius merito rationabiles hucusque tenuistis in parrochiis, in processionibus, in ordinationibus, inconuulsas uobis manere sancimus. Crisma uero, oleum sanctum, consecrationes altarium, ordinationes clericorum*f* qui ad sacros ordines fuerint promouendi, a quocumque malueritis suscipietis episcopo, *g*sicut est hactenus obseruatum,*g* *h*dummodo episcopus catholicus sit*h* et gratiam atque communionem *i*apostolice sedis habeat*i* et ea gratis et absque prauitate uobis uelit exhibere.

335. Statuimus etiam ut Wigornenses episcopi a uobis aliquid iniuste

a xlxl V   *b-b* insuper uobis V H   *c-c* illarum ecclesiarum V   *d* V; om. R
e ipsius V   *f* interlined V   *g-g* order reversed with h–h below in V   *h-h* see previous
note   *i-i* habeat sedis apostolice V

[1] Benedictine houses normally had cemeteries for the burial of lay persons, especially

and unimpaired for you and your successors. As for the tithes of your crops canonically and constantly held by your church for forty years for the relief of the poor, or for the buildings and ornaments of the churches, we grant you free licence to distribute these in accordance with the regular custom hitherto practised among you. You are also to be permitted, without hindrance from anyone, to receive into the religious life clerks or free laymen abandoning the world, and they are to surrender for the use of the monastery the things they have lawfully brought with them which are rightfully theirs. We forbid anyone to take away or impair the altars, cemeteries, tithes, or any other things that rightfully belong to that monastery. We also grant free burial in the monastery, so that no man may hinder the devotion or the last wishes of those who have resolved to be buried there, unless they have been excommunicated or are under interdict, saving however the canonical rights of those churches from which the bodies of the dead have been taken.[1] When a general interdict has been placed upon the land, you are to be permitted to celebrate divine services with subdued voices, but you must close your doors, refrain from ringing the bells, and exclude those who are under excommunication or interdict.

333. When you, the present abbot of this place, die or any of your successors, let no successor be proposed there through any sort of underhand chicanery or force but only a man whom the brethren of the monastery by common consent or whom that part of the brethren of wiser counsel have taken measures to elect in the fear of God and in accordance with the Rule of the blessed Benedict.

334. Furthermore, we decree that you should continue to enjoy undisturbed all the honours and liberties granted by the apostolic see to St Ecgwine, bishop and founder of that place and later abbot, and confirmed in writing, as well as the special customs in his honour which you have hitherto regularly maintained in the parishes, in processions, and in ordinations. You will receive from any bishop of your choice, as has been the practice hitherto, chrism, holy oil, the consecration of altars, and the ordination of clerks who are to be promoted to holy orders, provided that the bishop is catholic and enjoys the approval and communion of the apostolic see, and is willing to provide these services for you free and without simony.

335. We also declare that the bishops of Worcester should make no

those in towns. The question of to whom the mortuaries were payable (normally the parish priest) was therefore often a disputed one.

non exigant, set hiis tantum contenti sint que antecessores uestros antecessoribus suis constat rationabiliter exhibuisse. Decernimus ergo ut nulli omnino hominum liceat supradictum monasterium temere perturbare, aut eius possessiones auferre uel ablatas retinere, minuere, seu quibuslibet uexationibus fatigare, set illibata omnia et integra conseruentur, eorum pro quorum gubernatione et sustentatione concessa sunt usibus omnimodis profutura, salua sedis apostolice auctoritate.

336. Si qua igitur in futurum ecclesiastica secularisue persona hanc nostre constitutionis paginam sciens contra eam temere uenire temptauerit, secundo tercioue commonita nisi presumptionem suam congrua satisfactione correxerit, potestatis honorisque sui dignitate careat, reamque se diuino iudicio existere de perpetrata iniquitate cognoscat. Et a sacratissimo corpore *et a* sanguine Dei et domini nostri redemptoris Iesu Christi aliena fiat, atque in extremo examine districte ultioni subiaceat. Cunctis autem eidem loco sua iura seruantibus sit pax Domini nostri Iesu | Christi, quatinus*b* hic fructum bone actionis percipiant et apud districtum iudicem premia eterne pacis inueniant. Amen. Amen. Amen.*c*

fo. 164*rb*

+ Ego Alexander catholice ecclesie episcopus subscribo.*d*

+ Ego Hubaldus Hostiensis episcopus subscribo.[1]

e+ Ego G. Albanensis episcopus subscribo.*e*[2]

f+ Ego Henricus presbiter cardinalis subscribo.*f*[3]

+ Ego Iohannes presbiter cardinalis*g* subscribo.[4]

+ Ego *h*presbiter W. cardinalis subscribo.*h*[5]

+ Ego Iacinctus diaconus cardinalis sancte Marie in Cosmidin subscribo.[6]

+ Ego Odo diaconus cardinalis sancti Nicholai in Carcere Tullii subscribo.[7]

+ Ego Iohannes diaconus*i* sancte Marie in Porticu subscribo.[8]

*j*Datum Turonis*j* per manum Hermanni sancte Romane ecclesie

---

a-a om. V; ac for et H   *b* et add. V   *c* Amen written once V, Triple Amen om. H
d subscripsi V, and in all cases throughout the cardinals' subscriptions   *e-e* om. V
f-f om. H (which places this subscription after presbiter W. cardinalis below; titulus sanctorum Nerei et Achilles add. V   *g* titulus sancte Anastasie add. V   *h-h* Willelmus presbiter cardinalis tituli sancti Petri ad uincula subscripsi followed by Walterus Albanensis episcopus subscripsi V; H adds Henricus here, before Walterus   *i* card. add. V; this subscription om. H   *j-j* Dat' Turon' V

[1] Later Pope Lucius III, he was created bishop of Ostia by Pope Adrian IV in 1158, subscribed between 1159 and 1181, and died in 1185; see Zenker, *Kardinalkollegium*, pp. 22–5. He and the following cardinals who subscribe are some of the most influential of the curial cardinals.

unjust demands of you but should be content solely with those things which it is accepted your predecessors had regularly provided to their predecessors. We therefore decree that no man whatsoever be permitted arrogantly to disturb the above-mentioned monastery, to remove its possessions, to hold on to them if he has removed them, to demean the monastery or to weary it with any sort of harassment, but all things are to preserved unimpaired and intact which belong to those men for whose governance and succour those things are likely to be beneficial in various ways, saving the authority of the apostolic see. **336.** Should therefore any person, ecclesiastical or lay, knowing of this document containing our decree, attempt arrogantly to oppose it, let him, unless he amends for his presumption by giving appropriate satisfaction, after a second or third warning lose the dignity of his position and power, and understand that he stands guilty of eternal sin at the divine judgment. Also let him be deprived of the most sacred body and blood of God and our redeemer Jesus Christ, and be liable to the severest punishment at the Last Judgment. But may the peace of our Lord Jesus Christ be with all who preserve the rights of that place that they may see the fruit of their good works and at the awful Judgment discover the rewards of eternal peace. Amen, amen, amen.

+ I, Alexander, bishop of the catholic church, subscribe.

+ I, Ubaldus, bishop of Ostia, subscribe.[1]

+ I, G. [Walter], bishop of Albano, subscribe.[2]

+ I, Henry, cardinal priest, subscribe.[3]

+ I, John, cardinal priest, subscribe.[4]

+ I, W[illiam], cardinal priest, sign my name.[5]

+ I, Hyacinth, cardinal deacon of St Mary in Cosmedin, subscribe.[6]

+ I, Odo, cardinal deacon of St Nicholas in carcere Tulliano, subscribe.[7]

+ I, John, [cardinal] deacon of St Mary in Porticu, subscribe.[8]

Dated at Tours by the hand of Herman, subdeacon of the holy

---

[2] Succeeded Nicholas Breakspear (Pope Adrian IV) as bishop of Albano; Zenker p. 39.

[3] A Cistercian cardinal, from Pisa, cardinal priest of SS. Nereo and Achilleo, 1151–5; Zenker, pp. 96–101.

[4] From Naples, cardinal priest of S. Anastasia; Zenker, pp. 73–7.

[5] Cardinal priest of S. Pietro in Vincoli, 1158–76; Zenker, pp. 118–23.

[6] 1144–91, later Pope Celestine III; Zenker, pp. 161–7.

[7] 1152–74; Zenker, pp. 171–4.

[8] 1158–67, Bishop of Palestrina from 1190; Zenker, pp. 168–70.

subdiaconi*a* et notarii, nonas Iunii, indictione undecima, incarnationis dominice anno millesimo centesimo sexagesimo tercio, pontificatus uero*b* domini*c* Alexandri pape tercii anno quarto. *d*Amen. Amen. Amen.*d*

337. *Indulgentia Clementis Pape*
Clemens episcopus, seruus seruorum Dei, dilectis filiis Ade*e* abbati et fratribus sancti Ecgwini Eueshamensis monasterii salutem et apostolicam benedictionem.

338. Largitione nostri muneris et gratie eos duximus decorandos quos fidei meritum ac deuotionis constantia nobis reddunt acceptos, et qui, nullo mediante, ad iurisdictionem beati Petri et nostram specialiter pertinere noscuntur. Hac itaque ratione inducti et deuotionis et fidei uestre intuitu prouocati, tibi, fili abbas, sicut ex gratia et liberalitate sedis apostolice tu et successores tui usum cirotecarum et anuli habetis, ita quoque usum mitre, dalmatice, tunice et sandaliorum*f* de consueta clementia et benignitate eiusdem*g* sedis apostolice duximus concedendum. Indulgentes ut hiis omnibus in sollempnibus diebus infra monasterium tuum et obedientias eius, in processionibus quoque ipsius monasterii, in conciliis Romani pontificis et legati eius, atque in sinodis episcoporum *h*incunctanter utaris.*h* Datum Lateran' sexto idus Iulii pontificatus nostri anno secundo. Amen. Amen. Amen.*i*

fo. 164*va* 339. | *Indulgencia Celestini pape*
Celestinus episcopus, seruus seruorum Dei, dilectis filiis Rogero abbati et fratribus sancti Ecgwini Eueshamensis monasterii salutem et apostolicam benedictionem.

340. Largitione nostri muneris et gratie eos duximus decorandos quos fidei meritum ac deuotionis constantia nobis reddunt acceptos, et qui, nullo mediante, ad iurisdictionem beati Petri et nostram specialiter pertinere noscuntur. Hac itaque ratione inducti et deuotionis et fidei uestre intuitu prouocati, tibi, fili abbas, et successoribus tuis, sicut ex gratia et liberalitate sedis apostolice tu et successores tui usum mitre et anuli habetis, ita quoque usum cirotecarum, dalmatice, tunice, et sandaliorum necnon et uestimenta sacerdotalia benedicendi, de consueta clementia et de benignitate sedis apostolice duximus concedendum. Indulgentes ut*j* hiis omnibus in sollempnibus diebus

---

a subdiaconusi *V*   *b* om. *V*   *c* domni *V*   *d–d* om. *V*   *e* Rogero *V*
f necnon et uestimenta sacerdotalia benedicendi *add.* H, *V*   *g* om. *V*   *h–h* incunctante utamini *V*   *i* marg. Nota bene   *j* ut *interlined*

Roman church, and notary, on 5 June, the eleventh Indiction, in the
year of our Lord's incarnation 1163, in the fourth year of the
pontificate of Pope Alexander III. Amen, amen, amen.

337. *The Indult of Pope Clement*

Clement, bishop, servant of the servants of God, to the beloved sons,
Adam, the abbot, and the brethren of St Ecgwine's monastery of
Evesham, greetings and apostolic benediction.

338. We have decided that those whose faithfulness and steadfast
devotion render them acceptable to us, and who are known to belong
especially to the jurisdiction of the blessed Peter and ourself without
any intermediary, should be honoured with the generosity of our
bounty and grace. Motivated by this principle and stirred by an
awareness of your devotion and faith, we have decided, my son abbot,
that just as you and your successors, through the grace and generosity
of the apostolic see, have the right to use the gloves and ring, so we
should, with the usual clemency and kindness of the apostolic see,
bestow upon you the right also to use the mitre, dalmatic, tunic, and
sandals. We therefore give you permission to use these without delay
on all holy days within your monastery and its dependencies, also in
processions of the monastery itself, in the councils of the pope and his
legate, and in the synods of bishops. Dated at the Lateran on 10 July,
in the second year of our pontificate [1189]. Amen, amen, amen.

339. *The Indult of Pope Celestine*

Celestine, bishop, servant of the servants of God, to the beloved sons,
Roger, the abbot, and the brethren of St Ecgwine's monastery of
Evesham, greetings and apostolic benediction.

340. We have decided that those whose faithfulness and steadfast
devotion render them acceptable to us, and who are known to belong
especially to the jurisdiction of the blessed Peter and ourself without
any intermediary, should be honoured with the generosity of our
bounty and grace. Motivated by this principle and stirred by an
awareness of your devotion and faith, we have decided, my son abbot,
that just as you and your successors, through the grace and generosity
of the apostolic see, have the right to use the mitre and ring, so we
should also bestow upon you, with the accustomed clemency and
kindness of the apostolic see, the right also to use the gloves, dalmatic,
tunic, and sandals, as well as the right to bless priestly vestments. We
therefore give you permission to use these without delay on all holy

infra monasterium uestrum*a* et obedientias eius, in processionibus quoque ipsius monasterii, in conciliis Romani pontificis et legati eius, atque in sinodis episcoporum incunctanter utamini. Statuentes ut nulli omnino hominum liceat hanc paginam nostre concessionis infringere uel ei aliquatenus contraire.

341. Si quis autem hoc attemptare presumpserit, indignationem omnipotentis Dei et beatorum *b*Petri et Pauli *c*apostolorum eius se nouerit incursurum. Datum Rome apud sanctum Petrum, idus Ianuarii, pontificatus nostri anno primo. *d*Amen. Amen. Amen.*d* [1]

342. *Sentencia Innocencii pape tercii super exemptione Eueshamensis cenobii* [2]

Innocentius episcopus, seruus seruorum Dei, dilectis filiis abbati et fratribus Eueshamensis cenobii salutem et apostolicam benedictionem. Ex ore sedentis in throno procedit gladius bis acutus.[3] Quoniam ex ore Romani pontificis qui presidet apostolice sedi rectissima debet exire sententia, que contra iustitiam nulli parcat set reddat quod suum est unicuique.[4]

fo. 164*vb* 343. Cum igitur inter uos et uenerabilem fratrem | nostrum Wigornensem episcopum super monasterii uestri subiectione ac libertate controuersia uerteretur et nos eam examinandam commisissemus iudicibus delegatis. Ipsi eandem causam sufficienter instructam ad nostram presentiam remiserunt, certum partibus terminum prefigentes quo cum instrumentis et attestationibus nostro se conspectui presentarent sententiam recepture.

344. Partibus igitur in presentia nostra per procuratores*e* idoneos constitutis, audientiam prebuimus liberam et benignam. Et quidem monasterii uestri proposuit procurator quod idem monasterium ab ipsa sui fundatione liberum exstitit et exemptum, ad hoc probandum priuilegia predecessorum nostrorum inducens, duo uidelicet Constantini, unum Innocentii, et alterum Alexandri, nec non indulgentias

---

a om. V   *b* a Petri V   *c* a *before* apostolorum R   *d–d* om. H, V   *e* H. corr. procures *to* procuratores, *and ins.* rato

[1] Pope Celestine III issued a document on the same day, and in exactly the same form as this, for the abbot of Westminster; printed *PUE* i, no. 301. As copied into Harley MS 3763 fo. 99*r*, the Evesham document does not include the triple Amen.

[2] This letter was registered on fos. 62*v*–63*v* of the papal register for the eighth year of Innocent III and is printed in *Reg. Inn. III*, viii, no. 205 (204), pp. 351–7. On the significance of the letter, parts of which came to be incorporated in the *Decretales* (*X*. V. 33. 17,

days within your monastery and its dependencies, also in processions of the monastery itself, in the councils of the pope and his legate, and in the synods of bishops. We decree that no man at all be permitted to violate this document concerning our concession or to oppose it in any respect.

341. Should anyone presume to attempt this, let him know that he will incur the wrath of Almighty God and of the blessed Peter and Paul, His apostles. Dated at St Peter's, Rome, on 13 January in the first year of our pontificate [1192]. Amen, amen, amen.[1]

342. *The sentence of Pope Innocent III over the exemption of Evesham monastery*[2]

Innocent, bishop, servant of the servants of God, to the beloved sons, the abbot and brethren of Evesham monastery, greetings and apostolic benediction. From the mouth of the One who sits upon the throne proceeds a two-edged sword.[3] So the sentence that proceeds from the mouth of the Roman pontiff who sits upon the apostolic seat should be most just, a sentence that spares nobody who opposes justice, but renders to each his due.[4]

343. With regard to the dispute that existed between you and our venerable brother, the bishop of Worcester, over the subjection or the liberty of your monastery, we had entrusted this to judges delegate for them to examine it. When they had gathered sufficient material on the case they returned it to our court, and fixed a final date by which the parties were to present themselves before us with their documents and written evidence in order that they might receive sentence.

344. The parties have now been represented before us by suitable proctors, and we have given them a free and sympathetic hearing. The proctor representing your monastery has argued that the monastery has been free and exempt from its very foundation, and he has introduced the privileges of our predecessors to prove this, two of Constantine, one of Innocent, another of Alexander, as well as indults

Friedberg, ii cols. 862–4), see P. Landau, 'Papst Innocenz III. in der richterlichen Praxis Zugleich ein Beitrag zur Geschichte der Kooperationsmaxime', in *Festschrift für Rudolf Wassermann* (Darmstadt, 1985), pp. 727–33, and J. Sayers, 'The proprietary church in England: a note on "Ex ore sedentis" (*X. V.* 33. 17)', *Zeitschrift der Savigny-Stiftung für Rechtsgeschichte*, kan. abt. lxxiv (1988), 231–45.

[3] Cf. Rev. 19: 15.

[4] *Digest* 1. 1. 10pr: 'justice is the constant and perpetual wish to give each person his due.' This definition of Ulpian preoccupied the pre-Accursian glossators from Irnerius to Azo; see the discussion in Stein, *Teaching of Roman Law*, pp. lvi–viii. See also *Digest* 16. 3. 31.1, and *Institutes* 1. 1. 3.

Clementis et Celestini. Quorum usum continuum a longis retro temporibus per depositiones testium ostendere[a] nitebatur.

345. In primo siquidem priuilegio Constantini continebatur expressum quod sancte recordationis Ecgwinus Wigornensis episcopus ad apostolicam sedem accedens, uisionem quandam qua se beata Virgo Maria manifestauit eidem prefato predecessori nostro reuerenter exposuit. Et tunc temporis duo reges Anglorum Kenredus et Offa, cum quibus iam dictus episcopus apostolorum limina uisitauit, in loco uisionis ostense de bonis suis plurima beneficia in presentia eiusdem predecessoris nostri regia libertate[b] donarunt. Que ipse auctoritate apostolica confirmauit, quatinus in eodem loco monachorum congregatio secundum beati Benedicti regulam, que minus in illis partibus tunc uigebat, ad diuini nominis constitueretur honorem.

346. Vnde prefatus pontifex Brithwaldo Brittanniarum primati per apostolica scripta mandauit ut coadunato consilio constitueret ouile | diuinitus preostensum, apostolica auctoritate munitum, regia libertate donatum, sibi et successoribus suis, memorato Ecgwino episcopo assentiente, curam animarum eiusdem ecclesie precipue iniungendo, ut ab omni peruasorum impulsu et tirannorum incursu potestate sibi tradita defensaret. Si quid uero sinistre partis inibi comperiretur oriri, eiusdem primatis auribus potius[c] deferretur quam per alicuius occultam sententiam locus sanctus deprauaretur iniuste. Ipsum ergo locum quem antedicti reges libertati donarunt, idem predecessor noster apostolice sedis auctoritate donauit, ut nullus cuiuscumque ordinis homo quod ipse constituerat deprauare aut[d] diminuere attemptaret.

347. In secundo uero priuilegio eiusdem Constantini pape perspeximus contineri quod ipse prefato primati per apostolica scripta mandauit, ut ecclesias Dei per Brittanniam constitutas protegeret et foueret. Inter quas eam que nuperrime[e] tunc a uenerabili uiro Ecgwino episcopo apostolica et regia auctoritate fuerat constituta ditioni eius precipue submittebat, ut eam ab omni aduersariorum impugnatione liberam inperpetuum reddere procuraret. Constituens ut idem locus sub monarchia proprii abbatis ab omni tirannica exactione sit liber, et nullus cuiuscumque ordinis homo aliquod ibi inferre grauamen presumat. Abbas autem secundum auctoritatem

fo. 165ra

---

[a] *interlined V (in another hand?)*   [b] liberalitate *V*   [c] *interlined V*   [d] ac *H*
[e] nuperrime *corr. H*

of Clement and Celestine. Through the testimony of witnesses he has endeavoured to show that there has been continuous use made of these since the earliest times.

345. The first privilege of Constantine contained the statement that when Ecgwine of sacred memory, bishop of Worcester, visited the apostolic see he reverently described to our aforementioned predecessor a vision in which the blessed Virgin Mary revealed herself. At that time two kings of the English, Cenred and Offa, with whom Bishop Ecgwine was visiting the threshold of the apostles, had, in the presence of this predecessor of ours, bestowed with royal liberty many gifts from their own possessions on the place where the vision was manifested. Pope Constantine confirmed these gifts with his apostolic authority in order that a community of monks might be founded to the honour of the divine name in that place under the Rule of the blessed Benedict which at that time did not thrive in those parts.

346. Hence the said pope [Constantine], by apostolic letters, commanded Berhtwald, primate of Britain, to convene a council, and to establish the flock which had been signified in the divine vision. Now that this had been ratified by apostolic authority and endowed with royal liberty, and that the care of souls had been specifically laid upon him and his successors with the assent of Bishop Ecgwine, Berhtwald was to defend this church from every assault of assailants and tyrants by the power entrusted to him. Should any evil faction be found to appear there, then the primate should be informed of it to prevent that holy place being wrongly maligned through any underhand scandal. Accordingly, the very place to which the aforesaid kings gave liberty, our predecessor granted the authority of the apostolic see so that no man of any rank whatsoever should attempt to corrupt or demean what he himself had established.

347. We have also observed that the second privilege of Pope Constantine contains the command to the said primate made in apostolic letters to protect and cherish the churches of God established throughout Britain. Amongst these churches he gave him especial responsibility for the church which had only just been established by the venerable bishop Ecgwine with apostolic and royal authority, that he might take care to keep it free for ever from all assaults of its enemies. He decreed that the same place should be under the sole rule of its own abbot, free from all demands of tyrants, and that no man of any rank whatsoever should presume to trouble it in any way. The abbot was to be chosen by the brethren in

canonicam uel de ipso*a* monasterio uel de parrochia Wictiorum a fratribus eligatur. Qui libere ac canonice sine aliqua exactione in eadem ecclesia benedictus ob reuerentiam uenerabilis Ecgwini qui episcopali sede dimissa in eodem monasterio factus est abbas, anulo in celebratione solummodo missarum utatur, primumque locum semper obtineat post presulem Wictiorum.

348. Ex horum*b* priuilegiorum capitulis monasterii uestri procurator nitebatur ostendere quod ipsum monasterium a prima sui fun | da-
fo. 165*rb* tione ab omni episcopali iurisdictione fuit prorsus exemptum, tum quia dicitur apostolica tantum et regia auctoritate*c* constructum, unde non nisi ad apostolicam sedem in spiritualibus et regiam coronam in temporalibus intelligitur pertinere, cum summus pontifex non con-sueuerit aliquod monasterium ut sua construatur auctoritate mandare, nisi quod in fundo sibi*d* donato fuerit construendum; tum quia locum ipsum quem reges donasse dicuntur regie libertati et ipse donauit, ut, sicut illi donauerunt eum*e* libertati quantum ad temporalia, sic et iste quantum ad spiritualia intelligatur libertati donasse, cum ad illos utique temporalia, ad istum spiritualia pertinerent; tum etiam quia curam animarum eiusdem ecclesie precipue iniunxit Brittanniarum primati, quam et ditioni eius precipue dicitur submisisse. Vt siquid ibi oriretur sinistri per ipsius corrigeretur industriam et cautelam, unde uidetur correctionem ipsius loci ei solummodo commisisse sicque ad alium minime pertinere; tum quia prefatum locum sub monarchia proprii abbatis manere decreuit: unde cum monarchia interpretetur unicus principatus, uidetur quod abbas ipsius loci solus in eodem loco principalem obtinet potestatem.

349. Quod autem *f*priuilegiorum ipsorum uerba*f* intelligi debeant tali modo sequentia priuilegia manifestius declarare uidentur. Nam in priuilegio felicis memorie Innocentii continetur ne aliquis episcopus in ipsa abbatia uel in capellis ipsius sinodum uel capitulum, ordinationes aut missas pupplicas, nisi inuitatus ab abbate et fratribus ipsius loci celebrare presumat.*g* Et cum abbas in eodem monasterio fuerit electus absque omni exactione a quocumque maluerit episcopo in ipsa benedicatur ecclesia dum modo catholicus fuerit et gratiam

---

a om. V   *b* ergo *follows in* V   *c* *interlined* V   *d* *interlined* H   *e* *interlined* V
f-f uerba priuilegiorum ipsorum H V   *g* *marg.* episcopus missas nisi inuitatus ab abbate celebrare non potest (*s. xv*)

accordance with canonical authority from the monastery itself or from the diocese of the Hwicce. He was to receive blessing in the same church freely and canonically, without any payment, out of reverence for the venerable Ecgwine who had relinquished his episcopal see when he became abbot in the monastery, and he was to use the ring only when celebrating mass, and was always to occupy the first place after the bishop of the Hwicce.

348. From sections of these privileges the proctor of your monastery endeavoured to show that the monastery itself was from its earliest foundation entirely exempt from all episcopal jurisdiction. First, it is said to have been established by apostolic and royal authority alone: it is therefore perceived as dependent upon the apostolic see in spiritual matters, and upon the royal crown in temporal matters since the supreme pontiff did not usually command any monastery to be established by his authority unless established on territory which has been given to him. Secondly, the pope himself gave the very place which the kings are said to have given with royal liberty, on the understanding that he had given it its liberty so far as spiritual matters are concerned, just as the kings gave it its liberty so far as temporal matters are concerned, for temporal matters of necessity belong to kings and spiritual matters to the supreme pontiff. Thirdly, he gave a particular command to the primate of Britain to be responsible for the care of the souls of that church, which is said to have submitted especially to his authority. So if any evil occurred there it was to be corrected through the primate's diligence and care: hence, the correction of that monastery is seen to have been entrusted to him alone, and is accordingly the concern of nobody else at all. Fourthly, he decreed that the place should remain under the sole rule of its own abbot: since 'sole rule' means the 'leadership of one man', it appears that the abbot of the same place alone possesses supreme power in that place.

349. That the words of these privileges should be understood in the way we have stated, the following privileges seem to declare more clearly. The privilege of Innocent of happy memory contains the statement that no bishop should presume to celebrate in the abbey itself, or in its dependencies, a synod or chapter, ordinations or public masses, unless invited to do so by the abbot and brethren of the place. Furthermore, when an abbot has been elected in the monastery he may receive a blessing in that church, without payment, from any bishop of his choice provided the bishop is catholic and enjoys the

fo. 165ᵛᵃ habeat | apostolice sedis. Idem etiam Innocentius, Constantini uestigiis inherendo, decreuit ut solummodo penes abbatem ipsius loci tocius domus et ecclesie aliorumque locorum ad eandem ecclesiam pertinentium pastoralis cura consistat, et eorundem ordinatio tantum in ipsius potestate*a* permaneat, sicut est hactenus obseruatum. In priuilegio uero Alexandri pape perspicitur contineri: ut crisma, oleum sanctum, consecrationes altarium, ordinationes clericorum qui ad sacros fuerint ordines promouendi, a quocumque maluerint episcopo communionem et gratiam apostolice sedis habente, fratres eiusdem loci suscipiant, statuto ut Wigornenses episcopi aliquid ab eis iniuste non exigant, set hiis tantum contenti permaneant, que antecessores eorum antecessoribus suis constat rationabiliter impendisse. In fine uero subiungitur quod 'salua sit apostolice sedis auctoritas', nec dicitur quod 'diocesani episcopi canonica sit salua iusticia'; cum in monasteriis non exemptis secundum approbatam ecclesie Romane consuetudinem diocesanis episcopis canonica iusticia conseruetur. In indulgentiis autem bone memorie Clementis et Celestini patenter innuitur quod idem cenobium ad iurisdictionem beati Petri nullo pertineat mediante, cum hoc in proemio[1] premittentes sic inferant consequenter: 'hac itaque ratione inducti usum cirothecarum et anuli, dalmatice, tunice, sandaliorum et mitre tibi duximus concedendum.'

350. Per id ergo quod pastoralis cura tocius domus et ecclesie penes abbatem solummodo decernitur permanere, illud dilucidatur ab Innocentio quod fuerat a Constantino statutum, ut uidelicet idem locus sub monarchia proprii abbatis liber existat. Vnde cum pastoralis

fo. 165ᵛᵇ cura tocius domus | et ecclesie penes abbatem solummodo debeat permanere, patet profecto quod episcopus pastoralem ibi curam exercere non debet, cum et abbas illius loci absque omni exactione infra suam ecclesiam debeat benedici, unde nec professio nec obedientia debet ab illo requiri. Quia uero quedam ad pastoralem sollicitudinem pertinentia per se ipsum abbas exercere non potest, ut nichil ei desit quod pertineat ad plenitudinem libertatis, conceditur illi ab Alexandro ut ecclesiastica sacramenta libere percipiat a quocumque maluerit episcopo communionem et gratiam apostolice sedis habente. Per id autem quod idem locus asseritur ad iurisdictionem beati Petri solummodo pertinere, sicut innuitur in indulgentiis

---

a *V ends here*

---

[1] The prefatory remarks to the letter.

favour of the apostolic see. The same Innocent, following the example of Constantine, decreed that the pastoral care of the whole house, church, and other places belonging to that church be the sole responsibility of the abbot of the place, and that the ordering of the same remain solely in his power, as had hitherto been the case. Certainly in the privilege of Pope Alexander the following statement is seen to be contained: that the brethren of the place may receive chrism, holy oil, the consecration of altars, and the ordination of those clerks who are to be promoted to holy orders, from any bishop of their choosing, who is in communion and favour with the apostolic see, it being decreed that bishops of Worcester should not demand payments unjustly from the monks but remain content with those things only which it is agreed the predecessors of the monks regularly paid to their predecessors. A final clause, to be sure, is added which says, 'saving the authority of the apostolic see'; it does not say 'saving the canonical justice of the diocesan bishop', whereas in monasteries which are not exempt, canonical justice must be the preserve of the diocesan bishops in accordance with the approved custom of the Roman church. In the indults of popes Clement and Celestine of blessed memory it is clearly intimated that the same convent is under the jurisdiction of the blessed Peter without there being any other intermediary, for in their proem[1] they make the following statement, 'influenced by this reasoning we have decided to allow you to use the gloves and the ring, the dalmatic, tunic, sandals, and mitre.'

350. Hence, since it is decreed that the pastoral care of the whole house and church remain the responsibility of the abbot alone, Innocent clarifies what was decreed by Constantine, that the same place should be free and under the rule of its own abbot. Since then the pastoral care of the whole house and church must remain the responsibility of the abbot alone, it is certainly clear that the bishop must not exercise pastoral care there; and since the abbot of that place must receive blessing within his own church without having to make any payment, then neither profession nor obedience must be required from him. However, as the abbot cannot by himself exercise some duties pertaining to pastoral concerns, he is permitted by Alexander to receive the ecclesiastical sacraments freely from any bishop of his choice who is in communion and favour with the apostolic see, so that he should not lack anything which pertains to the full exercise of his liberty. While it is affirmed that the same place belongs to the jurisdiction of the blessed Peter alone, as the indults of Clement

Clementis et Celestini, uidetur illud manifestius declaratum, quod Constantinus papa dicitur locum ipsum libertati donasse, tutelam eiusdem Brittanniarum primati tanquam uicario suo uel legato committens.

351. Porro in priuilegio Constantini quiddam contineri perspicitur per quod idem cenobium uidetur ad iurisdictionem episcopi pertinere, uidelicet ut abbas eiusdem loci primum locum post Wictiorum presulem semper obtineat. Vnde cum locum istum optinere non possit in generali concilio, neque prouintiali, quoniam absonum esset ut abbas primum post illum super alios episcopos resideret relinquitur ergo quod locum istum in episcopali sinodo intelligatur habere quare tenetur ad sinodum episcopalem accedere, ac per hoc ipsius statuta recipere ac seruare.

352. In priuilegio uero Alexandri pape quiddam aliud continetur, per quod diocesanus episcopus in eodem cenobio iurisdictionem suam etsi non in omnibus in quibusdam tamen retinuisse uidetur. Cum in illo dicatur, ut Wigornenses episcopi a fratribus eiusdem loci aliquid fo. 166ra iniuste non exigant set tantum hiis contenti permaneant | que predecessores eorum antecessoribus suis constat rationabiliter impendisse. Vnde constat quod abbates episcopis aliquas de suis rationibus exhibere tenentur.

353. Nos igitur hiis et aliis diligenter auditis et perspicaciter intellectis. Cum a neutra parte per testes prescriptio sit probata, de communi fratrum nostrorum consilio[a] sentencialiter diffinimus quod Eueshamense cenobium liberum in capite est, tanquam ab episcopali iurisdictione prorsus exemptum, soli Romano pontifici et ecclesie Romane subiectum, tutela tamen ipsius Cantuariensi archiepiscopo reseruata.

354. In membris autem, uidelicet illis que non probantur exempta, diocesano episcopo ipsum decernimus subiacere propter que abbas ad sinodum eius debet accedere primumque locum post Wigornensem episcopum obtinere. Pro ipsis quoque membris, ut diximus, non exemptis, idem abbas tenetur Wigornensi episcopo exhibere reuerentiam, obsequium et honorem, quibus Wigornensis episcopus sibi competenter exhibitis debet manere contentus. Quia uero priuilegium meretur amittere qui concessa sibi abutitur libertate,[1] uolumus et

---

[a] *Macray p. 183, citing a confirmation of Innocent VI in H (dat. Avignon 13 Nov. 1360) prints* consensu *for* concilio

---

[1] *Decretum*, D 74. 7 (Friedberg, i col. 263), and C 11 qu.3 c. 63 (Friedberg, i col. 660), and C 25 qu.2 cc. 21, 23 (Friedberg, i cols. 1017, 1018). Innocent III referred to this rule in a letter of 1198 to the archbishop of Lund in Denmark, concerning the privileges of the

and Celestine intimate, it seems even more clearly confirmed as such in that Pope Constantine is said to have given the place itself with its liberty, entrusting its protection to the primate of Britain as his vicar and legate.

351. On the other hand one sees contained in Constantine's privilege a statement from which it is seen that the monastery belongs to the jurisdiction of the bishop, where it says that the abbot of that place should always occupy first place after the bishop of the Hwicce. Since he could not hold that position in the general council nor in the provincial council, as it would be unreasonable for the abbot to occupy the first place after him above other bishops, it must be concluded that he is understood to occupy that place in the bishop's synod, because he is bound to come to the bishop's synod to receive and thereby observe the bishop's statutes.

352. Pope Alexander's privilege contains another statement from which it is seen that the diocesan bishop retained his jurisdiction in that monastery in certain respects but not all. It states that the bishops of Worcester should not unjustly demand payments from the brethren of that place, but should remain content with those things alone which it is agreed the brethren's predecessors had reasonably rendered to their predecessors. From this it is agreed that the abbots are bound to make some reasonable renderings to the bishops.

353. We have listened intently to these and other arguments, and have a clear understanding of them. Since neither party has proved prescription through its witnesses, we confirm by this sentence, which is given with the counsel of our brethren, that the monastery of Evesham is itself free, wholly exempt from episcopal jurisdiction, and subject only to the Roman pontiff and the Roman church, its protection being entrusted to the archbishop of Canterbury.

354. In the case of its dependencies, however, which have not been proved to be exempt, we decree that they be subject to the diocesan bishop, and because of this, that the abbot must attend the bishop's synod and occupy the first place after the bishop of Worcester. On behalf of these dependencies also which, as we have said, are not exempt, the abbot is bound to show reverence, obedience, and deference to the bishop of Worcester, and the bishop must remain content with these attentions properly shown to him. As the man who abuses the freedom granted him deserves to lose this privilege,[1] we

Hospitallers, see Pennington, *Pope and Bishops*, p. 178 and n. 94, citing *Reg. Inn. III*, i, no. 450, pp. 673–4.

mandamus ut quanto liberiores estis a seruitiis secularibus, tanto uos arcius mancipetis diuine per omnia seruituti.

355. Decernimus ergo ut nulli*a* hominum liceat hanc paginam nostre diffinitionis infringere, uel ei ausu temerario contraire. Siquis autem hoc attemptare presumpserit, indignationem omnipotentis Dei et beatorum Petri et Pauli apostolorum eius se nouerit incursum. Datum apud sanctum Petrum quintodecimo kalendas Februarii pontificatus nostri anno octauo.

---

a *Macray, ibid., adds* omnino *after* nulli

desire and command that being all the more free of secular duties you be all the more strict in undertaking divine service in all you do.

355. We therefore decree that no man be permitted to violate this document containing our decision or arrogantly dare to dispute it. If any should presume to attempt this let him know that he will endure the wrath of Almighty God and of the blessed Peter and Paul, his apostles. Dated at St Peter's on 18 January in the 8th year of our pontificate [1206].

PARTICVLA QVARTA

356. *Incipit particula quarta, qualiter causa iurisdictionis Vallis fuit actitata*

Cum itaque talem sententiam apud nos quintodecimo kalendas Februarii haberemus bullatam, propter uarios huius seculi | casus timens tanti thesauri amissionem, cupiens habere duplicem, quamuis ad hoc exactissimam adhibuissem diligentiam nec profecissem, tamen caute feci ipsam sententiam et non sine magno labore executioni a capite usque ad finem interseri, et sic propositum habui.

fo. 166rb

357. Dum hec agerentur bis intra natiuitatem Domini misit michi dominus papa xenia de uenatione sua. Tandem transactis aliquot diebus post natiuitatem Domini, dictum est nobis ex parte domini pape ut in tercium diem compareremus coram eo litigaturi de ecclesiis de Valle. Et die statuto comparuimus et proposuit aduersarius noster ecclesias illas infra limites Wigornensis[a] diocesis esse sitas et ideo, de iure communi, Wigornensi episcopo lege diocesana esse subiectas, et ideo nos iurisdictionem ad episcopum de iure pertinentem iniuste in illis exercere.[1]

358. Igitur cum iam rediissent ad urbem mercatores Romani qui iuerant in Angliam cum abbate nostro pro quadringentis quadraginta marcis quas abbas mutuo acceperat nec recepissent eas sicut conuenerat. Et ego iam expendissem quinquaginta marcas quas mutuo acceperam, non inueni qui aliquid michi mutuo daret.[2] Immo me ipsum obseruabant Romani ut caperent me et mitterent in carcerem donec uniuersum debitum solueretur, sicut prius fecerunt Ermesfredum monachum qui in eorum custodia mortuus est.[3] Cum itaque

---

[a] *R consistently writes* Wigornensis

[1] X. III. 36. 8 (Friedberg, ii cols. 606–7; 4 *Comp.* 3. 13. 2; P 66) stated the accepted position that a monastery was concluded to be subject to the bishop in whose diocese it was sited unless it was proved to be exempt.

[2] The Evesham proctors had raised money from the Scarsi, a firm of Roman bankers who continued operations into the 1230s (see *Les Registres de Grégoire IX*, ed. L. Auvray, i (Bibliothèque des Ecoles françaises d'Athènes et de Rome 2nd ser. ix, 1896), nos. 845, 1462, and 1465; and below, **449**). There is also record of a loan of twenty marks from another Roman merchant banker, Peter Malialardus, which was made in the presence of John, bishop of Albano, in San Clemente, Rome, on 19 Dec. 1205, shortly before the settlement of the main suit on Christmas eve (printed in App. I, below). The proctors of

PART FOUR

356. *Here begins part four: how the case concerning jurisdiction over the Vale was transacted*

We received this same sentence that concerned us sealed with the *bulla* on 18 January [1206]; I was now afraid that because of the changes and chances of this mortal life we might lose this great treasure, wherefore I desired to have another copy. Although I had given the most demanding attention to this suit without success, I now gave careful consideration to the sentence itself, putting a great deal of work into scrutinizing it from beginning to end, and so I held to my purpose.

357. While I was engaged in this the pope sent me twice during Christmas gifts from his hunt. Several days after Christmas we at last received word in the name of the pope that we were to appear before him in three days' time to contest the case that concerned the churches of the Vale. When we appeared on the appointed day our opponent argued that those churches were situated within the boundaries of the diocese of Worcester and therefore, according to the *ius commune*, were subject to the bishop of Worcester by diocesan law, so we were wrongfully exercising the jurisdiction over them which belonged by right to the bishop.[1]

358. The Roman merchants who had gone to England with our abbot to be paid the 440 marks which the abbot had borrowed from them had not received the money as agreed, so they had now returned to Rome. I myself had now spent the fifty marks which I had borrowed and could not find anyone to lend me anything.[2] In fact the Romans were watching out for me to arrest me and send me to prison until the whole debt was paid, just as they had previously done to the monk Ermefred who died in their custody.[3] As I did not know where I could

---

the abbot and convent, Thomas of Warwick, the abbot's clerk and representative, and Thomas of Marlborough, for the convent, promised repayment by Whitsun (21 May 1206), otherwise they would be charged one mark for every ten owing, plus the expenses of the merchant, his servant, and a horse. The proctors also surrendered the bond that they had from the abbot and convent. It is impossible to separate the abbot's debts from those of the convent, though Marlborough is clear that it was the abbot who owed the 440 marks. The fact that the merchants increased their attentions, imprisoning the proctors (see below, **386**) shows that more repayments had not been made.

[3] For Ermefred, see above, **226**, **245**, and below, **432**.

hac de causa non haberem unde aduocatos conducerem, inuocantes auxilium de celo[1] in nos ipsos pondus litis suscepimus.[a]

359. Et dixi, 'Pater sancte, bene dixisset aduersarius noster nisi ecclesie ille per priuilegia Romanorum pontificum ab omni iurisdictione episcopali essent exempte, et nisi etiam in eisdem omne ius fo. 166[va] episcopale prescripsissent.[2] | Quod autem sint exempte ita probo. Matrix ecclesia, uidelicet Eueshamensis que est capud est exempta, ergo et capelle Vallis que sunt menbra', et ad hoc induxi leges et canones.[3]

360. Aduersarius uero dixit, 'Non sunt capelle set matrices ecclesie, ergo non quasi membra ratione capitis eximuntur', et ad hoc induxit leges et canones.[4] Tunc ego, 'Immo capelle sunt, quia crisma et oleum a nostra matrici ecclesia percipiunt, et parrochiani earum, immo magis ecclesie Eueshamensis, apud eam ecclesiasticam accipiunt sepulturam; ergo capelle sunt', et induxi ad hoc canones.[5] Tunc aduersarius, 'Pater sancte, in ecclesiis illis sunt fontes baptismatis et non in ecclesia Eueshamensi: ergo sunt baptismales et non capelle', et ad hoc induxit canones qui bene faciebant ad hoc.[6]

361. Tunc dominus papa intuens me dixit, 'Procurator, dic uerum, sunt apud uos fontes uel apud ecclesias illas?' Et ego, 'Non apud nos set apud ecclesias illas.' Et dominus papa, 'Dic aliud.' Et sic hec

---

[a] potest responderi(?) quod bene obiect' esset nisi (s. xiii[1])

[1] Cf. 1 Macc. 12: 15, and 16: 3.

[2] Prescriptive rights were known to the Roman Law; see *Code* 7. 33, 34, 35. They came to be defined as rights that had been held for a long time, ten, twenty, and then thirty or forty years (*Code* 7. 39). On the history and development of prescription in the canon law, see Noel Vilain,'Prescription et bonne foi du Décret de Gratien (1140) jusqu'à Jean d'André (1328)', *Traditio*, xiv (1958), 121–89. On the prescriptive rights (over a hundred years) of the Roman Church itself under Innocent III, see J. Petersohn, 'Kaiser, Papst und römisches Recht im Hochmittelalter', in *Medievalia Augiensia: Forschungen zur Geschichte des Mittelalters*, ed. J. Petersohn (Vorträge und Forschungen, liv: Stuttgart, 2001), pp. 307–48, at 337–41. The English payment of Peter's Pence was held to belong to the papacy in this way (p. 339). There is no doubt that there was an explosion of interest in prescriptive rights at this time.

[3] Thomas probably had in mind *Decretum*, C 16. qu.2 c.7 (Friedberg, i col.787), concerning chapels which were conceded to monks by bishops, with full rights, and D 70. 2 (Friedberg, i col.257), where it was stated that chapels were the responsibilty of the greater church. For Innocent's decisions on chapels, see Pennington, *Pope and Bishops*, pp. 170–1. In the case of the canons of Langres, Innocent declared in 'Cum capella' of 1206 (3 *Comp.* 5. 16. 6; *X.* V. 33. 16, Friedberg, ii col. 862) that canons who held parish churches were exempt from the diocesan only in churches for which they had specific exemptions, not generally. In another decretal of 1213 Innocent declared that if the archbishop of Lund's predecessor had exempted the monks of All Souls from paying tithes unconditionally, then the monks were exempt also on lands acquired in future (4 *Comp.* 5. 12. 5; *X.* V. 33. 22, Friedberg, ii cols. 865–6).

hire advocates for this case, I called upon aid from heaven[1] and took the weight of the suit upon my very own shoulders.

359. I began, 'Holy father, my opponent would have been right in what he said if those churches had not been exempted from all episcopal jurisdiction by the privileges of the Roman pontiffs and if prescriptive rights[2] against all episcopal jurisdiction had not been claimed in the case of those same churches. That they are exempt I shall prove. The mother church of Evesham, which is the head, is exempt, so, therefore, are the chapels of the Vale which are its dependencies', and I produced laws and canons to support this argument.[3]

360. Our opponent replied, 'They are not chapels but mother churches, and are therefore not exempt as dependencies on the principle that they are head churches', and he produced laws and canons to support that argument.[4] I then argued, 'But they are indeed chapels, because they receive chrism and oil from our mother church, and their parishioners, indeed, as parishioners of Evesham church, receive ecclesiastical burial at Evesham: they are therefore chapels', and I produced canons to support this argument.[5] But our opponent then said, 'Holy father, there are baptismal fonts in those churches, but not in the church of Evesham: they are therefore baptismal churches, and not chapels', and he produced canons which well supported this argument.[6]

361. The pope then looked at me and asked, 'Proctor, tell me the truth, are there fonts in your church or in those churches?' I replied, 'There are no fonts in our church, but there are in those churches.' The pope then said, 'Proceed to your next point.' So that argument

[4] The points are too general to say exactly what Master Robert cited. He was clearly emphasizing that these churches came under the bishop and hence under diocesan law. For the principle that chapels were subject to a mother church, see D 70. 2 (Friedberg, i col. 257) and C 16 q. 1 (cols. 761–85), and C 17. q. 4. c. 6 (col. 816) on chapels or minor churches.

[5] These arguments would appear to depend more on the recently declared exemption and on the earlier papal privileges of Popes Constantine, Innocent II, and Alexander III rather than on definable texts. On the procession to Worcester from Abbots Morton at Whitsuntide when the chrism was distributed, see below, **373**. If these churches received chrism and oil from Evesham and their parishioners were buried there they were clearly chapels. On monastic chapels, see Pennington, *Pope and Bishops*, pp. 164–6, and the texts cited there. Possibly Thomas was using some of the glosses of Rufinus to C 16 q. 2.

[6] Thomas here pays some tribute to the legal acumen of his adversary. If there were fonts then the assumption was that they were churches under the bishop and not chapels. On baptismal churches see C 25 qu. 2 c. 25 (Friedberg, i col. 1019) and C 16 q.1 c. 45 (col. 774), texts that Robert may have used with those on the status of chapels.

allegatio parum profuit michi, set si nos a quadraginta annis retro fontes[1] habuissemus et non capelle, sine dubio in causa obtinuissemus.

362. Tum ego, 'Pater sancte, in priuilegio Constantini pape continetur, "Ipsum ergo locum quem regia potestas regie libertati donauit et nos auctoritate Dei et sanctorum apostolorum et nostra donamus."[2] Locus iste non tantum monasterium set etiam omnes possessiones ecclesie nostre complectitur ut beneficium imperatoris amplissime et benignissime interpretetur.[3] Nec uerisimile est quod duo reges Romam iuerint ut tantillum locum quantus est situs abbatie nostre summo pontifici et ecclesie Romane conferrent et libertati donarent, cum in eodem priuilegio contineatur quod ipsi reges in loco ostense uisionis plurima de suis beneficiis in presentia summi pontificis regia libertate donata et apostolica auctoritate confirmata contulerunt. Ex quibus uerbis colligi potest quod non tantillus locus, |
fo. 166[vb] set magis ita ampliatus sit a summo pontifice libertati donatus. In cuius medio monasterium nostrum quasi cor in corpore situm est. Nam in priuilegiis regum, sicut ex eorum inspectione manifeste patebit, tota Vallis libertati donatur, et summus pontifex eundem locum dat libertati quoad spiritualia quem reges dederunt libertati quoad temporalia.'

363. Hec ideo dixi non tantum quia reuera ita se res habebat set etiam ut causa dilationem caperet donec priuilegia regum exhiberentur; quod et ita factum est. Et adieci, 'Quod autem hoc priuilegium ita intelligi debeat in priuilegio Innocentii pape manifeste declaratur, ubi dicitur, "Statuimus insuper ac predecessoris nostri, felicis memorie Constantini pape, uestigiis inherentes decernimus ut solummodo penes te et successores tuos tocius domus et ecclesie tue et aliorum locorum ad eandem ecclesiam pertinentium, pastoralis cura consistat, et eorundem ordinatio in tua et successorum tuorum tantum potestate permaneat."[4] Ecce, manifeste ostenditur quod non tantum monasterium set etiam menbra sunt exempta. Hoc idem etiam in eodem priuilegio alibi patenter ostenditur ubi dicitur, "Statuimus etiam ne in uestra abbatia aut in capellis uestris aliquis episcopus sinodum aut capitula, aut ordinationes aut missas publicas nisi inuitatus ab abbate

[1] Alexander III had decreed that to uphold a prescriptive right it was necessary to prove that it had been exercised for forty years; *X.* II. 26. 4 (Friedberg, ii col. 383). On the *prescriptio longissimi temporis*, see Falkenstein, *La Papauté et les abbayes françaises*, pp. 94 (and n. 2), 135.
[2] See above, 322.

was of little benefit to me, though, if we had had fonts forty years before[1] instead of the chapels having them, we would undoubtedly have won our case.

362. I then continued, 'Holy father, the following is contained in the privilege of Pope Constantine: "The very place to which royal power has granted the royal liberty we also grant liberty by the authority of God and the holy apostles and by our own authority."[2] The word 'place' embraces not only the monastery but also all the possessions of our church, so this 'imperial' gift should be interpreted as fully and as benevolently as possible.[3] It is not likely that two kings went to Rome to bestow upon the high pontiff and the Roman church so tiny a place as the site of our abbey, and to grant it liberty, when contained in that same privilege is the statement that in the presence of the high pontiff those very kings bestowed many things from their bounty upon the place where the vision was seen, things given with royal liberty and confirmed by apostolic authority. From these words it can be gathered that it was not the tiny place itself, but rather a larger region to which the high pontiff granted liberty. Our monastery is situated in the middle of this region like the heart in the middle of the body. Indeed, in the privileges of the kings, as an inspection of them will make abundantly clear, the whole Vale is granted its liberty, and the high pontiff gives the same place liberty in respect of its spiritualities, just as the kings do in respect of its temporalities.'

363. I said these things not only because this was the true state of affairs but also to delay proceedings until the privileges of the kings could be produced; and I was successful in this. I further added, 'That this privilege should be so understood is clearly affirmed in the privilege of Pope Innocent (II) when it says, "Furthermore, adhering to the decisions made by our predecessor, Pope Constantine of happy memory, we further command and decree that the pastoral care of your entire house, church, and other places belonging to the same church should rest solely with you and your successors, and that the ordering of those places should remain your prerogative alone and that of your successors."[4] Surely, then, it is clearly shown that not only the monastery but also the dependencies are exempt. This is also made abundantly clear elsewhere in the same privilege when it says, "We also command that no bishop should presume to celebrate a synod, chapters, ordinations, or public masses in your abbey or your

[3] For the *beneficium imperatoris*, see above, 289 and n.
[4] See above, 330.

illius loci uel a fratribus celebrare presumat."[1] Cum itaque in ecclesiis non priuilegiatis hec diocesanis episcopis exercere non possit dene- gari, constat quod capelle ille eodem gaudent priuilegio quo et matrix ecclesia cum qua hoc priuilegium sunt adepte et infra limites parrochie eius constitute. Preterea tam ab Innocentio quam ab Alexandro conceduntur et confirmantur nobis peculiares consuetu- dines quas habemus in parrochiis, in processionibus, in ordinationi- bus, ut sicut hucusque | consueuimus eas teneamus.[2] Set in parrochiis omnium ecclesiarum de quibus agitur, sicut in possessorio iudicio pro nobis est sentenciatum, hucusque tales habuimus pecu- liares consuetudines quod decanus ecclesie nostre ab abbate nostro de consensu nostro constitutus de omnibus causis tam maioribus quam minoribus in eis emergentibus cognoscit, et abbas noster publicas penitencias iniungit.

fo. 167ʳᵃ

364. 'Processionem etiam Pentecostalem, que tantum est cathedra- lium ecclesiarum, hucusque ab illarum ecclesiarum parrochianis in ecclesia Eueshamensi auctoritate istorum priuilegiorum annuatim suscipimus, peculiari quadam consuetudine, more cathedralium ecclesiarum. Ordinationes etiam earundem ecclesiarum habemus quia in eis personas et uicarios instituimus. Que omnia per testes omni exceptione[3] maiores non tantum ex parte nostra productos set etiam per clarissimos et autenticos uiros ex parte episcopi productos, nos auctoritate horum priuilegiorum hec fecisse probatum est. Cum igitur hec iura episcopalia auctoritate ecclesie Romane in hiis ecclesiis habeamus, nichil potestatis uel iurisdictionis episcopalis relinquitur episcopo. Quare eas sicut menbra cum capite suo, ecclesia scilicet Eueshamensi, dico exemptas.

365. 'Verum adhuc alia in priuilegio Alexandri pape continentur per que manifeste ostenditur ecclesias illas simul cum monasterio ab omni iurisdictione episcopali esse exemptas. Dicit enim, "Crisma uero, oleum sanctum, consecrationes altarium, ordinationes clericorum qui ad sacros ordines fuerint promouendi a quocumque malueritis susci- piatis episcopo."[4] Set cum in maiori ecclesia nostra tantum simus monachi nec crismate nec oleo sancto nec ordinatione clericorum

---

[1] See above, 329.

[2] See above, 330, 334.

[3] 'omni exceptione' seems to mean here that the witnesses were accepted by both sides as irreproachable. They could be objected to on certain canonical grounds, as partisan and so forth.

[4] See above, 334.

chapels, unless invited to do so by the abbot of the monastery or by the brethren."[1] Therefore, since in churches not so privileged diocesan bishops cannot be prevented from exercising these powers, it follows that our chapels rejoice in the same privilege as the mother church, having acquired this privilege at the same time as the mother church did, and been established inside the bounds of its parish. Moreover, both Innocent and Alexander have granted and confirmed that we should retain our own peculiar customs which we enjoy in our parishes in the case of processions and ordinations, as we have hitherto been accustomed to practise them.[2] However, in the parishes of all the churches which are the subject of legal action, as in the case of the possessory trial when sentence was passed in our favour, we have hitherto freely enjoyed our own peculiar customs, for the dean of our church, appointed by our abbot with our agreement, takes cognizance of all cases, both large and small, which arise in them, and our abbot imposes public penance.

364. 'Every year we have engaged in the annual Whitsuntide procession, a practice of cathedral churches alone, and hitherto we have been joined in the church at Evesham by the parishioners of those churches. We have done this on the authority of those privileges by our own peculiar custom in the manner of a cathedral church. We are also responsible for the ordering of those churches because we institute the parsons and the vicars in them. And it has been proved by the witnesses, who were major witnesses accepted by the parties,[3] produced not only by our side, but also by those—distinguished men of authority—called on the bishop's side, that we did all these things with the authority of these privileges. Since therefore we possess these episcopal rights in these churches on the authority of the Roman Church, no episcopal power or jurisdiction whatsoever remains for the bishop. I say then that those churches as dependencies enjoy exemption along with their mother church, the church of Evesham.

365. 'But there are still other things contained in the privilege of Pope Alexander by which it is clearly demonstrated that those churches as well as the monastery are exempt from all episcopal jurisdiction. For it says, "You may receive from any bishop of your choice chrism, holy oil, the consecration of altars and the ordination of clerks who are to be promoted to sacred orders."[4] But since in our church alone, which is the head church, we are monks, and do not need for ourselves chrism, holy oil, or the ordination of clerks but

propter nos nisi ratione subditorum indigeamus, relinquitur quod ratione ecclesiarum aliarum et rectorum et parrochianorum hec fo. 167[rb] percipiamus, sicut | dicit Innocentius, qui peculiares consuetudines in crismate accipiendo et per ecclesias nostras distribuendo nobis confirmat. Quod cum secundum ius canonicum non exemptis nisi a suo episcopo[1] hec accipere non liceat, sequitur quod tam clerici quam laici qui hec a nullo specialiter episcopo suscipere tenentur nullo diocesano subiciantur, set magis cum illa eccclesia a qua hec percipiunt ab omni diocesani episcopi iurisdictione sint exempti. Cum et, secundum idem priuilegium, altaria earundem ecclesiarum a quocumque maluerimus possint consecrari episcopo, quod secundum canones in ecclesiis non exemptis non licet. Preterea cum ex hiis ecclesiis maxima libertatis nostre utilitas oriatur et dependeat, ex quarum fructibus maxime sustentamur,[2] quid proderit nobis hec libertas si illas amiserimus ex quibus emolumentum[a] libertatis suscipimus, cum ex earum amissione pauperes efficiamur.

366. 'Preter hec, pater sancte, uehementer admiror qua fronte episcopus adhuc petit sibi subici duas ecclesias Eueshamie, quas constat esse sitas infra ambitum monasterii nostri et muros cimiterii nostri, quarum una non distat a matrici ecclesia nisi per nouies uiginti pedes, altera uero tantum per quadraginta sex pedes.[3] Cum iam uestri gratia per sentenciam uestram declaratum sit saltem illum tantillum locum ubi situm est monasterium nostrum esse liberum et exemptum, quare illas ut in loco libero sitas dico exemptas.'

367. Tunc dominus papa conuersus ad aduersarium dixit ei, 'Responde hiis.' Et aduersarius, 'Pater sancte, ego nunquam in uita mea amplius super priuilegiis summi pontificis disputabo, set uos cuius est condere pro uoluntate uestra interpretamini ea.'[4] Tum dominus papa, qui multum fauorabilis erat episcopo in hac ultima causa, dixit, 'Videtur prima facie quod priuilegia Innocentii et fo. 167[va] Alexandri | dependeant ex priuilegio Constantini, et sub tali

[a] emolimentum *R*

---

[1] Cf. *X.* III. 36, 8 (Friedberg, ii cols. 606–7); and see *X.* III. 37. 2 (Friedberg, ii cols. 607–8; P 1523; 3 *Comp.* 3. 29.1), where Innocent III stated in 1201 that all churches were subject to the diocesan unless exempted by a special privilege or by legitimate prescription.

[2] The income from the Vale churches, listed in the Taxatio of Pope Nicholas IV of 1291 (*Taxatio Ecclesiastica Angliae et Walliae auctoritate P. Nicholai IV circa A.D. 1291* (Record Commission: London, 1802), p. 219 col. b), amounted to about £80. Other churches which the abbey claimed would have doubled this income.

[3] St Laurence and All Saints; cf. the two surviving churches within the enclave of the

only for our dependents, the explanation is then that we receive them
on behalf of the other churches, and their rectors and parishioners, as
Innocent says, who confirms our own peculiar customs in the
receiving of chrism and in our distribution of it throughout our
churches. According to canon law, these things may not lawfully be
received by those who do not enjoy exemption except from their own
bishop:[1] it follows, therefore, that clerks as well as laity who are not
bound to receive these from any specific bishop are not subject to any
diocesan, but rather are exempt from all diocesan jurisdiction along
with that church from whom they receive these things. Furthermore,
according to that same privilege the altars of the same churches are
able to be consecrated by any bishop of their choice, whereas
churches not enjoying exemption are not so permitted by the
canons. Hence, since the greatest benefit arising from our liberty
originates from and depends upon these churches—for we are
particularly sustained by the income we receive from them[2]—what
advantage would this liberty be to us if we lost those churches from
whom we receive the benefit of our liberty and so be made paupers as
the result of that loss?

366. 'In this connection, Holy Father, I am very much surprised at
the bishop's boldness in continuing to seek the subjection to himself
of the two churches of Evesham, which he admits are situated within
the boundary of our monastery and the walls of our cemetery, for one
of them is 180 feet from the mother church and the other only forty-
six feet away.[3] Since you have already graciously declared in your
sentence ['Ex ore sedentis'] that that tiny area at least, where our
monastery is situated, is free and exempt, I say that as those churches
are situated within that free area they also are exempt.'

367. Then the pope, turning to our opponent, said to him, 'Make your
reply to these arguments.' Our opponent then said, 'Holy Father, I
shall never again in my life argue over the privileges of the high pontiff,
but it is for you, who have to draw them up, to interpret them as you
will.'[4] The pope, who had a good deal of sympathy for the bishop in
this second case, said, 'On the face of it, it seems that the privileges
of Innocent and Alexander are dependent upon the privilege of

great Benedictine monastery of Bury St Edmunds: St James' (now the cathedral) and St
Mary's, both of which are in close proximity to the abbey church.

[4] Cf. *Code* 1. 14. 12, and *Digest* 46. 5. 9. The medieval maxim, founded on the Roman
law notion, 'Eius enim est interpretari, cuius est condere', was employed by Innocent III,
see 3 *Comp.* 5. 21. 4 (*X.* V. 39. 31, Friedberg, ii cols. 901–2), cited by Pennington, *Pope and
Bishops*, p. 171.

conditione sint ecclesie Eueshamensi concessa si Vallis Eueshamie in qua site sunt ille ecclesie sit ille locus quem Constantinus papa dedit libertati.' Et data benedictione, precepit ut recederemus donec super prescriptione dicturi alias uocaremur.

368. Post aliquot dies iterum uocati comparuimus et dixi, 'Pater sancte, quod per priuilegia huius sancte sedis ecclesie Vallis Eueshamie ab omni iurisdictione episcopali sint exempte sufficienter, ut michi uidetur, pridie ostendi. Et quod similiter prescriptione tuti simus non credo aduersarium nostrum uelle inficiari, quia diutina possessio nostra, que memoria hominum excedit, non tantum per testes ex parte nostra productos, set etiam per uiros clarissimos et fidedignos ex parte episcopi productos sufficientissime probatur.' Et proferens rotulum nostrum incepi legere attestationes que ad hoc faciebant.[1]

369. Et dominus papa, tedio affectus, conuersus ad aduersarium nostrum dixit, 'Num opus est lectione attestationum? num prescripserunt?' Et dixit magister Robertus, 'Reuera prescripserunt.' Et dominus papa, 'Vt quid ergo laboramus?' Et aduersarius, 'Pater sancte, nos didicimus in scolis, et hec est opinio magistrorum nostrorum, quod non currit prescriptio contra iura episcopalia.' Et dominus papa, 'Certe et tu et magistri tui multum bibistis de ceruisia Anglicana quando hec didicistis.'[2] Et cum magister Robertus adhuc idem affirmaret, iterum idem audiuit responsum. Et cum adhuc magister Robertus idem probare niteretur per quosdam canones qui hoc dicere uidebantur, et per quandam sentenciam domini pape quam iam triduo transacto tulerat contra canonicos Cenomannie de capella domini regis pro episcopo Cenomanensi,[3] respondi | ego, 'Pater

fo. 167ᵛᵇ

[1] Alexander III, in defining the length of time required for the proof of a prescriptive right, had accentuated the importance of witnesses in determining the point (*X*. II. 26. 8, Friedberg, ii col. 384).

[2] A standing Bolognese joke; compare e.g. Ricardus Anglicus' preface to the Distinctiones '. . . resistentes atramento uelut anglicus inebriabo' (MS Vat. Lat. 2691, fo. 1), cited by Kuttner and Rathbone, *ANC*, p. 326 n. 40. And cf. the gloss of Casus Parisiensis on Lat. IV c. 15, 'On restraining the drunkenness of clerks'; printed in *Constitutiones concilii quarti Lateranensis una cum commentariis glossatorum*, ed. A. García y García, p. 469, 'A crapula: Reprehendentur hic Anglici, Poloni et Hungari qui se inebriant et se ad garsel inuitant.'

[3] Innocent's sentence in this case between the canons of the royal chapel of Saint-Pierre-de-la-Cour and the chapter of Le Mans (S. Julien) as to whether the canons were subject to an interdict which had been imposed on the city of Le Mans by the bishop was probably given on 1 Feb. 1206 when a letter was addressed to the canons (P 2675). On 3 Feb. 1206—the day on which he sent the Vale case to judges delegate for enquiry—he wrote to the dean and chapter of Le Mans (P 2679). His decision argued against the force of custom in claiming exemption and was incorporated in the first official canon law

Constantine, and on this basis they support the church of Evesham if the Vale of Evesham in which those churches are situated is the place which Pope Constantine granted its liberty.' After giving us his blessing he commanded us to depart until we were called at another time to speak on the subject of prescriptive right.

368. After several days we were again called, and when we appeared before him, I said, 'Holy Father, I have given sufficient proof, it seems to me, on the previous occasion that the churches of the Vale of Evesham have been given exemption by the privileges of this Holy See from all episcopal jurisdiction. I do not believe our opponent would want to deny that we are similarly protected by prescriptive right, for our long possession, which goes back beyond human memory, is thoroughly proved not only by the witnesses produced by our side but also by the distinguished and trustworthy men produced on the bishop's side.' I brought out our roll [of the attestations] and began to read the testimonies relating to this point.[1]

369. The pope, now weary of the argument, turned to our opponent and said, 'Surely there is no need for the testimonies to be read as to whether or not they have prescriptive right?' Master Robert replied, 'Certainly they have prescriptive right.' The pope went on, 'Why then are we labouring the point?' Our opponent replied, 'Holy Father, we learned in the schools—and this is the opinion of our masters—that prescriptive right does not preclude episcopal rights.' To this the pope replied, 'Without doubt you and your masters had drunk deeply of your English ale when you learnt that!'[2] When Master Robert continued to insist that this was so, he heard the same reply. And when he still endeavoured to prove the point from specific canons which seemed to say as much, and from a specific sentence of the pope which he had given three days before against the canons of Le Mans and in favour of the bishop of Le Mans in connection with the royal chapel,[3] I replied, 'Holy Father, there are some episcopal

collection, the so-called Compilatio Tertia (3 *Comp.*, I tit. 3 c.4) of Peter Collivaccinus of Benevento: from that source it was later included in the *Decretales* of Pope Gregory IX (*X.* I. 4. 5, Friedberg, ii cols. 37–8). The papal letters in the case are printed in the *Cartulaire du chapitre royal de Saint-Pierre-de-la-Cour* (Société des archives historiques du Maine. Archives historique du Maine, iv), ed. Le Vicomte Menjot d'Elbenne and l'Abbé L.-J. Denis (Le Mans, 1903–7), pp. 33, 40–5 (no. xxxiv) and 46–8 (no. xxxvi). The proctor of Saint-Pierre-de-la-Cour had argued that from its foundation the church was exempt, but he could show no documentary evidence of this. Instead he referred to gifts from the ancestors of King John and to the conferment of the deanship and the prebends by the king without need of the bishop's consent. The proctor of the bishop of Worcester obviously had knowledge of the case from the presence of the Le Mans representatives in

sancte, quedam sunt iura et officia episcopalia, ueluti dedicare
ecclesias, conficere crisma, conferre sacros ordines, et hiis similia
que a nemine possunt exerceri nisi ab episcopo, et ideo hec non
possunt ab aliis priuatis possideri, quare nec prescribi ut alie persone
quam episcopi unquam cohereant. Forte in tali casu locuntur canones
illi quos aduersarius noster allegauit. Nos uero non petimus quod hec
officia cohereant persone abbatis nostri, set ut alii quicumque episcopi
sicut consueuimus hec aput nos possint exercere, Wigornensis autem
non. Et cum sit instar sacrilegii de sentencia uestra disputare,[1] multo
grauius peccatum illam peruertere, *multum admiror quod* aduersarius noster sentenciam uestram aut peruertit aut male intelligit, quia
canonici Cenomanenses tantum diutinam possessionem absque bona
fide et iusto titulo contra iura episcopalia allegauerunt, et ideo non
prescipserunt. Nos uero ex priuilegiis nostris et bonam fidem et
iustum titulum habemus et diutinam possessionem, sicut aduersarius
noster confitetur, *et ideo prescripsimus'.

370. Tunc iratus* dominus papa eo quod magister Robertus tepide
allegasset in casu isto, multum enim fouit partem eius secundum
iusticiam in causa ista. Dixit, 'Audiuimus quod ecclesia Wigornensis
pluries uacauit quam aliqua alia ecclesia Anglicana,[2] unde fortassis
potest contingere quod subducto tempore uacationis minime sit
completa uestra prescriptio, et, sicut ex attestationibus uestris
audiuimus, multe intercesserunt interruptiones.' Et quamuis dominus papa ut iustus iudex hoc diceret quia odiosa est prescriptio,[3]
tamen dolui quod ita defectum aduersarii nostri suppleret, et non
potens cohibere linguam meam pre tristitia, dixi, 'Pater sancte, in
plenitudine potestatis[4] uocati estis, et ideo omnia licent uobis, set
fo. 168ra secundum iura ciuilia aliis iudicibus | non licet de hiis que desunt

---

a–a multum . . . quod *correction written over an erasure*   *b–b* et ideo . . . Tunc iratus
written over an erasure

Rome, and the decision would have been a matter of much interest to the Evesham and
Worcester proctors in particular.

[1] See above, 309 n.

[2] In the forty years before the consecration of Bishop Mauger in June 1200, there had
been seven periods of vacancy, the average length being one year, and the longest vacancy
taking place after the death of Bishop Alfred on 31 July 1160 and before the consecration
of Roger of Gloucester on 23 Aug. 1164 (four years). In particular, four vacancies had
occurred in the decade between 1190 and 1199, the last of which on the death of John de
Coutances (24 Sept. 1198), and before the consecration of Mauger (on 4 June 1200), lasted
for one year and eight months; see *HBC*, pp. 278–9.

[3] The description of prescription as 'hated' is an allusion to the Roman Law, *Code* 7. 40.
3. 2 and 3. In title 40 of the *Code*, dealing with exceptions and prescriptions, exceptions are

rights and duties, such as the dedication of churches, the consecration of chrism, the conferring of sacred orders, and other similar duties which can be exercised by nobody but a bishop and cannot therefore be possessed by other persons not holding the office, and no rule can be made that would ever allow them to be attached to any person other than a bishop. It happens that it is about such a case that those canons whom our opponent has mentioned are pleading. But we are not asking for these duties to be attached to the person of our abbot, only that other bishops of our choice may be able to exercise these duties amongst us, as has been the custom, and not the bishop of Worcester. Since it is tantamount to sacrilege to dispute your sentence[1] and a much more serious sin to misrepresent it, I am very surprised that our opponent either misrepresents or misunderstands your sentence, for the canons of Le Mans have without good authority or just title argued long possession against the rights of the bishop, and so do not have prescriptive rights. We, on the other hand, have good authority and just title on the basis of our privileges as well as long possession, as our opponent admits, and so have prescriptive rights.'

370. The pope was then angry that Master Robert had casually alluded to that case, for he greatly favoured that party in this case, as far as justice allowed. He then remarked, 'We have heard that the church of Worcester has had more vacancies than any other English church,[2] so it is perhaps possible that your prescriptive right was not fully maintained during the period of a vacancy and, as we have heard from your own evidence, many interruptions did occur.' Now although a pope as a just judge might say this on the grounds that prescription is hated,[3] yet I deplored the fact that he supplied the deficiencies in our opponent's argument in this way, and unable to curb my tongue in my frustration, I said, 'Holy Father, you are called to a plenitude of power,[4] so you may do anything you wish, but the civil law does not allow other judges to supply the deficiencies of

described as *odiose*. Gratian, *Decretum*, C16 qu. 3 p. c.15 (Friedberg, i cols. 794–5) esp. §2 ('hee prescriptiones sunt introducte fauore possidentis et odio petentis, quia lex fauet his, qui bona fide et iusto titulo, uel bona tantum fide possident, odit autem et punit circa rem suam negligentes et desides') proceeds from this; and perhaps 1 *Comp.* 2. 18. 7 = *X*. II. 26. 5 (Friedberg, ii col. 383; JL 14186). See also below, **382**.

[4] On the 'plenitude of power', see Pennington, *Pope and Bishops*, pp. 42–74. R. Benson, 'Plenitudo potestatis: evolution of a formula from Gregory IV to Gratian', in *Studia Gratiana*, xiv (1968), Collectanea Stephan Kuttner iv. 193–217, esp. 214–17, showed that Gratian elaborated this to show that the pope was the judge ordinary of all.

aduocatis supplere de facto, nisi tantum de iure.'[1] Et dominus papa, 'Falsum est; immo et de facto et de iure licet iudici supplere.'[2] Et compescui labia mea,[3] quamuis sentirem me grauatum, quia nisi dominus papa de facto ita suppleuisset, prescriptionem tuti sine dubio in causa obtinuissemus.

371. Tunc precepit dominus papa quod recederemus, et post paucos dies dedit nobis dominum Gualam diaconum cardinalem, inter cardinales in iure ciuili peritissimum,[4] super interruptionibus prescriptionis nostre auditorem.[5] In qua causa bene astitit michi magister Adam Sortes[6] quia in attestationibus erat ualde expeditus, ueluti qui interfuerat in Anglia disputationi super eisdem in iudicio possessorio. Cum uero per multos dies coram predicto auctore[a] litigassemus, inuente sunt multe interruptiones prescriptionis nostre in attestationibus nostris et scriptis allegationibus utriusque partis super eisdem et facta relatione ad dominum papam. Per ipsius interlocutionem date sunt nobis littere communes[7] sub hac forma.

372. *Forma literarum domini pape super iurisdictione Vallis*
Innocentius episcopus, seruus seruorum Dei, uenerabilibus fratribus Eliensi[8] et Rofensi[9] episcopis et [b]magistro B., canonico Londoniarum,[c][10] salutem et apostolicam benedictionem. Auditis et intellectis attestationibus, instrumentis et allegationibus in causa que uertitur[d] inter uenerabilem fratrem nostrum Wigornensem episcopum et

---

[a] *Probably a mistake for* auditore   [b] *H adds* dilecto filio *and* de *after* magistro
[c] Londonen' *H*   [d] *interlined H*

[1] The 'other judges' is probably a reference to *Digest* 5.1.79.1, concerning provincial governors, who have ordinary jurisdiction, and their judges delegate; viz.'Iudicibus de iure dubitantibus presides respondere solent; de facto consulentibus non debent presides consilium impertire, uerum iubere eos prout religio suggerit sententiam proferre. Hec enim res nonnumquam infamat et materiam gratie uel ambitionis tribuit.'
[2] On this instance of Innocent shaping the law, see P. Landau, in *Festschrift für Rudolf Wassermann* (Darmstadt, 1985), pp. 728, 730.
[3] This may be a quotation, but we have been unable to trace it.
[4] Guala (Bicchieri), from Vercelli, was created cardinal deacon of S. Mary in Porticu by Innocent III in Dec. 1204. His legal knowledge is likely to have been acquired in Bologna. He wrote a *libellus* 'on the forms of petitions according to the procedure of the Roman curia', which was completed probably close to 1226; see Sayers, *Honorius III*, pp. 21–2. In 1211 he was promoted cardinal priest of S. Martin and in May 1216 he was sent on legation to England, staying until Dec. 1218; Maleczek, pp. 141–6.
[5] On Innocent III's interpretation of the law on prescription and his and his agents' actions in this particular case, see J. Petersohn, 'Papst Innocenz III. und das Verjährungsrecht der römischen Kirche', *Sitzungsberichte der Wissenschaftlichen Gesellschaft an der Johann Wolfgang Goethe-Universität Frankfurt am Main*, xxxvii nr. 3 (1999), 65–90, at 84–5.

advocates on matters of fact, only on matters of law.'[1] The pope
retorted, 'That is untrue; a judge may indeed do this in respect of
matters of fact as well as of matters of law.'[2] I held my tongue,[3]
though I felt I had been wronged, for if the pope had not supplied
information on the facts of the case we would undoubtedly have kept
our prescriptive right intact in this suit.

371. The pope then ordered us to withdraw, and after a few days he
granted us the cardinal deacon Guala, the most learned of the
cardinals in civil law,[4] as auditor to investigate the interruptions in
our prescriptive right.[5] I was well assisted in this case by Master
Adam Sortes,[6] for he was very knowledgeable of the evidence, having
been present in the contest over the same matters at the possessory
trial in England. We argued the case for many days before the
auditor. The attestations revealed many interruptions of our prescriptive right, so written arguments on both sides about these
interruptions were made and a report was presented to the pope.
We then received a letter in common form[7] through his instigation in
the following terms.

372. *The terms of the pope's letter concerning jurisdiction over the Vale*
Innocent, bishop, servant of the servants of God, to the venerable
brethren the bishops of Ely[8] and Rochester[9] and Master Benedict,
canon of London,[10] greeting and apostolic benediction. We have
heard and understood the evidence, the documents, and the
arguments in the case which is proceeding between our venerable
brother the bishop of Worcester and the beloved son the abbot of

---

[6] See above, 275–8.

[7] Letters which were impetrated (or petitioned for) according to a common form and in
which set phrases were used; see Herde, *Audientia Litterarum Contradictarum*, ii. 548, 551,
552, 553, 586, 599, 604, 607, 608, 640.

[8] Eustace, bishop from 1198 to 1215, well known as a judge delegate and for his tireless
questioning of Innocent III which resulted in the decretal,'Pastoralis'. Previously treasurer
of York, archdeacon of Richmond and of the East Riding, and dean of Salisbury; royal
vice-chancellor and acting chancellor; see Greenway, *Fasti*, ii. 45; iv. 10, 111; and vi. 23–4,
41, 48, 111; and see *BRUO*, iii. 2173–4; and see above, 223 n. 3.

[9] Gilbert de Glanville, previously archdeacon of Lisieux and a clerk of Archbishop
Baldwin of Canterbury, elected to the see of Rochester on 16 July 1185, d. 24 June 1214,
succeeded by Master Benedict (see below); Greenway, *Fasti*, ii. 76.

[10] Master Benedict of Sawston was precentor of St Paul's, London, by 26 March 1204,
and a canon, by the date of this document (3 Feb. 1206); Greenway,*Fasti*, i. 23, 64. He had
been a clerk of Prince John, royal treasurer, and became a royal justice. In 1214 he was
lecturing in law in Paris (*ANC*, p. 289). A notable judge delegate, he heard cases as
precentor, and canon, of St Paul's (see Sayers, *PJD*, esp. pp. 130, 150, and 208), and after
Dec. 1214 as bishop of Rochester; Greenway, *Fasti*, ii. 76–7.

dilectum filium Eueshamensem abbatem super ecclesiis in Valle de
Eueshamia constitutis: quas episcopus asserit ad se diocesana lege
spectare, abbas autem eas esse ab eius iurisdictione prorsus exemptas.
Cognouimus euidenter ecclesias illas per priuilegia pontificum Romanorum non esse ab episcopali iurisdictione subtractas nisi forte Vallis
de Eueshamia sit ille locus quem a duobus regibus, Kenredo uidelicet
et Offa, libertati donatum bone memorie Constantinus papa libertati
donauit, sicut in ipsius priuilegio continetur. |

fo. 168rb **373.** Verum tanto tempore probantur per testes ab abbatibus
Eueshamie pleno iure possesse, ut uideantur in eis ius episcopale
legittime prescripsisse[1] nisi forte per tantum temporis Wigornensis
ecclesia interim uacauisset ut, tempore uacationis sublato,^a prescriptio minime sit completa. Licet autem sit utrimque in causa
conclusum, quia tamen utraque pars necessariam, ut asserit,
probationem omisit, nos attendentes quod utraque ecclesia fungitur
uice^b minoris,[2] equitate pensata, utramque restituimus contra
reliquam ad probandum rationem omissam, ne alterutra propter
huiusmodi negligentiam graui iactura ledatur. Quocirca discretioni
uestre per apostolica scripta mandamus quatinus inspectis priuilegiis
predictorum regum que abbas super predicta libertate asserit se
habere. Si per illa constiterit quod Vallis de Eueshamia sit ille locus
quem prefatus predecessor noster libertati donauit, absoluatis
Eueshamensem abbatem ab impetitione Wigornensis episcopi
super ecclesiis memoratis et, adiudicantes illas abbati pleno iure
subiectas, episcopo super illis perpetuum silentium imponatis.^c
Quod si abbas in hac probatione defecerit, audiatis probationes

---

^a subducto H   ^b uoce H   ^c im *interlined* H

[1] The source is the Roman law of Justinian, *Novels* 131. cap. 6: 'Pro temporalibus autem
praescriptionibus X et XX et XXX annorum sacrosanctis ecclesiis et aliis universis
venerabilibus locis solam quadraginta annorum praescriptionem opponi praecipimus; hoc
ipsum servando et in exactione legatorum et hereditatum quae ad pias causas relictae sunt.'
For the canon law, Gratian, *Decretum* C 16 q.3 p. c. 15 §6, and p. c. 16 ix pars 4; C 16 q. 4
p. c. 1, c. 2, p. c. 3 (Friedberg, i cols. 795–7).
[2] The Roman Law of guardianship, *Digest* 26 and 27, protected the minor. A church
was perceived as a minor, with the bishop, abbot, or parson acting as the tutor/protector,
or guardian, who had to see that the church or churches in his care were unharmed. See a
decretal of Alexander III, 1 *Comp.* 1. 32. 1, and 3. 11. 8, included in *X.* I. 41. 1, 'ecclesia
iure minoris debeat semper illesa servari' (Friedberg, ii cols. 222–3, JL 13737; and
W. Holtzmann, 'Kanonistische Ergänzungen zur Italia Pontificia', *Quellen und Forschungen
aus Italienischen Archiven und Bibliotheken*, xxxviii (1958), 67–175, at 139–40, no. 184). On
this point, usually cited when property or rents were at stake, see M. Cheney, 'Inalien-

Evesham concerning the churches established in the Vale of
Evesham: the bishop declares that they belong to him according
to diocesan law, the abbot that they are totally exempt from his
jurisdiction. It is our clear understanding that those churches are
not removed from episcopal jurisdiction by what is stated in the
privileges of the Roman pontiffs unless it is a fact that the Vale of
Evesham was the place given its liberty by the two kings Cenred
and Offa, and on that basis given liberty by Pope Constantine of
blessed memory as contained in his privilege.

373. Indeed, the evidence of witnesses proves that those churches
were over that long period possessed with full right by the abbots of
Evesham. They would therefore seem to have enjoyed lawful
prescriptive right against episcopal jurisdiction,[1] unless perhaps
over that long period of time the church of Worcester had a vacancy
so that, with allowance made for the vacancy, the term of prescriptive
right was not fulfilled. Although each side has concluded its case,
because each party has nevertheless failed to produce the proof which
it asserts is necessary, we observe that each church is functioning as a
minor.[2] So, having weighed up the justice of the situation, we are
restating the need for each side to produce evidence of proof against
the other, which they have failed to present, so that neither church
may suffer grave injury because of this negligence. Accordingly, by
apostolic letter we entrust to your good judgment the examination of
the privileges of the afore-mentioned kings which the abbot declares
he possesses in connection with the aforesaid liberty. If it is evident
from these that the Vale of Evesham is the place which our afore-
mentioned predecessor [Constantine] gave its liberty, you are to
absolve the abbot of Evesham from the claims of the bishop of
Worcester over the said churches and, judging them to be subject by
full right to the abbot, you are to command the bishop to be silent for
evermore about them. But if the abbot does not possess this proof,

---

ability in mid-twelfth-century England: Enforcement and Consequences', in *Monumenta
Iuris Canonici*, ser.2 Subsidia, vii (Città del Vaticano, 1985), 467–78. See also F. Pollock
and F. Maitland, *The History of English Law*, ed. Milsom, 2 vols. i (Cambridge, 1968),
503–4. The phrase occurs in a letter of Innocent III in *PL* 216 col. 518C, 'uel restituere in
integrum vice minoris idem monasterium dignaremur'. The church 'functioning as a
minor' also gets some attention in the much mutilated glossed text of one of the endpapers
(from the abbey of Evesham) of Wellcome MS 209, a 15th-cent. text of a medical treatise,
Constantine's *Viaticum*, possibly from Evesham. These endpapers concern legal cases,
including the Vale case. Unfortunately the text is too damaged to make more of, but it is
noteworthy that the question as to whether kings may give privileges in a synod is also
raised here, where the glossator is commenting on 'Auditis et intellectis'.

super tempore quo infra quadraginta annos sedes episcopalis uacauit. Et si per tantum temporis uacasse constiterit ut illo subducto non sit quadragenaria completa prescriptio,[1] uos in illis ecclesiis ius episcopale adiudicetis episcopo, et super illo perpetuum silentium imponatis abbati. Si autem exceptionem huiusmodi episcopus non probauerit, quia tamen interruptionem probauit circa processionem Pentecostalem in uilla et ecclesia de Mortune[2] et receptionem et procurationem archidiaconi, necnon solutionem denariorum beati[a] Petri in Valle de Eueshamia, circa cognitionem quoque causarum matrimonialium[3] et capellani sus|pensionem in predicta uilla de Morton et interdictum capellarum in prefata uilla de Eueshamia, uos super hiis ius episcopale adiudicetis eidem. Si tamen circa suspensionem et interdictum huiusmodi infra quadraginta annos interruptio facta fuit, in ceteris ei silentium imponentes quas abbas prescripsisse probatur.[4]

fo. 168[va]

374. Quod si forte noluerint sententiam diffinitiuam a uobis recipere, uos receptis probationibus prelibatis, eas nobis sub sigillis uestris fideliter destinetis, prefigentes partibus terminum competentem quo per procuratores idoneos recepture sentenciam nostro se conspectui representent. Testes autem qui fuerint nominati si se gratia, odio uel timore subtraxerint, per districtionem ecclesiasticam, appellatione remota, cogatis ueritati testimonium perhibere,[b] nullis litteris obstantibus si que apparuerint preter assensum partium a sede apostolica impetrate. Si uero non omnes hiis exequendis potueritis interesse, duo uestrum ea, sublato appellationis obstaculo, exequantur.[5] Datum Rome apud Sanctum Petrum tercio nonas Februarii, pontificatus nostri anno octauo.[c][6]

---

   [a] sancti *H*   [b] *followed by* Si uero non omnes hiis exequendis *expunged and* uacat
written above   [c] *H adds* Innocentii pape iii

---

[1] On the forty years' prescriptive right, see Alexander III's decretal, *X.* II. 26. 4 (Friedberg, ii col. 383, JL 14091, noted Holtzmann, 'Kanonistische Ergänzungen', at p. 133, no. 176i, 1 *Comp.* 2. 18. 6). Thomas has drawn attention to it above; 361 n. 1 (p. 348).

[2] Worcester (to which the Whitsuntide procession from Abbots Morton had gone) was about twelve miles away, Evesham about eight miles distance.

[3] Pope Clement III granted Abbot Samson of Bury St Edmunds the right to hear marriage cases in the abbey's subject parishes in 1189; *PUE* iii, no. 416. No licence of this kind survives for the abbot of Evesham, but it would be presumed that abbots of exempt houses had this right.

[4] Innocent's instructions in the case of the bishop of Lucca against the abbot and convent of S. Salvator de Ficheto super plebe Salamazanne (probably in, or close to Lucca, see Cottineau, ii, col. 1672), given in 1208 (*X.* II. 26. 18, Friedberg, ii cols. 389–91), also stressed the importance of witnesses' testimony as to what had happened in the last forty years in prescription cases, and on the possession of genuine privileges which conferred

you are to examine the evidence concerning the time when the episcopal see was vacant within the last forty years. If it is established that the vacancies amount to so great a period that the forty years needed for prescriptive right were not fulfilled,[1] you are to award episcopal rights over those churches to the bishop, and you are to command the abbot to be silent for evermore about that matter. But if the bishop does not prove a limitation of this length, nevertheless, because he has proved that there was an interruption [of prescriptive right] relating to the Whitsuntide procession in the town and church of Abbots Morton,[2] that the archdeacon was received and entertained, that Peter's pence was paid in the Vale of Evesham, that matrimonial suits[3] were heard and a chaplain suspended in Abbots Morton, and that an interdict was placed upon the chapels in the afore-said town of Evesham, you are to award episcopal rights over these churches to the bishop. If, however, in connection with the suspension and the interdict, there was an interruption within the last forty years in the other churches which the abbot is proved to have in prescriptive right, you are to impose silence upon him.[4]

374. However, should they refuse to accept a definitive sentence from you, after you have received the afore-mentioned evidence, you are to send it to us sealed, and fix a convenient date for the parties to present themselves before us by suitable proctors to receive sentence. If witnesses who have been named have withdrawn through favour, hate, or fear, you are to compel them to testify truthfully under pain of ecclesiastical censure, forbidding appeal, notwithstanding any letters unless they appear to have been obtained from the apostolic see with the agreement of the parties. If you cannot all take part in these proceedings then two of you are to proceed in these matters,[5] refusing any appeal which would hinder matters. Dated at St Peter's Rome on 3 February in the eighth year of our pontificate [1206].[6]

---

exemption. 'Auditis et intellectis' may be seen as a forerunner of this ruling: in Evesham's case, however, it was royal privileges that were at stake.

[5] This permission was usually included in the mandate; see Sayers, *PJD*, pp. 135–6.

[6] Sections of this important letter concerning prescriptive rights, the examination of privileges for authenticity, and their interpretation, were included in the collections of decretals formed by Alan, the Englishman (*c.*1206), Bernard of Pavia (1208), and Peter Beneventanus Collivaccinus (1210). From these sources they were selected for inclusion in Raymond of Pennaforte's *Decretales* (*X*) of 1234, where they appear under the titles 'De Prescriptionibus' (*X*. II. 26. 15, Friedberg, ii cols. 387–8) and 'De fide instrumentorum' (*X*. I. 41. 3, Friedberg, ii col. 224). The letter, listed by Cheney, *Letters*, no. 684 (P 2681), was registered, Reg. Vat. 7 fo. 63ᵛ (lib. 8 ep. 205), without place or pontifical year, and is printed in *Reg. Inn. III*, viii, no. 206 (205), pp. 357–60. It is likely that Alan and Gilbert,

375. Obtinuit etiam magister Robertus, me nesciente donec cum eis*a*
recessisset, tales litteras.

376. *Forma litterarum episcopi*[1] *super falsitate priuilegiorum regum*
Innocentius episcopus, seruus seruorum Dei, uenerabilibus fratribus
Eliensi et Roffensi episcopis et magistro B., canonico Londoniensi,
salutem et apostolicam benedictionem. Presentium uobis auctoritate
mandamus quatinus si in causa uenerabilis fratris nostri Wigornensis
episcopi et dilecti filii Eueshamensis abbatis, quam sub certa forma
uobis duximus committendam, falsi contigerit incidere questionem
super priuilegiis duorum regum Kenredi et Offe que preponitur idem
abbas habere, uos auctoritate nostra suffulti de ipsa, sublato cuiuslibet
fo. 168ᵛᵇ   appellationis et contradictionis | obstaculo, cognoscentes, eam fine
debito terminetis. Facientes quod statueritis per censuram ecclesiasticam firmiter obseruari, nullis literis etc.[2] Quod si non omnes etc.,
duo uestrum etc. Datum Rome apud Sanctum Petrum sexto idus
Februarii pontificatus nostri anno septimo.*b*[3]

377. Priuilegia regum hic non scribo quia sicut ex precedentibus
perpendere potestis, adhuc dubium est utrum nobis sint profutura
necne. Multa etiam scitu digna hic scribere pretermitto ne quocumque casu ad aduersarios nostros eadem peruemant. Quia quantum
prodesset nostrates ea scire, tantumdem obesset ad scientiam aduersariorum eadem peruenire.

378. *Consilium Thome prioris circa capellanos et decanatum et denarios
beati Petri et usum priuilegiorum et prescriptionem et interruptionem et
receptionem Wigornensium*
De hoc tamen omnes fideles et amicos Eueshamensis ecclesie
premunio, ut caueatis uobis de decano uestro et*c* capellanis uestris
et parrochianis uestris quia omnes predicte interruptiones per illorum
defectum, negligentiam et maliciam preter consensum et uoluntatem

---

a *interlined (s. xiii')*   *b* *followed by* Innocentius etc. *expunged*   *c* *interlined*

another English master at Bologna, were known to Thomas. See also Landau, in *Festschrift
Wassermann*, p. 730.

[1] This might be a reference to Innocent III as bishop (the pope's normal title) or it
might be to indicate that it was a letter impetrated for the bishop of Worcester by his
proctor, Master Robert.

[2] Thomas here abbreviates the common-form clauses, as was the usual practice for
entries in registers and letter collections.

[3] The seventh year is clearly a mistake for the eighth. Reg. Vat. 7 fo. 64 (lib. 8 ep. 206)
gives 7 id. Feb. (i.e. 7 Feb.), without place and pontifical year. The letter is printed in *Reg.*

375. In fact, Master Robert had obtained the following letters, though I did not know of this until he had returned with them.

376. *The [terms of the] bishop's letter[1] about the fraudulence of the kings' privileges*

Innocent, bishop, servant of the servants of God, to the venerable brethren the bishops of Ely [Eustace] and of Rochester [Gilbert] and Master B[enedict], canon of London, greeting and apostolic benediction. We command you on the authority of this present letter to see to it that, in the case between our venerable brother the bishop of Worcester and the beloved son the abbot of Evesham, which we have thought right to entrust to you under specific terms, if any question of fraud happens to arise in connection with the privileges of the two kings, Cenred and Offa, which it is claimed the abbot possesses, then, trusting on our authority, you are to forbid the hindrance of any appeal or any action to dispute it and, after hearing the evidence, are to make a final, just decision. You are to see that your decision is strictly observed under pain of ecclesiastical censure, no letters being withheld, etc.[2] If you cannot all take part, etc., two of you, etc. Dated at St Peter's Rome on 6th of the ides of February in the seventh year of our pontificate [7 or 8 Feb. 1206].[3]

377. I am not setting down in writing here the privileges of the kings because, as you can judge from my preceding narrative, it is still doubtful whether those privileges are going to be of any benefit to us or not. Indeed, I am here omitting many things that ought to be known, in case by some mischance this information reaches our opponents. Although this knowledge would be of great benefit to our side, it would be equally harmful to us if it were ascertained by our opponents.

378. *The advice of Prior Thomas about the chaplains, the deanery, Peter's Pence, the use of privileges, prescriptive right, interruption, and the receiving of the bishops of Worcester*

It is in this connection that I am warning all who are loyal and friendly to the church of Evesham to beware of your dean, your chaplains, and your parishioners, for the interruptions described occurred as the result of their ineffectiveness, neglect, and ill will. They acted without the agreement and permission of the abbot and

Inn. III, viii, the papal register for year 8, as no. 207 (206), pp. 360–1. Cal. Cheney, *Letters*, no. 685; P 2683.

abbatis et conuentus contigerunt, et tamen propter imperitiam et negligentiam nostram ac si nos ipsi ea commisissemus pro culpa nobis eadem reputantur. Capellani enim duarum ecclesiarum de Euesham citra consensum nostrum detulerunt suspensioni episcopi, et ecce! in dampnum ecclesie nostre eorum stult⟨it⟩ia redundat. Quia etiam capellanus de Mortune uisus fuit cum parrochianis cuiusdam uicini sui¹ in processione Pentecostali apud Wigorniam, in eadem processione facta est contra nos interruptio prescriptionis nostre. Dum etiam clerici essent decani Euesham' quia habebant redditus in episcopatu timentes episcopum, non compescebant per censuram ecclesiasticam, sicut debebant, parrochianos nostros quominus appellarent ab eis et irent ad episcopum pro quibusdam causis maioribus. Ideo, ut audistis, facta est interruptio prescriptionis nostre in quibusdam causis matrimonialibus.

379. Cum etiam episcopi Wigornenses teneantur soluere domino fo. 169ᵃ pape | undecim libras et quinque solidos pro denariis beati Petri annuatim et nos unam, decani, ut dictum est timentes episcopos, soluerunt episcopis libram quam debebant soluere domino pape pro denariis beati Petri omnium terrarum nostrarum, et episcopi, defraudantes ecclesiam Romanam, non ideo amplius soluerunt. ᵃQuam rationem cum audiret dominus papa multum motus fuit contra episcopum. Hoc ergo factum inter interruptiones non computaretur nisi nobis ad iacturam libertatis imputaretur. Magnum ergo periculum est ei soluere. Nam si ei deberet fieri solutio, ad solutionem faciendam eidem competeret cohercio. Quam si haberet, constat parochianos nostros non esse plene exemptos, cum episcopus posset eos excommunicare et etiam in solidum cogeret eos ad solutionem eorundem denariorum usque ad summam centum solidorum uel amplius, nacta qualicumque causa ut nos grauaret, nec posset aliquis ei resistere, cum ipse papa ad hoc nitatur omnes compellere. Et si tantum uiginti solidos contra nos obtineret, periculum nobis immineret ne tam domino pape quam illi soluere cogeremur eosdem.ᵃ ᵇEt quia hec mala et multa alia contigerantᵇ per clericos decanos,ᶜ² et quia timentes magnates terre non defendebant possessiones nostras et

---

ᵃ⁻ᵃ this passage is written over an erasure, in another hand, with numerous abbreviations, and replaces an earlier shorter one   ᵇ⁻ᵇ Item quia multa mala contra priuilegia huius ecclesie H   ᶜ H adds contigerant

¹ Abbots Morton, the northernmost of the Vale churches, lies about eight miles from Evesham: to the north-east of the church can be seen a sizeable mound surrounded by a moat of the abbot's house. The nearest neighbouring church would be Church Lench.

convent, yet we are blamed for our ignorance and negligence over what happened, as if we had actually done these things ourselves. The chaplains of two of the churches of Evesham submitted to suspension by the bishop without our agreement, and please note that their foolishness is causing our church harm. Also, because the chaplain of Abbots Morton was seen with the parishioners of a neighbouring church[1] in the Whitsuntide procession at Worcester, an interruption in our prescriptive right occurred to our detriment. Then, when clerks were deans of Evesham, because they were receiving an income in the diocese, out of fear of the bishop they did not prevent our parishioners—on pain of ecclesiastical censure, as they should have done—from taking their appeals away from them and going to the bishop over certain important issues. For that reason, as you have heard, interruption in our prescriptive right occurred in the case of certain matrimonial disputes.

379. Although the bishops of Worcester are under obligation to pay the pope £11 5s. Peter's Pence per annum, and we have to pay £1, the deans, out of fear of the bishops, as has been mentioned, paid to the bishops the £1 which they should have paid as Peter's Pence to the pope for the whole of our territory. So the bishops defrauded the Roman Church, for they did not thereby increase their payment. When the pope heard the account of this he was very angry with the bishop. This action should not therefore be counted amongst the interruptions, lest it should be regarded as a loss of liberty for us. There is therefore great peril in paying the bishop. For if we were under obligation to pay him, then he would have the right to demand that payment be made to him. And if he had this right, it follows that our parishioners would not enjoy complete exemption, for the bishop could excommunicate them and compel them collectively to pay Peter's Pence in full, which could be as much as 100 shillings or more, giving any reason he liked to burden us so, and nobody could stand up to him, as the pope himself tries to compel everybody to pay this money. If he were successful in forcing us to pay only twenty shillings, we should be in danger of being forced to pay as much again to the pope as we were paying to him. Deans who were clerks[2] had caused these and many other evils, and because they feared the magnates of the land they did not defend our possessions or our men,

---

[2] Thomas is making the point that these ills were caused by the deans because they were not monks.

homines nostros, nec in malefactores nostros, prout decano incumbit, per censuram ecclesiasticam ausi erant animaduertere. Immo homines nostros quando habebant coram eis causas magis spoliabant eos, inhiantes lucris temporalibus, et curam animarum in periculum[a] nostrarum animarum paruipendebant, [b]nam facti securi per cartam ecclesie[1] non poterant amoueri et ideo non timebant nos.[b] Et quia onerosi erant [c]ecclesie per omnia sicut senescaldus[c] in cotidianis procurationibus hominum et equorum, prouisum est et statutum ut monachi sint decani, sicut fuit prior Auicius et quidam alii[d] monachi post eum, qui ad uoluntatem abbatis et conuentus si male egerint uel tepide, possint amoueri, et qui ea que adquirunt ecclesie adquirant, et qui audacter in malefactores ecclesie animaduertant, et qui non sint magis oneri ecclesie quam simplex monachus preter procurationem apparitoris sui.

380. Et maxime hiis diebus necesse est ut monachi sint decani, quia si

fo. 169rb abbas discessisset[e] | nisi monachus esset decanus non esset aliquis qui ministros regis ausus esset excommunicare, si forte contra priuilegium nostrum manus ad diripiendos redditus officiis monachorum assignatos uellent apponere. Nec posset aliquis monachus hanc potestatem sibi assumere post mortem abbatis nisi eo uiuente illam habuisset.[f] Hiis de causis quendam magnum uirum, Rogerum scilicet filium Mauricii, canonicum Herefordensem,[2] cui abbas contulerat decanatum citra consensum conuentus, uiriliter ab ecclesiis Eueshamie ubi capitula uoluit celebrare expellendo eiecimus. Et etiam cum in domo sua uellet capitulum celebrare prohibuimus clericis et laicis ne ei obedirent, et coegimus eos inde recedere. Quo ita a decanatu amoto, factus sum ego decanus et functus sum officio illo omnibus diebus usque dum hec scripta sunt, etiam tempore prioratus mei.[3]

381. [g]Audistis etiam quod circa receptionem et procurationem archidiaconi facta est interruptio quamuis caritatiue eos receperimus. [h]Vnde ualde cauendum est ne unquam episcopum uel archidiaconum Wigorn' etiam caritatiue petentes, uel etiam cum

---

[a] periculo H   [b–b] om. H   [c–c] ecclesie . . . senescaldus written over an erasure R   [d] om. H   [e] decessisset H   [f] H ends here fo. 116   [g–g] Audistis etiam . . . extremo tempore (p. 370 (383)) written over an erasure R   [h–h] H resumes here with Item . . . permittetis (p. 370, end of 381)

---

[1] Thomas's comment implies that the appointment by charter was for life and without restriction.

[2] Clerk, and later canon of Hereford, he was a considerable landlord, owning much property in the city of Hereford. He had the church of Bacton (Herefs.) and successfully claimed the tithes of Hampton (Court, Herefs.); EEA 7: Hereford, 1079–1234, nos. 169,

nor had they dared to use ecclesiastical censure, as a dean should, to proceed against those who were harming us. In fact they preferred to plunder our men when they had cases before them, being greedy for this world's goods, and they showed little concern for the care of souls, so endangering our souls, for, safeguarded by their charter from the church they could not be moved and so were not afraid of us. [1] They also burdened the church by all they did like a steward in daily maintenance of men and horses. It was therefore resolved and instituted that monks should be deans as Prior Æfic was and certain other monks after him, who, if they acted with ill-intent or half-heartedly, could be removed at the desire of the abbot and convent: what they acquired would be acquired for the church; they would show no fear in punishing those who harmed the church; and they would be no more of a burden upon the church than a simple monk, except for the payment of their own apparitors.

380. It is very necessary these days for deans to be monks, for when an abbot dies, unless the dean is a monk, there will be nobody who would dare to excommunicate royal officials if such men desired at any time to take action against our privilege and plunder the revenue assigned for the duties of monks. No monk could appropriate this power for himself after the death of an abbot unless he had had it when the abbot was alive. Accordingly, when Roger fitz Maurice—an important man and canon of Hereford,[2] whom the abbot had appointed dean without the consent of the convent—wished to hold chapters, we forcibly expelled him and drove him out of the churches of Evesham. Even when he wished to hold a chapter meeting in his own house we forbade the clerks and laymen to obey him, and forced them to leave the house. When, as a result, he was removed from the office of dean, I was made dean, and have held that office continuously until the present time of writing this, even during my time as prior.[3]

381. You have heard that an 'interruption' occurred because of our reception and entertainment of the archdeacon, even though we did this in a spirit of friendship. In future we must be very careful never to make any request of the bishop or archdeacon of Worcester, even out of friendship; you must never admit them, even if they arrive with

267. The editor, J. Barrow (ibid., pp. 205, 308), says that it is likely that he died shortly after 1206. He had witnessed Hereford charters in the 1150s (no. 93). Probably well-connected, he is just the sort of man who would have appealed to Abbot Norreis.

[3] Thomas was made dean in 1206, and was prior from 1218 to 1229. For the date of the composition, see above, pp. xxiii–xxv.

legato Romano uel rege uel archiepiscopo uenientes, uel quocumque alio modo, admittatis ad cibum uel ad alia ad que alios admittimus, quia semper interpretandum est pro iure communi. Priorem uero Wigorn' et archidiaconum Glouc', nisi forte nomine officialium petierint, bene potestis admittere, nam nomine officialium neminem admittetis, nec quod aliquod officium infra Vallem etiam de suis parochianis exerceant permittetis.*h'*

382. *ᵃIgiturᵇ* cum ex priuilegiis et ex prescriptione omnis libertas huius ecclesie dependeat, cauete uobis, omnes filii huius ecclesie, ne unquam utamini iure communi ubi ius speciale habetis, nam de facili admittaturᶜ possessio libertatis quia exemptio contra ius commune est, et facillime interrumpitur prescriptio quia odiosa est.*ᵃ*[1]

383. Vos igitur quos huius litis de libertate Vallis discertatio et cause decisio expectat, adiuro per Ihesum Christum filium Virginis que elegit locum istum, ut, exemplo nostri qui tot mala, ut audistis, pro libertate huius ecclesie sustinuimus, uiriliter agatis. Nec aliquod discrimen huius seculi iacture libertatis reputetis comparabile, quia si Vallis libertatem amiseritis, ecclesias et decimas et cohercionem malefactorum, que pluris est, procul dubio amittetis. Et pauperes et miseri eritis et, quod absit, inuenient uos mala in extremo tempore.*ᵍ*[2] *ᵈ'*Quia uero, ut in premissis continetur, ᵉnon tantum ille priuilegium meretur amittere qui, omissis ui et*ᶠ* potestate priuilegiorum, utens iure communi concessa sibi non utitur potestate, set etiam ille qui non concessa sibi utitur potestate.[3] Cauete uobis ne unquam uim et potestatem priuilegiorum uestrorum excedatis, ordinando uidelicet alienos parrochianos ad ordinem subdiaconatus, diaconatus uel presbiteratus.[4] Alienum dico omnem qui non habet titulum ordinationis sue in parrochia uestra nisi de licentia sui diocesani.[5] Nec alienis excommunicatis post denuntiationem uobis factam communicetis. Nec crisma et oleum, si apud uos confecta fuerint, aliis quam uobis similibus, uidelicet priuilegiatis, prebeatis,*ᵍ* nisi de uoluntate diocesani episcopi petentis. Nec in aliis casibus qui infiniti sunt.*ᵈ'*

ᵃ⁻ᵃ Igitur . . . odiosa est *H fo. 116*   *ᵇ om. H*   *ᶜ corr. H to* amittitur   *ᵈ'⁻ᵈ'* Quia uero . . . infiniti sunt *lower marg. in second hand. This passage together with* Audistis . . . tempore (*ᵍ'⁻ᵍ', beginning p. 368*, 381–3) *replaces an earlier shorter one*   *ᵉ⁻ᵉ H continues here* Et quia non tantum ille . . . infiniti sunt   *ᶠ interlined*   *ᵍ om. H*

---

[1] See above, 370.   [2] Cf. Deut. 31: 29.

[3] See above, 354 and n., for the ruling concerning the abuse of privileges.

[4] Ordination could only be performed by a bishop, and this, therefore, means a bishop of Evesham's choice.

[5] Letters dimissory from the bishop allowed the candidate to seek ordination in a diocese other than his own.

the papal legate, the king, or the archbishop, or on any pretext whatever, whether it be for hospitality or for any other reason for which we admit others, for we must always interpret our action in the light of the *ius commune*. You can safely admit the prior of Worcester and the archdeacon of Gloucester, provided they do not demand entrance in an official capacity, for you should not admit anyone coming in their official capacity, nor allow them to exercise any official duty inside the Vale even if it concerns their own parishioners. 382. Since then the whole liberty of this church depends upon its privileges and prescriptive right, see to it, all you sons of this church, that you never apply the *ius commune* when you have a special right, for the possession of liberty is easily lost because exemption is inimical to the *ius commune*, and prescriptive right is very easily interrupted because it is hated.[1]

383. I therefore entreat all of you who await the outcome of this contentious lawsuit over the liberty of the Vale, and look for the settlement of the case, in the name of Jesus Christ son of the Virgin who chose this place, to follow the example of those of us who, as you have heard, have endured so many troubles in the pursuit of this church's liberty, and to act manfully. Do not consider any hazard in this world comparable to that of the loss of liberty, for if you lose the liberty of the Vale, then there is little doubt that you will lose the churches, the tithes and, what is worse, the power to restrain those who would harm you. You will become poor and wretched, and, God forbid! disaster will come upon you at the last.[2] However, as has already been stated, it is not only the man who disregards the force and authority of the privileges by applying the *ius commune*, and so fails to use the power granted to him, who deserves to lose the privilege, but also the man who uses power not granted to him.[3] See to it, therefore, that you never exceed the force and authority of your privileges by, for example, ordaining members of other parishes to the rank of subdeacon, deacon, or priest.[4] By this, I mean any member of another parish who does not have the right to be ordained in your parish, unless he has the permission of his diocesan bishop.[5] And you must not communicate with members of other parishes who have been excommunicated once you have been informed of the fact. You must not provide chrism or oil, if they have been consecrated in your church, except to others like you who are privileged, unless with the agreement of the diocesan bishop of the church making the request. The same goes for other cases too numerous to list.

384. *De prohibitione domini pape ne ab urbe recederemus cum priuilegiis, et de recessu magistri Ade cum executione et modo executionis facte in Anglia*

Completis itaque ut putabamus omnibus negociis nostris, mandatum domini pape, audientibus aduersariis nostris, recepimus ne ab urbe cum priuilegiis nostris recederemus. Igitur quamuis omnes infirmi essemus, locuti tamen sumus adinuicem ut aliquis nostrum maiori simulata infirmitate cum executione recederet, ad liberandum fratres nostros qui in Anglia quasi Egiptiaca seruitute[1] deprimebantur, quamuis hoc sine graui periculo propter prohibitionem domini pape facere non possemus. Et quolibet nostrum cupiente discedere, facta est contentio inter nos quis primo discederet. Allegaui pro me quia iam per annum et dimidium ibi moram feceram, clericus uero domini abbatis tantum per decem ebdomodas, magister autem Adam non nisi per sex ebdomodas.[2] Tandem quia magister Adam infirma-batur durius, cecidit sors super eum, et accepta executione et uiatico clam recessit. Et per gratiam Dei prospere dirigentis iter eius sanus et incolumis in Angliam est reuersus.

385. Et anno reuoluto, eadem die qua episcopus nactus est posses-sionem iurisdictionis monasterii nostri, scilicet Dominica qua canta-tur Misericordia Domini,[3] per abbates de Westmonasterio et de Stanleia facta est executio sentencie domini pape.[4] Et episcopo in perpetuum excluso, publice denunciatum est monasterium nostrum liberum et exemptum, et nos in plena possessione libertatis sumus constituti.

386. *Qualiter priuilegia sint tradita Romanis*

Cognito autem recessu magistri Ade comminati sunt nobis aduersarii nostri et Romani mercatores. Et uidentes Romani quia presumptuosi eramus qui hec contra prohibitionem domini pape feceramus, obser-uauerunt nos donec obtinuissent quod ex precepto domini pape omnia priuilegia nostra et instrumenta eis tradidimus loco pignoris pro quadringentis marcis quas eis debebamus.

---

[1] Cf. Deut. 16: 12.

[2] The abbot's clerk was probably Thomas of Warwick; see above, **261**. For Master Adam Sortes, see above, **275–8, 316, 371**, and below, **386, 435, 436, 446, 499, 525**.

[3] The second Sunday after Easter.

[4] The abbots of Westminster and Stanley promulgated the sentence on 16 Apr. 1206. The choice of promulgators of sentences is not always obvious. The selection of the

384. *The command of the pope not to leave the city with the privileges, and the departure of Master Adam with a mandate enforcing sentence and the manner in which it was to be enforced in England*

When all our affairs had been concluded, as we thought, we received a command from the pope, with the full knowledge of our opponents, not to leave the city with our privileges. Though all of us were ill, we agreed amongst us that one of us pretending to be more seriously ill should leave with the mandate to enforce the sentence, so that we might free our brethren who were being oppressed in England like the slaves in Egypt,[1] even though we could not do this without grave peril because of the pope's prohibition. As each one of us wanted to leave, a disagreement broke out amongst us as to who should leave first. I argued my own case that I had stayed in Rome for a year and a half, whereas the abbot's clerk had been there no more than ten weeks, and Master Adam only six weeks.[2] In the end Master Adam was chosen because he was suffering more than the others from his illness. He took the mandate of execution, received the sacrament, and then left secretly. By the grace of God who prospered his journey he reached England safe and sound.

385. After a year had passed, but then on the same day on which the bishop had obtained possession of jurisdiction over our monastery, the Sunday on which the Misericordia Dei is sung,[3] the pope's sentence was promulgated by the abbots of Westminster and of Stanley.[4] The bishop was excluded for ever, and a public proclamation was made that our monastery was free and exempt, and we were instituted into full possession of our liberty.

386. *Our privileges are handed over to the Romans*

On learning of Master Adam's departure, our opponents and the Roman merchants threatened us. When the Romans saw that we had thus acted in defiance of the pope's command not to leave, they kept us prisoner until they succeeded in getting us to hand over all our privileges and documents in accordance with the pope's command, as security for the four hundred marks which we owed them.

abbot of Westminster, however, as abbot of a prestigious Benedictine house (with a dependency at Great Malvern) would seem not unexpected, but that of the abbot of Stanley, a Cistercian house in Wiltshire not far from Malmesbury, is not so easily explained. The abbot of Westminster at the time was Ralph Arundel, abbot from 1200 to 1214, who had been prior of Westminster's dependency at Hurley: the abbot of Stanley was Thomas of Calstone, who had been prior of that house, and was elected abbot in 1205; *HRH*, pp. 77, 142.

fo. 169vb **387.** *Qualiter Thomas monachus liberauerit abbatem ne a domino papa per inquisitionem factam in Anglia deponeretur*

^{*a*}Postea uero cum^{*a*} aduersarius noster diceret se adhuc habere causam contra me cui respondere non possem. Indignatus sum et, quamuis nescirem quidnam loqueretur, more litigantium audacter et presumptuose respondi quod ad omne quare, sicut ex premissis iam mundo innotuit, ei responderem et uigilantius insidiatus sum ei. Cum igitur dominus papa, ut erat curialissimus, more suo liberalissimo oppressos consolans, ne uictus aduersarius noster dolens recederet, multas speciales indulgentias aduersario nostro indulsisset. Quadam die cum in publica audientia legerentur,¹ obieci me aduersarium et omnibus contradixi, quamuis de multis nichil ad me. Et cum in crastino ad audientiam contradictarum conuenissemus,² misertus aduersarii mei eo quod ualde tristis efficeretur. Dixi ei ut diceret michi quam causam haberet contra me et renuntiaret illi, et ego omnibus contradictionibus meis; et factum est ita.

388. Erat autem causa huiusmodi. Episcopus Wigornie nactus possessionem iurisdictionis monasterii nostri, cum monachi, ut sepe dixi uobis, nollent adquiescere ei ut per eos de persona abbatis fieret inquisitio. Fecit eam per compatriotas nostros sub testimonio omnium prelatorum episcopatus sui,³ et, sigillis eorum in ea appensis, misit eam domino pape. Huic cause renunciauit magister Robertus et fractis sigillis tradidit michi cedulam scriptam, nullo sciente preter me et ipsum. Et facti sumus amici adinuicem nec apposuimus amplius inuicem nos in aliquo grauare. Et sic ibi factum est ne abbas a domino papa deponeretur, quia si uidisset inquisitionem in qua multa enormia continebantur, sine dubio eum deposuisset. Ita et prius factum fuit in Anglia ne ab episcopo deponeretur.

389. *De recessu clericorum episcopi et postea clerici abbatis et ultimo de recessu Thome monachi a curia absque licencia domini pape*

fo. 170ra Post paucos uero dies recesserunt aduersarii^{*b*} | nostri, et tunc instanter petiuimus licentiam recedendi, nec impetrauimus. Et cum iterum super hoc sollicitarem dominum papam, precepit ut starem in

^{*a–a*} Postea . . . cum *written over an erasure*   ^{*b*} *catchword* nostri *in lower margin of col. b*

---

¹ See above, **268** n. 2 (p. 270).
² See above, ibid. Thomas of Marlborough is one of the first chroniclers to mention the two courts.
³ The sense here is of enquiry by local men. The prelates were presumably the higher clergy, namely archdeacons, abbots, and priors.

387. *Thomas the monk saves the abbot from being deposed by the pope in an inquiry held in England*

It was after this that our opponent said that he still had a case against me to which I could have no reply. I was angered by this, and although I did not know what reply I would make I answered him with confidence and self-assurance as though I were in court, saying that I would reply to every question in the way now well-known to everybody from previous occasions; and I carefully laid a trap for him. However, as the pope was a very courteous man who consoled the downcast in his most generous manner, he granted our opponent many special indults so that he should not depart feeling aggrieved. But one day when these were being read out in the public audience,[1] I stood up and opposed them, protesting against all the indults, though most of them were of no importance to me. On assembling the next day at the audience of contradicted letters,[2] I felt sorry for my opponent as he was very upset by the proceedings. I told him to tell me what case he had against me and to withdraw it and I would then withdraw all my objections. And that is what happened.

388. The case was as follows. When the bishop of Worcester had gained possession of the jurisdiction over our monastery, the monks, as I have frequently told you, were unwilling to agree to the bishop's request that an inquiry should be held by them into the character and behaviour of the abbot. He therefore had one conducted by our fellow-countrymen with evidence submitted by all the prelates of his diocese,[3] and when their seals had been affixed to this evidence he sent it to the pope. Master Robert renounced this case and after breaking the seals he handed me the document, but nobody knew of this apart from Robert and me. We became good friends, and pledged that we would never again attack each other on any matter. It was therefore settled there and then that the abbot should not be deposed by the pope, for without a doubt, if the pope had seen the record of an inquiry containing accounts of his many outrages, he would have deposed him. This was what was done previously in England to prevent his being deposed by the bishop.

389. *The return of the bishop's clerks, then of the abbot's clerk, and lastly of the monk Thomas from the curia without the pope's permission*

After a few days our opponents returned home, so we immediately asked permission then to return, but did not obtain it. I again pleaded with the pope to allow this, but he commanded me to stay in Rome

urbe nec apposuit causam quare. Post aliquot dies infirmabatur socius meus clericus domini abbatis,[1] et cum nollet amplius stare tradidi eum mercatoribus Romanis qui cum priuilegiis nostris ibant in Angliam pro pecunia quam eis debebamus, ut et ipsi inuenirent ei expensas itineris. Et recessit cum eis.

390. Et relictus sum ego solus ut uiderem finem, expectans auxilium de celo. Et iterum post aliquot ebdomadas circa mediam Quadragesimam[2] cum iam inciperet aeris intemperies, et plenissime constaret michi quod licentiam recedendi non impetrarem, nisi prius dominum papam et cardinales, sicut decet uictorem, uisitarem,[3] nec unde eis satisfacerem haberem, unde satis dolendum est, quia si eos uisitassem, omnium priuilegiorum nostrorum innouationem, et etiam nouorum capitulorum adiectionem, et litteras de expensis nobis ab episcopo refundendis,[4] et quecumque alia de iure uellem impetrassem. Accepta licentia a sanctis apostolis Petro et Paulo et aliis patronis urbis sacre, et cum benedictione apostolica cum populari multitudine accepta, clam recessi, per quinque uel sex dietas semper timens ne reuocarer. Et gratia Dei mecum comitante, quamuis graui febre in Francia a Domino essem correptus, prospero gressu in Angliam sum regressus. Fratribus congaudentibus et mecum gratias Deo agentibus quia saluum me receperunt.

391. *De triplicata depressione conuentus ab abbate post securitatem libertatis*

Abbas uero meus, licet actus mei eius essent successus, inuidens factis meis felicibus quia prospere agebam[5] in negotiis ecclesie, non omittebat persequi me, et non tantum me set uniuersum conuentum. Nec etiam illis pepercit quos aliquando, cum sibi timeret ut erroris sui haberet fautores uidebatur amasse. | Iam enim putauit se securum ne propter libertatem ecclesie ab alio quam ipso papa posset deponi, nesciens quia legati Romane sedis diligentius exemptorum quam non exemptorum, qui episcopos habent uisitatores, transgressus scrutantur et corrigunt, quia alium quam ipsos non habent correctorem. Noluit etiam intelligere quod dominus Cantuariensis ut tutor noster qui habet

fo. 170rb

---

[1] Thomas of Warwick; see above, 261, 263, 384.

[2] The middle of Lent means 'Letare Hierusalem' Sunday, the fourth in Lent, which fell upon 12 March in 1206.

[3] The use of 'uisitare' here is in the sense of a formal visit to take leave and give presents.

[4] Costs were usually awarded to the victor; see Sayers, *PJD*, pp. 80, 267–8.

[5] Cf. Gen. 39: 2.

and he did not add any reason why. Some days later my companion, the abbot's clerk,[1] fell ill, and when he refused to stay any longer I entrusted him to the Roman merchants who were travelling to England to collect the money which we owed them, so that they might also provide his expenses for the journey. So he returned with them.

390. I was now left alone to see the end of things, hoping for divine help. Several weeks passed again until the middle of Lent[2] when the weather was becoming stormy, and it was very clear to me that I would not obtain permission to leave unless I first gave the pope and the cardinals the presents that were expected from the winning party.[3] But I did not have the wherewithal to satisfy them. It is a matter of considerable regret that, had I given them the presents, I would have obtained the renewal of all our privileges, the addition also of new clauses, a letter requiring the bishop to refund our expenses,[4] and anything else I lawfully requested. When I had gained permission from the holy apostles Peter and Paul and the other patrons of the Holy City, and had received the apostolic blessing along with the multitude, I left in secret, and for five or six days of the journey I was fearful of being recalled. God's grace went with me, and although the Lord laid me low in France with a serious fever, I reached England after a successful journey. The brethren were overjoyed, and joined me in giving thanks to God that they had received me back safely.

391. *The oppression of the convent trebled by the abbot after the winning of our liberty*
However, although my deeds meant success for my abbot too, he was envious of my success in effecting a prosperous outcome[5] in the affairs of the church. He did not cease to persecute me, and not only me but the whole convent. In fact he did not even spare those whom, when he was fearful for himself, he sometimes seemed to like in order to secure accomplices in his misdoing. He now thought he was safe from being deposed by anyone other than the pope himself since the church had its liberty, for he did not know that legates of the Roman see scrutinize and correct the offences of the exempt more thoroughly than they do those of the non-exempt churches who have bishops as visitors, for exempt churches have no other to correct them than the legates themselves. He did not even wish to know that the archbishop of Canterbury, as our protector, who has

potestatem in capite libero haberet curam animarum nostrarum, et si quid sinistre partis apud nos oriri compertum fuerit per eius debeat corrigi cautelam et industriam, sicut in priuilegiis continetur.[1] Quod si forte facere non posset, facta inquisitione excessuum tam abbatis quam conuentus et cognita ueritate, debeat eam ad dominum papam referre, qui pro qualitate excessuum penam infligat. Qui etiam tanto magis rigorem in talibus exercet quanto scit se difficilius posse adiri. Et quanto ei specialius subicimur tanto magis ueretur excessus nostros impunitos relinquere, cum sciat in eius caput redundare quicquid a nobis delinquitur nisi per eum corrigatur. Hec et hiis similia non attendens, abbas noster quecumque uolebat faciebat, per libertatem factus securior, propter quam, ut dictum est, magis sibi debuit timere et, dupplicata tirannide, durius et crudelius tam circa nos quam sui ipsius custodiam cepit conuersari.

392. *Qualiter conuentus accusauerit abbatem coram legato Iohanne in Via Lata, et qualiter idem legatus redditus et consuetudines conuentus confirmauerit*

Interim missus est in Angliam dominus Iohannes diaconus cardinalis tituli sancte Marie in Via Lata, legatus tocius Anglie. Qui cum uenisset ad nos causa uisitationis, et nos in multis abbatem nostrum accusaremus et ipse nos.[2] Cepit dominus legatus per se ipsum et clericos suos facere singulare scrutinium de statu domus tam interiori quam exteriori. Et recedens inperfecto scrutinio, reliquit hic de Lileshulle et de Hagemon abbates[3] ad perficien|dum illud, nichilominus concedens ut pacem inter nos si possemus reformaremus, set tantum de temporalibus; de spiritualibus uero que ad salutem anime pertinebant sibi reseruauit correctionem.

fo. 170ᵛᵃ

393. Et tunc facta est compositio inter nos fere ad uotum nostrum. In qua omnes redditus officiis nostris assignati et omnes consuetudines de cellario in scripturam sunt redacta, et contra omnia in quibus

---

[1] See the first privilege of Pope Constantine, 321, for the archbishop's powers of correction.

[2] John of Ferentino, created a cardinal by Innocent in Dec. 1204, had been associated with the papal chancery and had held the title of chancellor for a year. He was designated legate on 1 Feb. 1206 and had arrived in England by the following May. His last recorded activity was the holding of the Council of Reading in October 1206; *C. & S.* ii pt 1, p. 4. He visited several Benedictine houses, including St Mary's abbey, York, for which he issued injunctions on 15 Aug., printed from Bodleian MS Digby 186 fo. 1 by C. R. Cheney, 'The papal legate and the English monasteries in 1206', *EHR*, xlvi (1931), 443–52, at pp. 449–52. It is not known when precisely he came to Evesham. For his previous career, see Maleczek, pp. 146–7, who says that he left England in Nov. 1206.

direct power in the case of a free church, would have the care of our souls, and that, if anything of an evil nature were discovered to have occurred amongst us, the archbishop would have to correct it with discretion and diligence, as the privileges state.[1] If it happened that he could not do this, then he had to hold an inquiry into the misdemeanours of both the abbot and the convent, and on discovering the truth was obliged to report this to the pope, who would inflict a punishment appropriate to the seriousness of the misdemeanours. The punishment he exacts in such cases is all the harsher, the more difficult he knows it to be to inflict it. Indeed, the more closely we are subject to him the more fearful he is of leaving our sins unpunished, knowing that whatever sin we commit recoils upon him if he does not correct it. Ignoring these facts and others like them, our abbot did whatever he liked, and feeling more secure on account of his liberty which, as has been said, ought to have made him more fearful for himself, he redoubled his tyrannical behaviour and began to act more harshly and cruelly both towards us and in the way he conducted himself.

392. *The convent accuses the abbot before the legate, John [cardinal deacon of S. Maria] in Via Lata, and the legate confirms the revenues and customs of the convent*

Meanwhile John, cardinal deacon of S. Maria in Via Lata, was sent to England as legate for the whole of the country. He came to us to carry out a visitation, and we made accusations against our abbot on many counts, and he against us.[2] The lord legate began to conduct an extremely careful scrutiny of the state of the house, both internal and external, and this was done by himself and by his clerks. However, he departed without finishing it, so he left the abbots of Lilleshall and Haughmond[3] here to complete the work, and gave us the task nevertheless of restoring peace between ourselves if we could, but only in connection with temporal matters; he reserved for himself the right to correct those spiritual misdemeanours that concerned the salvation of the soul.

393. An agreement was then made between us that almost entirely met our wishes. All the revenues assigned to our offices and all the customs relating to the cellary were put in writing, and we were

---

[3] Both were Augustinian houses in Shropshire about fifty miles from Evesham: it is not clear why these abbots in particular were chosen. The abbot of Lilleshall was possibly Ralph or Adam, the abbot of Haughmond perhaps Ralph, who occurs 1204×10: nothing more is known of either of them; see *HRH*, pp. 165, 171.

solebat nos grauare est in ea nobis cautum. Et misimus eam ad dominum legatum et confirmauit eam.[1]

394. Abbas autem timens adhuc inquisitionem circa spiritualia accessit ad dominum legatum in concilio Radingensi,[2] ubi fuit mitratus cum episcopis et gratiam domini legati ibi obtinuit, et dedit nepoti domini legati redditus decem marcarum.[3]

395. *Qualiter conuentus recesserit cum magistris Thoma de Norwich et Thoma de Merlebergia monachis quos abbas uoluit penitus expellere. Et qualiter bellum cum abbate commiserint et eum uicerint et confirmationem reddituum obtinuerint*

Cum igitur dominus legatus post consilium prepararet se ad transfretandum[4] et peteremus ab abbate nostro ut sigillum suum et nostrum, sicut conuenerat, scripto nostro appenderentur. Noluit adquiescere, set penitus a pacto recedens, auctoritate indulgentiarum quas cum Rome essemus, sicut dixi uobis, me ignorante adquisierat, uoluit quosdam fratres qui instanter scripti confirmationem petebant excommunicare et magistrum Thomam de Northuuic et me penitus a domo nostra expellere. Set fidelis et constans conuentus Eueshamensis cuius memoria in benedictione sit,[5] similis Ieremie fratrum amatori,[6] elegit magis nobiscum recedere quam permittere tantum nos duos periclitari. Igitur inito consilio tradidimus senibus et ualetudinariis reliquias et thesaurum ecclesie, sigillum in terra abscondimus.[7] Et ipsi sub periculo anime sue usque ad effusionem sanguinis hec receperunt obseruanda. Iniuncto etiam eis ut si abbas aliqua ex hiis uellet diripere, publicum inuocarent auxilium. Et accepta benedictione more iter agentium, in die sancte Katerine circa horam diei terciam recesserunt fo. 170vb nobiscum | triginta monachi omnes pedites, succinctis renibus,[8] baculos habentes in manibus,[9] per quosdam fratres appellantes

    [1] This is *Mon. Angl.* ii, num. xxvii and xxviii, pp. 23–5, said to be from the original in the Augmentations Office (not now traced), printed below, App. II A; and see C. R. Cheney, 'Cardinal John of Ferentino, papal legate in England in 1206', *EHR*, lxxvi (1961), 654–60, at p. 657 no. 5. The confirmation of the legate is at the end of the document, followed by clauses of corroboration on behalf of the abbot and convent. It appears that the seals of the abbot and of the convent were not yet attached to the agreement, see below, 397. It is perhaps not a coincidence that the legate provided similar customs for St Mary's York, with which Evesham had a close relationship, the two communities sharing confederate rights, see below, 504 and n., but there is no indication of a common *forma* having been used.

    [2] Little is known about the business of the Council which met at some date between 18 and 20 Oct. 1206. However the Peterborough chronicler comments that the complaint of the monks of Evesham against their abbot was aired there, but that the legate, bribed by money, left the matter unconcluded. He thus confirms Thomas's remarks; *Chronicon*

protected against all the things with which he used to oppress us. This document we sent to the legate and he confirmed it.[1]

394. The abbot still feared the inquiry into spiritual matters, so he met the legate at the Council of Reading[2] where he wore his mitre alongside the bishops. He won the legate's approval there, and made a gift of ten marks to the legate's nephew.[3]

395. *The convent quits the abbey with Masters Thomas de Northwich and Thomas of Marlborough, the monks whom the abbot wanted to expel permanently. The battle they engage in with the abbot, their victory over him, and the confirmation of their revenues obtained*

After the Council the legate was now preparing for his return voyage,[4] when we asked the abbot to have his seal and ours attached to our document, as had been agreed. He refused to give his assent to this, completely abandoning his pledge, and, on the authority of the letters which, as I have told you, he had acquired without my knowledge when we were at Rome, he decided to excommunicate those brethren who were seeking immediate confirmation of the document and to expel master Thomas de Northwich and me permanently from our house. However, that faithful and loyal convent of Evesham—may its memory be blessed[5]—like Jeremiah, the lover of his brethren,[6] chose rather to leave with us than to allow only the two of us to face danger. So, forming a plan, we handed over the sacred relics and the treasure of the church to the old and infirm monks, and buried the seal in the ground.[7] The old men at the risk of their lives accepted the responsibility of guarding these things, even if they had to spill their blood. They were told to call upon the help of the people if the abbot decided to seize any of these things. Then, after receiving a blessing like men setting out on a journey, thirty monks, all of them on foot, dressed for action[8] and their staffs in their hands,[9] left with us at about nine o'clock in the

---

Angliae Petriburgense, ed. J. A. Giles (Scriptores Monastici: London, 1845), pp. 114–15, also printed in *C. & S.* ii pt 1, pp. 4–5.

[3] The legate's nephew, possibly merely a kinsman (the word can be translated loosely), has not been identified.

[4] Oct. to Nov. 1206, see above, 392 n. 2.

[5] Cf. Ecclus. 45: 1; 46: 14.

[6] 2 Macc. 15: 14.

[7] This means the matrix of the seal, usually made of silver, which made the impression on the wax. By burying it, they sought to prevent possible misuse of it.

[8] Cf. 4 Kgs. (2 Kgs.) 1: 8.

[9] Cf. Exod. 12: 11.

coram abbate qui sedebat tunc pro tribunali in quadam causa in capella sancti Laurentii.[1] Et uidens nos recedere, conuocans quoscumque potuit amicos, sumptis armis et ascensis equis, cum armis et fustibus insecutus est nos.

396. Et cum iam ascendissemus collem[2] qui est in campo de Wikewone, uenit ad nos et iussit ut staremus. Et stetimus hinc et hinc, publica strata media, et crux posita erat in ea. Tandem allocutus est quosdam de senioribus qui uidebantur regere nos, et rogauit eos ut uenirent ad eum. Et primicerio nostro respondente, 'Ego uado ad abbatem meum', accensus est furor alterius senis quem uocauerat Willielmi, uidelicet de Lithun, cuius memoria sit in benedictione,[3] et quasi alter Mathathias increpans illum dixit, 'Absit a me et quolibet bono uiro quod ab unitate et ueritate et uniuersitate recedam.'[4] Et hoc sermone multos confortauit, alios confirmauit, quosdam ab errore reuocauit. Abbas uero uidens constantiam nostram precepit suis ut percuterent in gladio[5] et caperent nos, et congressi sumus habentes fiduciam in Domino,[6] inermes contra armatos. Illi uero extractis gladiis miserunt manus in quosdam ex fratribus. Alii uero fratres baculis quos tenebant in manibus uiriliter expugnabant eos[7] et, liberantes fratres suos a manibus eorum,[8] coegerunt eos retrorsum abire. Illis itaque fugatis in campum, omnes unanimiter iter quod inceperamus progressi sumus, gratias agentes Deo in quo omnem spem nostram posueramus,[9] quod nullum ex nostris amisimus quamuis aduersarii nostri illesi non abissent.

397. Et quam citius potuimus egressi sumus possessiones nostras, ut ab extraneis qui abbatem non timerent, si opus esset, publicum fo. 171ra inuocaremus auxilium, quamuis multi qui abbatem | corpore comitabantur, ueluti qui iure hereditario nobis seruiebant, magis nobiscum mente starent. Cum autem uenissemus in campum de Morcote, qui erat Willielmi de Bellocampo,[10] iterum insecutus est nos abbas. Et dolens quod potestatem eius euasimus, timens ne publicum inuocaremus auxilium, ex campo de Wikewone, uia media inter nos, allocutus est nos uerbis pacificis, spopondens se facturum quicquid uellemus si

---

[1] One of the two churches within the abbey's boundary, and a suitable place for the abbot to hold a court.

[2] This is Longdon hill: the plain is the area round Wickhamford and Childswickham, which took their names from Wickwane.

[3] Cf. Ecclus. 45: 1; 46: 14.

[4] Cf. 1 Macc. 2: 21, where Matthathias refuses to forsake the law and the ordinances.

[5] Cf. 1 Kgs. (1 Sam.) 31: 4; Judg. 9: 54; Job 1: 17.

[6] Cf. Prov. 3: 5.   [7] Cf. Exod. 12: 11.

morning of St Catherine's day [25 Nov.]. Certain brethren were appealing on our behalf before the abbot, who was then sitting in judgment upon a case in the chapel of St Laurence.[1] When he saw us leaving he summoned all the friends he could, and they took up arms, mounted their horses, and pursued us with arms and cudgels. **396.** When we had now climbed the hill[2] situated in the plain of Wickwane, he came to us and ordered us to halt. We did so as they did on their side, and there was a public highway between us where a cross stood. Finally, he addressed some of the older monks who seemed to be in control of us, and asked them to come to him. When our leader replied 'I am going to my abbot', the other elderly monk whom the abbot had called, William de Lithun—may his memory be blessed[3]—was furious and, like Mattathias, he rebuked him, saying, 'God forbid that I or any good man should abandon our unity, truth, and solidarity'.[4] With these words he put heart into many, reassured others, and stopped some from doing wrong. The abbot, seeing our determination, commanded his men to use their swords[5] and capture us, but we faced them with trust in the Lord,[6] the unarmed against the armed. They drew their swords and attacked some of the brethren. Other brethren fought them back manfully with the staffs they held in their hands[7] and, saving their brethren from capture,[8] they forced the abbot's men to retreat. We drove them into the plain and then all of us together continued the journey we had begun, giving thanks to God in whom we had placed all our hope,[9] for we lost none of our men while our foes had not departed unscathed.

397. We left our lands as quickly as we could so that, if necessary, we might seek help from people who did not fear the abbot. Indeed, many who were accompanying the abbot in body supported us more in mind, like men serving us by hereditary right. When we reached the plain of Murcot, the land of William Beauchamp,[10] the abbot began his pursuit of us again. He was annoyed because we had escaped his clutches, and afraid that we would call for the help of the people, so he addressed us in conciliatory terms from the plain of Wickwane, which was halfway between us, and he promised to do

---

[8] Cf. Dan. 3: 17; Ecclus. 51: 12; Exod. 18: 10.   [9] Cf. Ps. 72: 28 (73: 28).

[10] Murcot situated roughly between Wickhamford and Childswickham: it might be an alternative name for the plain of Wickwane. The William Beauchamp (of Elmsley) mentioned is presumably the William ('Wilekin') who died as a minor in 1210–11, see *The Beauchamp Cartulary Charters 1100–1268*, ed. E. Mason (PRS n.s. xliii: London, 1980), pp. xxii–iii and lviii. The Beauchamps had *nativi* in Murcot and Wickhamford (see ibid. no. 104).

reuerteremur.*ª* Et quamuis nos prudentiores certi essemus quod dispositio nostra quam dominus legatus confirmauerat in perpetuum esset duratura quamuis sigilla nostra tunc non appenderentur, et etiam non dubitaremus si processisemus ad dominum legatum, uel dominum papam si legatum non inuenissemus, et scrutinium quod tunc factum fuit publicaretur, quin abbas noster deponeretur. Tamen propter fratres pusillanimes petitioni abbatis adquieuimus, et iurauit nobis abbas quod omnia contenta in dispositione in perpetuum obseruaret. Et renunciauit in perpetuum impetratis et impetrandis contra nos, et resignauit nobis indulgentias. Per quarum unius auctoritatem uolebat nos duos expellere in perpetuum, et per alterius auctoritatem dicebat se posse aliorum fratrum delicta pro uoluntate sua punire. Quibus receptis statim demoliti sumus eas, et statim misimus propter sigillum nostrum. Et appensa sunt sigilla nostra[1] in eodem loco constitutionibus illis, et tam nos qui presentes eramus quam illi qui domi erant hec eadem ei iurauimus quam diu fideliter ea obseruaret. Et reuersi sumus cum gaudio[2] eadem die ad uesperam.

398. Ecce audistis quibus laboribus et periculis ad hanc dispositionem peruenimus, nunquam enim abbas noster aliquid nobis gratis fecit, set semper inuitus et coactus, et semper aduersitatibus uicimus et tribulationibus meliorati sumus et creuimus. Post exemptionis |

fo. 171ʳᵇ enim confirmationem est hec dispositio. Si quis ea bene utatur, unum de preclarissimis factis huius ecclesie, ad quod, ut audistis, tot iniuriis affecti uix attigimus. Hanc autem dispositionem successor eius dominus Rondulfus[3] non solum libenter confirmauit, set etiam multis reddittibus, ut ex eiusdem inspectione patet, ampliauit. Et

---

ª re *at the commencement of* reuerteremur *interlined*

[1] The abbot and convent attached separate seals, the abbot sometimes using a counter-seal in addition to his seal of office. Two fragments of a very fine and complex conventual seal of Evesham, from a 13th-cent. matrix, survive in the Public Record Office, where there are also impressions of an abbot's seal and counter-seal belonging to Abbot Randulf. See *Catalogue of Seals in the Public Record Office: Monastic Seals*, i, comp. R. H. Ellis (HMSO, 1986), pp. 33–4 and pl. 28 (the fragments of the conventual seal). We know of no surviving examples of Abbot Norreis's seal or counter-seal. It appears that Norreis did seal the 'dispositio' in the end.

[2] Cf. Tobias 5: 27.

[3] Randulf, known as Randulf of Evesham, was a native of Evesham. He became a monk at Worcester and was a leader of the party of monks from there who were sent to the curia in late 1202 with documentation for the canonization process of Wulfstan ('Annales prioratus de Wigornia', *Ann. Mon.* iv. 391). He was elected prior of Worcester on 24 Dec. 1203 and bishop of Worcester on the death of Mauger ten years later (2 Dec. 1213), but the

whatever we wanted if we would return. The wiser amongst us were convinced that our disposition which had been confirmed by the legate would be a permanent arrangement even though our seal had not yet been attached; and we were in no doubt also that if we approached the legate, or the pope if we did not find the legate, and the scrutiny, which had by then been completed, were to be published, the abbot would be deposed. However, we gave in to the abbot's request because of some weak-minded brethren, and he gave us his oath that he would ever more observe everything contained in the disposition. He renounced forever the things he had gained and intended to gain against us, and surrendered to us the letters. It was on the authority of one of these that he wanted to banish the two of us forever, and on the authority of the second, so he said, that he could punish the sins of other brethren in any way he liked. The moment we had them from him we destroyed them and immediately sent for our seal. We then attached our seals[1] to those statutes where we were, and those of us who were there, as well as those at home, made him the same promises on oath provided he faithfully kept his part of the agreement. We returned that same evening rejoicing.[2]

398. Now you have heard of the difficulties and dangers we had acquiring this disposition, for our abbot never did anything for us for nothing but always reluctantly and under pressure, yet we always prevailed in adversity, and prospered and flourished in tribulation. Hence this disposition followed the confirmation of the exemption. If good use is made of it, then our achievement has been one of the most outstanding of this church, though hard won by us, as you have heard, at the cost of much personal suffering. The abbot's successor, Randulf, not only gladly confirmed this disposition,[3] but even enhanced it with many additional revenues, as inspection of the documents reveals. Later when I was with him in Rome at the

election was quashed by the papal legate Nicholas, cardinal bishop of Tusculum. After Norreis's deposition he was elected abbot of Evesham in Jan. 1214 (*HRH*, p. 48 has the 22nd, Greatrex, *Biog. Reg.*, p. 804, and Greenway, *Fasti*, ii. 103, give the 20th). He died on 17 Dec. 1229, see Introduction, n. 92. He has been erroneously described as a monk of Evesham in the above three accounts. In fact he was only a monk of Evesham in the sense of being part of the confraternity that existed between the Benedictines of Evesham and the Benedictines of Worcester, which allowed monks of the other house to have a place in chapter and a stall in the choir in times of need. For further clarification of this practice, see above, pp. xlvi–xlvii, lxi, and for the account of Randulf's acts, see 510–15, below. For the first disposition approved by the legate, see below App. II A.

postea cum essem cum eo Rome in consilio generali,[1] a domino papa eam fecimus confirmari.[2] Est autem dispositio talis.

399. *Dispositio reddituum Eueshamensis cenobii et confirmatio consuetudinum*

Omnibus sancte matris ecclesie filiis ad quos presens scriptum peruenerit, Randulfus Dei gratia abbas Eueshamie et totus eiusdem loci conuentus salutem in domino.

400. Quoniam a domino Innocentio papa tercio dispositionis reddituum officiis nostris assignatorum confirmationem optinere meruimus, redditus, non tantum illos quos tempore confirmationis habuimus set et quos postea adquisiuimus cum ipsa eorum dispositione, ad posterorum noticiam profuturum, scripto commendare dignum duximus. Nam tam ab Innocentio papa secundo quam ab Alexandro tercio non solum redditus quos tempore eorum habuimus, set et illi quos postea quibuscumque iustis modis adquirere possemus, nobis conceduntur et confirmantur:[3] quod et ipsum nobis facere licere in hiis nostris constitutionibus et consuetudinibus continetur.

401. Sunt igitur consuetudines monasterii huiusmodi. Videlicet quod abbas infra septa monasterii existens inter fratres secundum antiquam domus illius consuetudinem conuersando regulariter uiuet, et exteriora pro uiribus suis ad utilitatem ecclesie prouide et fideliter dispensabit.

402. Prior uero, supprior, tercius prior, et alii custodes ordinis,[4] prior de Penwrtham, precentor, decanus, sacrista, camerarius, coquinarius, celerarius interior, | infirmarius, eleemosinarius, custos uinee et gardini, magister fabrice ecclesie, magister hospitum, de consilio et consensu conuentus uel maioris et sanioris partis in capitulo ab abbate de proprio conuentu creentur.[5] Qui si minus, quod absit, honeste uel minus prudenter in offitiis suis se habuerint uel male fratribus administrauerint, prius correpti regulariter,[6] si non emendauerint amoueantur in capitulo, et alii sub forma predicta in loco eorum in capitulo et incontinenti subrogentur. Ne aliquo

---

[1] The Fourth Lateran Council of 1215.
[2] See below, **431**.   [3] See above, **329** and **332**.
[4] Those in charge of discipline, the higher officials.
[5] *RSB* cap. 65 provides for the abbot taking advice in the appointment of the prior 'cum consilio fratrum timentium Deum'. The cellarer (cap. 31) was to be chosen out of the community, but nothing is said about the abbot taking advice: the other obedientiaries were not specified. Doubtless abbots expected to appoint them (see *Monastic Constitutions of Lanfranc*, pp. 108–9, where it states that a new abbot receives the resignations of

General Council[1] we had it confirmed by the pope.[2] The disposition is as follows.

399. *The disposition of the revenues of the monastery of Evesham and the confirmation of its customs*

To all the sons of holy mother Church to whom the present document shall come, Randulf, by the grace of God abbot of Evesham, and the whole of the convent of that place, greeting in the Lord.

400. Since we have been thought worthy by Pope Innocent III of obtaining confirmation of the disposition of the revenues assigned to our offices, we have thought it right to make a written record of them, not only of those revenues which we had at the time of the confirmation, but also of those we acquired afterwards, with their actual disposition, so that posterity will benefit from this knowledge. Pope Innocent II and Alexander III both granted us not only the revenues which we held in their time, but also those which we could acquire by just means after their time, and they confirmed these:[3] indeed, our constitutions and customs have clauses allowing us to do this.

401. The customs of the monastery are as follows. The abbot while he is present within the enclosure of the monastery shall live amongst his brethren in accordance with the Rule, following the ancient custom of that house, and will diligently and faithfully deal with external matters, to the best of his ability, to the benefit of the church.

402. The following officers are to be appointed by the abbot from amongst his own convent in chapter on the advice and with the assent of the convent or of a majority of brethren of wiser counsel: the prior, subprior, third prior and other masters of order,[4] the prior of Penwortham, the precentor, dean, sacrist, chamberlain, kitchener, internal cellarer, infirmarer, almoner, keeper of the vineyard and garden, master of the church fabric, and the guest-master.[5] Should these officers, God forbid, fail to conduct themselves honourably and wisely in carrying out their duties, or manage them badly for the brethren, they are first to be reproved in accordance with the Rule,[6] but then, if they do not mend their ways, they are to be removed at once from office in chapter, and others immediately substituted in the manner stated above. This is to prevent those

obedientiaries and reappoints them if he wishes), and it is not until later that communities began to demand some say in the choice.   [6] *RSB* cap. 32.

casu in manus regis deueniant ipsa officia, abbate forte discedente;[1]
uel per moram fiat deterioratio obedientiarum, aut aliquis defectus
propter moram emergat. Prior uero et predicti magistri ordinis
simul cum abbate ut ordo monasticus cum rigore discipline
secundum regulam beati Benedicti obseruetur summam diligentiam
adhibeant. Maxime autem operam prestent ne monachi aliquid sine
licentia habeant, et ne alias quam in refectorio sine licentia
comedant, et ut elemosina eorum per manus elemosinarii erogetur,[2]
et ne a claustro sine licentia exeant, et ut silentium locis et horis
statutis obseruetur, et ut fratres frequenter delicta confiteantur, non
tamen aliis quam hiis qui ad hoc deputantur. Alii uero predicti
officiales omnes qui redditus percipiunt quater in anno[3] coram
abbate, uel eo quem loco suo statuerit, priore et sex claustralibus,
tribus ab abbate et tribus a conuentu uocatis, de administratione sua
compotum reddant; coquinarius uero qualibet ebdomada.[4]

403. Isti officiales quociens domi fuerint in congregatione iugiter
fo. 171[vb] permaneant, et conuentum in ecclesia, in | capitulo, in claustro, in
refectorio sequantur, ut si, quod absit, in offitiis suis aliquis defectus
emerserit illi statim suppleant. Nulli duo officia assignentur, sed
cuilibet adiungatur socius, si opus fuerit, solatium et testis diligentie
sue. Si uero in aliquo officio propter temporis malitiam aliquid ultra
redditus offitio illi assignatos expensum fuerit, si in aliquo alio offitio
aliquid fuerit residuum, per illud defectus alterius offitii suppleatur.
Si autem nullum officium defectum alterius offitii supplere potuerit,
abbas per manum celerarii exterioris suppleat.[5] Preterea, si quodlibet
offitium sibi suffecerit et aliquid residuum fuerit, abbas de consilio

---

[1] On the death of an abbot, the king might fill the monastic offices, if they were vacant
at the time, possibly appointing monks from another house. For regalian right, see
M. Howell, *Regalian Right in Medieval England* (London, 1962), pp. 5–59.

[2] i.e. that the monks are not to earmark their leftovers for poor people of their own
choice; cf. *Documents illustrating the Activities of the General and Provincial Chapters of the
English Black Monks 1215–1540*, i, ed. W. A. Pantin (Camden 3rd Ser. xlv: London, 1931),
p. 10, the Statutes of the first Benedictine chapter, held at Oxford in 1218–19, which has
some echo of this: '*Vt pauperes debitis elemosinis non defraudentur*, firmiter preceperunt, ut
omnia apponenda sine fraude apponantur in conuentu et alibi ubi monachi reficiuntur, et
de omnibus appositis totum residuum sine diminutione in elemosinam cedat, *per
elemosinarium indigentibus fideliter erogandum*. Qui contrafecerint, in crastino sine dispensatione in abstinentia panis et aque permaneant: presidentem uero ab hac necessitate
exceperunt.' The italics are ours.

[3] This particular point was made by the legate, John of Ferentino, in his injunctions for
St Mary's abbey, York, printed Cheney, *EHR*, xlvi (1931), 450, from Bodleian MS Digby
186 fo. 1. The legate was clearly trying to reform the financial arrangements in monastic
houses and to make the officers more accountable for their departments. The four times in

offices, through some mischance, falling into the hands of the king as, for example, on the death of the abbot;[1] and to prevent a decline in the quality of the offices occurring through delay, or some other imperfection arising from delay. The prior and the other masters of order are, along with the abbot, to show the utmost diligence in ensuring that monastic order is observed with strict discipline in accordance with the Rule of St Benedict. They are to make it their special business to ensure that monks do not possess anything without permission, that they do not eat in any place other than the refectory without permission, that their alms are distributed by the almoner alone,[2] that they do not leave the cloister without permission, that silence is observed at the specified times and places, and that the brethen confess their sins frequently, but only to those who have been appointed to hear their confession. All the other officers mentioned who receive revenues are to render an account of their stewardship four times a year[3] before the abbot or the one appointed by him in his place, with the prior and six cloister monks in attendance, three appointed by the abbot and three by the convent. The kitchener shall submit accounts each week.[4]

403. These officers are always to remain in the congregation of the monks whenever they are in the house, and are to follow [the common life of] the convent in the church, in the chapter-house, in the cloister, and in the refectory so that if, God forbid, any failing occur in their duties they may immediately provide for it. Let none be assigned two offices, but let a fellow monk be appointed, if necessary, as a support and witness of his diligence. If in any office, because of bad times, an amount is spent that exceeds the revenue assigned to it, whereas in another office there is money left over, then let the deficiency in the one office be met by the excess in the other. If, however, no office can make up the deficiency of that other office, the abbot is to do so with funds from the external cellarer.[5] Moreover, if any office has sufficient for its own needs and something left over, the abbot, after consultation with the chapter or a

the year were presumably Michaelmas, Christmas, Lady Day, and Midsummer Day (the feast of the nativity of St John the Baptist). It is likely, but not certain, that these accounts were intended to be written, rather than continuing the old system of making oral declarations, supported by, in some cases, written schedules.

[4] Weekly kitchener's accounts survive, for example, for Westminster and Ely, but not from as early as this.

[5] For his duties, see below, 405.

capituli uel maioris et sanioris partis in eo offitio in quo in capitulo
iudicauerit utilius ecclesie expendat.

404. Si uero aliquid de redditibus monachorum officiis assignatis uel
in perpetuum, quod absit, uel ad tempus detineri contigerit, uel
aliquo modo euacuari uel diminui, abbas tantumdem de consilio
capituli ubi commode fieri poterit alibi eidem offitio assignet.
Liceat preterea monachis possessiones et redditus officiis suis assignatos, ueluti noualia faciendo et redditus augmentando, et nouos
adquirendo ampliare, seu quibuscumque aliis iustis modis meliorare.
Et alios pro aliis tantumdem ualentibus et utilibus, cum uiderint
expedire, uel ad tempus uel in perpetuum commutare.

405. Celerarius siquidem exterior talis de proprio conuentu et in[a]
fo. 172[ra] capitulo ab abbate creetur, qui, exceptis | redditibus monachorum
offitiis assignatis, ad preceptum abbatis, tocius abbatie curam gerens,
sciat et possit libere conuentui necessaria administrare, scilicet
panem, ceruisiam, duo pulmenta,[1] ignem et salem, et quedam alia
in consuetudinibus expressa. Hospitibus etiam iuxta facultatem
domus prouidebit celerarius; uiris tamen religiosis coquinarius que
de officio suo sunt, uidelicet personis eorum sicut et fratribus,
administrabit, exceptis abbatibus et capellanis eorum quibus non
inueniet aliquid nisi in diebus ieiunii, sicut nec ipsi abbati, nec illis
qui cum illo commedunt uel capellanis eius. Hoc dicimus nisi in
refectorio commedant, ut in profestis diebus. Seruientibus etiam
obedientiarum abbatie celerarius procurationem debitam et stipendia
iuxta consuetudinem domus administrabit.

406. Iste quidem celerarius de administratione sua non solum quater
superioribus set quociens ipse abbas uoluerit compotum reddat. Qui
nisi bene administrauerit, sicut de aliis obedientiariis dictum est, ad
iustam conquestionem conuentus et rationabilem uoluntatem abbatis
amoueatur, et alius statim loco ipsius subrogetur et in capitulo.
Numerum fratrum abbas integrum conseruet, nullum monachum
recipiat aut eiciat uel ad tempus uel in perpetuum nisi de consilio

---

[a] interlined (s. xiii[1])

[1] These were dishes of vegetables and/or cereals, more specific than the generic term
'pottage', but difficult to translate with exactitude; cf. RSB, cap. 39, where the two
cooked dishes are mentioned. For details and wider uses of the term, see B. Harvey,
Living and Dying in England 1100–1540: The Monastic Experience (Oxford, 1993), pp. 11–
12 and n. 15.

majority of the brethren of wiser counsel, is to spend that residue on the office in which the chapter judges the spending will most benefit the church.

404. If any part of the revenues which have been assigned to the offices of the monks happens to be withheld either permanently, God forbid, or temporarily, or happens to become exhausted or reduced in some way, the abbot is to assign, with the consent of the chapter, an equivalent amount elsewhere for that office, with the consent of the chapter, when this can be done to advantage. The monks are to be permitted, moreover, to increase their possessions and revenues assigned to their offices, for instance, by ploughing up new land, by augmenting rents, and by acquiring new possessions and revenue, or they may improve them by any other just means. They may exchange rents for others of equal value and use, should this seem desirable, either temporarily or permanently.

405. The external cellarer is to be appointed as such from his own convent and in chapter by the abbot, and is to be responsible, under the abbot's command, for the care of the whole abbey, save the revenues assigned to the offices of the monks. He is to know how to minister to the needs of the convent, and to be able to do so freely, with respect to bread, ale, the two dishes of pottage,[1] kindling and salt, and certain other commodities stated in the customs. The cellarer shall make provision for guests also to the extent that the resources of the house allow, though the kitchener shall provide for the personal needs of the religious as for the brethren, for this is part of his duty, but he shall not provide anything for abbots and their chaplains except on fast days, just as he does not do so for the abbot himself [i.e. of Evesham], or for those who eat with the abbot or for his chaplains. This does not apply if they eat in the refectory, as they do on the eves of festivals. The cellarer shall provide due maintenance for the servants of the abbey's obedientiaries and their stipends, in accordance with the custom of the house.

406. The cellarer must render an account of his stewardship not only four times a year to his superiors but as often as the abbot wishes. If his stewardship has not been good, as has been mentioned in the case of other obedientiaries, he is to be removed at the just complaint of the convent and the reasonable request of the abbot, and he is to be immediately replaced in chapter by another. The abbot is to maintain the full number of monks, and he is not to accept or expel any monk either temporarily or permanently without the consent of the convent

conuentus uel maioris et sanioris partis, et in capitulo. *Ecclesias autem uel alios redditus uel aliquas terras non nisi de consilio uniuersitatis uel maioris et sanioris partis¹ et in capitulo* *ᵇalicui conferat. Nec rusticos sine consensu eorundem manumittat.ᵇ

407. *De terris siquidem reuocandis pro uiribus suis, si que tempore suo uel predecessorum suorum alienate sunt, consilio conuentus sui utatur.ᶜ ᵈSimiliter in causis ecclesiasticis uel forensibus agendis uel fo. 172ʳᵇ terminandis capituli | sui utatur consilio. Seruientes autem qui monachis ministrare tenentur, scilicet de infirmaria, sartrina, lauendria, refectorio, sacristaria, locutorio, de consilio capituli secundum priorem formam constituantur et deponantur. Hec omnia intelligantur saluis in omnibus regularibus institutis.ᵈ

408. Hii sunt redditus officiis monachorum Eueshamensis cenobii assignati.

409. *Redditus prioratus*

Ad prioratum pertinent decime de Beningwrthe tam maiores quam minores² de omnibus terris et hominibus monachorum ad parcamenum et exhibitionem scriptorum pro libris scribendis. Pertinet etiam ad priorem curia nostra de Beningwrthe cum croftis ad eandem curiam pertinentibus cum gardino, uiuario et prato queᵉ sunt infra ipsam curiam, et omnibus masuagiis que sunt de croftis circa ipsam curiam, uidelicet a domo Thome Algar usque ad domum Walteri Ballard.³ De quibus debet prior pro tempore ᶠpascere uiginti quinque pauperes annuatim in anniuersario prioris Thome⁴ pro animabus priorum et omnium fratrum. Et inueniet unum cereum in die sancti Wistani et alium in die sancti Credani die ac nocte ardentes coram feretris eorum.ᶠ⁵ Nam idem prior Thomas quandam terram de Litletona quam emit a Radulfo dispensatore, de qua tempore

---

ᵃ⁻ᵃ *see note b–b, below*   ᵇ⁻ᵇ *a–a and b–b, passages marked* A *and* B *and reversed* ᶜ⁻ᶜ *marked* C   ᵈ⁻ᵈ *marked* D (*s. xiii¹*)   ᵉ *interlined* (*s. xiii¹*)   ᶠ⁻ᶠ *pascere . . . eorum written over an erasure*

---

¹ On the Roman law of consent, see *Code* 5. 59. 5. 2, and *Digest* 1. 3. 32. On 'wiser counsel', see above, **293** n. 1 (p. 294).

² The greater tithes were those of corn of every variety, the lesser those levied on every kind of natural commodity, hens, hay, hemp, wood, flax, honey, wax, salt, cabbages, fish.

³ Bengeworth lay just to the south across the River Avon. Evesham was by now a flourishing seigneurial borough and small market town with traders and craftsmen. For its development in the late 12th cent., see Slater, 'Medieval town-founding', pp. 78–81; and Hilton, 'Small town and urbanisation', p. 3, who relies heavily on this disposition of the revenues, which he calls '1206 rentals'. The date, however, can be given no more precisely than the date of the disposition: the text as given in the *History*, to which Hilton is

or of a majority of monks of wiser counsel, and this is to be dealt with in chapter. He is not to bestow churches or other revenues or any lands upon anyone, except with the consent of the whole convent or of a majority of monks of wiser counsel,[1] and this is to take place in chapter. He is not to free villeins without the same consent being given.

407. With regard to the recovery that is in his power of lands that have been alienated during his own time or during the time of his predecessors, he must take the advice of his convent. Similarly, in undertaking or terminating lawsuits, ecclesiastical or secular, he is to take the advice of his chapter. The servants who are kept to minister to the needs of the monks in the infirmary, the tailor's workshop, the laundry, the refectory, the sacristy, and the parlour, are to be appointed and dismissed on the advice of the chapter as previously specified. Let all these provisions be accepted, saving in all things the requirements of the Rule.

408. The following are the revenues assigned to the offices of the monks of Evesham.

409. *The revenues of the office of Prior*
To the prior's office belong the tithes of Bengeworth, the great as well as the small,[2] from all the lands and men of the monks, and these are for the parchment and the maintenance of the scribes who write the books. To the prior also belongs our court of Bengeworth with the crofts belonging to the same court, along with the garden, fishpond and meadow, which are within the court, as well as all the messuages which are part of the crofts that surround the court itself, that is, from the house of Thomas Algar right up to the house of Walter Ballard.[3] From these the prior, according to circumstances, is obliged to provide food for twenty-five paupers annually on Prior Thomas's anniversary,[4] for the souls of the priors and all the brethren. He is to provide one candle on St Wigstan's day and another on St Credan's day to burn day and night before their shrines.[5] The same Prior Thomas, with our consent, exchanged for land from our abbot, some land at Littleton which he bought from Ralph the steward, which was

referring, is later, see below, App. II B. There is little in the *History* about the development of the town, which was both stimulated and partially controlled by the monks, save for the details supplied in the customs and disposition of the revenues.

[4] Thomas was not made prior until 1218. He may have provided for his anniversary during his lifetime: on this practice see App. II B, p. 548 n. 1. This sentence and the one after next show that this document cannot be the actual one confirmed by Pope Innocent III.

[5] St Wigstan's day is 1 June, St Credan's 19 Aug.

commutationis plus redditus soluebatur quam de ista de Beningwrthe, pro ista a domino abbate nostro de consensu nostro commutauit. Debet etiam prior percipere duas marcas et dimidiam de ecclesia de Ambresleia de ueteri pensione sexaginta solidorum, et uiginti solidos de pensione ecclesie de Bradewelle, ut per manum refectorarii, quem ipse de consilio conuentus debet constituere, uel alterius obedientiarii de uiginti solidis fiat festum sancti Iohannis ante fo. 172ᵛᵃ portam Latinam,¹ et de decem solidis | anniuersarium abbatis Reginaldi, et de decem solidis anniuersarium abbatis Ade; de una uero marca anniuersarium abbatis Rondulfi.

410. *Redditus refectorarii*

Debet etiam iste refectorarius recipere et expendere in uino et medone redditus qui fuerunt ad pitanciariam qui pertinent ad potum: scilicet in Euesham de noua terra decem marcas, de Ulleberwe uiginti quinque solidos, de ecclesia de Hildendune unam marcam, de redditibus de Penwrtham unam marcam, de molendino de Withlakesfort dimidiam marcam, de molendino senescalli de Salford dimidiam marcam, de Ambresleia duodecim sextaria mellis.ᵃ²
Ad eum etiam pertinent minute decime³ de Wikewane, Baddeseia, et Aldintone ad reparationem et numeri conseruationem cocclearium, ciphorum, iustarum, manutergiorum, et aliorum utensilium, cum lampadibus et oleo earum. Et de hiis omnibus debet reddere rationem⁴ priori, adiunctis ei aliquibus fratribus, quociens opus fuerit.

411. *Redditus precentoris*

Ad officium precentoris pertinet quedam terra in Hamptona de qua percipit annuatim quinque solidos, et decime de Stokes,⁵ et quedam terra in Alincestre. De hiis debet inuenire precentor incaustum omnibus scriptoribus monasterii, et colores ad illuminandum, et necessaria ad ligandos libros, et necessaria ad organa.⁶

ᵃ *marg.* De terra quam R. Keche emit in noua terra xii d. (*in similar hand to rubricating hand?*) de terra portarii xii d. pro redditu duodecim denariorum quos dedimus Willelmo de Tywe qui fuerunt ad refectorium de quadam terra uersus molendinum que fuerat Acelote pro quieta clamatione terre Isabelle filie King (*in s. xiiiᵗ charter hand*)

---

¹ 6 May.
² *marg.* '12*d.* from the land which R. Keche bought as new land. 12*d.* from the land of the porter for a rent of 12*d.* which we gave to William de Tywe which was for the refectory

receiving at the time of the exchange more rent than the land at Bengeworth. The prior is also obliged to take two and a half marks from the church of Ombersley from an old payment of sixty shillings, and twenty shillings from a payment from the church of Broadwell [Glos.], to go through the hands of the refectorer—an arrangement that needs the consent of the convent—or through another obedientiary, so that he may arrange the festival of St John before the Latin gate[1] for twenty shillings, the anniversary of Abbot Reginald for ten shillings, the anniversary of Abbot Adam for ten shillings, and the anniversary of Abbot Randulf for one mark.

410. *The revenues of the refectorer*

The refectorer must receive and spend on wine and mead those revenues which have been assigned to the pittancery for drink: ten marks from new land in Evesham, twenty-five shillings from Oldberrow [Warws., formerly Worcs.], one mark from the church of Hillingdon [Middx.], one mark from the revenues of Penwortham [Lancs.], half a mark from the mill of Wixford [Warws.], half a mark from the steward's mill of Salford [Warws.], and twelve sextaries of honey from Ombersley.[2] Other revenues also belonging to the refectorer are the small tithes[3] of Wickhamford, Badsey, and Aldington for replacing and maintaining the number of spoons, cups, flagons, towels, and other necessaries, as well as lamps and their oil. The refectorer must render an account[4] of all these revenues to the prior and to any brethren acting in conjunction with him whenever required to do so.

411. *The revenues of the precentor*

To the office of precentor belong some land in Hampton, from which he receives five shillings per annum, the tithes of 'Stokes',[5] and some land in Alcester [Warws.]. From these revenues he must provide ink for all the scribes of the monastery, colours for illumination, and the things necessary for binding the books and for the organ.[6]

from certain land opposite the mill which was Acelot's for a quitclaim on the land of Isabel daughter of King.'

[3] See above, 409 n. 2 (p. 392).

[4] Cf. *RSB* caps. 2 and 65: the abbot is to render account to God on the day of Judgment for the souls of his monks.

[5] Probably Severn Stoke.

[6] It is not clear whether this means parts of the psalter or possibly books of organ music. It is unlikely to mean the organ as such.

412. *Pertinencia ad decanatum*

Ad decanatum pertinet corrodium[1] unius seruientis de cellario, et collecta denariorum beati Petri ubicumque episcopus non colligit, et uisitatio ecclesiarum Vallis, et ouentiones[2] causarum de quibus debet inuenire conuentui caritatem[3] Dominica qua cantatur Misericordia Domini.[4]

413. *Redditus sacristarie*

Ad sacristariam pertinent sex capelle in Valle, uidelicet due in Euesham, et due capelle de Lencwich et de Nortone, et una in Mortone, et una in Uffeham. Item de ecclesia de Baddebi percipit duas marcas. De capella de | Withlakesford et prato de Salford decem solidos, de ecclesia de Westune dimidiam marcam, de ecclesia de Stowe quinque solidos uel duas petras cere, de ecclesia sancti Albani in Wigornia quinque libras cere, de terris in eadem uilla tres marcas et dimidiam.

fo. 172ᵛᵇ (to the left of "duas marcas")

414. Pertinent etiam ad sacristariam in Euesham solda iuxta portam cimiterii, de fabrica Willelmi fabri quatuor denarii, de terra Nicholai Coci due libre cere, de terra Matildis in Merstowe[5] quinque denarii, de terra Nicholai sacriste in eodem uico sex denarii, de terra senescalli que fuit Geraldi sex denarii, de terra Bulet sex denarii, de terra Ferre triginta denarii, de terra le Hosiere in Brutstrete[6] duo denarii, de terra Willelmi de Tiwe proxima eidem sex denarii, de terra Willelmi de Tiwe in magno uico duo solidi et quatuor denarii, de terra dispensatoris proxima eidem quadraginta denarii, de terra que dicitur Gordani in Colestrete sexdecim denarii, de terra Reginaldi fabri duo solidi, de terra Walteri proxima eidem octo denarii, de terra Pate proxima eidem octo denarii, de terra Nicholai fullonis super aquam sexdecim denarii, de terra Henrici fabri uiginti denarii, de terra proxima Willelmi de Tiwe quatuor denarii, de terra Simonis fabri octo denarii, de terra Andree Coci octo denarii, de terra in Hamtone quinque solidi.

415. In Lench pertinent ad sacristariam tres hide et dimidia, in

---

[1] i.e. the allowance of board, etc., for a servant. Corrodies in the shape of food, ale, and the like could be purchased by lay people, fulfilling the same functions as a life insurance policy.

[2] Obventions are occasional revenues or rents, as distinct from oblations, offerings, for which see below, 415.

[3] The *caritas* was a pittance, consisting normally of a drink, probably wine, and a bun or the like, usually provided on days when there was no supper.

[4] The second Sunday after Easter.   [5] Merstow Green in Evesham.

412. *The appurtenances of the office of dean*

To the office of dean belongs the corrody[1] of one of the cellarer's servants, the collection of Peter's Pence wherever the bishop does not collect it, the visitation of the churches of the Vale, and the obventions[2] from lawsuits, from which he must provide a *caritas*[3] for the convent on the Sunday on which the Misericordia Domini is sung.[4]

413. *Revenues of the sacristy*

To the sacristy belong six chapels in the Vale, viz. two in Evesham and the two chapels of Lenchwick and Norton, one in [Abbots] Morton and one in Offenham. He also receives two marks from the church of Badby, ten shillings from the chapel of Wixford [Warws.] and from the meadowland of Salford [Warws.], half a mark from the church of Weston [Weston-upon-Avon, Glos. and Warws.], five shillings or two stones of wax from the church of Stow [Glos.], five pounds of wax from the church of St Alban in Worcester, and three and a half marks from the lands in the same vill.

414. To the sacristy also belong the shop by the gate of the cemetery, four pence from the forge of William the smith, two pounds of wax from the land of Nicholas the cook, five pence from the land of Matilda in Merstow,[5] six pence from the land of the sacrist Nicholas in the same neighbourhood, six pence from the land of the steward which was Gerald's land, six pence from the land of Bulet, thirty pence from the land of Ferre, two pence from the land of le Hosiere in Bridge street,[6] six pence from the land of William de Tiwe which is next to le Hosiere's land, two shillings and four pence from the land of William de Tiwe on the high street, forty pence from the land of the steward which is next to William's land, sixteen pence from the land which is called Gordan's in Cole street, two shillings from the land of Reginald the smith, eight pence from the land of Walter which is next to Reginald's land, eight pence from the land of Pate next to Walter's land, sixteen pence from the land of Nicholas the fuller above the river, twenty pence from the land of Henry the smith, four pence from William de Tiwe's land next that, eight pence from the land of Simon the smith, eight pence from the land of Andrew the cook, and five shillings from land in Hampton.

415. Belonging to the sacristy are three-and-a-half hides in Lench,

[6] The Cotton charter (see App. II B) has Bruggestrete from where no doubt came Brutstrete.

Brethfortona in uno campo quinquaginta quinque acre, in altero septuaginta sex in dominico, in uilinagio quinque uirgate terre et dimidia, et decime de eadem terra tam maiores quam minores, et de quatuor hidis in eadem uilla, duabus scilicet Hugonis, et duabus militis de Cocthuna;[1] et decime de nouem uirgatis terre Pagani in Litlethona tam maiores quam minores, et decime de quinque uirgatis terre | senescalli in Baddeseia, et decime de dominico cuiusdam liberi hominis in Pikeleia in Herefordsire, et omnes oblationes et omnia legata altaris[2] Eueshamie.

fo. 173ʳᵃ

416. *Redditus camere*

Ad cameram pertinent Malgaresburi et Swelle sicut antiquitus fuerunt, et loco Burthone, que fuit ad cameram,[3] assignata est Tetlestrope ita uidelicet quod abbas ex hac camera nec uestimenta nec hospitium, nec aliquid aliud percipiet sicut consueuit ex priori camera exigere. Hec autem maneria in perpetuum cum omni integritate sua ad uestimenta monachorum sunt assignata.

417. *Redditus infirmarie*

Ad infirmariam pertinent Biuintona cum bosco et omnibus aliis pertinentiis suis, et molendinum fullonum de Burthona cum una uirgata terre et aliis pertinentiis suis de quo percipit infirmarius tres marcas,[a 4] et duo molendina de Stowa, de quibus percipit sedecim solidos, et duo solidi de terra Towi in eadem uilla, et duo solidi de terra uicina eidem, et uiginti denarii in eadem uilla de terra Andree, et in Euesham de terra Ricardi Sperwe uiginti duo denarii. De terra Galfridi molendinarii decem et octo denarii, de terra Iohannis de Kent quadraginta denarii,[b 5] apud Penwrtham duo solidi de terra Stephani de More, et decem et octo de terra de Hotune Roberti Antigonie, et duodecim de terra Roberti le Sureis, et sex denarii de quadam terra de Farintona, et duodecim denarii de piscaria de Roberto Bussel, de Sulstan uero dimidia marca.

418. Iste etiam infirmarius debet recipere redditus qui fuerunt de

---

ᵃ *marg.* Pro hiis tribus marcis recipit duas et dimidiam de capella de Baddeseya et dimidiam de capella de Bretfortone (*in another s. xiii¹ charter hand, over a pencil guide for a rubric?*)   ᵇ *lower marg.* Memorandum non recip. nisi duos sol. usque post mortem relicte Iohannis (*s. xiii¹, same hand as of p. 400 n. e, below*)

---

[1] See above, 178 and n.
[2] Bequests to the priest for the services of the altar.
[3] See below, App. II B (pp. 554–5).

fifty-five acres in one field in Bretforton, seventy-six acres of demesne
land in another field, five-and-a-half virgates of land in villein tenure,
with both the great and small tithes from this land, four hides in the
same vill, two of Hugh and two of the knight of Coughton;[1] the tithes,
both great and small, from nine virgates of land of Pagan in Littleton,
the tithes from five virgates of the land of the steward in Badsey, the
tithes from the demesne of a certain freeman in Pixley in Herefordshire, and all the offerings and altar bequests[2] of Evesham.

416. *The revenues of the chamber*

To the chamber belong Maugersbury [Glos.] and Swell [Glos.], as
they have from of old, and in place of Bourton [Bourton-on-the-
Water, Glos.], which once belonged to the chamber,[3] Adlestrop
[Glos.] has been assigned, but on such terms that the abbot shall
receive from the chamber neither clothing, nor hospitality, nor
anything else that he used to demand from the chamber previously.
These manors have been permanently assigned in entirety to clothe
the monks.

417. *The revenues of the infirmary*

To the infirmary belong Binton [Warws.] with the woodland and all
other of its appurtenances, the mill of the fullers of Bourton-on-the-
Water with one virgate of land and other of its appurtenances from
which the infirmarer receives three marks,[4] the two mills of Stow
[Stow-on-the-Wold, Glos.] from which he receives sixteen shillings,
two shillings from the land of Towi in the same town, two shillings
from the land next to it, twenty pence in the same town from the land
of Andrew, and twenty-two pence from the land of Richard Sperwe
in Evesham. From the land of Geoffrey the miller eighteen pence,
from the land of John of Kent forty pence,[5] two shillings from the
land of Stephen de More at Penwortham [Lancs.], eighteen [pence]
from the land of Robert Antigonie of Houghton [Lancs.], twelve
[pence] from the land of Robert le Sureis, six pence from certain land
at Farington [Lancs.], and twelve pence from the fishery of Robert
Bussel, half a mark from Southstone [in Stanford-on-Teme].
418. The infirmarer must receive the revenues which used to belong

---

[4] *marg.* 'Of these three marks, he receives two and a half from the chapel of Badsey and
a half from the church of Bretforton.'
[5] *marg.* 'Memorandum that he did not receive more than two shillings until after the
death of the widow of John.'

pitanciaria, qui pertinent ad cibos, scilicet de Wortesleia et de Liuintona duas marcas, et de sacrista quinque marcas[a][1] quas sacrista dat annuatim pro hospitio quod[b] abbates consueuerunt extorquere iniuste ab eo. Set abbas Rondulfus, secundum priuilegia ecclesie et fo. 173[rb] statuta capituli generalis,[2] sacristariam | sicut et alias obedientias decernens liberam esse debere, illi hospitio et omnibus aliis exactionibus pro se et successoribus suis renunciauit ut in fratrum utilitatibus et ecclesie usibus ad quos deputati sunt redditus sacristarie, sicut et aliarum obedientiarum, libere et absque omni diminutione expendantur.[c][3]

419. *Redditus elemosinarie*

Ad elemosinariam pertinent duo furni in Euesham, et tercius in Beningwrthe,[d][4] de terra Iohannis de Kent in Euesham dimidia marca,[e][5] de solda Ade Credani ante portam cimiterii quatuor solidi,[f][6] de terra Iohannis portarii duodecim denarii,[g][7] de terra Godefridi Baggard sex denarii,[h][8] de terra Cranford cum soppa ferri duodecim denarii, de terra Cecilie retro furnum sex denarii,[i][9] de terra Rogel (*sic*) iuxta alium furnum uiginti[j] denarii. Ad eam etiam pertinet hospitalis iuxta pontem,[10] saluis octo denariis refectorario,[k][11] in Glocestria de

---

[a] *lower marg.* de hiis tamen percipit coquinarius xxti sol. ad faciendam terciam misericordiam uel dabit infirmario x sol. cum illis xx ut ipse faciat terciam (*in another s. xiii[t] charter hand*)   [b] *interlined*   [c] *marg.* et una marcha qua abbas Randulfus dedit ad emendationem diete monachorum prima die minutionis. Hanc percip(it?) de Stouua [d] *marg.* Et omnes furni Vallis. Et decem et octo denarii de decimis feni Willelmi de Tywe R[o]g[er]i Ællardi et Ernaldi Camberlagi   [e] *lower marg.* Memorandum non recip. nisi quatuor sol. et viii d usque post mortem relicte Iohannis (*s. xiii[t] as above p. 398 n. b*) [f] *marg.* De alia solda sita iuxta aliam soldam scilicet mar. (*sic*) dimid. marce (*sic*) [g] *marg.* Isti pertinent ad refectorium predicta ratione   [h] *marg.* De terra Rogeri de Persora in Merstowe ii sol. In noua terra de domo qua Reginaldus de locutorio dedit ii sol. [i] *marg.* hoc modo tota pertinet ad elemosinariam et reddit iiii sol. De terra Iohannis Bonpain in magno uico xii d. eadem (*inserted*) de terris que dicitur hospitalis iiii sol. [j] *written over an erasure*   [k] *marg.* De terra Randulfi textoris de feodo R. (St?)eche xx d. De terra quam dedit Isabella filia Henrici King xl. sol.

---

[1] *marg.* 'From this, however, the kitchener takes 20s. for a third allowance of food or gives the infirmarer 10s., in addition to the 20s., for him to make the allowance.'

[2] Following the decree of the Fourth Lateran Council of 1215, the Benedictines began to hold general chapters. The first for the southern province (Canterbury) was held at Oxford some time between Sept. 1218 and July 1219. Abbot Randulf played an important part in the early chapters as visitor in the second chapter of 1219 and as president at Northampton in 1225. For the chapters, see *Documents . . . of the General and Provincial Chapters of the English Black Monks*, i, ed. W. A. Pantin, pp. 7–24. This is probably a reference to the rather general statutes amongst those of 1218 against extravagance on the part of superiors.

to the pittancery for food, namely two marks from Wrottesley and Loynton [Staffs.], and five marks[1] from the sacrist—which the sacrist gives annually for lodging tax—which the abbots wrongfully used to demand from him. But Abbot Randulf, in accordance with the privileges of the church and the statutes of the general chapter,[2] deciding that the sacristy should be free like the other offices, rejected this money for lodging and all the other demands for himself and his successors, so that the revenues of the sacristy might be spent freely and without any diminution upon the needs of the brethren and the requirements of the church for which they were assigned,[3] as is the case of the other offices.

419. *The revenues of the almonry*

To the almonry belong two bakeries in Evesham and a third in Bengeworth,[4] half a mark from the land of John of Kent in Evesham,[5] four shillings from Adam Credan's shop by the gate of the cemetery,[6] twelve pence from the land of John the porter,[7] six pence from the land of Godfrey Baggard,[8] twelve pence from the land 'Cranford' with the iron-workshop, six pence from the land of Cecilia behind the bakery,[9] and twenty pence from the land of Rogel near another bakery. Also belonging to it is [land] of the hospital near the bridge,[10] except for eight pence belonging to the refectorer,[11] four shillings

---

[3] *marg.* 'and one mark which Abbot Randulf gave to supplement the diet of the monks on the first day of bloodletting. This comes from Stow.'

[4] *marg.* 'And all the bakeries in the Vale. And 18*d.* from tithes of hay of William de Tiwe, Roger Ællardi and Ernald Camberlag.'

[5] *marg.* 'Memorandum that he did not receive more than 4*s.* 8*d.* until after the death of the widow of John.'

[6] *marg.* 'from another shop sited beyond the other shop, that is, one and a half marks.'
The cemetery gate to the north of the convent gave access from the town and the market to the two churches (of All Saints and St Laurence) and the large surrounding cemetery, as well as to the abbey. The lower part of the present gate and gatehouse, built of stone, dates from the time of Abbot Reginald.

[7] *marg.* 'These belong to the refectory in the said amount.'

[8] *marg.* 'From the land of Roger of Pershore in Merstow 2*s.* In the new land of the house which Reginald of the parlour gave, 2*s.*'

[9] *marg.* 'Thus the whole of this belongs to the almonry and returns 4*s.* From the land of John Bonpayn on the main street, 12*d.* From the lands which it is said are the hospital's, 4*s.*'

[10] The date of the foundation of the hospital by the bridge as being before 1206 (KH pp. 320, 358) is based on a misunderstanding by R. M. Clay of Macray's printed text. Although it is likely that the hospital did indeed pre-date the early 13th cent., all that can be said from this evidence is that it was there by 1215, presuming no interpolation.

[11] *marg.* 'From the land of Randulf the weaver from/on the fee of R (Str?)eche 20*d.* From the land which Isabel, daughter of Henry King, gave, 40*s.*'

terra Iohannis Crume que data fuit cum Ada monacho quatuor solidi,*ᵃ*¹ et de terra Botilde que data fuit cum Roberto monacho octo solidi.*ᵇ*² Ad eam etiam pertinent due marce de ueteri pensione sexaginta solidorum de ecclesia de Ambresleia, scilicet uiginti solidi ad opus pauperum in Cena Domini ad mandatum, et dimidia marca ad opus pauperum in die Animarum et anniuersario abbatis Rondulfi.*ᶜ*³ De Aldintona nongenta oua. De toto eciam pane infra portam abbatie expenso uel liberato ibi cocto uel empto debet elemosinarius habere decimam, et curam orti monachorum ut inde habeat pulmentum ad refectionem pauperum.

420. *Redditus operis*

Ad fabricam ecclesie et domorum claustro adiacentium pertinent quindecim marce de ecclesia de Ambresleia: que si aliquo casu solute non fuerint abbas ecclesiam et domos cooperire debet. Pertinent etiam ad idem faciendum de | cime de terra Willielmi Burn in Uffeham et fabri eiusdem uille et predicatio et legata fidelium, et si que sunt alie gratuite obuentiones.

fo. 173ᵛᵃ

421. *Redditus celle hospitum*

Ad cellam hospitum pertinent minute decime de tribus Litlethonis ad emendum manutergia ciphos et bacinos hospitibus.

ᵃ *marg.* De terra que fuit Ade Hesegate xi sol.   ᵇ *marg.* De terra Rogeri Sewi quam Adam Botild dedit xii denarii   ᶜ *lower marg.* nam ille contulit has duas marcas elemosinarie ratione scripta interius de bonis operibus suis. Cum etiam idem abbas fecisset sex molendina in maneriis abbatie loco decimarum eorundem molendinorum contulit elemosinarie molendinum de Aldintun' quod ipse emerat de quo tempore collationis Odde d[?omus] et [?crof]ta ad idem molendinum pertinentibus recepit elemosinarius annuatim xvi sol. (*s. xiii med.*)

---

¹ *marg.* 'From the land which was Adam Hesegate's, 11*s.*' On donations given when a man entered a monastery, see next note.

² *marg.* 'From the land of Roger Sewi which Adam Botild gave, 12*d.*'

The custom of new recruits to a house bringing dowries with them was widespread: such gifts were necessary for early monasteries to function. The practice could be seen as close to simony and reformers began to condemn it. Twelfth-cent. legislation forbade compulsory dowries for canons, monks, and nuns, emphasizing that such donations must be voluntary; see c. 3 of the legatine council of Westminster, 1127 (*C. & S.* i pt 2, p. 747) and c. 8 of the archiepiscopal council of the southern province held at Westminster in 1175 (ibid., p. 987). Alexander III had defined entry into religion, accompanied by a gift, as simoniacal, at the Council of Tours in 1163, c. 6 (*X.* V. 3. 8, Friedberg, ii cols. 750–1), and this was repeated at the Third Lateran Council of 1179, c. 10 (*X.* V. 3. 9, Friedberg,

from the land of John Crume in Gloucester that was given with the monk Adam,[1] eight shillings from the land of Botild [in Gloucester] that was given with the monk Robert.[2] Also belonging to it are two marks of an old payment of sixty shillings from the church of Ombersley, of which twenty shillings is for the service of the poor on Maundy Thursday, and half a mark for the service of the poor at the feast of All Souls and the anniversary of Abbot Randulf.[3] From Aldington, ninety eggs. The almoner must also have a tithe from all of the bread consumed or given as livery inside the gate of the abbey whether baked there or bought, and he must look after the garden of the monks so that he may have pottage to feed the poor.

420. *Revenues of the fabric*

To the fabric of the church and of the houses adjoining the cloister belong fifteen marks from Ombersley church: if this money by any mischance is not paid, the abbot must keep the church and the houses roofed. For this same purpose belong the tithes from the land of William Burn in Offenham and from that of the smith of the same vill, as well as preaching collections, legacies of the faithful, and any other obventions freely given.

421. *Revenues of the guest-chamber*

To the guest-chamber belong the small tithes of the three Littletons for buying towels, cups, and basins, for the guests.

ii col. 751; Alberigo edn., p. 193). In answer to a question from the archbishop of Canterbury about simoniacs who were exposed at a visitation, Innocent III introduced definite sanctions for those guilty of this type of simony who were to be sent to do penance in a harsher monastery and suspended from orders (*X*. V. 3. 30, Friedberg, ii cols. 759–60; P 1403). At the Fourth Lateran Council of 1215, expulsion and penance, which was to be undertaken in a harsher monastery, were decreed for all those engaging in simoniacal practices (c. 64 = *X*. V. 3. 40, Friedberg, ii cols. 765–6). It is not possible to date when these gifts were made to Evesham nor when Adam and Robert entered the noviciate. Barbara Harvey surmises that the references suggest that these monks were some distance in the past, possibly mid or early 12th cent., and that the rents suggest smallish holdings.

[3] *marg.* 'He conferred these two marks on the almonry as recorded below in the account of his good works. When also this abbot had had six mills built on manors of the abbey, in place of the tithes of those same mills, he bestowed upon the almonry the mill of Aldington, which he had bought on the occasion of the collation of [Odda?], and? the houses and crofts belonging to the same mill. ?With the appurtenances ? the almoner received 16*s*. annually.'

422. *Redditus coquine*

Ad coquinam uero pertinet tercium uiuarium post fontem sancti Egwini, et uetus uilla et forum de Euesham de quibus percipit coquinarius qualibet die sabbati quinque solidos et tres obolos,[a][1] et molendina iuxta pontem, et molendina in Hamptona cum pertinentiis suis de quibus molendinis percipit qualibet die sabbati tres solidos, et sexaginta sticas[2] anguillarum annuatim,[b][3] et uilla de Stowe et forum, de quibus percipit qualibet die Dominica quatuor solidos, de Mortona sexaginta solidi, de Salford sexaginta solidi, de Withlakesford quatuor libre,[c][4] de molendino in eadem uilla uiginti quatuor solidi, et duodecim stice anguillarum annuatim, de molendinis senescalli in Salford uiginti solidi, de molendinis de Chedelesburi cum suis pertinentiis uiginti quinque solidi et quadraginta stice anguillarum, de molendinis de Twiford et Aldintona cum pertinentiis suis viginti octo solidi et quadraginta stice anguillarum, de molendinis de Vffeham cum pertinentiis suis decem solidi, de Fokemule[5] dimidia marca, et molendinum de Wikewane de quo non percipit modo nisi octo solidos. De Vudefe pertinent sexaginta solidi ad coquinam, de piscatione in Ambresleia uiginti tres solidi. In Glocestria de terra Roberti Botild tres solidi et obolus, de terra quadam in Winchelcumba et quodam furno duo solidi et una libra piperis. In Euesham de fo. 173ᵛᵇ quadam terra in Bruttestrete una | libra piperis. De terra Reginaldi filii Willelmi dimidia marca annuatim, de Penuurtham quatuor marce et una summa[6] salmonis,[d][7] de qualibet carrucata terre in ualle Eueshamie de dominico, excepta Aldintona, trecenta oua annuatim, et de quolibet manerio tres denarii ad discos et duodecim olle,[8] de Braduuelle nongenta oua et tres denarii et duodecim olle.

423. Item singulis diebus debet habere coquinarius feorragium ad unum equum, et prebendam uel duo prebendaria de furfure de granario, et duos porcos habere debet ad plancherum, et quociens

---

[a] *marg.* et annuatim in capite ieiunii quatuor milia alletium   [b] *marg.* Et decime molendinorum et feni pratorum ad eadem molendina pertinencium scilicet de Euesham et de Hamtona et de Hieffeham et de Fokemulle et de Twiford et de Chaldelbur' et de Baddeseia et de Wikewane hee(?) omnes decime deputantur ad allec monachorum in xl [c] *marg. add.* argenti   [d] *marg. add.* et duo milia allecium

[1] *marg.* 'and yearly at Ash Wednesday 4000 herrings.'

A thriving town had developed at Evesham by this time, with a broad marketplace in the High Street and a 'new borough' east of the High Street, see T. R. Slater, 'Medieval townfounding', pp. 78–9, and 80 for a plan of the town with the boundaries of the plots as in 1883.

[2] The stick was a measure of small eels, normally twenty-five.

422. *Revenues of the kitchen*

To the kitchen belong the third fishpond past the well of St Ecgwine, and the old town and market place of Evesham from which the kitchener receives five shillings and three halfpence every Saturday[1] and the mills near the bridge, the mills in Hampton with their appurtenances from which he receives three shillings every Saturday and sixty sticks[2] of eels annually,[3] the town of Stow [Glos.] and its market place from which he receives four shillings every Sunday, sixty shillings from Morton, sixty shillings from Salford, four pounds[4] from Wixford [Warws.], twenty-four shillings from a mill in the same vill, and twelve sticks of eels annually, twenty shillings from the steward's mills in Salford, twenty-five shillings from the mills of Chadbury with their appurtenances and forty sticks of eels, twenty-eight shillings from the mills of Twyford and Aldington with their appurtenances and forty sticks of eels, ten shillings from the mills of Offenham with their appurtenances, half a mark from 'Fokemille',[5] and only eight shillings from the mill of Wickhamford. To the kitchen belong sixty shillings from 'Wodefe', twenty-three shillings from the fishery in Ombersley, three shillings and a halfpenny from the land of Robert Botild in Gloucester, two shillings and one pound of pepper from some land and a bakery in Winchcombe [Glos.], one pound of pepper from some land in Evesham in Bridge street, half a mark annually from the land of Reginald son of William [in Evesham], four marks and one seam[6] of salmon from Penwortham,[7] three hundred eggs annually from every carrucate of demesne land in the Vale of Evesham, except Aldington, and three pence from each manor for bowls and twelve pots,[8] as well as nine hundred eggs, three pence, and twelve pots from Broadwell [Glos.].

423. Also every day the kitchener must have hay for one horse and one or two measures of bran from the granary, two pigs for the sty

---

[3] *marg.* 'And the tithes of the mills and of the hay of the meadows belonging to the same mills, that is of Evesham, Hampton, Offenham, Fokemille, Twyford, Chadbury, Badsey, and Wickhamford. All these tithes are assigned to herrings for the monks in Lent.'

[4] *marg.* 'of silver'.

[5] 'Fokemille' is unidentified: it might suggest a mill in which the villagers had certain rights.

[6] The seam was an unspecified load, perhaps a cart load, perhaps a pack-horse load.

[7] *marg. add.* 'and 2000 herrings'.

[8] This might mean the actual pot, or pail, or a measure of ale. Later, at Westminster, the *olla* was a pail of five-gallon capacity (see Harvey, *Living and Dying*, p. 58 n. 70). But, of course, one cannot be precise about the measure at a different date and in a different place.

emerit in uilla Euesham piscem ad totum conuentum debet habere de cellario panem et iustam[1] ad opus uendencium. Ad omnes etiam cibos qui condimento ceruisie indigent debet habere ceruisiam de cellario.[a][2]

424. *Consuetudines cellarii*

Hee etiam sunt consuetudines Eueshamensis cenobii ab antiquis temporibus statute et a celerario generali complende. A cellario igitur singulis diebus debent in refectorium uenire septuaginta duo panes monachiles, quorum quilibet erit ponderis sexaginta quinque solidorum ex quibus singuli monachi singulos percipient.[3] Prior semper duplum nisi cum abbate commederit, nichilominus qui ad superiorem mensam ut custos ordinis sederit duplum. Qui missam maiorem celebrauerint duos. Lector uero et seruientes unum et iustam. Elemosinarius autem septem de decima, et tres ad mandatum, et duos ad tritennales currentes percipiet.[4] Percipiet etiam quilibet fratrum cotidie duas iustas de ceruisia et certe mensure. Inueniet etiam celerarius salem, [b]ignem et summagium,[b] et duo pulmenta: ad unum, de fabis siccis unum prebendarium rasum uel de nouis cumulatum de granario; ad aliud uero pulmentum, decem panes fo. 174[ra] monachiles de cellario, singulis diebus, preterquam in Qua | drage-sima, in qua percipiet duodecim summas fabe de Huniburne ad unum pulmentum inueniendum per totam Quadragesimam. Et de auena duodecim summas, de eadem uilla ad gruellum faciendum, scilicet quarta et sexta feria per totam Quadragesimam, et farinam ad olera singulis diebus in Quadragesima.

425. Insuper habere debent monachi ad octo festiuitates prin-cipales[5] octo summas frumenti ad quamlibet festiuitatem unam summam ad frixuras de granario. Et in eisdem festiuitatibus singulos siffuls[6] de frumento ad wastellos[7] de granario, et in translatione sancti Ecgwini duos ad prandium scilicet et ad cenam. Preterea percipiet coquinarius ad Pasca tria prebendaria

---

[a] *marg. add.* Et caseum semel in die ad quem emendum si non detur de cellario assignauit abbas Randulfus capellam Breffertona   [b-b] ignem et summagium: ignem *and* sum *written over an erasure*

---

[1] The *iusta* is a measure of ale, a monastic allowance, sometimes reckoned by the flagon.

[2] *marg. add.* 'Abbot Randulf assigned the chapel of Bretforton to supply the cheese which he (the kitchener) has to buy once a day if it is not supplied by the cellarer.'

[3] For the monastic or conventual loaf, the daily ration of the monk, see Harvey, *Living and Dying*, p. 59.

[4] Trentals: a set of thirty masses for the repose of the soul were celebrated on a single day or over successive days.

and, whenever he buys fish in the town of Evesham for the whole convent, he must have bread from the cellarer and an allowance of ale[1] for the service of those selling the fish. He must also have ale from the cellarer for all the foods that need a seasoning of ale.[2]

424. The customs of the cellarer

These are the customs of the monastery of Evesham, established from of old, which must be maintained by the general cellarer. Each day the cellarer must deliver to the refectory seventy-two monastic loaves of bread, each of which shall weigh three pounds four ounces, and each monk shall receive one of these.[3] The prior shall always have two loaves unless he is eating with the abbot, but then whoever presides at the high table must have two. Those who are celebrating high mass must have two. The reader and the servers shall have one loaf and a flagon of ale. The almoner, however, shall receive seven out of every ten and three for Maundy, and two for successive trentals.[4] Each of the brethren shall also receive every day two flagons of ale of a fixed measure. The cellarer shall also provide salt, kindling, and the carriage, and the two dishes of pottage. For one he shall provide a razed measure of dried beans or else an allowance of new beans from the granary, for the other, ten monks' loaves daily from the cellar, except during Lent, when he shall receive twelve seams of beans from Honeybourne to provide one dish [per monk] for the whole of Lent. From the same vill he shall receive twelve seams of oats to make gruel on the Wednesdays and Fridays throughout the whole of Lent, and wheatmeal to add to the vegetables every day during Lent.

425. In addition, the monks must have eight seams of corn for the eight principal feasts,[5] and one seam from the granary for each feast for pancakes. During these feasts they must have one measure[6] of corn from the granary for each feast to make wastel-loaves,[7] and at the feast of the Translation of St Ecgwine, two for dinner and supper. Moreover, the kitchener shall receive three prebends of corn from the

---

[5] This may be a slip for the *seven* feasts recorded at Evesham and referred to just below, but, on the other hand, it might reflect a recopying by which time another major feast had been instituted and the scribe failed to correct the first entry. The 'Seven Feasts' (i.e. those of the top rank) at Evesham are recorded as Christmas, the deposition of St Ecgwine, Easter, Whitsun, the Assumption of the Blessed Virgin Mary, the translation of St Ecgwine, and All Saints; and see 425 n. 2 (p. 408), below.

[6] According to Macray, the *sifful* or *cyfolle* (Latin *scapha, scaphula*, and German *scheffel*) is a bushel. *Sciffus* can also mean a dry measure.

[7] See Harvey, *Living and Dying*, p. 59: 'a biscuity loaf, made from flour which had been refined with the aid of a bolting cloth, and baked in an exceptionally hot oven'.

frumenti de granario ad flaccones inueniendos, similiter et in Rogationibus ad festum sancti Odulfi unum prebendarium ad frixuras, similiter et in Septuagesima, et unum die Parasceue ad pulmentum. Ad formittas uero in Aduentu Domini debent habere quatuordecim summas, contra Natale tantumdem, contra Quadragesimam tantumdem, contra Pascha totidem, contra Pentecosten totidem, contra Assumptionem sancte Marie totidem, contra translationem sancti Egwini totidem; omnes scilicet percipiendas de horreis. Debent etiam habere de cellario singulis diebus sabbati caritatem ad collationem pro mandato,[1] et ad omnes collationes festiuitatum, tam in capis quam in albis,[2] in uigilia et in die. Exceptis collationibus septem festiuitatum principalium tam in uigilia quam in die, tunc enim refectorarius inuenire debet.

426. Debent etiam habere caritatem de cellario ad prandium singulis diebus octabarum principalium festiuitatum que octauas[3] habent, exceptis diebus quibus sunt in capis, tunc etiam refectorarius inueniet. Et ad collationem singulis diebus earumdem octabarum

fo. 174rb ha | bebunt de cellario, et a Natali Domini usque ad Epiphaniam simili modo habebunt de cellario. Et quandocumque potus est post nonam,[4] percipiet refectorarius duas iustas, ante collationem uero sex cotidie: item singulis diebus Dominicis in Quadragesima dimidium prebendarium frumenti de granario ad oblatas ad cenam, et dimidium similiter in Cena Domini ad idem. In minutionibus[5] uero et in misericordiis regularibus duo et duo unam iustam de cellario, tam ad prandium quam ad cenam, in uentositate uero unam. Seruiens uero qui fratres sanguinauerit panem et iustam percipiet de cellario si plures fuerint sanguinati. Quotiens etiam mappe de refectorio abluuntur seruientes de lauendrina panem monachilem de cellario habere debent.

427. Et tribus septimanis in Aduentu Domini et tribus ante Pascha,

---

[1] The evening reading which took place before compline (the collation) was accompanied by a drink allowance. The collation perhaps took its name from the Collations of the Fathers of John Cassian, a record of his conversations with the hermits of the Egyptian deserts which originally formed the texts used. For the institution of the practice, see RSB cap. 42. For the procedure, see Lanfranc, *Monastic Constitutions*, pp. 55–7.

[2] On the most important feasts both copes and albs were worn by the monks, but for lesser feasts just albs. At neighbouring Worcester (*c.*1230 and probably considerably earlier) more than forty days in the year were celebrated in copes and another eighteen in albs. The feasts were graded into (1) *septem festum*, (2) *solennis processio*, (3) *in capis*, (4) *in albis*, (5) *xii lectiones*, (6) *iii lectiones*, and (7) *commemoratio*. At Worcester and at Evesham *septem festum* meant the maximum solemnity, but while Evesham appears to have stuck to

granary for Easter Day to provide custard-tarts, similarly at Roga-tiontide, on the feast of St Odulf, one measure of corn for pancakes, the same on Septuagesima [the third Sunday before Ash Wednesday], and again one on Good Friday for pottage. Then at Advent the monks must have fourteen seams of corn for cakes, as many to provide for Christmas, Lent, Easter, Pentecost, the Assumption of St Mary, and the Translation of St Ecgwine; all to be taken from the barns. The monks must also have a *caritas* from the cellar every Saturday at the collation[1] as Maundy, and at every collation at festivals on days when copes as well as albs are worn,[2] on the vigil as well as the day of the festival. However, the collations of the seven principal festivals are excepted, the vigils as well as the days of the festivals, when the refectorer must provide for these.

426. The monks must also have a *caritas* from the cellar for dinner each day on the octaves of those principal festivals that have octaves,[3] except on days when copes are worn when the refectorer shall provide them. The cellarer shall provide the collation on each of those same octaves, and shall also do so from Christmas until Epiphany. Whenever wine is drunk after nones,[4] the refectorer shall receive two measures of ale, and six measures before the collation every day: similarly every Sunday during Lent he shall receive half a measure of corn from the granary for the wafer-cakes at supper, and again, half on Thursday in Holy Week for the same purpose. At blood-letting[5] and at other times of relaxation of the Rule, pairs of monks shall have one measure of ale between them from the cellar for both dinner and supper, and one at times of bleeding. The servant who has bled the brethren will receive bread and a measure of ale from the cellar if many brethren have been bled. Whenever table-cloths from the refectory are washed, the laundry-servants must have monks' bread from the cellar.

427. During three weeks in Advent and three weeks before Easter, on

---

the original seven such feasts, Worcester by the 13th cent. had thirteen. See *M. O.*, pp. 541–2; André Mocquereau, *Les Principaux Manuscrits de Chant: Antiphonaire Monastique . . . de Worcester* (Paléographie Musicale, xii: Tournay, 1922), pp. 48–52; and *The Customary of the Benedictine abbey of Bury St Edmunds in Suffolk*, ed. A Gransden (Henry Bradshaw Soc. xcix: London, 1973 for 1966), pp. 11, 22, 91–4, and the index, under feasts: *in albis, in cappis*.

[3] The octave was the eighth day from the feast counting the feast day itself in the reckoning.

[4] Nones took place at about 1.30 p.m. in winter and at 2.30 p. m. in summer.

[5] On blood-letting, undertaken for health reasons, see Harvey, *Living and Dying*, pp. 96–9.

singulis scilicet diebus quando fratres balneant, balneatores percipere
debent de cellario panem et iustam. *Item duo capellani, sancti
uidelicet Laurentii et Omnium Sanctorum, debent habere cotidie
de cellario panem et ceruisiam sicut monachi.* Debet etiam camerarius habere cotidie ad unum seruientem procurationem, et prebendam ad unum equum de granario, et feorragium de grangia; similiter
et sacrista. Item in anniuersariis, abbatum Reginaldi[1] scilicet et Ade,[2]
habere debent monachi singulos siffuls[3] de granario ad wastellos.[4]
Debet etiam in die Animarum elimosinarius recipere unam summam
frumenti de granario pauperibus erogandam. Similiter fiet in obitu
cuiuslibet monachi.

428. Abbates etiam et monachi eiusdem loci per totum annum post
obitum suum corrodium totum sicut in uita sua perceperunt, habere
debent, quod alicui indigenti pro anima sua erogabitur. Seruientes
etiam qui uigilant circa fratrem proximum morti panem et ceruisiam
fo. 174va habere debent de cellario. | Si uero obitus monachi uel abbatis
alterius domus, si fuerint de capitulo Eueshamensi,[5] euenerint, ad
annale pro abbate, et tritennale pro monacho de cellario panis et
ceruisia sicut et monacho alicui pauperi erogentur.[6] Debet etiam
celerarius dare singulis pauperibus in Cena Domini qui fuerint in
capitulo singulos panes et tria allecia, et de ceruisia quantum opus
fuerit.

429. Si quis uero hec conseruauerit uel adauxerit, adaugeat Dominus
dies eius et conseruet eum in uitam eternam. Si quis uero destruxerit
uel diminuerit, diminuat Dominus dies eius et destruat uitam eius
desuper terram. Amen.

430. *Confirmatio legati*
Confirmatio uero domini legati talis:
'Iohannes Dei gratia sancte Marie in Via Lata diaconus cardinalis,
apostolice sedis legatus, dilectis fratribus abbati et conuentui de
Eueshamia in uero salutari salutem. Ea que pro statu religiosorum
locorum et obseruantia regulari prouide statuuntur, firmiter et
inuiolabiliter uolumus obseruari. Ea propter uestris postulationibus

---

a–a marg. vacat

[1] 25 Aug. (1149).   [2] 12 Nov. (1189).
[3] See above, 425 n. 6 (p. 407).   [4] See above, 425 n. 7 (p. 407).
[5] See above, Introduction. Monks of confederate houses were to enjoy all the same
benefits, 'bodily and spiritual', as in the house of their profession. Although some of the

each of the days that brethren take a bath, the servants of the bath-house must receive from the cellar bread and a measure of ale. Similarly, the two chaplains of St Laurence and All Saints must have bread and ale every day from the cellar, like the monks. The chamberlain must also have a maintenance allowance every day for one servant from the granary, and an allowance of corn from the granary for one horse, as well as fodder from the barn; the same goes for the sacrist. On the anniversaries of abbots Reginald[1] and Adam,[2] the monks must each have a measure[3] of corn from the granary for wastel-bread.[4] On the feast of All Souls the almoner must receive one seam of corn from the granary to give to the poor. This should also be done on the death of any monk.

428. Furthermore, abbots and monks of the same place must have their corrody, just as they had in their lifetime, for the whole year after their death to be disbursed for the sake of their souls to some needy person. Servants who keep vigil around a brother who is close to death must have bread and ale from the cellar. If the death occurs of a monk or abbot of another house, who has belonged to the Evesham chapter,[5] bread and ale must be given from the cellar to some poor person, for a year on the abbot's behalf, and for thirty days on the monk's behalf.[6] On Maundy Thursday the cellarer must give to individual paupers who have been in the chapter-house a loaf each and three herrings, and as much ale as they need.

429. May the Lord add to the days of him who preserves or adds to this, and preserve him for everlasting life. But may the Lord shorten the days of him who destroys or subtracts from them, and destroy his life upon earth. Amen.

430. *The confirmation of the legate*
The confirmation of the legate is as follows.
John, by the grace of God cardinal deacon of St Mary in Via Lata, legate of the apostolic see, to the beloved brethren, the abbot and convent of Evesham, greeting in true salvation. We desire that those things which are prudently decreed for the good estate of religious places and for regular observance be steadfastly and inviolably observed. Therefore, assenting to your requests, and by the authority

privileges may never have been used, arrangements for the provision of masses and allowances from the refectory for deceased abbots and monks of the confederation and their entry on the obit rolls in 'twinned' houses, as described here, were definitely honoured.

[6] See Harvey, *Living and Dying*, p. 13, on these arrangements.

annuentes, constituciones quasdam pro statu monasterii et religionis obseruantia inter uos communi factas assensu et redactas in scripto, prout rationabiliter et regulariter facte sunt, et ab utraque parte sponte recepte, legationis auctoritate qua fungimur confirmamus, et presentis scripti patrocinio communimus.'[1] Domini autem pape confirmatio huiusmodi.

431. *Confirmatio domini pape*

'Innocentius episcopus seruus seruorum Dei dilectis filiis abbati et conuentui monasterii de Euesham salutem et apostolicam benedictionem. Cum a nobis petitur quod iustum est et honestum, tam uigor equitatis quam ordo exigit rationis ut id per sollicitudinem offitii nostri ad debitum perducatur effectum. Ea propter, dilecti in Domino filii, uestris iustis postulationibus grato concurrentes assensu, regulares dispositiones reddituum uestrorum qui de communi consensu fo. 174vb capituli | sunt ad officia uestri monasterii deputati; sicut prouide facte sunt, auctoritate apostolica confirmamus et presentis scripti patrocinio communimus. Inhibentes ne redditus ipsi contra regularem dispositionem uestram in usus alios transferantur. Nulli ergo omnino hominum liceat hanc paginam nostre confirmationis et inhibitionis infringere uel ei ausu temerario contraire. Si quis autem hoc attemptare presumpserit indignationem omnipotentis Dei et beatorum apostolorum Petri et Pauli eius se nouerit incursurum. Datum Laterani quartodecimo kalendas Martii, pontificatus nostri anno octauo decimo.'[2]

432. *Qualiter episcopus contra nos egerit per literas communes super iurisdictione Vallis, et utrum lis sit contestata uel non*

Post recessum legati uocauit nos in ius episcopus Wigornie auctoritate litterarum communium prescriptarum coram Rofensi et Elyensi episcopis et magistro Benedicto canonico Londoniensi.[3] Et cum pluries comparuissemus coram eis apud Sanctum Albanum tandem exhibita sunt ibi priuilegia regum et lecta in auditorio eorum. Hinc animaduertat prudens aduocatus quem causa hec expectat, quatenus uidelicet sit in causa processum, scilicet utrum in hac causa lis sit

[1] See above, 393 where his confirmation is referred to, and below, App. II A. Master Robert de Wlveia (? Wolvey, Warws.), Master Thomas of Warwick, and William the steward of Evesham were sworn as witnesses to the agreement on behalf of the abbot and added their seals.

[2] Cheney, *Letters*, no. 1054.

[3] See above, 372.

of the legation which we discharge, we confirm that certain statutes made among you by common consent for the good estate of the monastery and for the observance of religion, and put in writing, have been made reasonably and consonant with the Rule, and willingly accepted by both abbot and monks, and we ratify them with the protection of this present document [1206].[1] The confirmation of the pope is as follows.

431. The confirmation of the pope
Innocent, bishop, servant of the servants of God, to the beloved sons, the abbot and convent of the monastery of Evesham, greeting and apostolic benediction. Since the petition made to us is just and honourable, not only the strength of what is right but also the promptings of reason urge us to grant what is due by the grace of our office. Hence, beloved sons in the Lord, acceding to your just requests with our gracious consent, we confirm with apostolic authority and ratify with the protection of this present document the dispositions of your revenues as prudently made consonant with the Rule, and assigned by common consent of the chapter to the offices of your monastery. We forbid those revenues to be transferred to other uses contrary to your disposition which accords with the Rule. Therefore let no man whatsoever violate this written confirmation and prohibition of ours, or oppose it with bold presumption. Should any man presume to dispute it, let him know that he will incur the wrath of Almighty God and the blessed apostles, Peter and Paul. Dated at the Lateran on 16 February in the eighteenth year of our pontificate [1216].[2]

432. The bishop acts against us over the jurisdiction of the Vale on the basis of the letter in common form, and over the question whether the case has been contested or not
After the departure of the legate [autumn–winter 1206], the bishop of Worcester summoned us before the bishops of Rochester and of Ely and Master Benedict, canon of London, on the authority of the letter in common form written above.[3] After we had appeared before them several times at St Albans [Herts.] the privileges of the kings were at last produced there, and were read out for them in their audience-hall. Hence, let the shrewd advocate, which this case looks for, consider the nature of the proceedings in the case, whether the suit in connection with this case has been [already]

contestata coram domino papa per primos nuncios nostros Herme-
fredum et Ricardum, uel coram primis iudicibus nostris in Anglia, uel
iterum coram domino papa in litterarum istarum obtentu, uel hic
coram iudicibus nostris per talem instrumentorum lectionem, uel
nusquam. Hec ideo sub dubitatione posui quia pro qualitate litterarum per quas episcopus nos conuenerit, poterit nobis obesse uel
prodesse litem fuisse uel non fuisse contestatam, ut semper quantum
poterimus iudicium subterfugiamus quia possidemus.

433. *Qualiter locutum fuit de pace inter abbatem et episcopum*
Interim locutum fuit de pace sub hac forma. Quod nos renunciare
deberemus questioni duorum milium marcarum argenti petitarum
nomine expensarum factarum in iudicio petitorio super exemptione
fo. 175ʳᵃ monasterii nostri in quo obtinui|mus, quia in iudicio possessorio
fuimus uictores quoad Vallem set uicti quoad monasterium, episcopus uero e contrario. Et ideo neuter ab alio potuit petere expensas.
Deberemus etiam renuntiare questioni de iurisdictione nouem
ecclesiarum extra Vallem[1] quas dicimus esse sitas sicut ecclesias
Vallis in loco quem summus pontifex Constantinus libertati
donauit, sicut regia potestas regie libertati donauit, loco uidelicet
large accepto ut caput cum membris complectatur, et quod ita
intelligi debeat expresse continetur in priuilegio Innocentii secundi
ubi dicitur quod 'pastoralis cura tocius domus et aliorum locorum
ad eandem ecclesiam pertinentium penes abbatem permaneat'.[2] Et
in signum libertatis quibusdam earum conferimus crisma et oleum,
in quibusdam uero colligimus denarios beati Petri, et super hiis
duabus questionibus obtinuimus litteras domini pape quando
fuimus in generali consilio.[3] Deberemus insuper dare ei baroniam
nostram in Wigornia cum ecclesia sancti Albani et capella sancte
Margarete, et in Kinwerton' uel Westone uel alias extra dominicas
uillas nostras aduocationem ecclesie uel ecclesiarum ualentem
uiginti marcas.

434. Episcopus uero debuit renunciare omni questioni super iurisdictione Vallis, et concedere nobis ecclesias de Ambresleia et de

---

[1] Church Lench, Kinwarton (Warws.), Weston-upon-Avon (Warws.), Ombersley,
Willersey (Glos.), Broadwell (Glos.), Stow-on-the-Wold (Glos.), Bourton on the Water
(Glos.), and Upper Swell (Glos.).

[2] See above, 330.

[3] One of the letters referred to here as having been obtained by Abbot Randulf and
Thomas at the time of the Fourth Lateran Council is the forerunner of the forgery of Pope
Gregory IX's 'Licet singuli archiepiscopi' for Evesham, concerning the collection of

contested before the pope through our original representatives, Ermefred and Richard, and before our first judges [delegate] in England, and again before the pope on the basis of those letters, and here before our judges on the basis of this reading of the instruments, or whether it has not been contested at all. Considering the nature of the letter on the basis of which the bishop summoned us, I personally considered it doubtful that it could harm or benefit us that the suit had been contested or not contested, believing that we should always, to the best of our ability, avoid judgment over what we possess.

433. *Discussion between the abbot and the bishop on peace terms*
Meanwhile a discussion of the following nature about peace terms took place. We must give up our demand for two thousand marks of silver, requested as the expenses incurred in the petitory judgment over the exemption of our monastery, which we won, on the grounds that although we were the victors in the possessory judgment concerning jurisdiction over the Vale, we were defeated over the monastery, and the opposite was true for the bishop. Therefore, neither side could demand expenses from the other. We must also give up our demand for jurisdiction over nine churches outside the Vale[1] which we said were situated, as were the churches of the Vale, in the place which the pontiff Constantine gave its liberty, just as the royal power gave it its liberty, taking 'place' in its widest sense just as the limbs go with the head, and that it should be so understood as expressly stated in the privilege of Innocent II where it is said that 'the pastoral care of the entire house and of other places belonging to the same church is to rest solely with the abbot'.[2] As an indication of that liberty, we grant some of those churches chrism and oil, in others we collect Peter's Pence, and in connection with these two points at issue, we had obtained papal letters when we were at the General Council.[3] We must in addition give to the bishop our barony in Worcester with the church of St Alban and the chapel of St Margaret, as well as the advowson of any church or churches valued at twenty marks in Kinwarton [Warws.], Weston [Weston-upon Avon, Glos. and Warws.], and other places outside our demesne vills.
434. The bishop must give up all his demands for jurisdiction over the Vale, and must grant us the churches of Ombersley and Stow

Peter's Pence, for which see Sayers, '"Original", Cartulary and Chronicle', pp. 392–4 and pl. II.

Stowa in proprios usus de quibus habemus indulgentias domini pape,[1] quod ita sint licet forte minus sint sufficientes, salua ei in eisdem omni iurisdictione episcopali. Et debuit concedere quod Willerseia[2] esset omnino libera, sicut ecclesie Vallis.

435. *De recessu magistri Ade Sortes et morte magistri Thome de Norwich, et casu turris et reparatione eiusdem*

Set cum abbas hanc formam pacis conuentui retulisset noluit conuentus ei consentire quia labe simoniaca plena eis uidebatur. Et quia magister Adam Sortes prius et ceteris constantius ei contradixit, tantum odium, iram, et indignationem concepit abbas aduersus eum quod recto oculo ab illa die deinceps, quamuis forte nec prius, illum non respexit. Set in tantum eum est | persecutus quod simul non poterant commorari.[3] Ille uero tantam persecutionem sustinere non potens, omnimodis operam dedit ut a nobis recederet, et cum ab abbate impetrasset quod daret ei litteras dimissorias.[4] Nos tam nobilis menbri ecclesie iacturam non sustinentes, cum illum apud nos nequaquam possemus retinere. Concessimus ei litteras commendaticias [*sic*] sub tali forma quod quandocumque uellet posset redire. Et cum iam uellet recedere, tanti uiri periculo compassi, nec abbas uellet eum apud se moram facere. Obtinuimus ab abbate ut faceret eum priorem de Penwrtham[5] ut ita non uiderent se ad inuicem, quod et factum est. Et mansit ibi per septennium et amplius usque in quintum diem post depositionem abbatis.[6]

436. Eodem uero anno post recessum eius mortuus est ille in negotiis ecclesie constantissimus monachus, magister uidelicet Thomas de Northwich, pro quo omnibus huius ecclesie amicis est orandum. Et turris ecclesie cecidit et comminuit presbiterium et, exceptis feretris sancti Egwini, sancti Odulfi, et sancti Credani miraculose conseruatis, omnia quecumque erant preciosa in eo cum feretro sancti Wistani et aliis feretris et maiori altari et tabulis et aliis ornamentis circa illud existentibus. Quorum omnium maximam partem tam ante prioratum

fo. 175rb

---

[1] No such licences for the abbot and convent to appropriate have survived, but it is quite likely that they had such letters.

[2] Willersey (Glos.) is included in Cenred's gift to Evesham of 709 (the charter is regarded as spurious), see above, 117; and is mentioned below, 513, where it says that Abbot Randulf built a barn there. The bishop's jurisdiction over it was clearly in dispute at this time.

[3] This may be a classical quotation, but we have not been able to trace it.

[4] Letters dimissory from the abbot as superior which allowed a monk to leave.

[5] Penwortham was Evesham's dependency in Lancs., and see next note.

[Glos.] for our own uses for which we have licences of the pope,[1] though in fact it happens that they are inadequately funded, while he retains all episcopal jurisdiction in them. He must also concede that Willersey[2] be entirely free, like the churches of the Vale.

435. *The departure of Master Adam Sortes, the death of Master Thomas de Northwich, and the collapse and repair of the church tower*
When the abbot reported these peace terms to the convent, it refused to assent to them because the monks thought that they were very much tainted with simony. Because Master Adam Sortes was the first to oppose them and did so with greater determination than others, the abbot conceived such hatred, anger, and indignation against him that from that day onwards he was prejudiced against him, though in fact he had no proper regard for him even before this. Indeed, so fierce was his persecution of Adam that they could not dwell in the same house together.[3] Unable to endure such persecution, Adam sought every means he could to leave us, and so prevailed upon the abbot to grant him letters dimissory.[4] We could not bear losing so noble a member of the church, but we had no success at all in persuading him to stay with us. We accordingly gave him a letter of recommendation, phrased in such terms as to allow him to return to us whenever he wished. Then when he wished to depart, we were deeply conscious of the danger that such a man faced, but the abbot refused to let him stay any longer with him. We therefore persuaded the abbot to make him prior of Penwortham so that they would not see each other,[5] and that is what happened. And Adam remained there for seven or more years until five days after the abbot was deposed.[6]

436. During that same year [1207] there occurred, after Adam's departure, the death of Master Thomas de Northwich, a monk stalwart in the affairs of the church, for whom all his friends in this church must pray. Also, the church tower collapsed and, apart from the shrines of St Ecgwine, St Odulf, and St Credan, which were miraculously saved, it crushed the presbytery and all the precious things inside it along with the shrine of St Wigstan and other shrines, with the high altar, tables, and other ornaments around it. I restored the great majority of these things, partly before becoming prior,

---

[6] Abbot Norreis was deposed on 22 Nov. 1213. Five days later would make his appointment to Penwortham the 26th if the normal medieval practice of including the day itself in the reckoning was followed; see below, **496**. Adam is likely to have resigned and returned to his old convent at Evesham.

meum quam post prioratum expensis labore meo et industria adquisitis usque ad summam centum marcarum reparaui. Et alii fratres uiriliter mecum omnia in melius reformauerunt, quia redditus operis abbas sibi appropriauit, pro quorum defectu turris imperfecta cecidit.

437. *Qualiter episcopus propter exilium suum omiserit abbatem et conuentum uexare, et qualiter Romani creditores nostri fuerint priuilegiis nostris spoliati, et de regno a rege fugati*

Interim factum est generale interdictum tocius Anglie[1] quia dominus rex noluit admittere magistrum Stephanum de Longetone quem dominus papa ad electionem monachorum Cantuarie, rege non consentiente, consecrauerat in archiepiscopum.[2] Quare episcopus Wigornie[3] exulauit cum aliis episcopis Anglie, nec apposuerunt fo. 175[va] amplius ipse uel | successores eius Walterus,[4] Siluester,[5] Willelmus,[6] in eadem causa uexare nos usque ad tempus quo hec scripta sunt. Rex etiam pro predicto facto admodum turbatus fecit omnes Romanos quotquot erant in Anglia comprehendi. Et omnibus bonis que secum habebant spoliatos de terra sua fugari.[7] Inter quos et creditores nostri,[8] qui tunc temporis uenerant pro pecunia sibi debita.[a] Omnibus instrumentis suis et priuilegiis nostris a domino rege spoliati sunt, et posita sunt priuilegia nostra in thesauro regio, primum Londoniis, et postea aput castrum de Corf.[9]

---

[a] over an erasure or correction by the scribe

[1] On 23 March 1208.

[2] After the monks' election of their sub-prior, Reginald, and then of John de Grey, under pressure from the king in late 1205, Innocent III quashed both elections and encouraged the monks' representatives who were in Rome to elect Langton at the end of 1206. Langton was then consecrated by the pope at Viterbo on 17 June 1207. John refused to confirm the election, and the monks of Canterbury were expelled from their house by a writ dated 11 July (*Rotuli litterarum patentium*, ed. T. D. Hardy, i, pt. 1 (Record Commission: London, 1835), p. 74).

[3] Mauger is mentioned in the Annals of Dunstable (*Ann. Mon.* iii. 31) as going into exile with Geoffrey, archbishop of York, William, bishop of London, Eustace, bishop of Ely, and Giles, bishop of Hereford. He died on 1 July 1212.

[4] Walter de Grey was elected on 20 Jan., cons. on 5 Oct. 1214, and translated to York *post* Nov. 1215; *HBC*, p. 279.

[5] Silvester of Evesham was elected on 3 Apr. and cons. on 3 July 1216: he died on 16 July 1218; *HBC*, p. 279.

[6] William of Blois was elected *c*.25 Aug. and cons. on 7 Oct. 1218: he died on 17 or 18 Aug. 1236; *HBC*, p. 279.

[7] The arrest and banishment of the Romans and the seizure of their possessions are not recorded in any of the surviving royal records. (Lady Stenton in her introduction to *The*

partly afterwards, with funds acquired by my own hard work and industry amounting to a sum of one hundred marks. Other brothers helped me manfully to restore everything for the better, for it was because of the lack of fabric revenues, which the abbot had appropriated for himself, that the tower had become dilapidated and had collapsed.

437. *Because of his exile the bishop stops troubling the abbot and convent, while our Roman creditors are divested of our privileges and banished from the kingdom by the king*

Meanwhile a general interdict was pronounced over the whole of England[1] because the king refused to admit Master Stephen Langton, whom the pope had consecrated archbishop [of Canterbury] after his election by the monks of Canterbury without the king's agreement.[2] As the result of this the bishop of Worcester[3] was exiled along with other bishops of England, and neither he nor his successors, Walter,[4] Silvester,[5] or William,[6] took any further action to trouble us in this case up to the time this account was written. The king was furious at the pope's action, and had all the Romans in England arrested. He then deprived them of all the possessions they had with them and banished them from the country.[7] Amongst these were our creditors,[8] who had come at that time to collect the money owing to them. The king divested them of all their own documents as well as our privileges which were deposited in the king's treasury, first in London and later at Corfe Castle.[9]

Great Roll of the Pipe for . . . 1208 (PRS n.s. xxiii: London, 1947), p. xi, comments on the lack of evidence in the pipe rolls for the momentous events of this year.) The chronicler Roger of Wendover, however, describes the king's reaction when the bishops of London, Ely, and Worcester came to the king with the mandate to impose the interdict. John flew into one of his celebrated rages, swearing by God's teeth that he would despatch all the prelates and clerks of England to the pope, and confiscate their goods. The king added, for good measure, that all Romans and papal clerks on his territories would be sent to Rome with their eyes gouged out and their noses slit (Wendover, *Flores*, iii. 221–2, whence *Chron. Maj.*, ii. 521–2). Wendover goes on to record the actual confiscation of the goods of the higher clergy in England (*Flores* iii. 223–4, and *Chron. Maj.*, ii. 522–3), but Thomas of Marlborough may be the only source for the carrying out of King John's threat to arrest, seize the goods of, and banish the Romans.

[8] See above, 358 n. 2 (p. 344), for the Scarsi.

[9] In John's reign there was still a royal treasury at Winchester, although the London treasury, based at the New Temple, was becoming the major place of deposit. Both were under the control of the Exchequer; see T. F. Tout, *Chapters in the Administrative History of Medieval England* (5 vols., Manchester 1920–33), i. 97–8. The royal castle of Corfe was seen as a safe stronghold for prisoners, important persons, and documents. John kept his heir and the bulk of his treasure there towards the end of his reign; see S. Painter, *The*

438. *Iteratum consilium Thome prioris qualiter pro tempore causa Vallis sit agenda*

Quia in superioribus prout potui ea que in causa ista acta sunt scripsi. Necessarium michi uidetur ut aliqua que post hec reor agenda ad instructionem posterorum transcribam, quamuis quedam secreta stilo minime sint commendanda, que ideo scribere omisi ne ad aduerariorum peruniant instructionem.

439. *ª*Cum igitur*ª* allegationes meas superius scriptas et litteras domini pape communes ex eisdem allegationibus formatas ante oculos mentis reuoco, michi uidetur quod forma illa litterarum in grauamen ecclesie nostre maximum concepta est. Quia, ut alias scripsi uobis,[1] tempore huius actionis gratiam domini pape et tocius curie rationibus prius scriptis amiseramus, quare aduersarii nostri et nescio quibus aliis rationibus, ualde fauorabiles tunc temporis extiterant. Si igitur prudenti patrifamilias qui sciat de thesauro suo duppliciter proferre noua et uetera,[2] uisum fuerit sicut et michi, uel in ipsa cause uentilatione, in iudicio, uel ante actionem, querat gratiam domini pape et in integrum restitutionem ad dicendum rationes omissas in priori iudicio quando nos causam istam egimus coram domino papa, scilicet illas quas prescripsi uobis, et si quas ex priuilegiis nostris sciat elicere meliores. Omissas dico, quia etsi illas tunc dixerimus | tantum de duabus illarum facta est mentio in litteris domini pape. Quare prudens aduocatus dissimulabit eas tunc fuisse dictas de quibus in litteris nulla facta est mentio, ut ad eas dicendas restituatur.

fo. 175ᵛᵇ

440. Sic feci et ego in priori iudicio. Nam cum expresse innuant Innocentius secundus et Alexander quod alia loca sint exempta quam monasterium, sicut superius allegaui, dominus papa in litteris communibus tantum de priuilegio Constantini facit mentionem et ponit in questione quod expresse ab Innocentio exponitur.[3] Et sic, ut michi uidetur, si omnes rationes omnium priuilegiorum simul collecte attendantur, quod minime in litteris illis factum est, non poterit eis responderi quin ecclesie ille sint exempte. Preterea, cum per *ᵇ*attestationes, quas sub sigillis iudicum inclusas propter uarios casus qui

---

ª⁻ª Cum igitur *over an erasure*   *ᵇ⁻ᵇ¹* *this passage (ends p. 422) written over an erased one*

Reign of King John (Baltimore, 1949), p. 359, and *Rotuli litterarum clausarum in turri Londinensi asservati*, ed. T. D. Hardy, i (Record Commission: London, 1833), pp. 102 col. 1, and 241 col. 2, for Corfe as a prison in 1208 and 1215.

[1] See above, **384, 389–90**.
[2] Matt. 13: 52.
[3] See above, **372–4** and **367**.

438. *Prior Thomas repeats his advice on how the case concerning the Vale should be conducted at the appropriate time*

To the best of my ability I have described above what happened in this case. However, I consider it essential to pass on my advice to posterity on what action needs to be taken in the future, though there are some secrets that must not be committed to writing, and these I have refrained from recording for fear they should provide advice for our opponents.

439. When I recall to mind the arguments I have recorded above and the pope's letter in common form drawn up as the result of those arguments, I am convinced that the terms of the letter were so framed as to cause as much trouble as possible for our church. As I have informed you elsewhere,[1] at the time of the court proceedings we had lost the favour of the pope and the whole of the curia for reasons I have previously explained, whereas our opponents, for some unaccountable reasons, enjoyed considerable favour at that time. But just as the wise householder thought it right to know how to produce things new and old in double measure from his treasure-house,[2] so I thought it right both in the initial presentation of the case in court and before proceedings took place, first to seek the support of the pope for a complete restitution of the opportunity to present the arguments I described to you before, which were omitted in the former judgment when we pleaded our case before the pope, and secondly to draw better arguments from our privileges, if there were any. I say 'omitted' because, although we did present arguments at the time, reference was made to only two of them in the pope's letter. A wise advocate will pass over the fact that these arguments, which were brought up at the time, are not mentioned in the letter, so that he may restate them.

440. That is what I did in the first judgment. For although Innocent II and Alexander expressly allow, as I have argued previously, that other places as well as the monastery may be exempt, the pope makes mention in the letter in common form only of the privilege of Constantine, and casts doubt upon what is expressly stated by Innocent.[3] Therefore, in my opinion, if all the points of all the privileges were brought together and considered carefully—and this was not done in the pope's letter—the only conclusion that could be reached would be that those churches are exempt. Furthermore, it is absolutely clear from the attestations secured under seals of the judges which I have put under lock and key in the treasury because

possint contingere in thesauraria reseruaui, expresse patet, et adhuc, si prudens aduocatus magis putauerit expedire, per testes potest probari, quod bona fide et iusto titulo, sicut prius dixi, prescripserimus ius episcopale in eisdem ecclesiis per tantum tempus quanta est memoria hominum. Dominus papa per subductionem temporis uacationis ecclesie *bl* Wigornensis, si forte tantum fuerit quod eo subducto nostra prescriptio minime sit completa, nostram prescriptionem penitus euacuat. Set si restituti fuerimus ad dicendum rationem omissam non oberit nobis tempus uacationis, quia, sicut ex pluribus tam iuris ciuilis quam canonici locis colligi potest, tantum contra illa loca tempore uacationis non currit prescriptio que yconomum non habent uel defensorem qui causas eorum tempore uacationis exerceat uel defendat. Et ecclesia Wigornensis habet priorem qui fungitur uice decani,[1] habet et archidiaconum, quorum

fo. 176ra quilibet uacante sede uendicat sibi executionem omnium | officiorum episcopalium que per alium quam per ipsum exerceri possunt; ueluti institutiones clericorum, custodiam ecclesiarum uacantium, cognitionem et executionem omnium causarum ad episcopum pertinentium, et si que sunt similia. Et sic ecclesia Wigornensis quoad talia numquam uacat quin in hiis contra eam currat prescriptio, cum habeat tales per quos actiones eius possint exerceri et defendi, maxime cum archidiaconus hec eadem iura petat in ecclesiis nostris que et episcopus.

441. Et hec omnia parati sumus probare per testes omni exceptione maiores.[2] Et reuera a quocumque illorum fiant, sicut dixi, ista, uacante sede ab aliquo illorum exercentur, quia illa que sibi petit episcopus in ipsis ecclesiis competenter ab*a* illis possunt, exerceri. Si itaque hiis rationibus hec exceptio episcopi de tempore uacationis sedis Wigornensis quassata fuerit, liquidum est quod prescriptio nostra sit completa, saluis episcopo quibusdam capitulis in quibus uidetur interrupta. Set si circa interruptiones restituti fuerimus ad dicendum rationes pretermissas, bene constabit nullam factam fuisse interruptionem. Quia reuera quecumque facta sunt

---

a interlined

[1] On the exercise of jurisdiction by the prior of Worcester, as dean, over the churches of the convent, see *C. & S.* i pt 2, no. 100 ('Wulfstan's synod of 1092') at p. 639, and Sayers, 'Proprietary Church', pp. 234–5 n. 12. The prior also acted as official of the bishop in a vacancy, and it was Prior Randulf who thus served as official on the death of Bishop Mauger in 1212; see 'Annales prioratus de Wigornia, *Ann. Mon.* iv. 401, where it is recorded that the 'archiepiscopus [Stephen Langton] misit priori curam officialitatis'.

of various accidents which can happen—and moreover it can still be proved by witnesses if an astute advocate wishes to produce them—that it was in good faith and with just title, as I have said before, that we claimed prescriptive right against episcopal jurisdiction in those churches, a right which goes back far beyond human memory. However, the pope subtracted any period of vacancy in the church of Worcester, and if the period of the vacancy happened to be sufficiently long that when it was subtracted our prescriptive right was not sufficiently complete, the pope entirely annulled that prescriptive right of ours. But, if the opportunity is restored to us of stating the argument denied us, the period of vacancy will not prejudice our case, for many examples from both civil and canon law can be assembled to show that during a vacancy, only in those places which do not have a deputy or an advocate to undertake or defend their lawsuits during the vacancy does the prescriptive right not continue in force. But the church of Worcester has a prior who functions as a dean,[1] and it also has an archdeacon, each of whom, when the see is vacant, claims for himself the right to carry out those episcopal duties which can be undertaken as well by another as by the bishop himself—for example, the institution of clerks, the custody of vacant churches, court-hearings and sentencing in all cases belonging to the bishop, and similar duties. Hence, in these circumstances, the church of Worcester at no time had a vacancy during which the prescriptive right did not continue in force against it, for it had such men as could undertake and defend its lawsuits, especially as an archdeacon claims these same rights as the bishop in our churches.

441. We are prepared to prove all these facts by producing major and irreproachable witnesses.[2] In fact, when the see is vacant, those duties are undertaken, as I have said, by one or other of those men, because they have the legal competence to undertake in those churches the duties which the bishop claims as his own. Therefore, if on the basis of these arguments the bishop's objection over the period of a vacancy in the church of Worcester has been shattered, it is clear that our prescriptive right has been fully maintained, except in the case of some chapter-meetings when the bishop thinks it was interrupted. However, if the opportunity is restored to us of stating the reasons, which we were prevented from putting, for those interruptions, we shall establish firmly that there was no interruption. Indeed, those

[2] See above, **364** and n. 3 (pp. 350–1).

que uidentur facere interruptiones a non dominis, immo quasi a mercennariis, a uicariis annuis, et aliis huiusmodi, qui nichil horum in quibus uidetur facta interruptio possidebant, facta sunt. Quare que a talibus facta sunt quod nobis dominis non debeant preiudicare ex pluribus locis legum et canonum potest haberi.[1] Et etiam *nobis non con*sentientibus, immo ignorantibus hec facta sunt, que omnia per testes legittimos parati sumus probare. Si ergo hec sufficiunt ad interruptiones istas adnichilandas, relinquitur quod plene illas ecclesias prescripserimus.

442. Itaque quamuis hec omnia alias dixerim, laudo quod dissimuletur me hec dixisse, et quamuis non uideantur alicui ad propositum sufficientia, ut saltem per hec iterum, sicut prius fecit, capiat cause huius determinatio dilationem, quia possidemus. Si alicui uero

fo. 176rb uideantur cum melioribus rationibus a se adiectis ad propo|situm sufficientia, laudo quod huius in integrum restitutionis ad dicendum rationes omissas petitio non differatur usque dum uentum fuerit ad litem, set ut litem preueniamus impetrando restitutionem et reuocatorias. Nec timeatis clausulam illam, 'nullis litteris preter consensum partium impetratis preiudicantibus', quia in istis ultimis, si impetrantur, tam de hac clausula quam de tota forma litterarum primarum fiet mentio, et sic non nocebit clausula illa.[2]

443. Hoc autem sciatis quod si gratiam domini pape tempore huius actionis habuissemus sicut tempore alterius habuimus, in hac sicut in illa predictis rationibus obtinuissemus. Hoc etiam prouideatis ut si alias litteras impetraueritis quod in illis contineatur peticio expensarum factarum in prima lite ut predictum est. In illis etiam fiat peticio rationibus premissis exemptionis et iurisdictionis nouem ecclesiarum, scilicet de Chirchlench, Kyneuuertone, Westone, Ambresleie, Willerseie, Bradwelle, Stowe, Burthone, Swelle,[3] que omnes pertinent ad locum istum quem Constantinus dedit libertati. Et si forte preuenti fueritis ab episcopo et facti rei, sicut adhuc sumus,

---

a-a nobis non *written over an erasure and* con *inserted at the beginning of the next line*

[1] On the Roman Law of agency, see *Institutes* 3. tit. 26 'De mandato', and *Gaii Institutionum Iuris Civilis Commentarii Quattuor*, ed. and trans. E. Poste (Oxford, 1871), pp. 348–57.

[2] Thomas is speaking generally and does not appear to have any particular letter in mind, certainly nothing he cites.

[3] All these places (after Willersey) are in Glos.

things which were done, which seem to establish that there was an interruption, were done by men who were not men of authority, no, they were virtually paid servants, vicars on annual pensions, and others of this kind, who possessed none of the authority of those men whose action would establish an interruption. Hence, it can be established from many places in the laws and in the canons that those things carried out by such men must not count against us who have the authority.[1] We are also prepared to prove through sworn witnesses that all the things which were done by these men were carried out without our consent, in fact without our knowledge. If then these arguments are sufficient to demolish the charge of interruptions, it follows that our prescriptive right over those churches is fully intact.

442. Although I have said all these things elsewhere, I advise you to conceal the fact that I have said them, and although one may think them insufficient for proceedings to be taken, it may ensure that the need to determine the nature of this case may again cause, as it did before, a delay over what we possess. If, however, someone, giving some better reasons, thinks the things I have said sufficient for taking proceedings, then I advise you not to wait until the suit is resumed before petitioning for the restoration of the opportunity to state those reasons, but to anticipate the suit, by impetrating for restitution and revocatory letters. Do not be put off by the clause 'no letter obtained without agreement of the parties which is prejudicial', for on this last point, if letters are impetrated, mention will be made not only of this clause but also of the entire content of the letter, so that phrase will cause no harm.[2]

443. You should understand that if we had enjoyed the favour of the pope at the time of these proceedings, as we had enjoyed it at previous proceedings, we would have been allowed an opportunity to put these arguments on this occasion as before. You should also ensure that, if you are granted other letters, a request for the expenses incurred in the first lawsuit, as stated before, should be included in these. In those letters a petition should be made for the inclusion of the arguments put previously about the exemption and jurisdiction of the nine churches of Church Lench, Kinwarton [Warws.], Weston [upon-Avon, Warws. and Glos.], Ombersley, Willersey [Glos.], Broadwell, Stow, Bourton, and Swell,[3] all of which belong to the place which Constantine granted its liberty. Should the bishop happen to forestall you by laying claim to them first, as an accomplished fact, as is the

nichilominus per reconuentionem eadem petatis. Hec ideo uobis dixerim, quia mos curie Romane est ut pie matris, ut si quos uirga patris leserit eosdem uberibus matris si fieri potest consoletur. Vnde causas que in ea aguntur sepe diuidunt, sicut nostram fecerunt, ut pro utraque parte ferant sententiam, ut nullus tristis recedat. Pro magno enim reputabunt si episcopum ab impetitione nostra quoad nouem ecclesias absoluerint, et in expensis mitius cum eo egerint, et nobis ecclesias Vallis adiudicauerint.

444. Hec uobis scripsi ut cum uenerit hora eorum uiriliter agatis[1] et reminiscamini quia ego dixi uobis, orantes pro me.

---

[1] Cf. Deut. 31: 6; Ps. 30: 25 (31: 24); 1 Macc. 2: 64; 1 Cor. 16: 13.

case up till now for us, you should nevertheless make a counter-claim for them. My reason for saying this is that it is the custom for the Roman curia, like a good mother, to console by suckling, if she can, those whom a father's stick has harmed. Hence cases which are being pleaded in the curia are often divided up, as our case was, so that sentence may be pronounced on each part, and no party depart in sorrow. The court will consider it a great achievement if they dismiss our claim against the bishop for the nine churches and deal with him gently over the matter of expenses, but decree that the churches of the Vale be ours.

444. I have written this advice down for you so that when the time comes you may act manfully,[1] and remember that I have spoken to you about this, praying for me.

PARTICVLA QVINTA

445. *Incipit particula quinta de multiplicata tirannide abbatis et suprema depressione conuentus ab eo*

Nunc itaque ad alia circa statum ecclesie nostre procedam, ut discant successores nostri sicut in premissis ita et in aliis aduersa sustinere qualia | nos temporibus nostris pro ueritate et ecclesia ista sustinuimus.

446. Igitur mortuo magistro Thoma de Northwich et magistro Ada Sorte amoto,[1] et regno, ut predictum est, propter consecrationem archiepiscopi turbato, abbas noster ad uomitum reuersus[2] quecunque uolebat ueluti ut neminem timens faciebat, et facta sunt nouissima nostra peiora omnibus prioribus.[3] Nos uero de necessitate facientes uirtutem,[4] colla iugo submisimus et, uidentes quod non erat qui nobis iusticiam exhiberet, quantum humana fragilitas permittebat patienter omnes iniurias nobis ab abbate illatas; quas difficillimum esset enumerare, siue uolentes siue nolentes sustinuimus. Et habentes fiduciam in Domino, speciales cotidie fecimus orationes ut mitteretur nobis auxilium de celo.

447. *De aduentu domini Nicholai legati in Angliam et Romanorum creditorum Eueshamie, et compositione facta cum eis per Thomam monachum*

Tandem, cum per septennium 'in fame et siti',[5] in frigore et nuditate, tantam sustinuissemus penuriam, misertus est Dominus ecclesie Anglicane. Et uisitante nos oriente ex alto,[6] missus est in Angliam a domino papa dominus Nicholaus Tusculan' episcopus, apostolice sedis legatus[7] qui, archiepiscopo iam reuocato,[8] generale soluit interdictum. Venerunt etiam Romani creditores nostri, qui petebant a nobis quadringentas marcas nomine sortis, septingentas uero nomine penarum et expensarum. Super hiis litteras domini *a*pape

---

a–a1 *written over an erasure*

[1] Northwich died in 1207, the same year as Adam Sortes became prior of Penwortham; see above, **435–6.**

[2] Prov. 26: 11.

[3] Matt. 12: 45.

[4] *S. Hieronymi Presbiteri Opera* pars iii. *Opera Polemica* i. *Contra Rufinum*, ed. P. Lardet (Corpus Christianorum Series Latina, lxxix: Turnholt, 1982), Epistula cap. 2 l.11 (p. 74).

[5] 2 Cor. 11: 27.

PART FIVE

445. *The abbot's many acts of tyranny, and his extreme oppression of the convent*

I will now proceed to other matters that concern the state of our church, so that our successors may learn how to withstand adversities in the future, just as we withstood them in the past, for the sake of truth and the church itself.

446. After the death of Master Thomas de Northwich and the departure of Master Adam Sortes,[1] when, as has been said, the kingdom was in disarray over the consecration of the archbishop, our abbot, returning [like a dog] to his vomit,[2] began to do as he liked as if he feared nobody, and our last state was worse than our first.[3] Making a virtue of necessity,[4] we submitted to the yoke and, seeing that he was not the man to act with justice towards us, we patiently endured, either willingly or unwillingly as much as human frailty allowed, all the injustices committed against us by the abbot; and it would be difficult to list them. Putting our trust in the Lord, we said special prayers every day for help to be sent us from Heaven.

447. *The arrival in England of the papal legate Nicholas and of the Roman creditors of Evesham, and the settlement made with them by the monk Thomas*

Finally, after seven years of being 'hungry and thirsty',[5] naked and cold, during which we had endured so much penury, the Lord took pity on the church in England. The Dayspring from on high visited us,[6] for the pope sent Nicholas, bishop of Tusculum, and legate of the apostolic see, to England and he raised the general interdict,[7] as the archbishop had now been recalled.[8] Our Roman creditors also arrived, claiming from us the 400 marks as their due, and 700 marks as compensation and expenses. In addition they brought papal

---

[6] Luke 1: 78.

[7] The legate arrived in England on 20 Sept. 1213. He raised the interdict on 29 June or, more probably, 1 July 1214. His other tasks were to confirm King John's surrender of the kingdoms and bring those who had offended against the Church to justice. In the restoration of ecclesiastical order, he was to attend especially to supervising elections and filling vacant bishoprics and abbeys with suitable occupants. He stayed until Dec. 1214. *C. & S.* ii pt 1, pp. 20–1.

[8] Stephen Langton, archbishop of Canterbury, had landed on 9 July 1213 (Gervase ii. 108), and had absolved the king from personal excommunication on 20 July 1213.

deferentes^{a1} ad dominum Pandulfum, domini pape camerarium, qui dominum archiepiscopum reuocauerat.[1]

448. Et cum optinuissent Romani priuilegia nostra et omnia sua a domino rege, uocati fuimus edicto peremptorio[2] ut compararemus apud Eboracum. Et missus sum ego illuc procurator, et iterum Norhampton', et postea London'.[3] Et excepi contra eos[4] quod non debebant petere penas quia nos non fuimus in mora nec in culpa, ueluti non habentes aliquos redditus tempore intermedio, eo quod rex omnes possessiones ecclesiasticas^a Anglie tenuerit in manu sua tempore interdicti.[5] Et multis aliis modis excepi contra eos. Vnde tandem composuimus in uigilia omnium sanctorum apud Walingeford[6] quod deberemus dare eis quingentas marcas pro sorte penis et expensis.[7] Et multum placuit domino legato hec | compositio et domino archiepiscopo, qui tunc ibi erant presentes, et confirmata est a domino Pandulfo.[8] Et prefixus est dies solutionis infra octabas Epiphanie.[9]

fo. 176vb

449. *De motione dominorum legati et archiepiscopi contra abbatem eo quod nollet soluere Romanis quingentas marcas*

Cum autem retulissem hanc compositionem domino abbati et conuentui, placuit conuentui. Abbas uero respondit, iurans per reginam angelorum,[10] quod numquam redderet inde unum denarium, et uerum dixit, prophetans sibi malum, quia ante tempus solutionis depositus est. Set precepit quod ego qui eandem pecuniam Rome consumpseram, ut dixit, ipsam Romanis persoluerem. Cum tantum septuaginta marcas in biennio quo ibi steteram mutuo accepissem,[11] ille uero in sex septimanis quibus ibi fuerat quingentas et triginta marcas mutuo accepisset, de quibus omnibus tantum ducentas soluerat.

450. Ego itaque recessi, sicut iniunctum fuit michi, ut nunciarem responsum abbatis domino legato et domino Pandulfo et creditoribus Romanis. Et cum Londoniis illos inuenissem et nunciassem eis

---

^a *corrected from* ? ecclesias

[1] Pandulf, the pope's emissary, arrived in England on 2 July 1211, and then again on May 1213 (*C. & S.* ii pt 1, pp. 12–14).

[2] A final summons.

[3] This might have been at the first of the series of settlement meetings held from 30 Sep. to 2 Oct. (*C. & S.* ii pt 1, p. 21; Wendover iii. 275).

[4] An objection on a point of law.

[5] 1208–14.

[6] Wallingford in Berkshire on 31 Oct.

letters to Pandulf, the pope's chamberlain, who had recalled the archbishop.[1]

448. The Romans had regained possession of our privileges and all their property from the king, and we were then commanded by peremptory summons[2] to attend at York. I was sent there as proctor, then to Northampton, and afterwards to London.[3] I pleaded exception[4] against them on the grounds that they ought not to claim compensation as the delay was not our fault, pointing out that we had had no revenue during the intervening years as the king had held all the ecclesiastical possessions of England in his own hands during the time of the interdict.[5] And I claimed exception against them in many other matters. As a result, we reached agreement finally at Wallingford on the eve of All Saints[6] that we should pay them five hundred marks as their due for compensation and expenses.[7] The legate and the archbishop, who were present then, were very pleased with this settlement, and it was confirmed by Pandulf.[8] It was arranged for payment to be made during the octave of Epiphany.[9]

449. *The anger felt by the legate and archbishop towards the abbot because of his refusal to pay the Romans the five hundred marks*
When I reported this settlement to the abbot and convent, it received the approval of the convent. But the abbot swore by the Queen of the angels[10] that he would never pay them a single penny (and he spoke the truth, prophesying his own downfall, for he was deposed before payment was made). Instead, he commanded that I who had, as he put it, spent the money at Rome, should pay the Romans this sum. But I had received a loan of only seventy marks during the two years that I had stayed there,[11] whereas he had received a loan of five hundred and thirty marks in the six weeks he was there, and had paid back only two hundred marks of the total sum he had received.

450. I left, as ordered, to convey the abbot's reply to the legate as well as to Pandulf and the Roman creditors. I found them in London and gave them his reply. They were very angry, but kept

---

[7] The assembly at Wallingford was held as one of a series of meetings to consider ways to compensate the clergy for their losses. It is recorded that the legate effected a reconciliation there between the king and the northern barons in Nov. 1213; see 'Annales de Dunstaplia', *Ann. Mon.* iii. 40; also Wendover iii. 276, and *Chron. Maj.* ii. 570.

[8] Pandulf, as papal chamberlain, would have had a close relationship with the Roman bankers, and he was therefore the obvious person to ratify the arrangement.

[9] 6 to 13 Jan., presumably 1214.

[10] The blessed Virgin Mary.

[11] For the bonds of twenty and fifty marks, see above, **358** and n.

responsum abbatis. Valde moleste illud tulerunt,[a] conseruantes omnia uerba illa, conferentes ea in corde suo.[1] Nullum tamen certum responsum michi dederunt, set preceperunt ut sequerer eos. Et cum diu moram facerem Londoniis, quadam die post cibum clam recessi apud Croindenn',[2] accipiens mecum fratrem meum uterinum,[3] dicens quod pro negociis eius recederem. Et reliqui Londoniis seruientes abbatis qui semper insidiabantur michi, et locutus sum cum domino Cantuariensi super responsione abbatis. Et cum tunc esset cum eo magister Ricardus decanus Sareberiensis, postmodum episcopus eiusdem loci, et essem ei notissimus quia discipulus fueram quondam archiepiscopi et conscolaris decani,[4] usque ad mediam fere noctem habuimus tractatum super statu et agendis ecclesie nostre.

451. Cum enim adhuc nescirem uoluntatem domini legati, procuraui quod dominus Cantuariensis, ut tutor noster et legatus perpetuus, accederet ad domum nostram et cogeret abbatem ad solutionem predicte pecunie, uel deponeret eum, et proposui ei satis liquidas manifestas et sufficientes rationes ad eius depositionem.

452. *De questione habita coram archiepiscopo super potestate eiusdem in abbatem Eueshamie*

fo. 177[ra] Orta est autem ibi | maxima questio inter nos de potestate domini Cantuariensis in nobis. Ex una parte, propositum fuit quod tutor[5] habet potestatem in capite libero, non ut pupillum exheredet uel in aliquo ledat uel dampnificet, set ut ipsum et patrimonium eius conseruet et tueatur. Non ergo potuit abbatem deponere, set magis, ut in priuilegio continetur, 'si quid sinistre partis inibi compertum fuerit oriri, per ipsius corrigatur industriam et cautelam'.[6] Non ergo per sententiam, set facta inquisitione super eo quod per eius cautelam corrigi non potest, fiat relatio ad dominum papam ut ipse per sententiam corrigat. Non enim aliter esset cenobium Eueshamense

---

[a] *corrected from* retulerunt, *with* re- *expunged*

[1] Luke 2: 19.

[2] On November 7×?18 1213. The archbishop had a manor and a house at Croydon in Surrey. The reference in Langton's itinerary for the archbishop being at Croydon at this time, *Acta Stephani Langton*, ed. K. Major (Canterbury and York Soc. l: London, 1950), p. 144, given as *Ann. Mon.* iv, is incorrect. The source is in fact this text and, so far as we know, it is the only known source.

[3] i.e. they shared the same mother; for example, Aymer de Valence was the uterine or half-brother of King Henry III, as their mother, Isabel of Angoulême, married Hugh X, count of La Marche, after the death of her first husband, King John; GEC x, col. 377.

all those words and pondered them in their hearts.[1] They gave me no
definite reply, but commanded me to follow them. I stayed in
London for some time, but one day after I had eaten, I left secretly
for Croydon,[2] taking with me my uterine brother,[3] saying that I
would go back to deal with his business. In London I left behind the
abbot's servants who were always lying in wait for me. I spoke to the
archbishop of Canterbury on the subject of the abbot's reply. It so
happened that Master Richard [Poore], the dean of Salisbury, and
later its bishop, was with him at that time. He knew me well, as I had
once been a pupil of the archbishop and a fellow-student with him.[4]
We had a discussion that lasted almost till midnight about the state of
our church, and what action needed to be taken.

451. As I still did not know the will of the legate, I made sure that the
archbishop, as our protector and as perpetual legate, should go to our
house and compel the abbot to pay the stated sum of money, or to
depose him, and I provided him with very clear evidence and
adequate reasons for deposing him.

452. *A debate held before the archbishop into the question of his power
over the abbot of Evesham*

A major discussion was begun there amongst us into the question of
the archbishop of Canterbury's power over us. On the one hand, the
argument was put that, as our protector,[5] he has full power in chief,
not to disinherit his 'ward' nor harm or damage him in any way, but
to save and protect him and his patrimony. He could not, therefore,
depose the abbot, but rather, as is stated in the privilege, 'if anything
of an evil nature was found to have occurred there, it was to be
corrected through his diligence and care'.[6] Hence, it is not for him to
pronounce sentence, but to hold an inquiry about a matter that cannot
be corrected by his care, so that he may make a report to the pope for
the pope himself to correct it by sentence. For if the abbot could be
deposed by any other than the Roman pontiff himself, then the

---

[4] Richard Poore, dean of Salisbury, 1197 to 1214, bishop of Chichester 1215; trans. to
Salisbury 1217, to Durham 1228, d. 15 Apr. 1237. A noted theologian, administrator, and
reformer, he was probably responsible for the final stages in the composition of Osmund's
Institutio, when dean of Salisbury; see Greenway, *Fasti*, iv. *Salisbury*, pp. 10–11. As bishop
of Durham, see *Fasti*, ii. *Monastic Cathedrals*, pp. 30, 31. On his episcopate at Salisbury,
see B. Kemp, 'God's and the King's Good Servant: Richard Poore, bishop of Salisbury,
1217–28', *Peritia*, xii (1998), 359–78. Both Thomas and Richard Poore had been pupils of
Archbishop Stephen Langton at Paris.

[5] See above, 255, 391.

[6] Cf. above, the first privilege of Pope Constantine, 295, 321.

solo Romano pontifici et ecclesie Romane subiectum, si abbas ab alio quam ab ipso posset deponi.

453. Ex aduerso autem dictum fuit quod quamuis dominus archiepiscopus sit tutor ecclesie Euesham, nichilominus tamen dominus papa curam animarum eiusdem loci ei ut suo uicario uel legato commisit, sicut in eodem priuilegio continetur.[1] Ergo, clarescentibus culpis, uidetur habere potestatem deponendi abbatem sicut habet ipse delegans. Ad quod fuit responsum quod fortassis hoc locum haberet nisi eius specialis legatio per presentiam*a* generalis legati esset suspensa.

454. Ex aduerso uero fuit dictum e contrario quod generalis legatio non extendebat se ad Eueshamensem ecclesiam, quia in ea de speciali nulla facta fuit mentio. Nobis itaque in hunc modum altercantibus et dubitantibus, nulla super hiis certa habita diffinitione, non proficiens in proposito meo recessi. Et secutus sum dominum legatum, sepe sollicitans eum super cogendo abbatem ad solutionem predicte peccunie, nullum tamen certum responsum potui ab eo recipere donec uenissemus Oxoniam.

455. *Qualiter legatus preceperit Thome monacho quod statum ecclesie Eueshamensis ei intimaret, increpans eum quod absque iussione hoc non fecerit*

Cum igitur esset sero die una sabbatorum[2] postquam uenimus Oxoniam, assidente ei predicto decano Saresbirriensi[3] et domino Pandulfo, uocauit me dominus legatus. Et oculo obliquo et uultu toruo respiciens me, dixit michi, 'Miserrime hominum, qui tantus habebaris in curia Romana, quomodo nunc conuersus es in tantam perfidiam ut, qui tunc tam fideliter tam constanter stetisti pro ecclesia tua, nunc uides eam subuerti et non compateris? Vt quid liberasti eam | a seruitute seculari si non liberes eam a peccatis et seruitute diabolica? Putasne nos nescire quod periit apud uos religio, et quod in tantam incidisti miseriam quod non habetis iam ubi caput reclinetis,[4] et tu negligenter agis? Immo malitiose, quia faues abbati tuo et agis cum eo qui est scandalum tocius religionis.' Et adiecit, 'Per beatum Petrum, ueniemus ad uos in uirga furoris,[5] et ita primo puniemus te

fo. 177rb

---

a per pres *written over an erasure* (*s. xiii'*)

[1] See above, 321.
[2] The nearest Saturday before the deposition on 22 Nov. was the 16th; see below, 500 n. 4, for the date of the deposition.

convent of Evesham would not be subject to the Roman pontiff and the church of Rome alone.

453. On the other hand, it was said that although the archbishop is protector of the church of Evesham, the pope has nevertheless entrusted him with the care of souls in that place as his vicar and legate, as is stated in the privilege.[1] Therefore, when the abbot has clearly committed offences, it appears that the archbishop has the power to depose the abbot, just as he who delegates has. The reply to this was that perhaps he did have this right, except when his special legation was suspended by the presence of a general legate.

454. Against this the contrary argument was put that the jurisdiction of a general legate did not extend to Evesham church, because no mention had been made of special jurisdiction in that church. No definite decision was reached on this question after all this debating and indecision, and I left without making any progress in my proposal. But I pursued the legate, urging him again and again to force the abbot to pay the stated sum of money, but I could get no definite response from him until we arrived at Oxford.

455. *The legate commands Thomas the monk to inform him of the state of the church of Evesham, and rebukes him for not doing this before being commanded to do so*
One Saturday evening[2] after we came to Oxford, the dean of Salisbury already mentioned[3] and Pandulf were sitting beside the legate when he called me to him. Looking askance at me angrily, he said 'What a knave you are! How is it that a man who was so highly regarded as you at the Roman curia can have become so disloyal that, having stood up so faithfully and resolutely for your church, you can now watch it being ruined and be unmoved? To what purpose have you set it free from earthly slavery if you have not freed it from sin and slavery to the devil? Do you think we are not aware that religion has perished among you, that you have plunged into such misery that you have nowhere to lay your heads[4] and are so neglectful in your behaviour? No, rather are you sinful in your behaviour, for you are supporting your abbot and associating with a man who is a scandal to the whole of religion.' He further added, 'By the blessed Peter, we shall come to you with the rod of anger,[5] and will punish you first for

---

[3] Richard Poore, see above, 450 and n. 4.
[4] Matt. 8: 20.   [5] Isa. 10: 5.

eo quod hec nobis non reuelasti, quod ceteri timebunt quicumque audierint uerbum hoc.'

456. Ego uero cum hec audissem magis timui, et uoce flebili respondi, 'Domine, quid me uis facere? Deo teste, ego non faueo abbati meo, teste domino decano, qui aliquando audiuit me pro posse meo impugnare facta eius.' Et cum perhibuisset michi testimonium decanus, quasi per hoc mitigatus, legatus dixit michi suppressa uoce, quia fere omnia alia audierat clericus abbatis, qui tunc aduenerat ut michi insidiaretur: 'Vade et confirma fratres tuos, et non timeas, quia in spiritu mansuetudinis ueniemus ad te.[1] Set caueas tibi quod per te sciamus ueritatem status interioris et exterioris ecclesie uestre, et bene tibi erit. Si autem per alium, male tibi erit, quia nouimus te omnia bene nosse.' Et subiecit, 'Vide ne aliquis sciat uerbum istud preter te solum.'

457. Ego uero gaudens recessi, et mane[2] ueni Bradewellam. Et inuento ibi abbate nuntiaui ei probra que dixerat michi legatus, uerumptamen aduentum legati non reuelaui ei. Et cum clericus eius perhibuisset michi testimonium super hiis que audierat, abbas suscepit me quasi in ampliorem gratiam, quia probra illa uidebar pro eo sustinuisse. Et cum uellem recedere Eueshamiam, non permisit, audierat enim quod dominus legatus transitum faciens per partes illas iturus esset Bristollum. Die autem sequenti[3] audiuimus quod ueniret Brueriam[4] et iuimus[a] ei obuiam. Et recepit nos uerbis pacificis, et cum audissemus sermonem eius in capitulo, licentiati ab eo recessimus, adhuc putantes quod Bristollum tenderet. Et ecce nobis egredientibus per portam abbatie, uenit quidam nuncius deferens abbati litteras domini legati continentes | quod in crastino ueniret Eueshamiam.[5] Quas cum audisset dominus abbas statim concidit cor eius, et dixit, 'Quid sibi uult tam subitum mandatum cum nichil inde dixerit nobis legatus in recessu nostro?'

fo. 177[va]

458. Et conuersus ad me, dixit me omnia ista machinatum fuisse, et iuimus Bradewellam. Cum uero comedissemus apud Bradewellam festinanter, iam inclinata die, iuimus Eueshamiam, et[b] semper in itinere conferentes adinuicem de iis que accidere poterant,[6] abbate

---

[a] Brueriam et iuimus *written over an erasure* (iuimus *extends into the margin*)   [b] et *expunged*

---

[1] 1 Cor. 4: 21.   [2] 17/18 Nov.
[3] 18/19 Nov.
[4] A Cistercian house in Oxfordshire, about six miles from Broadwell, five miles north of Burford, and one mile north-west of Lyneham.

having failed to reveal to us what is happening, so that others who hear this story will be afraid.'

456. When I heard this I was much alarmed, and replied tearfully, 'My lord, what do you wish me to do? As God is my witness, I do not support my abbot, and the dean, who has heard me time and again censure his deeds with all the power in me, can testify to this.' The dean bore witness to what I said, and the legate, apparently mollified by this, addressed me with a softer voice, for the abbot's clerk, who had heard almost everything else, had just arrived to spy on me: 'Go and encourage your brethren, and do not be afraid, for we shall come to you in a spirit of gentleness.[1] But for your own sake see to it that we learn from you the truth about the inner and outer state of your church, and all will be well with you. If we learn about it from another, it will be the worse for you, for we know that you are in possession of the facts.' He added, 'See that no one else knows of our conversation.'

457. I was well pleased when I left him, and the following morning[2] I went to Broadwell [Glos.]. Finding the abbot there, I told him truthfully what the legate had said to me, but did not inform him that the legate was coming. When the abbot's clerk had presented evidence of what he had heard concerning me, the abbot appeared to receive me with better grace, as he thought I had withheld the truth for his sake. I now wanted to return to Evesham, but he would not permit this, for he had heard that the legate was travelling in the vicinity, and was likely to go to Bristol. The following day[3] we heard that he was going to Bruern [abbey][4] and we went to meet him. He received us amiably, and when we had heard his address in chapter, we left with his permission, still thinking that he was making for Bristol. In fact, as we were leaving the gate of the abbey [of Bruern], a messenger brought the abbot a letter from the legate stating that he would be coming to Evesham the next day.[5] As soon as the abbot heard this his heart sank, and he said, 'What does he want with so sudden a command when he said nothing of this to us when we left him?'

458. Turning to me, he accused me of having plotted it all, and we made for Broadwell. When we had dined hastily at Broadwell, the day now declining, we went to Evesham, always conversing with each other on the journey about those things which could happen,[6] with

---

[5] 19/20 Nov.   [6] Cf. Luke 24: 14.

crebro increpante me de subito aduentu legati. Et quamuis constanter negarem hoc per me factum non fuisse, sepe comminatus est michi, unde ualde timui ne occideret me,[1] erat enim nox. Et uenimus Eueshamiam.

459. In crastino uero circa horam terciam[2] uenit dominus legatus, et recepto eo cum sollempni processione, ea die non est ingressus capitulum. Interim tam ex parte abbatis quam ex nostra uaria facta sunt conuenticula et consilia. Ego uero paucos ex fratribus, quos noui fidelissimos, de uoluntate legati consolatus sum, non tamen aperte alicui uoluntatem legati reuelaui.

460. Altera autem die[3] ingressus est dominus legatus capitulum cum magno comitatu clericorum suorum et plurimorum abbatum.[4] Et primum facto sermone, dixit: 'Multa mala audiuimus de domo ista et, Deo teste, ad hoc uenimus ut statum eius corrigamus. Surgat ergo aliquis*a* uestrum et dicat nobis statum huius ecclesie tam interiorem quam exteriorem. Nec parcat alicui, et si quid forte minus dixerit, precipimus, sub pena excommunicationis, quod alii suppleant.' Nullo itaque ad hanc iussionem surgente, timui michi. Erant enim oculi eius, et fere omnium fratrum, intenti in me, supersedi tamen, secundam expectans iussionem.

461. *Qualiter Thomas monachus accusauerit abbatem coram legato*
Tunc conuersus ad me dominus legatus dixit, 'Tu qui stetisti in curia Romana pro ecclesia ista, surge.' Et cum stans, excusarem me per insufficientiam et ignorantiam, adiciens quod multi erant seniores me et qui melius nouerant statum ecclesie quam ego, | cunctis fere fratribus acclamantibus ut preciperet michi quod loquerer. Precepit ut procederem in medium, et dixit michi, 'Nemini os tuum nec capiti nec menbris parcat, quia,*b* per beatum Petrum, si cuiquam peperceris non parcemus tibi.' Ego uero quamuis bene premeditatus, sepius enim super hiis mecum deliberaueram, tamen, quia ambigua sunt fata causarum, timens exitum cause nostre, tremens et stupefactus flendo etiam in hunc modum assumpsi parabolam meam, dicens: 'Quamuis

fo. 177ᵛᵇ

---

a ex *erased after* aliquis   *b* parcat quia *written over an erasure, and extending into the margin*

[1] Cf. Acts 23: 25.
[2] 19/20 Nov.
[3] 20/21 Nov.
[4] Wendover (iii. 274–5, *Chron. Maj.* ii. 569) comments on his large retinue and household, saying that he arrived in England with seven mounted attendants who soon became fifty in number. This was, of course, a common complaint. The attendant abbots

the abbot frequently reproaching me about the sudden arrival of the legate. Although I constantly denied that I had had any hand in it, I kept threatening me, and I was very much afraid that he would murder me,[1] for it was night-time. We then arrived at Evesham.

459. Around nine o'clock the next morning[2] the legate arrived, and he was received in solemn procession, but he did not that day enter the chapter-house. Meanwhile there were various assemblies and meetings held not only on the abbot's part, but on our's too. I reassured a few of the brethren, whom I knew to be very loyal to me, about the legate's intentions, yet I did not openly reveal them to anyone.

460. On the second day[3] the legate entered the chapter-house with a large retinue of his own clerks and several abbots.[4] He first addressed us in these words: 'We have received many bad reports about this house and, God being our witness, we have come here to correct the state of affairs in this place. Therefore, let one of you stand up and tell us about the state of this church, not only the inner state but also the outer. Spare no one, and if anything by chance is omitted, we command, under pain of excommunication, that others supply the omissions.' When no one stood up in response to this command, I feared for myself. The eyes of the legate, and of almost all the brethren, were focused on me, but I sat tight, awaiting a second command.

461. *Thomas the monk accuses the abbot before the legate*
Turning to me, the legate said, 'You who stood up in the Roman curia on behalf of this church, stand up now.' I did so, excusing myself on the grounds of weakness and ignorance, adding that there were many brethren senior to me who had better knowledge than I of the state of the church, but almost all the brethren cried out that he should command me to speak. So he commanded me to stand before him, and said to me, 'Let your lips spare no one, whether he be a superior or subordinate, for by the blessed Peter, if you spare anyone we shall not spare you.' Although I had given much thought to this beforehand, for I had often pondered over it in my mind, yet, because the outcome of cases is never sure—and I feared the outcome of this case—I began my story tearfully in fear and trembling: 'Although

on this occasion were the abbots of St Mary's, York, and Selby (both Benedictine), and the abbot of S. Martino al Cimino in Tuscany, diocese of Viterbo; see below, **488** and nn. 5–7 (p. 460).

secundum iura ciuilia et canonica non liceat subditis prelatos suos passim accusare,[1] tamen ex certis causis accusare eos conceditur eisdem. De quibus causis aliquas in medium deducam que dominum abbatem nostrum et nos ad presens contingunt.

462. 'Si igitur uita prelati tam inhonesta sit qualis est uita abbatis nostri, quod per subsequentia, Deo fauente, omnibus luce clarius liquere faciam, quod non tantum subditis, set etiam aliis prope positis, scandalum ex ea generetur. Locus est subditis accusationi, ne si forte uitia eius non impugnauerint, uel uitiis eius consentire uel eisdem ipsi laborare credantur. Et quia iuris periti estis, non est necesse me circa huiusmodi iura allegare, ne tedio uos afficiam, quamuis ad excusationem michi sufficiat quod licet monachis iura ignorare. Licet etiam subditis prelatos accusare quando per eorum accusationem graue periculum uitatur, uel maxima utilitas adquiritur, aut si non accusauerint ipsis uel ecclesie graue incommodum uel periculum imminet, uel maxima utilitas amittitur.[2] Que omnia in casu presenti locum habere per subsequentia manifeste probabo. Quamuis hec omnia ex habundanti premiserim, cum iussio superioris non tantum ab omni culpa in hac parte me excuset, set etiam agendi contra abbatem necessitatem ingerat.

463. 'Igitur quia scriptum est quod iustus in principio accusator est sui,[3] salua pace quorundam fratrum nostrorum quorum mens ita in ordine solidata est quod nullo terrenorum impulsu ab eius obser-

fo. 178ra uatione possunt separari, monasticus ordo |[a] deperiit fere apud nos, et, ut uerum fatear, sicut ex subsequentibus patebit, ob defectum administrationis exteriorum humanitati fragilitati et infirmitati nostre necessariorum. Cum enim silentium quod est cultus religionis locis et horis statutis obseruare deberemus, fame et siti afflicti non tantum conquerentes loquimur tempore et loco silentii, uerum etiam, quod beatus Benedictus maxime prohibet, incessanter fere murmuramus.[4] Per multos enim dies, quorum numerum non memoriter teneo, in

---

[a] Nota istam columpnam *top marg.*(?s. xiv)

---

[1] *Code* 9.1, 'Qui accusare non possunt'; *Decretum*, C 2 qu. 7 cc. 10–12 (Friedberg, i col. 485), condemns accusations against superiors. Cf. Matt. 10: 24 ' the disciple is not above his master', and W.Hartmann, 'Discipulus non est super magistrum (Matth.10, 24). Zur Rolle Laien und der niederen Kleriker im Investiturstreit', in *Papsttum, Kirche und Recht im Mittelalter: Festschrift für Horst Fuhrmann zum 65. Geburtstag*, ed. H. Mordek (Tübingen, 1991), pp. 187–200, who traces the general conception that superiors should not be accused by inferiors, e.g. bishops by the people (p. 191 n. 22, citing Anselm of Lucca) or clerks by laymen (p. 188 n. 6, citing Burchard of Worms).

[2] See *Decretum*, C 2 qu. 7 (Friedberg, i cols. 483–502).

civil and canon law forbid subordinates to accuse their leaders indiscriminately,[1] nevertheless they are permitted in certain cases to do so. I shall therefore present some of these cases that concern our abbot and ourselves at the present time.

462. 'If the life of a prelate is as dishonourable as that of our abbot— and with God's help I shall make it abundantly clear from the following evidence that it is—then not only his subordinates, but also those near him in rank, are involved in the disgrace. There is a place therefore for subordinates to accuse him, in case they should be thought to acquiesce in his vices or to be labouring under the same vices themselves, if they are not seen to be condemning them. Since you are men who are learned in the law, it is unnecessary for me to argue my rights in this sort of case, and I do not wish to bore you, but it would be sufficient excuse that monks are allowed to be ignorant of the law! Subordinates are also permitted to accuse superiors when serious peril is prevented by their accusations, or great benefit accrues from them, or, when serious harm or peril threatens them or their church, if they do not accuse them, or indeed great benefit is lost thereby.[2] I shall give clear proof in the following arguments that all these circumstances pertain in the present case. I am saying more than I need in mentioning all these facts at the outset of my speech, as the command of a superior not only exonerates me of all blame in this respect, but also imposes upon me the necessity of proceeding against the abbot.

463. 'Scripture has it that he who accuses himself is just,[3] so I say that, apart from some of our brethren whose minds have always been so unshakeable in the Order that no earthly force can prevent them from holding it fast, monastic order has almost perished amongst us and, to speak the truth, as will become clear from the following, this situation has arisen from a lack in the provision of the material things necessary for our human life, and from our frailty and weakness. Although we ought to observe the silence which the practice of our religion requires at specified hours and places, yet, because we are suffering from hunger and thirst, we not only speak words of complaint at times and in places of silence, but also grumble almost incessantly, which the blessed Benedict particularly forbids.[4] For many days—I cannot remember the exact number—we spent our life

[3] Cf. Prov. 18: 17.
[4] *RSB* caps. 5 (on obedience), 6 (on silence), and 23 (excommunication for faults, including murmurers).

solo pane et aqua, ob defectum pulmentorum et quorumlibet aliorum ciborum et ceruisie, uitam duximus in refectorio.[1] Panis autem qui nos pascebat sepe talis erat de quo etiam minimi seruientes abbatis edere recusabant, cum ipse et seruientes sui pane per optimo et aliis cibis delicatissimis reficerentur. Et cum sepius abbas reficeretur ante capitulum, nos pro defectu cibariorum ieiunauimus usque ad meridiem estatis tempore, in hieme uero usque ad uesperam. Et, ut breuiter dicam, a multis annis retro raro contigit quod horis statutis simul haberemus panem, ceruisiam et pulmenta; immo fere nunquam contigit quin cum aliquo defectu ad mensam sederimus. Nam si aliquo casu, quod tamen raro contigit, esculentum et poculentum habuimus ut miseram uitam duceremus, quamuis rarissime secundum abusum[a] nostrum hec habuimus, fere semper contigit quod ligna ad coquendum cibum defuerunt uel sal ad condiendum. Proh dolor! Vnde sepissime contigit ut si quatuor oua habuimus quartum pro sale in uillam misimus.'

464. Et de omnibus hiis certos defectus, certos dies et horas certas expressi, quorum omnium modo expressos casus ponere esset tediosum et inutile. Quibus tunc expressis abbas non potuit eis contradicere, set ex paupertate hec omnia contigisse asserebat.'Preterea, pater sancte, opus Dei ad quod uenimus in ecclesia Dei fere apud nos defecit. Quia cum non sit nostre consuetudinis quod quis sine frocco uel cuculla uel aliis uestimentis ordinatis conuentum fo. 178rb sequatur, paucissimi sunt ex nobis, ut hic uidere potestis, | quibus non desint frocci uel cuculle uel alia uestimenta ordinata, unde pauci ex nobis ecclesiam, claustrum, uel refectorium sequuntur; set in infirmaria pro defectu uestimentorum morantur.'[2]

465. Vnde ad probandum uerbum istud, ut ego opinabar, capellanum abbatis uocauit ad se, et eo palpato inuenit eum in sola staminia[3] et cuculla, hyemis, ut erat tempore. 'Preterea, pater sancte, cum secundum traditionem nostram non liceat nobis absque femoralibus

---

a written over an erasure

[1] *RSB* (cap. 39) specified adequate food, although gluttony was to be avoided, and frugality was to be observed in all circumstances. Cap. 40 advocated a similar moderation in drinking wine—abstinence brought its own special reward. These regulations were scarcely followed by the 13th cent., but the point was clear; namely that St Benedict had not intended his monks to starve.

[2] *RSB* cap. 55 (on clothes and shoes) required basic clothing: tunics and cowls (thicker in winter), belts, shoes, and stockings. The frock (long with ample sleeves) and the cowl (also long, but sleeveless or with short sleeves) formed the two outer garments known as

in the refectory on bread and water alone, because of the lack of pottage and certain other foods and ale.[1] The bread which sustained us was often so poor that even the meanest servants of the abbot refused to eat any of it, whereas he and his servants regaled themselves on the very best bread as well as other delicious food. Although the abbot had often had his meal before the time for chapter, we went hungry until noon in the summer because of a lack of food, and even until evening in winter. In brief, for many years now it has been a rare occurrence for us to have bread, ale, and pottage together at the hours laid down; indeed, there has hardly ever been an occasion when we have not sat down at table without some food missing. If by some chance—and this rarely occurred—we ever had anything edible or drinkable to enable us to drag out our miserable existence, although we did have such things very rarely given the extent to which we had been abused, it was almost always the case that we had no wood with which to cook the food or salt to flavour it. Oh, what misery! Hence, it very often happened that if we had four eggs we sent the fourth one into the town in exchange for salt.'

464. Of all the things we suffered, I have given particular examples, particular dates and times, for it would be tedious and pointless now to give full details of all of them. Once they had been expressly mentioned, the abbot could not contradict them, but declared that they had all occurred because of poverty. I continued, 'Moreover, holy father, the work of God for which we entered the church of God has virtually ceased. It is contrary to our custom for any monk to follow conventual routine without wearing the frock, cowl, or other approved clothing, but there are very few of us, as you can see here, who do not lack frocks, cowls, or other approved clothing, so only a few of us go to the church, the cloister, or the refectory; most stay in the infirmary for lack of garments.'[2]

465. To establish the truth of what I said, in my view, the legate summoned to his presence the abbot's chaplain, and when he had examined him he found him to be wearing a single shirt of linsey-woolsey[3] and a cowl, in spite of it being winter-time. 'Furthermore, holy father,' I continued, 'our tradition does not allow us to celebrate

---

'the habit'. They were never worn together. Both of them had hoods. See B. F. Harvey, *Monastic Dress in the Middle Ages: Precept and Practice* (The Trustees of the William Urry Memorial Trust, Chapter Library of Canterbury Cathedral, 1988), pp. 14–15.

[3] A textile material of mixed flax and wool, a kind of serge.

missas celebrare,[1] et multi ex nobis eodem careant uestimento, ob defectum eorum multorum sacramentorum celebratio est omissa, quorum numerum propter multitudinem ignoro. Proh pudor! Capellanus etiam abbatis, non ille quem modo probastis, set ille alius', ex nomine illum designans cum esset ibi presens, 'cum missam coram abbate celebrare deberet et femoralibus careret, accommodauit ei abbas femoralia sua, cum missam celebrasset restituenda.

466. 'Ex hiis etiam defectibus, pater sancte, peiores exordinationes supradictis nobis contigerunt. Quia libere discurrebamus quocumque uolebamus, nec poterat prior uel alii custodes ordinis[2] nos libere corripere, nobis respondentibus quod non poterant nobis uictum et uestitum inuenire, et cum non haberemus quid in refectorio comederemus, in thalamis et angulis carnes comedimus. Et quidam, quasi "oues sine pastore"[3] errantes, discurrebant per patriam ad abbacias uicinas, alii autem ad cognatos et amicos, querentes ab eis aliquod miserie sue remedium, quorum ego primus sum. Et facti sumus quasi girouagi,[4] nemine prohibente quia necessitate cogente. Vnde pessimam notam infamie incurrimus, illis qui causam discursus nostri nesciebant dicentibus quod causa libidinis explende hec fecimus. Abbas uero et complices sui omnibus uiribus suis infamiam nostram aumentabant, nec abbas super hiis nos corripiebat, nescio quo ductus zelo, uel quia | non intellexit quod curam animarum suscepit, uel forte si aliquando super eodem uitio eum accusaremus obiciendo nobis idem ab hac accusatione nos repelleret; uel, quod melius credo, semel a facie Dei proiectus[5] uoluit et alios secum in intentum deuenire.

467. 'Vnde, ut michi uidetur, exordinationes nostre magis in capud eius debent redundare qui dedit occasionem delinquendi, nec impediuit cum posset nec prohibuit cum deberet, quam illorum qui deliquerunt. Ospitalitas, pater sancte, aput nos penitus deperiit, preterquam de diuitibus. "Quorum terror sibi exigit honorem", cum secundum regulam beati Benedicti pauperes "in quibus Deus magis suscipitur" suscipere et fouere deberemus.[6]

fo. 178[va]

---

[1] Drawers (like long johns; see Harvey, 'Monastic dress', p. 26) were specified in the Rule only for wear on journeys, but clearly by this time it was thought inappropriate to celebrate Mass without them.

[2] Prior, subprior, third prior, i.e. those in charge of discipline; see above, 402.

[3] Num. 27: 17.

[4] *RSB* cap. 1, where St Benedict discusses the four kinds of monks of whom the *Girouagi* are the worst, wandering from place to place, ever roaming and without stability. Only the first type, the Cenobites, received his approval and attention.

[5] Cf. 1 Kgs. (1 Sam.) 13. 12: 'And I have not pleased the face of the Lord'; and possibly

masses whout drawers,[1] so, as many of us are without that garment many masses have not been celebrated, though I cannot tell you the exact number for there were so many of them. The shame of it! Even the abbot's chaplain, not the one you examined just now, but another'—I indicated him by name, for he was present—'whose duty it was to celebrate mass before the abbot, lacked breeches, so the abbot lent him his own, to be returned when the celebration was over.

466. 'As a result of these deficiencies, holy father, we perpetrated worse infringements of the Rule than those just described. We roamed about freely wherever we chose, and neither the prior nor any other of the masters of order[2] found it easy to stop us, for our response was that they could not find us food or clothing, and as we had nothing in the refectory to eat, we ate meat in rooms and secluded spots. Some, wandering like "sheep without a shepherd",[3] roamed throughout the land visiting neighbouring abbeys, others went to relations and friends, seeking from them some relief for their misery, and I was amongst the first of these to do that. We became like itinerant monks,[4] nobody saying us nay, for necessity was the spur. So we earned ourselves a bad reputation, for those who did not know the reason for our roaming said that we were doing it to gratify our lust. The abbot and his associates did all they could to blacken our name more, but, motivated by some sort of envy, he did not rebuke us for what we were doing, either because he did not realize that he had taken on responsibility for our souls, or because, if at any time we should accuse him, he might successfully rebut any accusations on the same count; or, as is most likely I think, he wished intentionally to drag others down with him once he was banished from the face of God.[5]

467. 'In my opinion, therefore, our infringements of the Rule ought to be laid at his door rather than at the door of those who did wrong, for he was the cause of our wrongdoing in failing to prevent us when he could have done, and for not forbidding us when he should have done. Hospitality, holy father, utterly perished amongst us, except towards the rich. "The terror they inspired demanded our respect" for them, though, according to the Rule of the blessed Benedict, we should have welcomed and nurtured the poor, "amongst whom God is more welcome".[6]

Dan. 9. 3: 'And I set my face unto the Lord God.' Thomas probably has a scriptural allusion in mind for rejection from the face of God, but there seems to be no exact scriptural quotation.   [6] *RSB* cap. 53, of the reception of guests.

468. 'Et non tantum pauperibus, uerum etiam seruientibus nostris a multis annis retro debita alimenta subtraxit abbas noster, unde "multi fame perierunt".[1] Et non tantum seruientes set etiam monachi, ut ipsi ante mortem confitebantur, et dicebant quod si haberent sufficientem procurationem possent adhuc uiuere, set non erat qui daret eis',[2] et nomina eorum expressi. 'Quare etiam usque in hodiernum diem pauperes elemosina nostra defraudantur.[a] Nam de reliquiis ciborum nostrorum pascimus seruientes nostros sine quibus esse non possumus, quamuis tercia pars panis abbatie huius preter reliquias ad seruientes et pauperes ex antiquorum statutis[3] pertineat, due uero partes ad nos et ad hospites.

469. 'Sarta autem tecta, pater sancte, non habemus, unde si forte quacunque parua pluuia inundauerit nec ubi diuina celebremus extra uoltas habemus, que etiam iam ruinam minantur, nec ubi capud nostrum reclinemus.[4] Ad que nullam aliam probationem nisi fidem occulatam induco, et si ante recessum uestrum pluuia inundauerit sanctitas uestra experimento approbabit quod uerum dico. Redditum enim quindecim marcarum ad cooperiendam ecclesiam et domos ei
fo. 178vb adiacentes assignatarum, et etiam redditus centum marcarum |[b] officiis nostris deputatarum, a multo tempore retro annuatim nobis abstulit abbas noster, per quos omnes predicti defectus, ob quos predicte exordinationes oriuntur, deberent suppleri si eosdem redditus habuerimus.'

470. Et expressi quantum de cellario et quantum de coquina et quantum de aliis officiis nobis annuatim abstulit et quod hec omnia in suam abyssum conuertit,[5] et quod diceret iactitando quod ita prouidebit sibi quod numquam accusationem nostram coram aliquo iudice timebit. Et ad probationem ablatorum, cum testimonio fratrum, protuli scriptum in quo redditus offitiis nostris assignati continentur sigillo capituli et abbatis munitum.[6] Et cum legissem in eo quod abbas iuuerat se omnia in eodem contenta obseruaturum, adieci, 'Si predicta, pater sancte, ad abbatis depositionem non sufficiunt, que tamen michi sufficere uidentur, ego eum de periurio accuso, quod uidelicet contra iuramentum suum ueniendo predicta nobis abstulerit.'

---

[a] marg. defraudacio elemo[?sine] (s. xv)   [b] tempore deposicionis abbatis top marg.
(s. xv)

---

[1] 1 Macc. 13: 49.   [2] Cf. Luke 15: 16.
[3] This stipulation is not included in the Customs.
[4] Matt. 8: 20.   [5] Rev. 20: 3.

468. 'But it is not only from the poor that our abbot has withdrawn rightful sustenance for many years now, but also from our servants, so that "many have perished of hunger".[1] And it is not only the servants but also the monks, as they themselves admitted before they died, when they said that if they had had sufficient sustenance they could still live, but there was no one who would give to them'[2]—and I gave details of their names. 'So it is that the poor are still cheated of our alms even to the present day. For we feed our servants, without whom we could not exist, on the left-overs of our food, though a third of this abbey's bread in addition to the left-overs belongs by ancient statute[3] to the servants and the poor, and two-thirds to us and our guests.

469. 'Our roofs, holy father, are in a bad state of repair so that, if a shower of rain penetrates them, we have nowhere to celebrate the divine offices except in the vaulted parts of the church, and even these are now threatened with ruin, so we have nowhere to lay our heads.[4] I offer no other proof of this than that which you can see with your own eyes, and if the rain comes in before you leave, your Holiness will prove by experience the truth of what I say. The revenue of fifteen marks assigned to roof the church and the houses adjacent to it, and also the revenue of one hundred marks allocated to our obediences, have for a long time now been appropriated every year by our abbot for himself, when the deficiencies I have already mentioned (which have been the cause of the infringements of the Rule) should have been met by these revenues if we had received them.'

470. I detailed the amounts that the abbot had taken from us annually, from the cellar, the kitchen, and other offices, and said that he had diverted them to his own bottomless pit,[5] and had boasted that he would so provide for himself as never to have to fear any accusation of ours before any judge. As proof of what he had taken from us I produced, along with the testimony of the brethren, the document in which the revenues assigned to our offices were listed, ratified by the seal of the chapter and of the abbot.[6] After reading in it that the abbot had sworn to observe everything contained in that document, I added, 'If what I have previously stated is insufficient, holy father, to depose the abbot—though I think it sufficient—I charge him with perjury, in that he has broken his oath in divesting us of the revenues I have stated.'

---

[6] The 'dispositio' which both abbot and convent had sealed (see above, **395–7**), as approved by the legate John of Ferentino.

471. Et cum requireret dominus legatus ab eo quare hec ita fecisset, solam allegauit paupertatem ad sui excusationem. Ego uero e contrario euidenter monstraui ipsum omnibus bonis temporalibus habundare et deliciis affluere. Quibus cum respondere non posset precepit legatus ut ad alia procederem, et dixi, 'Sunt multe alie cause, pater sancte, quare deponi debet abbas noster. Primo, quia per hostium non ingressus est in ouile ouium, set aliunde.[1] Nam per regiam potestatem intrusit se, non electus a conuentu isto; sicut ipse sepe dicere consueuit quod non per nos, uocans nos canes,[2] adeptus est abbatiam istam, set quod rex dedit eam sibi pro seruitio suo. Quod non solum per nos sanctitati uestre patebit, set etiam per sacrum collegium ecclesie Christi Cantuarie, ubi aliquando fuit monachus. Set propter facinora sua ibi in carcerem est detrusus, a quo tandem liberatus per cloacas aufugit. Vnde domo illa priuatus, a nullo col|legio fuit requisitus uel assumptus. Set et postquam inde aufugerat per potestatem archiepiscopi possessiones monachorum illorum inuasit et bona diripuit. Vnde adhuc petunt ab eo monachi Cantuarie mille marcas. Et cum ita in *possessiones illorum se intrusisset dicens se ab archiepiscopo factum priorem, duos fratres missos ad archiepiscopum capi fecit et a se diuisos arctiori custodie mancipari.* Permisit hec omnia tunc temporis archiepiscopus Baldewinus quia maxima contentio fuit tunc inter illum et monachos suos pro capella de Hakentone.[3]

fo. 179ra

472. 'Est etiam, pater sancte, abbas noster simoniacus, nam decanatum huius ecclesie et duas capellas de Baddeseia et de Bretfortone cuidam capellano Alueredo nomine[4] uendidit, nobis ab inicio ignorantibus. Quod cum idem capellanus post aliquot annos nobis esset confessus, de consilio nostro illis renuntiauit. Et tunc uendidit abbas easdem capellas Galfrido de Oxonia, filio creditoris sui, nobis contradicentibus. Et cum post aliquot annos idem clericus moreretur, pater eius repetiit a nobis et adhuc repetit quinquaginta marcas quas dicit filium suum non percepisse de capellis illis. Obedientiarios etiam nostros palam pro pecunia instituit.' Et expressi quantum ab illo et quantum ab alio, immo a multis aliis, acceperat. Quod cum

---

a–a [posses]siones . . . mancipari *written over an erasure*

[1] John 10: 1.
[2] See above, 189.
[3] See above, 185–7, for a detailed account of Norreis's previous career and appointment as abbot of Evesham.

471. When the legate asked him why he had done this, he pleaded poverty alone as his excuse. To counter this I gave clear proof that he possessed an abundance of this world's goods and an excess of delicious food. When the abbot was unable to refute what I said, the legate commanded me to proceed to other matters, and I continued, 'There are many other reasons, holy father, why our abbot should be deposed. First, because he did not enter the sheepfold by the door, but by another way.[1] He forced his way in by using the power of the king, for he was not elected by this convent; as he himself often used to say, he obtained his abbacy not through us—"dogs" he called us[2]—but because the king gave it to him in return for his service. This will be made clear to your holiness not only by us, but also by the sacred college of Christ Church, Canterbury, where he was once a monk. Because of his misdeeds there he was imprisoned, but he gained his freedom by escaping through the sewers. Banished from that house, he was not offered sanctuary or admitted by any other community. However, after his escape from prison he appropriated possessions belonging to the monks of Canterbury and plundered their property on the authority of the archbishop [Baldwin]. Indeed, the monks are still claiming a thousand marks from him as compensation for his depredations. He had trespassed upon their possessions by saying that the archbishop had made him prior and, when two brethren were sent to the archbishop, he had them arrested, and after separating them he had each of them placed under close guard. The archbishop at that time, Baldwin, allowed all this because he was involved in a serious dispute with his monks over the chapel of Hackington.[3]

472. 'Secondly, holy father, our abbot is guilty of simony, for he sold the deanship of this church and the two chapels of Badsey and Bretforton to a chaplain called Alfred,[4] though from the beginning we knew nothing of this. Several years later the chaplain admitted this to us, and on our advice he gave up those benefices. Then, despite our objections, the abbot sold the same chapels to Geoffrey of Oxford, his creditor's son. Some years later this clerk died, and his father claimed from us, and he is still claiming, fifty marks which he says his son had not received from those chapels. He even pressed our obedientiaries openly for the money.' I gave details of how much the abbot had received from him and how much from another, indeed, from many

---

[4] He was called 'de Burchulle' when he witnessed a charter concerning the church of Kinwarton; H fo. 89ʳ.

abbas non inficiaretur dicens sibi hoc bene licere, ualde admiratus est dominus legatus super eius imperitia.

473. 'Homicidium etiam, pater sancte, non tantum, ut predictum est, de monachis et seruientibus quos fame peremit commisit abbas noster, uerum etiam quendam prepositum nostrum laicum originarium, Augustinum uidelicet de Salford.[1] Fecit in carcerem detrudi et flagellari donec fere spiritum exhalaret ut ab eo pecuniam extorqueret. Et cum uideret eum debere expirare, fecit eum a carcere extrahi et ad domum suam duci, et ibi cito mortuus est.

474. 'Manifestus etiam, pater sancte, possessionum huius ecclesie dilapidator est abbas noster'; et expressi possessiones, tam noualium fo. 179rb que | dederat nepoti suo et senescallo,[2] quam alias possessiones quas aliis contulerat, et personas. Que omnia abbas non est inficiatus, set respondit se posse pro uoluntate sua noualia cui uellet conferre, ueluti possessiones ab eo adquisitas; cum ipse non terram adquisisset, set tantum a domino rege licentiam colendi eam. Dixit etiam quod bene licuit ei seruientes bene meritos, ecclesie de *caducis et aliis immobilibus remunerare.* Quibus omnibus ego contradixi, et per leges et canones ostendi *quod ei non licuit uel noualia uel caduca que posset retinere alicui conferre, nec seruientes de hiis uel aliis* immobilibus remunerare.[3]

475. Quare legatus, adquiescens rationibus meis, omnes illas possessiones que solo titulo donationis abbatis possidebantur ab aliquibus reuocauit. Et adieci, 'Pater sancte, non tantum pro hiis possessionibus dilapidator est abbas noster, et debet deponi, set etiam cum quasdam alias possessiones potuisset defendisse et retinuisse, colludendo cum aduersariis nostris quibusdam eas in iure cessit. A quarumdam uero possessione cecidit per contumaciam, et facti sunt aduersarii nostri ueri possessores per eius contumaciam, sicut moris est in curia regia.' Et expressi possessiones ueluti Raggeleyam, et terram Walteri le Poer de Ambresleya, et terram Iohannis de Tethlestrope, et terram Hugonis Russel de Neweham, et multas alias, quas legatus reuocare non potuit quia alio titulo quam ex donatione abbatis possidebantur.

476. Et cum abbas respondisset quod non potuit eas defendisse, et

---

a–a [ca]ducis . . . re[munerare] *written over an erasure*   *b–b* quod . . . aliis *written over an erasure (s. xiii¹)*

---

[1] Probably Salford in Warwickshire.   [2] Probably Roger, see above, **227**.
[3] The points here seem to be general, rather than specific: (*a*) that the abbot did not have the right to the land, and (*b*) that the escheated land goes back to the lord, in this case the abbot *and* the convent, and that it could not be granted out without their consent.

others. The abbot did not deny this, but when he said that he was well within his rights, the legate was quite astonished at his ignorance.

473. 'Thirdly, holy father, our abbot has committed murder, not only, as has already been stated, of his monks and servants whom he starved to death, but also of a certain reeve of ours, originally a villein, Augustine, that is, of Salford.[1] He had him thrown into prison and flogged to the point of death so that he could extort money from him. When he saw that he would inevitably expire, he had him dragged from prison and taken home, where he died soon after.

474. 'Fourthly, holy father, our abbot is an open plunderer of this church's possessions', and I detailed the possessions, not only of tithes of newly cultivated lands which he had given to his nephew and steward,[2] but also other possessions which he had granted others, and I mentioned the persons concerned. The abbot denied none of these, but replied that he had every right to bestow the tithes of newly cultivated lands on anyone he liked since they were possessions which he himself had acquired; though, in fact, he had not acquired land, only permission from the king to cultivate it. He said he was well within his rights to remunerate servants who served him well, from the church's escheats and from other immoveable possessions. I rebutted all that he had said, and demonstrated by reference to laws and canons that he did not have the right to grant anyone the tithes of newly cultivated lands or the escheats which he could retain, nor to remunerate servants from these or other immoveables.[3]

475. The legate accepted my arguments, and called back from some men all those possessions which they held on the sole basis of being a gift from the abbot. I added 'Holy father, our abbot is a plunderer not only because of these possessions—and for that reason deserves to be deposed—but also because, when he could have protected and retained certain other possessions, he colluded with some of our opponents and surrendered property in a legal action. He lost possession of some of these properties because of contumacy, and our opponents therefore became the rightful possessors through his contumacy, as is the custom in the king's court.' I detailed the possessions at Ragley [in Arrow, Warws.], the land of Walter le Poer of Ombersley, the land of John of Adlestrop [Glos.], the land of Hugh Russel of Newnham [Northants.], and of much other, which the legate could not recover because the lands were possessed under a different title from that of being a gift of the abbot.

476. The abbot replied that he could not have protected those lands,

ideo pecuniam ab aduersariis nostris recepit ne totum amitteret; et reliquit eis terras. Ego[a] e contra, exposui domino legato ius nostrum tam possessionis quam proprietatis quod habuimus in terris illis, et expresse ostendi quod si abbas sapiens fuisset et uellet expendisse pecuniam ecclesie in tuitione possessionum eius, potuisset eas defendisse. [b]Quare dixi quod propter dilapidationem uel collusionem uel insufficientiam debuit deponi. 'Mobilia etiam ita dilapidauit quod uicesimam ⟨partem⟩ instau|ramentorum non habemus quibus deberemus et possemus precipue sustentari. Ere in super alieno ita nos onerauit quod uix liberabimur.'

fo. 179va

477. Et cum abbas diceret hec ita esse propter expensas litis. Respondi eum bene posse hec complesse in octo annis quibus a lite cessauimus.[b] 'Preterea, pater sancte, multum exordinatus est abbas noster quia lintheaminibus in lecto et caligis consutis eis pedulibus more militum et camisiis,[1] sicut statim probare potestis, utitur contra statuta ordinis nostri.' Que abbas non est inficiatus, dicens sibi hoc bene licere propter infirmitatem, et etiam quia dispensatio circa regulam esset in manu eius, sicut dicebat.

478. Cui ego expresse contradixi, 'Immo, sicut dicit beatus Benedictus de ordinando abbate, ipse precipue regulam obseruare tenetur,[2] quamuis, sicut sepius audiuimus, ipse se diceret non esse monachum.' Et prosecutus rationem meam dixi, 'Frocco etiam non utitur, set cappatus[3] in ecclesiam et per claustrum et capitulum incedit, quamuis a multis annis retro nullum capitulum tenuerit nec in claustro sederit, set in thalamo suo citra consilium et consensum fratrum et capituli monachos suspendit et excommunicat et statutis alimentis priuat, et obedienciarios pro sua uoluntate ibi instituit et destituit',[4] et expressi tempora et personas. Que omnia ipse non est inficiatus, set ea sibi licere est protestatus, quod ego sibi non licere per regulam beati

---

^a uero *expunged following* ego   ^{b–b} Quare dixi . . . cessauimus *written in a blacker ink in another s. xiii¹ hand over an erasure: the top four lines of fo. 179va being squeezed into the space of three lines using many abbreviations*

---

¹ *RSB* cap. 55, on clothing, includes details on bedding: a mattress, a blanket, a coverlet, and a pillow being allowed. It is not clear when shirts entered the monastic wardrobe: they were made of linsey-woolsey or serge (Harvey, *Monastic Dress*, pp. 18, 24), but Norreis's may have been of linen, which was expensive, like his sheets. The sewn footwear, as worn by knights, suggests something softer and more comfortable than the stock monastic shoe.

² *RSB* cap. 64, 'Et precipue, ut presentem regulam in omnibus conseruet.'

³ A long elegant robe, as worn by secular clergy and nobles, which was made to fit the body, unlike the shapeless and loose monk's frock.

and therefore accepted money from our adversaries so as not to lose the whole lot; so he left them the lands. Opposing what he said, I explained to the legate the right which we had both of possession and of ownership of those lands, and demonstrated clearly that if the abbot had been wise and willing to spend the money of the church to protect its possessions, he could have succeeded in doing so. I therefore declared that he should be deposed on the grounds of his dilapidation of property, his collusion with our opponents, and his incompetence. 'He has so squandered our moveable goods that we have less than a twentieth of the stock we ought to have and, most important of all, the stock with which we could sustain ourselves. Furthermore, he has so burdened us with debt that only with difficulty shall we be freed from it'.

477. The abbot blamed this state of affairs on the expenses of the lawsuit. My reply was that he was well able to have repaid them in the eight years that had passed since the lawsuit ended. 'Moreover, holy father, our abbot is in considerable breach of the Rule, for contrary to the ordinances of our Order, he uses linen sheets on his bed, wears sewn footware like the boots worn by knights, and shirts;[1] and you can prove this without delay.' The abbot did not deny any of this but said that he was allowed to do it because of a disability, and also, so he said, he had a dispensation with regard to the Rule.

478. I emphatically disputed this, 'Not at all', I said, 'for as the blessed Benedict says concerning the appointment of an abbot, he is himself especially bound to observe the Rule,[2] however much he may declare—as we have often heard—that he is not a monk.' I proceeded to give my reasons: 'He does not wear the frock, but enters the church and walks through the cloister and chapter-house wearing a cape,[3] though for many years now he has not held a chapter or sat in the cloister, but has suspended, excommunicated, and deprived monks of their rightful sustenance in his own chamber without the advice and consent of the brethren and of the chapter, and has appointed and dismissed obedientiaries there just as he pleased',[4] and I gave details of times and persons. He denied none of these charges, but protested that he was within his rights, but referring to the Rule of the blessed

---

[4] See the Customs of the Abbey and the Disposition of the Revenues (App. II A). Obedientiaries were to be appointed in chapter by the abbot with the counsel and consent of the convent or the greater and wiser part of it, and, if it proved necessary to remove them from office this was only to be done in chapter and with the agreement of the community. Nor were monks to be received into the community or dismissed from it, unless in chapter and with the consent of the convent.

Benedicti et leges et canones et consuetudines domus[1] scriptas ostendi.

479. Vnde legatus multum admirabatur, quod quasi iuris ignarus, abbas sepe confiteretur se contra iura facere posse, et quasi tedio affectus, protraxeram enim sermonem meum a mane ultra horam diei nonam, dixit michi ut de eius incontinentia loquerer. Ad quod respondi, 'Pater sancte, cum premissa ad eius depositionem sufficiant ut quid detegam ego pudenda patris mei?' Et iterum precepit ut loquerer. Et dixi, 'Pater sancte, cum crimen abbatis nostri de eius incontinentia sit notorium, si placeret sanctitati uestre, non oporteret in hiis multum immorari. Sed quia | apud plerosque iurisperitos solet dubitari quod crimen sit notorium, pauca de hiis que nobis et aliis prope positis manifesta sunt et notissima proponam, omissa ceterorum fere innumera multitudine de quibus etiam apud longe positos fama eius laborat et scandalum permaximum ortum est.

480. 'Solet igitur, pater sancte, abbas noster publice et manifeste, nobis uidentibus et aliis thalamum suum ingredientibus, mulierculas suas in thalamo suo a mane usque ad uesperam retinere. Et etiam estiuo tempore, aliis post prandium recedentibus, remanserunt cum eo per totam meridiem sole muliercule cum puero qui ostium thalami custodiebat. Vnde maxime scandalizati sumus, cum hora illa honestius et secretius quam nocturna, si fieri possit, a nobis in dormitorio cum summo silentio obseruari consueuerit. Percunctantibus etiam nobis cum summa diligentia ad uesperam recederent, hoc nequaquam aliquando perscrutari poteramus, set in crastino, hora qua abbas surgere consueuerat, sepius eedem ibi reperte sunt, et hoc sepissime non occulte set palam et impudenter facere consueuit. Et, quod magis dolendum est, hoc non tantum de illis et illis solutis'—et nominaui sex—'set etiam de illis matrimonialiter illis uiris copulatis'—et expressi nomina duarum—'facere consueuit. Quarum unam ipse nuptui dedit cuidam consanguineo suo infra tercium consanguinitatis gradum ei coniuncto.[2] Qui et eorum tante nequitie consentiens uxorem suam ad abbatem etiam nocturnis horis ducere et ab eo reducere consueuit. Et quod magis stupendum est et formidandum, etiam cum sanctimonialibus manifestius hec agere

fo. 179vb

---

[1] See App. II A.
[2] If the abbot had had intercourse with her, it would have provided an impediment to her marrying his kinsman.

Benedict, the laws, the canons and the written customs of this house,[1] I showed that he did not have such rights.

479. The legate was very surprised that the abbot so often declared that he could act contrary to the law, as if he were ignorant of it, and apparently wearying of this argument, for I had been speaking from early morning till three in the afternoon, he told me to speak about the abbot's incontinence. To this I replied, 'Holy father, since the charges I have made are sufficient to depose the abbot, what is the purpose of my revealing behaviour which will inevitably shame my father?' But he again commanded me to speak. So I said, 'Holy father, since the charge against our abbot of incontinence is well-known, if it please your holiness, it would be best not to dwell upon it for too long. But as it is the nature of most men learned in the law to doubt that a charge is well known, I will cite a few examples of his incontinence which are evident and very well known to us and to others who live in close proximity to him, but I will omit an almost countless number of other instances for which his reputation has suffered amongst those who live at a distance, and because of which a serious scandal has arisen.

480. 'Our abbot, holy father, is in the habit of keeping his concubines in his chamber from morning till night in full view of us and others who enter his chamber. Even in the summer, when others had left after luncheon, the concubines alone stayed with him throughout the midday break, and a boy was put on guard outside the door of his chamber. We are greatly scandalized by this, for it is our custom to observe that hour in our dormitory with greater respect and privacy, if such is possible, than we do the hours of the night, and to keep the utmost silence. As we remained conscientiously where we were, we could at no time discover in any way at all whether the women left in the evening, but on the following day, at the hour the abbot usually rose, the women were often found there, and this was how he most often behaved, and not secretly, but openly and brazen-faced. All the more deplorable is the fact that he behaved like this not only with those women who were unmarried'—and I gave the names of six such women—'but also with women who were married'—and I gave details of two. 'One of these women he himself gave in marriage to a man related to him in the third degree of consanguinity.[2] That man, consenting to such wickedness, used to take his wife to the abbot at night and then collect her again. What is more astonishing and dreadful, he even used to behave like this openly with nuns'—and

solet'—et nominaui tres—'sub specie religionis culpam tegens, quasi opus pietatis esset, ut ipse dicere consueuit. Tales specialius quasi in loco honestiori et digniori lateri suo in mensa et colloquio iungere, sicut consueuerunt beatus Benedictus et beata Scolastica soror eius facere.[1] Quod minime solum cum sola, sicut facere abbas consueuit, fo. 180ra beatum | Benedictum fecisse credo, quamuis tanta propinquitas et personarum sanctitas et collocutionis raritas, omnem suspicationem in illis debeat abolere.

481. 'Igitur, pater sancte, ex illis quare numerum non noui, paucas uobis nominaui. Cuius rei fere omnes fratres testes michi esse possunt, et precipue quinque quos secretius uobis nominabo. Et si testimonium aliorum quam monachorum habere uolueritis, cogite clericos et laicos quos uobis nominauero ad perhibendum testimonium ueritati, et quotquot uolueritis habebitis. Quamuis puplica fama et ipsa rei noticia et facti euidentia et argumenta super terram gradientia michi ad probationem sufficiant, uidelicet filii et filie muliercularum illarum, qui nullum alium se protestantur habere patrem nisi illum, nec unquam apud nos alius fuit habitus uel inuentus nec adhuc habetur nisi abbas. Ipse etiam muliercule hoc non tantum publice fatentur set etiam iactitant se esse concubinas baronis domini regis et non monachi, quod et ipse abbas eis suggessit, uidelicet, se non esse monachum, unde multas seduxit.

482. 'Super hiis fere omnibus, pater sanctissime, fere dico, quia de die in diem multiplicantur eius facinora, deposuimus querimoniam coram domino Cantuariensi tunc temporis apostolice sedis legato, a quo super hiis facta diligentissima inquisitione. Plures facte sunt constitutiones, que omnes postquam legatus insignia legationis deposuit, ad nichilum redacte sunt, et postmodum eodem Cantuariensi agenti in*a* transmarinis, facta sunt nouissima nostra peiora prioribus.[2] Iterum super eisdem conquesti fuimus domino Iohanni sancte Marie in Via Lata diacono cardinali tunc temporis apostolice sedis legato.[3] Qui, super hiis singularem faciens inquisitionem, iussit illam deponi et seruari penes abbates de Hawemon et de Lilleshulle qui eidem scrutinio interfuerant,[4] donec quid super hiis esset statuendum disponeret secundum quod prouideret.

---

a added in margin (s. xv)

[1] This is taken from Gregory the Great's Dialogues, see *Grégoire le Grand Dialogues* (3 vols., Sources Chrétiennes, ccli, cclx, cclxv: Paris, 1978–80), ii, ed. A. de Vogüé, translated P. Antin, caps. xxxiii–iv, pp. 230–5.

[2] Matt. 12: 45.

I named three—'concealing his sin under the cloak of religion, as if it were an act of piety, as he used to call it. More especially, he would invite such women to join him at table for conversation in a place of special honour and merit by his side, as the blessed Benedict and his sister the blessed Scholastica used so to do.[1] The blessed Benedict did not, I believe, dine with his sister entirely alone, as the abbot has been accustomed to do with his women, though such close kinship as theirs, as well as the holiness of their persons and the rarity of conversation between them, must remove all suspicion in their case.

481. 'So then, holy father, because I do not know the number of women involved, I have given you the names of a few of them. Almost all the brethren are able to be my witnesses of this, and there are five brethren in particular whose names I will give you in private. If you wish to have the testimony of men other than monks, assemble the clerks and laymen whose names I shall give you so that they may testify to the truth, and you shall have as many as you wish. His general disrepute and notoriety provide sufficient proof for me, as well as the evidence and proofs of his behaviour who, treading the land as they do in the sons and daughters of those concubines, declare that they have no other father but him, and indeed, no other father has ever been considered or discovered amongst us except the abbot, and this is still our belief. The abbot's women not only admit publicly but even boast that they are the concubines of a baron of the king and not of a monk, a notion which the abbot has himself put into their heads—that he is not a monk—and thus has seduced many of them.

482. 'In addition to almost all of these things, most holy father—I say "almost" because his crimes are increasing from day to day—we lodged a complaint before the archbishop of Canterbury, at a time when he was papal legate, and he conducted a strict inquiry into these matters. As a result, more statutes were made, but after he laid down the office of legate nothing came of any of them, and when the archbishop later went abroad on business, our last state became worse than our first.[2] We again complained to John, cardinal deacon of St Mary in Via Lata, when he was papal legate.[3] He, on holding a special inquiry into these matters, ordered it to be postponed and put into the hands of the abbots of Haughmond and Lilleshall who were involved in that inquiry,[4] until he made up his mind what decision he must make in accordance with the findings.

[3] See above, 392 and n.   [4] See above, 392 and n.

483. 'Quo recedente antequam super hiis aliquid statueret, usque in hodiernum diem peius quam unquam prius oppressit nos abbas.

fo. 180rb Dicens | quod propter querimoniam nostram expenderit in domino legato trecentas marcas, quas omnes dicit se uelle habere de bonis usui nostro assignatis; et quamuis tunc sibi timeret, nichilominus usque nunc factus est nouissimus error eius peior priore.[1]

484. 'Cum itaque, pater sancte, metu predictarum querimoniarum nostrarum et inquisitionum super hiis factarum abbas noster sepius tum coram predictis legatis, tum coram uicinis abbatibus, tam per scripturam quam iuramento, ut audistis, interposito, se omnia predicta in statum debitum reformaturum et post reformationem statum bonum conseruaturum promiserit. Nec aliqua uel uite sue uel status nostri subsecuta sit correctio; set potius de die in diem deterioratio, ut uerbis Abner utar, quia "periculosa est desperatio".[2] Scientes quod induratum est cor[3] abbatis nostri et quod auertit oculos suos ne uideat celum, si uos eo relicto abbate recesseritis, quotquot non obstante corporis imbecillitate pedem mouere possumus, exceptis tribus uel quatuor complicibus abbatis, proicientes habitus nostros ad pedes uestros,[4] uobiscum recedemus, redeuntes ad seculum, ut in die iudicii anime nostre a manibus uestris requirantur.'[5]

485. Et cum hec dixissem[6] cecessi ad locum meum. Dominus uero legatus conuersus ad abbatem nostrum, dixit ei, 'Quid respondes tibi obiectis?' Et dominus abbas, 'Iam pridem pluribus ex hiis respondi, aliis uero respondeo quia falsa sunt que michi obicit.' Dominus autem legatus allocutus pariter abbatem et conuentum, dixit, 'Mittite manus uestras ad pectora uestra et dicite in uerbo Domini quod stabitis iudicio nostro super obiectis et responsis.' Quo facto, excommunicauit omnes qui falsum dicerent uel uerum reticerent de hiis que requireret ab eis. Et incipiens a priore per singulos requisiuit, dicens, 'Dic si uera sunt que dixit frater Thomas.' Et cunctis respondentibus quod uera erant, exceptis tribus fratribus qui dicebant se super quibusdam dubitare, respexit abbatem dominus legatus et dixit ei, 'Audis quanta testimonia dicunt aduersum te? Quid respondes?'

---

[1] Cf. Matt. 12: 45.

[2] 2 Kgs. (2 Sam.) 2: 26.

[3] Cf. the hard-hearted Pharaoh in Exod. 7: 22, and see below, 495, for Roger Norreis described as Pharaoh.

[4] A symbolic gesture signifying renunciation of obedience. See above, 279.

[5] Cf. *RSB* cap. 2 'quia in die iudicii ipsarum omnium animarum est redditurus'. The abbot is repeatedly reminded in the Rule that he will have to answer for the souls in his care on the day of judgment. The fearful responsibiltiy is here transferred to the legate.

483. 'As the legate left before he could make any decision about these matters, the abbot has ill-treated us worse than ever before right up to the present day. He says that because of our complaint he spent 300 marks on the legate, and that he wants to have all this back from the property assigned to our use; and although he might then fear for himself, yet his latest deeds are now so far worse than his first.[1]

484. 'Holy father, it was because he was apprehensive of these complaints of ours and the inquiries made into them, that our abbot often promised, both before the said legates, and before neighbouring abbots, not only in writing but also on oath, as you have heard, that he would restore all things to their proper estate, and after restoring them would maintain that good estate. But in fact no amendment of his life or improvement in our condition has followed; rather has there been a daily deterioration, so, to use the words of Abner, "despair is a dangerous thing".[2] We know that our abbot is hard-hearted,[3] and that he averts his eyes so as not to see heaven, but if you depart, leaving him here as abbot, then, except for three or four of his accomplices, as many of us as can walk will, despite our physical weakness, cast our habits at your feet,[4] depart with you, and return to the world, that on the Day of Judgment our souls may be required of your hands.'[5]

485. After this speech[6] I returned to my place. The legate turned to our abbot and asked him, 'What is your reply to these charges made against you?' The abbot said, 'I have long since made my reply to many of these charges, but I will reply to other charges against me because they are false.' The legate then addressed the abbot and the convent alike, and said, 'Put your hands upon your hearts and swear by the Word of the Lord that you will stand by our judgment upon the charges and the response to them.' We did so, and he pronounced excommunication upon all who might speak falsely or keep silent about the truth of the matters upon which he would require answers from them. Then, beginning with the prior, he asked the question of the brethren one at a time, 'Tell me whether brother Thomas has spoken the truth on these matters.' When all replied that he had, that is, except for three who said that they had doubts about some points, the legate looked at the abbot and said, 'You hear how much evidence has been given against you? What is your reply?'

---

[6] On 20/21 Nov.

486. *Responsio abbatis contra sibi obiecta a conuentu per Thomam monachum et obiectio abbatis contra conuentum*

fo. 180va Et abbas,'Domine, ex hiis que | dicunt potestis scire quia conspirauerunt contra me, sicut ego manifeste probabo.'[1] Legatus uero dixit, quasi fauens ei, 'Si hoc probaueris, non debet testimonium eorum admitti contra te. Set quia aduesperascit et inclinata est dies, cras mane proba illud;[2] et habeas consilium tuum tecum, ut quecumque uolueris contra eos dicas.'

487. Quibus dictis, recessit dompnus legatus et comedit in refectorio cum abbatibus collateralibus suis et cum conuentu, cereis accensis. Abbas uero, consolatus de uerbis legati, commedit in thalamo cum clericis et familia domini legati. Ego siquidem seruiebam domino legato in mensa, ubi pluria uerba consolatoria[3] ab eo recepi, et certam spem de depositione abbatis.

488. Mane autem facto[4] conuenimus iterum in capitulo.*a* Dompnus uero legatus sedens pro tribunali, assidentibus sibi abbatibus de Eboraco[5] et de Seleby[6] et de Sancto Martino Tuscie Sisteriensis ordinis[7] collateralibus suis, et abbatibus Gloucestrie,[8] Winchelcumbie[9] ad hoc uocatis. Dixit abbati ut procederet in medium et staret ubi ego steteram eri, et responderet sibi obiectis et probaret nos conspiratores. Qui stans in medio obiecit nobis quod aliquando detuleramus brachium sancti Ecgwini in capitulum et iuraueramus super eo quod fideliter staremus simul in negotiis ecclesie nostre contra abbatem nostrum.[10]

489. Et quamuis difficilis esset responsio, quia factum ita se habebat, tamen respondi ita.

---

a legatus cum assessoribus in capitulo *marg.* (*s. xv*)

[1] On the penalties for clerks and monks found guilty of conspiracy, see Gratian, *Decretum*, C. 11 q. 1 cc. 21, 23, 24 (Friedberg, i cols. 632–3). Such offenders are to be demoted.

[2] 22 Nov.

[3] Cf. Zech. 1: 13.

[4] 22 Nov.

[5] Robert II, abbot of the Benedictine abbey of St Mary's, York, from 1197 to 1239. A brother of William de Longchamp, he had been prior of Ely before he was elected abbot of St Mary's on 17 March 1197; see *HRH*, p. 84.

[6] Probably Richard, prior of Selby (Benedictine, Yorks.) in 1195, then abbot from 1195 to 1214, when he resigned to become abbot of Ramsey; *HRH*, pp. 63, 69–70.

[7] This was Abbot John. The house, a daughter of Pontigny from 1207, was well-respected by Pope Innocent III who apparently used this abbot on curial business. As a

486. *The reply of the abbot to the charges made against him by the convent through Thomas the monk, and the abbot's charge against the convent*

The abbot began, 'My lord, you can be sure from what they say that they have conspired against me, as I will clearly prove.'[1] The legate replied, in an apparently encouraging tone, 'If you prove this, their testimony must not be admitted against you. However, as it is getting late and almost evening, prove your charge tomorrow morning;[2] take counsel with yourself, so that you can say whatever you wish against the brethren.'

487. Having said this, the legate departed, and dined in the refectory with his attendant abbots and the convent, and the candles were lit. The abbot, encouraged by what the legate had said, dined in his own room with the clerks and members of the legate's household. I waited on the legate at table, and there received more comforting words[3] from him, and a sure hope that the abbot would be deposed.

488. When it was morning[4] we met again in the chapter-house. The legate took his place on the judgment seat, with the abbots of York,[5] Selby,[6] and of S. Martino in Tuscany of the Cistercian order,[7] sitting beside him as his attendants, and the abbots of Gloucester[8] and Winchcombe[9] had also been summoned. He told the abbot to come forward and stand where I had stood the previous day, to reply to the charges made against him and to prove that we were conspirators. He stood before them and made the charge against us that we had once brought into the chapter-house the arm of St Ecgwine, and had sworn upon it that we would stand loyally together against our abbot in the affairs of the church.[10]

489. Though it was difficult to reply to this, because what he said was true, I nevertheless replied as follows.

---

result of this visit, King John, on 26 May 1214, granted the abbey an annual payment of thirty marks from the church of Holkham (Norf.); *Rotuli chartarum in turri Londinensi asservati*, ed. T. D. Hardy, i, pt. 1, 1199–1216 (Record Commission: London, 1837), p. 198b; Cheney, *Letters*, no. 1171; *Regesta Honorii III*, cal. P. Pressutti (2 vols., Rome, 1888–95), i no. 350 (confirmation).

[8] Henry Blont, abbot from 1205 to 1224. He had previously been prior of the house; *HRH*, p. 53.

[9] Master Robert of Hasleton, abbot 1196–1221; *HRH*, p. 79.

[10] On the arm-reliquary of St Ecgwine and its miraculous properties, see above, **95–7**. Swearing on relics by monks of the house to protect their rights was well known. Durham monks swore on the body of St Cuthbert in their struggle against the bishop; see *Records of Antony Bek*, ed. and cal. C. Fraser (Surtees Soc. clxvii, 1953 for 1957), no. 109.

490. *Responsio Thome monachi contra obiectionem abbatis*

'Quamuis tale factum non sufficiat ad probandum nos conspiratores, tamen ne ex hoc facto alicui rei uideamur, sciatis, pater sancte, quod abbas noster alias super hoc eodem facto coram domino Cantuariensi tunc temporis apostolice sedis legato nos accusauit. Qui tunc decreuit propter hoc factum nos non debere dici conspiratores, set tamen penitentiam cuilibet nostrum pro eodem facto iniunxit. Et cum non puniat deus bis[1] in idipsum, non debet nobis reputari ad culpam quod per sufficientem deletum est penam.'

491. *Iterata obiectio abbatis contra conuentum*

Cum itaque propter hanc causam dominus legatus fratres nostros a testimonio non repelleret, iterum ad eos repellendos a testimonio abbas cuilibet nostrum, | preterquam tribus qui contra eum testimonium non perhibuerunt, aliquod crimen obiecit, et precipue michi multa opprobia dixit. Super quo legatus corripuit eum, asserens quod coactus locutus sim contra eum et quod multum uerbis pepercerim in loquendo contra eum. Multum commendans me quod bone fame fuerim in curia Romana cum ibi sub alis eius stetissem.

492. Et cum nichil ex hiis que nobis obiecit abbas probare posset, nec sibi obiectis aliter quam predictum est respondere, precepit dominus[a] legatus ut tam ipse quam nos recederemus.

493. *Sententia legati super depositione abbatis*

Habito igitur tractatu et consilio cum suis, uocati fuimus abbas et nos, et assumens parabolam suam,[2] dominus legatus dixit, 'Domine abba, quia multa crimina ex hiis que tibi obiecta sunt in iure confessus es te commisisse, nec aliis que negasti te perpetrasse possis respondere. Et cum omnia que tibi obiciuntur contra te sufficienter sint probata; et quia odio habes conuentum, et ipsi te non diligunt. Non potestis simul morari quin multi scandalizentur. Et quia scriptum est "Ve homini illi per quem scandalum uenit":[3] tutius est et melius quod unus recedat quam omnes. Et ideo absoluimus te a cura pastorali huius ecclesie, et dicimus tibi ut surgas et, secundum statuta ordinis, ueniam petas et misericordiam de obedientia tibi iniuncta.'

---

[a] Depositio abbatis *marg.*, *pencil* (*?s. xiii*)

---

[1] Cf. Nahum 1: 9.
[2] Num. 23: 7.
[3] Matt. 18: 7.

fo. 180ᵛᵇ

490. *The reply of Thomas the monk to the abbot's charge*

'Such an oath is not sufficient to prove that we are conspirators, but lest that act of ours should in any respect make it appear that we are, you should know, holy father, that our abbot has on a previous occasion made this same charge against us before the archbishop of Canterbury when he was papal legate. The archbishop's judgment was that we should not be called conspirators on the basis of that oath, though he did decree that one of our number should do penance for this act. Since God does not punish twice[1] for the same sin, we should not be blamed for something which has been blotted out by sufficient penance.'

491. *The abbot's charge against the convent repeated*

As the legate did not reject the testimony of our brethren on the basis of the abbot's charge, the abbot accused each of us, except the three who had not testified against him, of something or other in order to secure the rejection of our testimony, and he was especially abusive towards me. The legate censured him for this, declaring that I had been forced to speak against him and had been very sparing in my condemnation of him. He spoke highly of my good reputation in the Roman curia when I had stood under his protection there.

492. Since the abbot could prove none of the charges he made against us, nor give any explanation for the charges against him other than that already given, the legate commanded both the abbot and ourselves to withdraw.

493. *The sentence of the legate deposing the abbot*

After conferring and deliberating with his fellow-judges, the legate summoned the abbot and us back again, and taking up his parable,[2] he said, 'My lord abbot, you have admitted in court that you have committed many of the crimes of which you have been charged, and have been unable to refute other crimes which you have denied committing. All the charges made against you have been adequately proved; furthermore you hate the convent, and the brethren have no love for you. Therefore it is not possible for you to stay there without causing great offence to many people. It is written, "Woe to that man by whom cometh offence":[3] it is therefore better that one man should depart than all. We discharge you accordingly from your pastoral care of this church, and command you to rise and, in accordance with the statutes of the Order, to ask forgiveness and mercy as obedience

Et cum ad hanc iussionem non surgeret, iterum precepit ei ut surgeret et peteret relaxationem officii sui. Qui tunc surrexit et, humi prostratus, uerba sibi iniuncta dixit, que predixerat ei legatus. Et surgens, tam curam animarum quam omnem aliam administrationem in spiritualibus et temporalibus cum pilliolo suo in manus domini legati resignauit, et omni iuri quod in ecclesia Eueshamensi habuit renuntiauit, sicut dominus legatus ei dictauerat.

494. *De restitutione bonorum, que habuit penes se, postquam fuit depositus*
Hiis igitur ita peractis, cum iterum sedisset iam exabbas, petii a domino legato ut cogeret eum ad restitutionem quorumdam bonorum ecclesie que habuit penes se, et expressi que illa erant. Et restituit ibi statim domino legato, secundum expressionem meam, clauem sigilli
fo. 181ra ecclesie et sigillum proprium: quo fracto legatus retinuit illud | penes se.[1] Restituit etiam nobis tres capas et unam casulam et unam albam et tunicam et dalmaticam et unum pallium,[2] omnes uestes auro textas, et baculum pastoralem argenteum. Que omnia ipse emerat, que etiam tunc estimabantur ad ualentiam quinquaginta marcarum. Restituit etiam nobis meliorem rubeam casulam huius domus de examito, et duos calices et tres anulos, et quasdam cartas, et quedam priuilegia nostra, tam summorum pontificum quam regum, que omnia sibi attraxerat ut ea a domo ista alienaret, ne alius illa post illum gauderet, sicut ipse sepe comminatus fuerat. Proposuerat enim, ut ipse sepe fatebatur, quod domum istam in quantum posset ere alieno oneraret, sicut fere iam fecerat, et quod priuilegia et ornamenta ecclesie quecumque posset pignori obligaret; et cum omnia in suam abissum[3] quecumque posset congregasset, recederet a domo ista ne inter nos canes, sic enim nos uocare consueuit, moreretur et sepeliretur. Et sic reuera prophetauerat sibi malum.[4]

495. Omnibus igitur hiis nobis restitutis, precepit dominus legatus abbati de Winchelcumba,[5] qui semper ei fauebat, ut illum irrediturum a capitulo educeret. Quod et factum est. Tunc consolans nos legatus precepit ut cogitaremus de abbate substituendo. Et, data benedictione,

---

[1] i.e. the key to the metal (latten or silver) matrix of the abbot and convent acting as a corporation. The abbot's own matrix was normally destroyed on his death or cession so that no further sealed documents could be issued in his name.

[2] In this context meaning either an altar-cloth or a funeral pall, not the symbolic narrow circular band of lamb's wool, with two bands at back and front, embroidered with six black crosses, worn by archbishops.

[3] Rev. 20: 3.

[4] Cf. 2 Chr. 18: 7, and 3 Kgs (1 Kgs) 22: 8 and 18.   [5] See above, **488** and n.

demands of you.' When the abbot did not rise at this command, the legate again commanded him to rise and to request release from his office. He then rose and, prostrating himself on the ground, repeated the words demanded of him, as the legate had told him to do already. Rising, he handed over to the legate both the care of souls and all other administration of spiritual and temporal things along with his cap of office, and he renounced all the rights he had had in the church of Evesham, as the legate had dictated.

494. *The restitution, after the abbot's deposition, of properties that he had in his possession*

After the proceedings had been thus concluded, and the ex-abbot had sat down again, I asked the legate to compel him to restore some of the properties of the church that he had in his possession, and I gave details of these. The abbot, in accordance with the details I gave, immediately restored to the legate the key to the church seal [matrix] and his own seal: the legate broke this latter and kept it in his own possession.[1] The abbot also restored to us three copes, a chasuble, an alb, a tunic, a dalmatic, and a pallium,[2] all the cloths being woven with gold, and a silver crozier. All of these he had purchased himself, and their value at that time was estimated at fifty marks. He also restored to us a red chasuble of superior quality belonging to this house which was made out of samite, and two chalices, three rings, some charters, and some of our privileges, both papal and royal, all of which he had appropriated in order to alienate them from this house, as he had often threatened he would, so that no other should have the benefit of them after him. Indeed, he had intended, as he often himself declared, to burden this house as much as he could with debt—which he almost succeeded in doing—and to pawn the privileges and such ornaments of the church as he could; and when he had gathered all he could into his own bottomless pit,[3] he had intended to leave this house so that he should not die and be buried amongst us 'dogs', as he used to call us. With those words he had actually prophesied his own downfall.[4]

495. When all these things had been restored to us the legate instructed the abbot of Winchcombe,[5] who had always supported our abbot, to escort him from the chapter-house, never to return again. And that is what happened. The legate then spoke words of encouragement, and commanded us to think about replacing the abbot. After receiving his blessing we all left the chapter-house,

recessimus omnes a capitulo, gaudentes quia perdidit Deus impium[1] et liberauerat nos de manu Pharaonis.[2]

496. *Qualiter legatus dederit exabbati prioratum de Penwrtham; et qualiter se habuerit post depositionem suam*

Quinta post hec die,[3] ad petitionem conuentus, misertus illius dominus legatus dedit ei prioratum de Penwrtham ad uite sustentationem, quem post quinque menses[4] propter excessus suos ei abstulit. Qui tunc Romam adiit, sed nec abbatiam nec prioratum nec etiam monacatum huius ecclesie optinere potuit. Reuersus igitur infecto negotio, adhesit Siluestro Wigornensi episcopo[5] et quecumque nobis et ecclesie nostre nocitura credebat ei subgessit, sed nichil nobis nocuit. Ad dominum etiam Walam, | tunc temporis apostolice sedis legatum,[6] apud Glouerniam cum episcopo accessit, et restitutionem abbatie petiit, set nichil ab eo optinuit, sicut nec prius a domino papa. Tunc, desperans de reformatione sua, petiit centum libras quas ab ecclesia Cantuariensi, ut dicebat, fraudulenter asportauerat eidem ecclesie ab ecclesia Eueshamensi debere restitui in cuius usus eas se expendisse asserebat. Set dominus legatus eius nudam assertionem in absentia nostra pro nichilo reputauit.

497. Tunc omnem malitiam suam et omne uenenum suum effundens,[7] humi prostratus, dixit quod contra conscientiam suam ecclesiam Eueshamensem a subiectione Wigornensis episcopi liberauerat, et omnia que circa libertatem nostram infirma putabat domino legato palam intimauit, set nulla fide digna proposuit. Vnde, dominus legatus qui tempore late sententie pro exemptione ecclesie nostre cum aliis cardinalibus domino pape assederat, ut inter cardinales in iure ciuili peritissimus, respondit, 'Non tu, miser, ecclesiam Eueshamensem liberasti; nec etiam tempore sententie late Rome fuisti, set dominus papa, inspectis et approbatis priuilegiis Romanorum pontificum, eam liberam per sentenciam suam declarauit. Et quia propriam turpitudinem allegas, non es audiendus', et iussit ut domum egrederetur. Et sic confusus, recessit.

fo. 181[rb]

---

[1] Cf. Ps. 100: 8.

[2] Exod. 18: 10.

[3] The date of Roger Norreis's deposition being 22 Nov., five days later would make it 26 Nov..

[4] Late April 1214.

[5] Silvester of Evesham, who had been prior of Worcester, was elected bishop on 3 Apr. 1216 in succession to Walter de Grey, who had been translated to York. He died on 16 July 1218; see Greenway, *Fasti*, ii. *Monastic Cathedrals*, p. 101.

rejoicing that God had destroyed a wicked man,[1] and freed us from the hand of Pharoah.[2]

496. *The legate gives the ex-abbot the priorate of Penwortham; his behaviour after his deposition*

Five days later,[3] at the request of the convent, and because he himself felt sorry for the abbot, the legate gave him the priorate of Penwortham to enable him to sustain his life, but five months later[4] he removed him again because of his intemperate behaviour. The abbot then went to Rome, but was unsuccessful in securing an abbey, priory, or even a place as a monk in this church. Returning therefore after achieving nothing, he attached himself to Silvester, bishop of Worcester,[5] and prompted him to do whatever he believed would harm us and our church, but he had no success in this. He then accompanied the bishop to Gloucester to see Guala, at that time papal legate,[6] and petitioned for the restoration of the abbey to him, but he gained nothing from him, just as he had gained nothing from the pope before this. Then, giving up hope of being restored, he asked for the hundred pounds which, so he said, he had dishonestly taken from the church of Canterbury and ought to be repaid to that church by the church of Evesham for whose benefit he declared he had spent the money. The legate paid no attention at all to this unsupported assertion made in our absence.

497. Then letting loose all his malice and venom,[7] he prostrated himself, declaring that against his own conscience he had freed the church of Evesham from subjection to the bishop of Worcester, and he clearly intimated to the legate all those arguments for our liberty which he regarded as weak, but nothing he said warranted belief. Hence, the legate who had sat with other cardinals alongside the pope at the time the sentence for the exemption of our church had been passed, being one of the most learned of the cardinals in civil law, replied 'It was not you, wretched man, who freed the church of Evesham; you were not even in Rome when the sentence was passed. No, it was the pope who, after scrutinizing the papal privileges and accepting that they were genuine, declared by his sentence that Evesham should be free. And because you admit your own shameful behaviour, you must not be listened to', and he ordered him to leave the house. Thus shamed, the abbot departed.

---

[6] For Guala, see above, 371 and n.

[7] This may be a quotation, but we have not been able to trace it.

498. Postmodum uero, elapsis fere quinque annis a tempore depositionis sue, misertus illius dominus Pandulfus, qui tunc legationis officio fungebatur in Anglia, ne esset girouagus omnibus diebus uite sue, restituit ei prioratum de Penwrtham.[1] Vbi quoscumque redditus potuit conuentui assignatos subtraxit.

499. Vixit autem ibi postea annis ferme sex.[2] Et quamuis pendente hoc tempore tam magister Adam Sortes uiua uoce quam ego prior, et per monacos et per uiros seculares consanguineos suos et alios, commonuissemus eum, immo consuluissemus et supplicassemus ei, quod scriberet conuentui ut utrimque omnis indignatio remitteretur, quamuis nos ex animo omnino remissemus, et etiam peteret a domino abbate et conuentu quod fieret monacus Eueshamie. Noluit adquiescere nobis, set mortuus est ibidem et sepultus in eodem loco. Quamuis itaque, ut dictum est, non esset monacus noster, tamen pie agentes cum eo dominus abbas et conuentus ita omnia pro eo tam in spirit⟨u⟩alibus quam temporalibus agi fecerunt, ac si Eueshamie apud nos monacus noster obiisset.[3]

fo. 181[va] **500.** | *Qualiter tractauerit conuentus cum legato de electione, confirmatione et benedictione abbatis, et custodia uacantis abbatie*

Deposito itaque abbate in die sancte Cecilie,[4] minuit sibi dominus legatus, et quarta die post hec[5] conuenit nobiscum in capitulo ut abbatem nobis eligeremus. Et super persona legittima nobis preficienda singillatim examinauit uniuersos, et dicta singulorum in scripturam redegit. Facta ergo examinatione secessit in conclauim, et habito cum suis super electione nostra tractatu, renunciauit nobis per dominum Pandulfum et alios collaterales suos quod cum multis interfuerit electionibus numquam in aliquo collegio tantam inuenit dissidentiam et contrarietatem quantam in nobis. Vnde idem collaterales eius dixerunt legatum ualde motum contra nos, et magnum periculum nobis imminere ne aut hominem reprobatum reformaret, aut aliquem alienigenam, quod maxime timebamus, cum et ipse Normannus esset,[6] nobis preficeret. Nos uero propter hec ualde

---

[1] A *girouagus*, wandering monk, see above, **466** n. 4. The restoration was in 1218×1219.

[2] He died on 19 July, probably in 1224.

[3] For some of the provisions on the death of a monk of the community, see above, **427–8**.   [4] 22 Nov. 1213.   [5] 25 Nov.

[6] Maleczek (p. 147) says that the name 'de Romanis' attached to Nicholas is not found in the sources and possibly does not make its appearance until Ciaconius's *Vitae*. 'De Romanis' might be a corruption of 'de Normannis'. Little is known about the cardinal's origins before he appears in the papal chapel and as penitentiary. On his way to England he

498. Later, nearly five years after his deposition, Pandulf, who was carrying out the duties of papal legate in England at that time, took pity on him, and so that he should not spend all the days of his life as a *girouagus*, restored to him the priorate of Penwortham.[1] Here he embezzled all the revenues he could which had been assigned to the convent!

499. After his restoration he lived there for almost six years.[2] During that time not only Master Adam Sortes, who spoke to him in person, but I myself, now prior, urged him—in fact, we counselled and implored him—through the mediation of monks and lay kinsmen of his and others, to write to the convent so that all the anger on both sides might be banished, though we had already banished it altogether from our hearts, and to request the abbot and the convent to allow him to become a monk of Evesham. Yet he refused to make peace with us, and died there, and was buried in the same place [at Penwortham]. Although, as has been said, he was not one of our monks, the abbot and convent acted dutifully towards him, and saw that everything was done for him in both spiritual and temporal concerns, just as though he had died as one of our monks of Evesham.[3]

500. *The convent's dealings with the legate over the election, confirmation, and blessing of the abbot, and the custody of the vacant abbey*

After the abbot had been deposed, on St Cecilia's Day,[4] the legate had himself bled, and four days later[5] met with us in chapter that we might elect an abbot for ourselves. He questioned every one of us individually over the right person to appoint over us, and he wrote down what each of us said. When he finished his examination he retired to his private chamber, and having conferred with his men about our election, he informed us through Pandulf and his other associates that although he had been involved in many elections he had never found as much dissention or antagonism in any other community as in ours. His associates told us that he was very angry with us, and that there was great danger that he would either settle upon a man of whom we did not approve, or that he would put a foreigner in charge of us, and we were very much afraid of this, as he was himself a Norman.[6] Greatly dismayed at this, we asked for their

had endeavoured to construct a truce between Philip Augustus of France and John, but was unsuccessful. Thomas may be the only source for his possible Norman origins.

consternati, super hiis consilium eorum requirebamus. Ipsi siquidem desolationi nostre compatientes, consuluerunt nobis ut de abbate nobis preficiendo in dominum legatum, si ei placeret, uota nostra conferremus. Quamuis hoc ipsum auctoritate priuilegii a domino papa eidem concessi facere potuisset, que indulgentia postea nobis fuit exhibita.

501. Nobis uero consilio eorum propter predictas rationes adquiescentibus, duxerunt dominum legatum iterum in capitulum, quia ipse ex ore nostro hoc audire uolebat. Et cum iterum sedisset, ex precepto capituli dixi ei, 'Pater sancte, confisi de sanctitate et iustitia uestra, scientes quia zelum Dei habes et secundum scientiam,[1] petimus ut, sicut liberastis nos a nostro oppressore et ecclesie huius subuersore, ita detis nobis aliquem uirum qui sciat huic domui disponere in abbatem et pastorem animarum nostrarum. Ita tamen quod iura ecclesie huius secundum priuilegia nostra conseruetis illesa, uidelicet, ne alium quam nominatum ab aliquibus fratribus sanioris consilii[2] nobis preficiatis, nec alium quam ex parrochia Wictiorum,[3] si forte, quod absit, nullus monachus huius capituli ad hoc officium sufficiens et idoneus sit inuentus et nominatus. Et etiam ut idem in ecclesia nostra a quo maluerimus episcopo absque | omni exactione professionis et obedientie benedicatur.' Et placuit domino legato peticio nostra, et dixit, 'Bene salua uobis erunt omnia hec. Immo, melius faciemus uobis, uos enim habetis pedem ᵃfixum in ecclesia Romana; et si quocumque modo, quod absit, illum ab ea retraxeritis, aut uix aut numquam ipsum in ea iterum figetis. Quare, cum de consilio nostro aliquem elegeritis, uel in illum quem uobis nominauerimus consenseritis, nos illum confirmabimus uice domini pape ut solo Romano pontifici et ecclesie Romane nullo mediante subiectum; quod de nullo adhuc fecimus in Anglia. Preterea, quamdiu uacauerit abbatia ista retinebimus custodiam eius in manu nostra ne, si in manus regis deuolueretur, omnia bona eius confiscarentur et a seruientibus regis diriperentur. Et sic, saluabimus uobis fortassis ad ualentiam quingentarum marcarum quas debetis Romanis.' Et tunc tradidit michi et cuidam seruienti suo custodiam abbatie et, data benedictione, recessit.

fo. 181ᵛᵇ

ᵃ pre *erased*

[1] Cf. Rom. 10: 2.
[2] See *RSB* cap. 64.
[3] i.e. Worcester.

advice in this matter. They certainly sympathized with us in our distress, and advised us to convey our wishes to the legate, if he was willing to listen, about the appointment of an abbot over us. They pointed out that he could make this appointment on the authority of the privilege granted him by the pope, and this empowerment was later shown to us.

501. We accepted their advice for the reasons they had given, so they brought the legate again to the chapter, as he wanted to hear this from our own lips. When he had taken his seat again, I addressed him in accordance with the instructions of the chapter: 'Holy father, trusting in your holiness and your sense of justice, and knowing that you possess a love of God according to knowledge,[1] we ask that, as you have freed us from our oppressor and destroyer of this church, so you may give us a man as abbot and shepherd of our souls who would know how to set this house in order. But so that you may preserve the rights of this church unimpaired and in accord with our privileges, do not put over us any man other than one nominated by brethren of wiser counsel,[2] or anyone outside the diocese of the Hwicce,[3] if it be, God forbid, that no capable or suitable monk of this chapter be found and nominated for this office. We also ask that he be blessed in our church by a bishop of our choice, but without any demand for profession of obedience.' Agreeing to our request, the legate said, 'All these requirements will be safeguarded for you. In fact, we shall improve your situation, for you hold a strong position in the Roman church; but if, God forbid, you backslide in any way at all, you will never, or only with difficulty, re-establish that position in the church. Therefore, since you will have elected a man on our advice, or will have accepted the man we nominate for you, we shall confirm on the pope's behalf that he be subject to the Roman pontiff alone and to the Roman church, with no intermediary; and we have up till now done this for no other in England. Moreover, as long as the abbacy is vacant we shall keep the custody of it in our hands lest, if it should fall into the king's hands, all its property be confiscated and plundered by the king's servants. So doing, we shall preserve for you property which may perhaps be worth the five hundred marks which you owe to the Romans!' He then handed over to me and one of his own servants custody of the abbey and, after giving us his blessing, he departed.

502. *De electione, confirmatione, et benedictione abbatis Randulfi*

In diebus illis fuit uir uite uenerabilis dominus Rondulfus prior Wigorn', natione Eueshamensis et etiam monachus capituli Eueshamie, quod tunc temporis bene licuit, uidelicet, quod monachus in pluribus monasteriis haberet locum in capitulo et stallum in choro.[1] Iste cum esset electus in episcopum Wigornie, persuadentibus domino rege et domino legato renuntiauit electioni sue, et electus est in episcopum Wigornie cancellarius domini regis.[2] Quibus ita peractis, uenit ad nos dominus legatus in die sanctorum Fabiani et Sebastiani[3] et consuluit nobis ut eundem priorem eligeremus. Dicens nichil obstare de petitione nostra quin illum haberemus abbatem, cum etiam plurimi ex nobis sanioris consilii in prima examinatione illum elegissemus.[a][4]

503. Et eligimus eum et dominus legatus confirmauit electionem eius. Et petiuimus eum a capitulo Wigornie, et uenit ad nos in die sancti Vincentii.[5] Tunc missus est a domino legato ut prior Wigornie ad dominum Cantuariensem ut peteret ab eo confirmationem electi fo. 182ra Wigornensis,[6] et optinuit. Factum est autem | [b] tunc ibi murmur,[7] eo quod non peteret proprie electionis confirmacionem, set audita ratione quare dominus legatus eum confirmasset, cessauit murmur et querimonia.

504. Deinde, ex precepto domini legati, processit Eboracum. Et benedixit ei ibidem dominus legatus et, post benedictionem, imposuit mitram capiti eius Dominica secunda mensis Martii[8] in ecclesie sancte Marie, quod monasterium a fundacione sua ita confederatum est monasterio Eueshamensi ut quasi unum corpus et una ecclesia reputentur.[c][9]

505. *De solucione quingentarum marcarum pro priuilegiis, et amissione unius priuilegii et duarum cartarum, et constitutione karitatis decani*

Venit autem ad nos in die sancti Gregorii,[10] et in proxima Pascha sequenti soluit Romanis quingentas marcas Londiniis.[11] Et liberauit omnia priuilegia nostra que eis pignori erant obligata, preter unum

---

[a] elegemus *corr. to* elegissemus [b] De gestis abbatum *top margin. This is a new quire and a 15th-cent. hand starts here* [c] *Four red dots here indicate that the rubricated heading in the top margin of fo. 182 should follow*

[1] See above, pp. xlvi–xlvii.
[2] Randulf was elected bishop on 2 Dec. 1213, but his election was quashed by the legate before 20 Jan. 1214, to make way for the king's candidate, the royal chancellor, Walter de Grey; see *HBC*, p. 279, and Greenway, *Fasti*, ii. 100–1.

502. *The election, confirmation, and blessing of Randulf as abbot*
In those days there was a man of holy life named Randulf, who was prior of Worcester, a native of Evesham, and also a monk of the chapter of Evesham, for at that time a monk was allowed to have a place in the chapter, and a stall in the choir, of several monasteries.[1] Randulf had been elected bishop of Worcester, but under pressure from the king and the legate he declined his election, and in his place the king's chancellor was elected as bishop of Worcester.[2] Having accomplished this, the legate came to us on SS Fabian and Sebastian's day[3] and advised us to elect the prior of Worcester as abbot. He said that to have him as our abbot was fully in accord with our request, since most of us brethren of wiser counsel had also elected him in the first scrutiny.[4]

503. So we elected him and the legate confirmed his election. We petitioned the chapter of Worcester for him, and he came to us on St Vincent's day.[5] The legate then sent him as prior of Worcester to the archbishop of Canterbury to request from him confirmation of the man elected bishop of Worcester,[6] and he obtained this. There was some grumbling there,[7] however, because he had not sought confirmation of his own election, but when the reason why the legate had confirmed him was heard, the grumbling and complaints ceased.

504. Next, on instructions from the legate, he made his way to York. There the legate blessed him and, after the blessing, placed the mitre upon his head on the second Sunday in March[8] in the church of St Mary, which monastery from its foundation was so joined in confederacy with Evesham monastery as to be thought one body and one church.[9]

505. *The payment of the five hundred marks in return for the privileges, the loss of one privilege and of two charters, and a ruling about the dean's* caritas *of wine*
The abbot came to us on St Gregory's day,[10] and the following Easter he paid the Romans five hundred marks in London.[11] So he secured the release of all our privileges that had been in pawn to the Romans,

---

[3] 20 Jan. 1214.   [4] See above, **293**.
[5] 22 Jan.
[6] Walter de Grey; see **502**, above.
[7] At Canterbury, or wherever Langton was.   [8] 9 March.
[9] For the confederation between Evesham and St Mary's abbey, York, see above, p. lxi.
[10] 12 March.
[11] The Roman merchant bankers conducted their business in London.

quod Romani amiserant in tribulacione illa quando a rege eisdem spoliati erant.[1] Quandam etiam cartam, sigillo communi signatam, super debito uiginti marcarum, quas ego a Petro Pauli ciue Romano in primo itinere meo mutuo accepi; et aliam signatam sigillo abbatis super debito quadraginta marcarum, scilicet de predictis uiginti marcis, quas abbas in eadem carta spopondit se soluturum, et de aliis uiginti marcis quas abbas ab eodem Petro mutuo accepit,[2] nobis non restituerunt Romani. Set super solucione eiusdem debiti specialiter, et omnium aliorum debitorum, duo paria instrumentorum, que dicuntur star,[3] nobis confecerunt signata sigillo Luce Scarsi generalis procuratoris omnium creditorum nostrorum Romanorum. Et detulimus priuilegia Eueshamiam Dominica qua cantatur Misericordia Domini.[4] Tum ego, gratias agens Deo, et gauisus quod priuilegia que ego pignori obligaueram salua ad nos peruenissent, impetraui ab abbate et conuentu ut statuerent quod de prouentibus decanatus, quos ego pro uoluntate mea consue|ui expendere, annuatim darem caritatem uini ea die conuentui, et alii decani post me in perpetuum.[a]

fo. 182[rb]

506. *Consilium Thome prioris circa electionem, confirmacionem, et benedictionem abbatum, et custodiam uacantis abbatie, et usum possessionis circa ea*

Igitur uobis quos aliorum abbatum Eueshamensis ecclesie expectat electio: immo et ipsis electis loquor. Ecce audistis, quamuis terror domini legati esset super nos, ita quod potestate sua, si uellet, multipliciter posset nos deprimere ut, ratione indulgencie sue, quem uellet nobis abbatem daret, tamen, quamuis in arto positi, priuilegiis nostris bene sumus usi ne in aliquo casu ab eorum possessione excideremus. Nam non alium quam monachum Eueshamensis capituli elegimus in abbatem.[5] Qui non a Wigornensi episcopo est confirmatus uel benedictus nec Wigornie; nec fecit ei obedienciam uel professionem que antecessores sui a multis temporibus retro facere consueuerunt.[6] Set a quo maluit episcopo, scilicet domino Tusculano, est benedictus, secundum formam priuilegiorum

---

[a] *Four red dots and the letters a and b indicate the placing of the rubricated heading which appears ten lines later on*

[1] See above, **437**, for the seizure of Evesham's newly obtained privileges by the king, who had them placed in his treasury and then sent to Corfe castle. It is not possible to say which the lost privilege was nor what it concerned.

[2] See above, **358** and n. 2.

except for one which they had lost during the time of troubles when they were stripped of their privileges by the king.[1] There was a further charter which the Romans did not restore to us, which was sealed with the common seal, held for the debt of twenty marks which I had borrowed from Peter Pauli, a Roman citizen; and another one sealed with the abbot's seal, held for a debt of forty marks, comprising the twenty marks which the abbot promised in the charter itself that he would pay, and twenty marks which the abbot had borrowed from the same Peter.[2] With regard to the payment of this debt in particular, and of all other debts, they produced two pairs of documents called 'starr',[3] sealed with the seal of Luke Scarsi, general proctor of all our Roman creditors. We brought our privileges to Evesham on the Sunday on which the Misericordia Domini is sung.[4] Then, giving thanks to God, and glad that the privileges which I had pawned had come back to us safely, I persuaded the abbot and convent to make a ruling allowing me on this day every year to give a *caritas* of wine to the convent from the revenues of my office as dean, which I was accustomed to spend as I thought right, and to allow succeeding deans to do the same for ever.

506. *The advice of Thomas the prior concerning the election, confirmation, and blessing of abbots, the custody of the abbey when vacant, and the right of possession in connection with it*

I now address you who face future elections of other abbots of the church of Evesham: indeed, my words are also for those who will be elected. Look now, you have heard that, though we were very fearful of the legate's anger against us, whose power was such that he could have dealt severely with us in many ways, if he had wished, in his kindness he gave us an abbot of his choice, and that though placed in a difficult situation, we made good use of our privileges so as not to be deprived of the possession of them through any mischance. Indeed, we did not elect a man as abbot who was not a monk of the Evesham chapter.[5] He was not confirmed by the bishop of Worcester, nor blessed at Worcester, neither did he swear obedience or make profession to him as his predecessors had done on many occasions in the past.[6] No, he was blessed by a bishop of his own choice, the bishop of Tusculum [Nicholas], in accordance with the terms of our

---

[3] The starr was a Jewish deed or bond but the term was also used for an indenture (non-Jewish). [4] 13 Apr.

[5] See above, **502**, and n. 1, for the meaning of this. [6] See above, **304**.

nostrorum, et in propria ecclesia, quia in ab[b]atia Eboracensi, et murmurante propter hoc archiepiscopo, a domino eciam legato est confirmatus.[1]

507. *Nota de archiepiscopo*

Vnde uos premunio quod si aliquando dominus Cantuariensis hoc sibi ut domini pape uicario uel legato competere uendicauerit, non ei adquiescatis. Quia cum in concilio generali sit statutum de pena indigne confirmantis electionem, quod illi qui nullo mediante ad Romanam pertinent ecclesiam uel eant uel mittant ad Romanum pontificem propter confirmacionem, si electus noster ad Romanum pontificem nec iret nec mitteret propter confirmacionem, sequeretur quod non pertineret ad Romanam ecclesiam nullo mediante.[2] Immo eciam, si benedictionem susciperet non confirmatus a domino papa, et sua sequeretur depositio et tocius libertatis et exempcionis ecclesie fo. 182[va] nostre | immineret subuersio. Ipse enim qui ei non confirmato benediceret penam non effugeret, eo quod in messem domini pape falcem misisset.[3] Littere tamen domini Cantuariensis ut tutoris nostri ualde necessarie sunt ad dominum papam de canonica electione nostra.

508. Preterea, cum in eodem capitulo contineatur quod illi qui eunt uel mittunt ad sedem apostolicam propter confirmacionem statim post concordem electionem administrent in temporalibus et in spiritualibus, si electus noster nec iret nec mitteret illuc illo careret priuilegio, et sic remanente uidelicet abatia in custodia domini regis et omnibus eius confiscatis donec confirmaretur electus; maximum dampnum in temporalibus incurremus. Quamuis ad dominum regem eius custodia non uideatur pertinere set magis ad dominum papam quia in solo sibi donato[a] est fundata, sicut ipse per sentenciam suam manifeste declarat. Quam rationem secutus dominus legatus, post depositionem abbatis, retinuit eam in manu sua et nostra. Vel si forte non fuerit generalis legatus[4] in Anglia abbate decedente, ut

---

[a] *marg.* Oct? (Ott? *or* Ett?)

---

[1] The legate had episcopal orders, and the privilege allowed the newly appointed abbot to be blessed by a bishop of his own choosing. For St Mary's abbey, York, being regarded as 'his own church', see above, **504**. The archbishop of Canterbury was clearly mindful of his rights as provincial.

[2] Thomas apparently had in mind ch. 26 of the decrees of the Fourth Lateran Council. His worry is that if blessing were to be received from the archbishop, then Evesham's privilege, stating that it was subject to the Roman church, *without intermediary*, would be at risk.

privileges, and in his own church, for he was confirmed in York Abbey by the legate, even though the archbishop of Canterbury demurred at this.[1]

507. *Note concerning the archbishop*
Hence, I forewarn you that if at any future time the archbishop of Canterbury claims the competence to undertake this duty as the pope's vicar or legate, do not acquiesce in this. Since a statute has already been passed in the General Council about the penalty of confirming an election when not entitled to do so, that those who belong to the Roman church without any intermediary should go, or send, to the Roman pontiff for confirmation, if a man elected in our church were not to go, or to send to the Roman pontiff for confirmation, it would follow that he did not belong to the Roman church without an intermediary.[2] Furthermore, if he received the blessing without being confirmed by the pope, his deposition would also follow, and the overthrow of the whole of the liberty and exemption of our church would be threatened. The man responsible for blessing someone who had not been confirmed would not escape punishment, for he would have put his sickle in the pope's harvest.[3] However, letters from the archbishop of Canterbury as our protector concerning our canonical election are very necessary for the pope.
508. Furthermore, since that same statute contains the statement that those who go or send to the apostolic see for confirmation are to administer the temporalities and spiritualities immediately after an agreed election, if our elected man were not to go or to send to the apostolic see, he would lose that privilege, and so the abbey would remain in the custody of the king and all its possessions be confiscated until the elected man was confirmed; and we should incur a very great loss of our temporalities. Yet custody of the abbey should not be seen as belonging to the king, but rather to the pope, because it was founded on the territory granted to him, as the pope clearly states in his sentence. On the basis of this principle the legate, after the deposition of the abbot, kept the abbey in his own hands and in ours. Furthermore, should a general legate [4] not happen to be in England when an abbot

---

[3] Cf. Joel 3: 13.
[4] The term seems to be used for a legate *a latere*. On the dual allegiance of the bishop-elect (in this case the abbot–elect) see in general R. Benson, *The Bishop-Elect: A Study in Medieval Ecclesiastical office* (Princeton, New Jersey, 1968), pp. 315–30, on the canonists' discussion on the bishop's prior duty to the prince, when he is a legate of the pope, rather than to the metropolitan.

michi uidetur, debet eius custodia deuolui ad dominum Cantuariensem sicuti in hac parte domini pape legatum uel uicarium uel
ipsius abbatie tutorem, sicut in eius sentencia continetur, et ad nos ut
speciales filios domini pape.

509. Set que cura cuius sit custodia cum quasi momentanea sit? Nam
si fratres in concordi fuerint electione, statim post electionem
canonicam, requisita prius a domino rege licencia eligendi, habebit
electus administrationem in spiritualibus et in temporalibus, auctoritate concilii, sicut superius dictum est,[1] quod electis in episcopos
deocesanos uel in abbates subiectos episcopis non conuenit. Hic
tamen subsisto, et dubito an ita circa confirmationem sit faciendum.
fo. 182ᵛᵇ Nam cum abbates be|nedicti a domino papa consueuerint uisitare
papam de triennio in triennium, sicut facit abbas sancti Augustini
Cantuarie,[2] timeo ne hec consuetudo trahatur ad confirmatos a
domino papa. Quod si factum fuerit melius esset quod abbas a
domino Cantuariensi confirmaretur, si tamen pericula imminentia
possemus euadere. Set et nunc hesito utrum sumptus uisitationis
debeant comparari bonis que ecclesia Romana consueuit conferre
specialibus filiis suis exemptis, quamuis pericula que imminent si
domino papa subtraxerimus confirmacionem milies grauiora sint
quam sumptus uisitationis et confirmacionis. ᵃNam dominus papa
de iure posset nos priuare priuilegiis nostris in illa parte in qua faciunt
pro nobis si nos abstulissemus ei confirmacionem que facit pro eo et
eius dignitate. Et Wygornences episcopi, qui semper insidiantur
nobis, hoc sine dubio nunciarent domino pape ut ita eis subiceremur.
Igitur, cum sitis in plena possessione electionis, confirmacionis,
benedictionis et custodie uacantis abbatie, secundum formam priuilegiorum nostrorum, caueatis ne ab eorum usu decidatis. Quod si
feceritis, quod absit, in seruitutem detrudemini et in perpetuum eritis
miseri.ᵃ³

ᵃ⁻ᵃ *bracketed together: the* Nota bene (*?the same hand found in the earlier section*) *in the top marg., may refer to this*

---

[1] IV Lateran c. 26.

[2] Both Roger and Master Alexander, elected abbots of St Augustine's, Canterbury, respectively in 1175 and 1213, had been blessed by the pope; *HRH*, p. 36. The dispute between Archbishop Richard and Abbot Roger over the blessing of the abbot of St Augustine's by the archbishop of Canterbury, and whether it entailed a profession of obedience to the archbishop, simmered on during the late 12th cent.; see D. Knowles, 'Essays in Monastic History. IV. The Growth of Exemption', *Downside Review*, l (1932), 201–31, 396–436, at pp. 411–15. For the privilege of Pope Alexander III allowing the abbot

dies, then in my opinion the custody of the abbey should devolve, as the pope's sentence states, upon the archbishop of Canterbury who is on the spot as the pope's legate, or vicar, or protector of the abbey itself and of us who are the special sons of the pope.

509. But why worry who has custody of the abbey when it is only temporary, as it were? Surely, if the brethren have agreed over the election, after permission has first been requested from the king to elect, the man elected will, immediately after the canonical election, have the administration of the spiritualities and temporalities on the authority of the Council, as has been stated above,[1] whereas this does not apply to those elected as diocesan bishops or to abbots subject to bishops. Here I beg to differ, and doubt whether this should be done in the case of confirmation. For abbots who have been blessed by the pope have been in the custom of visiting the pope every three years, as the abbot of St Augustine's, Canterbury, has,[2] and I fear that this custom may become restricted to those confirmed by the pope. If this happens it might be better for the abbot to be confirmed by the archbishop of Canterbury, provided that we could avoid the dangers contingent upon doing so. But even now I hesitate as to whether the cost of the visit should be compared with the good things which the Roman church has been accustomed to bestow upon its special sons who enjoy exemption, though the dangers which threaten us if we withdraw confirmation from the pope might be a thousand times worse than the cost of the visit and the confirmation. For the pope could rightfully deprive us of that part of our privileges which benefit us if we deprived him of confirmation which benefits him and the dignity of his office. The bishops of Worcester, who are ever lying in wait for us, would undoubtedly proclaim to the pope that we should therefore be subject to them. Therefore, as you are in full possession of the right of election, confirmation, blessing, and custody of the abbey when vacant, in accordance with the terms of our privileges, see that you do not lose the benefit of them. If you do so, God forbid, you will be reduced to slavery, and be for ever wretched.[3]

---

to receive blessing from the archbishop of Rouen, and, if that was not acceptable, from the pope himself, see Thomas of Elmham, *Historia Monasterii S. Augustini Cantuariensis*, ed. C. Hardwick (RS viii, 1858), pp. 428, 432, and for similar concessions of Popes Lucius III and Urban III, ibid., pp. 452, 469.

[3] This marks the end of what can be certainly attributed to Thomas's authorship.

510. *De operibus Randulphi abbatis*

Iste abbas Randulphus in conuentu suo mitissimus apparuit. Cuius primum bonum opus fuit, ut predictum est, solucio quingentarum marcarum Romanis, quarum pene multum erant timende nisi tunc soluerentur.[1]

511. Secundum uero quod cum predecessores sui consueuerint conferre consanguineis et clericis suis *a* ueterem pensionem sexaginta solidorum de ecclesia de Ambresleya, et illa consuetudo per tantum tempus durasset quod dominus legatus et clerici eius iam assererent constantissime quod abbas non potuit eam in manu sua retinere. |

fo. 183ra Vnde instanter petebant et uolebant quod eadem pensio uni eorum conferretur, quod nobis facere renuentibus, dominus legatus potestate sua contulit eam cuidam clerico Runfredo uocato,[2] nomine personatus eiusdem ecclesie. Qua per commutacionem reuocata abbas, de licencia legati, sicut superius in consuetudinibus est expresse distinctum,[3] eandem pensionem in usus pauperum et conuentus conuertit. Et sic euasit periculum predictum scilicet perpetuam amissionem illius pensionis, et eciam liberauit se ab onere mandati in Cena Domini ad quod ante assignationem istam consueuerunt abbates inuenire denarios quotquot erant necessarii ad opus pauperum.

512. Tertium uero bonum opus eius fuit. Quod cum predecessor eius, inter cetera mala que fecit in domo Eueshamie, consueuisset per extorsionem semel in anno hospitari apud Bratforton'; et ibi una die cum luxuriosis et ebriosis in commessacionibus et ebrietatibus, bona sacristarie multis ecclesie membris per totum annum sufficiencia consumere. Iste abbas, uidens hec in multarum fieri periculum animarum et enormem ecclesie lesionem, de consilio uirorum prudentum, huiusmodi abusum decreuit abolendum. Set quia quosdam defectus in quibusdam officiis monasterii iam cognouerat, uidens redditus sacristarie habundare ueluti tempore suo aumentatas, ad petitionem fratrum, predictas expensas inutiles et superfluas in usus

---

a *interlined*

[1] It had already increased by 100 marks.

[2] Cf. below, 540 and App. II B, where he occurs as Humfredus. According to V fo. 65^r, this same clerk Rumfredus had been given the church of Weston-on-Avon (Warws.), which Abbot Roger had conveyed to Hugolinus, bishop of Ostia, when he was cardinal deacon (of S. Eustachio, 1198–1206), to assign to one of his clerks. The cardinal then conferred it on Rumfredus, who was to have 8 silver marks annually from the convent until the church of Weston became vacant. Abbot Roger's original grant is likely to have been made when the abbot and convent were pressing their case at the curia. See above, 274, for

510. *The deeds of Abbot Randulf*

Abbot Randulf seemed a mild man in his dealings with the convent. His first good deed was the payment to the Romans of the five hundred marks previously mentioned, for the penalty for not making immediate payment was one to be greatly feared.[1]

511. His second good deed was this. His predecessors had been accustomed to assign to their relatives and clerks an ancient payment of sixty shillings from the church of Ombersley, and that custom had prevailed for so long a time that the legate and his clerks now made a firm declaration that the abbot could not keep personal possession of it. The result was that they [the relatives and clerks] expressed a strong request and desire for the payment to be granted to one of them. When we objected to this the legate used his authority to grant it to a clerk called Runfredus,[2] in the name of the parsonage of the same church. The abbot now reclaimed this payment by an exchange, and with the permission of the legate, as clearly specified above in the Customs, diverted it to the use of the poor and the convent.[3] So he avoided the risk we have mentioned of losing the payment for ever, and he also released himself from the burden on Maundy Thursday, when the abbots, before the transfer of the payment, had been accustomed to provide as much money as was necessary for the service of the poor.

512. His third good deed was as follows. His predecessor, amongst other evil deeds perpetrated in the house of Evesham, had been in the habit of forcibly obtaining lodgings once a year at Bretforton, and of feasting and drinking there with lechers and drunkards; with these men he would consume as much of the provisions of the sacristy in one day as would suffice many members of the church for a whole year. The new abbot saw that this was endangering the souls of many men and causing great harm to the church, so after consulting men of good sense he decided to abolish such an abuse. He had by now noticed that some departments of the monastery had deficiencies, and saw that the sacristy had superfluous revenues, for they had been increased in his own time, so, in response to a request of the brethren, he diverted to the necessary purposes of the brethren those extra

Thomas's description of Hugolinus as 'the guardian and protector of our church and cause'. For Evesham's portion in the church in 1281, see *Taxatio Ecclesiastica Angliae et Walliae . . . 1291* (1802), p. 223. For the legate Nicholas's provision for his nephews and clerks in England, including a Master Gratian and a Master Hugolinus, see Maleczek, pp. 149–50, but nothing more is known of Humfrey.

[3] For the 60s. from Ombersley see above, **409.**

fratrum necessarios conuertit. Et secundum antiquam domus consuetudinem, per habundantiam unius officii defectus aliorum officiorum quos necesse habuit supplere, sicut superius est constitutum,
suppleuit.[1] Et de redditibus sacristarie tres marcas ad infirmariam et
duas ad refectorium deputauit, quas duas postea conuentus cum
fo. 183[rb] reliquis tribus ad | pitanciariam assignauit, reformata pitanciaria ex
predictis duabus obedienciis.

513. Iste eciam abbas fecit apud Ambresley uiuarium de Linholt et
duo ultima uiuaria subtus curiam et uiuarium de Lenchwyc. Et
redemit molendinum eiusdem uille, saluo redditu coquine, et uiuarium de Honyborne, et fecit super eo[a] molendinum et columbarium,
et tria columbaria de Offenham, Hamton' et Wickewane, et uiuarium
de Bradewelle, et super eo molendinum, et secundum et tertium
uiuarium apud Euesham, nam primum prius fuit. Fecit eciam domos
de Ambresley et columbarium, et domos de Honyborne, tamen
tempore eius fuerunt combuste domus de Offenham et de Bradewelle. Et non reedificauit eas, nisi tantum grangias. Fecit eciam
grangiam de Willarsey et de Alditon' et de Wykewane et de Euesham
et de Lenchwych, multum meliores quam prius essent. Fecit eciam
speculam abbatis iuxta aulam in curia de Euesham, set tamen
destruxit aulam hospitum et stabulum nobile edificium, uolens re-
edificare, set non reedificauit. Fecit eciam magnum assartum de
Lenchwic; destruxit tamen Langabeiam, boscum de Somborne, in
enorme dampnum ecclesie quia erat extra rewardum, et medietatem
bosci de Baddeby, et magnum boscum de Ambreslei qui dicebatur
Chatteley, uolens in hiis facere assarta. Set non potuit propter
communam pasture hominum nostrorum et uicinorum.

514. Dedit tamen pro licencia assartandi omnibus liberis hominibus
nostris terras ualentes annuatim centum solidos si fuerint culte, in
magnam lesionem ecclesie, quia Walterus de Bellocampo[2] illam
licentiam impediuit, et segetes assartorum nostrorum pluries consumpsit. Cito etiam post ingressum suum in abbatiam tradidit
fo. 183[va] Iohanni de Thettllestropp' sex uirgatas terre et | dimidiam in
Theccllestropp', et per cartam conuentus eidem et heredibus suis
confirmauit.

---

[a] *eum* R

---

[1] See above, 403.
[2] Walter (II), d. 1236, sheriff of Worcs., and a considerable landowner in the area; see

funds which were not being used. In so doing he was following an
ancient custom of the house, and in accordance with the Ordinance
mentioned above, he was supplementing from the abundant revenues
of one department the deficiencies of other departments that were in
need of extra funds.[1] So, from the revenues of the sacristy he
allocated three marks to the infirmary and two marks to the refectory,
then later the convent assigned these two marks with the other three
to the pittancery, the pittancery being re-formed from the two
obediences [infirmary and refectory] just mentioned.

513. At Ombersley the abbot made the fishpond of 'Linholt', the two
furthest fishponds below the court, and the fishpond of Lenchwick.
He bought back Ombersley mill, [thus] saving the revenue of the
kitchen, and the fishpond of Honeybourne, and built a mill and a
dovecot by it, constructed three dovecots at Offenham, Hampton,
and Wickhamford, made the fishpond of Broadwell [Glos.] and the
mill above it, and the second and third fishponds at Evesham (the first
was already there). He also built houses at Ombersley and the
dovecot, and houses at Honeybourne, though it was in his time
that the houses of Offenham and Broadwell were burnt down. He did
not rebuild these, only the barns. He also built a barn at Willersey
[Glos.], at Aldington, at Wickhamford, at Evesham and at Lenchwick, and they were much better than the previous barns. He built an
abbot's watch chamber next to the hall in the court at Evesham, but
pulled down the guest-hall and stable, which was a fine building,
intending to rebuild this, but he never did. He made the large assart
of Lenchwick, but destroyed 'Langaby', the wood of Sambourne
[Warws.] (to the great detriment of the church because it was outside
the jurisdiction of the forest), half of Badby wood [Northants.], and
the large wood at Ombersley known as Chatteley wood, as he wished
to make assarts in these. But he could not do this, as they were
common pasture-land of our men and the men of the district.

514. To the great detriment of the church, he gave lands to all our
freemen, which when cultivated would be worth 100 shillings a year,
instead of licence to assart, because Walter de Beauchamp[2] prevented
them enjoying that licence and often destroyed the crops of our men's
assarts. Soon after the abbot entered his office he handed over to John
of Adlestrop six and a half virgates of land in Adlestrop [Glos.] and
confirmed it to him and his heirs by a charter of the convent.

Beauchamp Cartulary, ed. E. Mason (PRS xliii, 1980), pp. xxiii, lviii, and nos. 61, 104,
148, 154.

515. Ditauit nos tamen nobili anulo ad missam, et una mitra, et de duabus albis auro textis, et de una capa de rubeo examito auro super intexto, et de tribus tunicis. Contulit etiam altari sancte Marie unum uestimentum sacerdotale cum casula de rubeo examito. Reliquit eciam ad discum in refectorio unam cuppam argenteam et alteram de mazere, cuius cooperturam prior Thomas circulo argenteo deaurato circumdedit. Reliquit eciam conuentui alios ciphos de mazere et coclearia argentea et duos anulos aureos. Et emit molendinum de Aldinton' et dedit illud ad elemosinariam, saluo redditu dominorum. Obligauit tamen medietatem pratorum de Bradewelle et de Burton',[1] et accepit pre manibus a Templariis de Gutingens,[2] scilicet pro quolibet anno duodecim marcas: et cum mortuus esset adhuc supererant de termino Templariorum octo anni. Emit autem minus uas Eucaristie et duo magna puluinaria cerica, et fecit tres sedes abbatum.

516. *De operibus Thome Marlebarwe decani et sacriste*[a]

Anno tercio monachatus istius[b] Thome, eo quod esset iurisperitus adquieuerunt consilio eius, licet tarde, abbas et conuentus, et reppulerunt episcopum Wygornen' uolentem uenire Eueshamiam causa uisitacionis. Quod a tempore Alurici abbatis nulli ausi erant facere. Et tunc factus est decanus Christianitatis Vallis Eueshamie, quod a tempore Auicii et Alurici priorum nullus monachus erat.

517. Et ipso existente procuratore in curia Romana, precipue per eius industriam et laborem, cum Dei auxilio et consilio ceterorum fratrum lata est sentencia a pontifice Romano pro exempcione et libertate ecclesie Eueshamie contra episcopum Wygornie,[3] sicut in libro fo. 183vb superius quem idem prior de eadem causa com|posuit plenius continetur.

518. Per huius eciam cautelam cum instancia aliorum fratrum sunt certi redditus in pluribus officiis monasterii assignati, et in aliis augmentati et quidam reuocati: sicut in eodem libro continetur. Iste eciam Thomas,[c] post reditum suum a curia Romana, sicut in curia didicerat in pluribus ecclesiis alibi factum, dedit consilium quod consuetudines monasterii et redditus ad conuentum pertinentes scriberentur, et per sigilla abbatis et conuentus et legati sedis

---

[a] De bonis operibus prioris Thome *V*   [b] prioris *subst. V*   [c] prior *subst. V*

---

[1] Both are in Glos.
[2] In Glos. Founded *c.*1150 by Gilbert de Lacy; KH, p. 296.

515. However, he enriched us with a fine ring for Mass, and a mitre, with two albs woven with gold, a cope of red samite embroidered with gold, and three tunics. For the altar of the Lady Chapel he gave a priest's vestment and a chasuble of red samite. For the high-table of the refectory he left a silver cup and another of maple-wood which Prior Thomas had plated with silver-gilt. He also left the convent other bowls of maple-wood as well as silver spoons and two gold rings. He bought the mill of Aldington and gave it to the almonry, saving the rent of the lords [of the manor]. But he mortgaged half of the meadows of Broadwell and Bourton,[1] receiving twelve marks in cash from the Templars of Guiting[2] every year: when he died there were still eight years to go before the mortgage matured. He had also bought a small eucharistic vessel and two large silk cushions, and he had three abbatial seats made.

516. *The deeds of Thomas [of] Marlborough as dean and sacrist*
In Thomas's third year as a monk, because he was learned in the law the abbot and convent accepted his advice, though reluctantly, and refused to admit the bishop of Worcester who wanted to come to Evesham to carry out a visitation. No bishop of Worcester had dared to do this since the time of Abbot Ælfric. Thomas became dean of Christianity of the Vale of Evesham, an office that no monk had held since the time of the priors Æfic and Ælfric.

517. When he was proctor at the Roman curia, the Roman pontiff passed a sentence against the bishop of Worcester in favour of the exemption and liberty of the church of Evesham:[3] this result was achieved mainly through Thomas's diligence and toil, but with God's help and the counsel of the rest of his brethren, as is fully described above in the book which the prior composed about the case.

518. As the result of his prudence and the steadfastness of other brethren, fixed revenues were assigned to many offices of the monastery and in others revenues were either increased or reclaimed: details are recorded in the same book. When Thomas returned from the Roman curia he gave advice about something which he had learned was practised in numerous churches elsewhere, and this was that the customs and revenues belonging to the convent should be put in writing and confirmed with the seals of the abbot, the convent and

---

[3] Innocent III's 'Ex ore sedentis' of 18 Jan. 1206; see above, **342–55**.

Romane et eciam ipsius Romani pontificis confirmarentur.[1] Quod uix et cum multo labore et periculo fuit optentum. Et nisi diuina gratia conuentui subuenisset, in ipso optentu multorum monachorum sanguis effusus fuisset, sicut in predicto libro habetur.

519. *ᵃPost primum eciam casumᵃ* turris[2] cum omnes fratres de reparatione ecclesie et eorum que per casum turris erant confracta desperarent. Ad peticionem fratrum et iussionem abbatis idem Thomas misertus ecclesie sue apposuit manum ad predictorum reparacionem. Et licet redditus *ᵇad hoc non haberet assignatos,ᵇ* de pecunia labore suo et prudencia adquisita, exceptis tingnis presbiterii, que conuentus pro maiori parte emit.[3] Muros presbiterii in modum pinnacularum ad deambulandum circa presbiterium, quod prius*ᶜ* factum non fuit; et ipsum presbiterium cum tectis criptarum presbiterio adiacentibus, et amplius quam medietatem tingnorum turris, infra biennium reparauit.

520. Cum eciam abbas, per exemptionem factus securus, quod a nullo nisi a domino papa uel legato eius posset deponi, multa immobilia dilapidasset et ecclesiam ere alieno ad mille marcarum onerasset. Et in tantum conuentum depressisset quod multi unde se cooperirent honeste, uel inundante pluuia ubi caput suum reclinarent, non haberent,[4] et multi fame et inedia afficerentur. | Iste Thomas decanus, nondum prior, opposuit se murum pro domo Domini,[5] et cum legatum Romane sedis pro quibusdam negociis ecclesie adisset, ex precepto eiusdem legati statum monasterii Eueshamie ei retulit. Et postea, cum uenisset legatus Eueshamiam, coram eo abbatem accusauit et super septem uel octo criminibus per abbatis confessionem, et per rei euidenciam et per fratrum testimonium, eum conuicit. Et ita, sub discrimine habitus et ordinis ipsius Thome decani—talionem reportaturi si eum non conuicisset—depositus est abbas Rogerus in maximam Eueshamie ecclesie utilitatem. Nam eo deposito, reuocata sunt immobilia ab eo diuersis titulis alienata usque ad redditum uiginti marcarum, tum tempore uacacionis tum tempore abbatis Rondulphi,*ᵈ* qui eciam omnia priuilegia que idem decanus Romanis

fo. 184ʳᵃ

ᵃ⁻ᵃ Post casum eciam, *omitting* primum V   *ᵇ⁻ᵇ* ad hoc assignatos non habere(?n)t V
ᶜ in monasterio *add.* V   *ᵈ* Randulfi V

---

[1] See above, **393**, **395**, **397**, and **430**, the legate's confirmation; and **431**, for the pope's later confirmation.   [2] The tower collapsed in 1207, see above, **436**.
[3] As monks were not permitted ownership of private property (*RSB* cap. 33), this is likely to refer to funds attached to the office of dean which Thomas held.
[4] Luke 9: 58.   [5] Cf. Ezek. 13: 5.

the papal legate, and even of the pope himself.[1] He got this done, but only with difficulty and hard work, and at personal risk. Had not divine grace come to the assistance of the convent, the blood of many monks would have been shed in achieving this, as is shown in the above-mentioned book.

519. When the church tower first collapsed[2] all the brethren despaired of being able to repair the church and the property that had been damaged by the collapse of the tower. Thomas was asked by the brethren, and instructed by the abbot, to do something about it, and having a deep feeling for his church he set himself the task of repairing the damage. Except for the timber for the presbytery, which was bought in the main by the convent, no revenue had been allocated for this work, but he used money that he had acquired by his own prudent management.[3] Within two years he renewed the walls of the presbytery and built them with pinnacles to provide an ambulatory around the presbytery, a feature not existing previously; he repaired the presbytery itself along with the ceilings of the crypt adjoining the presbytery, and replaced more than half of the timbers of the tower.

520. The previous abbot, made bold by the exemption, in the knowledge that he could not be deposed by anyone except the pope or his legate, had ruined much of the immoveable property and burdened the church with a debt totalling a thousand marks. He had dealt the convent such a crushing blow that many had no means of clothing themselves decently and nowhere to lay their heads[4] when the rain poured in, and there were many who suffered from hunger and fasting. Thomas was not at that time prior, but dean, and he set himself up as a wall for the house of the Lord,[5] for when he went to see the papal legate on certain church business, at the request of the legate he reported to him on the state of the monastery at Evesham. Afterwards, when the legate came to Evesham, he accused the abbot to his face, and convicted him of seven or eight crimes admitted to by the abbot, and proved by the evidence of his behaviour and the testimony of the brethren. So it was that, at the risk of Thomas the dean losing his habit and status—for he would have suffered the retaliation of the abbot if he had not secured his deposition—Abbot Roger was deposed to the very great gain of the church of Evesham. Indeed, after Roger had been deposed, immoveables, which had been alienated by him under various pretexts and had brought him an income of twenty marks, were reclaimed not only during the time of the vacancy but also during Abbot Randulf's time, who secured, at

obligauerat pro quingentis marcis liberauit. Ob eorum igitur liberacionis gaudium, fecit*a* idem decanus *b*constitui ut in die qua cum processione receperunt priuilegia,*b* de obuentionibus decanatus annuatim detur caritas conuentui.

521. Secundo anno abbatis Rondulphi iuit idem decanus cum eo Romam ad concilium generale.[1] Vbi, de eius consilio et industria, confirmacionem dispositionis reddituum et multa alia necessaria impetrauerunt. Secundo uero anno reditus a curia, factus est sacrista,[2] et fecit lectricium[3] retro chorum: quod prius factum non erat in ecclesia Eueshamie, set legebantur lectiones iuxta tumbam sancti Wlsini.[4] Fecit eciam *c*caminum in ecclesia*c* cum pede orilogii, et albas duodecim. Et omnes fenestras uitreas que confracte erant per casum turris et omnia feretra confracta reparauit. Et feretrum sancti Wistani nouum fecit, et tres tabulas maioris altaris reparauit et illam

fo. 184*rb* ante maius altare cum ipso al|tari ampliauit, *d*in quorum reparacione expendit plusquam decem marcas.*d e*Nam omnia hec per casum turris usque ad desperationem reparacionis erant demolita.*e f*Quinque eciam arcus presbiterii et unum ante hostium criptarum opturauit.*f* Redditus etiam sacristarie usque ad summam duarum marcarum adauxit, ueluti ecclesiam de Norton *g*et decimas de dominico de Lench in proprios usus reuocando.*g* Iste eciam sacrista *h*primo optinuit uiuum auerium*h* secundo melius*i* mortuorum cum corporibus eorum et denarium offerendum ad missam mortuorum. *j*Pro quorum augmentatione,*j* fecit constitui in capitulo quod lampas ante maius altare et lampas in criptis ante altare sancte Marie iugiter essent ardentes. Hec omnia fecit infra unum annum et, relicto officio omnibus bonis pleno,*k* factus est prior.[5]

---

a subiit *V*   *b–b* honus pro se et successoribus suis ut *subst. V*   *c–c* piscinam in claustro extra hostium ecclesie et caminum in ecclesia *V*   *d–d* que omnia per casum turris usque ad desperationem reparationis erant demolita in quorum reparationis expendit plusquam x marc. *subst. V*   *e–e om. V*   *f–f* Et v arcas presbiterii obturauit et .i. ante hostium (criptarum?) *V*   *g–g* in proprios usos reuocando et decimas de dominico de Lench *V*   *h–h* primus obtinxit bouem *V*   *i* meliorem *V*   *j–j* De quibus omnibus *V*   *k* repleto *V*   *l V is followed here by* Iste prior sepeliuit . . . profuturis *fo. 185ra–rb* (528 *k–k*)

---

[1] The Fourth Lateran Council of 1215.

[2] 1217.

[3] The fine lectern, which was found at Evesham in 1813, now at Norton, would appear to be *c.*1180 and so earlier than this, and is most likely to be associated with Abbot Adam. See above, **182** and n. 2 (p. 186). Houghton ('Stone lecterns', p. 4) supposed that the Crowle lectionary is Thomas's, but there is no stylistic support for that conjecture.

the cost of five hundred marks, the release of all the privileges which the dean [Thomas] had pawned to the Romans. In celebration of their release, the dean established that every year on the same day that they had celebrated receiving their privileges with a procession a *caritas* of wine should be given to the convent from the income of the dean's office.

521. In Abbot Randulf's second year of office the same dean [Thomas] went with him to the General Council at Rome.[1] There, as the result of Thomas's advice and exertions, they petitioned for confirmation of the disposition of the revenues and many other necessary benefits. Two years after his return from the curia, Thomas was made sacrist,[2] and he had a lectern[3] made behind the choir: there had not been one in the church of Evesham before, but lessons used to be read by the tomb of St Wulfsige.[4] He also put a stove in the church at the base of the clock, and had twelve albs made. He replaced all the glass windows that had been broken when the tower collapsed, and repaired all the damaged shrines. He renewed the shrine of St Wigstan, repaired the three high-altar tables, and enlarged the space in front of the high altar as well as the altar itself, spending more than ten marks on the restoration of all these things. In fact, the damage to these things resulting from the collapse of the tower had been such that there had been no hope of their restoration. Then Thomas blocked up five of the arches of the presbytery and one that was in front of the entrance to the crypt. He increased the revenue of the sacristy to a total of two marks, by recovering for the monastery's own use the church of Norton and the tithes of the demesne of Lench. When men died, as sacrist he was the first to obtain the second-best of their draught animals at the time the monastery received their bodies and the penny offered for the mass of the dead. From the increase in these benefits, he had it decreed in chapter that lamps should be kept perpetually burning before the high altar and in the crypt before the altar of St Mary. He did all these things within the span of one year and, after relinquishing an office that had abounded in all these good acts, he was made prior.[5]

---

[4] For Wulfsige, or Wulsi, a saintly hermit attached to the abbey at Evesham, and brother of Æfic, see above, 146. He was confessor of Earl Leofric and Lady Godgifu and adviser to Wulfstan of Worcester. He died 1097/1098 and was buried in the abbey at Evesham.

[5] In 1218.

522. *De operibus Thome de Marlebarwe prioris*

Iste prior in ingressu suo attulit secum libros[1] utriusque iuris, canonici scilicet et ciuilis, per quos rexit scolas ante monachatum apud *ª*Oxoniam et Exoniam.*ª*[2] Et libros phisice,*ᵇ* scilicet librum Democriti[3] et librum Antiparalenionis[4] et librum Graduum secundum Constantinum,[5] et Ysidorum*ᶜ* de Officiis,[6] et Quadriuium Ysidori,[7] Tullium de Amicitia[8] et alterum librum Tullii, et Tullium de Senectute,[9] et Tullium de Paradoxis,[10] et Lucanum[11] et Iuuenalem,[12] et multos alios auctores, et multos sermones et notas et questiones theologie, et multas notas artis gramatice cum uerbis preceptiuis et libro accentuum.

523. Post prioratum fecit magnum breuiarium quod melius tunc fuit in monasterio, et Haymonem super Apocalipsim et uitas et gesta*ᵈ* patronorum et abbatum*ᵉ* Eueshamie*ᶠ* in uno uolumine,[13] et iterum easdem uitas et eadem gesta seorsum in alio uolumine. Fecit | eciam magnum Psalterium quod tunc fuit*ᵍ* melius*ʰ* in monasterio, exceptis glosatis, *ⁱ*ut semper habeant illud priores ad opus suum. Et de grossa littera librum de ordine officii abbatis a Purificacione sancte Marie usque ad Pentecosten, et de professione monachorum,[14] et lectiones de Pascha et Pentecosten fecit scribi et ordinauit in uno uolumine: item in alio predictum officium, quod officium non prius erat ordinate

fo. 184ᵛª

ª⁻ª Exoniam et Oxoniam *V, where the whole line has been squeezed in.* Exon et *is added before* Oxon *in H*   *ᵇ* fisice *V*   *ᶜ* Ysodorum *V*   *ᵈ* et gesta *om. V*   *ᵉ* et abbatum *om. V*   *ᶠ* ecclesie de Eueshamensis cum gestis omnium bonorum et malorum ecclesie Eueshamens' *subst. for* Eueshamie *V*   *ᵍ* tunc fuit *om. V*   *ʰ* fuit *add. V*   *ⁱ⁻ⁱ* *om. V*

---

[1] For identification of all the named books and whether there are editions of them, see *English Benedictine Libraries: the Shorter Catalogues*, ed. R. Sharpe, J. P. Carley, R. M. Thomson, and A. G. Watson (Corpus of British Medieval Library Catalogues, iv, 1996), pp. 136–8.

[2] See above, Introduction, p. xviii. Exeter is likely to be a mistake due to a miscopying or a mishearing.

[3] Pseudo-Democritus, *Liber medicinalis*, ed. in Latin, J. Heeg, *Abhandlungen der. K. Preussischen Akademie der Wissenschaften*, phil.-hist. Classe (1913), iv. 46–59. Listed by L. Thorndike and P. Kibre, *A Catalogue of Incipits of Mediaeval Scientific Writings in Latin*, 2nd edn. (London, 1963), 364G, and G. Sabbah *et al.*, *Bibliographie des textes médicaux latins* (Paris, 1987), 68.

[4] Whether this work was by Galen or not is in doubt as it is also attributed to Hippocrates. It is probably related to Galen's *De succedaneis*. Listed Thorndike and Kibre, *Catalogue of Incipits*, 317k, 1128i, 1130b, 1278j (with attribution), and 1128k, 1210h, 1260i (without attribution). It is a short text, usually found bound up with other texts, as in Bethesda, Nat. Lib. Of Medicine, MS 8, a mid-12th cent. manuscript from an English monastic house.

[5] A text attributed to Constantine the African who had translated the work of Isaac

522. *The deeds of Thomas of Marlborough as prior*

On entering office as prior Thomas brought with him books[1] of both branches of the law, canon and civil, which he had used before becoming a monk, when he lectured as a master in the schools at Oxford and Exeter.[2] And there were books on medicine, namely, Democritus [*Liber medicinalis*],[3] the *Liber Antiparalenionis* [Galen, *Antibalomenon*],[4] the *Liber graduum* according to Constantine,[5] Isidore's *De Officiis*[6] and *Quadrivium*,[7] Cicero's *De Amicitia*,[8] with another of his books, his *De Senectute*[9] and *De Paradoxis* [*Paradoxa stoicorum*],[10] Lucan [*De bello civili*],[11] Juvenal [*Saturae*],[12] and many other classical authors, many sermons, commentaries and disputations on theology, many commentaries on grammar with words of explanation, and a book on intonation.

523. After his priorate he had made a large breviary which was the best copy at that time in the monastery, and he had bound Haymo's *Super Apocalypsim* and *The Lives and Deeds of the Patrons and of the Abbots of Evesham* in one volume,[13] and also the same *Lives and Deeds* separately in another volume. He also had made a large Psalter, which, except for the glosses, was the best at that time in the monastery, so that the priors might always have it available for their own service. He also had the following produced and written in large script, and in one volume: a book on the office of the abbot covering the period from the Feast of the Purification of St Mary to Pentecost, a book on the profession of monks,[14] and a book of readings on Easter and Pentecost. He also had the office of the abbot written in another book, for this had not previously been part of

Judaeus. Listed in Thorndike and Kibre, *Catalogue of Incipits*, 115j, in a BN MS (6891), where the text is immediately followed by the Antibalomenon. It has been edited by M. McVeagh (from Oxford, All Souls MS 69), '"Apud antiquos" and mediaeval pharmacology' *Medizinhistorisches Journal*, i (1966), 16–22 (text 18–22).

[6] Isidore, *De ecclesiasticis officiis*. E. Dekkers, *Clavis Patrum Latinorum*, 2nd edn. (Steenbrugge, 1961), 1207; ed. C. M. Lawson, Corpus Christianorum, Series latina, cxiii (1989).

[7] R. Sharpe *et al.* (*English Benedictine Libraries*, p. 137), suggest that this may have been a part of Isidore's *Etymologiae*, for which see Dekkers, 1186.

[8] Ed. K. Simbeck (Teubner: Leipzig; Stuttgart, 1917).

[9] Ed. K. Simbeck, ibid. (1917).

[10] *Paradoxa stoicorum*, ed. O. Plasburg (Teubner, 1908), and R. Badali (Milan, 1968).

[11] Ed. A. E. Housman (Oxford, 1926).

[12] Ed. W. V. Clausen (Oxford Classical Texts, 1959).

[13] The present Rawlinson MS A 287, though re-bound.

[14] This might be construed as meaning a book in which monks wrote their professions, but that interpretation seems less likely because the singular 'de professione' is used, not 'de professionibus'.

scriptum apud nos.[il] [1] Inuenit eciam omnia necessaria ad quatuor antiphonaria cum ipsis notariis, excepto quod fratres monasterii scripserunt ea,[a] [b]et duo communia sanctorum in ueteribus antiphonariis. Emit eciam quatuor Euangelia glosata, et Ysaiam et Ezechielem glosatos, et postillas super Mattheum, et allegorias super Vetus Testamentum,[2] et Trenas Ieremie glosatas, et Exposicionem Misse secundum Innocencium papam,[3] librum eciam Alexandri Nequam, qui dicitur Corrogaciones Promethei, de partibus Veteris Testamenti et Noui.[b4] [c]Plures eciam alios libros, quos[d] bone memorie Willelmus de Lith[5] inceperat, perfecit, ueluti martilogium et Expositionem[e] Misse, et quasdam notas egregias super Psalterium.[cl]

524. Fecit eciam duas albas cum apparatibus auro textis, et ornauit duas nigras capas floribus auro textis. Turres eciam presbiterii fecit et quinque tabellata lapidea super quinque tecta criptarum. Et illam partem ecclesie que[f] super altare sancti Iohannis Baptiste reparauit post secundum casum turris, et fecit eam in modum pinnaculorum ad deambulandum circa illam partem ecclesie [g]cum tabellatu et turribus petrinis. Et[g] fenestram uitream in presbiterio de historia sancti Egwini, et duas uitreas[h] in fronte occidentali ecclesie. Fecit eciam[i] thronum feretri sancti Egwini et ipsum feretrum floribus et lapidibus preciosis, per casum turris mutilatum, reparauit. Fecit eciam quatuor

fo. 184[vb] pri|mas sedes de choro prioris et formas in eodem choro.

525. Iste eciam[j] prior [k]omnes fenestras magne infirmarie ferreis obstaculis muniuit. Et duas areas seldarum in medio magni uici Eueshamie emit a Ricardo, filio Hugonis de Warwic, et dedit eas ad

---

[a] eos V   [b-b] et due communia . . . Testamenti et Novi *and*   [c-cl] Plures eciam alios . . . egregias super Psalterium *reversed V, but with notes* a *and* b *to correct so as to read as in the main text*   [d] ins. V   [e] exceptionem! V   [f] *followed by* est *in V*   [g-g] V substitutes et duas turres fecit super eandem partem ecclesie cum tabulatu petrino. Fecit etiam   [h] ueteres! V   [i] Et *for* Fecit etiam V   [j] *om.* V   [k-kl] *om.* V, *subst.* emit decem acras annuas (*inserted*) terre de Randulfo dispensatore in Litlethon' in adiutorium prioratus et anniuersarii eiusdem H. prioris uidelicet quod idem prior (pro tempore?) pascat eadem die uiginti quinque pauperes et commutauit acras easdem pro terra de Benigwrthe. Emit etiam terra in Merstowe de Hugone de Warwic et aliam de filia serganti ad anniuersarium suum et boscum de Petro de Lenc ad idem faciendum ut habeat pitanciarius ad(?) nutrimentum animalium. Capitulum etiam pro maiori parte depinxit.

[1] This probably formed the basis of Bodleian Library MS Barlow 7 (*Officium Ecclesiasticum Abbatum*, ed. H. A. Wilson, Henry Bradshaw Soc. vi: London, 1893, a late 13th- or early 14th-cent. manuscript, written in all likelihood for Abbot John of Brockhampton (1282–1316)).

[2] Sharpe *et al.* (*English Benedictine Libraries*, pp. 137–8), suggest that this might be *ps.* Hugh of Saint-Victor, *Allegorie in Vetus testamentum* (*PL* clxxv. 633–750) or Richard of Saint-Victor, *Liber exceptionum*, commonly called *Allegorie*. This text is printed in *PL* 177,

the written offices amongst us.[1] He further provided everything
needed for the writing of four antiphonals complete with musical
notation (though the brethren of the monastery did the copying) as
well as for two sets of services for saints' days from ancient books of
antiphons. He bought the four Gospels glossed and Isaiah and Ezekiel
also glossed, commentaries on Matthew, a book of allegories in the
Old Testament,[2] a glossed Lamentations, the *Exposition of the Mass*
according to Pope Innocent [III],[3] and the book of Alexander
Nequam, called the *'Corrigationes' of Prometheus*, on parts of the
Old and New Testaments.[4] He completed many other books, which
William de Lith[5] of blessed memory had begun, for instance, a
calendar of saints and benefactors, and an exposition of the Mass, as
well as some excellent commentaries on the Psalter.

524. Thomas had two albs made with ornamentation woven in gold,
and two black copes adorned with flowers woven in gold. He built the
towers of the presbytery and five stone floors above the five ceilings of
the crypt. After the second collapse of the tower he restored that part
of the church which is over the altar of St John the Baptist, and built
it with pinnacles to provide an ambulatory around that part of the
church, with the floor and towers of stone. He put a glass window in
the presbytery illustrating the story of St Ecgwine, and two glass
windows in the west front of the church. He built a throne for the
shrine of St Ecgwine and restored the shrine itself, which had been
badly damaged by the collapse of the tower, renewing its flowers and
precious stones. He had four front seats made for the prior's choir
and put benches in the same choir.

525. It was when he was prior that he protected all the windows
of the great infirmary with iron bars. He bought from Richard,
son of Hugh of Warwick, two sites for shops in the centre of
Evesham's main street, and used their income for the altar-lights

191–184, part I only, and ed. J. Châtillon, Textes philosophiques du moyen âge, v (Paris,
1958).
    [3] This is presumably the 'De sacro altaris mysterio' in six books of *c.*1195. The text is
printed in *PL* ccxvii. 773–916, and Thomas's *Expositio* may have included the *Ordo Missae*
(*PL* ccxvii. 765–74). D. F. Wright, 'A medieval commentary on the mass: particulae 2–3 &
5–6 of the *De Missarum Mysteriis* (ca. 1195) of Cardinal Lothar of Segni (Pope Innocent
III)', Ph.D. thesis, Notre Dame Univ. 1977, discussed part of the text. C. Egger of the
University of Vienna is working on a critical edition.
    [4] Excerpts ed. P. Meyer in *Notices et extraits*, 35 (2) (1896), pp. 641–82. See R. W.
Hunt, *The Schools and the Cloister: The Life and Writings of Alexander Nequam*, ed. M. T.
Gibson (Oxford, 1984), pp. 131–4, 138–9. Nequam was abbot of the Augustinian house at
Cirencester: he died in 1217.   [5] See above, 396.

luminaria sancte Marie in criptis. Procurauit etiam quod Muriella filia auunculi sui dedit ad elemosinariam post mortem suam et filiorum suorum domum quam emit in Euesham a prefato Ricardo. Capitulum pro maiori parte depinxit.[kl 1] Fecit eciam lauatorium ante hostium ecclesie in claustro.[a] In plumbo [b]et in stagno[b] et operariis[c] magni lauatorii in claustro expendit xv solidos. Hic enim semper fuit modus istius prioris, quod[d] circa reparacionem et conseruacionem bonorum ecclesie multum sollicitus fuit, et bene operantes libenter adiuuit. Ad magnum etiam campanile quod magister Adam Sortes incepit,[2] dedit plusquam ad ualenciam unius marce. Muros eciam cimiterii mona- chorum magnis sumptibus reparauit et priuatum dormitorium minans ruinam tribus arcubus suffulcit in quibus arcubus expendit plusquam quatuor marcas. Arcum eciam nobiliorem noue infirmarie fecit, ubi expendit plusquam quatuor marcas, et multa alia cum magna diligen- cia operi illi impendit. In tingnis eciam plumbo et operariis ad cooperturam unius anguli magne[e] turris ecclesie expendit xx[f] solidos. Omnia eciam uestimenta capelle superioris infirmarie fecit cum hostio specule eiusdem. Minus eciam uas eukaristie appendit cum cathenula argentea et tintinnabilum in refectorio ad discum cum cathena ferrea appendit.[g] Et textum maioris altaris sine libro reparauit. Mos enim semper eius fuit huiusmodi paruos defectus supplere.

526. Iste eciam prior emit quandam terram de Ada Peterel, et dedit fo. 185[ra] medietatem ad elemosi|nariam et alteram medietatem ad luminaria sancte Marie in criptis. [h]Magnas eciam fenestras misericordie ferreis obstaculis ab ingressu hominum muniuit. Et magnam diligenciam apposuit apud abbatem Rondulphum[i] ut ortus infirmarie ampliaretur ad latitudinem coquine, et magnos sumptus in fossato et muris clausure eius fecit; eciam hostium misericordie uersus eundem ortum positum[j] ubi fuit tempore huius scripti.

527. Laudabilem eciam consuetudinem fecit constitui: uidelicet,

---

[a] ante hostium *add. V*   [b-b] etiam et stagno *V*   [c] ad reparacionem *add. V*
[d] quod *add. V*   [e] *V; incorrectly* magni *R*   [f] uiginti *V*   [g] suspendit *V*
[h-h] (*p. 496*) *This passage,* Magnas eciam fenestras . . . maius luminare uestiarii, *on fo. 5 of V, is repeated again at the bottom of fo. 6. It is followed by* Preterea librum de ordine officii abbatis a purificatione sancte Marie usque ad sanctum Pascha et lectiones de Pascha et de Pentecost' et de benedictione fontium baptismatis et de professione monachorum in uno uolumine de grossa litera fecit et in alio de gratiliori litera; que omnia non erant prius scripta apud nos ordinate.   [i] Randl' *V*   [j] posuit *V*

---

[1] V 'He bought ten acres of land [which were rented] yearly from Randulf the steward in Littleton to support the office of prior and the anniversary of the same H. the prior, so that on that occasion the prior of the time might feed twenty-five poor people, and he

of St Mary in the Undercroft. He made arrangements with his cousin Muriel [of Chepstow] for the house, which she had bought in Evesham from the above-mentioned Richard, to be given to the almonry after she and her sons had died. He had most of the chapter-house painted.[1] He had a washing place built in the cloister in front of the entrance to the church. He spent fifteen shillings on the lead, the pit, and the labour-costs of the 'great' wash place in the cloister. This prior was always as generous, for he was very concerned about the repair and maintenance of the church's property, and gladly assisted those who worked well. He contributed more than a mark towards the great bell-tower which Master Adam Sortes had begun.[2] He repaired the walls of the monks' cemetery at great expense and, at a cost of more than four marks, he had three arches built to support the private dormitory which threatened to collapse. He had a magnificent arch built for the new infirmary, which cost him more than four marks, and he spent money on many other items for the infirmary, taking great pains over it. He also spent twenty shillings on the beams, lead, and labour-costs required to roof one corner of the great tower of the church. He provided all the vestments for the chapel of the upper infirmary at the same time as he had the entrance of the watch chamber of the same [chapel] made. He had a silver chain attached to a small eucharistic vessel and also an iron chain to the bell at the high table in the refectory. He restored from memory the text that was on the high altar. But it was always his way to make good any minor imperfections of this kind.

526. It was when he was prior that he bought some land of Adam Peterel, and he gave half of this to the almonry and the other half for the altar-lights of St Mary in the Crypt. He protected the large windows of the misericord from burglary by fitting iron bars. He made great efforts during the time of Abbot Randulf to have the infirmary garden enlarged to the width of the kitchen, and spent a considerable sum on the ditch and walls necessary to enclose it; he also put a door in the misericord to face this garden, and this still remains at the time of writing.

527. Furthermore, Prior Thomas had the following commendable

---

exchanged those same acres for land in Bengeworth. He also bought land in Merstow from Hugh of Warwick and other land from the daughter of the serjeant for his [own] anniversary and woodland from Peter of Lench for the same purpose, so that the pittancer might have help for feeding the animals. He also had most of the chapter house painted.'

[2] See above, **275** and n., and **499**.

quod feretrum*a* sancti Wistani*b*1 et feretrum sancti Credani*c*2 in
festiuitatibus eorum ante altare ponerentur, et tunc inueniet prior
de terra de Bengeworthe,*d* *e*quam prior Thomas adquisiuit,*e* cereum
per diem et noctem iugiter ardentem coram reliquiis eorundem
sanctorum. Et trabem ante altare sancti Petri cum cruce et ymagini-
bus reparauit et exaltauit ad maius*f* luminare uestiarii.*h*13 Fecit eciam
tabellatum locutorii super capellam sancte Anne ad occidentem.
Postquam eciam altare sancte Marie in criptis a furibus secundo*g*
spoliatum fuit libris et uestimentis ad ualenciam decem marcarum,*h*
iste prior ad restauracionem uestimentorum beate Marie emit unam
albam cum apparatu, auro super intexto. Dedit eciam dimidiam
marcam pro carta confirmacionis terre de Radeforde ad luminaria
eiusdem altaris, et tres solidos in auxilium precii dalmatice de rubro
examito quam abbas Rondulphus*i* emit.*j*4 Dedit eciam dimidiam
marcam pro carta confirmacionis et warentizacionis terre precentoris
in Alincestria iuxta pontem.

528. Insuper *k*iste prior sepeliuit predecessorem suum, priorem
Iohannem, in mausoleo nouo lapideo, et Iohannem cognomento
Dionisium similiter, de quo idem prior Thomas dicere consueuit
quod nunquam uidit hominem tam perfecte omne genus penitencie

peragere | sicut idem Iohannes peregit triginta annos et amplius, 'in
ieiuniis et oracionibus',5 in lacrimarum effusione et uigiliis, in
corporalibus cruciatibus et frigoribus, in uestimentorum uilitate et
asperitate, et ultra modum aliorum fratrum corporalium sustenta-
cionum subtraxcione, cunctis sibi subtractis bonis usibus et pauperum sustentacionibus profuturis.*k*

529. Emit eciam iste prior redditum duodecim denariorum a
Ricardo iuuene filio Richardi claudi de domo illorum que est in
magno uico Eueshamie, et redditum nouem denariorum a Willelmo
de Ponte, de terra quam Eua filia eiusdem Willelmi tenet de eo in
maritagio in Alincestria, et dedit eos idem prior ad elemosinariam
Eueshamie. Fecit eciam thronum feretro sancti Wistani et ymaginem

---

a fetrum *V*   *b* Credani *V*   *c* Wistani *V*   *d* Beningewrth' *V*   *e–e* *om.* uel de
Luthlet' unum *subst. V*   *f* magis *V*   *g om. V*   *h* librarum *V*   *i* Randulfus *V*
j Hic enim fuit mos istius monachi quo pro posse suo semper suppleuit defectus ne negotia
ecclesie relinquerentur infecta *add. V which ends here*   *k–k* V (*see note l, above on p. 488,*
end)

---

1 1 June.
2 19 Aug.
3 V at this point gives roughly the account in **523** with the addition of a work on the

custom established: during the festivals of St Wigstan[1] and St Credan[2] their reliquaries were to be placed in front of the altar, and the prior was to provide from the land in Bengeworth, which he had acquired, a candle to burn perpetually before the relics of these saints day and night. He restored the [rood] beam in front of St Peter's altar together with the cross and images and raised the vestry altar-light to a higher level.[3] He had flooring put in the parlour above the chapel of St Anne on the western side. After the altar of St Mary in the Crypt had been twice robbed by thieves of its books and vestments to the value of ten marks, this prior purchased an alb with ornamentation interwoven in gold thread as a replacement for the vestments of the blessed Mary. He gave half a mark to pay for the charter of confirmation of the land in Radford, the income from which was for the lights of the same altar, and three shillings as a contribution towards the cost of the dalmatic of red samite that Abbot Randulf purchased.[4] He also gave half a mark to pay for the charter of confirmation and warranty of the land belonging to the precentor by the bridge in Alcester [Warws.].

528. As prior, Thomas buried his predecessor, Prior John, in a new stone tomb. He did the same for John, surnamed Dionysius, of whom he used to say that he had never seen a man who fulfilled every kind of penance so impeccably as John Dionysius had done over thirty or more years, 'in fasting and in prayer,'[5] in shedding tears and in vigils, in mortifying the flesh and enduring the cold, in the raggedness and coarseness of his clothing, in depriving his body of sustenance beyond the endurance of other brethren, and in depriving himself of every good thing which could be used for the sustenance of the poor.

529. As prior, he procured a rent of twelve pence from the young man Richard, son of Richard the lame, in respect of their house situated in the main street of Evesham, and a rent of nine pence from William de Ponte, in respect of the land which William's daughter Eva held of him in Alcester on her marriage, and this rent Thomas gave to the almonry of Evesham. He also had a throne made for the shrine of St Wigstan

---

blessing of baptismal fonts: 'Moreover he provided in one volume of large script, and in another of finer script, a book on the order of the office of abbot for the period from the purification of St Mary to the feast of Easter, and readings for Easter, for Pentecost, for the blessing of baptismal fonts, and for the profession of monks; all these things were not previously written down for regular use among us.'

[4] V 'This was the custom of that monk, always to the best of his ability to make good any deficiencies so that the business of the church should not be left unaccomplished.'

[5] Judith 4: 12.

regiam eidem throno proposuit, quam perfecerat postquam factus est abbas.

530. Hec uobis minuta facta cum maioribus istius Thome monachi scripsimus, ut exemplo eius saltem paruos defectus suppleatis, quia qui minora contempnit paulatim decidit.[1]

531. *De operibus Thome de Marlebarwe abbatis*

Abbate Rondulpho defuncto[2] misit rex ad abbatiam duos clericos et unum militem. Qui, nec libere tenentibus nec uillanis parcentes, ceperunt ab eis ad opus domini regis trecentas marcas, et tenuit rex abbatiam in manu sua per tres partes anni, et omnes prouentus in usus suos conuertit, exceptis redditibus specialiter ad obediencias monachorum assignatis.[3]

532. Interim statim missi sunt duo fratres cum litteris conuentus ad dominum regem. Qui impetrauerunt licenciam eligendi abbatem et, redeuntes quinto die, scilicet in uigilia sancti Thome apostoli, statim elegerunt Thomam priorem suum.[4] Et in crastino Natalis Domini presentauerunt eum domino regi qui tunc age|bat apud Eboracum.[5] Cui reuertenti occurrit electus, et in Epiphania Domini ab eo est admissus, qui litteras domini regis ibi optinuit de consensu regio directas domino pape ut ab eo confirmacionem impetraret.[6] Et tunc missi sunt duo fratres Romam, qui in curia per octo ebdomadas moram facientes non poterant impetrare confirmacionem. Set tandem, quamuis domino pape et curie nollent seruire,[7] impetrauerunt litteras a domino papa in hac forma:

533. 'Gregorius episcopus, seruus seruorum Dei, uenerabili*ᵃ* fratri episcopo[8] et dilecto filio priori de Conuent'[9] salutem et apostolicam

fo. 185ᵛᵃ

ᵃ uiro *expunged*

---

[1] Cf. Ecclus. 19: 1.

[2] On 17 Dec. 1229; see above, Introduction, p. lvii n. 92.

[3] This is a classic description of the king's actions when a vacancy occurred in an abbey and underlines the importance of separating the abbot's income from that of the monks. The king committed the custody of the abbey to his chancellor the bishop of Chichester, Ralph Neville, and ordered all the tenants to report to Peter de Bedinton, the bishop's clerk. Furthermore, the sheriff of Worcester was ordered to give Peter de Bedinton full possession of all the things belonging to the abbey in his county, and similar orders were sent to the sheriffs of Northants., Glos., Lancs., and Warws.; *Patent Rolls of the reign of Henry III, 1225–32* (HMSO: London, 1903), p. 320.

[4] The two brethren who reported the death of Abbot Randulf, and who obtained the licence to elect on 19 Dec., were Adam, the subprior, and Walter, the cellarer; *Patent Rolls, 1225–32*, p. 320 In fact the eve of St Thomas the Apostle (20 Dec.), when they returned, was the fourth day and not the fifth.

and conceived the design for the royal image for this throne, which he had made after he became abbot.

530. We have combined the less important deeds of Thomas the monk with our description of his major deeds, so that you may by his example remedy at least minor faults, for he that condemneth small things shall fall little by little.[1]

531. *The deeds of Thomas of Marlborough as abbot*
When abbot Randulf died[2] the king sent two clerks and a knight to the abbey. These spared neither freemen nor villeins, but took three hundred marks from them for the king's purposes, and the king took possession of the abbey into his own hands for three-quarters of the year, and appropriated all the abbey's income for his own uses, except for the revenues specifically assigned to the obediences of the monks.[3]

532. Meanwhile, two brethren were immediately sent to the king with a letter from the convent. They obtained licence to elect an abbot and, returning five days later, on the eve of the feast of St Thomas the apostle, they immediately elected their prior, Thomas.[4] The day after Christmas they presented him to the king who was at that time staying at York.[5] After he had been elected, Thomas met the king on his return journey, and was admitted by him at Epiphany, when he obtained from him letters of royal assent which were directed to the pope to obtain his confirmation.[6] Two brethren were then dispatched to Rome, but although they spent eight weeks in the curia they could not obtain this confirmation. However, at last, despite their refusal to pay service dues to the pope and the curia,[7] they obtained a letter from the pope written in the following terms.

533. 'Gregory, bishop, servant of the servants of God, to the venerable brother bishop of Coventry,[8] and the beloved son, the prior of Coventry,[9] greeting and apostolic benediction. When our

[5] This does not mean that they presented Thomas physically at York, but that they notified the king of his election.

[6] *Patent Rolls, 1225–32*, p. 321. The king wrote to the pope on 7 Jan. from Newark (Notts.), approving the election of Thomas, and asking for papal confirmation.

[7] This was apparently a customary payment rather than a compulsory tax; cf W. E. Lunt, *Financial Relations of the Papacy with England to 1327* (Studies in Anglo-Papal Relations during the Middle Ages, i: Cambridge, Mass., 1939), pp. 461–2, and p. 681 for the amount paid by Evesham in 1317.

[8] Alexander Stavensby, who had been a royal proctor, was provided by the pope before 13 Apr. 1224, cons. 14 Apr. 1224 to 26 Dec. 1238; *HBC*, p. 253.

[9] Geoffrey II, prior from 1216 to 1235. He had been elected bishop in 1223, but the

benedictionem. Cum dilecti filii monachi monasterii de Euesham presentassent nobis electionem quam de persona Thome prioris eiusdem monasterii duxerant faciendam, humiliter supplicantes ut dignaremur electionem eandem tamquam celebratam de persona idonea confirmare, nos, eius examinato processu aliisque negocii circumstanciis attente pensatis, supplicacionem eorum non duximus admittendam. Ne uero dictum monasterium longa uacatione graue dispendium patiatur, discretioni uestre per apostolica scripta mandamus quatinus, si prefati monachi infra mensem post monitionem uestram ad electionem duxerint procedendum, uos electionem eorum, si fuerit canonica et electi persona idonea, autoritate apostolica confirmetis, tuque, frater episcope, munus electo benedictionis impendas. Alioquin, uos eadem auctoritate prouideatis de persona litterata que laudabilis sit conuersationis et uite, de gremio eiusdem ecclesie si ibi inuenitur idoneus, alioquin de alia, prefato monasterio in abbatem. Dat' Lat', vi nonas Maii, pontificatus nostri anno quarto.'

534. Et nos statim celebrauimus electionem, set tamen sub alia forma quam prius. Nam cum prius omnes una uoce et uoto concordi fo. 185vb fecissent electionem; tunc contulerunt | potestatem eligendi quinque fratribus, qui eundem priorem elegerunt quem omnes prius elegerant.[1] Qui missus, cum litteris continentibus formam electionis et quinque fratribus qui eandem formam probarent, ad predictos episcopum et priorem Conuent'.[2] Ab eis est confirmatus, habita prius de persona electi et de eligendi forma et de zelo et racione eligencium diligentissima examinatione. Et a prefato episcopo in ecclesia sancti Iohannis apud Cestriam benedictionis munus in crastino translacionis sancti Benedicti[3] est adeptus.[4]

535. Et statim missus est abbas ad dominum regem et ad cancellarium,[5] cui statim post mortem prioris abbatis commissa est custodia abbatie, cum litteris predictorum episcopi et prioris ut optineret possessionem abbatie. Et non potuit optinere a cancellario set

---

election was quashed. In 1232 he was suspended by the bishop for refusing to allow him to bring members of another Order on his visitation of the priory, and following this he appealed to Rome. He was author of a lost chronicle covering the bishop's expulsion of the monks in 1191; see Greatrex, *Biog. Reg.*, p. 356, and the references cited there.

[1] The form of election, known as *per compromissum*, made by a selected number of monks, acting as electors, and not by the whole community; see *DDC* v cols. 242–5.

[2] See above, 533.

[3] 12 July.

[4] The blessing by the bishop thus both accorded with the terms of the pope's mandate (533) and with the abbot of Evesham's privilege to be blessed by a bishop of his choice and not at Worcester.

beloved sons monks of the monastery of Evesham presented us with the election which they had thought right to make in favour of the person of Thomas, prior of the same monastery, and humbly begged that we should approve the same election as one celebrated of a suitable person, having examined the procedure undertaken and considered carefully other particulars of their action, we decided that we should not assent to their request. However, in order that the said monastery should not suffer heavy loss of revenue because of a long vacancy, we order you by this apostolic mandate to act as follows: if the aforesaid monks decide, within a month of being given formal notice by you, to proceed to an election, then you are to confirm their election on apostolic authority, provided it has been done canonically and the person elected is suitable, and you, brother bishop, are to bestow the grace of your blessing upon the man elected. If they do not so decide, then on the same authority you are to appoint from within the same church an abbot who is an educated person, and whose life and behaviour are commendable, if a suitable man is found there, otherwise you are to appoint a man from another church. Dated at the Lateran, on 2 May, in the fourth year of our pontificate [1230].'

534. We celebrated the election without delay, but we adopted a different procedure this time. On the previous occasion all the monks had made the election with one voice and in full agreement; this time the monks empowered five brethren to make the election, and they elected the same prior [Thomas] as they had all elected before.[1] He was sent to the bishop and prior of Coventry[2] with a letter outlining the procedure that had been taken for the election, and with the five brethren who had approved that procedure. They first closely examined the person of the man elected, the procedure of the election, and the piety and discretion of those who conducted it, and then they confirmed the election of Thomas. On the day after the feast of the translation of St Benedict,[3] he received the gracious blessing of the bishop of Coventry in the church of St John, Chester.[4]

535. He was then sent without delay to the king and to the chancellor,[5] to whom the custody of the abbey had been entrusted immediately after the death of the previous abbot, with a letter from the bishop and the prior of Coventry requesting that Thomas be given possession of the abbey. As he could not obtain this from the

---

[5] Ralph Neville.

missus est ad regem, qui tunc agebat in transmarinis, cum predictis litteris et cum litteris cancellarii. Et cum abbas nollet transfretare, missus est unus*a* ex monachis qui fuerant Rome cum duobus seruientibus in Pictauem ad dominum regem, qui statim optinuerunt litteras de habenda possessione.[1]

536. Quibus prospere reuersis, per graciam Dei, optinuit abbas a cancellario litteras de possessione abbatie aput Conuent' in die translacionis sancti Egwini.[2] Et cum predicto episcopo, conuocatis multis abbatibus, prioribus, clericis et magnatibus et militibus, quoscumque abbas habere poterat, adepta possessione abbatie, in die sancti Michaelis[3] cum solempni processione in abbatia est receptus et a prefato episcopo installatus.

537. Iste abbas quamuis in abbatia nichil preter solam frugem et fenum et duas partes carucarum, tertia parte deficiente boum, inuenisset, in breui tamen postea domino regi soluit quadraginta tres marcas et domino pape uiginti sex marcas, et hominibus de Euesham de minutis debitis satisfecit de quadraginta marcis, et creditoribus | propriis de expensis quas ipse fecerat soluit quinquaginta marcas; et clericis de pensionibus preteriti temporis decem marcas, et adhuc tenebatur clericis de pensionibus in quinquaginta marcis; et Romanis creditoribus ad minus in trescentis, et cuidam creditori de expensis in uiginti marcis, et aliis, parum de nouo et multum de ueteri debito, usque ad summam uiginti marcarum.

538. Et quamuis ita ere alieno oneratus esset et multo se exonerasset, tamen toto eo anno, per gratiam Dei, uixit sine nouo mutuo. Et in Morton' et Lenchwic et Somborne emit centum acras terre ad opus abbatum, et instaurauit carucas de Valle et de Ambresleg' et Morton' et Sompburne et Baddeby, ad fortitudinem boum et numerum qui numquam prius fuerat in terris illis.

539. Sculpsit etiam super duas tumbas predecessorum suorum ad honorem et ostensionem dignitatis ecclesie ymagines episcopales. Et sibi ipsi cum eisdem fecit mausoleum et incidit in lapide marmoreo superposito ymaginem episcopalem ad honorem ecclesie.[4] Et assignauit conuentui redditus uiginti solidorum de terris

fo. 186ra

---

a interlined

[1] From Tournai, on 19 Aug. 1230, the king issued a letter ordering the knights, freemen, and all the tenants of the abbey of Evesham, to answer to Thomas as the new abbot of Evesham; *Patent Rolls, 1225–1232*, p. 392.

[2] 10 Sept. 1230.   [3] 29 Sept. 1230.

[4] The two tombs of his predecessors are likely to be those of Abbot Randulf and, probably, Abbot Adam. The word used to describe the effigies is *episcopalis*, which

chancellor he was sent to the king, who was then busy overseas, with the aforesaid letter and a further letter from the chancellor. As the abbot did not wish to travel abroad, one of the monks who had been in Rome was sent with two servants to the king in Poitou, and they immediately obtained letters of possession.[1]

536. After they had returned from their successful mission, the abbot obtained, by God's grace, at Coventry, on the feast of the translation of St Ecgwine,[2] a letter from the chancellor granting possession of the abbey. At Michaelmas,[3] in the presence of the bishop of Coventry and of as many abbots, priors, clerks, magnates, and knights as the abbot could assemble, he took possession of the abbey, and in solemn procession he was received in the abbey and installed by the aforementioned bishop.

537. The abbot discovered that there was nothing in the abbey but corn and hay, and only two-thirds of the abbey's ploughlands in use, the other third having no oxen. Yet, soon after he took office he paid forty-three marks to the king and twenty-six marks to the pope, made a settlement with the men of Evesham of forty marks in connection with some small debts, and paid fifty marks to his own creditors in connection with expenses he himself had incurred; he paid ten marks to clerks in respect of payments relating to the time before he took office, but still remained in debt to them to the tune of fifty marks for payments due; he owed his Roman creditors at least three hundred marks, a single creditor twenty marks for expenses, and others a little in new debt and much in old debts amounting to twenty marks.

538. However, though he was burdened in this way with debt and had discharged much of it, yet during the whole of that year he lived, by the grace of God, without taking out a new loan. In Morton, Lenchwick and Sambourne [Warws.] he bought one hundred acres of land for the abbots' purposes, and restored the plough-teams in the Vale, Ombersley, Morton, Sambourne and Badby [Northants.] to bring the complement of oxen up to a number such as had never before worked in those lands.

539. He enhanced the dignity and appearance of the church by having effigies clad in pontifical vestments carved above two tombs of his predecessors. Alongside these tombs he built a tomb for himself, and had an effigy dressed in pontifical vestments carved in marble to be placed on it to dignify the church.[4] He also assigned to the convent

Knowles, *M. O.*, p. 342, took to mean effigies of abbots dressed in pontifical vestments. This makes better sense than any other rendering. Of surviving tombs of abbots of the

quas emit a liberis hominibus abbatie ad faciendum inperpetuum anniuersarium suum in die benedictionis sue usque ad obitum suum, et deinde annuatim in die obitus sui x solidos.[a]

540. Et cum sic ditasset abbatiam de centum acris, et conuentum de redditu uiginti solidorum, omnia de terris emptis: preterea secundo anno assartauit in Ambresley duas carucatas terre de Chattesley, adquisita licencia a Waltero de Bellocampo.[1] Qui prius semper impedierat illud assartum pro communa pasture quam ibi habuerat. Cum eciam conuentus haberet tres marcas de ecclesia de Bratforton' ad caseum, et non sufficerent, iste abbas ad supplementum casei et fo. 186rb aliorum defectuum dedit residuum ecclesie conuentui: | scilicet, dimidiam marcam ad infirmariam, et dimidiam marcam ad salsas coquine, et dimidiam marcam ad uinum in die sancti Vincencii,[2] et dimidiam marcam ad uinum in die sancti Odulphi,[3] et residuum ad festum Reliquiarum.[4] Iste eciam abbas redemit redditum quinque marcarum a Stephano de Fossonouere domini pape subdiacono,[5] quas predecessor eius dederat ei, timens ne eodem Stephano mortuo, dominus papa, sicut tunc mos erat ecclesie Romane, conferret eundem redditum alteri clerico.[6] Sicut prius fecerat redditum decem marcarum annuarum quas prius habuerat Umfredus clericus domini pape,[7] quo mortuo dominus papa contulit easdem Hugucioni Frapein, scilicet cuidam capellano suo.[8] Iste eciam abbas reuocauit in proprios usus molendinum de Haddeley in Ambresley. Et funditus nouum reparauit, quod modo ualet triplo plusquam prius ualuit cum

---

[a] x. s[olidos] *interlined*

late-12th and early 13th centuries, those at Peterborough are perhaps the finest; see B. R. Kemp, *English Church Monuments* (London, 1980), pl. 5 for Abbot Benedict (d. 1193), and Abbot Alexander of Holderness (d. 1226), mentioned on p. 25. The mention of the effigies as *above* (*super* and *superposito*) the tombs makes it clear that these were tomb chests with the figures superimposed on them, and not the slab effigies of the late 12th century. See also the tomb of Bishop William of Blois at Worcester (d. 1236).

[1] See above, 514 and n.

[2] 24 May.

[3] 12 June.

[4] Celebrated on different days in different churches.

[5] This is likely to be Stephen of Fossanova, the nephew of Stephen of Fossanova, cardinal priest of the basilica of the SS. XII Apostoli (called of Ferentino until the death of his uncle in 1227); see Sayers, *Honorius III*, pp. 185–6, and the references cited there. The date of the grant of the rent was, therefore, before 1229, and probably nearer 1214.

[6] The 'ancient custom' of the pope conferring a benefice (or rent) when it was vacated in the Roman curia, sometimes, but not always, due to death, was fostered on one occasion at least by Pope Innocent III. In 1205, when Peter des Roches vacated the church of Kirby Underdale on his consecration in Rome as bishop of Winchester, the pope declared his

rents of twenty shillings from the lands that he had bought from
freemen of the abbey so that they might celebrate his anniversary in
perpetuity on the day of his blessing until his death, and then ten
shillings to celebrate the day of his death annually.

540. He endowed the abbey with one hundred acres of land, and the
convent with a rent of twenty shillings, all from lands he had bought:
in his second year he assarted two carucates of land at Chattesley in
Ombersley, after obtaining licence from Walter de Beauchamp.[1]
Walter had previously always opposed that assart in order to maintain
the [right of] common pasturage that he had had there. Furthermore,
although the convent received three marks from the church of
Bretforton to provide cheese, this amount was insufficient, so the
abbot gave the surplus income of that church to the convent to
supplement the income for cheese, and for other deficiencies: namely
half a mark to the infirmary, half a mark to the kitchen for salt, half a
mark for wine on St Vincent's day,[2] half a mark for wine on St
Odulf's day,[3] and the remainder for the Feast of Relics.[4] The abbot
also redeemed from Stephen of Fossanova, papal subdeacon,[5] a rent
of five marks which Stephen had received from Thomas' predecessor,
for he feared that when Stephen died the pope, following the
prevailing practice in the Roman church, would give that rent to
another clerk.[6] Indeed, this had happened previously, for the annual
rent of ten marks received by the papal clerk, Humfrey,[7] had on his
death been given by the pope to Huguicio Frapein, one of his
chaplains.[8] The abbot also restored Hadley mill in Ombersley to
full ownership of the abbey. He completely renovated it, and it now
has a value of more than three times its previous value, since

right to provide, but there is no record that he did so to Peter's other benefices; see
Cheney, *Innocent III*, pp. 82, 86–7. The exclusive right of the papacy to provide to
benefices vacated in the Roman curia was not expressed in legal terms until Pope Clement
IV's decretal 'Licet ecclesiarum' of 17 Aug. 1265; see G. Barraclough, *Papal Provisions*
(Oxford, 1935), pp. 8–9. At the time under discussion it was still in process of definition.

[7] See above, 511.

[8] In 1249 Pope Innocent IV granted the abbot of Evesham a faculty to confer the church
which the late Huguicio, papal subdeacon and chaplain, had held, on any fit person; *CPL* i.
254, *Reg. Inn. IV*, ii (1887), no. 4445. On the same day (4 Apr.) a similar faculty was
granted to the abbot of St Mary's, York, for him to confer Huguicio's church of Croft
(Yorks. NR) (ibid., no. 4446). Frapein is likely to be a corruption of the name of the
Roman family of Frangipani. In the case of Ombersley, the papal chamberlain, Master
Martin, declared in 1249 that it was worth between 30 and 40 marks sterling a year. Papal
clerks, Marinus, Innocent IV's vice-chancellor, and then Tedisius de Lavagna, a papal
scribe, canon of Beauvais, and the pope's nephew, maintained their hold (most probably
with Evesham's connivance); see BL Harley MS 3763 fos. 13^{r-v}, and 20^{r-v}.

a tempore fundationis sue prius esset ad firmam. Retinuit eciam in proprios usus molendinum de Wykewane, cuius possessor moriebatur tempore quo rex habuit custodiam abbatie. Dedit, tamen, regi quandam summam pecunie ne traderet idem molendinum quibusdam qui illud petebant iure hereditario. Concessit eciam ecclesiam de Morton' in proprios usus ad sacristariam, de qua sacrista prius habuit tantum tres solidos annuatim. Dedit tamen pro bono pacis tres marcas de camera annuatim cuidam clerico domini regis, cui rex dederat beneficium siquod uacaret tempore custodie domini regis de abbatia. Iste eciam abbas secundo anno installacionis[1] sue satisfecit omnibus creditoribus, et clericis pensionariis de preteritis, usque ad summam septuaginti marcarum, Romanis tamen creditoribus non satisfecit eo anno.

fo. 186va 541. Fecit eciam in naui ecclesie altare sancte crucis, su | perposito ei lapide marmoreo, et erexit super illud egregiam crucem Dei ymaginibus sancte Marie et sancti Iohannis.[2] Fecit eciam unam de uoltis ecclesie retro hostium processionis de claustro. Et cum abbas Rondulphus fecisset simplicem thalamum iuxta aulam abbatis, iste abbas ut esset thalamus congrue habitabilis, apposuit ex una parte eiusdem thalami capellam et subtus eam uoltam optimam; et ex altera parte thalami optimam domi necessariam. Suffulcit eciam ipsam aulam arcu lapideo.

542. Et cum incendio amisisset decem equos suos meliores, et alia ad summam centum librarum, intra bertonam, cito post annum reparate sunt domus loco combustarum triplo meliores quam erant priores. Fecit eciam aput Sompburne et apud Morton' domos satis habitabiles quando uenerint illic abbates. Emit eciam capam de examito auro super intextam. Cum eciam ecclesia de Weston prope finem secundi anni benedictionis abbatis uacasset, et abbas multos haberet aduersarios et potentes petentes ius patronatus eiusdem ecclesie, abbas tandem optinuit cum sumptibus tamen plusquam centum marcarum, et institutus est in eadem ecclesia clericus ad presentacionem abbatis.[3]

543. Set quamuis ita liberasset monasterium omni ere alieno, sic quod nullus peteret aliquid ab eo in fine secundi anni installacionis

---

[1] 1231–2.

[2] There were nave altars (for the use of the laity) dedicated to the Holy Cross in many of the great Benedictine houses, cf. Bury St Edmunds, Canterbury, Christ Church and St Augustine's, Ely, Winchester, and Westminster. The rood above the pulpitum, or screen separating the monks' choir from the nave, usually had the two figures of the Virgin Mary and of St John on either side of the cross; see W. St John Hope, 'The twelfth century pulpitum . . . of Ely; with some notes on similar screens . . . monastic churches',

formerly, from the time of its foundation, it was leased out to farm. He retained in his ownership the mill of Wickhamford whose occupier had died during the time the king had had custody of the abbey. However, he gave the king a sum of money so that he would not hand the mill over to those who were claiming it as theirs by hereditary right. He appropriated to the sacristy the church of Morton, from which the sacrist had previously received no more than three shillings annually. To keep the peace he gave three marks annually from the chamber to one of the king's clerks, to whom the king had granted a benefice if a vacancy occurred during the time of his custody of the abbey. During the second year after he had been installed[1] he paid up all his creditors, as well as clerks who had previously received payments, at a total cost of seventy marks, though he did not pay up his Roman creditors that year.

541. In the nave of the church he built an altar of the Holy Cross, covered with marble, and upon this he erected a magnificent cross of our God, with statues of St Mary and St John.[2] He also built one of the vaults of the church behind the processional entrance from the cloister. Abbot Randulf had had a simple inner chamber built next to the abbot's hall, but Thomas, in order to make the chamber more commodious, annexed a chapel to one side of it and built a fine vault below it; he also put a very convenient privy on the other side of the chamber. He supported the hall itself with a stone arch.

542. He lost ten of his best horses in a fire in the barton [at Evesham], and other things valued at a hundred pounds, but after no more than a year he had replaced the houses destroyed by the fire with new ones that were three times better than the previous houses. At Sambourne [Warws.] and at Morton he built houses suitable enough for abbots to stay in when they visited there. He also bought a cope made of samite, interwoven with gold. When a vacancy occurred in the church of Weston-upon-Avon [Glos. and Warws.] towards the end of his second year as abbot, despite the fact that he had many powerful opponents claiming the right of patronage of that church, he held on to the patronage at a cost of more than a hundred marks, and a clerk was instituted in that church on his presentation.

543. However, although he had freed the monastery of all debt, as described, so that by the end of his second year as abbot no one was

Proceedings of the Cambridge Antiquarian Society, xxi (Cambridge, 1919), 19–73, at pp. 43, 51, 55, 58, 63, 71.

sue cuius eris partes et quantitatem non memoriter retinuit, Romanis
tamen creditoribus non satisfecit, quia nullus debitum illud petiit nec
sciuit abbas cui illud deberet. Sciuit tamen quod siquis petens
instaret, peteret ab eo plusquam trecentas marcas, et quamuis
conseruaret ecclesiam sic ab ere alieno, tamen ad huc non redierunt
fo. 186[vb] in manus suas, nec multis annis | postea redirent, prata de Burton' et
de Bradewelle,[1] que abbas Randulphus pro ducentis marcis et
pluribus impignorauit Templariis de Gutinges.[2]

544. Hic eciam abbas tercio anno installacionis sue,[3] tercio kalendas
Marcii, fecit dedicari capellam sancti Wistani quam ipse construxerat,
ut prius dictum est; et dati sunt quadraginta dies relaxationis
annuatim in anniuersario eiusdem dedicacionis et per octo dies
sequentes ab episcopo Iohanne qui eam dedicauit.[4] Qui tunc temporis
per multos annos suppleuit uices episcopi Wyntoniencis et aliorum
episcoporum[5] caritatiue petentium.[6] Idem eciam episcopus die pre-
cedenti[7] ordinauit ibi septem monachos Eueshamie in presbiteros et
unum diaconum, et duos accolitos, et quosdam monachos Cistercien-
cium de Wallia.[a][8] Nullos uero clericos nisi in Valle Eueshamie
beneficiatos uel monachos nisi exemptos aliquando permisit iste
abbas in ecclesia Eueshamie ordinari. Pridie uero kalendas Marcii
dedicauit idem episcopus capellam sancti Michaelis in firmaria, cuius
altari idem abbas lapidem marmoreum superposuit. Et totidem dies
relaxacionis dati sunt in dedicacione eiusdem capelle sicut et prioris.

545. Fecit eciam iste abbas colere in dominico apud Baddesey
quasdam particulas terrarum ad ualenciam quinque acrarum, que
supra memoria hominum uel numquam prius fuerunt culte. Dedit
eciam Waltero de Bellocampo uiginti quatuor marcas pro licencia
faciendi fossatum inter Prestemede et quasdam alias terras in
Wikewaneforde, et pratum de Morcote, et pro licencia colendi

---

[a] *marg.* Nota de collatione ordinum in mon' etc.

[1] Both are in Glos.

[2] See above, 515 n.

[3] 1233.

[4] This grant of an indulgence by Thomas is of interest as being a singular example of an abbot using this power which was normally reserved for bishops.

[5] A suffragan could perform all the episcopal functions but had no see of his own. The term suffragan also means all the bishops subject to the metropolitan who might summon them to give their support in synods. It is used in the former sense here.

[6] John, bishop of Ardfert, a Benedictine, was consecrated before July 1219, but deprived of his see on 18 June 1224, after allegations of his intrusion into the see by Geoffrey Marsh, justiciar of Ireland. He acted as a suffragan by papal licence of 25 Feb. 1225; *CPL*

claiming from him the repayment of any debt of which he had any recollection of the amount or details, yet he had not repaid the Roman creditors, as no one had demanded payment of that debt nor did he know to whom he owed the money. However, he did know that if anyone pressed the claim for payment, he would have to pay more than three hundred marks, so, although he was keeping the church out of debt, as described, he did not yet take back ownership of the meadows of Bourton and Broadwell[1] which abbot Randulf had mortgaged to the Templars of Guiting[2] for two hundred marks or more, nor would they be taken back for many years to come.

544. On 27 February, during his third year as abbot,[3] he had the chapel of St Wigstan dedicated, which, as has been said, he himself had had built; and he granted forty days' release from penance every year on the anniversary of this dedication, and a further eight days' release were granted by Bishop John who had dedicated it.[4] Bishop John was at that time, and for many years, suffragan of the bishop of Winchester, and of other bishops[5] who requested his service in a spirit of friendship.[6] On the day before,[7] he ordained in the chapel seven monks of Evesham to the priesthood, one monk as a deacon, and two as acolytes, and he also ordained some Cistercian monks from Wales.[8] The abbot allowed no clerks to be ordained at any time in the church of Evesham unless they held a benefice in the Vale of Evesham and no monks unless they enjoyed exemption. On 28 February the bishop dedicated the chapel of St Michael in the infirmary, whose altar the abbot (had) covered with marble. The same number of days of release from penance on the dedication of this chapel were granted as on the dedication of the chapel of St Wigstan.

545. Abbot Thomas had some plots of land in his demesne at Badsey amounting to five acres cultivated, which had never been cultivated before, or not within human memory. He gave Walter de Beauchamp twenty-four marks for permission to dig a ditch between Preste Mede and some other lands in Wickhamford and the meadow of Morcote, for

i. 100, 68, and 98. He had already acted as an auxiliary of Archbishop Langton in 1222 and was to deputize for Archbishop Edmund. He issued indulgences for those visiting the shrine of St William of York, and for religious foundations in the diocese of Winchester, as well as consecrating altars. He retired to St Albans abbey and died in 1245; see *EEA 9: Winchester, 1205–38*, ed. N. Vincent (1994), pp. xxxiv–xxxv for references.

[7] 26 Feb., a Saturday after the first Sunday in Lent, which, as an ember day, could be used for ordinations.

[8] The Cistercians were permitted to seek ordination from bishops of their choice and therefore not necessarily from the diocesan; see J.-B. Mahn, *L'Ordre Cistercien et son gouvernement des origines au milieu du xiiie siècle (1098–1265)* (Paris, 1951), pp. 88–90.

easdem terras et faciendi sibi in hoc quotienscumque abbates uoluerint, et pro licencia imparcandi aueria eiusdem Walteri et hominum suorum si inuenta fuerint in dampno abbatis tempore fo. 187ʳᵃ quo terre | ille fuerint inbladate.[1] Que predicta a nullo abbate prius, quamuis sepius attemptata, poterant consumari, cum super hiis supra memoriam hominum fuerit inter eos lis et contencio. Iste eciam abbas assignauit conuentui redditus decem solidorum de dimidia uirgata terre in Luctultone, quam Adam le Boteler tenet de conuentu pro secta de Bratforton' facienda ad comitatum Wygornie: quos sacrista pro eo soluet infirmario. Et quia decem solidi predicti assignantur ad misericordias faciendas, oportet quod conuentus assignet alios decem solidos de bursaria ad anniuersarium predicti Thome faciendum.

546. Cum autem iste abbas fere per septem annos suam rexisset ecclesiam, pridie idus Septembris in Domino obdormiuit, anno uidelicet Domini millesimo ccxxxvi.

---

[1] For Walter de Beauchamp, see above, 514 and n., and for his lands at Wickhamford and Morcote, esp. *Beauchamp Cartulary*, no. 104.

permission to cultivate those lands and for succeeding abbots to do the same if they wished, and finally for permission to empark this property of Walter's and his men, if it was found that the abbot lost out when these lands were brought under cultivation.[1] No abbot before Thomas had been able to achieve such arrangements, though they had often tried, for either a lawsuit or a quarrel was going on over these issues between Walter and the abbey for longer than men could remember. The abbot also assigned to the convent rents of ten shillings from half a virgate of land in Littleton, which Adam the Butler held of the convent for carrying out suit and service for Bretforton at Worcester county court: these rents the sacrist was to pay on his behalf to the infirmary. As these ten shillings were assigned to almsgiving, it was necessary for the convent to assign another ten shillings from the bursary for celebrating the anniversary of Thomas.

546. Thomas ruled the church for almost seven years as abbot, and fell asleep in the Lord on 12 September 1236.

APPENDICES

APPENDIX I

A BOND OF THE PROCTORS OF EVESHAM

BL, Cotton MS Vespasian B xxiv fo. 52^v (V)

Iohannes Dei gratia Albanen' episcopus omnibus ad quos litere iste peruenerint salutem in domino. Nouerit uniuersitas uestra quod T. de Marleb. et T. de Warewic. clericus nuncii et procuratores abbatis et conuentus de Euesh⟨am⟩ confessi sunt coram nobis se tantam pecuniam recipisse mutuo pro utilitate ecclesie de Euesh[am] a Petro Malialordo mercatore Rom'. Pro qua debent ei uel eius nuntio soluere xx marcas bonorum et legalium sterlingorum ei,^{a} xiii solidos et quatuor denarios pro qualibet marca computatos, ad festum Pentecostes in nundinis ^{b} proximum. Quod nisi facerent, promiserunt eidem nomine pene pro singulis x. marcis unam marcam de nundinis in ⟨n⟩undinas et expensas competentes sibi ⟨et cum?⟩ ⟨ser?⟩uiente et equo uno. Pro qua pecunia concesserunt eidem mercatori literas abbatis et conuentus de mutuo quas habebant et quod bona fide laborabunt peccuniam supradictam solui iuxta promissionem factam tactis sacrosanctis euangeliis ^{c} iurauerunt nuncii memorati. Dat. apud S. Clementem xiiii kal. Ianuarii pontificatus domini Innocencii tercii pape anno septimo et cuius rei testimonium rogati presentes literas sigillo nostro duximus concedendas.

---

^{a} *Interlined: a repetition of* ei *in the previous line* ^{b} *MS* mundinis ^{c} *MS* euangiis

APPENDIX I

A BOND OF THE PROCTORS OF EVESHAM

John, by the grace of God, bishop of Albano, to all those whom this letter reaches, greeting in the Lord. Let it be known to all that T. of Marlborough and T. of Warwick, clerk, messengers and proctors of the abbot and the convent of Evesham, have confessed before us that they received a large sum of money using a bond for the business of the church of Evesham from Peter Malialordus, merchant of Rome. For this they are under obligation to pay him or his messenger twenty marks of good and legal sterling, thirteen shillings and four pence reckoned for every mark, at the fair at the next feast of Whitsun. Should they fail to do this, they have promised him by way of a penalty one mark for every ten from fair to fair and adequate expenses for him and a servant and a horse. As surety for this money thay have surrendered to the same merchant the letters of the abbot and convent which they had as a bond, and the said messengers have sworn on the holy Gospels that they will make the effort for that money to be paid in accordance with the promise made. Dated at San Clemente on 19 December in the seventh year of the pontificate of Pope Innocent III, and in witness of this as requested we have granted this present letter under our seal. [Rome, S. Clemente, 19 Dec. 1205]

APPENDIX II

THE CUSTOMS OF THE ABBEY AND THE DISPOSITION OF ITS REVENUES

A. AS CONFIRMED BY THE PAPAL LEGATE IN 1206

The agreement made before the legate, John of Ferentino, cardinal deacon of S. Maria in via Lata, between the abbot of Evesham and the convent (see above, 392–3), and confirmed by him in 1206 (see above, 397, 430). The original, now lost, survived amongst the records of the Court of Augmentations until the early nineteenth century. The following text is based on *Monasticon*, ii, num. xxvii, pp. 23–5, and has been given the siglum M. For its relationship with Abbot Randulf's disposition (above, 399–429, and below, App. II B), see App. II C. Full historical annotation is provided above, 399–429.

Cum I. Dei gratia Marie in Via Lata diaconus cardinalis apostolice sedis legatus, officio legationis sibi iniuncte in Anglia fungeretur, et orta esset controuersia inter me abbatem et nos conuentum Eouesham super statu domus nostre coram eo; tandem amicabiliter hoc modo sopita est: uidelicet quod abbas infra septa monasterii existens, inter fratres secundum antiquam domus illius consuetudinem conuersando regulariter uiuet, et exteriora pro uiribus suis ad utilitatem ecclesie prouide et fideliter dispensabit. Prior uero, subprior, tercius prior, et alii custodes ordinis, prior de Penuertham, precentor, sacrista, camerarius, celerarius exterior, coquinarius, pitanciarius, infirmarius, elemosinarius, custos uinee, gardinarius, magister fabrice ecclesie, magister hospitum, de consilio et consensus conuentus uel maioris et sanioris partis in capitulo ab abbate creentur. Qui si minus honeste, quod absit, uel minus prudenter in officiis suis se habuerint, uel male administrauerint, a fratribus prius correpti regulariter,[a] si non emendauerint, in capitulo amoueantur, et alii sub forma predicta in loco eorum in capitulo incontinenti[b] subrogentur, ne aliquo casu in

---

[a] regulenter *M*   [b] in contuenta *M*

APPENDIX II

THE CUSTOMS OF THE ABBEY AND THE DISPOSITION OF ITS REVENUES

A. AS CONFIRMED BY THE PAPAL LEGATE IN 1206

When J., by the grace of God, cardinal deacon of [St] Mary in the Via
Lata, legate of the apostolic see, was exercising the legation with
which he had been entrusted in England, a controversy arose between
me the abbot and us the convent of Evesham in the presence of the
legate over the state of our house, at length it was amicably settled in
this way: viz. that the abbot shall live within the enclosure of the
monastery amongst his brethren in accordance with the Rule,
following the ancient custom of that house, and will diligently and
faithfully deal with external matters to the best of his ability, to the
benefit of the church. The following officers are to be appointed by
the abbot in chapter, on the advice and with the consent of the
convent or of a majority of brethren of wiser counsel: the prior,
subprior, third prior, and other masters of order, the prior of
Penwortham, the precentor, sacrist, chamberlain, external cellarer,
kitchener, pittancer, infirmarer, almoner, keeper of the vineyard,
gardener, master of the church fabric, and the guest-master. Should
these officers, God forbid, fail to conduct themselves honourably and
wisely in carrying out their duties, or manage them badly, they are
first to be reproved by the brethren in accordance with the Rule, but
then, if they do not mend their ways, they are to be removed at once
from office in chapter, and others immediately substituted in the
manner stated above. This is to prevent those offices, through some

manum regis deueniant ipsa officia, abbate forte decedente, uel per moram fiat deterioratio obedientiarum, aut aliquis defectus propter moram emergat. Prior uero et predicti magistri ordinis simul cum abbate, ut ordo monasticus cum rigore discipline secundum regulam beati Benedicti obseruetur, summam diligentiam adhibeant. Maxime autem opera prestent ne monachi aliquid proprium habeant, et ne alias quam in refectorio sine licencia comedant, et ut elemosina sua per manus elemosinarii erogetur; et ne a claustro sine licencia exeant, et ut silencium locis et horis statutis obseruetur, et ut fratres frequenter delicta confiteantur, nec tamen aliis quam hiis qui ad hoc deputantur. Alii uero supradicti officiales omnes qui redditus percipiunt, quater in anno coram abbate, uel eo quem loco suo statuerit, priore, et sex claustralibus, tribus ab abbate et tribus a conuentu uocatis, de administratione sua computum reddant, coquinarius uero qualibet ebdomada.

Isti uero officiales, quotiens domi fuerint, in congregatione iugiter permaneant, et conuentum in ecclesia, in capitulo, in claustro, in refectorio sequantur, ut si, quod absit, in officiis suis aliquis defectus emerserit, illi statim suppleant. Nulli duo officia assignentur, sed cuilibet adiungatur socius testis diligentie sue.

Si uero in aliquo officio propter temporis malitiam aliquid ultra redditus officio illi assignatos expensum fuerit, si in aliquo officio aliquid fuerit residuum; per illud defectus alterius officii suppleatur. Si autem nullum*a* officium defectum alterius officii supplere potuerit, abbas per manum celerarii exterioris suppleat. Preterea si quodlibet officium sibi suffecerit, et aliquid residuum fuerit, abbas de consilio capituli, uel maioris et sanioris partis in id quod in capitulo iudicauerit utilius ecclesie expendat.

Si uero aliquid de redditibus monachorum officiis asignatis, uel in perpetuum, quod absit, uel ad tempus detineri contigerit, uel aliquo modo euacuari, uel diminui, abbas tandem de consilio capituli ubi

---

a ullum *M*

mischance, falling into the hands of the king as, for example, on the death of the abbot; and to ensure that no deterioration in the obediences should occur through delay, or any other type of defect arise from delay. The prior and the other masters of order are, along with the abbot, to show the utmost diligence in ensuring that monastic order is observed with strict discipline in accordance with the Rule of St Benedict. They are to make it their special business to ensure that monks do not possess anything of their own, that they do not eat in any place other than the refectory without permission, that their alms are distributed only through the almoner, that they do not leave the cloister without permission, that silence is observed at the specified times and places, and that the brethren confess their sins frequently, but then only to those who have been appointed to hear their confession. All the other officers mentioned who receive revenues are to render an account of their stewardship four times a year before the abbot or the one appointed by him in his place, with the prior and six cloister monks in attendance, three appointed by the abbot and three by the convent. The cook shall submit accounts each week.

Furthermore, these officers are always to remain in the congregation of the monks whenever they are in the house, and are to follow [the common life of] the convent in the church, in the chapter-house, in the cloister, and in the refectory, so that if, God forbid, any failing occurs in their duties they may immediately provide for it. Let none be assigned two offices, but let a fellow monk be appointed as a witness of his diligence.

If in any obedience, because of bad times, an amount is spent that exceeds the revenue assigned to it, whereas in another office there is money left over, then let the shortfall in the one office be met by the excess in the other. If, however, no office can make up the deficiency of that other office, the abbot is to do so with funds from the external cellarer. Moreover, if any office has sufficient for its own needs and something left over, the abbot, after consultation with the chapter or a majority of the brethren of wiser counsel, is to spend the residue on that office in which the chapter judges the spending will most benefit the church.

If any part of the revenues which have been assigned to the offices of the monks happens to be withheld either permanently, God forbid, or temporarily, or happens to become exhausted or reduced in some way, then the abbot is to assign, with the consent of the chapter, an

commode fieri poterit alibi in eodem officio assignet. Liceat preterea monachis possessiones et redditus officiis suis assignatos, ueluti noualia faciendo, et redditus augmentando et nouos adquirendo ampliare, seu quibuscunque aliis iustis modis meliorare.

Celerarius siquidem exterior talis de proprio conuentu et in capitulo ab abbate creetur, qui exceptis redditibus monachorum officiis assignatis, ad preceptum abbatis totius abbatie curam gerens, sciat et possit conuentui necessaria ministrare, scilicet panem, ceruisiam, duo pulmenta, ignem et salem, et quedam alia in consuetudinibus expressa. Hospitibus autem iuxta facultatem domus prouidebit celerarius. Viris tamen religiosis, qui de officio suo sunt, uidelicet personis eorum sicut et fratribus administrabit, exceptis abbatibus et capellanis eorum, quibus non inueniet aliquid nisi in diebus ieiunii, sicut nec ipsi abbati, nec illis qui cum eo comedant uel capellanis eius, hoc dicimus nisi in refectorio comedant. Seruientibus etiam obedientiarum abbatie, celerarius procurationem debitam et stipendia iuxta consuetudinem domus administrabit.

Iste quidem celerarius de administratione sua, non solum quater superioribus, set quotiens ipse abbas uoluerit compotum reddat, qui nisi bene administrauerit, sicut de aliis obedientiariis dictum est, ad iustam conquestionem conuentus et rationabilem uoluntatem abbatis amoueatur, et alius statim loco eius subrogetur et in capitulo. Numerum fratrum abbas integrum conseruet, nullum monachum recipiat aut eiciat uel ad tempus uel in perpetuum nisi de consilio conuentus uel maioris et sanioris partis, et in capitulo. Ecclesias autem uel alios redditus uel aliquas terras, non nisi de consilio uniuersitatis uel maioris et sanioris partis, et in capitulo alicui conferat. Nec rusticos sine consensu eorundem manumittat.

De terris siquidem reuocandis, si que tempore suo uel predecessoris sui alienate sunt, pro uiribus suis, consilio conuentus sui utatur. Similiter in causis ecclesiasticis uel forensibus agendis uel terminandis, capituli sui utatur consilio. Seruientes autem qui monachis

equivalent amount for that office, when this can be done to advantage. The monks are to be permitted, moreover, to increase their possessions and revenues assigned to their offices, for instance, by ploughing up new land and by augmenting rents, and by acquiring new possessions and rents, or they may improve them by any other just means.

Let the external cellarer be appointed from within the convent by the abbot in chapter, such a man as can be responsible under the abbot's command for the care of the whole abbey, save the revenues assigned to the offices of the monks. He is to know how to minister to the needs of the convent, and to be able to do so, with respect to bread, ale, the two dishes of pottage, kindling and salt, and certain other commodities stated in the Customs. The cellarer will make provision for guests also, according to the ability of the house to do so. He will minister to the needs of visiting religious, in matters which belong to his office, and look after their persons as he does his own brethren, though he will not provide anything for abbots and their chaplains except during fast days, just as he does not do so for the abbot [of Evesham] nor for those who eat with the abbot or his chaplains, that is, unless they eat in the refectory. The cellarer will provide due maintenance for the servants of the abbey's obedientiaries and for their stipend in accordance with the custom of the house.

The cellarer must render an account of his stewardship not only four times a year to his superiors but as often as the abbot wishes. If his stewardship has not been good, as has been mentioned in the case of other obedientiaries, he is to be removed at the just complaint of the convent and the reasonable request of the abbot, and he is to be immediately replaced in chapter by another. The abbot is to maintain the full number of monks, and he is not to accept or expel any monk either temporarily or permanently without the consent of the convent or of a majority of monks of wiser counsel, and this is to be dealt with in chapter. He is not to bestow churches or other revenues or any lands upon anyone, except with the agreement of the whole convent or of a majority of monks of wiser counsel, and this is to take place in chapter. He is not to free villeins without the same consent being given.

With regard to the recovery that is in his power of lands that have been alienated during his own time or during the time of his predecessor, as far as he is able he must take the advice of his convent. Similarly, in conducting or terminating lawsuits, ecclesiastical or secular, he is to take the advice of his chapter. The servants

ministrare tenentur, scilicet, de infirmaria, sartrina, lauandaria, refectorio, sacristaria, locutorio, de consilio capituli secundum priorem formam constituantur et deponantur. Hec omnia intelligantur saluis in omnibus regularibus institutis.

Hii sunt redditus officiis monachorum Eoueshamensis coenobii assignati
Ad prioratum pertinent decime de Beningwrthe, tam maiores quam minores, de terris monachorum, ad pergamenum et exibitionem scriptorum pro libris scribendis.

Precentor
Ad officium precentoris pertinet quedam terra de Hamptona, de qua percipit precentor annuatim quinque solidos, et decime de Stokes, et de quadam terra de Alnecestre decem et octo denarios. Ex his debet inuenire precentor incaustum omnibus scriptoribus monasterii, et pergamenum ad breuia, et colores ad illuminandum, et necessaria ad ligandum libros, et necessaria ad organa.

Sacrista
Ad sacristariam autem pertinent sex capelle in Valle, uidelicet due in Euesham, ex quibus percipit sacrista annuatim decem marcas et candelas que offeruntur in illis, due etiam capelle de Lenchwic, et de Nortona, de quibus percipit decem solidos annuatim, et una in Mortona, de qua percipit tres solidos annuatim, et una in Vffeham, de qua percipit decem et octo denarios. Item de ecclesia de Baddebi percipit duas marcas, de capella de Wihtlakeford decem solidos, de ecclesia de Westona dimidiam marcam, de ecclesia de Stowa quinque solidos uel duas petras cere, de ecclesia sancti Albani in Wigornia quinque libras cere. De burgagio in uilla Eouesham uiginti solidos. De burgagio in Wigornia quinquaginta solidos. De terra in Hamptona quinque solidos. In Lench pertinent ad sacristariam tres hide et dimidia, in Bretfortona in uno campo quinquaginta quinque acre, in altero septuaginta sex in dominico, in uillenagio quinque uirgate terre et dimidia, et decima de eadem terra, in garbis, linis, et agnis, et decime de quatuor hidis in eadem uilla, duabus scilicet hidis Hugonis, et duabus Willielmi de Cairdino, et decime de nouem uirgatis terre Pagani in Litleton, et decime de quinque uirgatis terre senescalli in Baddeseia, et decime de dominico de Pikesleia in Herefordiascire. Omnes etiam oblationes et legate omnia altaris de Eouesham.

who are kept to minister to the needs of the monks in the infirmary, the tailor's workshop, the laundry, the refectory, the sacristy, and the parlour, are to be appointed and dismissed on the advice of the chapter as previously specified. All these ordinances are to be understood saving in all things the provisions of the Rule.

The following are the revenues assigned to the offices of the monks of Evesham
To the prior's office belong the tithes of Bengeworth, the great as well as the small, from the lands of the monks, and these are for parchment and the maintenance of the scribes who write the books.

The Precentor
To the office of precentor belong some land in Hampton, from which he receives five shillings per annum, the tithes of 'Stokes', and eighteen pence from some land in Alcester. From these revenues he must provide ink for all the scribes of the monastery, parchment for writs, colours for illumination, and the things necessary for binding the books and for the organs.

The Sacrist
To the sacristy belong six chapels in the Vale, that is, two in Evesham, from which the sacrist receives yearly ten marks and the candles that are offered in them, also the two chapels of Lenchwick and of Norton, from which he receives ten shillings annually, one in Morton, from which he receives three shillings yearly, and one in Offenham, from which he receives eighteen pence. He also receives two marks from the church of Badby, ten shillings from the chapel of Wixford, half a mark from the church of Weston, five shillings or two stones of wax from the church of Stow, and five pounds of wax from the church of St Alban in Worcester. Twenty shillings from burgage tenure in the town of Evesham. Fifty shillings from burgage tenure in Worcester. Five shillings from land in Hampton. Belonging to the sacristy are three and a half hides in Lench, fifty five acres in one field in Bretforton, in another field seventy six acres of demesne land, five and a half virgates of land in villein tenure, and the tithes of sheaves of corn, flax, and lambs from the same land, and the tithes of four hides in the same vill, two of Hugh and two of William de Cairdino; the tithes of nine virgates of land of Pagan in Littleton, the tithes of five acres of land of the steward in Badsey, and the tithes of the demesne of Pixley in Herefordshire, and all the offerings and altar bequests of Evesham.

Camerarius

Ad cameram pertinent Meilgaresbrai et Suella, sicut antiquitus fuerit, et loco Burhton que fuit ad cameram assignata est Theclesthropa, ita uidelicet quod abbas ex hac camera nec uestimenta, nec aliud percipiet, sicut consueuit ex priori camera exigere. Hec autem maneria imperpetuum cum omni integritate sua ad uestiendum fratres permanere debent.

Coquinarius

Ad coquinam uero pertinent de uilla et foro de Eouesham qualibet die sabbati quinque solidi et tres oboli. De molendinis eiusdem uille iuxta uineam cum pertinentiis suis quinque marce annuatim terminis suis soluende. De molendinis iuxta pontem et de molendinis in Hamptona cum pertinentiis suis qualibet die sabbati triginta denarii et sexaginta stice anguillarum annuatim. De uilla de Stowa et foro, qualibet die dominica quatuor solidi, de Mortona sexaginta solidi, de Saltford sexaginta solidi, de Wihtlakesford quatuor libre, de molendino in eadem uilla uiginti solidi et duodecim stice anguillarum annuatim, de molendino senescalli in Saltford uiginti solidi, de molendino de Chadelberia, cum suis pertinentiis, uiginti quinque solidi et quadraginta stice anguillarum, de molendino de Twiford, et de Aldington, cum pertinentiis suis, uiginti octo solidi et quadraginta stice anguillarum, de molendino de Vffeham decem solidi cum pertinentiis suis, de Fokemulna dimidia marca, de molendino in Wikewon octo solidi. De Wdefeo pertinent sexaginta solidi ad coquinam. De piscatione in Ambresl. uiginti tres solidi. In Glouc. de terra Roberti Bould tres solidi et obolus, de terra quadam et quodam furno in Wincelcumb duo solidi et una libra piperis. In Euesham de terra uxoris Iohannis Grene una libra piperis, de terra Reginaldi filii Willielmi in eadem uilla dimidia marca annuatim, de Pennertham una summa salmonis, de qualibet carucata terre in Valle Eouesham de dominico, excepto Aldington, trecenta oua annuatim, et de quolibet manerio tres denarii ad discos, et duodecim olle, de Bradewella uiginti oua et tres denarii, et duodecim olle. Item singulis diebus habere debet coquinarius forragium ad unum equum et prebendam, uel duo prebendaria de furfure de granario, et duos porcos habere debet ad plancherum et quotiens emerit in uilla de Euesham piscem ad totum conuentum, debet habere de cellario panem et iustam ad opus piscatorum. Ad

The Chamberlain

To the chamber belong Maugersbury and Swell, as they have from of old, and in place of Bourton, which once belonged to the chamber, Adlestrop has been assigned, but on such terms that the abbot will receive from the chamber neither clothing nor anything that he was accustomed to demand from the chamber previously. These manors should be retained permanently and in their entirety for providing clothing for the monks.

The Kitchener

To the kitchen belong five shillings and three halfpence every Saturday from the town and market place of Evesham. From the mills of the same town near to the vineyard, with their appurtenances, five marks are to be paid yearly at the customary terms. From the mills near the bridge and from the mills of Hampton with their appurtenances, thirty pence every Saturday and sixty sticks of eels yearly. From the town of Stow and its market place four shillings every Sunday, sixty shillings from Morton, sixty shillings from Salford, four pounds from Wixford, twenty shillings from a mill in the same vill, and twelve sticks of eels annually, twenty shillings from the steward's mill [sic] in Salford, twenty five shillings from the mill of Chadbury with its appurtenances, and forty sticks of eels, twenty eight shillings from the mill of Twyford and of Aldington, with their appurtenances and forty sticks of eels, ten shillings from the mill of Offenham with its appurtenances, half a mark from 'Fokemulna', eight shillings from the mill in Wickhamford. Sixty shillings from 'Wodefe' belong to the kitchen, twenty three shillings from the fishery in Ombersley. Belonging to the kitchen in Gloucester are three shillings and a halfpenny from the land of Robert Bould, two shillings and a pound of pepper from some land and a bakery in Winchcombe, one pound of pepper from the land of the wife of John Grene in Evesham, half a mark yearly from the land of Reginald son of William in the same town, one seam of salmon from Penwortham, three hundred eggs annually from every carucate of demesne land in the Vale of Evesham except Aldington, and three pence from each manor for bowls and twelve pots, as well as twenty eggs, three pence, and twelve pails from Broadwell. Also every day the kitchener must have hay for one horse and one or two measures of bran from the granary, two pigs for the sty, and whenever he buys fish in the town of Evesham for the whole convent he must have bread from the cellarer and an allowance of ale for the service of those selling the fish.

omnes etiam cibos qui condimento ceruisie indigent debet habere ceruisiam de cellario.

Pitanciarius

Ad pitanciariam etiam pertinent in Euesham de noua terra decem marce. De Wrotesleia due marce. De Vleborga uiginti quinque solidi. De ecclesia de Hildendon una marca. De ecclesia de Leilond una marca. De molendino de Withlakesforth dimidia marca. De molendino senescalli in Saltforth dimidia marca. De Ambresl. duodecim sextarii mellis.

Infirmarius

Ad infirmariam pertinent molendinum fullonum de Burhtona, cum pertinentiis suis, de quo percipit infirmarius tres marcas, et duo molendina sub Stowa, de quibus percipit quatuordecim solidos. In eadem uilla de terra Towa duos solidos. De terra eidem uicina duos solidos. De terra Sowi in eadem uilla duodecim denarios. In uilla de Euesham de burgagio triginta duos denarios. De Sulstano quatuor solidos et quatuor denarios, et candelas que offeruntur in capella sancti Iohannis.

Elemosinarius

Ad elemosinariam pertinent duo furni in Eouesham et redditus de Penuertham, scilicet quatuor marce in Eouesham de terra portarii duodecim denarii, de terra ei contigua sex denarii, de terra Cranforth cum soppa ferri duodecim denarii. In Glouc. de terra data cum Rodberto monacho quatuor solidi. In eadem uilla de terra Johannis Crume quatuor solidi. De Aldintona nonaginta oua. De toto etiam pane infra portam cocto uel empto, debet elemosinarius habere decimam. Abbas etiam in cena Domini debet inuenire dimidiam marcam ad mandatum, per manus elemosinarii liberandam fratribus ut distribuant pauperibus, et de cellerario cellarius debet dare singulis pauperibus singulos panes, et tria allecia, et de ceruisia quantum opus fuerit. Debet etiam elemosinarius curam habere orti monachorum.

Magister fabrice

Ad fabricam ecclesie et domorum claustro adiacentibus pertinent decem libre de ecclesia de Ambresl': que si aliquo casu solute non fuerint, abbas ecclesiam et domos cooperire debet. Et decime de terra

He must also have ale from the cellarer for all the foods that need a seasoning of ale.

The Pittancer

To the pittancery belong ten marks from new land in Evesham, two marks from Wrottesley, twenty-five shillings from Oldberrow, one mark from the church of Hillingdon, one mark from the church of Leyland, half a mark from the mill of Wixford, half a mark from the mill of the steward in Salford, and twelve sextaries of honey from Ombersley.

The Infirmarer

To the infirmary belong the mill of the fullers of Bourton with its appurtenances from which the infirmarer receives three marks, and two mills below Stow, from which he receives fourteen shillings, and two shillings in the same town from the land 'Towa', two shillings from the land next to it, twelve pence from the land of Sowus in the same town, in the town of Evesham from a burgage thirty-two pence, from Southstone [in Stanford-on-Teme] four shillings and four pence and the candles which are offered in the chapel of St John.

The Almoner

To the almonry belong two bakeries in Evesham, and the rent from Penwortham, that is, four marks, twelve pence from the land of the porter in Evesham, sixpence from the land next to it, and twelve pence from the land 'Cranforth' with the iron-workshop. In Gloucester four shillings from the land which was given with the monk Robert, and in the same town four shillings from the land of John Crume. Ninety eggs from Aldington. The almoner must receive a tithe from all the bread within the gate, whether cooked or bought. The abbot also has to find half a mark on Maundy Thursday for the maundy, to be distributed by the almoner alone to the brothers for distribution to the poor, and the cellarer must provide from the cellary separate loaves for each of the poor, and three herrings, and ale as they need. The almoner also must look after the garden of the monks.

The Master of the Fabric

To the fabric of the church and the houses adjoining the cloister belong ten pounds from Ombersley church: if this money is by any mischance not paid, the abbot must keep the church and the houses roofed. For this same purpose belong the tithes from the land of

Willielmi Beorn et fabri in Vffeham et legata et si que sunt alie
gratuite obuentiones.

Celerarius

Hee sunt consuetudines Eoueshamensis coenobii, ab antiquis temporibus statute, et a celerario generali complende. Celerarius itaque
qui totius abbatie curam geret, exceptis redditibus assignatis officiis
monachorum, hospitibus iuxta facultatem domus necessaria administrabit, omnibus uidelicet, excepto eo quod coquinarius que de
officio suo sunt uiris religiosis inuenire debet. Debet etiam idem
celerarius ea que inferius annotata sunt de officio suo fratribus per
manus subcelerarii administrare. A cellario igitur singulis diebus
debent uenire in refectorium septuaginta et duo panes monachiles,
quorum quilibet erit ponderis sexaginta quinque solidorum. Ex
quibus singuli monachi singulos percipient, prior et per duplum
nisi cum abbate commederit, nichilominus qui ad superiorem
mensam et custos ordinis sederit duplum, qui missam maiorem
celebrauerit duos, lector uero et seruitores unum ad mixtum,
elemosinarius autem sex de decima, et tres ad mandatum et duos
ad triennales currentes. Percipiet etiam quilibet fratrum cotidie duas
iustas de ceruisia, et certe mensure. Inueniet etiam celerarius salem et
ligna ad ignem, et singulis diebus duo pulmenta: ad unum, de fabis
siccis unum prebendarium rasum uel de nouis cumulatum de
granario, ad aliud uero pulmentum, decem panes monachiles de
celerario singulis diebus, preterquam in Quadragesima in qua
percipient duodecim summas fabarum de Huniburn ad unum
pulmentum inueniendum per totam Quadragesimam. Et de auena
duodecim summas de eadem uilla ad gruellum faciendum scilicet
quarta et sexta feria per totam Quadragesimam, et farinam ad olera
singulis diebus in Quadragesima. Insuper debent*a* habere monachi ad
octo festiuitates principales octo summas frumenti ad quamlibet
scilicet festiuitatem unam summam ad frixuras de granario. Et in
eiusdem festiuitatibus fiffuls [*sic*] de frumento ad wastellos de
granario, et in translatione sancti Ecguini duos ad prandium scilicet
et ad cenam. Preterea percipiet coquinarius ad Pasca tria prebendaria
frumenti de granario ad flathones inueniendos, similiter et in
Rogationibus, ad festum sancti Odulfi, unum prebendarium ad
frixuras, similiter in Septuagesima, et uno die parasceue ad pulmentum. Ad formittas uero in Aduentu Domini debent habere quatuordecim summas, contra Natale Domini, contra Quadragesimam

---

a debet *M*

William Beorn and from that of the smith in Offenham, and the legacies and any other obventions freely given.

The Cellarer

These are the customs of the monastery of Evesham, established from of old, which must be maintained by the general cellarer. The cellarer shall have charge of the whole abbey, except for the revenues assigned to the monks' obediences; he shall make provision for the needs of the guests to the extent that the resources of the house allow; however, the kitchener must provide for visiting religious from his office. The cellarer must also provide from his office those things which are noted below to be delivered to the brothers by the sub-cellarer. Each day the cellarer must deliver to the refectory seventy-two monastic loaves of bread, each of which shall weigh sixty-five shillings. Each monk shall receive one of these, and the prior double the number unless he is eating with the abbot, but then whoever presides at the high table must have double. Those who are celebrating high mass must have two, the reader and the servants one, and an allowance of food; the almoner, however, will receive six out of every ten, and three for Maundy and two for successive trentals. Each of the brethren shall also receive every day two flagons of ale of a fixed measure. The cellarer shall also provide salt and kindling, and the two dishes of pottage daily. For one he will provide a measured allowance of dried beans or, as a change, a rased measure from the granary, for the other ten monks' loaves daily from the cellar, except during Lent, when he will receive twelve seams of beans from Honeybourne to provide one dish [per monk] for the whole of Lent. From the same vill he shall receive twelve seams of oats to make gruel on the Wednesdays and Fridays throughout the whole of Lent, and wheatmeal to add to the vegetables every day during Lent. In addition, the monks must have eight seams of corn for the eight principal festivals, one seam from the granary for each festival for pancakes. During these festivals they must have one bushel of corn from the granary for each festival to make wastel-loaves, and at the feast of the translation of St Ecgwine two for dinner and supper. Moreover, the kitchener will receive three measures of corn from the granary for Easter day to provide custard tarts, similarly at Rogationtide, on the feast of St Odulf, one measure of corn for pancakes, the same on Septuagesima, and again one on Good Friday for pottage. Then at Advent the monks must have fourteen seams of corn for cakes, as many to provide for Christmas,

tantundem, contra Pasca totidem, contra Pentecosten totidem, contra Translationem sancti Ecguini totidem, omnes scilicet percipiendas de horreis. Debent etiam habere de celerario singulis diebus sabbati caritatem ad collationem pro mandato, et ad omnes collationes festiuitatum tam in capis quam in albis, in uigilia et in die, exceptis collationibus septem principalium festiuitatum, tam in uigilia quam in die, tunc enim pitanciarius inuenire debet. Debent etiam habere caritatem de cellario ad prandium singulis diebus octabarum principalium festiuitatum que octabas habent, exceptis diebus quibus sunt in capis; tunc enim pitanciarius inueniet. Et ad collationem singulis earundem octabarum, et a natali Domini usque ad Epiphaniam, simili modo habebunt de cellario. Et quandocunque est potus post nonam, percipiet refectorarius duas iustas de cellario, et ad mixtum unam: item singulis diebus dominicis in Quadragesima dimidium prebendarium frumenti de granario ad oblatas ad cenam, et dimidium similiter in cena Domini ad idem. In minutionibus uero et misericordiis regularibus duo et duo, unam iustam de cellario tam ad prandium quam ad cenam, in ⟨uentositate⟩ uero unam. Seruiens uero qui fratres sanguinauerit panem et iustam recipiet de cellario, si plures fuerint sanguinati. Quotiens etiam mappe de refectorio abluuntur, seruientes de lauendaria panem monachilem de cellario habere debent. Et tribus septimanis in Aduento Domini et tribus ante Pascha, singulis scilicet diebus quando fratres balneant, balneatores percipere debent de cellario panem et iustam. Item duo capellani, sancti uidelicet Laurentii et Omnium Sanctorum, debent habere cotidie de cellario panem et ceruisiam sicut et monachi. Debet etiam camerarius habere cotidie de cellario ad unum seruientem procurationem, et prebendam ad unum equum de granario, et forragium de grangia: similiter et sacrista. Item in anniuersariis abbatum, Reginaldi scilicet et Ade, habere debent monachi singulos siffuls de granario ad wastellos, et uiginti solidos de ecclesia de Buldewellei ad pitanciam et caritatem. In die Animarum recipere debet elemosinarius unam summam frumenti de granario pauperibus erogandam. Similiter fiet in obitu cuiuslibet monachi Euesham. Abbas et monachi eiusdem loci per totum annum post obitum suum totum conredium sicut in uita sua perceperint habere debent; quod alicui indigenti pro anima sua erogabitur. Seruientes etiam qui uigilant circa fratrem proximum morti panem et ceruisiam habere

Lent, Easter, Pentecost, and the translation of St Ecgwine; all to be
taken from the barns. The monks must also have a *caritas* from the
cellar every Saturday at the collation for the maundy, and at every
collation at festivals when copes and albs are worn, on the vigil as well
as the day of the festival. However, the collations of the seven
principal festivals are excepted, the vigils as well as the days of the
festivals, when the pittancer must provide for these. The monks must
also have a *caritas* from the cellar for dinner every day on the octaves
of those principal festivals that have octaves, except on days when
copes are worn when the pittancer shall provide them. The cellarer
will provide the collation on each of the same octaves, and will also do
so from Christmas until Epiphany. Whenever wine is drunk after
nones, the refectorer will receive two flagon measures from the cellar,
and a food allowance: similarly every Sunday during Lent he shall
receive half a measure of corn from the granary for the wafer-cakes at
supper, and again half on Thursday in Holy Week for the same
purpose. At blood-letting and at other times of relaxation of the Rule,
pairs of monks will have one measure of ale from the cellar for both
dinner and supper, and one at times of bleeding. The servant who has
bled the brethren shall receive bread and a measure of ale from the
cellar if many brethren have been bled. Whenever tablecloths from
the refectory are washed, the laundry-servants must have monks'
bread from the cellar. During three weeks in Advent and three weeks
before Easter, on each of the days that brethren take a bath, the
servants of the bath-house must receive from the cellar bread and a
measure of ale. Similarly, the two chaplains of St Laurence and All
Saints must have bread and ale every day from the cellar, like the
monks. The chamberlain must also have a maintenance allowance
every day for one servant from the cellar, and an allowance of corn
from the granary for one horse, as well as fodder from the barn; the
same goes for the sacrist. On the anniversaries of Abbots Reginald
and Adam, the monks must have one measure of corn from the
granary for a wastel cake each, and twenty shillings from the church
of Broadwell for a pittance and a *caritas*. On the feast of All Souls the
almoner must receive one seam of corn from the granary to give to the
poor. This should also be done on the death of any monk of Evesham.
The abbot and monks of the same place must have their corrody, just
as they had in their lifetime, for the whole year after their death, to be
disbursed for the sake of their souls to some needy person. Servants
who keep vigil around a brother who is close to death must have bread

debent de cellario. Si uero obitus abbatis uel monachi alterius domus, si fuerint de capitulo Euesham, euenerit, ad annale pro abbate et tritennale pro monacho de cellario panis et ceruisia, sicut et monacho alicui pauperi, erogabuntur.

Vt autem hec in posterum obseruentur, prefatus legatus ea sub hac forma confirmauit.

Iohannes Dei gratia sancte Marie in via lata diaconus cardinalis, apostolice sedis legatus, dilectis fratribus abbati et conuentui de Eouesham in uero salutari salutem. Ea que pro statu religiosorum locorum et obseruantia regulari prouide statuuntur, firmiter et inuiolabiliter uolumus obseruari. Eapropter uestris postulationibus annuentes, constitutiones quasdam pro statu monasterii et religionis obseruantia inter uos communi factas assensu, et redactas in scripto, prout rationabiliter et regulariter facte sunt, et ab utraque parte sponte recepte, legationis auctoritate qua fungimur confirmamus, et presentis scripti patrocinio communimus. Huius auctoritate confirmationis auctenticum sub communi custodia cum sigillo ecclesie nostre seruandum posuimus: et hec omnia sigillorum nostrorum appositione roborauimus.

Et ut hec omnia imperpetuum immutilata firmiter obseruentur, magister Rodbertus de Wlueia,[1] et magister Thomas de Warewic,[2] et Willielmus senescallus de Eouesham, ad petitionem et instantiam domini R. abbatis, eo presente, in animam ⟨iurauerunt⟩ ipsius abbatis, ipsum abbatem premissa omnia pro posse suo obseruaturum, et nos paterna dilectione tractaturum, et consilio conuentus sui se usurum. Tactis sacrosanctis euangeliis iurauit, et nos conuentus singuli et uniuersi hoc idem nos obseruaturos sub eadem cautela promisimus, et domino abbati, ut patri et domino reuerendo, obedientiam et reuerentiam exhibituros, quamdiu nos paterna tractauerit affectione. Et predicti Rodbertus, Thomas et Willielmus iurati in testimonium premissorum simul nobiscum sigilla sua apposuerunt.

---

[1] Warws.; clerk of Abbot Norreis. See above, 235.

and ale from the cellar. If the death occurs of a monk or abbot of another house, who has belonged to the Evesham chapter, bread and ale must be given from the cellar to some poor person, for a year on the abbot's behalf, and for thirty days on the monk's behalf.

In order that these things shall be observed in future, the legate has confirmed them as follows:
John, by the grace of God cardinal deacon of St Mary in the Via Lata, legate of the apostolic see, to the beloved brethren the abbot and convent of Evesham, greeting in true salvation. We desire that those things that are prudently decreed for the good estate of religious places and for regular observance be steadfastly and inviolably observed. Therefore, assenting to your requests, and by the authority of the legation which we discharge, we confirm that certain statutes made among you by common consent for the good estate of the monastery and for the observance of religion, and put in writing, have been made reasonably and consonant with the Rule, and willingly accepted by both abbot and monks, and we ratify them with the protection of this present document. By the authority of this confirmation we have placed the original with the seal of our church to be kept in common custody, and we have corroborated all this by the addition of our seals.

And so that these statutes shall be faithfully observed in perpetuity without alteration, Master Robert of Wolvey,[1] and Master Thomas of Warwick,[2] and William, the steward of Evesham, on the petition and request of R. the abbot, swore upon the soul of the abbot himself, in his presence, that the abbot would observe all these arrangements to the best of his ability, that he would treat us with fatherly affection, and would act only with the advice of the convent. He [the abbot] swore this on the holy Gospels, and we the convent, individually and collectively, promised that we would observe the same with that same provision, and would show obedience and reverence to the abbot, as to a father and revered lord, as long as he treated us with fatherly affection. The said Robert, Thomas, and William, sworn as witnesses of these arrangements added their seals with ours.

---

[2] Also a clerk of Abbot Norreis, see above, 261, 384, 389.

B. AS IN THE CHARTER DRAWN UP
UNDER ABBOT RANDULF

The words, phrases, and sections printed in italic are omitted in the version in Thomas's *History* (R).

BL, Cotton MS Aug. II. 11.

Omnibus sancte matris ecclesie filiis ad quos presens scriptum peruenerit Rondulfus Dei gratia abbas Eueshamie et totus eiusdem loci conuentus salutem in Domino. Quoniam a domino Innocentio papa tertio dispositionis reddituum officiorum nostrorum confirmationem*a* optinere meruimus, redditus, non tantum illos quos tempore confirmationis habuimus set et quos postea adquisiuimus cum ipsa
l.2 eorum dispositione, ad posterorum | noticiam profuturum, scripto commendare dignum duximus. Nam tam ab Innocentio papa secundo quam ab Alexandro tercio non solum redditus quos tempore eorum habuimus, set et illi quos postea quibuscumque iustis modis adquirere possemus, nobis conceduntur et confirmantur: quod et ipsum nobis facere licere in hiis nostris constitutionibus et consuetudinibus continetur.

Sunt igitur consuetudines monasterii huius. Videlicet quod abbas
l.3 infra septa | monasterii existens inter fratres secundum antiquam domus illius consuetudinem conuersando regulariter uiuet, et exteriora pro uiribus suis ad utilitatem ecclesie prouide et fideliter dispensabit. Prior uero, subprior, tercius prior, et alii custodes ordinis, prior de Penwrtham, precentor, decanus, sacrista, camerarius, coquinarius, celerarius interior, infirmarius, eleemosinarius, custos uinee et gardini, magister fabrice ecclesie, *pitanciarius*,
l.4 magister hospi|tum, de consilio et consensu conuentus uel maioris et sanioris partis in capitulo ab abbate de proprio conuentu creentur. Qui si minus, quod absit, honeste uel minus prudenter in officiis suis se habuerint*b* uel male fratribus administrauerint, prius correpti

----

a *corrected and squeezed in*   *b* se *squeezed in*

B. AS IN THE CHARTER DRAWN UP UNDER ABBOT RANDULF

For full historical annotation, see above, **399–429**, and for the charter's relationship with the version in Thomas's *History* (**399–429**), see the Introduction, pp. lvi–lix, and App. II C.

To all the sons of holy Mother Church to whom the present document shall come, Randulf, by the grace of God abbot of Evesham, and the whole convent of that place, greeting in the Lord. Since we have been thought worthy of obtaining from Pope Innocent III confirmation of the disposition of the revenues assigned to our offices, we have thought it right to make a written record of them, not only of those revenues which we had at the time of the confirmation, but also of those which we acquired afterwards, with their actual disposition so that posterity will benefit from this knowledge. Pope Innocent II and Alexander III both granted us not only the revenues which we held in their time, but also those which we could acquire by just means after their time, and they confirmed these: indeed, our constitutions and customs have clauses allowing us to do this.

The customs of the monastery are as follows. The abbot shall live within the enclosure of the monastery amongst his brethren in accordance with the Rule, following the ancient custom of that house, and will diligently and faithfully deal with external matters, to the best of his ability, to the benefit of the church. The following officers are to be appointed by the abbot from amongst his own convent, in chapter, on the advice and with the assent of the convent or of a majority of brethren of wiser counsel: the prior, subprior, third prior, and other masters of order, the prior of Penwortham, the precentor, dean, sacrist, chamberlain, kitchener, internal cellarer, infirmarer, almoner, keeper of the vineyard and garden, master of the church fabric, pittancer, and the guest-master. Should these officers, God forbid, fail to conduct themselves honourably and wisely in carrying out their their duties, or manage them badly for

regulariter, si non emendauerint amoueantur in capitulo, et alii sub forma predicta in loco eorum in capitulo et incontinenti subrogentur, ne aliquo casu in manus regis deueniant ipsa officia, abbate |

l. 5 forte discedente, uel per moram fiat deterioratio obedientiarum, aut aliquis defectus propter moram emergat. Prior uero et predicti magistri ordinis simul cum abbate ut ordo monasticus cum rigore discipline secundum regulam beati Benedicti obseruetur summam diligentiam adhibeant. Maxime autem operam prestent ne monachi aliquid sine licencia habeant, et ne alias quam in refectorio

l. 6 commedant sine licencia, et ut eleemosina eorum per | manus eleemosinarii erogetur, et ne a claustro sine licencia exeant, et ut silencium locis*a* statutis obseruetur, et ut fratres frequenter delicta confiteantur, non tamen aliis quam hiis qui ad hoc deputantur. Alii uero predicti officiales omnes qui redditus percipiunt quater in anno coram abbate, uel eo quem loco suo statuerit, priore et sex claustralibus, tribus ab abbate et tribus a conuentu uocatis, de administratione sua compotum reddant; coquiniarius uero qualibet ebdomada. |

l. 7 Isti officiales quociens domi fuerint in congregatione iugiter permaneant, et conuentum in ecclesia, in capitulo, in claustro, in refectorio sequantur, ut si, quod absit, in officiis suis aliquis defectus emerserit illi statim suppleant. Nulli duo officia assignentur, set cuilibet adiungatur socius, si opus fuerit, solatium et testis diligencie sue. Si uero in aliquo officio suo propter maliciam temporis aliquid

l. 8 ultra redditus officio illi assignatos expensum fuerit, si in aliquo | alio officio aliquid fuerit residuum, per illud defectus alterius suppleatur. Si autem nullum officium defectum alterius officii supplere potuerit, abbas per manum celerarii exterioris suppleat. Preterea, si quodlibet officium sibi suffecerit et aliquid residuum fuerit, abbas de consilio capituli uel maioris et sanioris partis in eo officio in quo in capitulo iudicauerit utilius ecclesie expendat.

Si uero aliquid de redditibus monachorum officiis suis assignari

---

a et horis *add.* R

the brethren, they are first to be reproved in accordance with the Rule, but then, if they do not mend their ways, they are to be removed at once from office in chapter, and others immediately substituted in the manner stated above. This is to prevent those offices, through some mischance, falling into the hands of the king as, for example, on the death of the abbot; and to ensure that no deterioration in the obediences should occur through delay, or any other kind of defect arise from delay. The prior and the other masters of order are, along with the abbot, to show the utmost diligence in ensuring that monastic order is observed with strict discipline in accordance with the Rule of St Benedict. They are to make it their special business to ensure that monks do not possess anything without permission, that they do not eat in any place other than the refectory without permission, that their alms are distributed by the almoner alone, that they do not leave the cloister without permission, that silence is observed in all the regular places, and that the brethren confess their sins frequently, but only to those who have been appointed to hear their confession. All the other officers mentioned who receive revenues are to render an account of their stewardship four times a year before the abbot or the one appointed by him in his place, with the prior and six cloister monks in attendance, three appointed by the abbot and three by the convent. The kitchener shall submit accounts each week.

These officers are always to remain in the congregation of the monks whenever they are in the house, and are to follow the common life of the convent in the church, in the chapter-house, in the cloister, and in the refectory so that if, God forbid, any failing occurs in their duties they may immediately provide for it. Let none be assigned two offices, but let each be joined by a colleague, if necessary, as a support and witness to his diligence. If in any office, because of bad times, an amount is spent that exceeds the revenue assigned to it, whereas in another office there is money left over, then let the deficiency in one office be met by the excess in the other. If, however, no office can make up the deficiency of that other office, the abbot is to do so, with funds from the external cellarer. Moreover, if any office has sufficient for its own needs and something left over, the abbot, after consultation with the chapter or of a majority of the brethren of wiser counsel, is to spend that residue on the office in which the chapter judges the spending will most benefit the church.

If any part of the revenues which have been assigned to the offices

l. 9 uel | imperpetuum, quod absit, uel ad tempus detineri contigerit, uel aliquo modo euacuari uel diminui, abbas tantumdem de consilio capituli ubi commode fieri poterit alibi eidem officio assignet. Liceat preterea monachis possessiones et redditus officiis suis assignatos ueluti noualia faciendo et redditus aumentando et nouos adquirendo ampliare, seu quibuscumque aliis iustis modis meliorare, l. 10 et alios pro aliis tandumdem ualentibus et utili|bus, cum uiderint expedire, uel ad tempus uel imperpetuum commutare.

Celerarius siquidem exterior talis de proprio conuentu et in capitulo ab abbate creetur, qui, exceptis redditibus monachorum officiis assignatis, ad preceptum abbatis, tocius abbatie curam gerens. Sciat et possit libere conuentui necessaria administrare, scilicet panem, ceruisiam, duo pulmenta, ignem et salem, et quedam alia in consuetudinibus expressa. Hospitibus etiam iuxta l. 11 fa|cultatem domus prouidebit celerarius, uiris tamen religiosis coquinarius que de officio suo sunt, personis eorum sicut et fratribus, administrabit, exceptis abbatibus et capellanis eorum quibus non inueniet aliquid nisi in diebus ieiunii, sicut nec ipsi abbati, nec illis qui cum illo comedunt uel capellanis eius. Hoc dicimus nisi in refectorio comedant, ut in profestis diebus. Seruientibus etiam obedienciarum abbacie celerarius procurationem debitam et stipendia l. 12 iuxta | consuetudinem domus administrabit.

Iste quidem celerarius de administratione sua non solum quater superioribus set quociens ipse abbas uoluerit compotum reddat. Qui nisi bene administrauerit, sicut de aliis obedienciariis dictum est, ad iustam conquestionem conuentus et rationabilem uoluntatem abbatis amoueatur, et alius statim loco ipsius subrogetur et in capitulo. Numerum fratrum abbas integrum conseruet, nullum monachum l. 13 recipiat | aut eiciat uel ad tempus uel imperpetuum nisi de consilio conuentus uel maioris et sanioris partis, et in capitulo. Ecclesias autem uel alios redditus uel aliquas terras non nisi de consilio uniuersitatis uel maioris et sanioris partis et in capitulo alicui

of the monks happens to be withheld either permanently, God forbid, or temporarily, or happens to become exhausted or reduced in some way, the abbot is to assign, with the consent of the chapter, an equivalent amount elsewhere for that office, when this can be done to advantage. The monks are to be permitted, moreover, to increase their possessions and revenues assigned to their offices, for instance, by ploughing up new land and by augmenting rents, and by acquiring new possessions and rents, or they may improve them by any other just means. They may also make some of their revenues available for other equally valid or beneficial purposes, when they think it right to do so, either temporarily or permanently.

The external cellarer is to be appointed as such from his own convent and in chapter by the abbot, and is to be responsible, under the abbot's command, for the care of the whole abbey, save the revenues assigned to the offices of the monks. He is to know how to minister to the needs of the convent, and to be able to do so freely, with respect to bread, ale, the two dishes of pottage, kindling and salt, and certain other commodities stated in the Customs. The cellarer will make provision for guests also to the extent that the resources of the house allow, though the kitchener will provide for the personal needs of the religious from other houses as for the brethren, for this is part of his duty, but he will not provide anything for abbots and their chaplains except on fast days, just as he does not do so for the abbot himself or for those who eat with the abbot or for his chaplains. This does not apply if they eat in the refectory, as they do on the eves of festivals. The cellarer will provide due maintenance for the servants of the abbey's obedientiaries and their stipends in accordance with the custom of the house.

The cellarer must render an account of his stewardship not only four times a year to his superiors but as often as the abbot wishes. If his stewardship has not been good, as has been mentioned in the case of other obedientiaries, he is to be removed at the just complaint of the convent and the reasonable request of the abbot, and is to be immediately replaced in chapter by another. The abbot is to maintain the full number of monks free of office, and he is not to accept or expel any monk either temporarily or permanently without the consent of the convent or of a majority of monks of wiser counsel, and this is to be dealt with in chapter. He is not to bestow churches or other revenues or any lands upon anyone, except with the agreement of the whole convent or of a majority of monks of wiser counsel, and

conferat. Nec rusticos sine consensu eorundem manumittat. De terris siquidem reuocandis pro uiribus suis, si que tempore suo uel predecessorum suorum alienate sunt, consilio conuentus sui utatur.

l. 14 Similiter | in causis ecclesiasticis uel forensibus agendis uel terminandis capituli sui utatur consilio. Seruientes autem qui monachis ministrare tenentur, scilicet de infirmaria, sarterina, lauenderina, refectorio, sacristaria, locutorio, de consilio capituli secundum priorem formam constituantur et deponantur. Hec omnia intelligantur saluis in omnibus regularibus institutis.

l. 15 Ad prioratum pertinent *ouentiones de communi sigillo*[1] *et* | *omnes* decime de Benigwrthe tam maiores quam minores de omnibus terris et hominibus *abbatis et* monachorum ad *emendum* parchamenum pro libris scribendis. Pertinent etiam ad priorem curia nostra de Benigwrthe cum croftis ad eandem curiam pertinentibus *et* cum gardino, uiuario et prato que sunt infra ipsam curiam, et *cum* omnibus mesuuagiis de croftis que sunt circa ipsam curiam, uidelicet a domo

l. 16 Thome Algar usque ad domum Walteri Bellard. | Nam prior Thomas quandam terram de Littlintona quam emit a Radulfo dispensatore, de qua tempore commutationis plus redditus soluebatur quam de ista de Benigwrth', pro eadem a domino abbate de consensu communi commutauit. Quare constitutum est quod supprior pro tempore in anniuersario prioris Thome pascat triginta pauperes *in locutorio* pro animabus priorum et omnium fratrum, et inueniet

l. 17 cereum in die sancti Wistani et alium in die sancti Credani | ardentes coram feretris eorum die ac nocte.

Ad decanatum pertinet corredium unius seruientis de cellario et collecta denariorum beatri Petri ubicumque episcopus non colligit *de quibus soluit annuatim domino pape uiginti solidos.* Et uisitatio ecclesiarum Vallis et ouentiones causarum *et omnium pertinentium ad decanatum* de quibus debet inuenire conuentui caritatem dominica qua cantatur misericordia Domini.

l. 18 Ad officium precentoris pertinent | decime de Stokes[2] et quedam terra in Hamtona de qua percipit annuatim quinque solidos, et alia in Alencestria de qua tantumdem percipit. De his debet inuenire

---

[1] Persons acquiring documents sealed with the convent's seal were required to pay for them.
[2] ? Severn Stoke.

this is to take place in chapter. He is not to free villeins without the same consent being given. With regard to the recovery that is in his power of lands that have been alienated during his own time or during the time of his predecessors, he must take the advice of his convent. Similarly, in undertaking or terminating lawsuits, ecclesiastical or secular, he is to take the advice of his chapter. The servants who are kept to minister to the needs of the monks in the infirmary, the tailor's workshop, the laundry, the refectory, the sacristy, and the parlour, are to be appointed and dismissed on the advice of the chapter as previously specified. Let all these provisions be accepted, saving in all things the Rule.

To the prior's office belong the proceeds from the common seal[1] and all the tithes of Bengeworth, the great as well as the small, from all the lands and men of the abbot and of the monks, and these are for buying parchment for writing books. To the prior also belong our court of Bengeworth with the crofts belonging to the same court, with the garden, fishpond, and meadow, which are within the court, as well as all the messuages which are part of the crofts which surround the court itself, that is, from the house of Thomas Algar right up to the house of Walter Bellard. For Prior Thomas, with common consent, exchanged for land from the abbot some land at Littleton which he bought from Ralph the steward, which was receiving at the time of the exchange more rent than the land at Bengeworth. Wherefore it was decreed that the subprior should feed thirty poor people in the parlour on the anniversary of Prior Thomas for the sake of the souls of the priors and all the brethren, and that he should provide a candle on St Wigstan's day and another on St Credan's day to burn before their shrines day and night.

To the office of dean belongs the corrody of one of the cellarer's servants, the collection of Peter's Pence wherever the bishop does not collect it, of which he pays twenty shillings per annum to the pope, the visitation of the churches of the Vale and the obventions from lawsuits and everything pertaining to the deanery, from which he must provide a *caritas* for the convent on the Sunday on which the Misericordia Domini is sung.

To the office of precentor belong the tithes of 'Stokes'[2] and some land in Hampton from which he receives five shillings per annum, and some land in Alcester [Warws.] from which he receives the same amount. From these the precentor has to find parchment for

precentor *parchamenum ad breuia*[1] *et ad cartas signandas sigillo communi et ad breuia mortuorum fratrum et*[2] incaustum omnibus scriptoribus monasterii, et colores ad illuminandum et necessaria ad ligandos libros et necessaria ad organa.

l. 19 Ad sacristariam pertinent | sex capelle in Valle, scilicet de Nortona, de Lenchewike, de Mortona et Vffeham, et due in Euesham *quarum duarum capellarum sacerdotes, scilicet sancti Laurentii et omnium sanctorum debent habere cotidie de cellario panem et ceruisiam sicut monachi. Debet etiam sacrista habere cotidie ad unum seruientem procurationem sicut seruientes abbatis habent et prebendam ad unum*
l. 20 *equum de granario et foragium de grangia.* Percipit etiam | sacrista de ecclesia de Baddebi annuatim duas marcas. De capella de With-lakesford et prato de Salford decem solidos. De ecclesia de Westona dimidiam marcam. De ecclesia de Stowa quinque solidos uel duas petras cere. De ecclesia Sancti Albani in Wigornia quinque libras cere. De terris in eadem uilla tres marcas. Pertinent etiam ad sacristariam in Eouesham solda iuxta portam cimiterii. De fabrica |
l. 21 Willelmi fabri quatuor denarii. De terra Nicholai coci due libre cere. De terra Matilldis in Merstowe quinque denarii. De terra Nicholai sacriste in eodem uico sex denarii. De terra senescaldi que fuit Geraldi sex denarii. De terra Bulet sex denarii. De terra Ferre triginta denarii. De terra le Hosiere in Bruggestrete duo denarii. De terra Willelmi de Tywe in magno uico duo solidi et quatuor |
l. 22 denarii. De terra Willelmi de Tywe proxima terre le Hosiere in Bruggestrete sex denarii. De terra dispensatoris proxima terre Willelmi de Tywe quadraginta denarii. De terra que dicitur Gordani in Colestrete sexdecim denarii. De terra Reginald fabri duo solidi. De terra Walteri proxima eidem octo denarii. De terra Pate eidem proxima octo denarii. De terra Nicholai fullonis super aquam
l. 23 sexdecim denarii. De terra Henrici fabri | uiginti denarii. De

---

[1] The writer presumably means the writs or mandates issued by the abbot and convent in the course of their conduct of business. He carefully avoids the use of *littere*, and he does not mean mortuary notices or death-bills (*breuia*), as these are distinguished further on in the sentence.

[2] Such mortuary notices were short documents announcing the death of a member of the community and seeking prayers for the deceased, which were carried by messengers to the houses within the confraternity; for the practice at the time of Lanfranc, see *Monastic Constitutions of Lanfranc*, ed. D. Knowles, revised C. N. L. Brooke, pp. 46–7, 122–3, 128–9, 130–1, 136–7. They were frequently entered on rolls and circulated amongst religious houses; see Jean Dufour, 'Les rouleaux des morts', *Codicologia* iii (1980), pp. 96–102; C. R. Cheney, 'Two mortuary rolls from Canterbury: devotional links of Canterbury with Normandy and the Welsh March', in *Tradition and Change: Essays in honour of Marjorie*

writs[1] and for charters sealed with the common seal, as well as for the mortuary writs,[2] ink for all the scribes of the monastery, colours for illumination, and the things necessary for binding the books and for the organs.

To the sacristy belong six chapels in the Vale, namely Norton, Lenchwick, Morton and Offenham, and two in Evesham, of which two chapels the priests, that is, of St Laurence and All Saints, should have every day from the cellarer bread and ale, as do the monks. The sacrist should also have daily maintenance for one servant, such as the abbot's servants have, and an allowance for one horse from the granary, and forage from the grange. The sacrist also receives two marks per annum from the church of Badby [Northants]. Ten shillings from the chapel of Wixford [Warws.] and the meadow in Salford [Warws.]. Half a mark from the church of Weston-on-Avon [Glos.]. Five shillings or two stones of wax from the church of Stow-on-the-Wold [Glos.]. Five pounds of wax from the church of St Alban in Worcester. Three marks from the lands in the same town. To the sacristy also belong the shop next to the gate of the cemetery, four pence from the forge of William the smith, two pounds of wax from the land of Nicholas the cook, five pence from the land of Matilda in Merstow, six pence from the land of Nicholas the sacrist in the same neighbourhood, six pence from the land of the steward that had belonged to Gerald, six pence from the land of Bulet, thirty pence from the land of Ferre, two pence from the land of le Hosiere in Bridge Street, two shillings and four pence from the land of William de Tywe in the High Street, six pence from the land of William de Tywe next to the land of le Hosiere in Bridge Street, forty pence from the land of the steward next to the land of William de Tywe, sixteen pence from the land which is called Gordans in Cole Street, two shillings from the land of Reginald the smith, eight pence from the land of Walter next to the same, eight pence from the land of 'Pate' next to the same, sixteen pence from the land of Nicholas the fuller above the stream, twenty pence from the land of Henry the

Chibnall, ed. D. Greenway, C. Holdsworth, and J. Sayers (Cambridge, 1985), pp. 103–14, esp. 104–5; and the pioneering work of Léopold Delisle, in *Bibliothèque de l'École des Chartes*, 2nd ser. iii (1847), pp. 361–412, and the same author's edition, *Rouleaux des morts du ixe au xve siècle* (Soc. Hist. France cxxxix, 1866). Neil Ker commented on mortuary 'briefs' in *Miscellany*, i (Worcestershire Historical Soc. n.s. [I], 1960), pp. 53–9. Payment of 18*d*. for 'writs' for dead brothers appear on the precentor's account for 1482–3 at Worcester, see *Compotus Rolls of the Priory of Worcester of the xivth and xvth centuries*, i, trans. and ed. S. G. Hamilton (Worcestershire Hist. Soc. xxvi: Oxford, 1910), p. 49.

terra proxima Willelmi de Tywe quatuor denarii. De terra Symonis fabri quatuordecim denarii. De terra Andree coci octo denarii. De terra in Hampton' quinque solidi. In Lench pertinent ad sacristariam tres hide et dimidia. In Bratfortona in uno campo quinquaginta quinque acre, in altero septuaginta sex in dominico. In uilinagio quinque uirgate terre et dimidia, et decime de eadem terra tam

l. 24 ma|iores quam minores. Et de quatuor hidis in eadem uilla duabus scilicet Hugonis et duabus militis de Coctona, et decime de nouem uirgatis terre Pagani in Littletona tam maiores quam minores, et decime de quinque uirgatis terre senescalli in Baddeseia, et decime cuiusdam liberi hominis de dominico in Pikeleia in Herefordesyre et omnes oblationes et omnia legata altaris Eoueshamie.

l. 25 *Ad altare sancte Marie in criptis perti|nent de sacristaria septem cerei cotidie ardentes dum missa gloriose Virginis domine nostre ibidem celebratur, quorum duos ab antiquis temporibus inuenerunt sacriste, et unus cereus die et nocte iugiter ardens. Ad cuius sustentationem cum quinque superioribus assignauit magister Adam Sortes sacrista*[1] *dimidiam uirgatam terre quam redemit de Petro de Lenz, et minutas decimas de*

l. 26 *nouem uirgatis terre in Littletona | quas idem sacrista euicit de rectore ecclesie de Littletona, et etiam decimas de assartis de Lenz quorum licenciam assartandi idem sacrista a participibus commune pasture multa pecunia redemit. Et unus crassetus*[2] *tantum de nocte ardens quem sacriste ab antiquo inuenerunt, et una lampas iugiter ardens de decimis de dominico de Lenz quas prior Thomas primus sacris[ta]*[a][3] *percepit et ad hoc*

l. 27 *assignauit. Et ne sacrista predictis grauetur, | prouisum est quod custos altaris eiusdem inueniat uestimenta et alia necessaria eidem altari que sacriste prius consueuerunt inuenire. Idem etiam custos altaris eiusdem inuenire triginta lampades ardentes dum missa ibidem celebratur et septem cereos. Ad quod faciendum assignata tota sinapis de omnibus grangiis sacristarie, et omnes ouentiones altaris eiusdem et duo solidi in Eouesham de terra Walteri Per iuxta pontem, et decem et nouem denarii de terra*

l. 28 *Willelmi | carpentarii super Runhulle,*[4] *et duodecim denarii de terra Willelmi Ouri in noua terra que est inter terram*[b] *Albini de Capis et*

---

[a] *damaged: supplied from R*   [b] inter terram *squeezed in*

[1] For numerous mentions of him, see the Index. Thomas was sacrist from 1217 to 1218. Sortes, after he had been driven from the house by Abbot Norreis, was made prior of Penwortham in 1207: he may have been appointed sacrist on his return in 1213. Alternatively he could have been sacrist before the litigation in Rome.

[2] A vessel for holding grease or oil which was then burnt to provide light.

smith, four pence from William de Tywe's land next to that, fourteen pence from the land of Simon the smith, eight pence from the land of Andrew the cook, five shillings from land in Hampton. Belonging to the sacristy are three-and-a-half hides in Lench, fifty-five acres in one field in Bretforton, in another field seventy-six acres of demesne land, five and a half virgates of land in villein tenure, with both the great and small tithes from this land, four hides in the same vill, two of Hugh and two of the knight of Coughton, the tithes, both great and small, from nine virgates of the land of Pagan in Littleton, the tithes from five virgates of the land of the steward in Badsey, the tithes from the demesne of a certain freeman in Pixley in Herefordshire, and all the offerings and altar bequests of Evesham.

To the altar of St Mary in the Crypt belong seven candles daily from the sacristy, to burn when the mass of our Lady the glorious Virgin is celebrated here, two of which are found by the sacrist from time immemorial, and one of which burns perpetually both day and night. In order to maintain this, with the five candles above, Master Adam Sortes, when sacrist,[1] assigned half a virgate of land which he redeemed from Peter of Lench, and the small tithes of nine virgates of land in Littleton which the same sacrist acquired from the rector of the church of Littleton, also the tithes from the assarts of Lench, for the same sacrist bought permission to assart at a high price from those sharing the common pasture. The sacrist is also to provide one cresset[2] to burn only during the night which the sacrists provided from of old, and one lamp to burn continuously from the tithes of the demesne land of Lench which Prior Thomas was the first sacrist[3] to receive and which he assigned for this purpose. So that the sacrist should not be overburdened by the aforesaid expenses, provision was made for the warden of the same altar to provide altar-cloths and other necessaries for the same altar which the sacrists had previously been accustomed to provide. This warden of the same altar is to provide thirty lamps to burn while mass is being celebrated, and seven candles. For this purpose the following are assigned: the whole of the mustard from all the sacrist's granges, and all the obventions of the same altar, and two shillings in Evesham from the land of Walter Per near the bridge, and nineteen pence from the land of William the carpenter above Rynehill,[4] and twelve pence from the land of William Ourri in the new land which lies between the land of Albinus de Capis

---

[3] He became sacrist in 1217.   [4] Rynehill (Rynal Street).

terram Iohannis Gnaueston et terra uxoris Iohannis Caperim, que est inter
terram Philippi sacriste et terram eiusdem Iohannis [1] *et domus fundate*
super spacia duarum soldarum et dimidie uersus portam cimiterii ecclesie,
et domus fundate super areas trium soldarum et dimidie magno uico iuxta
murum cimiterii uersus portam abbacie. Et due solde quas Adam Sortes |
l. 29   *emit. Et due quas prior Thomas emit iuxta eas de Ricardo de Warwic. Et*
terra quam M. relicta Credani dedit. Et omnes terre in Eouesham que
fuerunt Ricardi de Kent. Et quedam terra de Stretford, [2] *et duo solidi de*
terra de Radeford, [3] *et de terra de Strengesham duo solidi, et de terra de*
Martleia duo solidi.

Ad elemosinariam pertinent duo furni in Eouesham [et] [a] tercius in
Benigwrthe et omnis furni Vallis in quibus consuetudinarii
l. 30   consuescunt | coquere panem, et decime feni Willelmi de Tywe et
Rogeri Alardi, et Ernaldi Cambralangi. De terra Iohannis de Kent in
Eouesham dimidia marca. De soldis Ade Credani in magno uico iuxta
soldas sancte Marie, quatuor solidi. *De aliis soldis sitis iuxta aliam*
sancte Marie dimidia marca. De terra Cramfot cum solda ferri
duodecim denarii. De terra Godefridi Bagart sex denarii. De terra
l. 31   Cecilie retro furnum quatuor solidi. De terra Rogel | iuxta alium
furnum uiginti denarii. Et terra que dicitur Hospitale uersus pontem,
saluis octo denariis pitanciario. De terra Rondulfi textoris de feudo
Streche uiginti denarii. De terra quam Isabella filia Henrici King
dedit quadraginta solidi. *De terra Ricardi de Piplintona duo solidi; de*
terra le Burimon duo solidi. De terra Ricardi Eadmundi sexdecim denarii.
De terra Bonpain duodecim denarii. *De terra Stephani presbiteri*
l. 32   *quadraginta denarii.* | *De terra Lilie sex denarii. De terra Ricardi*
iuuenis duodecim denarii, et terra Murielle de Strigul. De R. Ywain et
heredibus suis annuatim sex denarii pro licentia colendi Chiteham. [4] In
Gloucestria pertinent ad elemosinariam de terra Iohannis Croume
quam contulit secum Adam monachus quatuor solidi. De terra Botild
que data fuit cum Roberto monacho octo solidi. De terra Rogeri Sewi
l. 33   quam Adam Botild dedit duodecim denarii. *De terra* | *que fuit Esegar*
undecim solidi. Ad eam etiam pertinent due marce de pensione

---

[a] *damaged: supplied from R*

---

[1] Presumably John Gnaveston.   [2] Stratford-on-Avon, Warws.
[3] ? in Rous Lench.   [4] ? in Evesham.

and the land of John Gnaveston and the land of the wife of John Caperim which is between the land of Philip the sacrist and the land of the same John,[1] and the houses built over the space of two and a half shops facing the gate of the cemetery of the church, and the houses built above the spaces occupied by three and a half shops in the High Street by the wall of the cemetery facing the gate of the abbey. And the two shops which Adam Sortes bought. And the two that Prior Thomas bought next to those of Richard of Warwick. And the land which M. the widow of Credan gave. And all the lands in Evesham which were Richard of Kent's. And certain land at Stratford,[2] and two shillings from the land at Radford,[3] and two shillings from land at Strensham, and two shillings from land at Martley.

To the almonry belong two bakeries in Evesham and a third in Bengeworth, and all the bakeries of the Vale in which the customary tenants are accustomed to cook their bread, and the hay tithes of William de Tywe, Roger Alard and Ernald Cambralang. Half a mark from the land of John of Kent in Evesham. Four shillings from the shops of Adam Credan in the High Street next to the shops of St Mary's. Half a mark from other shops situated next to another shop of St Mary's. Twelve pence from the land of Cramfot with the ironwork shop. Six pence from the land of Godfrey Bagart. Four shillings from the land of Cecilia behind the bakery. Twenty pence from the land of Rogel near another bakery. And the land which is called 'Hospital' facing the bridge, except for eight pence to the pittancer. Twenty pence from the land of Randulf the weaver from the fee of Streche. Forty shillings from the land which Isabel daughter of Henry King gave. Two shillings from the land of Richard de Piplintona; two shillings from the land 'le Burimon'. Sixteen pence from the land of Richard Edmund. Twelve pence from the land of Bonpain. Forty pence from the land of Stephen the priest. Six pence from the land of Lilia. Twelve pence from the land of the young man, Richard, and from the land of Muriel of Chepstow. Six pence per annum from Richard Ywain and his heirs for permission to cultivate 'Chiteham'.[4] In Gloucester four shillings belong to the almonry from the land of John Croume which Adam the monk brought with him. Eight shillings from the land 'Botild' which was given with Robert the monk. Twelve pence from the land of Roger Sew which Adam Botild gave. Eleven shillings from the land which was Esegar's. Also belonging to it are two marks from a pension of sixty shillings from

sexaginta solidorum de ecclesia de Ombresleia, scilicet uiginti solidi ad opus pauperum in Cena Domini ⟨ad Mandatum, et dimidia⟩*a* marca in anniuersario abbatis Rondulfi. Nam idem abbas contulit has duas marcas elemosinarie ratione scripta in capitulo de bonis operibus abbatis Rondulfi.[1] Cum etiam idem abbas fecisset sex molendina in

l. 34 maneriis abbacie | contulit elemosinarie loco decimarum de eisdem molendinis, molendinum de Aldintona quod ipse emerat de quo cum croftis et domibus ad idem molendinum pertinentibus recepit elemosinarius tempore donationis annuatim sexdecim solidos. De eadem etiam uilla percipit elemosinarius nongenta oua. De toto etiam pane infra portam abbacie expenso uel liberato ⟨ib⟩*b*i cocto uel empto

l. 35 debet elemosinarius habere decimam et curam orti monachorum | ut inde habeat pulmentum ad refectionem pauperum, *et collectam ceruisie ad secundum cibum uel potum.*[2] *Debet etiam elemosinarius percipere in die animarum unam summam frumenti de granario. Similiter fiet in obitu cuiuslibet monachi Eoueshamie. De terra filie Willelmi de Ponte in Alincestria nouem denarii.*

Ad refectorarium pertinent minute decim[e] de Wikewane, Baddeseie et Aldetone, ad reparationem cloclearium cyphorum | ius-

l. 36 tarum fenestrarum uitrearum et uasorum salis et aliorum utensilium cum duodecim lampadibus et oleo earum de quibus respondet priori qui eum de consilio fratrum preficit. Pertinet etiam ad eum collecta ceruisie post primum cibum et cotidie sex iuste[3] de cellario de quibus dat caritatem conuentui post collationem dominicis diebus et omni septimana semel quando ⟨cantatur⟩ de sancta Maria. Et inueniet

l. 37 potum ante collationem quando non est potus | post collationem et multa alia onera. Et statuta circa minutos et alios fratres de hiis sustinet et supplet. Et quoties potus fuerit post nonam habebit refectorarius duas iustas de cellario.

Ad infirmariam pertinet Biuintone cum bosco et dimidia marca de assarto de Sauford et cum omnibus aliis pertinenciis suis. Debet etiam

---

a supplied from R   *b* abraded

[1] The provisions made by Abbot Randulf are referred to in the chapter on his 'good works' (see above, **510–15**). His 'second good work' (**511**) was that he had diverted a pension from the church of Ombersley to the use of the poor (and incidentally released himself from considerable expenditure on Maundy Thursday). The twenty shillings and the half mark specified here add up to the two marks, but the sixty shillings mentioned in the good deeds is more, that is, four and a half marks. The half mark was presumably not paid until his death. It was not unusual to provide for an anniversary during lifetime; see *The Chartulary of the High Church of Chichester*, ed. W. D.Peckham (Sussex Rec. Soc. xlvi,

the church of Ombersley, twenty shillings for the service of the poor
on Maundy Thursday, and half a mark on the anniversary of Abbot
Randulf. For the same abbot bestowed these two marks upon the
almonry as written in the chapter on the good works of Abbot
Randulf.[1] When that abbot had done this, he bestowed upon the
almonry six mills on the manors of the abbey in place of the tithes
from the same mills, the mill of Aldington, which he himself had
bought, from which with the plots and the houses belonging to the
same mill the almoner received sixteen shillings annually at the time
of the donation. The almoner also receives ninety eggs from the same
vill. The almoner must also have a tithe from all of the bread
consumed or given as livery inside the gate of the abbey, whether
baked there or bought, and he must look after the garden of the
monks so that he may have pottage to feed the poor, and a collation of
ale for the second food or drink.[2] The almoner must also receive on
All Souls' day one seam of corn from the granary. It must similarly be
done on the death of any monk of Evesham. Nine pence from the land
of the daughter of William de Ponte in Alcester [Warws.].

To the refectory belong the small tithes of Wickhamford, Badsey,
and Aldington, for the repair of spoons, cups, flagons, glass-windows,
salt-cellars, and other utensils, with twelve lamps and their oil, for
which he is answerable to the prior who appoints him with the advice
of the brethren. It is also the refectorer's responsibility to provide a
collation of ale after the first meal, and six flagons[3] of ale from the
cellarer every day, from which he gives a *caritas* to the convent after
the collation on Sundays, and once a week when the Magnificat is
sung. He will also provide a drink before the collation when there is
no drink after the collation, and will be responsible for many other
requirements. He will also maintain and fulfil the regulations about
those who have been bled and other brethren who are concerned with
this. Whenever there is a drink after nones the refectorer will have
two flagons of ale from the cellarer.

To the infirmary belong Binton [Warws.] with the woodland and
half a mark from the assart of Salford with all of its other

1942–3), nos. 408, 420, and 595, examples from the late 12th to the mid-13th cent., most
vividly no. 595, Dean Geoffrey of Gloucester, who made provision for his anniversary in
1247, and did not die until at least October 1254. Abbot Randulph died on 17 Dec. 1229.
The reference to the chapter of the 'good deeds' must mean, however, that this document
has had additions and cannot be considered as the original.

[2] Perhaps meaning supper.

[3] The *iusta* was often taken to equal a flagon measure.

habere infirmarius unam suem cum nutrimento unius anni, uel duos
l. 38 porcos ad | plancherum et unum truncum de celerario contra Natale
qualem fert una biga curie. Et molendinum fullonum de Burtona cum
una uirgata terre et ferragio unius equi et ferragio certe quantitatis ad
calefaciendum aquam ad pannos,[1] et cum aliis pertinenciis suis de quo
percipit infirmarius annuatim tres marcas. Set propter predictas
consuetudines tediosas et onerosas de curia assignet ei abbas alibi
l. 39 illas tres marcas ubi | uoluerit. Pertinent etiam ad idem officium duo
molendina de Stowa de quibus percipit sexdecim solidos, et duo solidi
de terra Towi in eadem uilla, et duo solidi de terra uicina eidem, et
uiginti denarii de terra Andree in eadem uilla. In Eouesham uero de
terra Ricardi Sperwe xxii denarii. De terra Galfridi molendinarii
decem et octo denarii. De terra Iohannis de Kent quadraginta denarii.
Apud Penwrtham de terra Stephani de More duo solidi. De terra |
l. 40 Roberti Antigonie apud Hotune decem et octo denarii. De terra
Roberti Sureis xii denarii. De quadam terra in Fariton' sex denarii.
De Roberto Bussel de piscaria xii denarii. De Sulleston uero dimidia
marca. Et una marca ad munitiones quam abbas Rondulfus dedit de
ecclesia de Huniburne.

Ad pitanciariam pertinent de noua terra in Eouesham decem
marce. De Ambresleia duodecim sextaria mellis. De Vlleberewe |
l. 41 uiginti quinque solidi. De ecclesia de Hildendune una marca. De
redditibus de Penwrtham una marca. De molendino senescalli de
Sauford dimidia marca. De terra inter terram Henrici King et
Alexandri Fossard quadraginta duo denarii. De terra Iohannis portarii
duodecim denarii.

Ad refectionem fratrum in infirmaria pertinent de Wrottesleia et de
Liuintone due marce; *de coquinario uero decem solidi quia parcitur*
l. 42 *coquine | per misericordiam.*[2] De sacrista autem quinque marce quas
sacrista dat annuatim pro hospitio.[3] Quod abbates consueuerunt
extorquere iniuste ab eo. Set abbas Rondulfus, secundum priuilegia
ecclesie et statuta capituli generalis, sacristariam sicut et alias obedientias, decernens liberam esse debere, illi hospitio et omnibus aliis
exactionibus pro se et successoribus suis imperpetuum renunciauit ut

---

[1] The heating of water means that the cloth was dyed. *Pannus* may mean cloth in a
general sense or it might be taken to mean more specifically cloth for the monks' habits or
for bedclothes.
[2] Probably meaning here for the eating of flesh-meat by perfectly healthy monks, which
took place in the infirmary before special rooms were constructed for this purpose.
[3] See above, 512, for the history of these five marks.

appurtenances. The infirmarer must have one sow with feed for a year, or two pigs for a sty and one carcass of pig from the cellarer for Christmas, such as one manorial cart can carry. To the infirmarer also belong the fulling-mill of Bourton-on-the-Water [Glos.] with one virgate of land, and straw for one horse, and straw of a certain quantity for heating water for cloth,[1] with other of its appurtenances from which the infirmarer receives three marks annually. But on account of the aforesaid wearisome and burdensome customs of the court, the abbot will assign to him those three marks from elsewhere when he wishes. There belong also to the same office two mills at Stow from which he receives sixteen shillings, and two shillings from the land 'Towi' in the same town, and two shillings from the land adjoining it, and twenty pence from the land of Andrew in the same town. In Evesham twenty-two pence from the land of Richard Sperwe. Eighteen pence from the land of Geoffrey the miller. Forty pence from the land of John of Kent. In Penwortham [Lancs.] two shillings from the land of Stephen de More. Eighteen pence from the land of Robert Antigonie at Houghton [Lancs.]. Twelve pence from the land of Robert Sureis. Six pence from certain land in Farington [Lancs.]. Twelve pence from the fishpond of Robert Bussel. From Southstone half a mark. And one mark for hedging which Abbot Randulf gave from the church of Church Honeybourne.

To the pittancery belong ten marks from new land in Evesham. Twelve sesters of honey from Ombersley. Twenty-five shillings from Oldberrow [Warws.]. One mark from the church of Hillingdon [Middx.]. One mark from rents at Penwortham. Half a mark from the mill of the steward of Salford. Forty-two pence from the land between Henry King's land and that of Alexander Fossard. Twelve pence from the land of John the porter.

Two marks from Wrottesley and Loynton [both Staffs.] are to be used for the refreshment of brethren in the infirmary; from the kitchener also ten shillings because this is allowed to the kitchen on account of the *misericordia*.[2] From the sacrist come five marks that he gives annually for lodging, which sum the abbots used to demand wrongfully from him.[3] But Abbot Randulf, in accordance with the privileges of the church and the statutes of the general chapter, deciding that the sacristy should be free like the other obediences, rejected this money for lodging and all the other demands for himself and his successors for ever, so that the revenues of the sacristy might

in fratrum utilitatibus et refectionibus quas abbates solent inuenire
l. 43 redditus | sacristarie sicut et aliarum obedienciarum libere expen-
derentur. Ne autem pitanciarius mendicet pasturam ad oues, boues et
porcos, dedit prior Thomas ad pitanciariam in auxilium anniuersarii
sui boscum in Eche Lenz quem emit de Petro*ᵃ* de Lenz. Per quem
boscum habebit pitanciarius per cursum tempore glandis ad porcos
usque ad portam de Bordesleye et communam pasture omnium
l. 44 uicinorum ad omnia genera animalium adeo libere sicut | sacrista
pro Lenz et infirmarius pro Biuintona habent. Assignauit etiam idem
prior Thomas ad anniuersarium suum terram in Merstowa quam
emit de Hugone de Warwich et terram iuxta eam quam emit de filia
Rondulfi Sergant. Ad festum etiam sancti Iohannis ante portam
Latinam faciendum assignauit abbas Rondulfus uiginti solidos de
pensione sexaginta solidorum de ecclesia de Ambresleia quam, quia
l. 45 abbates dederant clericis, legatus dedit eam Humfredo¹ | clerico suo
qua reuocata pro alia. Assignauit etiam abbas unam marcam de eadem
pensione ad anniuersarium suum. Abbas uero Adam assignauit
decem solidos de redditu ecclesie de Braddewelle ad anniuersarium
Reginaldi abbatis et alios decem solidos de eadem pensione ad
proprium anniuersarium.

Ad coquinam pertinet tertium uiuarium post fontem sancti
Ecgwini, et uetus uilla et forum de Eouesham de quibus percipit
l. 46 coquinarius qualibet die sab|bati quinque solidos et tres obolos, et
annuatim in capite ieiunii quatuor millia alletium, et molendina iuxta
pontem et molendina in Hamptona cum pertinenciis suis de quibus
molendinis percipit qualibet die sabbati tres solidos et sexaginta stikas
anguillarum annuatim, et decime molendinorum et feni pratorum ad
eadem molendina pertinencium, scilicet de Eouesham, et de Hamptone et de Huffeham et de Fokemulne, et de Twiford et de
l. 47 Chadel|buri et de Baddeseie et de Wikewane. Hec omnes decime
deputantur ad allec monachorum in Quadragesima. Et uilla de Stowa
et forum de quibus percipit qualibet die dominica quatuor solidos. De
Mortona sexaginta solidi. De Sauford sexaginta solidi. De With-
lakesford quatuor libre. De molendino de eadem uilla uiginti quattuor
solidi et duodecim stice anguillarum annuatim. De molendinis
l. 48 senescalli in Sauford uiginti solidi. De molen|dinis de Chedelburi
cum pertinenciis suis uiginti quinque solidi et quadraginta stice

---

ᵃ de Petro *repeated*

be spent freely, as is the case of the other obediences, on the needs and refreshment of the brethren for which the abbots are accustomed to make provision. So that the pittancer should not have to beg pasture for his sheep, cattle, or pigs, Prior Thomas gave the pittancery to help with his own anniversary a wood in East Lench that he bought from Peter of Lench. Throughout this wood the pittancer will have in the course of time acorns for his pigs all the way to the gate of Bordesley, and the common pasture of the whole neighbourhood for animals of all kinds as freely as the sacrist has at Lench and the infirmarer at Binton. Prior Thomas also assigned for his anniversary land in Merstow that he bought from Hugh of Warwick and land adjoining it that he bought from the daughter of Randulf the serjeant. Abbot Randulf assigned twenty shillings for the celebration of the feast of St John before the Latin gate from the pension of sixty shillings from the church of Ombersley, which, because the abbots had given this to their clerks, the papal legate gave to his own clerk Humfrey[1] in place of another. The abbot also assigned one mark from the same pension for his anniversary. Abbot Adam assigned ten shillings from the revenue of the church of Broadwell for the anniversary of Abbot Reginald and another ten shillings of the same pension for his own anniversary.

To the kitchen belong the third fish-pond past the well of St Ecgwine, and the old town and market-place of Evesham from which the kitchener receives five shillings and three half-pence every Saturday, and four thousand herrings annually at the beginning of Lent, the mills by the bridge and the mills in Hampton with their appurtenances from which he receives three shillings every Saturday and sixty sticks of eels annually, and the tithes of the mills and the hay of the meadows belonging to the same mills, that is of Evesham, Hampton, Offenham, 'Fokemulne', Twyford, Chadbury, Badsey, and Wickhamford. All these tithes are allotted for the herrings of the monks during Lent. And the town of Stow and its market-place from which he receives four shillings every Sunday. Sixty shillings from Abbots Morton. Sixty shillings from Salford. Four pounds from Wixford [Warws.]. Twenty-four shillings and twelve sticks of eels annually from the mill of the same town. Twenty shillings from the mills of the steward in Salford. Twenty-five shillings and forty sticks of eels from the mills of Chadbury with its appurtenances.

---

[1] Humfrey, clerk of Nicholas of Tusculum, and of Pope Innocent III, see above, 511.

anguillarum. De molendinis de Twiford et Aldintone cum pertinenciis suis uiginti octo solidi et quadraginta stice anguillarum. De molendinis de Offeham cum pertinenciis suis decem solidi. De Fokemulne dimidia marca, et molendinum de Wikewan de quo non percipit modo nisi octo solidos. De Wodefe pertinet sexaginta solidi l. 49 ad coquinam. De piscatione in Ambresleia | uiginti tres solidi. In Gloucestria de terra Roberti Botild tres solidi et obolus. De terra quadam in Winchelcumba et quodam furno duo solidi et una libra piperis. In Eouesham de quadam terra in Brutstrete una libra piperis, de terra Reginaldi filii Willelmi dimidia marca annuatim. De Penwrtham quatuor marce et una summa salmonis, et duo milia allecium. De qualibet carucata terre in Valle Eoueshamie de dominico excepta l. 50 Aldintona | trescenta oua annuatim, et de quolibet manerio tres denarii ad discos et duodecim olle. De Bradewella nonginta oua et tres denarii et duodecim olle. Item singulis diebus debet habere coquinarius foragium ad unum equum et prebendam, uel duo prebendaria de furfure de granario, et duos porcos habere debet ad plangerum, et quociens emerit in uilla de Eouesham piscem ad totum conuentum l. 51 debet habere de cellario panem et iustam ad opus uenden | tium. Ad omnes etiam cibos qui condimento ceruisie indigent debet habere ceruisiam de cellario, et caseum semel in die ad quem emendum, si non detur de cellario assignauit abbas Rondulfus capellam de Bretfordtone. *Habebit etiam coquinarius ad septem festiuitates principales septem summas frumenti de granario ad frixuras, et in festo sancti Iohannis ante Portam Latinam unum prebendarium et aliud in festo sancti* l. 52 *Odulfi, et tercium in Septuagesima,*[1] *et quartum in die Pa | rasceue ad pulmentum, et tria ad Pascha ad faciendum flacones et totidem in Rogationibus*[2] *ad idem.*

Ad cameram pertinent Malgaresbur' et Swelle sicut antiquitus fuerunt, et loco Burntone, que fuit ad cameram, assignata est Tatelestroppe.[3] *Et abbas habet Burittonam*, ita uidelicet quod abbas ex hac camera nec uestimenta nec hospicium nec aliquid aliud percipiet sicut consueuit ex priori camera exigere. Hec autem maneria l. 53 imperpetuum cum omni integritate | sua ad uestimenta monachorum sunt assignata. Debet etiam camerarius habere cotidie ad unum seruientem procurationem et prebendam ad unum equum de granario et foragium de grangia, sicut seruientes et equi abbatis habent.

---

[1] The third Sunday before Ash Wednesday.
[2] The Monday, Tuesday, and Wednesday before Ascension Day.
[3] All these places are in Glos.

Twenty-eight shillings and forty sticks of eels from the mills of Twyford and Aldington with their appurtenances. Ten shillings from the mills of Offenham with their appurtenances. Half a mark from 'Fokemulne', and the mill of Wickhamford from which he receives only eight shillings. To the kitchen belong sixty shillings from 'Wodefe', twenty-three shillings from the fishery in Ombersley, three shillings and a halfpenny from the land of Robert Botild in Gloucester, two shillings and one pound of pepper from some land and a bakery in Winchcombe, one pound of pepper from some land in Bridge Street in Evesham, half a mark annually from the land of Reginald son of William. From Penwortham, four marks and one seam of salmon, and two thousand herrings. From every carucate of land in the Vale of Evesham, on the demesne, except for Aldington, three hundred eggs yearly, and from each manor three pence for dishes and twelve pots. From Broadwell ninety eggs, and three pence and twelve pots. Also every day the kitchener must have hay for one horse, and one or two measures of bran from the granary, and two pigs for the sty and, whenever he buys fish in the town of Evesham for the whole convent he must have bread from the cellarer and a flagon of ale for the service of those selling the fish. He must also have ale from the cellarer for all foods that need a seasoning of ale, and Abbot Randulf assigned the chapel of Bretforton to supply the cheese that he has to buy once a day, if it is not supplied from the cellar. On the seven principal festivals the kitchener shall have seven seams of corn from the granary for pancakes, and on the feast of St John before the Latin Gate one measure of corn, and another on the feast of St Odulf, a third at Septuagesima,[1] and a fourth on Good Friday for pottage, and three at Easter for making cakes and three again on Rogation days[2] for the same purpose.

To the chamber belong Maugersbury and Swell as they have from of old, and in place of Bourton-on-the-Water, which once belonged to the chamber, Adlestrop has been assigned.[3] The abbot has Bourton, but on such terms that the abbot will receive from the chamber neither clothing, nor hospitality, nor anything else that he used to demand from the chamber previously. These manors have been permanently assigned in entirety for the monks' clothing. The chamberlain must every day have a maintenance allowance for one servant and provender for one horse from the granary and forage from the grange, as the servants and horses of the abbot do.

Ad fabricam ecclesie et domorum claustro adiacentium pertinent quindecim marce de ecclesia de Ambresleia que, si aliquo casu solute non fuerint, abbas ecclesiam et domos cooperire debet. Pertinent l. 54 etiam ad idem faciendum decime Willelmi Beorin in Offeham, | et fabri eiusdem uille et predicationes[1] *abbacie* et legata fidelium, et si que sunt alie gratuite ouentiones.

Ad cellam hospitum pertinent minute decime de tribus Littlintonis ad emendum manutergia, cyphos et bacinos hospitibus.

Hee etiam sunt consuetudines Eoueshamensis cenobii ab antiquis temporibus statute et a celerario generali complende.

A cellario igitur singulis diebus debent uenire in refectorium l. 55 septuagin|ta duo panes monachiles, quorum quilibet erit ponderis sexaginta quinque solidorum, ex quibus singuli monachi singulos percipiant. Prior semper duos nisi cum abbate comederit, *et unum ad cenam et iustam nisi cum abbate uel in refectorio cenauerit.* Nichilominus qui ad superiorem mensam ut custos ordinis sederit duos habebit, *scilicet unum de pasta abbatis et unum cyphum uini de abbate*, qui missam l. 56 uero maiorem celebrauerit duos. Lector *etiam coquina|rius* et seruitores unum *admixtum* et iustam *in hyeme*. Elemosinarius autem septem pro decima et tres ad Mandatum, et duos ad tritennales currentes percipiet. Percipiet etiam quilibet fratrum cotidie duas iustas ceruisie *ᵃquarum quelibet continebit duas caritates quarum caritatum sex faciunt sextarium regis.ᵃ* Nichilominus prior unam ad nouum tractum, et qui sederit ad discum unum cyphum ad cibum et alium ad l. 57 uesperam. In|ueniet etiam celerarius salem *et ligna ad* ignem et summagium *ad cibum et potum monachorum* et duo pulmenta. Ad unum, scilicet de fabis siccis unum prebendarium rasum, uel de nouis cumulatum de granario; ad aliud uero pulmentum decem panes monachiles *uel unum prebendarium rasum de frumento.* Singulis diebus preterquam in Quadragesima in qua percipiunt monachi duodecim summas fabe de Huniburne ad unum pulmentum per l. 58 totam Quadrage|simam, et de auena duodecim summas de eadem uilla ad gruellum faciendum, scilicet quarta et sexta feria per totam Quadragesimam, et farinam ad olera singulis diebus in Quadragesima. Insuper habere debent monachi ad septem principales festiuitates septem cyffoles[2] de frumento ad wastellos de granario, et in

---

ᵃ⁻ᵃ *R subst.* et certe mensure

[1] Collections were made at sermons.

To the fabric of the church and of the houses adjoining the cloister belong fifteen marks from Ombersley church: if this money is by any mischance not paid, the abbot must keep the church and the houses roofed. For this same purpose belong the tithes of William Beorin in Offenham and of the smith of the same vill, as well as preaching collections[1] of the abbey, and legacies of the faithful, and any other obventions freely given.

To the guest-chamber belong the small tithes of the three Littletons for buying towels, cups, and basins, for the guests.

These are the customs of the monastery of Evesham, established from of old, which must be maintained by the cellarer general.

Each day the cellarer must deliver to the refectory seventy-two monastic loaves of bread, weighing sixty-five shillings, and each monk shall receive one of these. The prior shall always have two loaves unless he is eating with the abbot, and one for supper as well as a flagon measure of ale unless he is either dining with the abbot or in the refectory. But then, whoever presides at the high table must have two, one of the abbot's pastries and one cup of the abbot's wine; the celebrant of high mass shall have two. The reader, also the kitchener, and the servers, shall have a cup of wine mixed, and a flagon of ale in the winter. The almoner, however, shall receive seven out of every ten, three for Maundy, and two for successive trentals. Each of the brethren shall also receive every day two flagons of ale, each of which shall contain two *caritates*, six of these making a royal sester. Nevertheless the prior shall receive one *caritas* when there is a new draught, and whoever sits at the high table shall receive one cup at dinner and one at the evening meal. The cellarer shall also provide salt and wood for kindling, and carriage for the monks' food and drink and the two dishes of pottage. For one he shall provide a rased allowance of dried beans or, as a change, a heaped measure from the granary, for the other, ten monk's loaves or one rased allowance of corn. These he shall provide every day except during Lent when the monks receive twelve seams of beans from Honeybourne for one dish of pottage throughout the whole of Lent, and twelve seams of oats from the same vill to make gruel on the Wednesdays and Fridays throughout the whole of Lent, and wheatmeal for the vegetables every day during Lent. In addition, the monks must have seven measures[2] of corn from the granary for wastel-loaves at the seven principal feasts, and

---

[2] On *cyfolles* and *sciffol*, see above, **425** and n.

translatione sancti Ecgwini octauum ad cenam sicut ad prandium, *et in festo sancti Iohannis ante portam Latinam unum sciffol ad wastellos,* |

l. 59 et in festo sancti Odulfi unum, et in die Omnium Animarum unum, *et in anniuersario beati Wlsini unum, et in anniuersario regum Ethelredi, Kenredi et Offe unum,* et in anniuersario abbatis Reginaldi[1] unum, et in anniuersario abbatis Ade[2] unum, *et in anniuersario abbatis Rondulfi*[3] *unum.* Ad formittas uero in Aduentu Domini debent habere monachi quatuordecim summas, et contra Natale totidem, et contra Quadragesimam totidem, et contra Pascha totidem, ⟨et contra⟩[a] | Pente-

l. 60 costen totidem, contra Assumptionem beate Marie totidem, contra translationem sancti Ecgwini totidem: omnes scilicet percipiendas de horreis. Debent etiam habere monachi de cellario singulis diebus sabbati caritatem ad collationem pro mandato, et ad omnes collationes festiuitatum tam in capis quam in albis in uigilia et in die. Exceptis collationibus septem festiuitatum principalium tam in uigilia quam in die, tunc enim pitanciarius inuenire debet.

l. 61 Debent etiam habere | caritatem de cellario ad prandium singulis diebus octabarum principalium festiuitatum que octabas habent, exceptis diebus quibus sunt in capis, tunc enim pitanciarius inueniet. Set ad collationem singulis diebus earumdem octabarum habebunt de cellario et a Natali Domini usque ad Epiphaniam simili modo habebunt de celario. Qualibet etiam die in misericordiis regularibus

l. 62 habebunt duo fratres unam iustam de cellario. In minutionibus | uero unam ad prandium et alteram ad cenam. Qui uero uentosatus fuerit, tantum ea die habebit unam iustam de celario. Seruiens uero qui fratres sanguinauerit habebit panem et iustam de cellario si plures fuerint sanguinati. Quociens etiam mappe obluuntur[b] de refectorio, ablutores habebunt panem monachilem de cellario. Balneatores etiam quando fratres balneant habebunt de cellario panem et iustam |

l. 63 singulis diebus per tres ebdomadas ante Natiuitatem Domini et per tres ante Dominicam in Ramis Palmarum.

Abbates etiam et monachi Eoueshamie debent habere corredium suum sicut habuerunt in uita sua per totum annum post obitum suum, quod alicui indigenti pro animabus eorum erogabitur. Seruientes etiam qui uigilant circa fratrem proximum morti debent habere

l. 64 panem et ceruisiam de cellario. Quando uero obitus | abbatis uel monachi euenerit alterius domus, si fuerint de capitulo Eoueshamie,

---

[a] *damaged: supplied from R*   [b] abluuntur *R*

[1] 25 Aug. 1149.   [2] 12 Nov. 1189.   [3] 17 Dec. 1229.

for the octave of the translation of St Ecgwine at dinner as at supper, and on the feast of St John before the Latin gate one measure for wastel-loaves, and one on the feast of St Odulf, and one on All Souls day, and one on the anniversary of the blessed Wulfsige, and one on the anniversary of kings Æthelred, Kenred and Offa, and one on the anniversary of Abbot Reginald,[1] and one on the anniversary of Abbot Adam,[2] and one on the anniversary of Abbot Randulf.[3] The monks must have fourteen seams of corn for frumenty at Advent, and the same number for Christmas, Lent, Easter, Whitsun, the Assumption of the blessed Mary, and the translation of St Ecgwine: all these to be received from the barns. The monks must also have a *caritas* from the cellar every Saturday at the collation as Maundy, and at every collation at festivals, on days when copes as well as albs are worn, on the vigil as well as the day of the festival. However, the collations on both the vigils and the days of the seven principal festivals are excepted, for then the pittancer must provide for these.

The monks must also have a *caritas* from the cellar for dinner each day on the octaves of those principal festivals that have octaves, except on days when copes are worn when the pittancer shall provide them. But for the collation every day of those same octaves, and from Christmas until Epiphany, they shall receive the same from the cellar. Every regular penitential day one flagon of ale shall be provided between two brethren by the cellarer. During blood-lettings there shall be one for dinner and another for supper. Those brethren who have been bled, shall have one flagon of ale from the cellar, but only on that day. The servant, however, who has bled the brethren shall have a loaf and a flagon measure of ale from the cellar if many brethren have been bled. Whenever refectory table-cloths are washed, the launderers shall have a monk's loaf from the cellar. Also the servants of the bath-house, whenever the brethren take a bath, shall receive from the cellarer bread and a flagon of ale every day for the three weeks preceding Christmas and the three weeks before Palm Sunday.

Also abbots and monks of Evesham must have their corrody, just as they had in their lifetime, for the whole year after their death, to be disbursed for the sake of their souls to some needy person. The servants who keep vigil around a brother who is close to death should have bread and ale from the cellar. When the death of an abbot or monk of another house occurs, who has belonged to the Evesham

ad annale pro abbate, et tricennale pro monacho panis et ceruisia de cellario sicut uni monacho alicui pauperi erogentur. Debet etiam celerarius dare singulis pauperibus qui fuerint in capitulo in Cena Domini singulos panes et tria allecia, et de ceruisia quantum opus fuerit.

l. 65   Si quis uero hec conseruauerit uel adauxerit, adaugeat | Dominus dies eius, et conseruet eum in uitam eternam. Si quis uero destruxerit uel diminuerit, diminuat Dominus dies eius et destruat uitam eius desuper terram. Amen, Amen, Amen.

chapter, bread and ale should be given from the cellar to some poor person as to a monk, for a year on the abbot's behalf, and for thirty days for a monk. The cellarer must give to each poor person who has been in chapter on Maundy Thursday a loaf and three herrings, and as much ale as he needs.

May the Lord add to the days of him who preserves or adds to this, and preserve him for everlasting life. But may the Lord shorten the days of him who destroys or subtracts from them, and destroy his life upon earth. Amen, Amen, Amen.

C. COMPARATIVE TABLE OF THE ENTRIES AS IN THE AGREEMENT MADE BEFORE THE LEGATE (M); THE AGREEMENT AS RECORDED IN THOMAS'S *HISTORY* (R); AND THE AGREEMENT AS RECORDED IN THE COTTON CHARTER (C)

M	R	C
Date		
before Nov. 1206 Confirmed by legate 1206	post 1218: not the document confirmed by Innocent III, Feb. 1216	After d. of Abbot Randulf (17 Dec. 1229) and before election of Abbot Thomas
Prior	Cellarer exterior	Cellarer exterior
Precentor	Prior (25 paupers to be fed on Prior Thomas's anniversary)	Prior (subprior to feed 30 paupers in the parlour on Prior Thomas's anniversary)
Sacrist	Refectorer (includes some of Pittancer)	Dean
Chamberlain	Precentor (parchment for writs & mortuary rolls not mentioned)	Precentor (parchment for writs and mortuary rolls)
Cook	Dean	Sacrist
Pittancer (no Refectorer)	Sacrist	Altar of S. Mary in the Crypt (pertinent de sacristaria)
Infirmarer	Chamberlain	Almoner

Almoner	Infirmarer—wearisome customs gone	Refectorer (for last sentence see Cellarer in R)
Master of the Fabric	Almoner (in marginalia some of Text of C)	Infirmarer—wearisome customs at Bourton-on-the-Water
Cellarer: Customs 20s. from church of Broadwell	Master of the Fabric	Pittancer (parts under Refectorer and Infirmarer in R) The legate's clerk Humfrey mentioned
Guest House		Kitchen
Kitchen (in marginalia some of text of C)		Chamber (part of last sentence under Cellarer in R)
Cellarer: Customs (includes sections under Sacristy and Chamber in C)		Fabric
		Guest House
		Cellarer: Customs
Anniversaries of 12th-cent. abbots (Reginald and Adam) only	8 principal feasts (but on fo. 174ra, 7 feasts, and then substitutes refectorer for pittancer)	7 principal feasts (according to *Mon. Angl.* ii p. 39, num. xxxvii, from Cotton MS Vit. E XVII fo. 252, reference fails: 1. Christmas; 2. Deposition of the blessed Ecgwine; 3. Easter; 4. Whitsun; 5. Assumption of the BVM; 6. Translation of St Ecgwine; 7. All Saints)

APPENDIX III

A LETTER OF ABBOT REGINALD TO GILBERT, ABBOT OF GLOUCESTER

The letter can only be dated by the terminal dates of Gilbert Foliot as abbot of Gloucester (1139–48). It provides important evidence of the continued aggression of the bishops of Worcester and Evesham's adherence to what it supposed to be its ancient rights. Reginald himself had been a monk of Gloucester before he became abbot of Evesham in 1130.

R fo. 148ᵛ (in the lower margin). Printed Macray in a footnote to pp. 112–13.

Domino medullitus dilecto Gil⟨berto⟩ ᵃscilicet Foliotᵃ abbati Glou-cestrieᵇ frater Reginaldus abbas Eueshamie, germen odoris Israel hebetudini mee imputo quod uobis parcius innotesco, licet et hebetudo per se citius innotescat. Lippus solis iubare delector, nec solis uitium est prauitas oculorum. Montem sole illustratum aspicio, sed eger procul solem campestria reuisentem opperior. Quorsum hec? Dum nostrum triste uiuere deploro, gaudeo Tullium in hec tempora reseruatum, Tullium in quam, qui urbem prouidentia reseruauit et peritia superbis ora reclusit. Vos ego Ciceronem, uos etiam rigidum Catonem, uos Augustum farriferum dixerim; Marcum seueritate, Catonem equitate, Augustum frugalitate.
Cumque hee uirtutes trifarie sint morum nitore uelut argento uermi-culate, gaudemus uos uelut optato sidere nubila nostra interpolare.

Huc ueniant fessi, rogitent discrimineᶜ pressi.
Omnibus ipse bonus alleuiabis onus.
Vita dabit meritum, fugiet fraus queque peritum.
Nec ledi poterit qui tibi fisus erit.
Alterutre litis compescis iurgia mitis.
Quemuis causa grauet, pars tibi queque fauet.

Quum igitur pretium de peritia habeatis ut recta dirigatis et praua corrigatis et in omnibus auctoritatem habeatis, meminisse uos libeat auunculi uestri[1] uos carne et spiritu pre omnibus diligentis,

---

ᵃ⁻ᵃ *interlined*   ᵇ *interlined*   ᶜ *MS* discrimini

[1] On the relationship, see A. Morey and C. N. L. Brooke, *Gilbert Foliot and his Letters* (Cambridge, 1965), pp. 36–8, 51, and 78.

APPENDIX III

A LETTER OF ABBOT REGINALD TO GILBERT, ABBOT OF GLOUCESTER

Brother Reginald, abbot of Evesham, to our deeply beloved Gilbert Foliot, abbot of Gloucester, I impute it to my own dullness, as a scion of Israel's bad repute, that I am too little known to you, though my dullness by itself may very soon be known by you. Being poor of sight I delight in the radiance of the sun, though the dimness of my eyes is no fault of the sun. I notice a mountain lit up by the sun, but in my weakness I wait at a distance for the sun to visit the plain again. Why is this so? When I bewail the grim life of our age, I rejoice that Cicero has been preserved for these times, Cicero I say, who saved his city by his foresight, and with his wisdom shut the mouth of the proud. I call you Cicero, but also harsh Cato and grain-giving Augustus: Cicero with his severity, Cato in his justness, Augustus in his frugality.

Since these are three kinds of virtue, ornamented with the lustre of character like silver, we rejoice that you, [Gilbert], are making your presence felt in our gloomy skies like a hoped-for star.

Let the weary come here, let those oppressed by trouble ask their eager questions. You are the man who in your goodness will lighten the burden for all. Life will grant its reward, and all deceit will abandon the advocate. And he who trusts in you cannot be harmed. You, kindly man, restrain the quarrels of each party in a suit. No matter whomsoever a case may harm, each side will favour you.

Since therefore you have the reputation of experience to direct things aright and to correct the wrong, and have authority in all things, it should please you to remember your uncle[1] who loved you above all

scilicet ne ueritas cause nostre, tam antiquis et probabilibus
munimentis fulta, uoluntario uel casuali iudicio uacillet. Iuuantes
nos ueritas iuuabit, quia quicquid contra nos emuli nostri emendi-
cant superbie et fraudulentie est. Iuuat nos annosa possessio,
antiqua regum et procerum collatio, tum denique Romana con-
scriptio.[1] Rome me nemo interpellauit, coram legato[2] nullus
appellauit, qui semper in palam ueni. Quid me retro lacessunt?
Wigornia nos colliberales, nunquam seruos, habuit; et que nunquam possederunt cur de possessore queruntur? Libuit cuilibet
fidem dare; fecit quod uoluit. Nescio conscientiam. Ego, in
libertate ecclesie natus, debeo liberam ancillam facere? Libertatem
nostram sacramento, armis, manu, quauis ratione, tuebimur. Vt a
nostris accepi 'nemini seruiuimus unquam'.[3]

> Vos nisi tederet, me scribere multa liberet.
> Sed tu multa brevi percipis aure leui.
> Pectore sincero sociari te michi quero:
>   nam quocunque uoles uertere fata soles.
> Linea sit stabilis consanguinitatis herilis.
>   Iamque memento mei conditione spei.

Vale.

---

[1] This is more likely to refer to the papal letter,'Sicut iniusta poscentibus', of 16 Apr.
1139, which Abbot Reginald had obtained from Pope Innocent II at the time of the Second
Lateran Council in Rome, than to one of the two papal privileges granted by Pope
Constantine.

[2] It is not clear to whom this refers. There was a legation to England in 1138–9, and the

things in body and spirit, so that the truth of our case, supported by both ancient and proved documents, may not be weakened through any judgement willingly given or unintentional. The truth will help those who help us, because whatever lies our opponents tell against us is an indication of their pride and deceitfulness. Ancient possession helps our case, ancient endowment of kings and nobles help us, then finally the Roman document.[1] No one obstructed me at Rome, no one accused me before the legate,[2] and I always acted openly. Why do they attack me about past proceedings? Worcester has treated us as free citizens, never as slaves. And why do they complain about the owner of things which they never possessed? Everyone was willing to give a pledge; what he did, he did voluntarily. I know no guilt. Born in the freedom of the church, must I make her who is free into a slave? We shall protect our freedom with oaths, with arms, by force, by every kind of argument. As I have learned from our scriptures 'I have never been in bondage to any man'.[3]

If it were not wearisome for you, I would have gladly written much more. But you will soon perceive many things with your ready ear. I ask you to be my ally with sincerity of heart; for you will be accustomed to turning Destiny into whatever direction you choose. May the line of our noble kinship be strong. And now remember the nature of my hopes.

Farewell.

---

legate, Alberic cardinal bishop of Ostia, held a council at Westminster in Dec. 1138 at which Abbot Reginald may have been present, and at which he may have raised the matter of the status of the abbey of Evesham; see C. & S. i. 2, pp. 768–9.

[3] John 8: 33.

APPENDIX IV

THOMAS, ABBOT, AND THE CONVENT OF EVESHAM, SUBMIT TO YEARLY VISITATION BY THE ARCHBISHOP OF CANTERBURY OR HIS DELEGATES. EVESHAM 17 APRIL 1233

Lambeth Palace Library MS 1212 fo. 48ᵛ (p. 92) (also in Bodleian Library, Oxford, MS Tanner 223 fo. 53ᵛ)

Vniuersis ad quos presentes littere peruenerint Thom' dei gracia abbas de Evesham et totus eiusdem loci conuentus eternam salutem in domino. Vniuersitati uestre publice protestamur nos illius qui pro tempore fuerit Cant' archiepiscopi uisitationem absque omni contradictione paratos esse suscipere, ut possit idem archiepiscopus singulis annis monasterium nostrum uel ipse personaliter uisitare uel uisitationem ipsam quibus uoluerit personis ecclesiasticis uiris prudentibus demandare necnon, et in ipsa uisitatione tam in capite quam in membris[1] corrigenda corrigere ipsum etiam ordinem nostrum, prout expedire uiderit, regulariter reformare. In cuius rei testimonium presentes literas inperpetuum ualituras sigillis nostris duximus consignandas. Act' apud Evesham xv. kalend. maii anno domini m. cc. xxxiij.

---

[1] Cf. above, 196 n. 7 (p. 203), and 283 n. 1 (p. 282).

APPENDIX IV

THOMAS, ABBOT, AND THE CONVENT OF EVESHAM, SUBMIT TO YEARLY VISITATION BY THE ARCHBISHOP OF CANTERBURY OR HIS DELEGATES. EVESHAM 17 APRIL 1233

To all to whom the present letter shall come Thomas, by the grace of God, abbot of Evesham, and all the convent of the same place, eternal greeting in the lord. To all of you we declare publicly that we are prepared to accept visitation by the archbishop of Canterbury, whoever he shall be at the time, without any contradiction, so that he can come annually to our monastery to carry out a visitation either in person or to ask other prudent ecclesiastics he chooses to do so, and that he may during the same visitation correct what needs correcting 'both in the head and in the limbs',[1] and that he may reform our order, as will seem expedient to him, according to the Rule. In witness of this we have drawn up this letter, appending our seals to give it lasting validity. Executed at Evesham 17 April 1233.

APPENDIX V

THE NUMBER OF MONKS IN THE ABBEY

The *History* tells us that there were twelve monks when Æthelwig became abbot in 1059 and that by the time of his death in 1077 Æthelwig had increased that number to thirty-six. Under Abbot Robert of Jumièges, in the early years of the twelfth century, according to the cartularies (H and V), that number had risen to fifty-five (printed below from H).[1] At the time of Abbot Roger Norreis's attempt to expel Thomas of Marlborough and Thomas de Northwich in 1206, thirty monks left with them on 25 November in that year. As they left behind them the sacred relics and the treasure of the church in the care of the old and infirm monks, we may presume the full number of the community to have been in the region of forty, perhaps fifty, monks.

H fos. 171^v–2^r

Tempore istius abbatis fuerunt in Euesham lxvii monachi et ex hiis fuerunt xii in Denemarcia, quos rex Willelmus iuuenis illuc transmisit,[2] et v moniales, tres pauperes ad mandatum, tres clerici qui omnes habent tantum quantum monachi. Item lxv seruientes fuerunt in monasterio, scilicet v in ecclesia, duo in domo informorum, ii in cellario,^{a} v in coquina, vii in pistrino, quatuor qui faciunt ceruisiam, quatuor seruitores in balneario, ii sutores, ii in pomerio,^{b} iii ortolani, i ad hostium^c claustri, ii ad magnam portam, v ad vineam, iiii qui seruiunt monachis quando^d pergunt foras, et^e quattuor piscatores, iv in camera abbatis, iii in aula, ii uigilantes.[3]

At the time of this abbot there were sixty-seven monks at Evesham, and of these twelve were in Denmark, where King William the younger [William Rufus] had sent them,[2] and five nuns, three Maundy men, and three clerks who all have the same allowances as the monks. There were sixty-five servants in the monastery, that is, five in the church, two in the infirmary, two in the cellary, five in the kitchen, seven in the bakehouse, four who make beer, four servants in the bath-house, two shoemakers, two in the orchard, three gardeners,

one at the entrance to the cloister, two at the great gate, five in the vineyard, four to serve the monks who travel, four fishermen, four in the abbot's chamber, three in the hall, and two watchmen.[3]

---

[a] cancellario *BL, Cotton MS. Vespasian B xv fo. 17*   [b] pannerio *ibid.*   [c] ostium *ibid.*   [d] qui *ibid.*   [e] et *om. ibid.*

---

[1] The text is in V on fo. 41[v] with minuscule and unimportant differences. *Mon. Angl.*, ii, p. 37 (in num. xxxvi) printed the text from BL Cotton MS Vespasian B xv fo. 17 where the only noteworthy variant is *cancellario* for *cellario*.

[2] King Eric 'Evergood' of Denmark, with the permission of William Rufus, and on the advice of Hubald the first bishop of Odense, imported Evesham monks to colonize Odense; see Macray, p. 325 (prologue to the Life of St Wigstan), and P. King in *Journal of Ecclesiastical History*, xiii (1962), 145–55, at p. 149.

[3] The number of servants actually specified in H comes to sixty-one, in V to sixty-three.

INDEX OF QUOTATIONS AND ALLUSIONS

Numbers in bold type refer to the paragraphs of the Text and Translation above

A. BIBLICAL ALLUSIONS

B. ALLUSIONS TO OTHER SOURCES

GENERAL INDEX

Numbers in italic are page numbers. *All* other numbers are paragraph numbers, given everywhere else in bold type.

ABBREVIATIONS

abb(s).	abbot(s)	ch(s).	church(es)
abp	archbishop	dau.	daughter
archdcn	archdeacon	k.	king
bp	bishop	OT	Old Testament
br.	brother	pr.	prior
cdnl bp	cardinal bishop	pst	priest
cdnl dcn	cardinal deacon	subdcn	subdeacon
cdnl pst	cardinal pst	unid.	unidentified